# THE MARKET MAKERS

# The Market Makers

*Creating Mass Markets for Consumer Durables in Inter-war Britain*

PETER SCOTT

**OXFORD**

UNIVERSITY PRESS

# OXFORD
### UNIVERSITY PRESS

Great Clarendon Street, Oxford, OX2 6DP,
United Kingdom

Oxford University Press is a department of the University of Oxford.
It furthers the University's objective of excellence in research, scholarship,
and education by publishing worldwide. Oxford is a registered trade mark of
Oxford University Press in the UK and in certain other countries

First Edition published in 2017

Impression: 1

Published in the United States of America by Oxford University Press
198 Madison Avenue, New York, NY 10016, United States of America

British Library Cataloguing in Publication Data
Data available

Library of Congress Control Number: 2017935735

ISBN 978-0-19-878381-7

Printed and bound by
CPI Group (UK) Ltd, Croydon, CR0 4YY

This book is dedicated to the memory of my parents, Eric and Vanda Scott, who—bringing up a family on the wages of an unskilled labourer—understood the realities of living on tight budgets and making difficult choices between competing priorities.

# Preface

This book is the outcome of more than a decade of research on how producers, retailers, and consumers interacted to create 'value' for new consumer durables, by imbuing them with various functional, psychological, and status characteristics. As such, it is an attempt to depart from both the approach of much traditional economic history—that focuses on production, to the neglect of distribution and, especially, consumption—and the traditional approach of much historical work on consumption, which is based in social and cultural history and tends to neglect the supply side. The more integrated framework of this study—viewing production, distribution, and consumption as interdependent processes, subject to cumulative causation—reflects a growing trend, evident from the late twentieth century and reflected in the work of scholars such as Avner Offer, Paul Johnson, Sue Bowden, and Frank Trentmann. It has perhaps been most fully developed by Francesca Carnevali, whose later work explored how goods with high status value, such as jewellery, were made available to a wider public without undermining traditional elite markets. She identified processes of mediation between producers, retailers, and consumers, to create new markets without undermining existing ones, a research agenda which was still in progress at the time of her early death.[1]

I chose high value consumer durables for my study as these were the goods that could be least easily absorbed into the weekly household budgeting cycle of most working-class families. Moreover these had major, and rapidly evolving, status and lifestyle connotations. As novel goods (at least for the mass market) they also required considerable efforts on the part of producers and retailers to reach lower-income groups—by 'selling' both the value and legitimacy of the physical products and of the financial (consumer credit) products that were often essential to extending the market.

Inter-war Britain was chosen as it was a key transition era. Incomes for those in work were markedly higher than in 1914, there was some blurring between working- and lower-middle-class lifestyles and aspirations, and a rising proportion of consumer expenditure was being devoted to consumer durables and related goods. Furthermore, this era witnessed rapid technological development of new consumer durables, especially those associated with the new technologies of electricity and the internal combustion engine. Nevertheless, household incomes were much lower, and less secure, than during the post-war era of the fully employed welfare state, and many families—both in the working classes and the lowest income

---

[1] See, for example, Francesca Carnevali, 'Fashioning Luxury for Factory Girls: American Jewelry, 1860–1914', *Business History Review*, 85 (2011), 295–317; Francesca Carnevali and Lucy Newton, 'Pianos for the People: From Producer to Consumer in Britain, 1851–1914', *Enterprise and Society*, 14 (2013), 37–70.

segments of the middle classes—faced tight budgets and difficult choices between competing priorities.

The research underpinning this book was developed through a number of smaller projects, involving fieldwork throughout Britain and in the United States and the Netherlands. I owe a great debt of thanks to the many archives, museums, specialist libraries, and individuals who were generous in giving me access to archival resources; to the various agencies that provided me with financial assistance; to those scholars who collaborated with me on papers connected with the project; and to the journal referees and editors who pushed me to do better work. My colleagues—at the University of Reading and in the wider world—have also been extremely generous with advice, constructive criticism, and time. But my main debt is, as always, to my wife Fong, for her continued love, support, and for putting up with me.

# Acknowledgements

The research for this project has involved significant resources in terms of research travel, the compilation of statistical datasets, and dissemination of preliminary findings through conference and seminar presentations. I have been privileged to receive financial support from the ESRC (Grant RES-000-22-0152); the Nuffield Foundation Social Sciences Small Grant Scheme (Project Number: H502620); and the Economic History Society. I am particularly indebted to the University of Reading's Henley Business School for its generous and consistent support for my research. I was also very fortunate to receive a Douglas Byrne Marconi Fellowship, administered by the Bodleian Library, Oxford, for my research into the British radio industry that formed the basis of Chapters 6 and 7. My research on the US radio industry was assisted by a Smithsonian Lemelson Center travel to collections award.

Many archives, museums, and research libraries provided generous assistance with my research, including the Bank of England Archives; Barclays Bank Group Archive; Bexley Local Studies and Archives Centre; Bodleian Library; Boots plc Archives; British Library (St Pancras and Colindale); BT Archives; Building Societies Association Library; Centre for Oxfordshire Studies; Clarks Archive; Construction Industry Resource Centre Archive; EMI Group Archive Trust; Essex Record Office; Geffrye Museum Library; Guildhall Library, London; Gunnersbury Park Museum; Harrods Company Archive; HBOS Archives; Hertfordshire Archives; Lloyds Bank Archives; London Metropolitan Archives; Manchester Museum of Science and Industry; Mass Observation Archive; Modern Records Centre, Warwick; Museum of Domestic Design and Architecture; Museum of London Archive; National Archive for Electrical Science and Technology; National Art Library; National Gas Archive, Manchester; National Media Museum, Bradford; Nuffield College, Oxford, Archives; Philips Company Archives, Eindhoven, Netherlands; Royal Mail Archives; Royal Pharmaceutical Society Library Archives; Southend Museum; The National Archives, Kew; University of East Anglia Archives; University of Reading's Museum of English Rural Life; and the Women's Library, London.

My research on comparisons with developments in the United States also benefited hugely from the help of a number of archives and specialist libraries, including: Hagley Museum Library; Hoover Historical Center; Library of Congress; McLean County Museum of History; Smithsonian National Museum of American History, Lemelson Center Archives; and US National Archives. I also owe an enormous debt to many individuals not known to me, whose dedicated efforts had led to the deposit of the above collections in publicly accessible archives. Without them, much of the historical record for consumer durables (and consumer goods in general) would have been lost forever.

Particular thanks are due to the colleagues who collaborated with me on papers related to this project, including Lucy Newton, Anna Spadavecchia, Peter Walsh, Nicolas Ziebarth, and, especially, James Walker—who has collaborated with me extensively both on this project and other related research. I have also received valuable comments and advice when presenting papers at various conferences and seminar series, particularly those of the Association of Business Historians; Business History Conference; Economic History Association; Economic History Society; and European Business History Association, together with seminars at the universities of Glasgow, Manchester, Lancaster, and Oxford. The Henley Business School's seminar series has also proved an exemplary forum for discussing my research in progress, providing a combination of lively, forthright, discussion with an openness to alternative research perspectives and approaches.

Many individuals have also given me valuable advice, ideas, and criticism. I doubt whether my memory (never perfect, even over the short run) will provide anywhere near a full list, but I would like to thank Gerben Bakker, Mike Best, Stephen Broadberry, Peter Burton, Mark Casson, Harold Cones, Jack Copp, Roy Edwards, Claude S. Fischer, Mike French, Christos Genakos, Dave Grant, Leslie Hannah, Howell Harris, Peter Hart, Sheldon Hochheiser, Dan Nunan, Avner Offer, Andrew Popp, Paul Rhode, Teresa Da Silva Lopes, Frank Trentmann, Chris Vickers, James Walker, John Wilson, and several anonymous referees of research articles for their help and advice. My research on the early radio industry was greatly assisted by the late Gordon Bussey, who was also responsible for saving several of the most important radio company archives used in my research.

Special thanks are due to Mike Ashworth, Neil Baylis, BT Archives, Dave Grant, Joe Haupt, Museum of Domestic Design and Architecture, Punch Ltd., and Southend Central Museum, for permission to reproduce images. I am also very grateful to Natalie Anderson, Nat Ishino, and Fatima Cardias Williams for excellent research assistance.

# Contents

PART I. 'NECESSITIES OF LIFE'—CREATING
MASS MARKETS IN NEW FURNITURE
AND OWNER-OCCUPIED HOUSING

## PART IV. BRITAIN'S MASS MARKET 'FAILURES'—CARS AND TELEPHONES

# List of Illustrations

# List of Tables

# List of Abbreviations and Note on Currency

| | |
|---|---|
| BCGA | British Commercial Gas Association |
| BSA | Building Societies Association (or, in Chapter 12, Bulk Supply Agreement) |
| BTH | British Thomson-Houston |
| BVA | British Radio Valve Manufacturers Association |
| EAW | Electrical Association for Women |
| EDA | British Electrical Development Association |
| FBI | Federation of British Industries |
| FTC | Federal Trade Commission |
| GPO | General Post Office |
| HP | Hire Purchase |
| MTA | Mutual Trading Agreement (or, in Chapter 11, Motor Trade Association) |
| Northmet | North Metropolitan Power Supply Co. |
| PEP | Political and Economic Planning |
| RCA | Radio Corporation of America |
| RGD | Radio-Gramophone Development Co. |
| RMA | Radio Manufacturers Association |
| SMMT | Society of Motor Manufacturers and Traders |
| TCMA | Telephone Cable Manufacturers Association |
| TDA | Telephone Development Association |
| VCMA | Vacuum Cleaner Manufacturers Association |

## Note on Currency

In this text pre-decimal currency is used: £1 = 20 shillings (s) = 240 old pence (d). In contemporary writings shillings were sometimes denoted by the symbol /-. This is not used in the general text, but is retained when it appears in direct quotes.

# 1

# Introduction

During the twentieth century 'affluence' (both at the level of the individual household and society as a whole) became intimately linked with the ownership of a range of prestige consumer durables. Success at both levels came to be measured through the yardstick of personal transport (particularly the car); 'white goods' (the washing machine, refrigerator, and vacuum cleaner, and later the dishwasher); entertainment durables (radios, televisions, and various incarnations of machines for playing recorded music); and—the most important durable 'good'—owner-occupied housing, incorporating modern utilities.

By the late 1950s diffusion rates for cars, refrigerators, and similar durables were being used as proxies for national differences in living standards.[1] In the United States the mass diffusion of durables was seen as both a vindication of the free-enterprise system and a weapon for winning hearts and minds during the Cold War. For example, when Richard Nixon confronted Nikita Khrushchev in front of the world's press at the 1959 American Exhibition in Moscow, he chose a 'typical American house' exhibit, featuring a modern kitchen, with built-in washing machine, as his backdrop. Nixon pointed out that, contrary to the Russian press's derision of the American claim that such standards of domestic luxury were within the means of ordinary US workers, a government guaranteed veteran's mortgage enabled a steelworker earning $3 an hour to buy this $14,000 house for $100 a month.[2]

Making consumer durables available to the masses typically entailed producing them in very large quantities. Many new household durables involved significant research and development costs. Some, such as the telephone and car, were dependent on complementary investments in infrastructure. All required intensive marketing to establish strong brand loyalty and 'educate' the public regarding their merits. This involved expensive advertising in national newspapers and magazines, which was only cost-effective if offset against large sales. Technical economies of scale from 'mass production' are also emphasized in many accounts though, as this study will show, their importance during the pre-1939 era is often exaggerated. While the manufacture of most electrical or transport consumer durables involved production methods popularly associated with 'mass production'—such as moving assembly lines—these could be efficiently employed by both large and relatively

---

[1] See Jonathan Rees, *Refrigeration Nation: A History of Ice, Appliances, and Enterprise in America* (Baltimore, MD: Johns Hopkins University Press, 2013), 179.
[2] William Seafire, 'The Cold War's Hot Kitchen', *New York Times* (24 July 2009), A25.

small firms. Conversely true 'Fordist' mass production also involved the substitution of skilled workers by dedicated machine tools—an innovation that could only be efficiently employed by giant firms, as developing and installing such machine tools was extremely expensive. Virtually all British consumer durables manufacturers found such costs prohibitive throughout the inter-war period, even in the car industry (which, owing to the skilled nature of many processes, offered the greatest cost advantages for such substitution).

This book charts the origins of trends that would eventually transform these objects of modern life from being 'luxuries' to 'necessities' for most British families. We examine how producers and retailers of durable goods succeeded in creating 'mass' (though not universal) markets for products such as new suites of furniture, radios, modern housing, and installed electrical or gas appliances. Although inter-war Britain failed to match the diffusion rates of the United States or Canada—where refrigerators, telephones, and cars were also viewed as 'necessities' by a large proportion of households by the late 1920s—it nevertheless experienced a 'consumer durables revolution' compared to the Edwardian period. By the late 1930s, many working-class families might boast a relatively new three-piece suite and radio in the living room, a modern gas (or, very occasionally, electric) cooker in the kitchen, running hot water, electric lighting, and a substantially larger proportion of coordinated, modern furniture than would have been found in the homes of their parents' generation. Furthermore, a substantial proportion (around a quarter of non-rural workers) would be living in modern semi-detached housing, with built-in utilities, mainly located in the suburbs.

White-collar workers' families were the most active participants in this new world of consumer durables. These often had insufficient income to employ a live-in servant, given the increasing range of job opportunities open to single women after the First World War and the fact that most women preferred factory, shop, or office work to the long hours, low pay, and restricted freedom of the live-in servant. A variety of commentators, not least the expanding women's press, advised middle-class housewives to overcome this new incarnation of the 'servant problem' by employing labour-saving durables in modern, labour-saving homes (together with, perhaps, the help of a charlady for a few hours, or days, each week). Such families might have coordinated suites of furniture throughout the house, a vacuum cleaner and wash boiler to help with housework, and a modern, 'labour-saving' home, which they would be more likely to own (or be purchasing on mortgage) than their working-class counterparts. Yet only those towards the top end of the white-collar spectrum would be likely to own a car or phone, while refrigerators remained confined to a very small number of 'early adopters'.

Working-class families faced a more difficult challenge in accessing these consumer goods, given their much lower and less stable incomes and larger average numbers of dependent children, but were nevertheless active participants in the inter-war consumer durables revolution. By the late 1930s most working-class households had a radio (licensed or unlicensed), many had new suites of matching furniture, at least in the front room, and a large proportion—especially in urban areas—had access to mains electricity. Few owned a vacuum cleaner or electric washing machine, while (with the exception of a few men who used their mechanic skills to keep second-hand vehicles going) working-class car ownership was almost unknown. However, there was widespread ownership of cheaper labour-saving and transport durables, such as modern gas cookers, carpet sweepers, sewing machines, electric lamps and mantel clocks, bicycles, and (less commonly) motorcycles. Moreover, the expansion in modern suburban housing (both municipal and, to some extent, owner-occupied) to working-class families brought with it a range of consumer durables that were integral to the structure of the new houses, including electric wiring, internal plumbing and water heating systems, fitted baths, and indoor toilets.

## CREATING MASS MARKETS

Rising incomes during the 1920s and 1930s (for those in work), opened up new possibilities for mass markets in consumer durables. However, in order to capitalize on the potential demand for these new products, manufacturers and retailers had to overcome entrenched consumer resistance, based on widely accepted social norms and practices. Even 'respectable' Edwardian working-class families were typically content to confine their 'smart' furniture to the parlour, while home-ownership was not then seriously considered by most members of the working, or even lower-middle, classes. Both new furniture and house purchase typically required buying on 'credit'—a term which carried strong social stigma, particularly in respectable working-class communities. Moreover, while many families might wish to engage in 'conspicuous consumption', via one or a few prized possessions, such as a piano or gramophone in the parlour, few considered furnishing the house with new, coordinated goods as being a significant priority, or even a practical possibility. In an era before the welfare state the spectre of destitution was always present for such families, should an unexpected turn of fortune lead to a major interruption to their income. Extravagant spending on luxuries was thus seen as the antithesis of the self-reliance and prudence which underpinned 'respectable' Victorian families.

These values were transformed, in a relatively short space of time, by an inter-war 'consumer durables marketing revolution'. The opening salvo of this revolution was fired by Benjamin Drage in 1922, with the launch of an ambitious, visionary marketing strategy to sell suites of new furniture to 'Mr Everyman'—including generous credit terms and guarantees against the perceived risks of buying on credit. Drage's strategy, discussed in Chapter 2, had a major impact on both con-sumer durables advertising and credit provision. Drage's example influenced other firms seeking to create a mass market, both in furniture and in a range of high-ticket consumer durables. Another key influence on the new marketing techniques was the example of America, a country where popular attitudes towards instalment credit were rapidly transformed during the 1920s, from being the refuge of the profligate and reckless to providing an acceptable and rational way of 'getting ahead'. American influence was particularly important for goods such as radios and vacuum cleaners—where marketing innovations in the United States are discussed in separate chapters so that their impacts on British practice can be fully explored. New marketing approaches, which included lifestyle marketing, leisure- and event-orientated marketing, relationship marketing, door-to-door canvassing, and cross-promotions with related goods, collectively played a major role in both accelerating the diffusion of consumer goods and changing working-class attitudes and lifestyles.

## UNPICKING THE CHAIN OF DESIGN, PRODUCTION, MARKETING, AND PROFITS

The four case-study sections of this book explore the production and marketing process for different classes of consumer durables—'necessities of life' (housing and furniture); entertainment durables; white goods; and durables which reached the mass market in the United States, but not in Britain. Each section opens with a brief overview of the common characteristics of the class of goods under review and how this impacted on the challenge of marketing them to a mass public. This is followed by several sector-specific chapters, each having the same basic structure. After a brief outline of changes in production technology over this period, the 'value chain' for each sector is examined. The value chain concept illustrates the various stages of value-adding links during the production and distribution process for a good or service and the distribution of 'rents' between these stages. Key players at one stage of the chain (normally either manufacturing or retailing) typically take responsibility for coordinating the sequence of activities that comprise the overall production and marketing process; exert some degree of 'governance' over the chain's operation; and benefit from improving its systemic efficiency by building barriers to competition from firms outside the value chain and by accruing much of the increased profits that these barriers generate.[3]

*Rents* (defined as abnormally high profits, arising through scarcity) are typically generated through the development of barriers to entry which prevent them being bid down by competitors. *Governance* concerns the ability to exert control over other stages of the value chain so as to efficiently coordinate its activities, upgrade the outputs of the chain, and prevent actions that might threaten the rents of the key players. For example, Chapter 3 shows how the big inter-war furniture manu- facturers dictated designs to their suppliers and blocked manufacturer branding— a strategy which both ensured that design responded to retailers' perceptions of changing customer tastes and prevented any branding or product differentiation strategies by their contractors—that might have weakened retailers' dominance over the chain.

---

[3] See Raphael Kaplinsky, 'Globalisation and Unequalisation: What can be Learned from Value Chain Analysis?', *Journal of Development Studies*, 37 (2000), 117–46; Raphael Kaplinsky and Mike Morris, *A Handbook for Value Chain Research* (Brighton: Institute of Development Studies, 2002) <http://www.ids.ac.uk/ids/global/pdfs/VchNov01.pdf>.

Value chain analysis identifies the key players involved in organizing the production process so as to bring the good to the consumer in a particular format, quality, and price. Moreover, it sheds light on factors that might raise the price of the good beyond that which would prevail in truly competitive markets. For example, leading firms might employ high-cost marketing strategies to deter competitors, or, in cases where they enjoyed monopoly positions (through, for example, control over key patents) might seek to extract high profit margins on each good sold, rather than employing a mass marketing strategy. The early radio industry was subject to a monopoly exploitation strategy by Marconi, which had control over British radio patents. Marconi imposed a patent licensing system that allowed it to accrue a substantial part of the value-added on each set manufactured in Britain. This both substantially raised retail prices and had another, unintended, consequence—encouraging product innovation that succeeded in reducing patent fees, but raised manufacturers' component costs. Meanwhile a classic high-cost marketing strategy was employed in the vacuum cleaner sector, where Hoover introduced a 'push' strategy of intensive door-to-door selling, which was copied by other major manufacturers and rapidly became the industry norm.

Value chain governance is typically exerted either by producers (generally those commanding strategic technologies)—*producer-driven chains*; or by firms responsible for the final distribution of the good—*buyer-driven chains*. The buyer-driven model is more common for labour-intensive industries lacking firms with key technological advantages, such as furniture. Retailers in such chains have been described as 'manufacturers without factories', using unique combinations of research, design, sales, marketing, and financial services to act as strategic brokers between producers and consumers.[4] Producer-driven chains are more likely to be dominated by technology and/or scale-intensive firms.[5] For example, as discussed in Chapter 6, British vacuum cleaner production was dominated by two overseas multinationals—Hoover and Electrolux—which controlled not only design and production, but marketing and distribution, of their products. These firms largely integrated manufacture and sales, the role of the retailer often being relegated to inventory and credit provision.

For some sectors, such as house-building, radio manufacturing in the 1930s (after Marconi's fundamental patents had expired) and, to some extent, white goods, rents, and governance were exerted at multiple stages of the chain by different players—a pattern also commonly found in modern value chains.[6] In such cases, value chain control was often vigorously contested. For example, in the 1930s radio valve manufacturers sought to dominate the radio value chain, though major independent manufacturers resisted this and were ultimately successful in gaining the balance of power. Similarly in house-building, the building societies—which

[4] Gary Gereffi, 'A Commodity Chains Framework for Analysing Global Industries', in Institute of Development Studies, *Background Notes for Workshop on Spreading the Gains from Globalisation* (Brighton: Institute of Development Studies, 1999), 1–2 <http:www.ids.ac.uk/ids/global/conf/wkscf.html>.

[5] Kaplinsky, 'Globalisation and Unequalisation', 125.

[6] Kaplinsky and Morris, *Handbook for Value Chain Research*, 33.

controlled the all-important mortgage finance—sought to exert a degree of control over the chain through establishing a cartel that would enforce a 'code' of terms on house-builders. However, the very large number of building societies, together with competitive tensions between them, led to the eventual breakdown of this strategy. In each case the ultimate victors were those firms who controlled branding and marketing, rather than the providers of the intermediate goods—components and retail credit.

This outcome is in line with research on modern value chains, which finds that the stage of the chain which controls marketing (either at the point of sale or through strong producer branding and advertising) is typically able to both dominate the chain and to capture a disproportionate share of the profits from the overall production and distribution process. As Paul Duguid has shown, brands (including retail brands) play important roles in competition between firms at different vertical stages of the same value chain, in seeking to control the overall chain and the profits generated from it.[7] For example, in the housing market both building societies and house-builders engaged in substantial consumer advertising, while in white goods both manufactures and retailers—particularly power supply companies—developed strong consumer brands. However, in each case the brands which had greatest resonance for the consumer at the point of sale—those of the house-building firms and the power companies—gained the upper hand in the struggle for value chain dominance.

## THE STRUCTURE OF THIS BOOK

Value chains are influenced both by the production technology for the good in question and by the value and nature of the services it provides to the consumer. These factors are key to determining both the practicality of creating a mass market and the marketing strategies that might realistically be employed to this end. The sector-specific chapters are organized with this in mind, being grouped into four separate sections—to show how different product and production process characteristics influence both value chains and marketing strategies. Part I covers 'necessities of life'—furniture and housing. Both were 'essentials'; nevertheless, consumers were not obliged to engage in the market for new goods, owing to the existence of close substitutes. Furniture and housing enjoyed active 'second-hand' markets, while renting was regarded as the standard (and, for many people, the only) way of securing accommodation. Moreover, these were high-cost goods—furnishing a house throughout with new suites of furniture would cost several months' wages, while buying a new house would typically require a sum equal to more than two years' income.

Such purchases generally entailed credit agreements spanning several years—a practice that initially encountered strong consumer resistance, as both working- and

---

[7] Paul Duguid, 'Brands in Chains', in Teresa Da Silva Lopes and Paul Duguid (eds.), *Trademarks, Brands, and Competitiveness* (London: Routledge, 2010), 138–64.

many middle-class families regarded debt as 'a millstone round your neck'. The story of mass marketing in these sectors is thus not just one of convincing people of the inherent value of the products, but of creating a desire for ownership and persuading purchasers that taking on extensive debts to achieve this was both practicable and worthwhile. Marketers devoted much time to portraying such investments as safe, morally acceptable, and as integral to providing a better future, both for the purchasers and their children.

Part II looks at the principal entertainment consumer durable of the era, radio. Radio achieved extremely rapid diffusion compared to the other products discussed in this book, despite the fact that radios typically cost the equivalent of around two weeks' wages for a skilled manual worker. Entertainment radio offered extremely valuable services relative to its cost, constituting a classic 'counter-status luxury'—a good which is more highly prized by those on low incomes, as they are less able to afford the more expensive entertainment services it substitutes for.[8] As many of the key marketing innovations in radio were pioneered in the United States, this section starts with a chapter on how radios were marketed there. Both Britain and America witnessed rapid household diffusion of radios, though in the United States higher incomes and cheaper motorized transport gave rise to a marketing device which was not significantly used in Britain (for radio): door-to-door canvassing. Meanwhile, as discussed in the following UK chapters, the British radio market was tightly controlled by trade associations and patent pools—particularly (prior to the early 1930s), Marconi's patent monopoly. This imposed high prices on consumers, though—given the immense popularity of radio—people were prepared to pay the substantial cost of a 'wireless' and the radio rapidly became ubiquitous in middle-class (and, by the late 1930s, working-class) homes.

Part III examines the marketing of 'white goods'—labour-saving electric and gas appliances. These constituted a much lower priority for households than radios; thirty minutes of entertainment was considered more valuable than reducing the time taken for housework by thirty minutes; especially given that the work white goods substituted for was typically done by the housewife rather than the husband, who, as 'breadwinner' had considerable influence over decisions involving large purchases, especially on credit. Moreover, while the radio was typically situated in the 'lounge' or 'parlour' and constituted a major status symbol, akin to the piano of the Edwardian house, a vacuum cleaner under the stairs or a washing machine in the kitchen was much less visible to visitors and thus provided little social kudos.

White goods thus required a much stronger element of 'push' marketing. For power-hungry appliances such as wash boilers, electric fires, and refrigerators, electricity and gas supply undertakings proved the key actors in the value chain—vigorously promoting appliance ownership in an effort to expand power sales (and counter competition from the rival utility). Such competition included particularly generous hire purchase (HP) terms and heavy investment in promotion and canvassing. Yet they still found it difficult to overcome consumer resistance for

---

[8] D. S. Landes, *The Unbound Prometheus: Technological Change and Industrial Development in Western Europe from 1750 to the Present* (Cambridge: Cambridge University Press, 1969), 428.

goods that were expensive (both in terms of purchase and running costs), had close substitutes, and offered relatively low status benefits. The first chapter in this section looks at white goods in general, while the following two discuss an alternative strategy adopted by vacuum cleaner manufacturers—raising and mobilizing an army of door-to-door salesmen. Chapter 9 looks at the United States, where the door-to-door selling system was pioneered prior to the First World War, while Chapter 10 examines its introduction in Britain during the 1920s and the notoriety which it came to enjoy by the 1930s.

Two classes of product that diffused very slowly in Britain, compared to North America—cars and telephones—are examined in Part IV. In each case the product was conceived as a 'luxury' in Britain, while becoming a 'necessity' for many people in the United States and Canada. The slow diffusion of cars in Britain is a complex story, involving both supply and demand constraints. The British motor trade viewed the car as a luxury product with a market effectively confined to the middle class, in contrast to Henry Ford's visionary approach of producing a standardized car within the financial reach of the typical American family. However, there is some justification to the British manufacturers' viewpoint. Given a smaller population and lower average household incomes, the potential market for cars was too small to sustain the high fixed costs of the specialist machine tools required for Fordist mass production, raising minimum unit production costs. Cars were thus less 'affordable' in Britain, despite more generous credit terms than in the United States.

Moreover, cars were less inherently desirable in Britain than in the United States, where households were often prepared to spend a substantial proportion of their incomes on them, prioritizing automobiles over other consumer durables. Britain was a much smaller, more densely populated, and urbanized country, with a highly developed public transport system. America had a large number of farmers and rural families who were attracted to the Model T, both as a way of freeing them from their isolation and as a 'work-horse' to take products to market or themselves to work. Conversely, the main customers for lower-priced cars in Britain were the professional classes, who often preferred using taxis to bearing the stigma of only being able to buy a 'utility' car.

The British state, specifically the Treasury, also successfully restricted car ownership, through high petrol and vehicle taxation. While these formed major sources of government revenue, the Treasury was chiefly concerned about minimizing any continuing and growing government commitment to roads expenditure that might threaten its policy of minimum, balanced government budgets. Meanwhile, the overriding wish of the Treasury to constrain public expenditure, even on remunerative infrastructure investments, forms the central reason for Britain's failure to develop a mass market in the final class of good examined in this study—the telephone. Treasury opposition to investment in the nationalized telephone network, or on marketing the telephone service, resulted in Britain having both one of the most poorly developed telephone networks of any industrialized country during the 1920s, together with some of the highest phone charges anywhere in the world (again, in a deliberate attempt to delay the growth of the network). The Treasury's habit of depressing sales of durable 'luxury' goods, in order to achieve its wider macroeconomic objectives, was to resurface after the Second World War, with devastating consequences for Britain's consumer durables industries.

Finally this study concludes by examining the implications of the 'consumer durables marketing revolution' for suppliers and consumers, together with the impacts of the marketing techniques developed during the 1920s and 1930s on the longer-term evolution of British economic development, living standards, and mass consumption. The inter-war period is shown to be an important first stage in the development of a 'mass market' for the types of goods which came to be considered as key symbols of the post-war 'affluent society'. The social consequences included the growing acceptability of buying on credit; new, more materially orientated norms for status and respectability—based around the ownership and coordinated display of prestige durables; and lifestyles increasingly based around the home and family. As such, the inter-war years are shown to represent a key transition phase from the Victorian era of sharp class divisions in purchasing habits, possessions, and aspirations, to the post-war model of a more mobile, aspirational society; a process in which these attempts to create mass markets for consumer durables played no small role.

## RECONSTRUCTING THE INTER-WAR CONSUMER DURABLES REVOLUTION

The last fifty years have witnessed a dramatic decline in Britain's consumer durables industries, in a process of liquidation, takeover, and merger that has generally not been kind to their corporate archives. Thus many firms that were once household names, such as Electrolux, Hotpoint, Drage's, Smart Brothers, and Times Furnishing Co., have left no significant archival records of their inter-war activities. For these sectors and for house-building (where firm survival has been better, but few companies have significant accessible archives) the main corporate documents used for this study are often published brochures, catalogues, adverts, and other marketing materials.

Corporate archives for radio manufacturers have better survival, largely owing to the efforts of a small group of dedicated enthusiasts, such as the late Gordon Bussey. This study has drawn on a number of valuable collections, including the Marconi Archives (at Oxford's Radcliffe Science Library), the corporate archives of Philips and EMI, together with museum-based records for Pye (National Media Museum, Bradford), Ferranti (Manchester Museum of Science and Industry), and Ekco (Southend Central Museum). I have also utilized a number of US-based radio industry archives, including the Smithsonian Museum's George H. Clark Radioana Collection and the Hagley Museum's archive for RCA-Victor. Motor vehicle manufacturers' archives have also been relatively well preserved (again partly thanks to the efforts of enthusiasts), with the development of archival centres with a specific remit for this sector, such as the University of Warwick's Modern Records Centre. The BT Archives hold an extremely rich collection of material for the Post Office's telecommunications activities, while other archives that I found particularly useful include the National Gas Archives and the Manchester Museum of Science and Industry's electricity supply sector archival collections.

Trade journals such as *Cabinet Maker* and *Wireless and Gramophone Trader* provided valuable information on their industries, while collections of marketing ephemera, such as the Bodleian's John Johnson Collection and the National Library of Art's Trade Catalogues collection also proved extremely useful. However, industry data only tell one side of the story. This study also benefits from extensive analysis of first-hand testimonies of people who lived through the period under discussion, preserved in oral history archival collections, or in published autobiographies. These mainly record people's experience as consumers though, in the case of the vacuum cleaner sector, I drew extensively on testimonies for people who had worked as door-to-door vacuum salesmen. Social surveys constituted a further source of much useful information, providing a contemporary commentary on both patterns of consumer durables ownership and their motivations. Most of these sources are available thanks to individuals who realized their historical importance and secured their preservation in archives, museums, or libraries. I owe them a great debt, as without their efforts this study would not have been possible.

# 2

# The Economic and Social Background to the Consumer Durables Revolution

## INTRODUCTION

On the eve of the Second World War, those families who had been lucky enough to avoid long-term unemployment typically enjoyed substantially higher living standards than their parents' generation had endured in the years before 1914. Their improved lifestyles included access to an array of durable goods that many people regarded as 'necessities' in 1939, but would have been beyond the dreams of their parents twenty-five years earlier. This was partly the result of the interaction between three interrelated trends: rising real wages; falling fertility rates; and an expansion and liberalization of consumer credit—to make goods that cost several weeks', months', or (in the case of housing) years' income 'affordable'.

This chapter examines each of these trends. It then discusses their impacts on household demand for durable goods; goods that are technically not classified as durables but have broadly similar characteristics (such as housing); and substitutes for durables, such as domestic servants. Demand for durable goods is shown to have risen substantially faster than incomes, producing a major rise in their share of total consumer expenditure. Moreover, there is no simple linear relationship between movements in durables' consumption and incomes. For some classes of goods, such as radios and motor vehicles, technological change also played a key role. However, for others, such as furniture, the timing of the consumer boom can only be fully explained in terms of successful marketing, which changed consumer attitudes both towards the product itself, and towards the moral propriety of purchasing it on credit (and thereby going into debt).

## REAL WAGES AND HOUSEHOLD INCOMES

Late Victorian Britain had already witnessed significant growth in living standards. Real wages rose by an estimated 1.58 per cent per annum over 1882–99, subsequently slowing to 0.29 per cent per annum over 1899–1913. Meanwhile white-collar workers' incomes rose faster, raising total annual incomes growth (for wages and salaries) to 1.71 per cent over 1882–99 and 0.58 per cent from 1889–1913.[1] Real

[1] C. H. Feinstein, 'What Really Happened to Real Wages? Trends in Wages, Prices, and Productivity in the United Kingdom, 1880–1913', *Economic History Review*, 43 (1990), 329–55 (344–6).

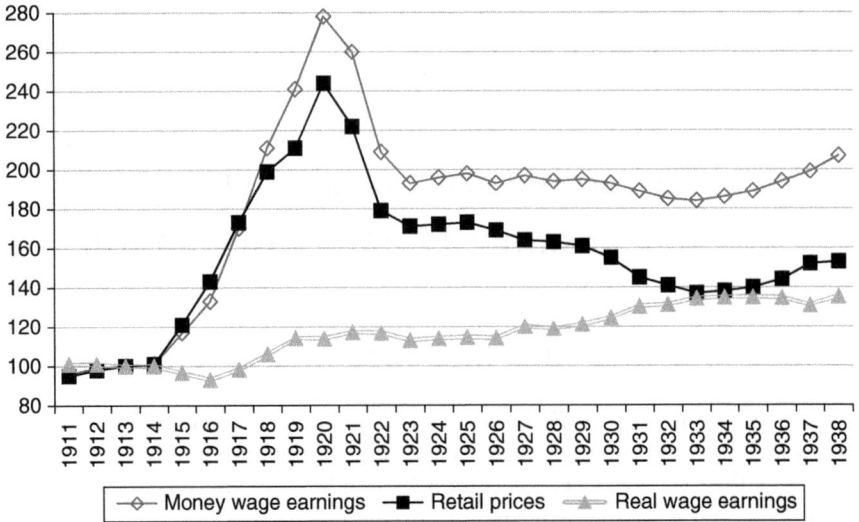

**Fig. 2.1.** Money wage earnings, retail prices, and real wage earnings, 1913–38 (1913 = 100)

*Source*: C. H. Feinstein, *National Income: Expenditure and Output in the United Kingdom 1855–1965* (Cambridge: Cambridge University Press, 1972), Table T140.

*household* income growth was markedly lower, however, owing to declining labour force participation rates for women and children.

The period from 1914–38 witnessed further substantial, though uneven, rises in real incomes. Figure 2.1 illustrates movements in weekly wage earnings (i.e. manual workers' incomes) over 1911–38: showing indices of money earnings; retail prices; and real (inflation-adjusted) earnings; all three series being set at 100 for 1913. The First World War witnessed rapid inflation, with earnings struggling to keep pace with prices over 1915–17. However, retail prices peaked in 1920 and then experienced a long-term fall until the mid-1930s. Money wages also fell, though less steeply, with real wages being broadly stable over 1919–26 at around 14 per cent above 1913 values. Thereafter real wages rose substantially, peaking at 35 per cent above 1913 levels in 1934. Despite a resumption of inflation after 1933, they remained at this level (apart from the 1937 recession) until 1938.

These averages exclude salaried workers and mask significant changes in the distribution of earnings for manual workers with different skill levels. On the eve of the First World War unskilled workers' earnings had averaged around 64 per cent of those of skilled manual workers while semi-skilled workers earned around 70 per cent of skilled workers' wages. Clerks' earnings were roughly on a par with skilled manual workers (though clerks benefited from much greater stability and security of employment). Meanwhile foremen earned around 14 per cent more than skilled workers managerial workers, around twice as much, and lower professionals around 55 per cent more.

The First World War witnessed substantial redistributions of income, both from the upper and middle classes to the working class and from skilled to less skilled manual workers. The war economy produced a shortage of skilled labour that was addressed largely through the substitution of skilled workers by machinery manned by semi-skilled workers or virtually unskilled machine minders. Thus, while reduced wage differentials between skilled and less skilled workers over the war years reflected flat-rate wage increases that had the largest proportionate impact on those with the lowest wages, there was an underlying rationale for this in that traditional skills were becoming less important and the productivity gap between skilled and less skilled workers (with the new machinery) had narrowed.[2] Unskilled male workers' earnings were around 17 per cent higher in real terms by 1922/24 compared to 1913/14, while skilled and semi-skilled male workers' earnings had increased by only 5 per cent. Clerks had done little better, with an average real earnings increase of 6 per cent.[3]

Wage rises during the war years also had a significant long-term impact on over-all working-class living standards, raising the average growth of real wages from 0.9 per cent per annum over 1920–38 to 1.21 per cent over 1913–38.[4] Meanwhile war production also boosted the growth of a number of key industries that were to play important direct or indirect roles in inter-war consumer goods provision, such as road transport, electricity supply, electrical machinery, and wooden goods, while also stimulating cost-reducing innovations to economize on scarce skilled labour.

Narrower income differentials between skilled and unskilled workers persisted during the 1920s and 1930s, compared to 1914, though skilled and semi-skilled workers made up some of the differential lost during the war years. By 1935/36 unskilled male workers' real earnings were around 45 per cent in excess of 1913/14 levels, compared to gains of 37 per cent for semi-skilled workers and 39 per cent for skilled workers. Clerks had only managed to increase their wages by 37 per cent, though two other classes of salaried male workers had done substantially better: administrators and managers (with a 56 per cent gain in real earnings between 1913/14 and 1935/6) and foremen (with a 71 per cent gain).[5]

The inter-war years are often depicted as an era of depression and stagnation for the working class, characterized by mass unemployment, especially during the early 1920s and early 1930s. There is a great deal of truth in this, though it masks considerable regional and local differences, together with important variations between sectors. While regions dominated by staple export industries and agricul-ture had high unemployment throughout this period, with the jobless total rising to more than 25 per cent in some regions during the worst depression years, unemployment in London, and in the rest of the South East, stood at 13.5 and 14.3 per cent respectively at the trough of the depression in 1932 and had fallen

[2] Sidney Pollard, *The Development of the British Economy 1914–1950* (London: Edward Arnold, 1962), 86.

[3] Sources: earnings, Guy Routh, *Occupation and Pay in Great Britain 1906–60* (Cambridge: Cambridge University Press, 1965), 104; retail prices, C. H. Feinstein, *National Income, Expenditure, and Output in the United Kingdom, 1855–1965* (Cambridge: Cambridge University Press, 1972), T140.

[4] George R. Boyer, 'Living Standards 1860–1939', in Roderick Floud and Paul Johnson (eds.), *The Cambridge Economic History of Modern Britain*, vol. II: *Economic Maturity, 1860–1939* (Cambridge: Cambridge University Press, 2004), 280–313 (284).

[5] Sources: earnings, Routh, *Occupation and Pay*, 104; retail prices, Feinstein, *National Income*, T140.

to less than 7 per cent by 1937.[6] The South East and West Midlands had high concentrations of expanding industries mainly serving domestic demand, such as motor vehicles, electrical engineering, and branded food, drink, toiletries, and other fast-moving household products. Greater London benefited from the rapid growth of both these sectors and more traditional light consumer goods industries such as clothing, furniture, printing, and leather goods.[7] London and its hinterland were also the main beneficiaries of the major expansion in inter-war service sector employment, in areas such as transport, utilities, retailing, and, above all, clerical work.

The period from 1913–38 thus witnessed both a substantial increase in real incomes for those lucky enough to avoid long-term unemployment and some reduction in income differentials among the largest groups of male employees (manual and clerical workers). Meanwhile, the effects of rising real earnings on discretionary incomes (that proportion of income left over after meeting the cost of necessities such as food, clothing, and shelter) were reinforced by a trend towards smaller families. A long-term fertility decline had been initiated by the middle classes in the third quarter of the nineteenth century and by the 1870s had already diffused to most sections of the working class.[8] Fertility is commonly measured using the *total fertility rate*—the average number of children that would be born to a woman over her lifetime, assuming that she survived until the end of her reproductive life. In the first half of the 1870s a woman in England and Wales who survived through her childbearing years would have an average of 4.81 children, though by 1911–15 this had fallen to only 2.83 (compensated for by a substantial rise in the probability of each child living to adulthood). Simon Szreter has convincingly argued that this can be explained in terms of the rising perceived relative (material and non-material) costs of childbearing. For the middle classes these costs were measured against the need to maintain a certain observed standard of living, while for the working classes they were dominated by the chronic economic uncertainty which characterized the lives of the vast majority of households.[9]

Declining fertility continued over the inter-war period. A woman marrying in 1921–5 would, on average, have had 2.39 children. This fell to 2.00 during 1926–30 and 1.79 during 1931–8. In other words, the number of births had fallen to a level insufficient to maintain the population at its current level. In 1920 children under 15 comprised 28.2 per cent of the UK population; by 1938 this had fallen to 21.9 per cent.[10] As in previous decades, fertility rates were inversely related to income. Fertility rates for women under 45 at the time of their first marriage, who married during 1930–4, were estimated to vary from 1.38 for salaried employees

[6] W. R. Garside, *British Unemployment 1919–1939: A Study in Public Policy* (Cambridge: Cambridge University Press, 1990), 10.

[7] See Peter Scott, *Triumph of the South: A Regional Economic History of Early Twentieth Century Britain* (Aldershot: Ashgate, 2007), 121–60.

[8] Robert Woods, *The Demography of Victorian England and Wales* (Cambridge: Cambridge University Press, 2000), 116–22.

[9] Simon Szreter, *Fertility, Class and Gender in Britain, 1860–1940* (Cambridge: Cambridge University Press, 1996).

[10] Feinstein, *National Income*, T121–3.

to 2.27 for manual wage-earners (excluding unskilled labourers), 2.33 for agricultural workers, and 3.01 for unskilled labourers. Nevertheless, manual wage-earners (excluding unskilled labourers and agricultural workers) had the most rapid inter-war fertility decline of any occupational group in the 1946 Family Census other than salaried employees.[11]

The reasons for such a sharp decline in fertility are unclear, though, in common with the late Victorian and Edwardian periods, the rising perceived costs of child-bearing appear to have been a key factor. Absolute costs were raised both by rising expectations regarding standards of child care (a trend already clearly evident in the late Victorian period) and by a 1918 increase in the minimum school-leaving age from 12 to 14, which increased the time over which each child would have to be entirely supported by their parents by 16.7 per cent. However, there is evidence that at least some working-class families were beginning to view the costs of child rearing from the perspective of seeking to maintain a certain minimum acceptable standard of living. This was strongly associated with the adoption of new, suburban lifestyles, as shown by a recent study of working-class migrants to owner-occupied suburban housing during the 1930s.[12]

Low fertility rates for salaried employees facilitated occupational mobility between the manual working class and salaried (principally clerical) occupations. Clerical employment was undergoing rapid expansion, the number of male clerks rising by 4 per cent from 1911–21 and a further 11 per cent from 1921–31, by which time they numbered around 817,000. There was no census in 1941, though it appears likely that a large proportion of the 21 per cent increase in clerical employment from 1931–51 occurred in the 1930s.[13] As the army of clerks grew faster than the entry of clerks' children into the workforce, much of the deficit was drawn from the ranks of the working class (especially skilled workers' children). Growing numbers of clerks formed part of a broader trend for the expansion of the middle classes to occur mainly towards the lower end of its income spectrum— which was accessible to those with the education levels provided to some working-class children, especially when they faced limited numbers of competitors from the more generously resourced offspring of salaried employees.

## MAKING HIGH VALUE DURABLES 'AFFORDABLE': THE EXPANSION OF 'EASY TERMS'

One major obstacle to expanding the market for consumer durables was the shame and secrecy associated with debt—particularly for 'luxury' and high value goods.

---

[11] D. V. Glass and E. Grebenik, *The Trend and Pattern of Fertility in Great Britain: A Report on the Family Census of 1946*, Papers of the Royal Commission on Population, Volume 6 (London: HMSO, 1954), 110 and 207. Based on fertility after twenty years of marriage (which approximates to completed fertility. Data involve an element of projection.

[12] See Peter Scott, 'Did Owner-Occupation Lead to Smaller Families for Interwar Working-Class Households?', *Economic History Review*, 61 (2008), 99–124.

[13] Routh, *Occupation and Pay*, 25.

This was not unique to Britain; in the United States instalment purchase had been widely viewed as not being 'respectable', though it appears to have been more so than in Britain—being accepted as a necessary evil for high value items such as pianos, sewing machines, or furniture. Moreover, credit achieved respectability somewhat more rapidly than in the UK—a process said to have helped fuel the US consumer durables revolution of the 1920s.[14] This transformation in popular attitudes was achieved through a major propaganda campaign by American manufacturers and retailers of high-ticket durables that sought to replace the traditional depiction of instalment purchase as embodying recklessness, lack of self-control, and a short-term outlook, with a new story of credit being a rational and respectable form of budgeting. Thus terms such as 'easy payments' were replaced by 'budget plans', 'thrift accounts', and 'preferred buyer plans'.[15]

Despite their misgivings, many British working-class families also found it necessary to use some form of consumer credit in an era when manual workers (and many low-salaried white-collar employees) did not have access to overdrafts or bank loans. For small durables, such as glassware, crockery, cutlery, and pocket watches, 'draw clubs' were already popular before 1914. These were effectively rotating credit vehicles, where a group of twenty people might agree to each pay in, say, a shilling per week for twenty-one weeks—each weekly take being assigned to one member via a lottery. After twenty weeks everyone would have received £1 and the person running the club would get the twenty-first payment (the 'poundage') as a reward for their effort.

Clubs were vigorously promoted by retailers, mail order firms being particularly active. Many mail order retailers traced their origins to Victorian watch, clock, and jewellery manufacturers, who set up 'watch clubs' (typically draw clubs) to market their products—later extending their geographical reach via club catalogues.[16] By the inter-war period these sold a wide range of merchandise; for example, John Noble Ltd of Manchester's 1935 'Ideal Club' catalogue ran to 434 pages and included clothing and footwear, carpets, rugs, and linoleum, and a broad assortment of household goods and equipment.[17] Mail order houses relied on community-based (often female) organizers, who recruited and vetted membership and policed payments. This policing function became more important when some mail order firms moved from draw clubs to clubs where customers only had to make the first payment to take receipt of goods—i.e. outright credit sales. Yet the fact that the two mail order firms that came to dominate the market by the late 1930s, Littlewoods and Great Universal Stores, used draw clubs points to the continued vitality of this system—possibly reflecting the fact that working-class households

[14] Martha L. Olney, *Buy Now, Pay Later: Advertising, Credit, and Consumer Durables in the 1920s* (Chapel Hill, NC: University of North Carolina Press, 1991), 86.

[15] Lendol Calder, *Financing the American Dream: A Cultural History of Consumer Credit* (Princeton, NJ: Princeton University Press, 1999), 180–204.

[16] Richard Coopey, Sean O'Connell, and Dilwyn Porter, *Mail Order Retailing in Britain: A Business and Social History* (Oxford: Oxford University Press, 2005), 16.

[17] Peter Scott collection, John Noble Ltd, *John Noble's Ideal Club Catalogue* (Manchester: John Noble Ltd, 1935), 1.

who viewed credit as disreputable did not perceive draw club membership as debt.[18] Clubs were also extensively used by stores and other traders (such as coal merchants).

The club system appears to have been free of any significant problem of bad debts and was particularly popular with working-class families. Club credit avoided the stigma associated with other forms of credit, owing to its 'associational' element (in common with friendly society and trade union saving schemes) and the fact that clubs combined credit with saving—indeed many families did not regard their use as going into debt. Interest rates were lower than for other forms of retail credit, as the 5 per cent poundage fee was paid only at the end of the loan term. Using community-based part-time organizers also mitigated the risks of mounting indebtedness, associated with the high pressure sales tactics often attributed to check trading and hire purchase agents.[19]

Check trading was a form of voucher credit, whereby borrowers received 'checks' (vouchers) for use in a range of specified local shops, which they repaid in weekly instalments. Customers paid a 5 per cent poundage fee with their first instalment, while check traders also received further income from retailers, as checks were redeemed from them at a discount to their face value.[20] Unlike clubs, which were typically organized by community-based part-time agents, check traders used full-time canvassers/collectors, the cost of which made checks more expensive than the club system. Stores which accepted checks offset heavy commissions to check providers by increasing their price mark-ups, further increasing the effective interest rate.[21] Again, there are no estimates of the annual volume of check credit, though this was clearly substantial; the largest check trader, Provident, loaned £18.1 million annually by 1939, with a customer base equivalent to just over 2 per cent of the UK population, and agreements with 14,000 retailers.[22]

However, for most of the goods considered in this study hire purchase (HP) was the dominant form of instalment credit. This was generally considered the most suitable credit mechanism for expensive durables with a substantial second-hand value. HP differed from conventional instalment credit in that goods were technically 'hired' until final payment was received and could thus be immediately repossessed following a missed payment. Thus, while retailers using other forms of credit had to sue defaulters in the courts as ordinary debtors, HP traders could simply repossess the goods, which remained their property until the end of the contract.[23] Like instalment credit in the United States, it thus both avoided the legal protections

[18] Coopey, O'Connell, and Porter, *Mail Order*, 92–3 and 98.

[19] Peter Scott and James T. Walker, 'Working Class Household Consumption Smoothing in Interwar Britain', *Journal of Economic History*, 72 (2012), 797–825 (800–1).

[20] Paul Johnson, *Saving and Spending: The Working-Class Economy in Britain 1870–1939* (Oxford: Oxford University Press, 1985), 153; Sean O'Connell and Chris Reid, 'Working-Class Consumer Credit in the UK, 1925–60: The Role of the Check Trader', *Economic History Review*, 58 (2005), 378–405 (394–5); Margaret Bondfield, *Our Towns: A Close-Up* (London: Oxford University Press, 1944), 58.

[21] Bondfield, *Our Towns*, 58.

[22] O'Connell and Reid, 'Working-Class Consumer Credit', 380–7.

[23] V. R. Fox-Smith, *Hire Purchase Organization and Management* (London: Pitman, 1932), 3.

accorded to those who used conventional retail credit and enabled the vendor to repossess following a missed payment, without having to pay any compensation.

HP had been used in Britain since around the second quarter of the nineteenth century and was adopted by Singer to market its sewing machines from the 1860s. However, it was only during the inter-war years that it became a central element in working-class credit for durable goods. One contemporary study claimed that the volume of HP trading had increased some twenty-fold between 1918 and 1938.[24] Trade sources suggest that by the late 1930s HP accounted for more than 70 per cent of sales for cars and bicycles, working-class furniture, electrical household equipment, pianos, and sewing machines. A Board of Trade document put the annual value of consumer HP sales in the late 1930s at around £100–120 million, or about half of all consumer credit.[25]

HP had a number of attractive features. It enabled consumers to match the stream of utility derived from durable goods with the stream of payments and assisted them in committing a set portion of income to such expenditure, by imposing the external discipline of contract.[26] However, the system was subject to widespread condemnation, on account of the abuses with which it was rife. One common criticism involved its typically high interest costs. HP interest rates were in excess of 25 per cent in many cases (and sometimes considerably higher), though weekly charges were kept 'affordable' by extending contracts over increasingly long periods. While bad debts were relatively low, dealing with large numbers of payments of relatively small value, from people who generally did not have bank accounts, together with chasing up arrears, imposed heavy collection and clerical costs that inevitably made HP a costly form of credit.[27] High interest rates were often disguised by quoting a rate based on the original cost, rather than the diminishing balance. This might make the real interest rate double, or more, the 'headline' rate, depending on the length of the agreement.[28]

HP constituted a substantial and inflexible commitment of future income and thus made customers extremely vulnerable to poverty in the event of illness or unemployment—which was a significant risk over the lifetime of the loan.[29] This, together with high interest rates, made it a less-than-ideal credit vehicle from the customer's perspective. Yet in both respects it was not clearly more onerous than, say, American instalment finance contracts. The most objectionable feature of the system was its abuse by unscrupulous traders to perpetrate various (often perfectly legal) 'cons' on unsuspecting consumers. Many HP contracts were deliberately written using phraseology so obscure that even well-educated people had great difficulty

[24] John Hilton, *Rich Man Poor Man* (London: Allen & Unwin, 1938), 133.

[25] The National Archives London [hereafter TNA], BT64/3430, 'Hire purchase and consumer goods'. Board of Trade memorandum, 12 Nov. 1943. It is not clear whether this would include draw clubs or informal credit at local shops.

[26] C. L. Bolling, *Hire Purchase Trading* (London: Pitman, 1935), pp. 5–6; Johnson, *Saving and Spending*, 221.

[27] Bolling, *Hire Purchase Trading*, 10.

[28] 'Hire Purchase Finance-II', *Economist* (14 Apr. 1934), 819–20.

[29] Peter Scott, 'The Twilight World of Interwar Hire Purchase', *Past & Present*, 177 (2002). 195–225 (208–10).

understanding them. For example, a defendant who appeared before Bedford County Court in 1937 was asked by the registrar if he understood the HP agreement he had signed and lightly replied, 'Yes.' 'That's funny', said the Registrar, 'because I have read it too, and I did not understand it at all'.[30] Furthermore, as it was common practice for traders not to give copies of HP contracts to customers, it was difficult for purchasers to check their contractual obligations during the course of the agreement.[31]

Such obfuscation opened the door to a number of common abuses. These were assisted by the primacy given to freedom of contract in English private law, underpinned by the fiction that equal bargaining power must normally be assumed to exist in all commercial transactions.[32] It was possible to write clauses into contracts which would appear extortionate to most observers yet were perfectly legal. One example concerned 'depreciation clauses', under which HP customers who then changed their minds and returned the goods had to pay a charge for depreciation, sometimes equal to 75 per cent or more of the total HP price.[33] For example, in 1926 Electrolux brought a case against the Revd W. H. Lloyd Oswell at Westminster County Court. Lloyd Oswell, who was over 80 and in very poor health, had been pressed to sign an agreement for two domestic appliances, but had repudiated it on the same day; nevertheless the machines were sent. Despite the fact that they had not been used, the firm claimed a total of £27 10s depreciation. The judge noted scathingly: 'You have only got to look at these machines and they depreciate. They are as delicate as a woman's reputation.'[34]

Agreements also often included clauses designed to remove or weaken customers' legal rights. For example, contracts usually granted owners a licence to enter the hirer's premises, sometimes even authorizing them to break in and forcibly remove valuables following default.[35] Most also contained a clause along the following lines: 'The owners do not give any warranty as to fitness or condition of the said goods, and any implied warranty is hereby expressly excluded.'[36] Where an HP finance company was the legal owner a longer clause was used, both exempting the firm from warranty and from liability for any claims made by the retailer. Such clauses exempted dealers both from promises made by their salesmen and from the implied warranty that would otherwise exist under the Sale of Goods Act, 1893, other statutes, and the common law, that goods should be fit for the purposes intended and of merchantable quality.[37] In one county court case, the judge

---

[30] 'The Hire Purchase Bill: Different Viewpoints', *Hire Purchase Journal*, 2 (Jan. 1938), 16–18.

[31] For discussion of this point in a contemporary court case, see 'Major and H.-P. Judge Speaks of Repudiated Contract', *Hire Traders' Record* (Oct. 1935), 4–5.

[32] David Sugarman and G. R. Rubin, 'Towards a New History of Law and Material Society in England 1750–1914', in G. R. Rubin and David Sugarman (eds.), *Law, Economy and Society, 1750–1914: Essays in the History of English Law* (Abingdon: Professional Books, 1984), 1–186 (12).

[33] E. S. Watkins, *Credit Buying* (London: Laidlaw & Laidlaw, 1939), 31.

[34] 'Judge on Canvassers', *Hire Traders' Record* (May 1926), 2.

[35] Bolling, *Hire Purchase Trading*, 100.

[36] C. B. Minshull, 'The Importance of the No Warranty Clause in Agreements', *Hire Purchase Trading* (July 1934).

[37] F. E. Sugden, 'Hire Purchase and the Law', *Hire Purchase Journal*, 1 (1937), 6–7.

interpreted the clause as: 'In other words, "we will sell you rubbish and you shall have no remedy".'[38]

Collecting payments was also rife with abuses; as a Lord Chancellor's Office memorandum noted: 'debtors are bullied and threatened...wives are terrorised with threats of their husbands being told, documents as much like county court documents as the firms dare to make them are sent to debtors...and...possession of the goods is often retaken without any compensation when large instalments have been paid'.[39] This last abuse, known as the 'snatch-back', was one of the most notorious features of the HP system. While most firms wanted payment in full rather than repossession, there was a significant proportion—including some who engaged in considerable advertising—that specialized in repossessing goods after most payments had been made. As goods were legally merely under hire until final payment was made, breach of contract allowed the vendor to summarily repossess them, with the purchaser having no legal right to any allowance for previous payments. By 1937 the number of repossessions was estimated at 600 per day.[40]

Firms commonly seized not only the goods on HP but additional goods, to cover alleged repossession costs.[41] For example, in 1928 Tottenham Magistrate's Court heard the case of a woman who, through illness, had got into arrears after £53 2s (out of £62 15s originally due) had been paid. While she was out the trader stripped her house of its possessions, with the exception of an overlay and two pillows. She was charged an additional £1 11s for the repossession, and offered an option to pay £3 11s to regain the goods, and then 15s a week until the debt was cleared—terms which led the magistrate to brand the firm 'robbers of the meanest order'.[42] The slightest delay could trigger repossession; many cases were reported of debtors who had almost completed contracts having their goods snatched within hours of missing a single payment.[43] A variation of the snatch-back was the 'linking-on' agreement, where hirers were approached towards the end of a contract and persuaded to buy more goods on the same terms. These were then added to the earlier agreement and, in the event of default, both the new and the earlier goods could be legally seized.[44] Allegations of forcible entry and trespass were common.[45] Many firms were said to employ 'bruisers' and there were numerous cases where traders or their henchmen were convicted of assault during repossessions, or hirers were convicted for assault in their attempts to stop them.[46]

---

[38] 'Scathing Comments by Judge', *Hire Purchase News* (22 Jan. 1931), 2; 'H.P. Firm Denies Responsibility', *Hire Purchase News* (26 Feb. 1931), 1.

[39] TNA, LCO2/1511, memorandum on HP regulation by Pritt, n.d., *c.*1937.

[40] House of Commons, *Parliamentary Debates*, CCCXXX (1937), col. 740.

[41] 'Hire Purchase Abuses', *The Times* (11 Dec. 1937), 9.

[42] A. Vallance, *Hire Purchase* (London: Thomas Nelson, 1939), 61–2.

[43] B. E. Astbury, 'The "Snatch-Back" System Menace', [letter] *The Times* (16 Dec. 1937), 15.

[44] 'Hire Purchase Bill – 1. Case for the Bill', *Economist* (16 Apr. 1938), 145–6; House of Commons, *Parliamentary Debates*, CCCXXX (1937), cols. 731–2.

[45] Bolling, *Hire Purchase Trading*, 101; Vallance, *Hire Purchase*, 68–9; House of Commons, *Parliamentary Debates*, CCCXXX (1937), col. 731.

[46] See, for example, *Hire Traders' Record* (Jan. 1923), 3; *Hire Traders' Record* (June 1932), 2; 'Hire Purchase Abuses', *The Times* (11 Dec. 1937), 9.

Organized HP interests appreciated that negative publicity acted to perpetuate the social stigma surrounding HP and thus constrain its growth.[47] Furthermore, 'responsible' firms resented what they saw as unfair competition from unscrupulous traders who could advertise better terms, such as a lower 'headline' interest rate, using the methods discussed above to hide the true cost. The industry's trade association, the Hire Traders' Protection Society, thus welcomed the opportunity of participating in an initiative launched by social reformers to get a private members bill before Parliament to counter some of the most notorious abuses. This initiative was also welcomed by government. Between 1931 and 1936 judgement summonses, largely (but not wholly) on account of HP agreements had risen from 267,000 to 327,000 a year,[48] while many customers had goods repossessed and were pressed for further payment without reference to the courts. Given the volume of cases and the publicity they received, pressure for reform was viewed as irresistible, government being on the point of setting up a committee of inquiry when news reached them of the bill.[49]

The 1938 Hire Purchase Act introduced various safeguard for consumers. While traders subsequently found ways of circumventing some of them, they were viewed at the time as important reforms. The Act sought to ensure that the hirer was given appropriate information, such as a copy of the agreement and written details of the cash price and the amount and date of instalments. Purchasers were also given more legal rights, such as the right to free themselves of liabilities under the contract (with some exceptions) if the goods were returned and half the purchase price had been paid; protection from repossession (in the absence of a court order) once a third of payments had been made; and the right to have any court case heard in the area where the purchaser lived. Other provisions addressed certain abuses by vendors; for example by prohibiting the notorious clauses which allowed the owner to forcibly enter the hirer's dwelling to repossess goods, and which obviated liability for any statements or promises made by the retailer.[50]

Both HP and other forms of consumer credit, such as clubs, were used most intensively by families towards the bottom end of the working-class income spectrum, for whom even relatively low value items, such as a pair of shoes, might strain weekly finances. However, their use was substantial for all sections of the working class. Evidence for middle-class credit use is much sparser, though HP appears to have been used extensively by the lower-middle classes. Meanwhile the high proportion of cars purchased on HP suggests that higher income groups also utilized this form of credit extensively for particularly expensive durables.[51]

---

[47] For example, Sean O'Connell's analysis of the inter-war motor vehicle market suggests that suspicion of, and embarrassment about, HP may have been a significant factor inhibiting the diffusion of car ownership during this period: Sean O'Connell, *The Car and British Society: Class, Gender, and Motoring, 1896–1939* (Manchester: Manchester University Press, 1998), 31.

[48] Vallance, *Hire Purchase*, 58.

[49] TNA, LCO2/1513, Lord Chancellor's Office memorandum, 25 Apr. 1938.

[50] E. Westby-Nunn, 'The New Hire Purchase Law Based on the New Hire Purchase Act, 1938', *International Accountants Journal*, 9 (1939), 13–20; Vallance, *Hire Purchase*, 123–30.

[51] See Scott, 'Twilight World', 201–3.

Consumer credit constituted one of several forms of 'committed' expenditure that families faced each week before further purchases were considered. Families also typically had various contractual savings and insurance policies against risks such as disruptions to income through unemployment, illness, or old age, together with the costs of medical expenses and funerals. As one report noted, 'Not only may sums be due to the moneylender, tallyman, clothing club, hire-purchase agent, etc., but also and at the same time to the insurance agent, Christmas club, hospital savings, and savings club.'[52] Analysis by Scott and Walker, using surviving returns from the Ministry of Labour's 1937–8 working-class household expenditure survey, estimated that consumer credit payments, together with contractual savings/insurance, accounted for 47 per cent of working-class income that was already 'committed' at the start of the week—the balance being made up of accommodation and travel to work costs. Total committed expenditures were found to account for 28.5 per cent of household income for families living on less than 50 shillings per week, the ratio declining for higher-income working-class families, to 23.6 per cent for those with household incomes over 120 shillings.[53] The greater commitments of lower-income families had an important impact on 'discretionary' expenditures, as these devoted a markedly higher proportion of their income to 'basic needs', such as food, shelter, fuel, and light. As Figure 2.2 shows, after committed expenditures and food costs, low-income families had only a relatively small proportion of their income left over for other expenses, though the proportion rose rapidly with income.

Consumer credit indebtedness was generally heaviest in the early years of the family life cycle. Starting a new household (typically on marriage, or after the arrival of the first child) constituted a major 'crisis' of expenditure, mainly owing to the costs of furnishing the home. Heavy HP costs for furniture and furnishings could extend over several years, significantly restricting the family's ability to make further durables purchases. However, HP enabled such families to deal with the expenditure 'crisis' that new household formation constituted, by spreading the costs over time.

HP and other credit mechanisms were relatively effective means of extending the availability of high-cost durables (subject to the problems outlined above), but were inefficient, in as much as they incurred high interest rates of around 25 per cent or more, reflecting heavy administrative costs. True interest costs were sometimes even greater, as prices for goods on HP and checks were said to be often substantially higher than for equivalent goods sold for cash (the evidence for clubs is less conclusive). High interest rates were inevitable; credit providers in the United States and France during the early post-1945 decades also found that the high administration costs of monitoring, collecting, and chasing up instalments made consumer credit unprofitable except at such rates.[54] Yet for poorer families, inflating the costs of durables and semi-durables by 25 per cent or more had a significant

[52] Women's Library, London Metropolitan University, Women's Group on Public Welfare, Box FL568, 5WFM/D/11, 'Enquiry into working-class credit', progress report, 1945.

[53] Scott and Walker, 'Working Class Household Consumption Smoothing in Interwar Britain', 816.

[54] J. G. Trumbull, 'Regulating for Legitimacy: Consumer Credit Access in France and America', paper presented at 2011 Economic History Association meeting, Boston, 6–16.

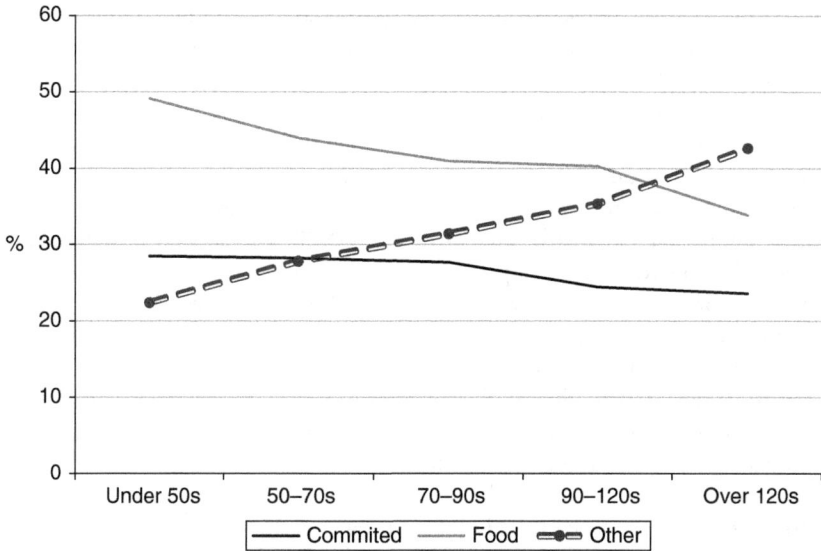

**Fig. 2.2.** The proportion of weekly household spending devoted to 'committed expenditures', food, and other expenditure, for working-class families, classified by weekly income, 1937–8

*Note:* Based on a sample of households that participated in the Ministry of Labour's 1937–8 working-class expenditure survey.

*Source:* Peter Scott and James Walker, 'Working Class Household Consumption Smoothing in Interwar Britain', *Journal of Economic History*, 72 (2012), 797–825 (818).

impact on quantities purchased, given that food and rental costs already tightly constrained available budgets for these items. HP and other forms of instalment credit thus substituted the constraint on consumption imposed by the lumpiness of expenditure with the weaker, but substantial constraint of higher effective prices. Meanwhile interruptions to earnings could often threaten both current consumption and accumulated 'investments' in goods purchased some months or years previously, for which final payment had not yet been made.

## A PROFILE OF THE BRITISH INTER-WAR 'CONSUMER DURABLES REVOLUTION'

A widely used definition of consumer durables is that of Simon Kuznets, who divided consumer goods into perishables (with an expected life of less than six months), semi-durables, which typically remain in service for six months to three years, and durables, which are typically employed in the use for which they were designed for more than three years.[55] Housing is typically treated as a service and is included in consumer expenditure data as annual accommodation costs. However, from a consumer's perspective, housing (especially owner-occupied housing) shares

[55] Simon Kuznets, *National Income and Capital Formation 1919–1935* (New York: NBER, 1937), 36.

many of the characteristics of a durable good and is examined alongside other consumer durables in this study. Indeed conceptually, housing is no different from consumer durables in that its demand is 'derived demand', derived from the stream of services it provides.

Table 2.1 shows estimates of consumer expenditure on housing, durables and related goods, and domestic service, in real (1938) prices, and as a proportion of total consumer expenditure. Average values for 1911–13 are shown, together with annual figures (at two-yearly intervals) from 1920–38. Housing expenditure is shown to have increased by 42.8 per cent from 1911–13 to 1938 and by 34.2 per cent over 1920–38. The increase was, however, much more modest in terms of housing's proportion of total consumer expenditure, which remained broadly stable from 1920 to the mid-1930s.

Yet these figures belie the rapid expansion in house construction and purchase over this period (and particularly in the 1930s). This reflects the nature of housing as both a necessity and a stock of very durable assets. During periods of very limited housing development—such as the Edwardian house-building slump, or the First World War—rents can be pushed up by a progressive failure to increase the housing stock in line with the number of households. Conversely, the major expansion in the housing stock from the mid-1920s to the late 1930s reduced the housing shortage and thus contributed to a faster decline in new housing prices than in general prices. Changes in building practices and building materials technologies reinforced this downward trend in house prices, as is discussed in Chapter 4. By 1939, Britain's 1914 housing stock had been increased by around 50 per cent, involving a considering upgrading of average housing dimensions, plot sizes, and amenities, though this translated into only a small increase in consumers' accommodation expenditure.

Two aggregate British data series are available for durable goods in this period, covering motor vehicles and household durables respectively. From 1920 household durables expenditure is further disaggregated, into major durables (such as furniture, floor coverings, and electrical appliances), and minor durables (such as household textiles and hardware). Vehicle running costs are also included in the table, given that these were integral to motor vehicle ownership and, typically, outweighed the annualized capital costs of vehicles during this period. Expenditure on motor vehicle purchases is shown to have risen by more than six-fold from 1911–13 to 1938, and to have reached 3.3 times its 1920 value in 1938. This is not surprising, given the limited technical development and slow diffusion of motor vehicles prior to the First World War. Vehicle running costs also rose sharply (partly owing to heavy taxation, as is discussed in Chapter 11), contributing to a major expansion in overall spending on personal transport.

Expenditure on household durables more than doubled in real terms between 1911–13 and 1938, while increasing by around 46 per cent over the inter-war years. Household durables' share of consumer expenditure peaked at 7.28 per cent in 1936, compared to only 3.85 per cent in 1913.

Table 2.1. Consumer expenditure at constant (1938) prices, 1911–13 to 1938 (£M and % of total)

| Year | | 1911–13 | 1920 | 1922 | 1924 | 1926 | 1928 | 1930 | 1932 | 1934 | 1936 | 1938 |
|---|---|---|---|---|---|---|---|---|---|---|---|---|
| A: Housing | (£M) | 319 | 339 | 343 | 349 | 359 | 375 | 388 | 399 | 412 | 434 | 455 |
| | (%) | 9.16 | 10.14 | 10.54 | 10.18 | 10.27 | 10.16 | 10.15 | 10.39 | 10.17 | 10.13 | 10.36 |
| B: Durables & related | | | | | | | | | | | | |
| Motor cars & motorcycles | (£M) | 6 | 13 | 11 | 21 | 26 | 28 | 27 | 25 | 36 | 48 | 43 |
| | (%) | 0.17 | 0.39 | 0.34 | 0.61 | 0.74 | 0.76 | 0.71 | 0.65 | 0.89 | 1.12 | 0.98 |
| Household durables: | (£M) | 134 | 186 | 178 | 193 | 206 | 233 | 247 | 261 | 294 | 312 | 272 |
| | (%) | 3.85 | 5.56 | 5.47 | 5.63 | 5.89 | 6.31 | 6.46 | 6.80 | 7.26 | 7.28 | 6.19 |
| Furniture, floor covering, electrical | (£M) | n.a. | 89 | 95 | 103 | 114 | 130 | 141 | 159 | 179 | 195 | 174 |
| | (%) | n.a. | 2.66 | 2.92 | 3.00 | 3.26 | 3.52 | 3.69 | 4.14 | 4.42 | 4.55 | 3.96 |
| Household textiles, hardware, etc. | (£M) | n.a. | 97 | 83 | 90 | 92 | 103 | 106 | 102 | 115 | 117 | 98 |
| | (%) | n.a. | 2.90 | 2.55 | 2.63 | 2.63 | 2.79 | 2.77 | 2.66 | 2.84 | 2.73 | 2.23 |
| Vehicle running costs | (£M) | 17 | 19 | 23 | 30 | 39 | 49 | 56 | 57 | 64 | 78 | 88 |
| | (%) | 0.48 | 0.57 | 0.71 | 0.88 | 1.12 | 1.33 | 1.47 | 1.48 | 1.58 | 1.82 | 2.00 |
| Total (durables & related) | (£M) | 157 | 218 | 212 | 244 | 271 | 310 | 330 | 343 | 394 | 438 | 403 |
| | (%) | 4.50 | 6.52 | 6.52 | 7.12 | 7.75 | 8.40 | 8.63 | 8.93 | 9.73 | 10.22 | 9.18 |
| C: Domestic service | (£M) | 194 | 82 | 85 | 88 | 91 | 94 | 97 | 100 | 104 | 107 | 110 |
| | (%) | 5.59 | 2.45 | 2.61 | 2.57 | 2.60 | 2.55 | 2.54 | 2.60 | 2.57 | 2.50 | 2.50 |
| Total consumer expenditure | (£M) | 3,479 | 3,343 | 3,254 | 3,428 | 3,496 | 3,690 | 3,822 | 3,839 | 4,051 | 4,285 | 4,392 |

Note: Data for 1911–13 include southern Ireland.

Source: C. H. Feinstein, *National Income: Expenditure and Output in the United Kingdom 1855–1965* (Cambridge: Cambridge University Press, 1972), T65–7.

This rise cannot be explained in terms of falling relative prices for durable goods; as Figure 2.3 shows, household durables witnessed lower price falls than for total retail goods and services over this period. After moving in line with general retail prices over 1911–13, household durables witnessed markedly higher inflation during the First World War and its immediate aftermath, as would be expected, given the diversion of output for many consumer durables manufacturers from civilian to munitions production. From around 1922 they again moved closely with retail prices and over 1922–38 their price decline of 14 per cent was only marginally less than that for all goods in the retail prices index (14.5 per cent). However, the apparent price stability of durable goods may reflect changes in the composition of the bundle of goods included in this category (such as a shift in expenditure towards more expensive classes of durables, or more expensive models within each class). In order to determine what really happened to durables' prices, analysis is required at the level of individual consumer durables sectors.

When the household durables series is diasaggregated into major and minor durables, divergent trends emerge. Spending on furniture, floor coverings, and electrical goods increased by 95 per cent over 1920–38, substantially raising their share of consumer expenditure. Conversely, spending on minor durables actually fell significantly as a proportion of total expenditure (but not in real terms) over this period. A similar trend is evident in the United States, where household expenditure on major durables expanded rapidly during the 1920s, while the share

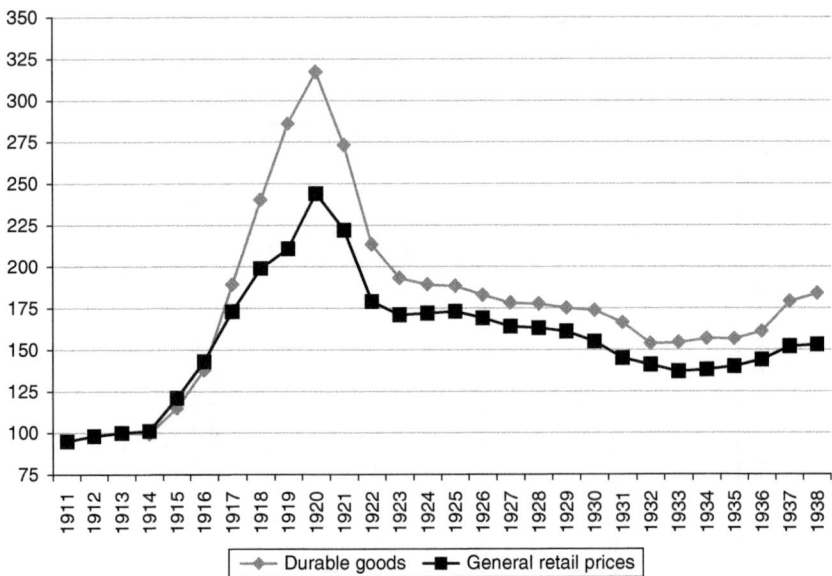

**Fig. 2.3.** Price indices for durable goods and general retail prices, 1911–38 (1913 = 100)

*Source: C. H. Feinstein, National Income: Expenditure and Output in the United Kingdom 1855–1965* (Cambridge: Cambridge University Press, 1972), Table T140.

of consumer expenditure devoted to minor durables declined from the turn of the century to the 1930s.[56]

The relatively sluggish performance of minor durables may at least partially reflect a change in home decor fashion. The overcrowded sitting room of the typical Victorian middle-class house, packed with furniture, ornamentation, and curiosities, was much less attractive to the inter-war housewife, who now generally had to do at least some of her own cleaning. Meanwhile magazines aimed at middle-class women, and the interior designers who contributed to the women's press, now typically promoted relatively simple, 'restful' room designs, which reflected mainstream tastes rather than individuality.[57] For the working classes there may also have been some element of switching from relatively cheap status symbols such as ornaments, prints, and mirrors, to more expensive ones such as new sets of furniture, radios, and linoleum.

Real expenditure on durables (including vehicle running costs) is shown to have increased by 157 per cent over 1911–13 to 1938 and by 85 per cent over the inter-war period. These goods also markedly increased their share of total consumer expenditure, from 4.5 per cent in 1911–13 to 8.40 per cent in 1928 and then, more modestly, to a peak of 10.22 per cent in 1936, before declining somewhat in the late 1930s. This cannot be explained simply in terms of rising incomes and high income elasticities of demand for these goods. In 1926, while real wage earnings stood only 14 per cent above their 1913 levels, real consumer expenditure on durable and related goods had risen by 73 per cent. Nor can it be explained in terms of a switch in spending from paid domestic help to durable goods. After declining sharply over the First World War the share of consumer expenditure on domestic servants remained quite stable over the inter-war period.

Aggregate figures tell us relatively little about the spending patterns of different classes and income groups. Unfortunately, most pre-1945 household expenditure surveys are not sufficiently large or detailed to capture spending on durables (which typically constitute lumpy, infrequent purchases). Two notable exceptions provide unique snapshots of working- and middle-class household spending towards the end of our period. The Ministry of Labour conducted a major working-class expenditure survey, covering the year from October 1937, for families headed by manual workers, or non-manual workers with incomes under £250 per annum. These were surveyed for four separate weeks (spaced at quarterly intervals). Households headed by people in long-term unemployment were excluded from the initial survey sample; however, those who became unemployed over the course of the survey were included. No full study of the survey's findings was ever published, though a 1949 report provided a detailed analysis of the expenditures of non-agricultural workers, who comprised 8,905 of the 10,762 households surveyed.[58] A counterpart 'middle-class' household survey was conducted in 1938/39

[56] Olney, *Buy Now, Pay Later*, 23–6.

[57] Deborah Cohen, *Household Gods: The British and their Possessions* (New Haven, CT: Yale University Press, 2006), 188–9.

[58] TNA, LAB17/7, 'Weekly expenditure of working-class households in the United Kingdom in 1937–38', Ministry of Labour and National Service, July 1949.

by the Civil Service Statistical and Research Bureau, for 1,360 civil servants, local government officers, and teachers, using a similar methodology, but including some extra classes of expenditure, such as motor vehicles.

Table 2.2 presents data from the working-class survey. Six of the survey's household income categories are shown, ranging from families on 40–50 shillings per week (which comprise households in the bottom 8.7 per cent of the survey's income distribution, excluding those in the bottom 2.7 per cent of the distribution), to families on over 140 shillings (comprising the top 7.3 per cent of the survey's income distribution). A notable feature of working-class households is that total income was mainly determined by the number of wage-earners, which varied from 1.19 for the bottom income group shown in the table to 2.91 for the top income group. In other words, prosperous working-class families tended to be those with several people in employment (which also tended to be relatively large families).

The proportion of home owners/purchasers is shown to be strongly related to income, ranging from 3.7 per cent of families on 40–50 shillings a week to 37.2 per cent for the most affluent households in the survey. Yet the average size of house varies less sharply and is roughly constant for families on over 110 shillings. Indeed households on 40–50 shillings and 80–90 shillings have just over one room per person, while those on over 120 shillings have significantly less than one room per person.[59] This may reflect the fact that many working-class districts had a relatively homogeneous housing stock, comprised of two- or three-bedroom houses.

The table then shows spending on accommodation, durables and related goods, and on domestic help and commercial laundries, for each income group. These data are also shown, as a proportion of total expenditure, in Table 2.3. The percentage of income devoted to accommodation declines as income rises, from 15.6 per cent for the lowest income group shown to 7.6 per cent for the highest. This is consistent with other pre-1945 working-class surveys and reflects a general tendency for poor people to have high accommodation costs relative to their income. The table also shows spending on fuel and light and, in particular, on electricity and gas. These are included in order to provide an indication of the use of electrical and gas durables such as cookers, lighting, and water and space heaters. Electricity consumption increases markedly with income in real terms, but remains roughly constant as a proportion of income. Meanwhile gas expenditure declines substantially as a proportion of income for better-resourced households. Nevertheless, gas consumption is substantially higher in absolute terms for higher-income groups within the working class, suggesting that the extent of substitution of gas by electricity remained limited for all groups.

Expenditures on various classes of durables are also shown. All rise markedly with income. However, the biggest changes (especially for furniture, carpets and linoleum, and other utensils and equipment) occur only at the very top end of the income distribution, where there appears to be a distinct 'jump' in expenditure.

---

[59] Defined so as to include kitchens, but not sculleries, bathrooms, and so forth.

**Table 2.2.** Household income and expenditure for non-agricultural working-class families surveyed by the Ministry of Labour in 1937/8

| Total expenditure (shillings) | 40–50 | 60–70 | 80–90 | 100–110 | 120–130 | 140+ | All |
|---|---|---|---|---|---|---|---|
| **Household composition** | | | | | | | |
| Sample size | 131 | 349 | 284 | 171 | 101 | 162 | 2,225 |
| % of income ranking | 2.8–8.7 | 19.0–34.7 | 49.4–62.2 | 71.7–79.3 | 85.0–89.6 | 92.7–100 | 0–100 |
| Average household size | 3.21 | 3.49 | 3.8 | 4.24 | 4.56 | 4.71 | 3.79 |
| Average no. of wage/ salary earners | 1.19 | 1.35 | 1.69 | 2.15 | 2.71 | 2.91 | 1.76 |
| Rooms per household[a] | 3.3 | 3.8 | 3.9 | 4.4 | 4.6 | 4.4 | 4.0 |
| Percentage owning/ buying their home | 3.7 | 13.0 | 17.4 | 22.2 | 30.6 | 37.2 | 18.9 |
| **Household expenditures (d per week)** | | | | | | | |
| Accommodation | 85.5 | 110.6 | 138.2 | 150.6 | 156.4 | 165.2 | 129.6 |
| Fuel & light | 53.2 | 67 | 76.4 | 94.3 | 105.2 | 120.8 | 78.2 |
| Electricity[b] | 4.5 | 9.9 | 11.7 | 15.0 | 14.8 | 19.7 | 11.7 |
| Gas[b] | 11.1 | 14.9 | 18.2 | 20.1 | 24.0 | 24.2 | 17.6 |
| Ironmongery, holloware, cutlery, tools, brushes/ brooms, pottery & glass | 1.7 | 3.8 | 5.4 | 6.9 | 11.7 | 16.1 | 5.8 |
| Drapery and haberdashery | 1.9 | 3 | 7.3 | 9 | 19.3 | 33.5 | 8.6 |
| Furniture | 3.6 | 7.7 | 10.5 | 12.2 | 16.3 | 84 | 15.1 |
| Carpets, linoleum, mats, etc. | 2.5 | 2.6 | 4.8 | 9.3 | 10.2 | 58.9 | 9.5 |
| Other utensils and equipment | 0.3 | 1.3 | 2.5 | 5.8 | 4.3 | 26.3 | 4.8 |
| Domestic help & laundries | 2.2 | 5 | 8.9 | 9.2 | 16.5 | 22.8 | 8.6 |
| Food | 247.5 | 336.6 | 409.1 | 489.3 | 593.2 | 666.1 | 412.4 |
| Clothing & footwear | 43.7 | 66.2 | 93.7 | 121.3 | 150.9 | 212.8 | 97.1 |
| Other | 107.4 | 180.0 | 261.2 | 352.8 | 412.1 | 763.0 | 286.2 |
| Total | 549.5 | 783.8 | 1,018.0 | 1,260.7 | 1,496.1 | 2,169.5 | 1,055.9 |

*Notes*: Final column includes all income ranges covered in the survey, not just those separately enumerated in the table. [a] For households renting their accommodation. Excludes any rooms sublet. Includes kitchens, but not sculleries or bathrooms. [b] Also includes meter rent and fittings.

*Source*: TNA, LAB17/7, 'Weekly Expenditure of Working-class Households in the United Kingdom in 1937–38', Ministry of Labour and National Service, July 1949.

This group is also categorized by a markedly higher proportion of expenditure on 'other' items not listed separately in the table, such as transport, precautionary contractual savings, and leisure. Domestic help also rises as a proportion of total expenditure for higher income groups, though this probably at least partly reflects a trade-off between their higher proportion of family members in paid work and the consequent need to buy in household labour.

**Table 2.3.** Household expenditures as a proportion of total weekly spending for non-agricultural working-class families surveyed by the Ministry of Labour in 1937/8

| Total expenditure (shillings) | 40–50 | 60–70 | 80–90 | 100–110 | 120–130 | 140+ | All |
|---|---|---|---|---|---|---|---|
| Accommodation | 15.6 | 14.1 | 13.6 | 11.9 | 10.5 | 7.6 | 12.3 |
| Fuel & light | 9.7 | 8.5 | 7.5 | 7.5 | 7.0 | 5.6 | 7.4 |
|   Electricity[a] | 0.8 | 1.3 | 1.1 | 1.2 | 1.0 | 0.9 | 1.1 |
|   Gas[a] | 2.0 | 1.9 | 1.8 | 1.6 | 1.6 | 1.1 | 1.7 |
| Ironmongery, holloware, cutlery, tools, brushes & brooms, pottery & glass | 0.3 | 0.5 | 0.5 | 0.5 | 0.8 | 0.7 | 0.5 |
| Drapery and haberdashery | 0.3 | 0.4 | 0.7 | 0.7 | 1.3 | 1.5 | 0.8 |
| Furniture | 0.7 | 1.0 | 1.0 | 1.0 | 1.1 | 3.9 | 1.4 |
| Carpets, linoleum, mats, etc. | 0.5 | 0.3 | 0.5 | 0.7 | 0.7 | 2.7 | 0.9 |
| Other utensils and equipment | 0.1 | 0.2 | 0.2 | 0.5 | 0.3 | 1.2 | 0.5 |
| Domestic help & laundries | 0.4 | 0.6 | 0.9 | 0.7 | 1.1 | 1.1 | 0.8 |
| Food | 45.0 | 42.9 | 40.2 | 38.8 | 39.6 | 30.7 | 39.1 |
| Clothing & footwear | 8.0 | 8.4 | 9.2 | 9.6 | 10.1 | 9.8 | 9.2 |
| Other | 19.5 | 23.0 | 25.7 | 28.0 | 27.5 | 35.2 | 27.1 |
| Total | 100.0 | 100.0 | 100.0 | 100.0 | 100.0 | 100.0 | 100.0 |

*Note:* [a] Also includes meter rent and fittings.

*Sources:* See Table 2.2.

Tables 2.4 and 2.5 provide a similar analysis for the middle-class survey. Middle-class families were concentrated in the £250–500 income range. There were some 1,890,000 incomes of £250–500 in 1938, which (assuming each was a head of household) would represent 15 per cent of UK households, together with a further 390,000 incomes of £500–750, equivalent to 3.1 per cent of households. Incomes above the range covered in the table (assuming that the top group's income has an upper bound of £750) number some 437,000, or only 3.5 per cent of all households, comprising the upper-middle and upper classes.[60] For the middle-class groups shown in the table, there is a much weaker relationship between household income and the number of wage/salary earners, as the head of household's income generally comprised most or all family income. The number of rooms occupied is markedly higher for households in the lowest middle-class income group than for the highest-income group of working-class households in Table 2.2, despite the fact that the highest-income working-class group has a higher mean household income and a larger family size. Moreover, the share of household income devoted to rent by the lowest middle-class income group is 13.97 per cent, compared to only 7.6 per cent for the most affluent working-class

---

[60] Income data are from Robert Bacon, George S. Bain, and John Pimlott, 'The Economic Environment', in A. H. Halsey (ed.), *Trends in British Society since 1900* (London: Macmillan, 1972), 64–96 (91). The number of UK households is based on Marion Bowley's estimate for England and Wales in 1939 (*Housing and the State 1919–1944* (London: George Allen & Unwin, 1945), 269), grossed up by the ratio of UK population to that of England and Wales.

**Table 2.4.** Household expenditures for a sample of middle-class households in 1938

| Annual income of household head (£) | £250–350 | £350–500 | £500–700 | £700+ | All |
|---|---|---|---|---|---|
| **Household composition** | | | | | |
| Sample | 598 | 507 | 186 | 69 | 1,360 |
| Household size | 2.98 | 3.39 | 3.56 | 3.97 | 3.27 |
| No. of wage/salary earners | 1.17 | 1.25 | 1.26 | 1.3 | 1.22 |
| **Accommodation[a]** | | | | | |
| Renting (%) | 36.4 | 34.1 | 29.7 | 42.4 | 35.0 |
| Buying (%) | 47.4 | 46.9 | 48.7 | 30.1 | 46.5 |
| Owning (%) | 16.0 | 18.2 | 21.6 | 27.5 | 18.2 |
| Number of rooms occupied | 5.1 | 5.6 | 6.0 | 7.6 | 5.5 |
| **Household expenditures (d per week)** | | | | | |
| Accommodation (all) | 228.0 | 240.5 | 309.0 | 418.3 | 253.5 |
| Accommodation (renters) | 226.3 | 236.3 | 317.3 | 497.0 | 257.3 |
| Fuel & light | 101.5 | 121.3 | 154.5 | 194.0 | 121.0 |
| Electricity[b] | 22.8 | 26.8 | 33.0 | 42.0 | 26.8 |
| Gas[d] | 18.3 | 20.0 | 23.5 | 41.5 | 20.8 |
| Coke | 3.8 | 6.0 | 15.0 | 23.8 | 7.3 |
| Ironmongery, holloware, cutlery, tools, brushes & brooms, pottery & glass | 15.0 | 22.3 | 25.5 | 29.8 | 19.8 |
| Drapery and haberdashery | 29.8 | 37.3 | 39.5 | 57.5 | 35.3 |
| Furniture | 39.3 | 50.5 | 80.5 | 111.5 | 52.8 |
| Carpets, linoleum, mats, etc. | 22.0 | 17.0 | 26.3 | 17.3 | 20.5 |
| Other utensils and equipment | 7.8 | 14.3 | 7.5 | 10.0 | 10.3 |
| Telephones & telegrams | 5.5 | 14.8 | 32.0 | 71.5 | 16.0 |
| Domestic help & laundries | 34.5 | 53.3 | 100.3 | 214.0 | 59.8 |
| Personal transport[c] | 40.0 | 56.8 | 123.8 | 284.5 | 70.0 |
| Radio[d] | 13.3 | 18.5 | 10.5 | 17.8 | 15.0 |
| Watches, clocks, jewellery, & repairs | 3.3 | 4.3 | 5.8 | 14.5 | 4.5 |
| Food | 462.0 | 556.0 | 688.0 | 809.0 | 492.0 |
| Clothing & footwear | 149.0 | 184.0 | 245.3 | 319.5 | 186.3 |
| Other | 481.0 | 690.3 | 885.5 | 1291.8 | 709.3 |
| **Total expenditure** | 1631.8 | 2080.8 | 2733.8 | 3860.8 | 2065.8 |

*Notes:* [a]A very small proportion of households who are provided with 'rent-free' accommodation are not shown separately, as they contribute 0.8 per cent or less of households in each income group. Rooms occupied are defined as in Table 2.2. [b]Also includes meter rent and fittings. [c]Cars, motorcycles, bicycles, including fuel, oil, etc., but not licences or insurance premiums. [d]Excluding licences.

*Source:* Philip Massey, 'The Expenditure of 1,360 British Middle-Class Households in 1938–39', *Journal of the Royal Statistical Society*, 105 (1942), 159–96 (181).

households. These differences reflect the fact that white-collar workers were expected to live in a particular kind of house, in a particular kind of neighbourhood, and such housing was expensive for those at the bottom of the middle-class income spectrum.

As with working-class households, the ratio of accommodation costs to total expenditure for middle-class households falls with income, but much less steeply. This is particularly evident when families renting their accommodation are examined (to control for the high proportion of outright home ownership among

**Table 2.5.** Household expenditures as a proportion of total weekly spending for the middle-class households analysed in Table 2.4

| Annual income of household head (£) | £250–350 | £350–500 | £500–700 | £700 + | All |
|---|---|---|---|---|---|
| Accommodation (all) | 13.97 | 11.56 | 11.30 | 10.83 | 12.27 |
| Accommodation (renters) | 13.87 | 11.35 | 11.60 | 12.87 | 12.45 |
| Fuel & light | 6.22 | 5.83 | 5.65 | 5.02 | 5.86 |
|   Electricity[a] | 1.39 | 1.29 | 1.21 | 1.09 | 1.29 |
|   Gas[a] | 1.12 | 0.96 | 0.86 | 1.07 | 1.00 |
|   Coke | 0.23 | 0.29 | 0.55 | 0.62 | 0.35 |
| Ironmongery, holloware, cutlery, tools, brushes & brooms, pottery & glass | 0.92 | 1.07 | 0.93 | 0.77 | 0.96 |
| Drapery and haberdashery | 1.82 | 1.79 | 1.44 | 1.49 | 1.71 |
| Furniture | 2.41 | 2.43 | 2.94 | 2.89 | 2.55 |
| Carpets, linoleum, mats, etc. | 1.35 | 0.82 | 0.96 | 0.45 | 0.99 |
| Other utensils and equipment | 0.47 | 0.68 | 0.27 | 0.26 | 0.50 |
| Telephones & telegrams | 0.34 | 0.71 | 1.17 | 1.85 | 0.77 |
| Domestic help & laundries | 2.11 | 2.56 | 3.67 | 5.54 | 2.89 |
| Personal transport[b] | 2.45 | 2.73 | 4.53 | 7.37 | 3.39 |
| Radio[c] | 0.81 | 0.89 | 0.38 | 0.46 | 0.73 |
| Watches, clocks, jewellery & repairs | 0.20 | 0.20 | 0.21 | 0.38 | 0.22 |
| Food | 28.31 | 26.72 | 25.17 | 20.95 | 23.82 |
| Clothing & footwear | 9.13 | 8.84 | 8.97 | 8.28 | 9.02 |
| Other | 29.48 | 33.17 | 32.39 | 33.46 | 34.33 |
| Total expenditure | 100.00 | 100.00 | 100.00 | 100.00 | 100.00 |

*Notes*: [a] Also includes meter rent and fittings. [b] Cars, motorcycles, bicycles, including fuel, oil, etc., but not licences or insurance premiums. [c] Excluding licences.

*Source*: See Table 2.4.

higher-income middle-class groups). It thus appears that higher-income middle-class households placed a much greater premium on a larger, more prestigious, house, to distinguish themselves from less affluent sections of their class, than was the case for high-income manual workers.

Spending on minor durables (proxied in the table by the two categories ironmongery etc., plus drapery and haberdashery) is shown to be markedly higher, in relation to income for middle-class, compared to working-class, households. However, across the middle-class income spectrum proportionate expenditure on these items falls as income rises, in contrast to working-class households, where expenditure rises with income. Meanwhile the lowest-income middle-class group in Table 2.5 spends a substantially larger proportion of income on minor durables than the highest-income working-class group in Table 2.3. For major durables, only furniture is a uniformly 'superior good'—with a share of total household expenditure that generally rises with income for both the working and middle classes. Spending on carpets etc., and on other utensils and equipment (including white goods), as a proportion of household expenditure, is generally higher for more affluent working-class families, but does not rise with income for the middle classes.

However, Table 2.4 and 2.5 also show four classes of durables that were not disaggregated in the working-class survey—expenditure on telephones and telegrams; personal transport; radios; and watches, clocks, and jewellery. With the exception of radios, these are shown to be superior goods, with a marked jump in their contribution to total expenditure for the highest middle-class income group. Telephones and cars were characterized by both high acquisition and running costs and, in contrast to the United States, experienced very low diffusion before the Second World War. A similar discontinuity between the top middle-class income group (and, to a lesser extent, the second highest) and the others is evident for domestic help and commercial laundries. It thus appears that households on over £700 enjoyed a different mode of life from lower-income middle-class groups, a trend corroborated by their substantially larger houses (with an average of 7.6 rooms, compared to 5.1–6.0 for the other middle-class groups).

## DRIVERS OF DURABLES SPENDING—STATUS, 'RESPECTABILITY', AND CONSPICUOUS CONSUMPTION

Considerations of status had long exerted a powerful influence over household spending and credit decisions, families organizing their finances not only to make ends meet, but to defend and enhance their social position.[61] During the inter-war years increasing social and geographical mobility, for those fortunate enough to be in secure employment, gave the ownership of consumer durables a particularly important status role. Many people were moving to new communities, where status could be asserted through material display, rather than being based on the broader 'life portrait' criteria used in longer-established neighbourhoods—encompassing not only visible possessions but one's family connections, background, and work, social, and leisure activities.[62]

While high unemployment in the staple export industries produced depression and economic stagnation in the industrial heartlands of northern and western Britain, much of the Midlands and South experienced relative prosperity. For many people in these areas, falling prices and family sizes boosted real incomes per head and provided access to modern semi-detached housing and durables

[61] Johnson, *Saving and Spending*, 5–6; Robert Roberts, *The Classic Slum: Salford Life in the First Quarter of the Century* (Manchester: Penguin, 1971), 17.
[62] Michael Young and Peter Willmott, *Family and Kinship in East London* (Harmondsworth: Penguin, 1957), 162.

such as new suites of furniture, radios, bicycles, and some electrical appliances.[63] Higher living standards and rising home ownership contributed to the emergence of more 'home-centred' lifestyles, while the growth of suburban private and council estates brought large numbers of people into new communities where displays of affluence became particularly important as a means of asserting social status.[64] For skilled manual and white-collar workers, moving to the suburbs offered an opportunity to distance themselves from those who could not afford the move, in terms of both physical distance and type of community. Part of this process involved emulation of the longer-established members of their new suburban neighbourhoods.[65] Meanwhile trends towards suburbanization and its accompanying lifestyle were much more strongly and generally evident among the middle classes.[66]

This fed into a growing blurring between the aspirations of the lower-middle class and the more affluent sections of the working class, influenced both by rising living standards and by the cinema and other developments in mass media that targeted the broadest possible number of consumers in order to maximize their audience.[67] For example, women's lifestyle magazines such as *Woman's Own*, which enjoyed both a substantial middle- and working-class readership, promoted domesticity and consumerism through the idealized 'professional' housewife, who achieved the perfect domestic environment with the assistance of labour-saving consumer durables.[68] Such influences were reflected in trends towards working-class emulation of middle-class standards in dress and (when circumstances allowed) other areas of consumption and in the growth of multiple retailers that served a wide income spectrum.[69]

Rising living standards for those in work, and the expansion of social welfare provision, tempered the perceived insecurity of some sections of the working class—especially in the Midlands and South—and enabled those with relatively secure jobs, or jobs in expanding high-wage sectors, to adopt new norms and values regarding lifestyles and consumption patterns. This new, aspirational, respectability emphasized high standards of personal and domestic hygiene, 'privatized' family- and

---

[63] J. K. Walton, 'Towns and Consumerism', in Martin Daunton (ed.), *The Cambridge Urban History of Britain*, vol. III: *1840–1950* (Cambridge: Cambridge University Press, 2000), 715–44 (718–28).

[64] Melanie Tebutt, *Making Ends Meet: Pawnbroking and Working-Class Credit* (London: Methuen, 1983), 165–6.

[65] Gary S. Cross, *Time and Money: The Making of Consumer Culture* (London: Routledge, 1993), 169–70.

[66] Walton, 'Towns and Consumerism', 728.

[67] Wilfrid Mellers and Rupert Hildyard, 'The Interwar Years', in Boris Ford (ed.), *The Cambridge Cultural History*, vol. VIII: *Early Twentieth-Century Britain* (Cambridge: Cambridge University Press, 1992), 27–45 (31–5).

[68] Jill Greenfield and Chris Reid, 'Women's Magazines and the Commercial Orchestration of Femininity in the 1930s: Evidence from *Woman's Own*', *Media History*, 4 (1998), 161–74.

[69] As an executive of W.H. Smith stated, 'all classes—even the Queen herself—have patronised Woolworths': Charles Wilson, *First With the News: The History of W.H. Smith 1792–1972* (London: Jonathan Cape, 1985), 326. See also John Benson, *The Rise of Consumer Society in Britain, 1880–1980* (London: Longman, 1994), 217.

home-centred lifestyles, and an increased commitment of resources to the welfare and material advancement of the next generation.[70] As De Vries noted, together with improved diets, these preferences formed a 'complex of consumption goals' which required clear household strategies to deliver them. Their importance as a 'cluster' of preferences was not due to each element being, 'equally essential to achieve the ultimate goal of a longer, healthier, more comfortable life but because they were perceived to facilitate these goals and to signal to others the commitment to achieve them'.[71]

According to Tedlow, during the early twentieth century the US economy moved from an initial phase of marketing, with geographical fragmentation and small firms pursuing high-margin, low-volume business strategies—to a second phase—where integrated markets became dominated by national firms which had succeeded in organizing and educating a mass market.[72] In Britain the main dimension of fragmentation during the first phase was economic rather than geographical, arising from much greater income disparities and social stratification. Reductions in income inequalities over the First World War had significantly lowered the economic barriers to mass marketing, but major social barriers remained. For example, until the development of 'popular' department stores, many working- and lower-middle-class customers avoided department stores—as they found facing the scrutiny of the floor walker, followed by the sales assistant, too daunting.[73] Extending HP sales also involved overcoming major social barriers, as HP was widely regarded by these groups as a disreputable and profligate way of financing a lifestyle beyond one's real means.[74]

As Susan Strasser has noted, effective marketing campaigns generally encourage new needs and desires, 'not by creating them out of whole cloth, but by linking the rapid appearance of new products with the rapid changes in all areas of social and cultural life'.[75] Contrary to some traditional depictions, the inter-war years, and particularly the 1930s, witnessed a marked expansion in working-class occupational, geographical, and (within certain limits) social mobility. Baines and Johnson found that occupational mobility for men was substantially higher during this period than in the nineteenth century, while research on young inter-war women, by Selina Todd, found a high level of occupational and geographical mobility,

[70] A. Hughes and K. Hunt, 'A Culture Transformed? Women's Lives in Wythenshawe in the 1930s', in A. Davies and S. Fielding (eds.), *Workers' Worlds: Cultures and Communities in Manchester and Salford, 1880–1939* (Manchester: Manchester University Press, 1992), 74–101 (92); Szreter, *Fertility, Class and Gender*, 528; Diana Gittins, *Fair Sex: Family Size and Structure, 1900–39* (London: Hutchinson, 1982), 175–6.

[71] Jan De Vries, *The Industrious Revolution. Consumer Behaviour and the Household Economy, 1650 to the Present* (Cambridge: Cambridge University Press, 2008), 189.

[72] Richard S. Tedlow, *New and Improved: The Rise of Mass Marketing in America* (Oxford: Heinemann, 1990), 4–12.

[73] S. F. Lomax, 'The Department Store and the Creation of the Spectacle, 1880–1940' (unpublished PhD thesis, University of Essex, 2005), 55–66.

[74] For a discussion of the social stigma surrounding HP, see Scott, 'Twilight World'.

[75] Susan Strasser, *Satisfaction Guaranteed: The Making of the American Mass Market* (New York: Pantheon, 1989), 95.

together with rising social aspirations—within constraints imposed by their material circumstances and class position.[76]

This new model of working-class respectability was based around 'privatized' family- and home-centred lifestyles, an increased commitment of monetary and psychological resources to the welfare and material advancement of children, and asserting status through the display of material goods and high standards of domestic hygiene and associated behaviour.[77] This period witnessed the diffusion of a powerful 'ideology of domesticity', which had begun to influence a substantial section of the working class by the 1930s, promoted through the new mass-circulation women's magazines, women's sections in national newspapers, the BBC, other media, health professionals, the Ideal Home Exhibition (and its local and regional counterparts), and advertisements for new consumer durables.[78] These idealized the married woman's role as 'professional housewife', providing a happy, clean, home environment for her family via labour-saving devices and efficient household management practices.[79] Women's magazines and women's sections of newspapers were particularly keen on promoting these new aspirational lifestyles, which appealed both to the desires of their readers and to the marketing needs of their advertisers.

However, considerable consumer resistance remained, especially among working-class families, who were particularly averse to buying 'luxury' goods on HP contracts that would commit them to weekly payments for several years. Such fears were accentuated by (often essentially true) popular 'myths' surrounding consumer credit—that it was rife with abuse or (at best) harsh treatment for customers who found themselves temporarily unable to meet the weekly payments. This problem was recognized by consumer durables producers and retailers, which reacted by trying to replace these myths with new ones that associated consumer credit with aspirational lifestyles, 'getting ahead', middle-class values, and (paradoxically) thrift, as discussed in the following chapters.

## CONCLUSIONS

Was there a 'consumer durables revolution' in inter-war Britain? Economic theory suggests that an increase in consumer expenditure can be explained due to three

[76] Dudley Baines and Paul Johnson, 'In Search of the "Traditional" Working Class: Social Mobility and Occupational Continuity in Interwar London', *Economic History Review*, 52 (1999), 692–713; Selina Todd, *Young Women, Work, and Family in England 1918–1950* (Oxford: Oxford University Press, 2005), 113–44.

[77] Hughes and Hunt, 'A Culture Transformed?', 92; Szreter, *Fertility, Class and Gender*, 528; Gittins, *Fair Sex*, 175–6, notes the importance of these new family-centred lifestyles as a factor encouraging family limitation.

[78] Deborah, Ryan, 'The Daily Mail Ideal Home Exhibition and Suburban Modernity, 1908–1951' (unpublished PhD thesis, University of East London, 1995), 92.

[79] Gittins, *Fair Sex*, 182–3; Margaret Judith Giles, 'Something That Bit Better: Working-Class Women, Domesticity, and "Respectability", 1919–1939' (unpublished DPhil thesis, University of York, 1989), 108–9.

factors. The first is a reduction in price (relative to other goods), which may lead to a more than compensating increase in purchases, if consumer expenditure is particularly price-sensitive (high 'own-price elasticity'). The second is an increase in incomes, which may lead to an increase in the proportion of income devoted to a particular good if it has high 'income elasticity'—the responsiveness of the quantity demanded to a change in income. The final factor is a change in preferences, which would increase demand at every price level, even if incomes are static. The debate on whether the United States experienced a consumer durables revolution in the 1920s has defined such a 'revolution' as a structural shift in demand, in other words a change in consumer tastes that accords higher priority to durables, relative to other goods and services (rather than a fall in the relative prices of durables or a shift driven purely by rising incomes).[80]

Rapidly expanding credit provision, together with the marked liberalization of credit terms for most durables, complicates the question of whether inter-war Britain experienced a consumer durables revolution (as defined in the American literature) not only empirically, but conceptually. Lower deposits and longer contracts can be interpreted as a fall in the 'price' of credit (if this is interpreted to mean the deposit and/or the weekly payment), arising from an increase in supply. This does not represent a shift in consumer preferences in favour of durable goods—which would imply that customers would buy more goods even at the same credit price. Moreover, the 'price' of credit, from the perspective of the household, is difficult to define.[81] The 'up-front' costs of purchase (the minimum deposit ratio and the size of each weekly/monthly instalment) fell markedly over this period owing to the liberalization of credit terms. Yet liberalization simultaneously raised the total price paid by the consumer, as interest was charged over a longer period. However, there is a strong consensus in academic studies that consumers generally place more importance on weekly instalments and, especially, minimum deposit ratios, than the cost of credit over the lifetime of the contract, with the deposit being particularly important—given that it represented a major constraint on 'affordability'.[82]

Distinguishing a shift in consumer tastes from changes in relative prices becomes even more problematic when we take into account the impacts of advertising. In contrast to the United States, where Martha Olney found that advertisements for consumer durables rarely mentioned credit terms,[83] in Britain some major durables suppliers used liberal credit as the cornerstone of their marketing strategy. If this was purely informational advertising—telling people of the new 'prices' of credit (in terms of up-front costs and instalment payments)—it would be of little relevance to the debate regarding whether there was a shift in consumer priorities in favour of durables. However, the adverts often presented 'easy terms' as the gateway to the sort of aspirational lifestyles which their products allegedly offered

---

[80] Olney, *Buy Now, Pay Later*, 61 and 76.    [81] Ibid., 112–13.

[82] See, for example, Peter Scott and James T. Walker, 'The Impact of "Stop-Go" Demand Management Policy on Britain's Consumer Durables Industries, 1952–1965', *Economic History Review* (forthcoming); Olney, *Buy Now, Pay Later*, 112–13.

[83] Olney, *Buy Now, Pay Later*, 160.

access to—an early form of 'lifestyle' marketing that was designed to shift consumer priorities by suggesting that these new lifestyles were now accessible. Thus identifying whether there was a clear shift in consumer preferences in favour of durables—after taking account of changes in the 'price' of credit and the purely informational role of advertising in making customers aware of more liberal credit terms—is a complex problem, that can only be solved by investigation on a product-by-product basis.

# PART I

# 'NECESSITIES OF LIFE'— CREATING MASS MARKETS IN NEW FURNITURE AND OWNER-OCCUPIED HOUSING

Furniture and accommodation (together with tools and pottery) are perhaps the oldest consumer durables, being present—in some form—since prehistoric times. However, these have always been costly items, owing to the large labour inputs required for their creation and for housing the growing scarcity of residential land. Moreover, rising living standards, in conjunction with the considerable utility and status value of accommodation and furniture, have led to growing expectations regarding their quantity and quality. Meanwhile technical innovation has had only a limited impact in reducing costs. The proportion of income devoted to these items has thus failed to fall substantially over time, in contrast to more novel consumer durables such as white goods, vehicles, or radios.

Moreover, their costs were strongly bunched at one stage of the family life cycle—new household formation. This was generally a time when household finances were coming under more general pressure, as it was often associated with the arrival of the first child and an (at least temporary) cessation of the housewife's paid work. Given that buying a new house would typically cost several years' wages, while furnishing it with entirely new items would take up the equivalent of several months' earnings, many families traditionally turned to close substitutes—mainly rented housing and second-hand furniture. These (particularly rented housing) offered further benefits during the pre-1914 era, when families often moved house frequently (partly in response to changing economic fortunes). Indeed, in Victorian Britain renting was the standard tenure for all but the very rich.

This section explores attempts to create mass markets in furniture and housing. Unlike most of the goods examined in Parts II–IV, these sectors were not significantly impacted by barriers to competition, such as patents, product differentiation through branding, retail price maintenance, or (as in telephones) government monopolies. However, they both faced similar marketing challenges—providing a suitable 'credit product' to make their physical products accessible to a mass market. Innovations in their credit products proved more important to creating mass markets than changes in the product characteristics and production processes of the physical products, given that both sectors were, and remain, labour-intensive industries offering little scope for radical price reductions through mass production.

The development of liberal credit terms in these sectors had wider long-term impacts on consumer credit and expenditure. There is a close correlation in modern societies between mortgage debt and other forms of consumer credit—with having a mortgage, rather than owning a home per se, being identified as a key determinant of consumer credit levels. This has been explained partly in terms of mortgages accustoming households to taking on large debts, a characteristic shared with furniture HP credit (which also involved large sums and diffused to lower-income groups faster than mortgage credit).[1]

The credit products these sectors developed also had major impacts on their industrial structure and stability. In furniture, credit terms were liberalized to such an extent that HP finance houses would not finance them, leading to dominance of the sector by a relatively small group of major retail chains which were able to fund their own credit—but at the cost of tying up an ever-increasing amount of capital in HP contracts. Conversely in speculative house-building there were a large number of building societies that were prepared to liberalize their mortgage lending along the lines demanded by housing developers and—despite attempts to develop a building society cartel—the mortgage market remained relatively competitive. This, in turn, meant that access to mortgage finance did not provide particular firms with major competitive advantages over their rivals—one of the reasons why, in contrast to the highly concentrated structure of furniture retailing, the speculative house-building industry remained very fragmented.

Overall, despite some problems of opportunism by providers of both the physical and the credit products, these sectors were among the most successful in meeting the challenge of the mass market. Chapters 3 and 4 explore how suppliers of the two most expensive classes of durable goods for most inter-war British households also became among the first to succeed in creating true mass markets.

---

[1] Frank Trentmann, *Empire of Things: How We Became a World of Consumers, from the Fifteenth Century to the Twenty-First* (St Ives: Allen Lane, 2016), 413.

# 3

## Furniture

### Britain's First Mass-Marketed Consumer Durable

#### INTRODUCTION

Our exploration of the inter-war consumer durables revolution starts with furniture, for a number of reasons. First and foremost, this was the sector where the first large-scale, concerted attempt was made to develop a true mass market in high-ticket consumer durables.[1] The explicit targeting of 'Mr Everyman' was the subject of much trade and popular discussion in the early 1920s, not just because of Drage's ground-breaking advertising campaign, but because the very idea of serving 'Everyman', especially for high-ticket products, was anathema to British retailing orthodoxy. Moreover, Drage's spectacular early success inspired emulation and adaption not just by furniture retailers, but by firms in other durable and semi-durable lines. It is dangerous to attribute the origins of a national trend to any single event—though by far the strongest contender for the launch of consumer durables mass marketing in Britain is the sudden and unexpected appearance of the large, eye-catching, 'Mr Drage, Mr Everyman' adverts in national newspapers from 1922.

Furniture is also interesting as a mass marketing challenge in its own right, owing to its demand and supply characteristics. Furniture, in some form, constituted a 'necessity' for all households and thus enjoyed high priority in family budgeting. Nevertheless, it also had particularly strong status connotations, on account of its considerable cost, high visibility, and great potential for differentiation via size, materials, and styling. For young working-class couples seeking to set up their own home, acquiring furniture typically represented their greatest financial challenge. However, there were viable and widely used alternatives to buying all, most, or even any, furniture new. Second-hand furniture enjoyed a ready market, given the extreme durability of furniture that was well-cared for. People might also pass on their old or surplus furniture to friends and relatives setting up home for the first time, while lower-income families might also improvise with furniture made from packing cases and other repurposed items.

During the inter-war years buying furniture 'new' began to be perceived as a 'necessity' by growing numbers of working- and lower-middle-class families. Moreover,

---

[1] It could be argued that the first mass marketed consumer durable was the sewing machine. However, sewing machines embodied elements of both 'consumer' and 'producer' durables—the 'producers' including women who worked from home on a part-time or casual basis.

people increasingly began to furnish their living, dining, and bedrooms with matching 'suites', rather than acquiring single items as and when finances allowed. This chapter shows how these trends were fostered by furniture retailers, especially a small group of rapidly expanding national furniture chains that marketed credit at least as much as the furniture it was used to buy, while also trying to persuade the public that 'furnishing out of income' was not only socially acceptable but constituted the cornerstone of modern, aspirational, lifestyles.

In the process, national furniture chains—most of which had been insignificant before 1914—gained virtually complete control over branding and design of the lines they marketed, effectively dictating terms to large numbers of small- and medium-sized manufacturers. Thus most furniture producers became mere contractors in value chains dominated and coordinated by the major retailers.

## PRODUCTION SYSTEMS AND VALUE CHAINS

The technological foundations of the furniture industry's rapid inter-war growth were laid during the First World War, which generated high demand for wooden goods in aircraft and other munitions sectors. An industry characterized in 1914 by simple, flexible machinery and vertically specialized production in craft-based industrial districts, saw the widespread introduction of new machinery that did not require craft skills and was best suited for standardized volume output.[2] This was accompanied by the introduction of electric motive power, which removed the constraints on machinery layouts imposed by overhead belts and enabled factories to reorganize on quantity production lines.[3] Electrical drives also offered major benefits to smaller manufacturers, as they reduced the heavy initial costs of the plant, shafting, etc. previously necessary for powered machinery, together with the space requirements of an on-site engine and transmission belts.

War production also led to the development of new materials. For example, while plywood was already in use in certain sections of the furniture trade, wartime technical advances—particularly improvements in adhesives for the aircraft industry—allowed it to be more generally applied after 1918 (together with other composite materials, such as laminates and blockboard). Following the war, wood-using munitions plants were sold off to the private sector and often ended up in the hands of furniture producers, facilitating the switch to new production methods.

Mechanization and new remuneration systems enabled semi-skilled workers to achieve much higher output than their craft-based colleagues in unionized factories. By the late 1930s, as the official history of the industry's union, NAFTA, notes, unionized workers in traditional factories making furniture for the high end of the market and employed on day rates were earning around 1s 9d an hour, compared

---

[2] London School of Economics, *The New Survey of London Life & Labour*, vol. II: *London's Industries* (London: P. S. King, 1931), 8.

[3] Interview reproduced in Pat Kirkham, Rodney Mace, and Julia Porter, *Furnishing the World: The East London Furniture Trade 1830–1980* (London: Journeyman, 1987), 123.

to 2s 6d or more for employees of mechanized plants producing for the mass market and operating payments by results systems (which were opposed by the conservative, craft-based NAFTA).[4]

Technical change was accompanied by geographical concentration. Production (which was already concentrated in the South East—in High Wycombe and Greater London) became further concentrated in London—which expanded its share of national employment from 36.7 per cent in 1923 to 42.5 per cent in 1938. Meanwhile the share of national furniture employment in the rest of the South East remained static and most provincial regions lost market share.[5] Within London there was considerable firm migration from traditional inner London industrial districts to new industrial areas of wartime munitions production with good arterial road access, such as the Lea Valley, Walthamstow, and Leyton.[6] Sourcing production in London minimized communication costs for retail chains headquartered in the capital. Furthermore, proximity to Britain's most prosperous consumer markets and London's good long-distance road links (which were particularly important given that furniture is not well-suited to rail transport, being easily damaged by scratching or rubbing in trans-shipment) made it particularly attractive from a distribution perspective.[7]

Furniture was a particularly strong growth industry—real net output rose by some 91.1 per cent over 1924–35, compared to 22.4 per cent for all manufacturing. This is a staggering rate of growth for a long-established industry and is of the same order of magnitude as that for the 'new' industries (for example net output in chemicals and electrical engineering expanded by 47.2 per cent and 104.9 per cent respectively over this period).[8] Yet despite rapid growth and technological change there was no significant trend towards true mass production methods; the technological revolution in furniture was essentially one of mechanization and deskilling, within small and medium plants producing relatively small production runs of each design. Average plant size remained below that for all British manufacturing; in 1935 some 36.3 per cent of employees in the industry proper worked in establishments of under fifty workers (compared to 22 per cent for all factory trades), while 51.8 per cent worked in establishments of below 200 workers (compared to 32.7 per cent for all factories).[9]

Developments in manufacturing technology offered only limited potential to expand sales through lowering production costs. Wooden furniture was, and

---

[4] Hew Reid, *The Furniture Makers: A History of Trade Unionism in the Furniture Trade* (Oxford: Malthouse, 1986), 134 and 152.

[5] Board of Trade Working Party Report, *Furniture* (London: HMSO, 1946), 48–9. Based on the Ministry of Labour's definition of the furniture trade, which is broader than that used by the Board of Trade Working Party.

[6] See Peter Scott and Peter Walsh, 'Patterns and Determinants of Manufacturing Plant Location in Interwar London', *Economic History Review*, 57 (2004), 109–41 (125–6).

[7] Board of Trade Working Party Report, *Furniture*, 50.

[8] Business Statistics Office, *Historical Record of the Census of Production, 1907–70* (London: HMSO, 1978), 2–33. Data deflated using retail price series in C. H. Feinstein, *National Income, Expenditure, and Output of the United Kingdom, 1855–1965* (Cambridge: Cambridge University Press, 1972), T133.

[9] Board of Trade Working Party Reports, *Furniture*, 51.

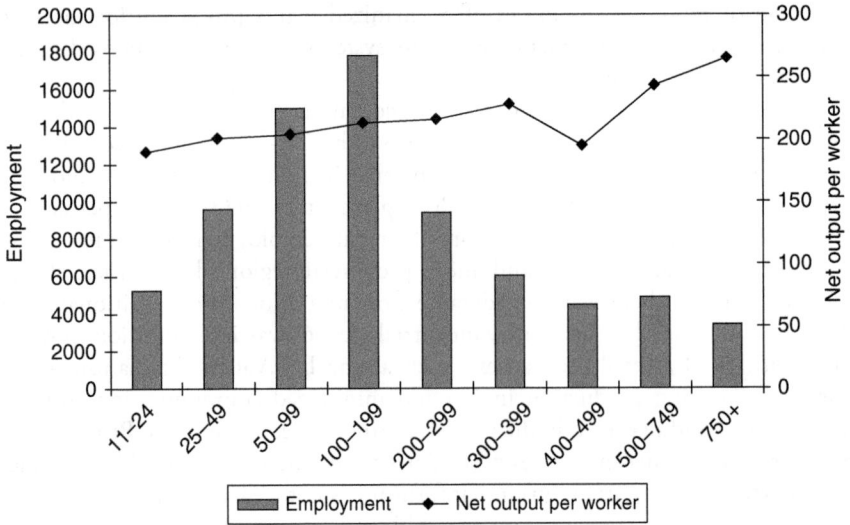

**Fig. 3.1.** Total employment and net output per worker in furniture establishments of various sizes, 1938

*Note:* Excludes firms with ten or fewer workers.

*Source:* Board of Trade Working Party Reports, *Furniture* (London: HMSO, 1946), 50.

remains, an industry which is not scale-intensive and has a relatively high representation of small and medium enterprises.[10] As Figure 3.1 demonstrates, the sector did not display particularly strong economies of scale and very large firms were exceptional. Furniture retailers did little to encourage larger factories or product standardization. The HP furniture multiples dealt with a mix of large and small manufacturers who had no say over design or branding and were forced to act as 'price-takers' (accepting the going price for their services). The main barrier to entry to the sector was at the retail level, imposed by strong retail branding, economies of scale from national advertising, and, especially, access to HP credit. Given that HP contracts ran for up to four years—much longer than was acceptable for the HP finance houses (that provided retail credit for other consumer durables sectors)—retailers who relied on liberal HP terms for their competitive advantage were compelled to finance them directly, which tied up a great deal of their capital.

Mass retailers successfully opposed producers' branding, generally removing manufacturers' labels to inhibit price comparisons.[11] Many sought to give the

---

[10] See Raphael Kaplinsky and Claudia Manning, 'Concentration, Competition Policy and the Role of Small and Medium-Sized Enterprises in South Africa's Industrial Development', *Journal of Development Studies*, 35 (1998), 139–61.

[11] Clive Edwards, *Turning Houses into Homes: A History of the Retailing and Consumption of Domestic Furnishings* (Aldershot: Ashgate, 2005), 187.

impression that they made their own furniture, despite most or all their stock being sourced externally. Producers' branding remained confined to specialist functional furniture not generally sold through HP furniture retailers, such as Minty and Globe-Wernicke sectional bookcases, Parker-Knoll and Berkeley easy chairs, and Compactom's fitted wardrobes.[12] Retailer control over branding also prevented manufacturers from imposing resale price maintenance; furniture became one of the least price-controlled consumer goods.[13]

The mass furniture chains claimed to gain economies of scale in purchasing.[14] Yet these do not appear to have been achieved through mass production—as evidenced by the fact that the chains frequently used both large and small contractors, even for the same designs.[15] The Board of Trade Furniture Working Party found that some retailers had established small manufacturers in business, who were entirely dependent on them for orders. These practices are characteristic of 'captive' value chains, where dominant firms contract out production to large numbers of smaller suppliers that undertake standardized tasks and have little or no input into product characteristics, design, and other specifications dictated by the buyer. Market power is thus retained by the retailer, who can easily switch between suppliers, based on price. Conversely, contractors are often highly reliant on an individual retailer for survival.[16]

Purchasing economies thus appear to have been accrued principally through exploiting the retailer's power over weak suppliers by forcing down manufacturers' prices.[17] Manufacturers also often found themselves obliged to give major retailers extended credit.[18] Squeezing manufacturers' margins was said to have depressed quality standards.[19] As representatives of the Lewis's of Liverpool department store group told the Board of Trade Furniture Working Party, shoddy furniture represented a substantial proportion of total output: 'considerable quantities were sold by hire-purchase shops, by West End stores, and by Lewis's Ltd themselves'.[20] Yet, despite this, their retail prices did not fall significantly in real terms; average prices for furniture and soft furnishings declined slightly more than general consumer prices over 1924–36, but slightly less if 1937 or 1938 is taken as the

---

[12] E. H. Pinto, *The Craftsman in Wood* (London: Bell, 1962), 129.

[13] J. B. Jefferys, *Retail Trading in Britain: 1850–1950* (Cambridge: Cambridge University Press, 1954), 422.

[14] TNA, BT64/2458, Board of Trade Furniture Working Party minutes, 2 Jan. 1946, evidence from Sir Isaac Wolfson.

[15] TNA, BT64/2458, Board of Trade Furniture Working Party minutes, 16 Jan. 1946, summary of evidence given by Messrs Hodkinson and Sawyer of Littlewoods.

[16] Gary Gereffi, John Humphrey, and Timothy Sturgeon, 'The Governance of Global Value Chains', *Review of International Political Economy*, 12 (2005), 78–104.

[17] Lynne Constable, 'An Industry in Transition: The British Domestic Furniture Trade 1914–1939' (unpublished PhD thesis, Brunel University 2000), 85.

[18] J. B. Jefferys, *The Distribution of Consumer Goods: A Factual Study of Methods and Costs in the United Kingdom in 1938* (Cambridge: Cambridge University Press, 1950), 271.

[19] Board of Trade Working Party Reports, *Furniture*, 33.

[20] TNA, BT64/2458, Board of Trade Furniture Working Party minutes, 24 Jan. 1946, summary of evidence given by Messrs Robinson and Breeze of Lewis's.

terminal year.[21] Thus, given the marked reduction in quality, it does not appear that gains from squeezing producers' margins were translated into lower real prices for the consumer.

Frequent change in styles, demanded by retailers so they could have new lines each season, hampered mass production and contributed to severe problems of seasonal unemployment and underemployment in manufacturing.[22] Firms partially overcame this by using standardized carcases and piece-parts, which were then differentiated by varying doors, bases, applied decorations, handles, and so forth.[23] For example, Great Universal Stores' 'designs' consisted chiefly of decorative panels and similar ornamentation, applied to standard furniture carcases, or variation in the shape of table legs and so forth.[24] Yet despite frequent design changes most new furniture was based on traditional designs, modified to suit the new production methods.[25] Estimates for the 1930s indicate that around 90 per cent of furniture represented period styles, modernist designs being generally confined to the higher end of the market.[26]

Table 3.1 shows an estimate of the value chain for multiple furniture retailers, in terms of each activity's contribution to the retail price. This assumes that multiple retailers' price mark-ups were 100 per cent over purchase costs (equivalent to 50 per cent of the final retail price); this is at the lower bound of available estimates—sources suggest that in the 1930s mark-ups of 125 or even 150 per cent were not unknown.[27]

**Table 3.1.** The value chain for the mass furniture sector

| Stages of value chain | Controlled by | % of retail price |
| --- | --- | --- |
| Design | Retailers | Negligible |
| Materials and power inputs | Market | 23 |
| Manufacture | Independent contractors | 27 |
| Marketing & distribution | Retailers | (50 |
| Consumer credit | Retailers | ( |
| Total | | 100 |

*Sources*: See text.

[21] Richard Stone and D. A. Rowe, *The Measurement of Consumers' Expenditure and Behaviour in the United Kingdom 1920–1938, Volume II* (Cambridge: Cambridge University Press, 1966), Tables 13 and 47.

[22] Board of Trade Working Party Reports, *Furniture*, 11.        [23] Ibid., 88.

[24] TNA, BT64/2458, Board of Trade Furniture Working Party minutes, 2 Jan. 1946; Constable, 'Industry in Transition', 193.

[25] Constable, 'Industry in Transition', 125 and 207.

[26] S. A. Worden, 'Furniture for the Living Room: An Investigation of the Interaction between Society, Industry, and Design in Britain from 1919 to 1939' (unpublished PhD thesis, Brighton Polytechnic, 1980), 12.

[27] Jefferys, *Distribution of Consumer Goods*, pp. 270–1; Board of Trade Working Party Reports, *Furniture*, 33.

## THE MARKET AND THE MULTIPLES

New furniture was the most important category of household durables. After falling back slightly in 1921, real consumers' expenditure on furniture and furnishings increased each year until 1936—at an average annual rate of 5 per cent (more than doubling over this period).[28] Jefferys estimated that consumers' expenditure on household furniture (excluding soft furnishings and floor coverings) in 1938 amounted to £63–64 million—more than twice the sum spent on household electrical goods and comfortably in excess of the £51–52 million spent annually by the public on new cars.[29]

The national household budget surveys of the late 1930s, discussed in Chapter 2, provide a snapshot of the composition of the furniture 'mass market' towards the end of our period, as shown in Table 3.2. Households with incomes in excess of £750 are excluded, as these typically frequented 'elite' retailers such as Maples and Heals, rather than the HP chains or other 'high street' outlets. In terms of aggregate purchasing power, the two most important socio-economic groups are shown to have been the non-agricultural working class, comprising 54.2 per cent of the mass market, and middle-class households with incomes of £250–500, comprising a further 31.9 per cent. Households with incomes of £500–750 per annum made a very small aggregate contribution to expenditure, on account of their very

**Table 3.2.** A profile of the UK 'mass market' for furniture in 1938

| | Households | | Annual expenditure on furniture per household | | Aggregate annual furniture expenditure | |
|---|---|---|---|---|---|---|
| | Number | % of total | % of household expenditure | £ | £ | % of total |
| **Working classes*** | | | | | | |
| Agricultural | 480,875 | 3.94 | 0.58 | 0.87 | 418,362 | 0.73 |
| Non-agricultural | 9,437,054 | 77.37 | 1.43 | 3.28 | 30,959,717 | 54.18 |
| **Lower-middle-classes** | | | | | | |
| £250–500 p.a. | 1,890,000 | 15.49 | 2.42 | 9.65 | 18,236,581 | 31.91 |
| £500–750 p.a. | 390,000 | 3.20 | 2.92 | 19.31 | 7,531,691 | 13.18 |
| **Total** | 12,197,930 | 100.00 | | | 57,146,350 | 100.00 |

*Notes*: * Working classes defined according to the Ministry of Labour 1937/38 budget survey definition of manual workers, plus non-manual workers with incomes under £250 per annum.

*Sources*: Expenditure: working-class households: TNA, LAB17/7, 'Weekly Expenditure of Working-Class Households in the United Kingdom in 1937–38', report, Ministry of Labour and National Service, July 1949, sections III and VI; middle-class households: Philip Massey, 'The Expenditure of 1,360 British Middle-Class Households in 1938–39', *Journal of the Royal Statistical Society*, 105 (1942), 159–96 (grossed up from England & Wales figure using ratio of UK/England & Wales population for 1941); A. H. Halsey (ed.), *Trends in British Society since 1900* (London: Macmillan, 1972), 91.

[28] Stone and Rowe, *Measurement of Consumers' Expenditure*, 14.
[29] Jefferys, *Distribution of Consumer Goods*, 269–300 and 350.

small numbers—despite their high spend per household. Meanwhile agricultural workers, who both formed a small proportion of households and had very low incomes, comprised less than 1 per cent of total expenditure.

Non-agricultural working-class households, which had hitherto often relied on second-hand or home-made furniture, thus made a major contribution to the expansion in national furniture consumption. This was facilitated by the growth in working-class incomes; yet despite an average rise in real wages of 1.21 per cent per annum over 1913–38, most working-class (and many lower-middle-class) families found it difficult to meet the costs of furnishing a house.[30] Furniture expenditure was strongly associated with new household formation and furnishing even a small house entirely with new items could cost as much as £100 or more. Even an exhibition by the Council for Art and Industry, showing how a small home could be furnished cheaply, proposed a budget of £50—for a two-bedroom house.[31] Furthermore, there was no strong tradition of working-class households buying new suites of furniture. While working-class families gained status from ownership of prestigious durables, they had generally focused on one or few prized possessions, such as a piano in the parlour, rather than a coordinated display of matching furniture and furnishings.[32]

This situation was transformed in the 1920s by a small group of furniture multiples that rapidly rose to national prominence. Jefferys found that multiple furniture retailing only began in around 1900, when there were some four firms with ten or more branches each, and that their growth was generally slow up to 1914.[33] Yet over the next twenty-five years, furniture multiples experienced meteoric growth, as shown in Table 3.3. By 1938 furniture was one of the sectors where multiples were most heavily represented, accounting for 28–32 per cent of retail sales (compared to around 18–19.5 per cent for all retail goods). Department stores were also over-represented, with 13–17 per cent of the trade, while co-ops had 6–8 per cent, leaving only 43–53 per cent of the market to independents (compared to around 63.5–67.5 per cent for all retail goods).[34]

Data on the inter-war furniture multiples are very sparse. However, monthly press advertising expenditure estimates for retailers and manufacturers that advertised nationally were published in the *Statistical Review of Press Advertising*. These probably omit some advertising in newspapers or magazines not monitored by the *Review*; conversely these data—based on standard newspaper rates—would not capture any discounts offered to major advertisers. Yet they are sufficiently reliable to rank the main advertisers and provide at least a rough estimate of their press advertising budgets.

---

[30] George R. Boyer, 'Living Standards 1860–1939', in Roderick Floud and Paul Johnson (eds.), *The Cambridge Economic History of Modern Britain*, vol. II: *Economic Maturity, 1860–1939* (Cambridge: Cambridge University Press, 2004), 280–313 (284–7).

[31] Alison Ravetz, *Council Housing and Culture: The History of a Social Experiment* (Abingdon: Routledge, 2001), 120; Peter Scott, 'Mr Drage, Mr Everyman, and the Creation of a Mass Market for Domestic Furniture in Interwar Britain', *Economic History Review*, 62 (2009), 802–27 (812).

[32] Robert Roberts, *The Classic Slum: Salford Life in the First Quarter of the Century* (Manchester: Penguin, 1971), 17; Joanna Bourke, *Working Class Cultures in Britain 1890–1960: Gender, Class and Ethnicity* (London: Routledge, 1994), 160–1.

[33] Jefferys, *Retail Trading in Britain*, 424. Jefferys defines multiples as firms with ten or more branches.

[34] Jefferys, *Distribution of Consumer Goods*, 73, 125, and 270.

**Table 3.3.** Estimates of the number of furniture multiples and their branches 1910–39

| Year | 10–24 branches | | 24–49 branches | | 50–99 branches | | 100+ branches | | Total | |
|------|-------|----------|-------|----------|-------|----------|-------|----------|-------|----------|
| | Firms | Branches | Firms | Branches | Firms | Branches | Firms | Branches | Firms | Branches |
| 1910 | 8 | 101 | 1 | 27 | 0 | 0 | 0 | 0 | 9 | 128 |
| 1920 | 10 | 131 | 2 | 65 | 0 | 0 | 0 | 0 | 12 | 196 |
| 1925 | 16 | 212 | 1 | 32 | 1 | 55 | 0 | 0 | 18 | 299 |
| 1930 | 20 | 254 | 2 | 51 | 2 | 126 | 0 | 0 | 24 | 431 |
| 1935 | 23 | 290 | 5 | 173 | 1 | 95 | 0 | 0 | 29 | 558 |
| 1939 | 24 | 334 | 3 | 106 | 1 | 73 | 1 | 175 | 29 | 688 |

*Source*: J. B. Jefferys, *Retail Trading in Britain: 1850–1950* (Cambridge: Cambridge University Press, 1954), 425.

Table 3.4 shows data for firms which spent £25,000 or more annually in either 1933 (the first full year for which data are available) or 1936, ranked according to 1933 advertising expenditure. Five 'hire purchase' retailers (i.e. firms which used generous HP terms as the basis of their marketing strategies) are shown to have dominated the sector, accounting for 57.8 per cent of national press advertising in 1933 and 47.9 per cent in 1936. Furthermore one of these—Woodhouse—was part of the British & Colonial Furniture group, which also included two smaller advertisers in the table: Cavendish-Woodhouse and Cavendish. The collective advertising for the five largest *groups* shown in the table would therefore amount to 60.3 per cent of the total in 1933 and 58.8 per cent in 1936.

Table 3.5 compares advertising expenditure with available data from the annual accounts of the four largest groups (the fifth, Times Furnishing Co., was not a public company). Such data have to be treated with caution; for example, Drage's HP debt portfolio is given net of an undisclosed figure for reserves against these debts. Nevertheless they suggest very high ratios of press advertising to turnover. By 1933 Smart Brothers' credit terms were based on forty monthly payments, with the first instalment acting as the deposit.[35] If it is assumed that sales were relatively stable over the previous forty months[36] and that bad debts had not been significant, then Smart Brothers' HP debt portfolio would represent a sum equal to twenty months' sales (as the average transaction would have repaid half the sum owed). Annual sales would thus be £827,203 and the ratio of advertising expenditure to sales would be 10.2 per cent (and 7.5 per cent for 1936).

Conducting a similar exercise for the British & Colonial Group (again assuming an average HP contract of forty months) would give a ratio of 13.1 per cent in 1933 and 12.0 per cent in 1936. Such calculations cannot be made for Drage's (given that its stated HP debts are reduced by an unknown amount of reserves) or Jays—as no HP debt figures are given.[37] However, as their advertising expenditures were

[35] Guildhall Library, London, bound volumes of London Stock Exchange company reports for 1933–4, Smart Brothers Ltd, AGM Chairman's speech, 11 Apr. 1934.

[36] National sales of furniture and furnishings are estimated to have fallen by 2.86 per cent over 1930–3 in nominal terms and increased by 12.38 per cent in real terms; Stone and Rowe, *Measurement of Consumers' Expenditure*, Tables 12–13.

[37] These were probably financed by an HP finance house, or a subsidiary firm.

**Table 3.4.** Furniture firms spending £25,000 or more on national advertising during 1933 or 1936

| Name | Type | Expenditure (£): | |
|------|------|------|------|
| | | 1933 | 1936 |
| Drage's Ltd | HP | 129,297 | 159,825 |
| Jay's | HP | 121,139 | 102,932 |
| Woodhouse* | HP | 114,784 | 100,160 |
| Smart Brothers Ltd | HP | 84,689 | 91,518 |
| Times Furnishing Co. | HP | 54,066 | 76,543 |
| Berkeley Chairs | Manufacturer | 44,801 | 43,171 |
| Campbell's | HP | 33,198 | 38,104 |
| Whiteley | Traditional | 28,676 | 25,983 |
| Gooch's | Traditional | 27,887 | 44,528 |
| Oetzmann | Traditional | 25,992 | 22,729 |
| Bolsoms | Traditional | 25,721 | 31,754 |
| Lawrence, Frederick Ltd | HP | 25,162 | 41,334 |
| Cavendish-Woodhouse* | HP | 14,463 | 65,646 |
| Hardy & Co. | HP | 11,911 | 42,120 |
| Cavendish* | HP | 7,118 | 54,732 |
| All listed retailers** | | 871,760 | 1,107,704 |
| Top 5 as % all listed | | 57.81 | 47.94 |
| Top 10 as % all listed | | 76.23 | 70.52 |

*Notes*: * These firms were part of the British & Colonial Furniture group. Advertising data for Cavendish and Cavendish-Woodhouse in 1933 are only given from October onwards. ** 31 firms were listed in 1933 and 33 in 1936.

*Source*: London Information Service, *Statistical Review of Press Advertising* (various issues).

**Table 3.5.** Advertising expenditure, HP debts owing, and net trading profit for the four largest furniture advertisers, 1933 and 1936

| Company | Advertising | HP debtors | Trading profit |
|---------|-------------|------------|----------------|
| **1933:** | | | |
| British & Colonial Group* | 136,365 | 1,730,964 | 166,916 |
| Drage's Ltd** | 129,297 | 1,126,414 | 86,580 |
| Jays Ltd*** | 121,139 | n.a. | 23,591 |
| Smart Brothers Ltd | 84,689 | 1,378,672 | 169,302 |
| **1936:** | | | |
| British & Colonial Group* | 220,538 | 3,052,423 | 338,273 |
| Drage's Ltd** | 159,825 | 1,492,781 | 90,349 |
| Jays Ltd*** | 102,932 | n.a. | 67,970 |
| Smart Brothers Ltd**** | 91,518 | 2,025,406 | 351,814 |

*Notes*: * Based on the reports and accounts for the British & Colonial Furniture Co. and the Cavendish Furniture Co. Both cover the year to 30 June following that shown in the table. HP debtors taken from item for: 'Goods on hire (less payments on account), sundry debtors, and pre-payments'. ** Reports and accounts cover year to 31 December. HP debtors figure taken from: 'Balance of HP contracts and sundry debtors, less reserves'. No figure given for reserves. 1933 trading profits taken from: 'Balance of trading account, including a proportion of reserves in respect of unexpired H.P. contracts for previous years'. 1936 trading profits figure is given before deducting transfer to reserves. *** Accounts cover year to 31 January. No figure is given for HP debtors. These may have been financed via an HP finance house. **** Accounts cover year to 31 December.

*Sources*: Advertising revenue—Table 3.4; other data—firms' annual reports and accounts for 1933/4 and 1936/7, held at the Guildhall Library.

substantially higher than Smart Brothers', and their net profits much lower, they can be expected to have at least as high ratios of advertising to sales. These ratios were far in excess of those for other retailers. Even department stores, which were among the most prolific advertisers, had average ratios of publicity expenditure (including both press advertising and other forms, such as direct mail and display) of only 3.05 per cent over 1931–8, while most retailers had markedly lower ratios.[38]

Indeed, despite comprising a very small proportion of household expenditure, furniture advertising accounted for a higher proportion of total retail advertising than any other commodity group. Furniture stores are estimated to have spent £2,039,000 on advertising in 1935, accounting for 21.9 per cent of all retailers' advertising; a particularly large figure given that a significant proportion of furniture was sold through outlets categorized separately, such as department stores and co-operatives.[39] High advertising spend was reflected in rapid stock-turn. Multiple furniture chains are estimated to have turned over their stock 4–5 times a year (and in some cases up to 6) by the late 1930s compared to 2.5–3 times for independent furniture retailers.[40]

Most national furniture chains developed from dedicated furnishing stores in the Tottenham Court Road/Holborn area of London. While their core business was furniture, many also diversified into other household goods, such as linoleum, carpets, and soft furnishings, while some also included lines such as bed linen and blankets, cutlery, china, glass, and silver ware, pictures, and even some electrical appliances and ironmongery.[41] As was the case with several other inter-war retail innovators which sought to create new mass markets, such as Montague Burton or Simon Marks, the national furniture multiples were dominated by Jewish entrepreneurs such as Benjamin Drage, Sampson J. Goldberg of Smart Brothers, and John Jacobs of the Times Furnishing Co. Furniture, like tailoring, was attractive to Jewish immigrants as it was a trade that could be entered on a small scale with little capital and the Jewish business community was already strongly established in the sector by 1914.

Financial constraints that prevented many households from purchasing new furniture were addressed via generous and aggressively marketed HP terms. HP had become an intrinsic feature of London's Tottenham Court Road furniture retailing district by the end of the Victorian period and on the eve of the First

---

[38] Source: Arnold Plant and R. F. Fowler, 'Operating Costs of Department Stores', reports for the Retail Distributors Association, Bank of England, and London School of Economics, final report for year ending 31 Jan. 1938 (1939), 44, and for year ending 31 Jan. 1939 (1940), 7. Data for 1931–7 refer to a constant sample of eighty-nine stores; 1938 data refer to all stores submitting returns in that year.

[39] Nicholas Kaldor and Rodney Silverman, *A Statistical Analysis of Advertising Expenditure and the Revenue of the Press* (Cambridge: Cambridge University Press, 1948), 10. The figures exclude hotels and restaurants (these were included in the original tabulation for the retail sector).

[40] Jefferys, *Distribution of Consumer Goods*, 271; W. R. Dunlop, 'Retail Profits', *Economic Journal*, 39 (1929), 357–70 (361–6); Royal Pharmaceutical Society Library Archives, IRA 1996.417, 'Survey of Retail Organisation and Trends', O. W. Roskill, 5 July 1939, 153.

[41] Geffrye Museum [hereafter GM], Times Furnishing Co., 'The Times Furnishing Company Ltd. Its History, its Service its Policy', brochure, *c.*1929; Hackney Furnishing Co., 'The Home Lover's Guide for Better Furnishing', n.d., *c.*1925.

World War at least a couple of central London furniture stores had begun to offer the kind of terms that were to revolutionize inter-war furniture retailing.[42] However, these were only to become extensively advertised to a national market from the early 1920s.[43] Estimates of the proportion of inter-war furniture sales to working-class customers conducted on HP vary from 65 per cent to as much as 90 per cent (the latter estimate being for furniture sold by the multiples).[44]

Furniture retailing became segmented both by the dominant types of store serving each income bracket and the HP terms they offered. Upmarket furniture and department stores such as Maples, Warings, and Harrods conducted only a small proportion of business on HP, usually on 12–24 month contracts. Meanwhile administrative costs were low, as careful selection of credit customers minimized risks and payments were usually made by monthly cheque or banker's order. Such firms were thus able to keep charges for HP down to around 10 per cent of the purchase price. Conversely, the specialist HP chains charged from 10–50 per cent (mainly towards the higher end of this spectrum), often via an additional price mark-up.[45] Jefferys found that HP retailers' margins were around 100–125 per cent, compared to an average of around 50–60 per cent for the cash trade, while the Board of Trade Working Party found margins of over 150 per cent in some cases.[46] Imposing an additional 50 per cent price mark-up to cover interest, for agreements involving equal monthly instalments over four years, would represent an implicit annual interest rate of around 24 per cent.

Yet retailers' net margins (after deduction of expenses) were much lower, reduced not only by their own interest costs but by the (much larger) administrative costs of recording and monitoring payments, inquiries into the status of customers, taking up references, and—for lower-income customers—door-to-door collectors. Such costs were inelastic with respect to the sum borrowed, being more strongly influenced by the length of the agreement, the frequency of payments, and whether these were made via collectors.[47] Costs were further inflated by the administrative expenses of dealing with arrears; it was estimated that 50 per cent of HP furniture customers from lower-income groups took longer than the agreed term to pay. Despite this the proportion of bad debts was relatively small—estimated by the Hire Purchase Traders' Association at less than 5 per cent—while sales of reclaimed

[42] Museum of Domestic Design and Architecture (hereafter MoDA), BADDA 553; Hackney Furnishing Co., 'British Homes: Their Making and their Furnishing' (1912); David Drage & Sons Ltd, 'Furniture of Quality and Distinction by Drage's, 230 & 231 High Holborn, brochure, n.d., c.1914.

[43] Pinto, *Craftsman in Wood*, 133; Clive Edwards, 'Buy Now—Pay Later. Credit: The Mainstay of Retail Furniture Business', in John Benson and Laura Ugolini (eds.), *Cultures of Selling: Perspectives on Consumption and Society since 1700* (Aldershot: Ashgate 2006), 127–52 (137).

[44] University of East Anglia Archives (hereafter UEA), Pritchard papers, memorandum by Cuthbert Greig, for Board of Trade Furniture Working Party, 28 Nov. 1945; Board of Trade Working Party Reports, *Furniture*, 145; Jefferys, *Distribution of Consumer Goods*, 270–1.

[45] UEA, Pritchard papers, Board of Trade Furniture Working Party minutes, 28 Nov. 1945.

[46] Jefferys, *Distribution of Consumer Goods*, 270–1; Board of Trade Working Party Reports, *Furniture*, 33.

[47] UEA, Pritchard papers, memorandum by Cuthbert Greig, for Board of Trade Furniture Working Party, 28 Nov. 1945.

goods reduced traders' losses to around 1 per cent.[48] Smart Brothers claimed in 1931 that its bad debt ratio had never exceeded 0.5 per cent at any time over the previous twenty years; an insurance policy with the Prudential guaranteed any bad debts over and above the first 2.5 per cent total loss on its HP portfolio of £704,650, for a single payment of £1,050.[49]

By the 1930s the phrase, 'furnishing out of income' had become a common slogan not only of furniture multiples, but of department stores and other furniture retailers. Meanwhile HP terms were being advertised openly even by prestige department stores. For example, a 1934 Harrods brochure prominently displayed its 'Convenient Furnishing Terms' on page 2, noting that, 'those desirous of furnishing without disturbance of capital may do so on exceptionally attractive terms'.[50] However, such stores rarely attempted to match the low deposits, or long repayment terms, of the furniture multiples.

Furniture multiples concentrated their marketing on suites of furniture for each room: the bedroom suite; the three-piece suite for the lounge/parlour; and the dining suite. Marketing suites provided larger unit sales to cover the administrative costs of HP instalment collections, together with the free carriage and other incentives commonly offered. Suites were also attractive to purchasers, as they were cheaper than buying individual items separately, provided a coordinated style, and had important status connotations.

The major obstacle faced by the multiples was consumer resistance to buying on HP. As a 1930 HP textbook noted: 'when a person furnished his house on credit he did so at the risk of endangering his social status, and consequently had to proceed under the cloak of secrecy'.[51] Many mass market retailers had traditionally avoided any mention of credit in their advertising, fearing reputational damage. Taking HP out from under the counter and promoting it as a legitimate means of furnishing entailed replacing the traditional stories surrounding HP (of borrowers' recklessness and lenders' predatory practices) with new stories based around responsible retailers offering those who wished to get ahead the opportunity to furnish 'out of income'.

## CREATING A MASS MARKET: 'MR DRAGE' MEETS 'MR EVERYMAN'

This problem was first successfully addressed by Benjamin Drage (originally Cohen, 1878–1952).[52] Today very few people have heard of Drage, but during the 1920s he was a household name, probably at least as familiar to the man in the

---

[48] Ibid.

[49] 'Smart Brothers Ltd', *The Times* (26 Mar. 1931), 23; 'Smart Brothers Ltd', *The Times* (9 Mar. 1927), 20.

[50] Peter Scott collection, Harrods, 'Home. Harrods', brochure (1934), 2.

[51] C. W. Aston, *Hire-Purchase Accounts and Finance* (London: Gee, 1930), 3; see also Roberts, *Classic Slum*, 17–18.

[52] Stephen Aris, *The Jews in Business* (London: Jonathan Cape, 1970), 137.

street as Gordon Selfridge or Lord Leverhulme. Drage's retail furniture empire was founded in 1908 in High Holborn. A 1914 catalogue shows that by this time the essentials of his marketing strategy were already in place, including the 'Drage's Way' of furnishing out of income, delivery in plain vans, and an assurance of secrecy with no references asked for.[53] However, it was only from the 1920s that this formula was to be taken to a national stage.

In 1922 a series of large display adverts appeared in national newspapers ranging from *The Times* to the tabloids, under the general title, 'The Drage Way of furnishing out-of-income'. These shared the common broad format of a conversation between Mr Drage and Mr (sometimes Mrs, Reverend, Captain, etc.) Everyman (Fig. 3.2). Each started with Mr Everyman explaining to Mr Drage that he had limited cash due to various circumstances, such as an officer who had given up his home during the war, or a man being about to get married. After praising the quality of Drage's furniture, they stated the value needed to furnish their house or flat (generally between £100 and £200) and asked how much they would need to pay as a deposit and instalments. Mr Drage's reply was along the lines of, 'That rests entirely with you. What can you conveniently pay now? We always try to agree with any reasonable suggestion.'[54] The customer invariably suggested a deposit of at least 10 per cent and monthly payments of around 2.5 per cent (implying a three-year repayment period, the maximum offered by Drage's at this time). When this was agreed, the question of references was broached by Mr Everyman, to which Mr Drage replied that these were not required.

Drage's advertisements sought to remove customers' fears of a negative reception, on account of either their class background or need for credit. In one Mr Everyman states: 'elsewhere we were treated almost as intruders. Here we were welcomed like old friends.'[55] As a Drage's brochure noted, 'Mr and Mrs Everyman…represent the average Englishman and his wife…You see them bringing their doubts, their difficulties and their troubles to Mr Drage, and how readily and pleasantly he finds them a way out.'[56] Mr Everyman spanned a broad class range, the public being informed that: 'All Classes Furnish at Drage's. Tinker, tailor, soldier, sailor—shopkeepers, clergymen, and railway men—solicitors and business women—professional men and artisans. All receive the same cordial welcome, the same courteous treatment, and the same generous terms.'[57] Nor did 'Everyman' imply a rejection of female customers. A 1926 Drage's brochure noted: 'Ladies Welcomed…Very often it is inconvenient for husband and wife to come together. But ladies may always rely on the most courteous and liberal treatment. Hundreds of business and professional ladies have their names on our books.'[58]

[53] GM, David Drage & Sons Ltd, *Furniture of quality and distinction by Drage's, 230 & 231 High Holborn*, brochure, c.1914.

[54] 'The Drage way', *The Times* (18 Sept. 1922), 5.

[55] 'You've Given a New Meaning to Credit Furnishing, Mr Drage', *The Times* (21 May 1924), 7.

[56] Peter Scott collection, Drages Ltd, 'Mr & Mrs Everyman Talk Things Over with Mr Drage', brochure, n.d., c.1926.

[57] Ibid.    [58] Ibid.

**Fig. 3.2.** An early (May 1923) Drage's advert featuring Mr and Mrs Everyman

*Source*: Peter Scott collection.

Drage also sought to reduce the perceived risks of HP. Fears of hidden costs were addressed via inclusive terms: furniture was delivered carriage-paid and linoleum and carpets laid free of charge. This was no small matter to people who lived in fear of being presented with a bill for a substantially larger sum than they believed they had agreed to, owing to the addition of 'extras'. Customers were also provided with a free fire and life insurance policy and assured that, 'The Drage Way provides the feeling of security, comfort, and safety, because in cases of unforeseen happenings—death, sickness, or unemployment—you can rely on the most generous treatment.'[59] By 1926 this had been replaced by a more explicit guarantee:

> The New Drage Way is entirely different from the usual hire purchase. Hitherto if a customer could not continue paying his instalments he would forefeit all he had paid and lose all the furniture into the bargain. Whereas under the New Drage Way each customer receives a written guarantee that if adverse circumstances keep him from going on paying he may keep all that he has paid for, less a fair and reasonable allowance for use and cartage.[60]

As Benjamin Drage explained in 1927, he wanted to remove customers' fears that in the event of some misfortune halting payments, the home would be broken up.[61] He claimed that by introducing a surrender value into HP contracts, Drage's had both extended the use of HP and improved its reputation—similar guarantee clauses having subsequently been adopted by most major furniture retailers.[62] These appear to have had some legal validity. For example, when the furniture chain Jay's brought a case to the Bow County Court in 1927—to recover £5 12s 6d outstanding on a set of repossessed furniture—the judge radically reduced the sum payable, in the light of the guarantee (which the defendant had earlier unsuccessfully tried to enforce).[63]

In a 1927 interview Drage claimed his trading policy had made a genuine contribution to reducing the risks facing lower-income families:

> The fear of the future is, with improved social legislation, becoming lessened...the need for close-fisted thrift has been considerably lessened...Nowadays, most of the great furniture dealers have incorporated in their Hire Purchase agreements the clause *that we first originated*, which gives the customer the right that, should unforeseen circumstances...prevent the continuation of payment...then after deduction of a reasonable charge for use and cartage the customer should retain all that has been paid for and only return what has not been paid for.[64]

Drage's 'Mr Everyman' campaign marked a watershed in furniture advertising. The furniture was never shown in detail, the focus instead being almost exclusively on the firm, the personal and confidential service offered by Mr Drage, and their

[59] 'Mr Everyman Comes up for the Derby', *The Times* (6 June 1923), 11.
[60] 'Crossing the Rubicon', *The Times* (17 Feb. 1926), 19. By this time Drage's conversational ads had been replaced by a series with illustrations of historical events, such as Caesar crossing the Rubicon, to signify the path-breaking character of the Drage way.
[61] Interview with Mr Drage by A. Warner Browne, reproduced in *Cabinet Maker* (5 Nov. 1927), 293.
[62] Ibid.     [63] 'Dispute over Hired Furniture', *Furniture Record* (18 Feb. 1927), 310.
[64] Interview of Mr Drage by A. Warner Browne, reproduced in *Cabinet Maker* (5 Nov. 1927), 293.

generous terms. Drage had substituted the traditional 'myth' of the unscrupulous HP furniture retailer with the new myth of 'Mr Drage' as philanthropist—helping those in need to furnish their homes on credit, guarding them from the risks traditionally associated with HP, and ensuring that their dealings with his firm were subject to the utmost secrecy.

The campaign was hailed in the advertising industry and furniture trade for its path-breaking approach to the customer.[65] It was perhaps the first British example of the 'conversational' style of advertising, offering the public an ever changing cast of characters visiting Mr Drage with each new advert. As such, the ads had what we would now call a 'viral' appeal, creating a genuine interest among readers regarding that week's Mr Drage story. They also had an element of 'relationship marketing', as people progressively came to perceive that they understood Mr Drage and his trading methods and could trust him. This approach was revisited by several firms during the following years, most notably by Murphy Radio, as discussed in Chapter 7.

However, others cast a more cynical eye on the ads and Drage's apparent philanthropy rapidly became something of a national joke. For example in the 1925 Norman Long music hall song *Drage Way*, a penniless Mr Everyman tells Mr Drage:

> See, I've only just got married, and I'm on the rocks and broke.
> He said, 'Don't let that worry you, why money is a joke!
> We only run our business to oblige you sort of folk,
> And we always lay your lino on the floor!'

> So I said 'That's very generous, but no reference I've got'
> He said 'we do not want them they're a lot of Tommy-rot.
> Why you needn't even give your name, if you would rather not
> And we always lay your lino on the floor!'

> Five hundred pounds in furniture, she spent did my Old Dutch;
> 'What deposit Mr Drage' said I 'would you require for such?'
> He simply smiled and said 'would two and sixpence be too much?
> And we always lay your lino on the floor!'

> ...

> And I said 'Mr Drage, suppose that I am taken ill
> And cannot keep my payments up.' He said, 'It costs you nil.
> We keep you while you're out of work and pay your doctor's bill
> And we always lay your lino on the floor!'[66]

Drage's financial performance suggests that the Mr Everyman campaign was initially very successful, net profits rising sharply from £71,569 in 1923 (the earliest year

[65] See, for example, Philip Kimber, 'Retailers! Look Natural Please!', *Advertiser's Weekly* (28 Feb. 1930), 316 and 348.
[66] Extract from Norman Long, 'The Drage Way', recorded 23 Oct. 1925. Reissued on Norman Long, 'My little Austin Seven' (CD, Windyridge CDs).

for which figures are available) to £146,722 in 1925.[67] Yet Drage's soon became a victim of its own success. There was nothing in the broad outlines of Drage's business model that could be protected by patents or copyrighting and he rapidly became subject to that most sincere form of flattery—emulation. Within a few years Drage's generous HP terms, secrecy, guarantees, free delivery and fitting services, and so forth featured prominently in the advertising of his main competitors (which—unlike Drage's—also had the advantage of extensive branch networks).

Moreover, Drage's campaign had not addressed the perceived shame associated with HP. The philanthropic tone of the Mr Everyman adverts, and references to plain vans, no references asked for, etc., only served to emphasize its dubious image. As *Cabinet Maker* noted in October 1925, prospective purchasers must not

> be made to feel that the advertiser is a wonderful philanthropist, and that out of his pity for the poverty of the would-be customer he proposes to do him the favour of letting him have goods for an initial payment of a tenth of their total cost... the aim should be to make readers think that to buy things in this way—out of income and without disturbing the capital which many of them never had—is quite a logical and rational proceeding.[68]

## THE 'SMART' ALTERNATIVE: LIFESTYLE MARKETING

The next big step in making furnishing on credit socially acceptable to the working and lower-middle classes was taken by Drage's competitor Smart Brothers, using an aspirational appeal. There had been elements of this in its advertising from the early 1920s; for example, a 1921 advert showed a young couple gazing longingly from the street into the windows of a luxurious home, with the tag line, 'Smarts' can bring this "HOME" to you.'[69] By the middle of the decade its approach had become more sophisticated; in October 1925 *Cabinet Maker* commended an advertisement showing 'a photo of a mature business man in conversation with a younger man the reason for a headline, "Don't break into your savings, my boy; do as I did."' This both created the impression that people used HP not because they could not afford to pay cash, but because it was the 'thing to do', and replaced the retailer as the exponent of this method by a prosperous-looking authority figure.[70]

Advertising agency chief A. J. Greenly (one of the pioneers of the modern British advertising industry, whose influence was cut short by his early death in 1933) had designed this new campaign specifically to counter Drage's conversational ads with a short-story format. As Greenly explained:

> The plots are extremely simple. There is the young man who has found at last a flat, and is only troubled about furnishing; the girl who finds her lover's home much better

[67] Drage's Limited, prospectus, *The Times* (15 Mar. 1926), 21, column A. The Mr Drage advertisements appeared in *The Times* from September 1922 to November 1924.

[68] 'Retail Advertising', *Cabinet Maker* (31 Oct. 1925), 195–6.

[69] '"Getting Across" in Advertising', *Furnishing Trades Organiser* (21 Nov. 1921), 421.

[70] 'Furnishing—out-of-income Ads', *Cabinet Maker* (10 Oct. 1925), 49–50.

than her own, and who tries to persuade her mother to refurbish the sitting-room; the young man who does not wish to spend all his little capital on furnishing; and the friend who tells him to get his home together without disturbing his savings.[71]

Smart Brothers thus moved the scene of the advert from the store to the home, yet in two important respects they built on Drage's example. First, they concentrated on converting a hesitant public to 'buying out of income', while never actually featuring the furniture. Second, they kept the reader's interest by always varying the script. As Greenly noted, 'The fundamental reason for the success of this type of advertising is the constant change of characters. There is always a new problem to be solved, a new story to be told, always fresh interest for the reader.'[72]

This strategy also underpinned their direct mail advertising, which pioneered a 'lifestyle' approach—emphasizing how they offered purchasers the chance to achieve the sort of aspirational, domestically orientated lifestyles being promoted in, for example, women's magazines. Large glossy brochures emphasized the glamour, luxury, and aspirational connotations of new suites of furniture. One eighty-page brochure included features such as 'Choosing Your Colour Schemes and Planning Your Room', and testimonials from movie stars. It also drew on the ideology of domesticity (a popular theme in women's magazines); for example, the section devoted to the nursery began, 'Your Baby! The most valuable thing in the world—a precious symbol of mutual love and understanding.'[73] Yet the short story format (here adapted for the women's magazine motif) was again used to deliver the main sales message. 'Honeymoon. A complete love story by Garth Preston', drew the reader in with the tag line, 'Sheila gets two surprises... they alter the whole course of her life! Thrill to this tender story of youthful love!' After a couple of paragraphs the predicament is set out:

> Gordon considered John and Arthur, now settled down with charming wives in beautiful new homes. Then he thought of his own position. Engaged to the most fascinating girl he'd ever met, and unable to marry her because he couldn't afford it. Even seeing Sheila seemed to be difficult. They couldn't be alone when he asked her to his house, because Mother and Dad were always there. It was the same at Sheila's. All they could do was go for walks or the pictures, or as they were doing to-morrow, to some dance. And these places he knew were unsatisfactory.[74]

Following the advice of a married friend, Gordon turns to Smart's furniture catalogue and their 'Easier to Pay—Smart's 4 Year Way System', which enables them to 'furnish the most beautiful home in the world without waiting another day!'[75] Smart Brothers were thus positioned as gatekeepers to the sort of aspirational

---

[71] Fernand A. Marteau, 'The Drage Way and the Smart Reply: Inside Story of Two Furnishing Houses' Campaigns', *Furniture Record* (19 Mar. 1926), 465.

[72] Ibid.

[73] GM, Smart Brothers Ltd, 'Smarts have Furnished a Million Homes and Won a Million Hearts', brochure, n.d.

[74] Ibid.     [75] Ibid.

**Fig. 3.3.** A section of an April 1934 Smart Brothers 'intimate' series advert

*Source*: Peter Scott collection.

lifestyles being promoted in the popular media and which many young lower-middle or working-class couples sought to buy into.

Smart Brothers' approach was copied by other HP furniture retailers. For example, the Times Furnishing Co. employed an advertising campaign where young, upwardly-mobile people emphasized the high priority they accorded to an attractive, well-furnished home. This drew on the lifestyle features type of women's magazine article. For example, in a May 1936 advert a middle-class woman explains that:

> Louis and I got married at Witsun last year... I kept on my secretarial post to help with the family budget... Before we married we both decided to start our lives together in a lovely home—even if it meant economising on other things... Certainly the greatest guarantee of happiness is a comfortable, attractive home. I am *absolutely sure* of that.[76]

Times Furnishing Co. also copied Smart Brothers' short story format, with stories carrying titles such as 'HIS FIRST NOTE TO HER WAS AN INSULT', and 'How Roger was convinced'.[77] Their brochures further developed a lifestyle appeal. For example, their magazine-style *Good Furnishing* booklet, edited by Christine Veasey of their 'Advisory Bureau', included items on weddings, film stars at home, health and beauty, and a knitting pattern, as well as 'What furniture means to your home', and planning various rooms.[78] Eventually Drage's produced its own 'lifestyle' brochure, 'Yours sincerely Jane & John'—the story of a couple who had bought their furniture from Drage's on marriage twenty-five years previously and now returned to help their daughters furnish their homes. They offered advice on what makes a happy marriage and emphasized the importance of new furniture in establishing the right domestic environment. The couple played a similar role to the knowledgeable advisers in the Smart Brothers adverts—as 'John' writes to his prospective son-in-law: 'If you, my young man, have not enough idle cash to buy, for the "only girl", the home she deserves, go and see Drages about it—as Jane and I did.'[79]

By 1934 Smart Brothers had taken their racy copy style further, with their 'Intimate' series of adverts (Fig. 3.3) that drew on the type of racy literature found in the expanding '2d libraries'. This echoed a growing trend in American consumer goods advertising (reacting to a 1931 Gallup magazine readership survey, which found that both men and women remembered ads featuring sex appeals more clearly than most other appeals, such as price or quality).[80] This drew sustained criticism from the advertising trade press, though not for lack of effectiveness. As *Advertising World* noted: 'Few advertising reviews... within the last six months have omitted at least one dig... Justifiably too. And in spite of the knowledge that this famous

---

[76] 'Married a Year...', Times Furnishing Co. advertisement, *Daily Mirror* (26 May 1936), 15.

[77] *Daily Mirror* (22 Feb. 1938), 6; (5 Apr. 1938), 6.

[78] National Art Library, Trade Catalogues Collection, Christine Veasey (ed.), *Good Furnishing*, Times Furnishing Co. (c.1935).

[79] MODA, BADDA.241, Drages Ltd, *Yours Sincerely Jane & John* (brochure, n.d., 1930s).

[80] Stephen Fox, *The Mirror Makers: A History of Advertising and its Creators* (New York: Morrow, 1984), 138–9.

campaign was created by one of the most competent agencies, and in spite of the fact that it has proved successful.' The campaign was viewed as, 'too "near the nuckle"...acknowledging the fact that here is a great campaign, let us say that to most of us it verges on the objectionable...the slogan "He's going to do the RIGHT THING." Oh, so there's been some scandal, has there, Messrs. Smarts? And now this unknown man about whom these two scantily dressed young things hold such happy converse, is about to put it right...Right appeal, but surely it could have been handled in a less suggestive manner.'[81]

The following month *Advertising World* attacked another Smart Brothers ad, showing two fashionable young women in conversation, with the slogan 'Darling—surely not *another* one!'. Although reading further produced a more innocent explanation to the phrase than the reader might initially imagine, the reviewer concluded: 'Gets *your* attention. Gets *their* pockets. Gets *many* goats.'[82] Yet their critic acknowledged that this was a successful pitch:

> At any time of the year there are always thousands of couples considering starting a home of their own. The market is there. All the competitive furniture advertisers know this. To find a means by which they could step in ahead of all their direct competitors was Smart's desire. They worked on the emotions of the males. Pretty, scantily dressed girls sometimes talking in slick terms of wedding joys, did the trick.'[83]

There were, of course, other ways of appealing to the newly married. A Drage's ad of the same period showed a young woman holding a baby high against her head, with the slogan, 'To a young lady in the seventh heaven'. This was acclaimed by *Advertising World* on both aesthetic and impact grounds: 'Behind those eight words there lies a whole wealth of domestic adventures and aspirations...They'll read every word of this advertisement, *and* of the other one in which we see the young father smiling all over his face, with a youngster on either side of him.'[84]

## IMPACTS ON CONSUMPTION AND WELFARE

It is notoriously difficult to find direct evidence of the impacts of specific advertising campaigns on consumer behaviour. However, the rise of intensive advertising by the furniture multiples during the 1920s was matched by a major expansion in sales, which cannot be explained in terms of factors such as rising incomes or new house-building. Household expenditure on furniture and furnishings rose sharply over 1924–30, from 1.12 to 1.50 per cent of total consumer expenditure, but then rose much more gradually, to 1.65 per cent of total consumer expenditure in 1935,

---

[81] 'You Saw These Too', *Advertising World*, 66, 2 (Oct. 1934), 42–8 (42).

[82] 'You Saw These Too', *Advertising World*, 67, 11 (Nov. 1935), 45–8 (45–6).

[83] 'Campaigns: In Furniture Field, Sex is Exclusively a Smart's Affair', *Advertising World*, 70, 3 (Mar. 1938), 55–6 (56).

[84] 'You Saw These Too!', *Advertising World*, 66, 3 (Nov. 1934), 33–40 (38–9).

despite the real rate of growth of consumer expenditure over 1930–5 being only 0.13 percentage points below that for 1924–30.

Similarly, furniture expenditure correlates very poorly with house-building. Real consumer expenditure on furniture and furnishings in 1931 was 76.8 per cent in excess of that in 1921, while the housing stock of England and Wales had expanded by only 17.8 per cent. Conversely a 19.8 per cent increase in the housing stock over the period 1931 to March 1939 was accompanied by only a 7.9 per cent increase in national furniture expenditure from 1931 to the end of 1938.[85] However, it is possible that wider post-1914 changes in the housing market, particularly increased stability of tenure (a product of rent control, greater legal rights for tenants, and improvements in transport, which made it easier to travel longer distances to work), may have had a significant impact in encouraging households to accumulate more furniture.

As noted earlier, family expenditure surveys show that working-class households constituted a major section of the furniture market by the late 1930s and that most of their purchases involved HP. Contemporary trade sources also indicate that working-class customers made the most intensive use of the liberal credit facilities offered by the HP furniture chains and were thus the main group attracted to this type of retailer.[86] As in other sectors (such as house purchase), the importance of the working-class market is obscured by the fact that advertisements generally showed prosperous young professionals, giving the impression that the furniture chains served an overwhelmingly middle-class market. However, depicting a higher social setting than that of the target customer was common practice in contemporary advertising, based on the premise that purchasers prefer to identify with people they aspire to be, rather than those who mirror their current circumstances.[87]

Oral history sources and contemporary social surveys suggest that the proportion of household income devoted to furniture was particularly high on new suburban estates, both owing to the relatively large sizes of suburban council and owner-occupied houses compared to inner-urban terraces and to strong social pressures to 'keep up with the Joneses', by projecting a coordinated display of material affluence.[88] For example, Jevons and Madge's survey of Bristol municipal estates found that the cost of equipping the house translated into weekly HP payments of around 2s 6d; while most families rejected the second-hand furniture collected for new tenants

---

[85] Sources: housing stock, Marion Bowley, *Housing and the State 1919–1944* (London: George Allen & Unwin, 1945), 269–71. The 1924 housing stock is estimated from the Census figure for 1921, plus new house-building for the years ending 31 Mar. 1922–5. Real furniture expenditure, Stone and Rowe, *Measurement of Consumers' Expenditure*, 26. Furniture and furnishings' consumption is deflated using Stone and Rowe's price index for this sector. Taking 1924, rather than 1921, as the starting point for the comparison produces very similar results.

[86] See, for example, UEA, Pritchard papers, memorandum by Cuthbert Greig, for Board of Trade Furniture Working Party, 28 Nov. 1945.

[87] Roland Marchand, *Advertising the American Dream: Making Way for Modernity, 1920–1940* (Berkeley: University of California Press, 1985), 166; Peter Scott, 'Marketing Mass Home Ownership and the Creation of the Modern Working Class Consumer in Interwar Britain', *Business History*, 50 (2008), 4–25 (15).

[88] Peter Scott, *The Making of the Modern British Home: The Suburban Semi and Family Life between the Wars* (Oxford: Oxford University Press, 2013), ch. 6.

by the Housing Committee.[89] Similarly, a 1939 survey of a Birmingham council estate found that more than half the families visited were buying furniture on HP.[90] Most accounts indicate that people generally welcomed the opportunity of buying their furniture on credit—mainly because they could not afford to pay cash.

## 'CUT-THROAT' COMPETITION, INSTABILITY, AND MIS-SELLING

The inter-war British furniture industry had strong similarities to the US furniture industry of the 1920s. In the United States buying furniture on instalments had also been regarded as disreputable, leading many credit furniture dealers at around the turn of the century to use plain wagons for delivery.[91] Yet, in common with other high-ticket durables, its acceptability had grown markedly by the early 1920s. A 1923 US government inquiry found that the majority of furniture stores relied on instalment business for 75 per cent or more of their sales, roughly on a par with the British figure for the 1930s.[92] The report also identified some of the key drawbacks of instalment finance. Those stores which used it most intensively typically had higher price mark-ups, higher operating expenses, and less frequent turnover of capital (which was tied up in credit contracts). Moreover, longer instalment contracts implied slower turnover of capital and greater capital requirements per dollar of business. This was not an onerous problem in the United States, where instalment contracts typically ran from ten months to two years in the early 1920s.[93] However, given Britain's lower average incomes, the creation of a mass market required the use of much longer credit terms, both necessitating higher price mark-ups to cover their costs and accentuating the retailer's capital problems.

The forms of credit agreement used by US furniture retailers also had striking similarities with British HP contracts, in that the balance of power was strongly weighted towards the retailer, providing significant opportunities for sharp practice. The most common American furniture credit plans were broadly similar to HP (using 'leases' with repayments treated as 'rental'). The next most common form, chattel mortgages, also shared the characteristic of HP that the retailer retained ownership until final payment had been made and the furniture could be repossessed if a payment was missed without any compensation.[94]

---

[89] Rosamond Jevons and John Madge, *Housing Estates: A Study of Bristol Corporation Policy and Practice between the Wars* (Bristol: Arrowsmith, 1946), 45.

[90] M. S. Soutar, E. H. Wilkins, and P. Sargant Florence, *Nutrition and Size of Family: Report on a New Housing Estate—1939* (London: George Allen & Unwin, 1942).

[91] Lendol Calder, *Financing the American Dream: A Cultural History of Consumer Credit* (Princeton, NJ: Princeton University Press, 1999), 180–1.

[92] U.S. Federal Trade Commission, *Report of the Federal Trade Commission on House Furnishing Industries*, vol. I: *Household Furniture* (Washington: USGPO, 1923), 12.

[93] Ibid., 18.

[94] Ibid., 12–18. The form of contract used by the remaining stores was not specified.

Competition between British HP retailers focused primarily on terms and advertising, rather than price. By 1927 *Furniture Record* was noting aggressive competition between retailers based around easy payments, including 'No Deposit' offers—led by the industry's 'trade giants' rather than, as in the past, small disreputable dealers. It viewed this as problematic: 'when everybody gives credit free and lays linoleum for nothing, what is to be the next move?'[95] Yet further liberalization followed; in 1927 it was still common to ask for a 10 per cent deposit and spread payments over 12–36 months; yet by July 1929 Drage's were advertising their 'famous 50 Pay Way terms...the longest and most liberal credit terms ever offered to the British public'.[96] This removed any deposit requirement, the customer instead paying 50 identical monthly instalments (the first on purchase). Pressure of competition led many independent retailers and even department stores to liberalize their HP terms; as *Cabinet Maker* noted in 1930, 'our successors will doubtless mark the present as a distinct "period" or phase in the selling of furniture through the newspaper...it will be known as the decade of "follow my leader"...suborned to the creed of "something for nothing", and "terms, terms, terms"'.[97]

HP finance houses, which provided much of the HP credit used by automobile and household durables retailers, would not accept such long contracts, thus forcing the HP multiples to rely on other sources of funding that did not involve the self-liquidating resale of their HP paper. This may have played a major role in the financial problems some of the largest HP retailers were to face as the scale of their credit business mushroomed.

Cut-throat competition fostered opportunistic behaviour by HP multiples, who had a bad reputation for selling shoddy goods to customers at inflated prices, using various devices to disguise quality and cost. As the Board of Trade Working Party noted, it was relatively easy to give a poor piece of furniture a 'showy appearance' so as to prevent customers from accurately assessing its true quality.[98] The concentration of purchases at the household formation stage of the family life cycle left customers particularly vulnerable to such sharp practice, as most purchasers were inexperienced furniture consumers.[99] HP chains suppressed price comparisons by refusing to display manufacturers' brands and by differentiating their products from their competitors using exclusive designs. Comparisons were also obstructed by aggressive salesmanship to try and close the sale and by the absence of clearly marked prices and credit terms in some shops.[100]

Misleading advertising further inhibited price competition. Misrepresenting furniture in press advertisements was said to be common practice, including such

[95] *Furniture Record* (27 Feb. 1927), 335.
[96] 'Hire Purchase. Systems to Meet a Growing Demand on the Part of the Public', *Cabinet Maker* (17 Sept. 1927), 621–2; 'Victory' (Drage's advert), *The Times* (9 July 1929), 21.
[97] 'Current Furniture Advertising', *Cabinet Maker* (23 Aug. 1930), 326–8.
[98] UEA, Pritchard papers, Board of Trade Furniture Working Party minutes, 28 Nov. 1945.
[99] Board of Trade Working Party Reports, *Furniture*, 11.
[100] Melanie Tebbutt, *Making Ends Meet: Pawnbroking and Working-Class Credit* (London: Methuen, 1984), 194.

fundamental characteristics as dimensions and materials, illustrations that did not match the products actually offered for sale, and a variety of other false statements.[101] There were also frequent claims of abuses regarding HP contracts, such as getting customers to sign blank agreements and then filling in a price much higher than that stated.[102] Even the Secretary of the Hire Purchase Traders' Association privately acknowledged that certain chains approached HP 'with the mentality of the worst type of moneylender... [and] sold furniture of bad quality and construction, but finished to catch the eye'.[103]

Sources examined for this study (including trade publications that regularly carried details of county court cases) suggest that while such practices were commonplace, there is little evidence of significant abuses on the part of the largest national HP chains—with the notable exception of Jay's. Jay's both featured in a disproportionate number of cases and came in for particularly strong judicial condemnation. For example, a May 1932 case brought before Yarmouth County Court by their Norwich branch—which was suing Mrs Eileen Clifton for the return of furniture—revealed that the defendant had not been given a reasonable chance to study the HP agreement, that the deposit was not credited to the customer's payments unless the purchase was completed, and that deductions from the surrender value of the furniture for 'depreciation' were excessive. Judge C. Herbert-Smith described the HP contract as 'the most one-sided agreement I have ever had to deal with' and advised the public to have nothing to do with Jay's, unless accompanied by a legal adviser. While he found against Mrs Clifton, he disallowed all costs to Jay's, whose behaviour he described as 'scandalous'.[104]

Competitive pressures intensified during the 1929–32 depression. Furniture sales were strongly influenced by the economic cycle, as new furniture constituted a major, postponable, and substitutable item of household expenditure. While the 2.48 per cent nominal fall in consumers' expenditure on furniture and furnishings over 1929–32 was matched by a 14.71 per cent fall in general retail prices, this period witnessed a significant slow-down in real sales growth compared to the 1920s.[105] Traditional furniture manufacturers and retailers fared particularly badly; by the end of 1932 some 30.4 per cent of NAFTA's members were out of work and several major department stores and house furnishers—including Gamages and Waring & Gillow—faced liquidation.[106] Smart Brothers' profits fell from £224,339 in 1929 to only £28,532 in 1932 (when no dividend was paid on their ordinary shares), mainly due to a sharp fall in the average size of

---

[101] Pinto, *Craftsman in Wood*, 133.

[102] 'Catchpenny Furnishing Offers. National Chains may Attempt to Stop Supplies', *Cabinet Maker* (24 July 1937), 103; see also Peter Scott, 'The Twilight World of Interwar Hire Purchase', *Past & Present*, 177 (2002), 195–225.

[103] UEA, Pritchard papers, memorandum by Cuthbert Greig, for Board of Trade Furniture Working Party, 28 Nov. 1945.

[104] 'Order for Return to Trader', *Hire Traders' Record* (2 May 1932), 3–4.

[105] Stone and Rowe, *Measurement of Consumers' Expenditure*, Tables 12–13.

[106] Constable, 'An Industry in Transition', 180 and 197.

order, together with many customers being unable to meet HP payments and either returning furniture or falling into arrears.[107] Yet during the following years the firm's profits recovered strongly—assisted by a further expansion in their branch network.[108]

Drage's fared less well, hampered by a business model based around selling from a single, heavily publicized London store. Despite announcing plans to establish a provincial branch network at the time of its public flotation in March 1926, Drage's only opened two branch stores—at Manchester and Birmingham.[109] Furthermore, though it had amassed an HP debt portfolio of £1,057,506 by the end of 1928 (after deductions of reserves for bad debts), Drage's sales pitch remained distinctly personal—based around the fiction that all customers seeking credit were granted a personal audience with 'Mr Drage', rather than having to broach the subject with a salesman.[110] As a brochure, of around 1929–30, stated:

> Buying furniture is peculiarly a personal matter. *Arranging the terms on a lengthy credit account is again personal and sometimes delicate.* It's better, far better to say to me, the man directly responsible, just how and what you can pay, rather than discuss the little secrets of your pocket and your purse with someone who is not directly and personally responsible.[111]

In December 1928 Drage's announced that they were to be taken over by the Drapery Trust (the main owner of Debenhams). This was justified to shareholders on account of their rapidly growing HP business having exhausted available capital. As part of the deal Benjamin Drage resigned from the chairmanship, taking on the role of technical adviser. Drage told disgruntled shareholders to 'Think yourself jolly lucky you have got what you have got...I have been in the hire purchase business all my life and I understand its peculiar finance. You cannot pay big dividends and maintain your business...Our share dividends were paid last year by the issue of more shares...There is no more money to pay you. We want all our profits to cope with the expanding business.'[112] Yet Drage's continued to struggle and in 1937—apparently unable to repay money borrowed from Debenhams—they were taken over by Isaac Wolfson of Great Universal Stores (which had already acquired the Midland and Hackney furniture groups in 1934).[113] Wolfson found it profitable to liquidate the company and realize its HP debt portfolio.[114]

---

[107] 'Smart Brothers', *The Times* (23 Mar. 1932), 24.
[108] 'Smart Brothers Ltd', *The Times* (24 Apr. 1936), 24.
[109] 'The Dawn of a New Era', *The Times* (16 Mar. 1926), 21.
[110] 'Drages Limited', *The Times* (27 Feb. 1929), 25.
[111] GM, Drages Ltd, 'Furniture of Quality and Distinction', brochure, *c*.1929–30.
[112] 'Drages. Acceptance of Drapery Trust Offer', *Financial Times* (15 Dec. 1928), 4.
[113] Edwards, *Turning Houses into Homes*, 204.
[114] Aris, *Jews in Business*, 138; Guildhall Library, London, bound volume of London Stock Exchange company reports for 1936–7, letter appended to Drage's 1937 annual report.

## CONCLUSIONS

Drage's 'Mr Everyman' campaign had indeed triggered a revolution in furniture marketing, being widely copied by the expanding major furniture chains, with consequences that dramatically boosted the market for new furniture during the 1920s. This, in turn, had a significant impact on how families furnished, and regarded, their homes. As Phyllis Willmott's account of growing up in working-class Lewisham noted, the arrival of The Times Furnishing Co. was to start a transformation of her parents' home, where the respectable, though antiquated, front room décor had hidden the spartan rooms beyond:

> Although we did not know it then, it was the death blow for Gran's front room, the piano, the solid Victorian furnishings and the aspidistras. It was also the end of Mum's solid Edwardian oak dressing table…bought secondhand in her early married years…she was only too glad to throw it out in favour of the new veneered walnut suite she could get—with matching wardrobe and chest of drawers—on the 'never never' of hire purchase.[115]

However, Drage's formula of expanding the market through liberalizing terms both led to his loss of control over his retail empire and, for HP furniture multiples in general, to increasingly onerous capital requirements that undermined their financial stability. Drage's revolutionary approach to furniture marketing was rapidly copied by competitors, launching an era of retailer competition via intensive promotion and liberal credit terms. Both raised costs, while lengthening repayment periods progressively slowed capital turnover. Rapid growth for the largest retail chains did provide some scale economies, though as far as production was concerned this generally involved squeezing the margins of their contractors, rather than assisting them in moving to true mass production (which was inhibited by manufacturers' requirements for frequent style changes and the simultaneous stocking of many different designs). Meanwhile cut-throat competition between retailers fostered opportunistic behaviour by some firms, which damaged attempts to improve the public's view of 'furnishing out of income'.

Nevertheless, the inter-war period witnessed a transformation in the furnishing of many working-class homes, with at least those rooms most visible to visitors becoming dressed with coordinated suites of new furniture. During a period when a substantial proportion of working- and lower-middle-class families moved from traditional inner-urban housing to new municipal or owner-occupied estates, the HP furniture multiples enabled many households to realize a higher standard of material comfort and display, if at a substantial cost—which was inevitably reflected in cut-backs to other areas of consumption.[116]

---

[115] Phyllis Willmott, *Growing Up in a London Village: Family Life between the Wars* (London: Owen, 1979), 133.

[116] See Scott, 'Marketing Mass Home Ownership'; Peter Scott, 'Did Owner-Occupation Lead to Smaller Families for Interwar Working-Class Households?' *Economic History Review*, 61 (2008), 99–124.

# 4

# A Home of One's Own
## Marketing Owner-Occupation

### INTRODUCTION

Prior to 1914 owner-occupation was unusual for both the working and middle classes, with even many landlords renting the houses they themselves lived in. Nor was there any great social kudos attached to owner-occupation per se. In this respect Britain was typical of most European countries. 'New world' countries generally had much higher levels of owner-occupation; by 1911 46 per cent of households in the United States and 50 per cent in Australia owned their own homes, while owner-occupation appears to have been even more prevalent in Canada and New Zealand.[1] However, even in these countries it is unclear whether there was any strong middle-class attachment to home-ownership during the early twentieth century. Richard Harris has persuasively argued that in the United States and Canada owner-occupation was most strongly associated with immigrants and blue-collar workers who built cheap wooden buildings (often 'shacks') in fringe areas of urban communities. Conversely, white-collar workers were often indifferent between home-ownership and renting.[2]

The inter-war years, and particularly the 1930s, witnessed both the start of a trend towards Britain becoming a nation of owner-occupiers and of a popular perception that ownership constituted a socially superior tenure to renting. Owner-occupied dwellings, conventionally put at around 10 per cent of the 1914 housing stock, rose to around 32 per cent by 1938, mainly due to new developments (an estimated 1.8 million new houses were built for owner-occupiers, compared to 1.1 million existing houses transferred from the privately rented to the owner-occupied sector).[3] This marked the start of a long-term transition in housing

---

[1] Herbert Hoover, opening address, President's conference on home building and home ownership, Washington, 2 Dec. 1931, cited in Niles Carpenter, 'Attitude Patterns in the Home-Buying Family', *Social Forces*, 11 (1932), 76–81 (76).

[2] Richard Harris, *Building a Market: The Rise of the Home Improvement Industry, 1914–1960* (Chicago, IL: University of Chicago Press, 2012), 24–7.

[3] The 1914 owner-occupation rate is subject to a substantial margin of error, as it is based on an assumption regarding the volume of pre-1914 housing transferred from the privately rented to owner-occupied stock by 1938, for which there are no direct estimates. Yet a low 1914 owner-occupation rate is strongly corroborated by contemporary household surveys. See Peter Scott, *The Making of the Modern British Home: The Suburban Semi and Family Life between the Wars* (Oxford: Oxford University Press, 2013), 7.

tenure that has culminated in a current owner-occupation rate around the new world, rather than the European norm.[4]

The 1930s owner-occupation boom has traditionally been portrayed as a process from which the working class were largely excluded. However, more recent research has shown that working-class families (particularly recently married couples) played a substantial role in this boom. The barriers to working-class participation had traditionally been formidable, including prohibitively high prices for new houses, onerous mortgage deposit terms, and relatively short mortgage contracts (generally no more than twenty years). Moreover, working-class cultural aversions to debt made taking on what would seem an enormous commitment to most working-class families (equivalent to several years' wages) an option they would not even consider. Many households headed by lower income white-collar workers, such as clerks (whose earnings were often no higher than those of some skilled manual workers), faced similar barriers.

This chapter shows how a process of interlinked economic and social changes following the First World War created a demand among lower-middle- and working-class people for modern suburban homes, similar in design to the early 'homes for heroes' council houses. However, it was only during the 1930s that this demand for a particular type of house became translated into a boom in owner-occupation. The housing boom was the product of falling building costs, mortgage liberalization, and an intensive marketing campaign by the two key players in the private house-building value chain—the house-building firms, which determined the character, design, and location of the final product—and the building societies, which provided the all-important mortgage finance.

These jointly developed a process whereby builders could offer 95 per cent mortgages, over twenty-five years, financed by building societies that reduced their risk by holding on to a proportion of the purchase money until around a third of the mortgage was paid off. Both groups had an incentive to expand the market and thus jointly engaged in an intensive and sophisticated marketing campaign to promote home-ownership as an integral element of the new, domesticated, family-centred lifestyles being advocated by a range of opinion-makers, from health professionals to the popular media. Meanwhile, despite building societies' efforts to exert some control over the value chain—by regulating the terms on which finance was provided to builders—competition between different elements of the building society movement frustrated their efforts. Only a high-profile mis-selling scandal allowed the largest building societies to gain the upper hand over both the builders and the smaller building societies, by influencing legislative reform of the sector to reflect their interests.

---

[4] Data collected by Maria Concetta Chirui and Tulllio Jappelli ('Financial Market Imperfections and Home Ownership: A Comparative Study', Università degli Studi di Salerno, Centre for Studies in Economics and Finance Discussion Paper No. 44 (2000), 27), give owner-occupation rates of 68.56 per cent for the UK, an average of 66.67 per cent for the United States, Canada, and Australia, and an average of 58.78 per cent for ten European nations.

## LAYING THE FOUNDATIONS OF THE 1930S HOUSING BOOM: THE FIRST WORLD WAR AND THE 1920S MUNICIPAL SEMI

As in many other areas of British life, the First World War proved a watershed in British house-building, with impacts that would not be fully evident for many years after the Armistice. The war accelerated the development of motorized transport and thereby substantially increased the viable radius of commuting into urban centres (for localities not on commuter train or tram routes). Thus large tracts of land which had previously only been seen as suitable for agriculture were suddenly transformed into potential suburban building plots. Agricultural depression following the brief post-war boom made land-owners enthusiastic to dispose of their land at a price greater than its agricultural value, while there were virtually no planning laws to impede such a transfer of use. Meanwhile, following the Armistice industrial workers were granted a forty-eight hour week, reducing the length of the average working day by about one hour.[5] White-collar workers also typically received a reduction in working hours of around the same magnitude. Thus an additional travel time to work of perhaps fifteen or twenty minutes appeared more practicable, given the shorter working day. The development of motor buses and cheaper and more efficient bicycles also made commuting easier and less fatiguing.

Towards the end of the war government policy for the transition to peace became increasingly focused on providing 'homes for heroes' via a major council housing programme. This was strongly influenced by fears of widespread social unrest, the Russian Revolution being seen as a threatening precedent for the potential consequences of trained soldiers finding that a return to civilian life meant unemployment. The 1918 Tudor Walters committee report on the provision of dwellings for the working classes set out the blueprint for the new council houses. They were to comprise self-contained semi-detached or short terraced houses—generally with at least three bedrooms, a bathroom, scullery kitchen, and, where possible, a parlour. Moreover, they were to be located in the suburbs, built at densities of twelve or fewer houses per acre (compared to the 40–50 per acre typical of pre-1914 urban terraces), and would include front gardens, together with larger rear gardens.[6]

The Tudor Walters house proved immensely popular, providing a practical, cost-effective model for low-density suburban housing. It drew on experience from earlier garden suburb and model workers village projects, together with housing estates for munitions workers. Reductions in building land costs arising from the agricultural depression and the extension in viable commuting distances brought

---

[5] Peter Scott and Anna Spadavecchia, 'Did the 48-Hour Week Damage Britain's Industrial Competitiveness?', *Economic History Review*, 64 (2011), 1266–88.

[6] Local Government Board for England and Wales, and Scotland, *Report of the Committee Appointed by the President of the Local Government Board and the Secretary of State for Scotland to Consider Questions of Building Construction in Connection with the Provision of Dwellings for the Working Classes in England and Wales, and Scotland...* (Cd. 9191 of 1918).

such housing within financial reach of a wider section of the public. Tudor Walters housing embodied some extremely important built-in 'consumer durables', such as gas and electricity supply and internal plumbing systems—including fitted baths, internal toilets, and integral water heating. In older terraces lacking internal plumbing a large proportion of the housewife's working day was taken up in moving water around the house and heating it for cleaning and bathing. Compared to such houses, Tudor Walters standards of plumbing and utilities (which were difficult, and extremely costly, to retro-fit into existing terraced housing) had a revolutionary impact on housework. Gardens constituted another highly prized utility of the Tudor Walters home, being used for a broad range of functions, including children's play, leisure gardening (one of the most popular pursuits of the era), growing produce, and storage.

Working-class families were attracted by their more spacious rooms, more hygienic conditions (free of damp and vermin infestation, and the high pollution levels of many inner-urban areas), modern utilities, and gardens. Inter-war Britain witnessed an intensification of propaganda in favour of greater priority being given to child care, family life, hygiene, and associated goods and services, via the expanding women's press, newspapers, radio, domestic education classes for girls, and a range of other channels. The building of several hundred thousand municipal suburban houses during the 1920s demonstrated to working-class families that they could access housing with this level of amenities and thereby played an important role in popularizing the modern suburban semi among manual workers.

Lower middle-class families also found that changes associated with the war made the Tudor Walters type suburban semi more attractive to them. War production had involved the recruitment of large numbers of young women into manufacturing (both for munitions and civilian goods) and had increased the respectability of factory work as a woman's occupation. Young women henceforth saw domestic service, with low wages, long hours, and restricted personal freedom, as a job they would only take if other work was not available. Meanwhile the standard rate of income tax had risen from 5.83 per cent on the eve of the First World War to 20–25 per cent over the inter-war years, while there had also been rapid rises in local rates and the cost of private education.

Many lower-middle class housewives found themselves unable to afford live-in servants and were forced to do their own housework—perhaps leaving the heavier and less pleasant tasks to a part-time 'daily'. The modern, labour-saving, compact Tudor Walters house thus looked particularly attractive, while the absence of a live-in maid also removed the need to provide a room for her. A similar trend was noted in the United States, where middle-class housewives found themselves able to dispense with some or all domestic help via a cluster of goods and services, including smaller homes, labour-saving devices, canned and other prepared foods, ready-made clothing, and easier-to-clean materials such as linoleum.[7]

[7] Robert S. Lynd and Helen M. Lynd, *Middletown: A Study in American Culture* (New York: Harcourt, Brace & Co., 1929), 171.

## THE HOUSING PRODUCTION PROCESS
### AND VALUE CHAIN

The value chain for house-building was markedly more complex than for furniture. It started with the land-owner and the producers of building materials and then moved on to the preparation of land. This was traditionally undertaken by land development companies, who would typically lay out the necessary roads, sewers, and other public utilities required for residential development, before subdividing the land for sale to speculative builders. However, it became increasingly common for large building firms to buy agricultural land directly and integrate the land developer's traditional functions. In either case the purchase was often dependent on loan finance, which might come from a bank, or a building society—the first point in the value chain where these key financial intermediaries appear.[8]

The housing development stage of the value chain was also subject to considerable variation. Site preparation and/or house construction was sometimes contracted out, as was, in some cases, site management—by employing estate agents to oversee operations. Furthermore, builders might be employed either on a 'labour only' basis, or on a contract where they undertook responsibility for providing both labour and materials. Some developers also preferred to divide up the site between several contractors, each of whom would be responsible for perhaps fifteen to twenty houses, while others employed their labour directly.[9]

While transport improvements accelerated by the First World War had reduced the cost of land inputs to the building process, other innovations connected with the war and its aftermath reduced the cost of building labour inputs. The disruption to the building labour force during the war years, together with the 'dilution' of traditional craft skill demarcations, led to a major increase in the employment of non-apprenticed building workers, particularly by speculative developers. Census data indicate an increase of the proportion of building employees who were unskilled labourers from 31.5 per cent in 1911 to 44 per cent in 1931, together with a decrease in the proportion of craftsmen from 48.6 to 39.8 per cent and a decline in apprenticeships.[10] This reduced restrictive practices and overall building costs, but had a negative impact on building quality (sometimes disguised by measures such as rendering over poor brickwork). Meanwhile the war and the post-Armistice building materials shortages accelerated the diffusion of building materials innovations such as the substitution of iron for lead piping (which greatly simplified plumbing work) and the introduction of plasterboard.[11]

---

[8] J. D. Bundock, 'Speculative Housebuilding and Some Aspects of the Activities of the Suburban Housebuilder within the Greater London Outer Suburban Areas 1919–1939' (unpublished MPhil thesis, University of Kent, 1974), 635–8.

[9] Ibid., 470–88.

[10] Ruth Issacharoff, 'The Building Boom of the Interwar Years: Whose Profits and Whose Cost?', in Michael Harloe (ed.), *Urban Change and Conflict* (London: CES, 1978), 280–325 (316).

[11] Ibid., 284–92.

The other main players in the value chain were the building societies. These had some role in providing finance to builders, as noted above, but their key contribution was the provision of the all-important house mortgage finance. Estate developers relied on building societies to make their houses 'affordable' to a significant market. During the 1920s and 1930s building society assets grew rapidly, from £107,400,000 in 1922 to £773,700,000 in 1939, almost all of which went into house mortgages.[12] Without this massive inflow of consumer credit, on very liberal terms, the inter-war speculative housing boom would not have been possible. Interest rates on mortgage finance were only a fraction of those for HP credit, reflecting both the relatively low administration costs of lending large sums, on collateral not subject to rapid depreciation, and the fact that building societies were not-for-profit institutions.

Inter-war Britain witnessed intense competition between expanding building societies. Prior to 1914 the movement's strongholds had been the industrial towns of northern England, with the six largest societies in 1922 all being located in the north.[13] Meanwhile even the largest, Halifax Permanent, operated only on a regional level until after the First World War. However, during the early 1920s the northern societies found it attractive to expand southwards, as they had excess funds available for mortgage lending. They had traditionally enjoyed a more important function as local savings banks than their southern counterparts, partly owing to their early development of branch networks, while depression in the staple industries of northern Britain sapped local demand for mortgages. Conversely, the southern societies enjoyed booming local mortgage markets and expanded northwards in search of more deposits to fund this demand. Southern societies had the upper hand in this competitive scramble for territory, as buoyant demand for mortgages in their traditional markets gave them a larger 'spread' between their deposit and lending rates, providing greater resources to support their expansion.[14]

The resulting competition changed the regional balance of the movement. In 1922 none of the eight largest building societies were based in London; yet by 1929 there were four, with Abbey Road (which had not even featured among the top ten in 1922) rising to second place. However, by this time those societies that had lost ground during the 1920s had woken up to the danger and began to copy their more aggressive counterparts. The 1930s thus saw much less change in the ranking of the top societies. Territorial expansion during the 1920s created a handful of truly national societies that were to dominate the movement until its demise, through privatization, towards the close of the twentieth century. By 1939 the twelve largest societies collectively controlled £411.3 million of the

[12] Herbert Ashworth, *The Building Society Story* (London: Franey, 1980), 81 and 114.

[13] E. J. Cleary, *The Building Society Movement* (London: Elek, 1965), 202.

[14] George Speight, 'Building Society Behaviour and the Mortgage Lending Market in the Interwar Period: Risk-Taking by Mutual Institutions and the Interwar House-Building Boom' (unpublished DPhil thesis, University of Oxford, 2000), 137–8.

movement's total assets of £758.9 million and dominated mortgage lending on speculative estates.[15]

Building societies needed effective house-building value chains to produce sufficient new housing for their ever-growing funds. They thus had strong incentives to work with house-builders to find a means of coordinating the value chain so as to boost supply. The private house-building sector was composed of family firms, almost all operating on a local or regional basis. Only around ten developers appear to have achieved an annual output of 1,000 or more units at any point during the 1930s and even at the height of the boom these were estimated to be developing only 16,000–18,000 private houses a year, or around 6–7 per cent of the national total.[16] As small, entrepreneurial firms, making substantial investments in land that took some time to develop, house-builders were thirsty for capital.[17] Building societies were usually happy to provide development finance and, until development was completed, only required payment of interest on the instalments advanced. This helped to cement close relationships with house-builders that would open the door to their lucrative house mortgage business.

There is relatively little evidence on the distribution of costs and profits in the house-building value chain. However, a document prepared by Wimpey in 1943 provides a detailed breakdown of their costs and margins on the eve of the Second World War. This suggests that land costs comprised just over 20 per cent of the retail price of houses and building costs just under 60 per cent. Legal and sales costs accounted for a further 5 per cent, leaving a profit of just over 15 per cent.[18] Alan A. Jackson estimated builders' profits (net of an allowance of around 6 per cent for interest on capital) to be in the region of about 10 per cent of turnover in the London region, while John Burnett estimated that net profits for speculative builders averaged around 10 per cent, with a range of between 7 and 14 per cent. A profit rate of 10–15 per cent is not particularly high, given the risks traditionally associated with the sector and the amount of capital tied up in land and work in progress at any one time. Profit growth was thus dependent on both rapid turnover of their properties and expansion of the number of houses under development.[19] The other key player in the value chain was, of course, the building societies. These provided mortgage finance for the vast majority of speculative houses, at an interest rate that fell from just under 6 per cent in the early 1930s to less than 5 per cent by the late 1930s.[20]

---

[15] 'Building Societies since 1925', *Economist* (1 July 1939), 10–11.

[16] Fred Wellings, *British Housebuilders: History & Analysis* (Oxford: Blackwell, 2006), 42 and 123–4.

[17] See Scott, *Making of the Modern British Home*, ch. 4.

[18] Circa Trust, George Wimpey archives, unsigned memorandum, 'Wimpey houses and land', 31 Aug. 1943. This is based on Wimpey's houses that remained unsold at the outbreak of war.

[19] Alan A. Jackson, *Semi-Detached London: Suburban Development, Life, and Transport, 1900–39*, 2nd edn. (Didcot: Wild Swan, 1991), 150; John Burnett, *A Social History of Housing 1815–1885*, 2nd edn. (London: Methuen, 1986), 263.

[20] Michael Ball, *Housing Policy and Economic Power: The Political Economy of Owner Occupation* (London: Methuen, 1983), 33.

## THE PRODUCT

Speculative housing developers drew extensively on the Tudor Walters housing standard, owing to its popularity and cost-effectiveness. Yet they took great pains to distinguish their estates from local authority housing. This was largely achieved via a focus on external architectural details such as bay and leaded windows, mock timbering, and gables to create both variegation between one pair of houses and the next and develop an Arts and Crafts (or, more negatively, 'Tudorbethan') style (Fig. 4.1). Meanwhile councils overwhelmingly used a grimmer 'neo-Georgian' or 'brick-box' style, to economize on costs and assert the collective identity of their estates.

Semis dominated the speculative market. These were built at slightly lower densities than municipal estates (typically eight to ten per acre, compared to twelve per acre for council houses). Yet they were fundamentally similar in basic design, typically being based on a rectangular 'universal plan', with two reception rooms of roughly equal size, placed back-to-back. A small staircased hall led from the front door of the typical speculative semi (at the side of the house furthest from the party wall)

**Fig. 4.1.** The new suburban streetscape, as envisaged by Davis Estates Ltd

*Source*: Image courtesy of The Museum of Domestic Design and Architecture, Middlesex University, BADDA 4932.1, Davis Estates Ltd, 'Builders of Homes, South Ruislip' brochure (n.d., *c*.1935).

and to the rear of this was a small working kitchen, often at the side of the rear reception room. This also had a window facing the back garden (partly so that the housewife could supervise children playing in the garden), while the bathroom was commonly placed above it, to minimize plumbing costs. Two reasonably sized bedrooms were provided, together with a smaller third bedroom, while the ground and first floors were equal in area.[21]

Post-Armistice building materials shortages led to very high house prices in the early 1920s, though these soon began a dramatic long-term decline. There are no price indices for speculative housing during this period and the best available data cover average building costs for a three-bedroom non-parlour council house.[22] This peaked at around £1,000 in the immediate post-Armistice period, then fell sharply to £510 during 1925 and 1926. By 1930 average council house costs had fallen to £411 and were to fall further in the early 1930s, to a low of £361 in 1934.[23] During the 1920s building costs for speculative housing were too high for virtually all working-class families and, while working-class mortgage borrowing did expand, this largely represented sitting tenants buying their houses from landlords who were eager to dispose of them, given the continuation of wartime rent controls.[24] George Speight estimated that the impact on working-class owner-occupation was modest, with a maximum of 8 or 9 per cent of working-class families owning or buying their own homes by 1931.[25]

Speculatively developed houses ranged in size and price, from a three-bedroom non-parlour terrace with a bath in the kitchen, marketed at from £395 in London (and perhaps £350 in the provinces) to around £1,500 (beyond which buyers generally sought architecturally designed houses)—though most were priced at £900 or less.[26] Middle-class households constituted the majority of new suburban owner-occupiers. However, working-class families were also important participants in this process during the 1930s and were targeted by many of the larger developers, in an effort to expand their market. Those fortunate enough to remain in regular employment were enjoying substantial long-term increases in real earnings. However, the terms on which houses were traditionally offered on mortgage—deposits of 20–25 per cent and repayments over eighteen to twenty years, were still beyond their reach. Thus the new physical product—the universal plan suburban semi—required a new financial product—the 5 per cent deposit, twenty-five-year mortgage.

---

[21] Gordon Allen, 'Building to Sell', in Ernest Betham (ed.), *House Building 1934–1936* (London: Federated Employers' Press, 1934), 145.

[22] However, building costs for speculative housing can be expected to have declined more steeply than council house costs—as speculative developers had greater scope for savings via cheaper materials, substituting unskilled labour on piecework for apprenticed building workers, and extensive subcontracting.

[23] Marion Bowley, *Housing and the State 1919–1944* (London: George Allen & Unwin, 1945), 30 and 278.

[24] Ashworth, *Building Society Story*, 70–2.

[25] George Speight, 'Who Bought the Inter-War Semi? The Socio-Economic Characteristics of New-House Buyers in the 1930s', University of Oxford, Discussion Paper in Economic and Social History No. 38 (Dec. 2000), 14.

[26] Burnett, *Social History of Housing*, 252; W. F. Stolper, 'British Monetary Policy and the Housing Boom', *Quarterly Journal of Economics*, 56, 1 (1941), 1–170 (20).

This was achieved (only for new houses) via the 'builders' pool' arrangement, where part of the mortgage advance was retained by the society, rather than being passed immediately to the builder. This retained sum was originally equal to the difference between the society's normal maximum ratio of mortgage to house price (typically 75 or 80 per cent) and the new ratio of, typically, 95 per cent. However, as competition between societies intensified, builders successfully renegotiated terms. Doing deals on a 'one in four' or 'four to one' basis (where the builder might be liable for, say, 20 per cent of the house's value but was only required to deposit a quarter of this sum with the society) soon became common.[27]

Pool deposits were to be repaid to the builder when the mortgage had been reduced to something between two-thirds and 70 per cent of the property's valuation. However, in practice builders would often press to have some of their pool funds released earlier, sometimes with success. Meanwhile they received interest on their pool deposits, usually at the current building society rate. Nevertheless, builders using the pool system faced a similar problem to the hire purchase furniture retailers discussed in the Chapter 3—their turnover of capital was slowed by funds being tied up in existing mortgage contracts, which placed a limit on their rate of growth. Speight found that builders dealt with this problem by increasing their house prices by an amount equal to the value of their pool deposits.[28] Government sources indicate that by 1938 between 40 and 60 per cent of current building society mortgage business was being conducted via pool schemes, while the proportion would be substantially higher for new speculative housing.[29]

Pool arrangements were already in use by the 1920s, but became much more widespread during the 1930s, particularly following the introduction of the government's cheap money policy from 1931, when building societies found themselves inundated with deposits that they struggled to place in mortgages. Given that they borrowed short and lent long—at fixed interest rates—they found it necessary to keep their rates relatively high.[30] Some were forced to put temporary restrictions on new deposits, though the problem was soon solved through expanding the mortgage market by liberalizing terms. Builders' pool arrangements allowed mortgage periods to be extended from eighteen to twenty to around twenty-five years, thereby substantially reducing weekly instalments. Meanwhile the minimum deposit requirement for new homes on pool mortgages was reduced to around 5 per cent of the purchase price.

Pool arrangements played a key role in opening up owner-occupation to manual workers. As one building society luminary noted, 'Innumerably more people can find a 5 per cent deposit than . . . 10 per cent . . . it is much easier to scrape together £25 than £50 and experience has shown us that ingenious methods of finding a

---

[27] Circa Trust, George Wimpey archives, G. W. Mitchell, letter file. 'Notes on private enterprise house-building', unsigned memorandum, 5 Feb. 1945.

[28] Speight, 'Building Society Behaviour', 94–5.

[29] TNA, CAB 27/645, Committee on Building Societies, meetings and memoranda, report of Cabinet Committee, 9 Dec. 1938.

[30] Interest rates on building society deposits generally moved in line with share rates and were about 0.6 per cent lower. Cleary, *Building Society Movement*, 190.

small deposit have certainly obtained.'[31] Making an initial payment of £25–£30 to secure a property was also more in keeping with working-class expectations, as it had a parallel in the house rental market, 'key money'—the money landlords sometimes demanded for handing over the keys to accommodation.[32] In some cases deposit requirements were reduced to below £25, through devices such as using a life assurance policy as additional collateral, or the developer loaning the purchaser part of the deposit.[33]

The liberality of British mortgage terms is illustrated by comparison with the United States, where—despite federal government support for mortgage liberalization in the aftermath of the depression—average loan to value ratios were still less than 70 per cent in the late 1930s. Meanwhile even insurance companies (which introduced the most liberal loan terms) increased average contract lengths to only around eighteen years.[34] In comparison, Britain's twenty-five-year, 95 per cent, mortgages were truly revolutionary. The ability of building societies to introduce such radical liberalization partly reflected the relative stability of Britain's domestic financial institutions and housing market during the early 1930s. Yet Britain's more generous terms were also necessitated by its higher land values and lower wages. 1939 US mortgage terms (which were broadly similar to those in Britain during the 1920s) would have left new houses beyond the reach of most working-class families.

From January 1919 to March 1931 only 1.3 per cent of new private sector houses in England and Wales were in the lowest rateable value band, equivalent to a sale value of below around £400 (or £600 in London), while almost a third were in the highest band (involving a sale price of over £750, or £1,000 in London). Yet over the subsequent eight years building in the highest value band stagnated, the lowest band expanded to 38.2 per cent of new construction, while building for the middle band underwent considerable absolute growth.[35] Working-class households accounted for virtually all houses in the lower value band, while also comprising a substantial proportion of the middle band.[36] This enabled building societies to expand their mortgage loan portfolios from £316 million in 1930, involving some 720,000 borrowers, to £636 million, and some 1,392,000 borrowers, in 1937.[37] Meanwhile, as shown in Figure 4.2, private-sector house-building in

---

[31] Frank L. Lee, 'The Changes in Building Society Practice to Meet Changed Business Conditions', *Building Societies Gazette* (Oct. 1936), 937.

[32] Howard Marshall, *Slum* (London: Heinemann, 1933), 52; Nuffield College, Oxford, Nuffield College Social Reconstruction Survey Archive (NCSRS), C5/12, M. P. Fogarty, 'Birmingham Housing', report, c.1939.

[33] TNA, HLG29/253, memorandum by joint committee of the Building Societies Association [hereafter BSA], National Federation of Building Societies (NFBS), and important unaffiliated societies, 12 Mar. 1938; Building Societies Association Library, London [hereafter BSA Library], bound volumes of circulated letters, Circular no. 4, 5 Aug. 1936, by R. H. Marsh; Gunnersbury Park Museum, Oral History Archive, GPM/OH70, interview with Edgar Wynn.

[34] Leo Grebler, David M. Blank, and Louis Winnick, *Capital Formation in Residential Real Estate* (Princeton, NJ: Princeton University Press, 1956), 234–57.

[35] Speight, 'Who Bought the Inter-War Semi?', 15.

[36] Scott, *Making of the Modern British Home*, 107.

[37] Bowley, *Housing and the State*, 279.

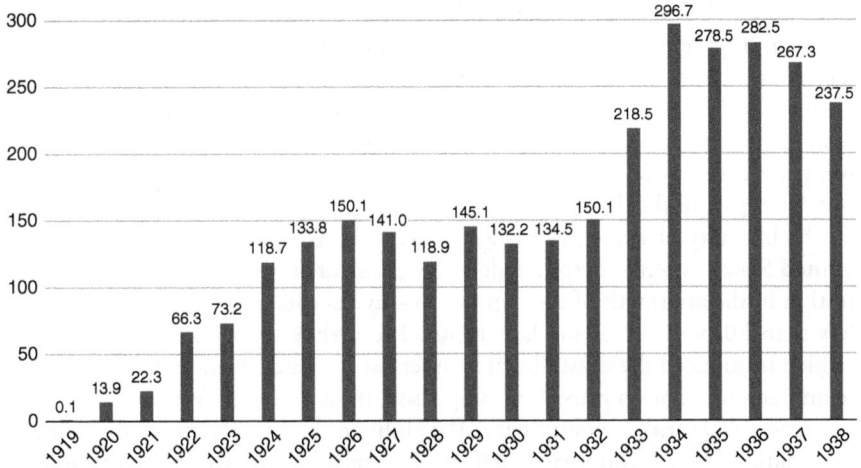

**Fig. 4.2.** New private house-building in Great Britain, 1919–38 (thousands)

*Note:* Data for England and Wales are for years ending 31 March of the following year.

*Source:* Peter Scott, *The Making of the Modern British Home: The Suburban Semi and Family Life between the Wars* (Oxford: Oxford University Press, 2013), 84.

Britain reached an all-time peak of almost 300,000 houses per year during the mid-1930s; almost twice the peak level of the 1920s. New private housing was both more plentiful and cheaper than at any time before or since; the cost of a new house during the mid-1930s has been estimated at around two and a half years' income for a man earning the average industrial wage.[38] Indeed it became generally cheaper (from the perspective of weekly payments) to buy a new house on mortgage than to rent it.[39]

## THE MARKETING CAMPAIGN

Like the furniture multiples, the house-builders' and building societies' problems did not end with making their product 'affordable'. They also had to deal with strong consumer resistance. In the early 1930s owner-occupation was still alien to most working-class families and ran counter to entrenched cultural orthodoxies. It involved dealings with middle-class professionals and institutions and entering into complex

[38] J. C. Weston, 'International Comparisons of the Cost of Housebuilding', *Journal of Industrial Economics*, 12, 1 (1963), cited in Burnett, *Social History of Housing*, 252.

[39] TNA, HLG56/157, Departmental Committee on Valuation for Rates, oral evidence from John Laing, Norman Wates, and Gilbert F. Armitage, 16 Mar. 1939; NCSRS, C5/12, M. P. Fogarty, 'Birmingham Housing', report, c.1939; BSA Library, verbatim reports of National Association of Building Societies' discussions, 1934–6, paper delivered at AGM, 2–5 June 1936, by R. Bruce Wycherley.

legal contracts—activities viewed with fear and suspicion by many working people.[40] The chief objection, however, was to taking on a massive and very long-term debt. Traditional 'respectable' working-class values emphasized keeping out of debt, which could greatly increase the risks of falling into destitution during periods of hardship.[41]

A mortgage was also much less flexible than a tenancy. There were heavy 'sunk costs' of the deposit, various transaction fees, and accumulated capital payments, plus a continuing legal liability to repay the loan (even if the house was surrendered to the building society). These made it difficult and expensive to switch to cheaper accommodation during periods of reduced income, or when a change of job required a new location. Many lower-middle-class people considering house-purchase for the first time also had anxieties, especially those towards the bottom end of the white-collar income spectrum, who were facing a real struggle to make ends meet given the need to maintain and project a middle-class lifestyle on incomes often little, if any, greater than those of skilled manual workers.

Marketing owner-occupation to lower-middle and working-class households (who were key to substantially expanding the market) was undertaken jointly by the house-builders and building societies. Building societies focused on the general merits of home-ownership, and the ease with which new housing could be obtained on mortgage, while builders placed more emphasis on the specific attractions of their houses and estates. However, there was a remarkable degree of conformity in building society and builders' advertising, which tended to stress the same key themes and make broadly similar marketing pitches, despite the fragmented nature of both industries.

Recent analysis found that building societies invested much more intensively in advertising during the 1930s than in previous decades, their average ratio of advertising expenditure to mortgage interest income (for all advertising, including savings as well as mortgages) rising from around 1 per cent over 1909–13 to around 2.8 per cent over 1929–38. However, their absolute advertising spend rose much more, owing to their rapidly growing asset base.[42] Compared to other financial institutions, building societies were particularly intensive advertisers, for both mortgage and deposit business. Indeed relative to the size of their assets, their 1935 advertising spend (including savings and 'goodwill', as well as mortgage advertising) was 3.8 times that of the insurance companies and around sixteen times that of the banking sector.[43]

Some of their marketing techniques were pioneered in the 1920s for middle-class housing, though during the 1930s the targeting of lower-income groups involved a

---

[40] For a discussion of British working-class attitudes to debt see Peter Scott, 'The Twilight World of Interwar Hire Purchase', *Past & Present*, 177 (2002), 195–225; Margot C. Finn, *The Character of Credit: Personal Debt in English Culture, 1740–1914* (Cambridge: Cambridge University Press, 2003).

[41] Simon Szreter, *Fertility, Class and Gender in Britain, 1860–1940* (Cambridge: Cambridge University Press, 1996), 528.

[42] Peter Scott and Lucy Newton, 'Advertising, Promotion, and the Rise of a National Building Society Movement in Interwar Britain', *Business History*, 54 (2012), 399–423.

[43] Ibid., 400.

much greater emphasis on 'easy terms' and the lifestyle benefits of modern suburban housing. There was also a general move towards more sophisticated marketing techniques, embodied, for example, in more extensive and lavishly illustrated brochures, with greater emphasis on emotive messages regarding the lifestyle advantages of owner-occupation and suburban living. Some large societies, particularly those based around London, began to employ leading advertising agencies. Woolwich hired the top London agency S. H. Benson,[44] while Abbey Road employed another prestigious London-based agency, Greenly's.[45] Advertisements were often placed alongside feature articles or regular columns on home-buying or savings—thus encouraging newspaper editorial coverage, which was further boosted via the use of public relations consultants to encourage editorial publicity.[46]

In addition to extensive advertising in newspapers, magazines, and professional journals, some of the largest building societies also ran their own in-house customer magazines—a strategy also used by some car companies, as discussed in Chapter 11. Halifax produced a quarterly *Home Owner* magazine, based on the popular *Ideal Home* type of magazine, with a print-run of 54,000 by 1939.[47] This was circulated to its members and distributed through branches, agencies, and exhibition stands. *Home Owner* included advice to house-buyers; house designs; housekeeping; hobbies; plus items such as 'health in the home', 'the young housewife', 'the art of furnishing', and on gardening. There were also articles on saving, insurance, etc., but these formed only a small part of the content. Abbey Road similarly produced the half-yearly *Abbey Road Journal*, issued free to members and depositors.[48]

Building societies also embraced 'outdoor' advertising via posters and enamel plates. These were particularly suited to mortgage advertising, as they could be targeted at locations such as building estates or commuter trains, where many viewers would be potential customers.[49] Builders and estate agents were usually prepared to display advertising boards for societies with whom they did business free of charge.[50] In October 1937 Woolwich had 131 boards on display at various estates, on free sites offered by builders. Societies also invested in display materials—such as posters, show cards, and window items—for their branches, agencies, and stands at the Ideal Home and other exhibitions. These also provided outlets for numerous

[44] Barclays Bank Group Archive [hereafter BBGA], Woolwich Building Society, Advertising Committee minutes, 1023/1209, 28 Jan. 1930.

[45] London Metropolitan Archives (LMA), Abbey Road Building Society, 30/32, Publicity committee minutes, advertising summary for financial year ended 31 Oct. 1935, 18 Nov. 1935.

[46] Scott and Newton, 'Advertising, Promotion', 408.

[47] HBOS Archives, Edinburgh, Acc. 04/13/31, Private and confidential report requested by Advertising committee from Chapman's, 11 July 1939; Ac. 2003/022, *The Home Owner* magazine, various issues.

[48] Harold Bellman, *The Thrifty Three Millions: A Study of the Building Society Movement and the Story of the Abbey Road Society* (London: Abbey Road Building Society, 1935), 239.

[49] Sydney J. Walter, 'British Building Society Methods of Publicity and Advertising', *Building Societies Gazette* (Sept. 1931), 664–9 (668).

[50] BBGA, Woolwich Building Society, Advertising Committee minutes, 1023/1209, 28 Jan. 1930.

booklets outlining home-buying and investing facilities.[51] Booklets and circulars were also used for direct mailings, enabling them to target adverts at districts whose inhabitants were particularly attractive mortgage prospects.

Analysis of building society press display ads in *The Times*, *Observer*, and *Manchester Guardian*, for 1925, 1932, and 1935, by Scott and Newton found that the most common appeals of their mortgage advertising involved attractive interest rates, liberal terms—often expressed as a statement that home-ownership was cheaper than renting—and the size of the society. The general merits of home-ownership (and the more specific claim that a house represented a good and secure investment) also featured heavily, collectively representing the most frequent type of appeal. As Sidney Walter, chairman of the Fourth City Building Society, noted in 1931, building societies were using mortgage advertising to communicate new messages based around the themes of 'home-ownership, self-help, thrift, and the road to independence'.[52]

One of the most innovative campaigns was the 'Mr Tenant' and 'Mr Owner' series, launched by Abbey Road in 1933. This was designed by Greenly's and had some similarities to the conversational advertisements they had used to promote the multiple furniture retailer Smart Brothers from 1925, though the Mr Tenant campaign added a strong element of humour. It sought to counter the common argument that a mortgage represented 'a millstone round your neck',[53] by claiming that home-ownership actually reduced anxiety. The ads, an example of which is shown in Figure 4.3, contrasted the miserable-looking Mr Tenant, constrained from making improvements to his house, as the financial benefits would accrue to his landlord, with the more prosperous Mr Owner, who is free to improve his home and enjoy the financial gains from home-ownership.[54]

Building society advertising tended to emphasize common themes, with relatively little brand differentiation. Key messages included the advantages of modern suburban housing, the superiority of owning over renting, the ease with which houses could be bought on mortgage, and the investment value of a home. Aspirational values were a central motif, linking owner-occupation with citizenship, domesticity, and a healthy, secure, and more prosperous future for one's family.[55]

Yet the building industry proved the key player in selling owner-occupation to a mass public. Building estate companies' direct advertising accounted for 1.08 per cent of press display advertising, while an unknown volume of additional advertising was conducted via estate agents.[56] Despite the limited size of even the largest

[51] HBOS Archives, Halifax Advertising Committee minutes, 'Suggested advertising budget for 1939', confidential report, Acc. 04/13/31, 15 Feb. 1939.

[52] Walter, 'British Building Society', p. 665.

[53] See Scott, *Making of the Modern British Home*, 109.

[54] Abbey Road advertisement in *The Times* (12 Oct. 1933), 11, col. E.

[55] J. R. Gold and M. M. Gold, '"Home at Last!" Building Societies, Home Ownership and the Imagery of English Suburban Promotion in the Interwar Years', in J. R. Gold and S. V. Ward (eds.), *Place Promotion: The Use of Publicity and Marketing to Sell Towns and Regions* (Chichester: Wiley, 1994), 75–92.

[56] Nicholas Kaldor and Rodney Silverman, *A Statistical Analysis of Advertising Expenditure and the Revenue of the Press* (Cambridge: Cambridge University Press, 1948), Table 69. This included advertising aimed at depositors as well as borrowers.

# Mr. TENANT  Mr. OWNER

lives in a pleasant little house—
but that doesn't make him any the
less miserable. It's at the end of
the month that the wrinkles on his
brow are at their worst. He
knows that another month's rent
is due—in advance. Hard earned
money slipping straight through
his fingers to swell another man's
bank balance. And Mr. Tenant is
full of ideas for increasing the
amenities of his house—but what's
the good of spending time and
money on a house which belongs
to another?

The "Abbey Road" makes
it easy for Mr. Tenant to
become Mr. Owner. He
can choose a house to be
his own anywhere in Gt.
Britain. The service is courteous and efficient and costs
are low. Write or phone
for the booklet "Home
Ownership"—it is free
and post free for the asking.

The Best Builders, the
most Reliable Agents,
the Discriminating
Public, use and recom-
mend the Abbey Road
Service.

did a few years ago what Mr. Tenant
will be doing to-morrow. He con-
sulted the 'Abbey Road' and realised how easy it is to avoid the
waste of paying rent and how much
better it is to become a house-
owner. Every cheque he sends
to the Abbey Road, in repayment
for their generous loan, brings him
nearer to that great day when his
home will be his own free and unen-
cumbered asset. In other words instead of spending money in rent, he
actually saves it by investing in his
own security and independence.

# ABBEY ROAD
## LONDON'S LARGEST BUILDING SOCIETY

Abbey House, Baker St., London, N.W.1.          Telephone: Welbeck 8282 (12 lines)

**Fig. 4.3.** A Mr Tenant, Mr Owner advert of February 1933
*Source*: Peter Scott collection.

house-building firms, the industry nevertheless collectively developed a sophisticated marketing appeal, with the messages of each builder again generally reinforcing those of their competitors to make the public more open to the idea of house-purchase. This apparent coordination of marketing messages probably involved emulation of those messages perceived to be effective, a process fostered through strong inter-firm marketing knowledge 'spillovers', via housing exhibitions, movement of sales staff, the activities of advertising agencies and estate agents as market intermediaries, and direct observation of competitors' estates and publicity material. Thus, despite its fragmented nature, best practice rapidly spread between firms, fostering similar and mutually reinforcing broad marketing pitches.

A barrage of advertising, including an increasing proportion of large, illustrated adverts, was brought into working-class homes via national, regional, and local newspapers, sometimes in the form of extensive property supplements.[57] Newspaper advertising covered a wide range of themes, though, in common with building society advertising, a number of key messages dominated, particularly the 'easy terms' on which attractive, modern houses could be purchased. Adverts became larger, more sophisticated, and more elaborately illustrated, including photographs, eye-catching slogans, and greater use of symbolism and emotional appeal, compared to the simple line-drawings or text announcements of the 1920s.[58] Moreover, they embraced new, emotive arguments regarding the benefits and superiority of owner-occupation and suburban life. Roadside hoardings were also widely used to alert local people to the presence of a new estate and to headline the easy terms on which the houses were available.

Having attracted the customer's initial interest, sales messages were delivered in a more elaborate form via the estate brochure. Brochures often ran to many pages and adopted a glossy format with large photographs or other good-quality illustrations. They were used to convey a number of messages, yet easy terms again typically featured prominently. For example, a New Ideal Homesteads brochure advised potential purchasers that: 'The deposit need no longer delay you from buying the modern home you have longed for. If you have an assurance policy you can buy it tomorrow—Yes, use the policy as deposit, don't wait a minute longer. If you can afford rent you can easily afford the weekly purchase-repayments.'[59] Brochures and advertisements further asserted affordability by portraying house-purchase as an investment—in effect suggesting that a mortgage made long-term savings less necessary.

Estate marketing also included one technique that has become more widespread in recent decades: incentivizing early purchasers to canvass their social networks.

[57] J. R. Gold and M. M. Gold, '"A Place of Delightful Prospects": Promotional Imagery and the Selling of Suburbia', in L. Zonn (ed.), *Place Images in Media: Portrayal, Experience, and Meaning* (Savage, MD: Rowman & Littlefield, 1990), 159–82.

[58] Ian Davis, 'A Celebration of Ambiguity: The Synthesis of Contrasting Values', in Paul Oliver, Ian Davis, and Ian Bentley, *Dunroamin: The Suburban Semi and its Enemies* (London: Pimlico, 1981), 93–8.

[59] New Ideal Homesteads Ltd, 'Homebuilders. New Ideal Homesteads. Britain's Best and Biggest Builders', brochure, n.d., 1930s, Peter Scott collection.

Several developers offered purchasers commission for introducing new customers, typically £5 (approximately 1 per cent of the purchase price). This practice appears to have been an important source of customers on at least some estates, as evidenced by developers who cited the large proportion of purchasers who were recommended by satisfied customers.[60]

Estate developers also followed Drage's practice of assuaging customers' fears that they might find themselves having to pay for hidden 'extras' which they had not budgeted for. Developers began to offer an 'all-in' product, which included arranging the mortgage and incorporating legal and other fees into the house price and, therefore, the mortgage. Some even offered free furniture removal over a certain distance.[61] It was also common for developers to reduce 'moving-in' costs by installing wallpaper and fittings for free; customers often being allowed to choose from a range of designs.[62]

Developers also relied heavily on 'event marketing'. Housing estates were vigorously promoted at exhibitions, including the hugely popular *Daily Mail* Ideal Home Exhibition, and similar regional or local events. Some London developers had their own permanent exhibitions, in the form of centrally located show houses, often alongside railway stations with heavy commuter traffic.[63] Such events generally used a low-pressure sales approach, with their publicity stressing that people would not be pressured into making a purchase.[64] This removal of a perceived obligation to buy reinforced the leisure aspect of the event, in keeping with the new low-pressure, leisure-orientated selling approach popularized by Gordon Selfridge from 1911, which had strongly permeated large sections of British retailing by the 1930s.

Estates were typically open on weekends (including Sundays) and evenings. Potential visitors might be offered a chauffeur-driven car to take them from the railway station to the estate, and live entertainment was frequently laid on, such as firework displays, concerts, visits from politicians, and launch events hosted by film or radio stars.[65] Visiting the various show houses, one for each 'model' of house available on the estate, also represented a leisure activity in its own right, as these were laid out with coordinated new furniture and modern consumer durables (typically provided by local retailers, whose representatives were on hand).

Sales were 'closed' by asking prospects who showed interest to pay an 'initial deposit'—typically £5, but in many cases only £1. This was sufficiently small for customers to be likely to be able to pay on the day, yet large enough to make them feel committed to the transaction. The balance of the deposit, typically £20–£25,

    [60] Scott, *Making of the Modern British Home*, 114–16.
    [61] Bexley Local Studies and Archive Centre, London, *Bexley Between the Wars*, unpublished two-volume collection of interviews with inter-war Bexley residents, *c.*1986–7, interview with Mr Bollon; A. D. McCulloch, 'Owner-Occupation & Class Struggle: The Mortgage Strikes of 1938–40' (unpublished PhD thesis, University of Essex, 1983), 214.
    [62] Ian Bentley, 'The Owner Makes his Mark: Choice and Adaption', in Oliver et al., *Dunroamin*, 136–53 (143).
    [63] Scott, *Making of the Modern British Home*, 116–17.        [64] Ibid., 117–18.
    [65] Gavin Weightman and Steve Humphries, *The Making of Modern London 1914–1939* (London: Sidgwick & Jackson, 1984), 114.

was not generally required until the customer took possession (though in some cases an intermediate deposit of £5–£10 was due after a week or so). Developers would often lend money to purchasers who could not find the full deposit; meanwhile customers who appeared interested but could not pay on the day of the visit were typically 'followed up' after a week or two, either via mail, or a personal call.[66]

Developers' marketing campaigns strongly emphasized the aspirational connotations of house-purchase, together with its lifestyle benefits. In so doing they both tapped in to the new, aspirational, family- and home-centred model of working-class respectability, discussed in Chapter 2, and played an important role in promulgating this model. Oral testimonies of people who bought houses during this period indicate that a modern suburban house was seen as offering the ideal environment for these new values, on account of its hygienic conditions, modern, labour-saving layout, more spacious rooms, front and rear gardens, and semi-rural setting. Many of these aspirational features, such as modern utilities, generously fenestrated rooms, front and rear gardens, and suburban location, were shared by both owner-occupied and council houses. Yet speculative estate developers successfully distinguished their product via various (often largely cosmetic) design features, aspirational street and estate names, and using advertising copy to assert a superior status.[67]

Both building society and estate developers' advertising typically showed much grander, often detached, houses than those purchased by their typical customers.[68] This was not atypical; contemporary advertising, in both Britain and the United States, often depicted a higher social setting than that of the target customer, based on the premise that people preferred to identify with portrayals of themselves as they aspired to be rather than as they currently were.[69] Developers also asserted status through emphasizing their estates' rural settings and scenic beauty. This both illustrated suburbia's advantages of clean air, space, and healthy living and tapped in to the upsurge in popular enthusiasm for the countryside.

Estate promotion also included a strong element of 'lifestyle marketing'. For example, a brochure for an estate in Edgware, Middlesex, set out a

DESIGN for LIVING.

What sort of home do you picture in your mind as a masterpiece of design, of planning and building—home to bring you the fullest enjoyment of living?

It is a house of health. A house cheerful and streaming with light, inviting the sun; where chill is impossible, where comfort is almost luxurious; where protection against the vagaries of the English weather is complete.

It is a house in which no work is created by the house itself, in which unnecessary toil is unknown, and necessary labour is reduced to its minimum by design afterthought.

---

[66] Anon, 'One Hundred Not Out: The First Century of Hilbery Chaplin 1894–1994', unpublished typescript, c.1994, 24.

[67] Scott, *Making of the Modern British Home*, 69–76.

[68] Gold and Gold, 'Place of Delightful Prospects', 173–5.

[69] Roland Marchand, *Advertising the American Dream: Making Way for Modernity, 1920–1940* (Berkeley: University of California Press, 1985), 166.

It is a house set in its surroundings that gives pleasure and rest, where gardens blend with the greenwood; and where, on the brink of the city, the countryside is unscarred....

It is not achieved in any sham-Tudor style, or by feeble acceptance of builders' ideas taken over from Victorian days—or even of twenty years ago. Nowhere has it been realised to such a degree, and made accessible to people of modest means, as in a Roger Malcolm home.[70]

The house's attractive modern fittings and 'labour-saving' features were often emphasized, appealing to the housewife—who was increasingly targeted by contemporary advertising as the key player in household expenditure decisions.[71] Thus New Ideal Homesteads marketed several estates with brochures entitled 'The Super Home. Designed by a *Woman* for the *Woman*'.[72] A Comben & Wakeling brochure noted that their kitchens' fittings and 'walls finished in white glazed tiling will appeal very strongly to the modern housewife. For the kitchen is the headquarters from which the housewife runs her home'.[73] Similarly Morrell's (developers of the Coney Hall Estate, Britain's most celebrated inter-war example of 'jerry building') collaborated with *Woman's Journal* to design 'The Bride's House', noting that: 'Happy indeed will be the bride who starts on life's greatest adventure in this thrilling house, for the many labour-saving improvements ensure that her home can be run efficiently and without too much hard work.'[74]

## THE BATTLE FOR CONTROL OF THE VALUE CHAIN AND THE CONSEQUENCES FOR THE CONSUMER

During the 1930s a group of large, predominantly southern-based building societies—generally those which had grown rapidly during the 1920s and had been early adopters of the builders' pool system—sought to coordinate the housebuilding value chain by regulating mortgage pool lending. This was to be achieved by imposing an industry-wide 'Code of Ethics', encompassing standard terms for mortgage interest rates, pool arrangements, commission payments, maximum mortgage durations and loan to value ratios, and minimum personal stakes for mortgage borrowers.[75] In May 1930 the chief executives of four major London-based building societies—Abbey Road, Westbourne Park, Woolwich, and the Co-operative—met to discuss a regulatory code, apparently prompted by surveys indicating that in

---

[70] MoDA, BADDA 4930, Roger Malcolm Ltd, 'Be Modern at St. Margaret's', brochure, n.d., c.1935.

[71] Marchand, *Advertising the American Dream*, 66–7.

[72] Bexley Local Studies, estate brochure collection.

[73] MODA, BADDA 4931, Comben & Wakeling Ltd, 'Beautiful Homes by Comben & Wakeling Ltd', brochure, 1935.

[74] MODA, BADDA 319, Morrell (Builders) Ltd, 'The Bride's Home. Built by Morrell (Builders) Ltd. Furnished & Decorated under the direction of *Woman's Journal*', brochure, n.d., c.1933.

[75] Martin Davis, *Every Man His Own Landlord: A History of the Coventry Building Society* (Warwick: Coventry Building Society, 1985), 67; Cleary, *Building Society Movement*, 212.

London and the south mortgage deposits had fallen to very low levels (making purchasers focus on deposits, rather than overall purchase costs), while certain districts were becoming 'over-built'.[76] Restrictions, including a maximum twenty-one-year mortgage term, were proposed.[77] By the end of the year the National and the Halifax building societies had joined the group and it appeared increasingly likely that these large building societies would succeed in strictly regulating competition on building society lending terms.[78]

The societies were effectively seeking to establish a cartel, which was then perfectly legal, and commonplace in a range of British industries. However, like many cartel arrangements, it fell foul of differences in the interests of various sections of the building society movement. For six years the advocates of the code failed to obtain national compliance—partly due to a wish on the part of societies which had been less aggressive during the 1920s to catch up by competing on terms. Dissension turned to crisis in 1936, when a group of societies, led by the Halifax, refused to comply with a decision by the large London societies to cut mortgage rates from 5 to 4.5 per cent, without first seeking agreement from the National Association of Building Societies. Supporters of the code then sought to impose compliance, reconstituting the National Association as the Building Societies Association, with the code written into its constitution. However, some fifty-five societies refused to accept the new conditions and formed a rival association.[79] When the movement later reunited in 1939, the code was formally abandoned.[80]

Ultimately, the building societies were in a weak position to exert control over the building value chain without near-unanimous support within their movement. While there were around a thousand building societies, the number of substantial builders was much smaller than the number of societies sufficiently large to meet their financial needs. As such, builders had the upper hand in negotiations and could generally find building societies prepared to offer more generous terms. Moreover, the house-building firms controlled a number of key 'assets' that were of considerable importance to expanding building societies. Pool arrangements (or other collateral guarantees) constituted the only means through which societies could offer 95 per cent mortgages, while the developer's retail role encompassed not only marketing the house but also, in many cases, the building society mortgage. Most building societies had limited branch networks and developers helped them to compensate for this by advertising the services of those building societies offering pool mortgages on their estates, negotiating mortgages with buyers, and, in some cases, even collecting their mortgage instalments. Their role as building

[76] LMA, Abbey Road Building Society, 7/32, Harold Bellman, 'Proposals for Co-operation', paper to be presented to Executive Committee of National Association of Building Societies, 3 Nov. 1931.

[77] LMA, Abbey Road Building Society, 7/32, Co-operation Group Committee minutes, 16 May 1930.

[78] LMA, Abbey Road Building Society, 7/32, Co-operation Group Committee minutes, details of agreements concluded up to 16 Dec. 1930, tabled at meeting of 20 Jan. 1931.

[79] Glyn Davies, *Building Societies and their Branches: A Regional Economic Survey* (London: Franey, 1981), 49–50.

[80] Davis, *Every Man His Own Landlord*, 67.

society agents was explicitly recognized via the payment of commission, typically 1 per cent of the value of each advance.[81]

Developers therefore largely retained their dominance over the house-building value chain, which had positive implications for purchasers, through encouraging competition on 'easy terms', but which may have also contributed to some negative features of the sector that attracted considerable publicity by the late 1930s. The builders' pool system contained a number of perverse incentives that encouraged builders to supply a low-quality product to high-risk customers, at an inflated price—problems that stronger governance by the building society movement might have mitigated.

This problem was accentuated by the absence of truly independent valuations, or legal advice, in the house mortgage system. Building societies conducted their own property valuations, rather than employing independent, qualified valuers.[82] The purchaser was not given access to the valuation report (or even the valuation figure), despite having paid for the 'survey'. Meanwhile the developer's solicitor typically also acted for the purchaser and building society.[83] Surveys offered no warranty and the surveyor owed no legal duty of care to the buyer (though builders sometimes encouraged buyers to believe otherwise). Building societies argued that, at the fee charged, no more robust survey could be provided, though the fee was typically two or three guineas—equivalent to over three days' wages for a highly skilled manual labourer or a low paid clerk.

By transferring risk from the builder to the building society (and the borrower), the builders' pool scheme encouraged jerry building—passing off shoddy building as good-quality houses.[84] Jerry building could push purchasers into financial difficulties, as the move from tenancy to house-purchase typically involved a substantial increase in the proportion of income devoted to accommodation, with little left over to meet unforeseen repairs. While weekly payments were lower for a mortgaged house than an *identical* rented house, the vast majority of, especially working-class, house-buyers did not move from similar properties, but from much cheaper inner-urban accommodation. By raising maintenance costs, jerry building intensified the precarious position of purchasers who had often already stretched themselves financially to meet mortgage payments on a larger house, thus contributing to rising mortgage defaults.

Buyers facing default had no real prospect of reselling their house for close to its purchase price, as 95 per cent mortgages—which underpinned the market for new homes—were only available on pool schemes.[85] A rise in mortgage defaults during the 1930s was hidden by the building societies, who ensured that official data—based on returns to the Chief Registrar of Friendly Societies—showed negligible

[81] John Laing, 'Increased Mortgages on Builders' Guarantees', in Ernest Betham (ed.), *House Building 1934–1936* (London: Federated Employers' Press, 1934), 86–91 (90).

[82] TNA, HLG29/253, Note, 31 May 1938, initialled B.W.G.

[83] McCulloch, 'Owner-Occupation', 171.

[84] Lee, 'Changes in Building Society Practice', 938.

[85] TNA, T161/945, letter by Inland Revenue official to H. E. C. Gatliff, 31 Mar. 1938; Lee, 'Changes in Building Society Practice', 938.

defaults. Such data were limited to mortgages over a year in arrears, or properties in the possession of the society for more than a year. However, societies took advantage of a general entitlement to sell houses when they had accumulated only three months' arrears, partly to keep them out of the returns.[86] Using holding companies and receiverships to manage properties in possession, or using builders' pool funds to reduce arrears to below twelve months, enabled them to further massage the data.[87] One consequence of this desire to minimize official default figures was harsh treatment of customers who fell into arrears. This problem was highlighted by senior judges as a dysfunctional characteristic of the system, leading to the repossession of houses from people who genuinely wanted to maintain payments but had run into temporary income difficulties.[88]

Negative publicity regarding jerry building eventually spurred leading housing developers to exert collective governance over the value chain, to mitigate this problem and protect themselves from competition from firms who undercut them via such practices. The National Federation of Master Builders established a Standards Board in 1936, to prescribe standard building specifications, and in January 1937 a voluntary builders' registration scheme was launched via a National House Builders Registration Council. Registered firms were obliged to allow the Council's officials to inspect developments at various stages of construction and to offer a two-year warranty on completion. By the eve of the Second World War many of the largest developers, including Wates, New Ideal Homesteads, Laing, and Wimpey, had signed up, together with large numbers of smaller firms.[89]

However, by this time events were already in train that would both intensify public disquiet about the current system and enable the major building societies to gain much of the regulatory control they had sought—via legislation. Elsy Borders, the wife of a London taxi driver, sued the Bradford Third Equitable Building Society, who had provided her mortgage for a house on the Coney Hall Estate, West Wickham, Kent, in 1934. In common with many houses on the estate, this soon developed serious building defects. Mrs Borders made various legal claims, but the two of greatest importance to the general relationship between building societies and speculative builders were that Bradford Third Equitable was a party to various fraudulent claims in the publicity material of the developers, Morrell's, and that pool arrangements were *ultra vires*—as building societies had no legal authority to accept non-property collateral security (while Bradford Third Equitable's rules also made no provision for such collateral).[90] By July 1938 Mrs Borders had also begun organizing a 'strike' on the estate—urging her fellow house-purchasers not to pay their instalments.[91]

---

[86] Speight, 'Building Society Behaviour', 93.

[87] Scott, *Making of the Modern British Home*, 222–4.

[88] TNA, CAB 27/645, memorandum by A. H. Holland, Chief Master, Chancery Division, for Cabinet Committee on Building Societies, 4 Apr. 1938.

[89] Jackson, *Semi-Detached London*, 128.

[90] See L. C. B. Gower, 'Building Societies and Pooling Agreements: The Borders Case and its Consequences', *Modern Law Review*, 3 (1939), 33–47.

[91] TNA, HLG29/253, Note for Minister [of Health?], 22 July 1938.

Mrs Borders's *ultra vires* claim threatened to make the bulk of existing mortgages on speculative housing null and void. Meanwhile, there were growing perceptions that London's speculative housing market had reached saturation and that there was a danger of a fall in property values, which a successful outcome to Mrs Borders's case might turn into a crash. Experts advised that this could threaten the financial stability of the building society movement and possibly even the clearing banks (which had made extensive loans to speculative developers). Government was sufficiently alarmed that a special Cabinet committee was convened. As the Chancellor of the Exchequer, Sir John Simon, informed the Cabinet, judgement in favour of Mrs Borders (who, government counsel advised, was almost certainly right in law) would invalidate a large proportion of mortgages, halt new house-building, produce heated political controversy, and, possibly, start a run on building society deposits.[92]

The building society movement pressed for a bill that would legalize both new pool advances and (retrospectively) existing ones, to prevent a crisis in the building industry and building society movement.[93] However, E. J. Cleary suggests that their major concern was that builders might take advantage of pool agreements being declared *ultra vires* by withdrawing their pool deposits with immediate effect and, possibly, successfully reclaiming any sums previously deducted by the societies in respect of mortgage defaults.[94]

The Borders case attracted considerable media coverage in Britain and overseas, with Mrs Borders being represented in court by the former Labour Solicitor General Sir Stafford Cripps. It went to the Court of Appeal and eventually to the House of Lords in May 1941, where Bradford Third Equitable was eventually victorious (though there are suggestions that this may have been influenced by political considerations).[95] Meanwhile a wave of 'rent strikes' by house-purchasers who, like Mrs Borders, found themselves in possession of defective houses, subsided following the onset of the Second World War. However, the initial trial had cast considerable doubt on the legality of builders' pool arrangements, leading the building societies to vigorously lobby for government action to legalize their position retrospectively.[96] The Building Societies Act, 1939, accomplished this end, though government, fearful of a negative public reaction, insisted on a number of safeguards for purchasers. Some of these were quietly welcomed by major building society figures, who were particularly active in advising and lobbying on the Act's provisions.[97]

The Act restricted mortgage terms to twenty-one years (except for houses built by National House Builders Registration Council members).[98] The collateral

---

[92] TNA, HLG29/253, memorandum to Cabinet by Chancellor of the Exchequer, 10 June 1938.

[93] TNA, HLG29/253, memorandum by joint committee of the Building Societies Association, the National Federation of Building Societies and important unaffiliated societies, 12 Mar. 1938.

[94] Cleary, *Building Society Movement*, 218–19.     [95] McCulloch, 'Owner-Occupation', 443.

[96] TNA, HLG29/253, note of meeting of representatives of government officials, later joined by building society representatives, 14 Feb. 1939.

[97] Cleary, *Building Society Movement*, 217–18.

[98] Speight, 'Building Society Behaviour', 227–8.

builders were required to deposit under pool schemes was fixed at the full difference between the societies' normal maximum loan to value ratio and the pool figure for the first five houses, with further houses then being funded with deposits on a 'one in three' basis. Meanwhile deposits would only be released when the outstanding debt fell below two-thirds of the valuation. Thus that section of the building society movement that had sought to regulate the sector, both to reduce risk and to protect their dominant position against competition from the rest, used a crisis to accomplish—via legislation—what they had not been able to achieve by consensus.

## CONCLUSIONS

The housing boom is widely recognized as having boosted economic growth and employment in the wake of the 1929–32 depression. House-building accounted for around 17 per cent of GNP growth from 1932–4, while if the expansion of construction materials is added it is estimated to have generated around 30 per cent of the increase in employment during the first three years of the recovery.[99] Moreover, given the close association between house-purchase and the acquisition of furniture and other household durables, these figures underestimate its true economic impact. Yet the macroeconomic effects of the 1930s housing boom were outweighed by its longer-term economic and social benefits for the people who moved into new suburban houses, their children, and subsequent owners of what many people still see as their 'ideal home'.

These impacts were most profound for those working-class families who typically moved from cramped inner-urban terraced or back-to-back housing to cheap suburban speculative houses. The 1937/38 Ministry of Labour household expenditure survey found that 17.8 per cent of non-agricultural working-class families either owned, or were purchasing, their own homes—at least double the proportion in 1930.[100] Such growth is dramatic—given that, according to an analysis of life histories for working-class house-purchasers in this period, most moved on, or within a few years of, marriage.[101] Working-class suburban owner-occupation rates were highest for skilled workers, but were nevertheless significant over a broad range of working-class incomes. However, there were strong regional variations, as shown in Figure 4.4, with depressed areas of northern Britain having markedly lower levels than the South East and West Midlands (the only two regions to enjoy higher house-building rates, per head of 1931 population, than England and Wales as a whole). Meanwhile Wales and, especially, Scotland, failed to participate in the private house-building boom to the same extent as any English region.

[99] Barry Eichengreen, 'The British Economy between the Wars', in Roderick Floud and Paul Johnson (eds.), *The Cambridge Economic History of Modern Britain*, vol. II: *Economic Maturity 1860–1939* (Cambridge: Cambridge University Press, 2004), 314–43 (334–5).

[100] TNA, LAB17/7, 'Weekly Expenditure of Working-Class Households in the United Kingdom in 1937–38', Ministry of Labour and National Service, July 1949; Speight, 'Who Bought the Inter-War Semi?'

[101] Scott, *Making of the Modern British Home*, 108.

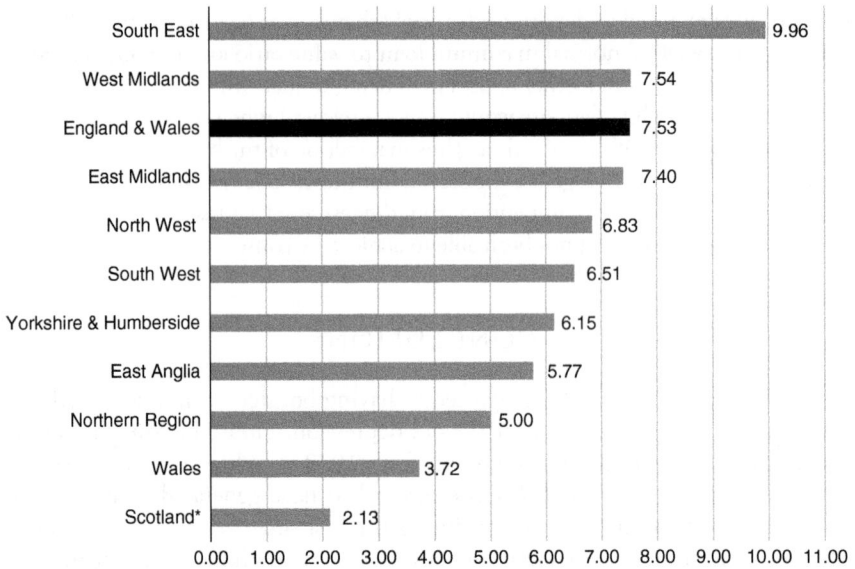

**Fig. 4.4.** A regional classification of new private sector house-building from the Armistice to 31 March 1940, as a percentage of the 1931 population

*Notes*: Regional classifications are UK Standard Economic Regions. *Data for Scotland only cover the period from 1919–38.

*Source*: Adapted from Peter Scott, *The Making of the Modern British Home: The Suburban Semi and Family Life between the Wars* (Oxford: Oxford University Press, 2013), 84–5.

A recent historical study of the social impacts of working-class migration to owner-occupied suburbia found that these moves had far-reaching effects on many aspects of family life.[102] Migration was strongly associated with the adoption of new, more 'domesticated' and 'privatized' family lifestyles, as evidenced by two ubiquitous phrases that people used to describe their new lives, 'keeping ourselves to ourselves' and 'keeping up with the Joneses'.[103] People who made this transition perceived it to have had a marked impact, encompassing how they dressed, furnished their homes, allocated their weekly finances, interacted with neighbours, socialized, and planned for their own, and their children's, future. Taking on a mortgage encouraged a longer-term planning horizon, reflected in, for example, smaller families (two or three children being viewed as the 'respectable' norm on the new estates).[104]

As such, moves to owner-occupation by working-class families during the 1930s can be seen as a key transition stage between 'traditional' working-class community life, based around the street, strong neighbourliness, and a status system based on a complex 'life portrait', to a characteristically 'modern' pattern, more based around the family, the home, and materially based status markers. Impacts on middle-class

---

[102] Ibid., ch. 6.      [103] Ibid.

[104] See Peter Scott, 'Did Owner-Occupation Lead to Smaller Families for Interwar Working-Class Households?' *Economic History Review*, 61 (2008), 99–124.

families moving to speculative suburban housing were generally much weaker, as many moved from relatively modern housing, with good utilities, often located in older suburbs.

The 1930s house-building boom was achieved through the building society movement and building industry collaborating to create both a new housing product, the cheap speculative suburban semi, and a new credit product, the 5 per cent deposit, twenty-five-year mortgage. The major London-based building societies which had been the main instigators of this new mortgage product were seeking to restrict its liberality in the 1930s, both to avoid excessive risk and to limit competition from their smaller rivals. Had their attempts at cartelization succeeded, some of the problems of jerry building might have been mitigated, but at the cost of restricting the market by tying up more builders' capital in pool deposits and reducing the number of people for whom mortgages were affordable. Overall, despite clear evidence of opportunistic behaviour by some builders (and some building societies) the 1930s speculative housing value chain appears to have been extremely successful in providing a quality product at a format and price suitable for the 'mass market'.

# PART II

# CREATING MASS MARKETS IN ELECTRONIC ENTERTAINMENT CONSUMER DURABLES

In contrast to most major labour-saving durables, entertainment durables have notoriously fast diffusion rates, being characterized by David Landes as 'counter-status luxuries', for which utility varies inversely with income (as higher income groups have more access to substitutes for their entertainment services).[1] With the exception of the cinema (with prices starting at as little as 3d for suburban 'fleapits') commercial entertainment was generally expensive relative to the leisure time purchased. Admission prices to league football games typically started at one shilling, and a pint of beer and admission to one of the cheapest dance halls, both cost around sixpence.[2] Moreover, with the exception of cinemas, which were sufficiently ubiquitous to be within walking distance of many urban dwellers, venue-based leisure entailed additional costs for transport. Such entertainments were also generally limited to specific times of the day and to consumption over particular time-spans, whereas even a few minutes of free time could be enjoyably spent listening to the radio—the first mass entertainment medium broadcast into people's homes—which could be enjoyed while doing the housework.

Radio had the further advantage over labour-saving durables in that while the washing machine would live in the kitchen, and the vacuum cleaner under the stairs, the radio typically took pride of place in the parlour or lounge, constituting a major status symbol. Radio prices reflected not only their electronics but the quality and styling of the cabinets—some of which, such as the Ekco circular radios or the Pye sunrise motif cabinets, remain iconic symbols of the inter-war era. As such, the radio rapidly began to displace the piano—the classic status symbol of the Edwardian parlour—which required skill and practice and thus had an

---

[1] David Landes, *The Unbound Prometheus: Technological Change and Industrial Development in Western Europe from 1750 to the Present* (Cambridge: Cambridge University Press, 1969), 428.

[2] Stephen G. Jones, *Workers at Play: A Social and Economic History of Leisure 1918–1939* (London: Routledge, 1986), 14; London School of Economics, *New Survey of London Life and Labour*, vol. IX: *Life and Leisure* (London: King, 1935), 52–6; Tony Mason, 'Football', in Tony Mason (ed.), *Sport in Britain: A Social History* (Cambridge: Cambridge University Press, 1989), 146–86 (152); James Walvin, *The People's Game: The History of Football Revisited* (Edinburgh: Mainstream, 2000), 123.

entertainment value for listeners limited by the competence of the player. It also had a severe impact on the market for phonograph/gramophone records, as it offered an endless sequence of the latest music, at lower cost and better sound quality, together with a range of non-music entertainment, including news, factual programmes, comedy, and drama.

Wireless ownership thus rapidly mushroomed in popularity, entertainment radio being unique among early high-ticket durables in reaching a mass audience within a few years of its launch. This posed major marketing challenges for the nascent radio industry, producers and retailers having to rapidly adapt to an explosion in demand. Radio was also distinctive in the nature of its production technology, for which Fordist 'mass-production' technologies were not appropriate—owing to highly unpredictable demand for new models, technical innovations that could suddenly render existing stock obsolete, and a form of assembly manufacture that lent itself to labour-intensive production methods.

Relatively small firms were able to compete with industry leaders, owing to both the barriers to Fordist mass production and three interrelated factors that made production extremely scale-flexible: simple assembly operations; modular components; and a technological standard that could accommodate innovations in individual components, or in their combinations, without simultaneous modifications to other elements. Production technology mainly involved mounting components onto 'boards' or 'chassis'—by hand or using simple generic tools. Components were 'modular' (compatible with a wide range of alternative components), giving assemblers the option of buying in standardized components cheaply, or producing customized ones directly. These characteristics were to become recurrent features of the electronics industry—most famously in the early microcomputer sector, where a wealth of small and medium assemblers competed through extensive use of bought-in standard components, while also often engaging in some degree of product differentiation.[3]

Chapter 5 examines how marketing radios was addressed in the United States. Major manufacturers sought to place large console radios in every home that could afford one, by developing strong relationships with independent distributors and retailers. Meanwhile manufacturers' promotional efforts were closely coordinated with dealers' marketing initiatives—including both conventional advertising and door-to-door canvassing. Chapter 6 discusses the different evolutionary path of the British market, where the smaller, table-top radio set became the standard model of the 1920s and sets were sold mainly in stores rather than door-to-door. Chapter 7 takes a detailed look at how radios were marketed by British manufacturers and retailers, while also examining other modes of providing radio reception to households without selling them a radio—radio relay services and rentals.

---

[3] Richard N. Langlois, 'External Economies and Economic Progress: The Case of the Microcomputer Industry', *Business History Review*, 66 (1992), 1–50; David P. Angel and James Engstrom, 'Manufacturing Systems and Technological Change: The U.S. Personal Computer Industry', *Economic Geography*, 71 (1995), 79–102.

Differences in the American and British socio-legal systems are shown to have played key roles in differentiating entertainment radio equipment markets in the United States and the United Kingdom. In the United States anti-trust legislation and anti-monopoly sentiment prevented the market leader and key patent owner, Radio Corporation of America (RCA) from retaining long-term control over the value chain, despite its ownership of key intellectual property rights. Conversely the British legal system was set up to protect the freedom of the individual (or, rather, a very particular type of individual—one with a lot of money) and thus upheld the rights of the British monopolist of fundamental radio patents—Marconi—to take full advantage of their position, even to the detriment of the industry. Britain's lack of anti-trust legislation also allowed radio valve manufacturers' cartels to exert a degree of governance over the value chain after the expiration of Marconi's fundamental patents, via a trade boycott of non-conforming firms.

These differences had a number of unforeseen consequences. British radio technology developed along a patent fee minimizing path which—owing to Marconi charging patent royalties based on the number of valves per radio—led to the development of expensive multi-functional valves, which economized on patent costs but raised direct costs. America, by contrast, continued producing simpler valves, which were much cheaper to produce, as they could operate at wider tolerances and were based on fewer, more standardized, designs. Then during the Great Depression the established structure of the US radio sector was shaken by the rapid growth of a new, low-cost, radio format, the 'midget radio' which the market leaders proved powerless to block. Conversely, the cartelized British industry successfully blocked this format throughout the 1930s, with consequences that were probably beneficial to the trade, but less so for lower-income consumers.

# 5

# America's Route to a Mass Market in Radio

## INTRODUCTION

Radio constitutes one of the key communications technologies that unified the United States. Indeed, its importance outweighed those of earlier transformative technologies—the telegraph, railroad, and telephone, or—arguably—even the early automobile. Radio's impacts were fundamental—projecting shared values to an ethnically and culturally diverse nation; introducing regional music styles to a national audience; and taking a new, intrusive, and inescapable form of advertising into people's homes. It provided entertainment and information that was accessible to almost all sections of society, including those with low incomes and education, while doing much to relieve the isolation of rural and small-town America. Housewives stuck at home during the day found it particularly valuable in alleviating their loneliness and the monotony of their domestic chores. As one listener reported, 'Oh, I tell you, it's company to me—someone with me all the time in the house.'[1] Radio even had a major influence on reducing linguistic diversity, establishing 'broadcast English' as the national popular norm.[2] These impacts were magnified by the explosive nature of its diffusion, reaching the majority of American homes within a decade of its launch as a commercial entertainment medium.

However, as with many new technology booms, most of the leading early radio equipment manufacturers failed to maintain their positions as key players in the market over the long term. Indeed radio's early growth spurt was characterized by high firm mortality for manufacturers (and, to a lesser extent, dealers). Moreover, the Great Depression witnessed the demise of several firms that appeared to have developed commanding positions, together with a huge number of smaller manufacturers and retailers. This chapter charts the early growth of the American radio manufacturing sector, the importance of intensive marketing and strong downstream value chains to developing and sustaining successful brands, and the reasons why—with one exception—the dominant set makers of the 1930s were not the big names of the 1920s. It also discusses the development of some of the

---

[1] A 1946 female Chicago interviewee, quoted in Frank Trentmann, *Empire of Things: How We Became a World of Consumers, from the Fifteenth Century to the Twenty-First* (St Ives: Allen Lane, 2016), 266.

[2] Michele Hilmes, *Radio Voices: American Broadcasting, 1922–1952* (Minneapolis: University of Minnesota Press, 1997), 5–20; Stephen Fox, *The Mirror Makers: A History of Advertising and its Creators* (New York: Morrow 1984), 150.

American techniques that proved important to the marketing of radio in Britain, together with others—such as door-to-door selling—that were less appropriate for British conditions.

## THE KEY ROLE OF PATENTS

Radio differs from the sectors discussed earlier in that patents played a crucial role in the development and cost structure of the industry. Numerous individuals and firms contributed to the process of cumulative technological innovation that made long-distance speech radio viable. The most important single innovator, however, was Guglielmo Marconi (1874–1937), an Italian who spent most of his working life in Britain. Innovation in the radio sector received an enormous boost during the First World War, on account of its key role in military communications. Radio's strategic importance cast a long shadow over the subsequent development of the American radio equipment industry. The US Navy took control over all domestic wireless communications shortly after it entered the war in April 1917 and thereafter sought to create a permanent solution to the current domination of American wireless communications by a 'foreign' company (Marconi's American subsidiary).

This involved both buying out American Marconi's assets and patents and bringing together all significant radio patents held by domestic companies under the control of a single national champion. The Navy's intervention led to the launch of Radio Corporation of America (RCA) as a sales company to market radios produced by the two main US-based patent holders—General Electric (GE) (producing 60 per cent of its sets) and Westinghouse (40 per cent).[3] RCA initially rejected licensing its patents to other manufacturers, aiming to control all American radio receiver production. Yet things didn't work out that way.

Failing to anticipate the massive growth in demand for household radios during the early 1920s, RCA produced insufficient numbers of sets, a problem compounded by delays in getting agreement on set specifications between RCA's sales department and the two manufacturing companies. These problems proved so severe that some small firms that had obtained 'amateur set' licences from Edwin Armstrong before he had sold his patents to Westinghouse were able to not only undercut RCA's price structure but also beat them to the market with technical improvements. Thus RCA found itself faced with stocks of outmoded sets during a period when rapid technical change required good logistics to avoid excessive depreciation. Despite being able to draw on the technical expertise of GE and Westinghouse, RCA also ran into continual technical problems and product launch delays during the 1920s, including being forced to release their first superhet radios late and with an unresolved thermal-hiss problem; subsequent problems of factory quality control and engineering design; a consequent buildup of obsolescent stock; and delays

---

[3] W. Rupert Maclaurin, *Invention and Innovation in the Radio Industry* (New York: Macmillan, 1949), 107; Robert Sobel, *RCA* (New York: Stein & Day, 1986), 21–35.

in launching new models.[4] Such problems were by no means unique to RCA, given the frenetic pace of technological change in radio—but nevertheless opened up a major gap in the market.

As a result of these problems, RCA gained less than a quarter of the receiver market during 1922–7.[5] Meanwhile American competition legislation undermined RCA's ability to leverage monopoly power through its control over radio's fundamental patents. The Sherman Anti-Trust Act of 1890 prohibited individual or collective actions aimed at creating monopolies, while the Federal Trade Commission Act and the Clayton Act subsequently empowered the Trade Commission to investigate restrictive practices that might violate the Sherman Act and enforce prohibitions against them.[6] When RCA sued over patent infringements, it found that the courts did not always support its position and even when it won, this was often at the expense of adverse publicity, damaged relations with the industry, and increased risk of anti-trust action.[7] It was therefore reluctantly forced to offer patent licences to its competitors from 1927, with royalties initially set at 7.5 per cent of the receiver's wholesale value. In 1932, following the expiry of some of its key fundamental patents, RCA reduced its licence fee to 5 per cent of the wholesale price (and 2.5 per cent for exported sets), while providing a licence bureau to assist with technical performance.[8] Meanwhile it retained its monopoly over radio patents by requiring licensees to offer it an option on any radio patents they developed—thus effectively creating a pool of all new radio patents.

RCA adopted package licensing, charging royalties on the total value of sets, despite the fact that not all components were covered by its patents. It even extended its licensing to radio tubes (known in Britain as valves). Despite the original De Forest 'audion' vacuum tube patent having expired in 1922, Clause 9 of RCA's 1927 licence agreement required licensees to purchase all tubes used as initial equipment in sets from RCA. RCA justified this on the grounds that tubes constituted integral parts of radio circuits and should thus be under the control of the circuit patent holder.[9] This point was contested in the courts by a group of independent tube makers and eventually settled in September 1931. RCA agreed to pay $1 million to the Deforest Co. and smaller amounts to some other litigants, in return for their acceptance of a 5 per cent licence fee to RCA (which might later be reduced to 2.5 per cent). Some tube manufacturers were said to have welcomed this, as a means of stabilizing an industry subject to relatively low entry barriers.[10]

---

[4] Alan Douglas, *Radio Manufacturers of the 1920's*, vol. III: *RCA to Zenith* (New York: Vestal, 1991), 29–43.

[5] Sobel, *RCA*, 84; Maclaurin, *Invention and Innovation*, 107–18; Leonard S. Reich, 'Research, Patents, and the Struggle to Control Radio: A Study of Big Business and the Uses of Industrial Research', *Business History Review*, 51 (1977), 208–35 (220–6).

[6] S. N. Broadberry and N. F. R. Crafts, 'Britain's Productivity Gap in the 1930s: Some Neglected Factors', *Journal of Economic History*, 52 (1992), 531–58 (547).

[7] Hugh G. J. Aitken, *The Continuous Wave: Technology and American Radio 1900–1932* (Princeton, NJ: Princeton University Press, 1985), 501.

[8] Sobel, *RCA*, 84–108; Maclaurin, *Invention and Innovation*, 132–6.

[9] 'What will the Tube Decision Mean to the Trade?', *Radio Retailing* (Mar. 1929), 52–3 and 83.

[10] 'Tube Suits Against RCA Settled by Cash and License Grants to 21 Claimants', *Radio Retailing* (Oct. 1931), 66; Alfred D. Chandler, *Inventing the Electronic Century: The Epic Story of the Consumer Electronics and Computer Industries* (New York: Free Press/Macmillan, 2001), 20.

Despite the price advantage it accrued from patent ownership, RCA never succeeded in dominating radio manufacture—though it was the only major set maker of the 1920s that remained a leading player in this market during the 1930s. Rather than developing along the lines of the highly concentrated US motor vehicle sector (the paradigmatic example of 'Fordist' mass production), radio remained an industry where small firms flourished alongside a small number of (often temporarily) major players, for reasons explained in the following section.

## PRODUCTION METHODS AND INDUSTRY STRUCTURE

Unlike the more extensively studied automobile sector, radio manufacture did not conform to the Chandlerian model of 'L' shaped cost curves—with costs per unit of production falling sharply as the scale of production increases until the 'minimum efficient scale' of mass production is reached, after which they become relatively stable.[11] Automobiles had very large numbers of moving parts, which had to be lubricated, powered, and cooled by various liquids without leakage. This necessitated production and fitting of interconnected components to very close tolerances, which made the substitution of highly skilled labour by dedicated machine tools attractive. Conversely, in common with most powered domestic appliances, radios had far fewer moving parts and did not require hydraulic systems. This had important implications for their production, most operations being characterized by repetitive assembly actions suitable for un/semi-skilled labour. 'Mass production' was employed only in basic form—using moving assembly lines to control the pace of work, with production flowing linearly across the factory floor at a predetermined speed. However, given the simple operations required—generally suitable for unskilled workers assembling components by hand or using basic, general-purpose tools—there was a much weaker cost imperative for the adoption of the expensive dedicated machine tools that characterized advanced Fordist mass production.[12]

Census data for 1939, shown in Figure 5.1, illustrates the striking contrasts between the radio and automobile industries. Scale economies are strongly evident for autos, though no clear positive relationship between plant size and value-added per worker is evident for radios and phonographs. Meanwhile plants with outputs of over $5 million constituted only 43 per cent of total employment in the radio sector, compared with 84.3 per cent of motor vehicle employment. Comparisons using such aggregate data potentially fall foul of Salter's 'index number problem'— mass produced goods (say Ford cars) are sold at much lower prices per unit than luxury cars produced using craft methods, thus biasing value-added per worker comparisons in favour of the high-end segment of the market.[13]

[11] Chandler, *Inventing the Electronic Century*, 21–8.

[12] Smithsonian National Museum of American History, Lemelson Center Archives, Clark Collection [hereafter Smithsonian, Clark], Box 111, W. S. Fitzpatrick, 'The Radio Manufacturing Industry', manuscript, 1932.

[13] See W. E. G. Salter, *Productivity and Technical* Change (Cambridge: Cambridge University Press, 1960), 151–2.

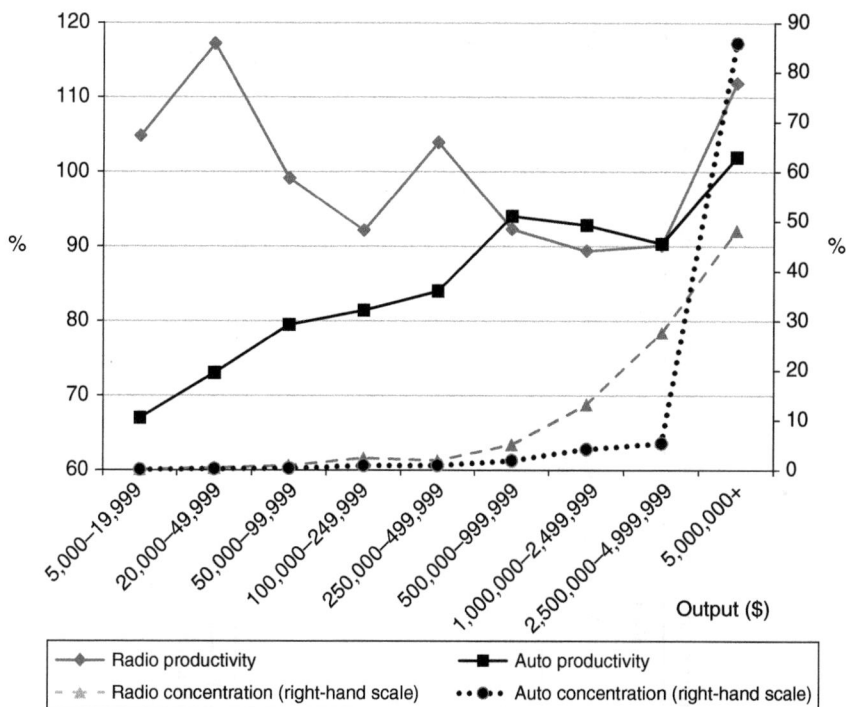

**Fig. 5.1.** Productivity by size of plant (value-added per wage earner, as a proportion of the average for each sector) and industrial concentration (proportion of total value-added) for radio, radio tube, and phonograph, and for motor vehicles, parts, and accessories, plants in 1939

*Source*: U.S. Department of Commerce, Bureau of the Census, *Sixteenth Census of the United States: 1940. Manufacturers 1939, Volume 1* (Washington, DC: USGPO, 1942), 190–214.

However, Scott and Zeibarth's recent analysis of Census of Manufacturing returns for US radio sector plants, for the years 1929, 1931, 1933, and 1935, found no significant trend towards plant-level scale economies. This is illustrated in Table 5.1, which shows labour productivity measures for the ten largest plants, by output, in 1935, together with figures for all radio and phonograph plants (from the Census). Several of the largest plants have outputs per wage-earner month, and/or per dollar of wages bill, below the industry average, including some of the very largest plants—such as RCA's receiver and tube plants. Several of these largest plants also fall below the industry average for value-added per wage-earner month, or per dollar of wages. Scott and Zeibarth also found that (contrary to the logic of the 'index number problem' scenario) small radio manufacturers were typically more focused on producing low-priced sets than their larger counterparts, while some of the leading radio manufacturers of the 1920s, such as RCA and Grigsby-Grunow, were strongly focused on the high end of the market.[14]

---

[14] Hagley Museum Library [hereafter Hagley], 2069/9/49, RCA Victor, 'Comparison RCAM Unit Sales since 1934 Against Industry Totals' (n.d. *c.*1940); Alan Douglas, *Radio Manufacturers of the 1920's*, vol. II: *Freed-Eisemann to Preiss* (New York: Vestal, 1989), 143.

**Table 5.1.** Labour productivity in the largest ten plants, together with aggregate radio and gramophone sector plant productivity, for 1935

| Firm | Plant | Class* | Output ($) | Ranking by: | | Output per: | | Value-added per: | |
|---|---|---|---|---|---|---|---|---|---|
| | | | | Value | Value-added | Wage-earner month | $ of wages | Wage-earner month | $ of wages |
| Philadelphia Storage Battery Co. | Philadelphia, Penn | R | 42,817,662 | 1 | 1 | 430 | 4.21 | 187 | 1.84 |
| RCA Victor Division | Camden, NJ | R | 29,065,617 | 2 | 2 | 333 | 3.67 | 213 | 2.34 |
| RCA Radiotron Division | East Newark, NJ | T | 9,886,216 | 3 | 3 | 199 | 2.64 | 100 | 1.33 |
| Zenith Radio Corporation | Chicago, Ill | R | 7,470,104 | 4 | 4 | 903 | 12.10 | 401 | 5.38 |
| Wells-Gardner & Co. | Chicago, Ill | R | 6,514,241 | 5 | 5 | 477 | 7.08 | 215 | 3.19 |
| Colonial Radio Corporation | Buffalo, NY | R | 6,305,542 | 6 | 6 | 458 | 5.64 | 195 | 2.40 |
| Crosley Radio Corporation | Cincinatti, Ohio | R | 4,923,000 | 7 | 21 | 372 | 6.00 | 72 | 1.15 |
| Atwater Kent Manufacturing Co. | Philadelphia, Penn | R | 4,634,770 | 8 | 9 | 326 | 4.24 | 156 | 2.02 |
| Hygrade Sylvania Corporation | Emporium, Penn | T | 3,577,461 | 9 | 10 | 198 | 3.25 | 121 | 1.99 |
| Ken-Rad Corporation | Owensboro, KY | T | 3,571,980 | 10 | 7 | 183 | 3.89 | 125 | 2.65 |
| All radio & phonograph | | | 200,972,523 | | | 374 | 4.68 | 181 | 2.27 |

*Notes*: * R = Radio receiver manufacturer; T = Tube manufacturer (based on at least 50 per cent of revenue being in that class).

*Source*: Peter Scott and Nicolas Ziebarth, 'The Determinants of Plant Survival in the U.S. Radio Equipment Industry During the Great Depression', *Journal of Economic History*, 75 (2015), 1097–127 (1106).

The weak scale economies underlying this industrial structure reflected highly unstable and unpredictable demand for any particular model of radio. Technical economies of scale are generally associated with steady operation and planned capacity, ensuring the full utilization of expensive machine tools. Conversely, highly variable output shifted competitive advantage towards more labour-intensive, scale-flexible production techniques, reducing both the optimal scale of plant output and the cost penalties from operating below that optimum.[15]

Even in the late 1930s, most firms were said to be still producing only for orders, hiring large numbers of workers during seasonal peaks, followed by heavy lay-offs during the slack season.[16] In order to avoid expensive machinery lying idle outside demand peaks, this strategy required the use of labour-intensive production methods, as illustrated by a 1926 description of radio assembly at one of America's largest manufacturers, Crosley. Some thirty-six women and six men contributed to the assembly of each radio, with work carefully subdivided by task. However, most functions involved either work by hand (mainly mounting components) or using simple generic tools (such as soldering).[17] Meanwhile economies of scope were obviated by many components being externally sourced from specialist firms.[18]

The automobile industry had responded to strong seasonal demand fluctuations with a strategy of building up massive inventories of completed cars in winter. They then required their franchised dealers to carry these stocks on their premises, in anticipation of the forthcoming seasonal upturn. Dealers' inventory costs were in turn covered by finance companies, who provided them with inventory loans and purchased their retail instalment sales contracts. Many of these finance companies were subsidiaries of the auto manufacturers, or had contractual agreements with them.[19] However, this strategy proved impracticable in radio, due to a different source of demand variability. In addition to a predictable seasonal pattern, radio suffered from less incremental annual model changes than cars, together with rapid and unpredictable technological obsolescence; factors which collectively prevented dealers from carrying substantial stocks over the slack season. As a 1931 report noted, overnight, 'a warehouse supply of stored radios [could be converted] into stock out of date and worthless in the eyes of the buying public, that will be satisfied with nothing but the latest model'.[20]

---

[15] Joe S. Bain, *Barriers to New Competition* (Cambridge, MA: Harvard University Press, 1962), 63.

[16] Gladys L. Palmer and Adam M. Stoflet, *The Labour Force of the Philadelphia Radio Industry in 1936* (Philadelphia Labour Market Studies Report No. P-2, Philadelphia, PA, 1938), 4–5.

[17] 'Combined Craftsmenship of 42 Men and Women Required in Assembling of One Crosley Five Tube Model 5-50', *Crosley Broadcaster* (15 Dec. 1926), 9.

[18] See Peter Scott and Nicolas Ziebarth, 'The Determinants of Plant Survival in the U.S. Radio Equipment Industry During the Great Depression', *Journal of Economic History*, 75 (2015), 1097–112.

[19] Martha L. Olney, *Buy Now, Pay Later: Advertising, Credit, and Consumer Durables in the 1920s* (Chapel Hill, NC: University of North Carolina Press, 1991), 119–30; Walter A. Friedman, *Birth of a Salesman: The Transformation of Selling in America* (Cambridge, MA: Harvard University Press, 2004), 209–24.

[20] Caroline Manning, 'Fluctuations of Employment in the Radio Industry', *Bulletin of the Women's Bureau*, 83 (Washington: USGPO, 1931), 32.

Even in the radio tube sector, where firms produced to common design standards and demand was more predictable (partly due to short tube lifespans, which generated a steady stream of replacement demand), the cost advantages of highly mechanized systems were not clear-cut. Such technologies left manufacturers extremely vulnerable to sudden downturns in demand.[21] For example De Forest, which had invested heavily in a highly mechanized tube plant, was forced to abandon mass production during the depression in favour of shorter production runs for a wider range of tubes.[22] Thus, as in radio set production, small firms continued to compete with large ones, even in manufacturing the same standardized tubes.

Survival and growth in the sector were determined principally by competitive advantages in product differentiation (branding), rather than production methods—a phenomenon evident in other manufacturing industries that lack substantial scale economies. These entailed cumulative investment in building up brand recognition, reputation, and goodwill among both dealers and final customers. Scott and Zeibarth's analysis of radio plant-level Census returns over the Great Depression found that ownership of a recognizable proprietary radio brand was a significant determinant of plant survival.[23] As the following sections will demonstrate, developing successful brands entailed exploiting complementarities between control over distribution networks, differentiation through design, and promotional activity.[24] This involved close cooperation with downstream distributors, forging value chains that also offered some measure of protection against new entrants with lower unit costs.

## ESTABLISHING VALUE CHAINS IN RADIO

The launch of entertainment radio was followed by a boom in equipment sales, unprecedented for any high-ticket household durable. The proportion of American households with radios rose from less than 1 per cent in 1922 to 16.0 per cent in 1926, 45.8 per cent in 1930, and 67.3 per cent in 1935, by which time a significant number owned more than one set.[25] Ownership greatly outpaced the diffusion of much longer-established appliances such as vacuum cleaners and washing machines, despite radios being initially very expensive and requiring costly external antennae and frequent servicing.

Demand was initially dominated by classic 'early adopters'—radio enthusiasts and home-constructors, who were more interested in the technical challenges of radio than in what was being broadcast. Homemade sets outnumbered factory-made

---

[21] Smithsonian, Clark, 37/7, De Forest bulletin to District Managers No. 59, 29 Apr. 1931, 'New Price and Commission Schedule'.
[22] Smithsonian, Clark, 108/2, Memorandum from D. E. Replogle, De Forest Radio Co., 27 Oct. 1931.
[23] Bain, *Barriers to New Competition*, 57.          [24] Ibid., 125.
[25] S. B. Carter et al., *Historical Statistics of the United States: Earliest Times to the Present. Millennial Edition* (Cambridge: Cambridge University Press, 2006), vol. I, 667; vol. IV, 1027.

receiver sales until 1925, while early listeners' first priority was often distance of reception.[26] However, by the mid-1920s mainstream users, who were chiefly interested in programme content, began to dominate the market. The advent of national programming also contributed to a decline in the importance listeners placed on distance, relative to characteristics such as tone, selectivity between stations, simplicity of operation, and appearance.[27]

The switch from kits to complete sets increased the importance of branding and effective downstream distribution systems. Manufacturers turned to retailers of musical or electrical goods, who were tasked to develop efficient local sales organizations to promote this new product, provide effective after-sales service, and organize instalment credit for what was a very high-ticket durable. As with production technology, much research on value chains for new consumer durables in this period has focused on the US automobile sector, where, as Tedlow noted, manufacturer–dealer relations were 'marked by often bitter conflict'.[28] Leading auto producers used their considerable market power over dealers to impose franchise contracts, which could be cancelled with little if any notice and without which continued activity in the sector was often not possible. This in turn assisted them in pressuring firms into both accepting close monitoring and coordination of their activities and taking on various costs, which they would otherwise have borne directly.[29] Examples include shipping stock that was either excess to dealers' requirements, was sent at the end of the production year for that model, or was packed with accessories, and pressure to use manufacturers' retail finance facilities.[30]

In contrast to the domination of the US automobile sector by the three leading firms, the absence of strong technical economies of scale in radio produced a fragmented and intensely competitive industry structure.[31] This, in turn, had important implications for downstream value chains, on account of both the weaker market power of individual manufacturers and the impracticality of manufacturers looking to dealers to hold their inventory over the slack season.[32] Most major manufacturers, including RCA, Crosley, Atwater Kent, and Zenith, adopted a distribution policy based on assigning territories to appointed wholesale distributors, who in turn supplied only authorized dealers (who nevertheless typically also sold

[26] Clayton R. Koppes, 'The Social Destiny of the Radio: Hope and Disillusionment in the 1920s', *South Atlantic Quarterly*, 68 (1969), 363–76 (364); Susan Smulyan, *Selling Radio: Commercialization of American Broadcasting, 1920–34* (Washington, DC: Smithsonian Institution, 1994), 12–31; Thomas Eoyang, 'An Economic Study of the Radio Industry in the United States of America' (unpublished PhD thesis, Columbia University, 1936), 72.

[27] 'What Does the Public Want?', *Radio Retailing* (Oct. 1929), 51.

[28] Richard S. Tedlow, *New and Improved: The Story of Mass Marketing in America* (New York: Basic Books, 1990), 358.

[29] Sally Clarke, 'Closing the Deal: GM's Marketing Dilemma and its Franchised Dealers, 1921–41', *Business History*, 45 (2003), 60–79 (62–3). For Ford before 1920, see Tedlow, *New and Improved*, 143–6.

[30] Clarke, 'Closing the Deal'; Tedlow, *New and Improved*, 155–64.

[31] Manning, 'Fluctuations of Employment', 32.

[32] Peter Scott, 'When Innovation Becomes Inefficient: Reexamining Britain's Radio Industry', *Business History Review*, 88 (2014), 497–521.

other makes of radio).[33] Some manufacturers, such as RCA, assigned sales quotas to each wholesaler.[34] A minority operated their own wholesale branches, while large retail customers such as mail-order houses, chain stores, and department stores often placed their orders directly with the manufacturer.[35]

Despite initial fears that there would be insufficient broadcast programmes to retain the interest of the nascent audience, in the event this was not problematic. During 1922 alone the number of licensed stations rose from twenty-eight to 570.[36] These were established by a variety of organizations, including newspapers, educational institutions, retailers, and municipalities. Start-up costs were low, as stations generally broadcast over relatively short distances and used either amateur performers, or professionals who could be persuaded to appear for free.[37] However, radio equipment manufacturers and dealers accounted for the largest single category of station owner by 1923.[38] Some large manufacturers also took the lead in developing regular national programming. In December 1923 the National Carbon Company launched what became the 'Eveready Hour' to promote its radio batteries, integrating music, drama, and talk into a single programme, later based around a weekly 'theme'.[39]

Eveready set a precedent for other major radio equipment manufacturers in sponsoring regularly scheduled programmes. In October 1925 the leading set manufacturer Atwater Kent launched the 'Atwater Kent Hour', which rapidly became the most popular US radio programme, featuring top musicians of the era and costing the firm $7,000 per week by the 1926–7 season.[40] In April 1928 RCA launched the 'RCA Demonstration Hour', breaking the tradition of prime programming being restricted to the evenings. Broadcast each Saturday at 2.30 p.m. EST, it enabled retailers to tune in to a quality music programme at their peak time.[41] RCA played a pivotal role in the development of national networked broadcasting, culminating in the launch of its National Broadcasting Company (NBC) network in the autumn of 1926.

Table 5.2 provides an estimate of the value chain in radio set manufacturing for 1928. Advertising expenditure is shown separately, as both manufacturers and retailers engaged in advertising to the final consumer (though, unlike the other

[33] Harold N. Cones and John H. Bryant, *Zenith Radio: The Early Years, 1919–1935* (Atglen, PA: Schiffer, 1997), 92; *Crosley Radio Weekly* (12 Oct. 1925), 3 <http://www.crosleyradios.com/pdf/CRW_October_12_1925.pdf>; store advertisement, *Spokane Daily Chronicle* (11 Oct. 1928), 13 <http://news.google.com/newspapers?nid=1338&dat=19281011&id=Q8tXAAAAIBAJ&sjid=rPQDAAAAIBAJ&pg=5617,2460983>.

[34] Hagley, 2069/9/38, RCA Victor, 'Merchandising Policy of the Radiola Division for the Year 1930–1931', 24 July 1930.

[35] Eoyang, 'Economic Study of the Radio Industry', 137.

[36] Douglas Gomery, *A History of Broadcasting in the United States* (Malden, MA: Wiley-Blackwell, 2008), 14.

[37] Smulyan, *Selling Radio*, 14 and 39.         [38] Hilmes, *Radio Voices*, 44–51.

[39] Ibid., 63–4; Smulyan, *Selling Radio*, 104–8.

[40] Alan Douglas, *Radio Manufacturers of the 1920's*, vol. I: *A-C Dayton to J. B. Ferguson Inc.* (New York: Vestal, 1989), 67.

[41] Smithsonian, Clark, 55, 108/2, Circular to RCA Distributors and Dealers from J. L. Ray, Sales Manager, 18 Apr. 1928.

**Table 5.2.** The value chain for US radio set manufacturers, *c.*1928

| Stages of value chain | Controlled by | % of retail price |
| --- | --- | --- |
| Patents | RCA | 4.1 |
| Design | Manufacturer | ( |
| Raw materials | Market | ( |
| Components | Market/manufacturer | (31.9 |
| Assembly | Manufacturer | ( |
| Tubes | Tube makers | 9.0 |
| Wholesale distribution | Distributors | 12.5 |
| Retail distribution | Retailers | 36.7 |
| Advertising | Manufacturer/retailer | 5.8 |
| **Total** | | 100 |

*Sources and notes*: Wholesaler and retailer margins—based on discounts on list prices offered by RCA in 1928 (Smithsonian, Clark 55, box 97, RCA Sales Dept. Retail Dealers Discount Schedules). Patents—based on RCA's 1927 patenting agreement, specifying royalties at 7.5 per cent of wholesale prices (Robert Sobel, *RCA* (New York: Stein & Day, 1986), 84–108; W. Rupert Maclaurin, *Invention and Innovation in the Radio Industry* (New York: Macmillan, 1949), 132–6). Advertising, based on a 1928 survey estimate of retailers' promotional expenditure as a proportion of net retail sales (S. J. Ryan, 'Expenses, 29.5%, Profit, 8.2%. Part II of Radio Retailing's Co-operative Industry Survey of the Costs of Selling Radio', *Radio Retailing* (Oct. 1929), 56–60 and 96) and a 1931 estimate of manufacturers' advertising expenditure as a proportion of sales to distributors (Association of National Advertisers Inc., *An Analysis of the Distribution Costs of 312 Manufacturers* (New York: The Association, 1931), 22, cited in Neil H. Borden, *The Economic Effects of Advertising* (Chicago, IL: Irwin, 1942), 67). Tube costs calculated using the data in Table 5.4, assuming the set has five valves, which are purchased by the final user (rather than being installed by the set maker) and that no RCA royalty is paid on them.

items in the table, the figure for advertising constitutes a pure cost, with no element of profit factored in). Tube costs are also shown (assuming the set in question to have five tubes)—though at this time tubes were still typically purchased by the final user rather than being installed by the manufacturer. The shares of retail value accounted for by other components, raw materials, and set assembly cannot be disaggregated, as set manufacturers varied widely in the proportions of components they sourced through the market, or produced in-house.

Value-chain governance was exerted principally by RCA (which controlled circuit patents and played a leading role in the industry's trade association, the Radio Manufacturers Association) and by the set manufacturers. Manufacturers had control over branding, cabinet design, and pricing, together with some technical features, such as tuning 'gadgets'. They also exerted considerable influence over downstream distribution, through their authorized distributors and dealers. Downstream distribution (including retailers' advertising spend) nevertheless accounted for more than half of retail prices—reflecting the high cost of the services that distributors and, especially, retailers were expected to provide. As the following discussion will show, this cost structure changed substantially during the 1930s, with the emergence of less uniform value chains (including some dominated by retailers), lower services inputs (and margins) for dealers, and new manufacturers who gained competitive advantage principally through lower prices.

## MANUFACTURERS' MARKETING AND DEALER SUPPORT STRATEGIES

During 1922 and 1923 David Sarnoff of RCA devoted considerable time to establishing an effective distribution network for their radios and educating dealers on how to market them, by addressing conventions of jobbers and retailers in the electrical goods and musical instrument trades and writing for their trade journals.[42] Sarnoff emphasized that the enthusiast home-constructor era was temporary and that radios would soon be sold as an entertainment device and a piece of furniture, rather than a machine. Distributors were told that their function was to sell 'a device which has a very important bearing on our home life, for its sphere is one of culture, education and entertainment... somewhat of the characteristics of the phonograph and other musical instruments... which is not a mere electrical utility but which also provides entertainment and enlightenment of a high order'. To achieve this, retailers should provide:

> an attractive store to fit in harmoniously with the accustomed methods of selling musical instruments... the adoption of intensive selling practices, such as special demonstrations, demonstrations in the home, a reasonable amount of local advertising, and inauguration of all those special methods, which have been found valuable in other business in carrying on intensive selling campaigns.[43]

Sarnoff urged dealers to make their stores attractive to women (whom, he said, accounted for 80 per cent of phonograph sales) and employ salesmen who could sell on the basis of appearance, simplicity of operation, and value for money. This might involve window displays showing home scenes with the radio taking pride of place in the living room, separate salesmen to deal with radio hams and mainstream customers, and crews of 'outside' salesmen, who would arrange home trials through door-to-door canvassing, to break down sales resistance and inertia (including fears that radios would be too complicated to operate).[44] He also emphasized the need for instalment purchase schemes to increase affordability.[45]

By the mid-1920s radio retailers were beginning to note this transition towards a new type of customer and, as Sarnoff had predicted, the need for retail practices that met (increasingly) her needs. Dealers characterized women as being more demanding customers than men, expecting a radio set to be reliable, easy to operate, and attractive in appearance. They were also said to purchase only after undertaking comparison shopping; 'for a woman largely sells the merchandise she buys to herself'.[46] However, the radio retailing sales force appears to have remained almost

[42] For details of Sarnoff's life and work, see Sopel, *RCA*.

[43] Hagley, David Sarnoff Technical Library [hereafter Hagley, Sarnoff], Publicity, Box 1, File B1F20, 'The Relation of the Jobber to Radio', article by David Sarnoff for the journal *Jobbers Salesman*, 14 Apr. 1923.

[44] Hagley, Sarnoff, Publicity, Box 1, File B1F20, David Sarnoff, 'Radio and the Electrical Dealer' draft article for publication in *Journal of Electricity*, 16 Apr. 1923.

[45] Hagley, Sarnoff, Publicity, Box 1, Folder BIF 8, 'Radio', informal address by David Sarnoff, before Electrical Supply Jobbers Association, 26 May 1922.

[46] Robert C. Planck, 'Her Ladyship, the Radio Customer', *The Radio Dealer* (Oct. 1925), 155–6 (156).

entirely male.[47] The absence (or invisibility) of female sales staff may reflect popular assumptions that technical competence in radio was a masculine characteristic, or the need for salesmen, on occasion, to deliver bulky console sets to households. However, during the 1920s men dominated most areas of direct sales (especially door-to-door), including sectors such as brushes, where women were the principal customers.[48]

Granting authorized dealerships limited local retail competition and thus constituted a 'carrot' to encourage dealers' conformance with the manufacturer's retail model. For example RCA, which moved to authorized dealerships in 1926, had the following requirements: a well-located store, with a well-appointed showroom providing booths for sound quality demonstration; window displays to promote their product; an 'energetic' sales organization; adequate servicing facilities; and 'An advertising policy which is as liberal as the dealer's circumstances will permit'.[49]

. Authorized distributors were rewarded with discounts from list prices that grew significantly over the 1920s. In August 1922 RCA offered dealers 25 per cent discounts for orders up to $499 and 33.3 per cent for larger orders, while their wholesalers received a 46 per cent discount (figures broadly in line with a December 1922 estimate for the sector as a whole).[50] Discounts were subsequently raised; by February 1928 RCA dealers and wholesalers received discounts of 40 and 52.5 per cent respectively.[51] Manufacturers also invested heavily in promoting their products, both directly and in cooperation with their retailers. Information on advertising expenditures for the radio industry is scarce for this period, though a 1931 survey estimated that (for radio equipment and supplies) manufacturers' direct advertising averaged 5.33 per cent of net sales.[52] Meanwhile fragmentary information for some of the largest manufacturers indicates that they supported their brands with proportionately larger advertising budgets than the sector average.[53]

Once retailers were secured, they had to be persuaded to hold significant stocks. This entailed substantial risks, as unstable market conditions often led to reductions in list prices, which eroded the value of their inventory and thus provided an incentive for under-stocking. RCA addressed this via a price protection policy; in the event of list price reductions, distributors and dealers were refunded the difference between the old and new price on each unsold set.[54] Meanwhile Zenith

[47] U.S. Department of Commerce, *Merchandising Problems of Radio Retailers in 1930* (Washington, DC: USGPO, 1931), 8–9.

[48] Friedman, *Birth of a Salesman*, 195 and 202–3.

[49] Smithsonian, Clark, 55, 239/1, Circular from E. E. Bucher, General Sales Manager, RCA, to authorized Radiola Dealers, 18 Jan. 1926.

[50] Smithsonian, Clark, 55, Box 97, RCA Sales Dept. Retail Dealers Discount Schedules; M. B. Sleeper, 'Distributing Problems of Radio Manufacturers', *Wireless World and Radio Review* (23 Dec. 1922), reprinted in Douglas, *Radio Manufacturers of the 1920's*, vol. I, viii.

[51] Smithsonian, Clark, 55, Box 97, RCA Sales Dept. Retail Dealers Discount Schedules.

[52] Association of National Advertisers Inc., *An Analysis of the Distribution Costs of 312 Manufacturers* (New York: The Association, 1931), 22, cited in Neil H. Borden, *The Economic Effects of Advertising* (Chicago, IL: Irwin, 1942), 67.

[53] Douglas, *Radio Manufacturers of the 1920's*, vol. I, 67 and 114.

[54] Smithsonian, Clark, 55, 108/2, circular from E. A. Nicholas, Manager, Radiola Division, RCA, to all RCA Radiola Distributors, 3 Dec. 1928.

and Philco achieved the same goal via an explicit policy of no price reductions, underpinned by careful 'production planning'.[55]

Maintaining capacity production was problematic in industries subject to strong seasonality and annual model changes. General Motors had pioneered production planning to address this, using information from their distributors and dealers to predict sales.[56] Zenith's spectacular success from the mid-1920s was attributed to a production and inventory planning system, based on distributors' purchase commitments—updated quarterly. By facilitating price stability, the system was also said to have built loyalty among their retailers.[57] Philco's entry into set manufacturing, from June 1928, was undertaken using a production control plan known as the 'Monday Morning Conference'. Each Monday morning wires were required from Philco's distributors, with details of their stocks and sales to dealers over the previous week. Together with information on their own inventories, Philco then predicted sales for the next five weeks and scheduled production and materials purchases accordingly. This scheme was said to have enabled Philco to end 1929 with a normal inventory, in contrast to their competitors, and built dealer loyalty by showing that Philco could maintain its promise not to dump surplus stock.[58]

However, production planning was not unproblematic. For example, RCA (which had introduced production planning by 1924 and moved to a more sophisticated system from around autumn 1930), nevertheless faced persistent problems in coordinating production and sales.[59] In addition to production or market volatility problems, an RCA review identified cases where they had over-sold dealers on likely sales, or where some smaller distributors had responded to RCA's 'pressure selling' by accepting larger stocks than they could move.[60]

An extensive volume of information also flowed downstream from manufacturers to distributors and dealers, via bulletins, national and regional sales conventions, and in-house journals. For example, Crosley Radio Corporation was producing the *Crosley Radio Weekly* by January 1924, later replaced by the *Crosley Broadcaster*. In addition to informing distributors and dealers about their general activities, these included information on marketing assistance, letters from dealers (generally supporting the company's marketing policy), and articles extolling the merits of activities such as direct selling.[61]

[55] Speech by Paul Klugh to annual meeting of Zenith stockholders, 25 June 1930, cited in Cones and Bryant, *Zenith Radio*, 92.

[56] Alfred D. Chandler, *Strategy and Structure: Chapters in the History of the Industrial Enterprise* (Cambridge, MA: MIT Press, 1962), 145–53.

[57] Cones and Bryant, *Zenith Radio*, 25.

[58] John Paul Wolkonowicz, 'The Philco Corporation: Historical Review & Strategic Analysis' (unpublished MSc dissertation, Alfred P. Sloan School of Management, 1981), 22–5.

[59] Smithsonian, 93/2, 'Radio Official Denies Tube Hold-up', press release by J. L. Bernard, Information Bureau, RCA, 1924; Hagley, 2069/9/41, circular to RCA Victor distributors by Roy A. Forbes, 15 Oct. 1930; Hagley, 2069/9/41, 'RCA Victor Production Control and Requisition Plan', 1 July 1931; Hagley, 2069/9/47, 'Seasonal Trend. RCA Radio Sets and Phonographs', RCA Victor memorandum, signed 'BLA', 15 Feb. 1943.

[60] Hagley, 2069/9/47, letter, 'BLA' to 'Tom', 6 Apr. 1943; Clarke, 'Closing the Deal', 62–3.

[61] Some surviving copies are available at <http://www.crosleyradios.com>.

Set makers also faced the problem, commonly found in situations where manufacturers rely on independent distributors, that levels of promotional and customer services considered optimal from the retailer's perspective will be lower than the optimal levels from the manufacturer's perspective. This is because while both manufacturer and retailer reap the benefits of such activity, it is the retailer who bears the costs. This problem is typically addressed by offering retailers appropriate incentives (or credible threats), to raise their provision of marketing and services to the manufacturer's desired level.[62] Lacking the market power to enforce retailer conformity primarily through the threat of 'exit' from their contractual relationship (as used in autos), radio manufacturers relied heavily on 'voice' strategies of cooperation and incentives.[63]

Major manufacturers made great efforts to develop strong relationships with retailers, partly in cooperation with local wholesalers. Authorized retailers were offered a variety of incentives to promote the firm's brand and conform to its retail policy, including cooperative and coordinated advertising, dealer educational activities, and a variety of other assistance with marketing and credit provision. In return, dealers were expected to follow the manufacturer's marketing policy and prioritize their brand over the others they stocked for activities such as door-to-door canvassing, window displays, or customer recommendation.

Cooperative advertising appears to have become popular in the late 1920s, as reflected in the advertising spend data for RCA in Table 5.3. This included a plan under which RCA paid half the costs of dealers' direct mailings featuring their products.[64] Crosley had initiated support for direct mailing by the start of the 1928/29 season, dealers being offered a set of three mailings for each potential customer, delivered to the dealer stamped and addressed for 15 cents, which they were advised to use in conjunction with a door-to-door sales campaign.[65] RCA's cooperative advertising appears to have grown considerably over the depression years. By the autumn of 1931 RCA Victor operated a plan whereby they and the local distributor each paid 25 per cent of a dealer's print advertising costs, providing certain conditions were met (including that at least 50 per cent of total advertising space was used to illustrate their merchandise and that the RCA Victor name featured at least as large as that of the store's).[66] For major accounts, such as chain stores, RCA offered to meet 50 per cent of advertising costs, for expenditures up to 5 per cent of the chain's purchases.[67]

Manufacturers also engaged in extensive advertising support activities for dealers, including the provision of 'ready-made' newspaper ads to which dealers could

[62] See Jean Tirole, *The Theory of Industrial Organization* (Cambridge, MA: MIT Press 1988), 177–9.

[63] See Susan Helper, 'Strategy and Irreversibility in Supplier Relations: The Case of the US Automobile Industry', *Business History Review*, 65 (1991), 781–824.

[64] Smithsonian, Clark, 55, Box 97, Memorandum to all RCA Radiola Distributors, 9 Oct. 1929.

[65] *Crosley Broadcaster* (1 Nov. 1928), 13.

[66] Hagley, 2069/10/14, 'RCA Victor Company Inc. Co-operative Advertising Plan, Oct 1st to Dec. 31, 1931', circular, c.Sept. 1931.

[67] Hagley, 2069/10/14, 'Special Discount and Cooperative Advertising Plan for Large Accounts, season 1931–32' (n.d., c.Sept. 1931).

**Table 5.3.** RCA's advertising expenditure as a percentage of sales, 1923–9

| Year | Space | Sales promotion | Cooperative | Broadcast | Total (%) | Total ($) |
|------|-------|-----------------|-------------|-----------|-----------|-----------|
| 1923 | 3.78 | 3.11 | 0.00 | 0.00 | 6.89 | 536,387 |
| 1924 | 2.59 | 1.65 | 0.00 | 0.00 | 4.24 | 1,058,640 |
| 1925 | 5.30 | 2.59 | 0.00 | 0.00 | 7.89 | 1,595,772 |
| 1926 | 7.01 | 2.95 | 0.00 | 0.00 | 9.96 | 2,257,859 |
| 1927 | 5.40 | 1.78 | 0.17 | 0.30 | 7.65 | 1,783,365 |
| 1928 | 4.47 | 2.20 | 0.00 | 0.47 | 7.13 | 2,556,828 |
| 1929 | 9.57 | 3.10 | 1.02 | 0.66 | 14.35 | 3,294,191 |
| Total | 5.29 | 2.30 | 0.17 | 0.24 | 7.99 | 13,083,037 |

*Notes*: Total sales figure for 1923 excludes tubes. Total sales for 1925 excludes $913,139 of component parts supplied to Brunswick and Victor, as attribution between firms not known.

*Source*: Data sheet on RCA advertising expenditure, n.d., *c*.1930, RCA, Victor Division, 2069/2/2, Hagley Museum Archives.

add their own details. Other aids included billboard posters, window display material, store interior displays, electric signs, and advertising novelties.[68] Some also provided sales training. For example, by 1925 De Forest's sales department was running a radio salesmanship and service correspondence course, which around 800 dealers had completed, involving a combination of home study and store-based discussion meetings.[69]

Manufacturers also sought to coordinate their own customer advertising with that of their dealers. As Table 5.3 shows, direct space advertising over 1923–9 was equivalent to around 5.3 per cent of RCA's sales revenue and accounted for two-thirds of its advertising expenditure. Adverts typically trumpeted key product characteristics, with an emphasis on technical superiority. By 1927 RCA was supplementing its national magazine advertising with newspaper advertising in major cities, while urging its distributors to encourage dealers in these communities to arrange tie-in promotions, such as set demonstrations.[70]

Manufacturers' brand recognition was further emphasized by the adoption of distinctive cabinet designs. Such cosmetic differentiation increased in importance over the inter-war period, as differences in performance between brands diminished. Firms began to employ artists and industrial designers to develop radio cabinets which were both attractive and distinctive. As leading industrial designer Ruth Gerth noted, this served to emphasize branding and differentiation:

> Our machine age makes possible for many factories to produce similar articles with similar machines and similar conditions. With so many factors being equal in manufacturing,

[68] Hagley, 2069/10/5, W. H. Stellner, 'Radio and Phonograph Sales Promotion and Advertising', in RCA, 'The Field Representative's training course 1935–36' (1935), 42–6 (42–4); Smithsonian, Clark, 55, Box 97, Memorandum to all RCA Radiola Distributors, 9 Oct. 1929.

[69] Smithsonian, Clark, 55, 104/4, Minutes of De Forest Interdepartmental Committee, 28 May 1925; 110/3, 'Course in Radio Salesmanship and Service. Manual for Discussion Meetings', De Forest Radio Institute (n.d., 1920s).

[70] Smithsonian, Clark, 55, Box 97, RCA circular to all RCA Radiola distributors, 8 Jan. 1927.

competition is levelled. Radio manufacturers present to the consumer products of similar character, performance, and price. So the main basis of differentiation is in the appearance.[71]

## THE RADIO DEALER

By the mid-1920s radio was becoming a mass-market product. A 1926 *Radio Retailing* survey estimated that the American radio audience had grown to 20,000,000, listening to 5,000,000 receivers, while the total 1925 retail value of radio equipment sales was estimated at $450 million and the average price of a receiver at $80. Some 31,000 radio retailers and 1,000 wholesalers were estimated to serve around 2,000 manufacturers.[72] An alternative estimate, for January 1927, put the number of radio retailers at 29,000, selling sets supplied by 2,550 manufacturers, via 985 wholesalers and distributors.[73]

Despite the rapidly growing market, there was significant dealer mortality. The National Electrical Manufacturers Association sponsored a Department of Commerce survey of dealers (defined as any retailer who carried an average stock of $500 or more in radio merchandise), covering the three quarters from 1 October 1927. Of the 31,000 dealers identified in each quarter, over 1,000 had gone out of business by the next quarter—suggesting an annual failure rate of about 13 per cent.[74]

Dealers were required to carry significant stocks of expensive and rapidly depreciating equipment. A 1930 national survey found that retailers typically stocked around five different brands of radio and that stocking an excessive range contributed to failures, by accentuating stock obsolescence risks.[75] Dealers also faced business risks from being obliged to accept trade-ins, estimated to account for at least 40 per cent of radio sales by the late 1920s. These both reduced effective margins and created the dilemma of either selling used radios in competition with new stock or otherwise disposing of trade-ins—either at a total loss, or at a price which would make only a small contribution to the trade-in allowance.[76] Yet this also provided a means for dealers to engage in price competition without openly flouting manufacturers' list prices.

Business risks were further accentuated by the need for retail credit. Radios were relatively expensive household durables in the 1920s. As Table 5.4 shows, the average 1924 retail price of a home radio was around $67, to which had to be added

[71] Ruth Gerth, 'The Rational Approach to the Problem of Radio Design', *R.M.A. Engineer*, 2 (1937), 27–30 (27).

[72] *New York Times* (14 Feb. 1926), cited in Leslie J. Page Jr, 'The Nature of the Broadcast Receiver and its Market in the United States from 1922 to 1927', in Lawrence W. Lichty and Malachi C. Topping (eds.), *American Broadcasting: A Source Book on the History of Radio and Television* (New York: Hastings House, 1975), 467–72 (470).

[73] Page Jr, 'The Nature of the Broadcast Receiver', 472.

[74] National Electrical Manufacturers Association, *The Radio Market* (New York: NEMA, 1928), 3.

[75] U.S. Dept. of Commerce, Bureau of Foreign and Domestic Commerce, 'Merchandise Problems of Radio Retailers in 1930', *Travel Information Bulletin No. 778* (Washington: USGPO, 1931), 4–5.

[76] 'Your Sales Program for 1929', *Radio Retailing* (Feb. 1929), 36–7.

**Table 5.4.** Sales of home radio apparatus in the United States, units and dollar values, 1922–34

|      | Radio sets* | | | Radio tubes | | All equipment | |
|------|-------------------|-----------------|------------|-------------------|-----------------|---------------|-----------------|
|      | Units (thousands) | Value ($ million) | Unit price | Units (thousands) | Value ($ million) | Unit price | Value ($ million) |
| 1922 | 100.0   | 5   | 50  | 1.0  | 6.0   | 6 | 60.0  |
| 1923 | 250.0   | 15  | 60  | 4.5  | 17.0  | 4 | 136.0 |
| 1924 | 1,500.0 | 100 | 67  | 12.0 | 36.0  | 3 | 358.0 |
| 1925 | 2,000.0 | 165 | 83  | 20.0 | 48.0  | 2 | 430.0 |
| 1926 | 1,750.0 | 200 | 114 | 30.0 | 58.0  | 2 | 506.0 |
| 1927 | 1,350.0 | 169 | 125 | 41.2 | 67.3  | 2 | 425.6 |
| 1928 | 3,281.0 | 388 | 118 | 50.2 | 110.3 | 2 | 690.6 |
| 1929 | 4,438.0 | 592 | 133 | 69.0 | 172.5 | 3 | 842.5 |
| 1930 | 3,827.8 | 332 | 87  | 52.0 | 119.6 | 2 | 501.0 |
| 1931 | 3,420.0 | 212 | 62  | 53.5 | 69.6  | 1 | 309.3 |
| 1932 | 2,620.0 | 125 | 48  | 44.3 | 48.7  | 1 | 196.0 |
| 1933 | 3,806.0 | 131 | 34  | 55.6 | 56.6  | 1 | 212.0 |
| 1934 | 4,084.0 | 151 | 37  | 55.2 | 56.6  | 1 | 235.0 |

*Notes*: Based on *Radio Retailing* data, shown at retail values. *Excludes cost of tubes.

*Source*: Thomas Eoyang, 'An Economic Study of the Radio Industry in the United States of America' (unpublished PhD thesis, Columbia University, 1936), 3–85. Corrected using original data from *Radio Retailing* (Mar. 1933), 17–18; (Mar. 1932), 18–19; (Mar. 1931), 20–1.

the cost of four or five tubes (sold separately), each costing around three dollars, plus batteries and other accessories.[77] As radios became grander and more complex, prices rose further, peaking at $133 in 1929 (again, net of tubes). Not surprisingly, credit facilities rapidly became integral to retail success.

In 1928 RCA reported estimates that approximately 70 per cent of radios were sold on deferred payments, while an estimate for 1930 put the figure at 75 per cent, on a par with other high-ticket consumer durables.[78] Of thirty-three dealers surveyed by the Department of Commerce in 1930, only one conducted business on a cash-only basis and the rest made an average of 80 per cent of radio sales on credit. Most financed deferred payments using their own funds or bank loans; only 21 per cent relied exclusively on a finance company. The most common terms involved a 10 per cent down-payment with the balance payable monthly over ten to twelve months, typically at 6 per cent annual interest.[79]

[77] The earliest estimate of tubes sold for use in new equipment, for 1927, indicates that each set required around six tubes: Smithsonian, Clark, 207/3, 'Broadcast: Published for the Radio Industry. An Analysis of the Radio Market', leaflet, presumably included with a copy of the trade magazine *Radio Broadcast* (n.d., c.1929).

[78] Smithsonian, Clark, 55, 103/3, booklet, 'The RCA–C.I.T. Finance Plan', 10 Sept. 1928; Friedman, *Birth of a Salesman*, 196–7.

[79] U.S. Dept. of Commerce, Bureau of Foreign and Domestic Commerce, 'Merchandise Problems of Radio Retailers', 12.

Several manufacturers arranged credit plans for their dealers. For example, by September 1928 RCA was advertising a plan run by Commercial Investment Trust, which provided dealers with an immediate advance of 90 per cent of the unmatured face value of their paper, less a discount charge. The remaining 10 per cent was then deducted from the final payment on the contract. Under this scheme the only cost to the dealer was the service charge, which could be passed on to the purchaser by adding 0.5 per cent per month to the cash price.[80]

Unlike in autos, where dealers claimed to be coerced into using finance companies tied to manufacturers,[81] even facilities promoted by the set makers typically involved independent finance companies. This reflected the weaker market power of individual manufacturers in radio and the impracticality of dealers holding large inventories, given highly unpredictable obsolescence. However, the absence of manufacturer-tied credit removed a potential source of cyclical demand stabilization. One justification for tied finance in autos was that it would be maintained during hard times, when independent finance companies might pull out.[82] Indeed, during the depression the availability of radio time-payment paper tapered off, becoming practically non-existent by 1932 according to *Radio Retailing*. Dealers were thus forced to finance credit provision directly, which gave better-capitalized firms a competitive edge. It was not until the mid-1930s that finance companies again began to show interest in this sector.[83]

## TAKING RADIO TO THE PROSPECT'S HOME

Canvassing was already a proven sales method for phonographs and was quickly adopted by the radio trade.[84] One common method was offering to set up a radio in the prospect's home and leave it for several days on trial. This was a relatively novel innovation, though it had been employed by the Hoover and Eureka vacuum companies in the 1910s and was widely used by refrigerator manufacturers during the 1920s.[85] Home demonstration had a number of important attractions for radio—it allayed fears that operation might prove too complex, or that reception would be too weak, and had the further advantage of introducing the family to the entertainment available from the radio over a period of several days. Buyers often perceived home demonstrations as a good way of testing a set's performance, though from the dealer's perspective it was seen primarily 'as a lever to accelerate

[80] Smithsonian, Clark, 55, 103/3, booklet, 'The RCA–C.I.T. Finance Plan', 10 Sept. 1928.
[81] Martha Olney, 'Credit as a Production-Smoothing Device: The Case of Automobiles, 1913–1938', *Journal of Economic History*, 49 (1989), 377–91.
[82] Ibid., 388–90.
[83] 'Finance Companies Re-enter the Field', *Radio Retailing* (Oct. 1935), 20.
[84] Powel Crossley Jr, 'Ten Commandments to 16,000 dealers', *The Radio Dealer* (Apr. 1926), 52–3.
[85] Harold Barger, *Distribution's Place in the American Economy since 1869* (Princeton, NJ: NBER, 1955), 32; Borden, *Economic Effects of Advertising*, 402–3; McLean County Museum of History, Bloomington, Illinois, Eureka Williams Electrolux archive, Box 3, copies of Eureka adverts in the *Saturday Evening Post*, 9 March 1912, and for 1914 (exact date not recorded).

the normal process of the realization of the *need*... to stimulate desire'.[86] It also avoided price comparison with cheaper models, boosting the sale of large console sets.

A 1925 *Radio Merchandising* survey found that 38 per cent of radio dealers in the United States and Canada used door-to-door canvassing.[87] A 1929 *Radio Retailing* article suggested that most radio dealers employed at least two outside salesmen full-time, with more recruited for special campaigns. Where merchants supervised their own salesmen, a straight commission of 15 per cent or less (with salesmen paying their own expenses) was considered most satisfactory.[88]

Major radio manufacturers vigorously encouraged their retailers to adopt door-to-door selling. For example, in February 1929 *Crosley Broadcaster* informed dealers that, 'During 1928 the sale of Crosley sets was built up to record-breaking proportions by means of home demonstration.'[89] Yet the independent trade journals were receiving a growing volume of complaints from dealers, arguing that direct sales were of limited, if any, long-term attraction.

Dealers found direct selling difficult to manage, expensive, and—given the rapidly growing proportion of replacement sales—a high-cost means of fighting for people who were already in the market, rather than creating a new market. One problem was that the minimum efficient scale for direct selling—a team of four or five salesmen working from a single vehicle—would require a much larger geographical area for year-round employment than the catchment areas of most dealers.[90] Personnel problems represented another key obstacle; a 1930 survey noted that, 'many store managers have found it impossible to secure men who are intelligent and sufficiently aggressive... More than two-thirds... definitely stated that the problem of securing the right type of men... was continually bothering them'.[91]

By the late 1920s Victor's Talking Machine Division was seeking to establish an outside sales organization in each of their wholesalers, to be put at the disposal of successive dealers for short periods of intensive selling. Where circumstances warranted, the wholesaler might turn over one or two experienced salesmen to the dealer on a permanent basis. It was anticipated that this would boost sales both directly and by encouraging retailers to intensify their own direct sales efforts.[92] The 'Victor Resale Plan' followed the broad outlines of established resale plans in other industries, such as vacuum cleaners (see Chapters 9 and 10), with the manufacturer running the direct sales operation and the dealer being responsible for itinerary, instalment credit, and paying a 10 per cent commission on sales (which,

---

[86] H. U. Mann, 'Selling in the Home Multiplies Desire', *Radio Retailing* (May 1930), 22–4 (23).

[87] 'Does House-to-House Selling Really Pay?', *Radio Merchandising* (July 1925), 57–8.

[88] 'Your Sales Program for 1929', *Radio Retailing* (Feb. 1929), 36–7.

[89] *The Crosley Broadcaster* (1 Feb. 1929), 5.

[90] Hagley, 2069/9/36, R. A. Forbes, 'Building', Victor Talking Machine Division, memorandum (n.d., *c.*1928); 'The Victor Resale Plan' (n.d., *c.*1928).

[91] U.S. Dept. of Commerce, Bureau of Foreign and Domestic Commerce, 'Merchandise Problems of Radio Retailers', 8.

[92] Hagley, 2069/9/36, R. A. Forbes, 'Building', Victor Talking Machine Division, memorandum (n.d., *c.*1928).

together with a further 2.5 per cent commission from the wholesaler, would fully finance the programme).

Based on experience in the South, crews of five salesmen were expected to close thirty sales per week (ten radiograms and twenty radios), remunerated via a drawing account of $30 per week against 5 per cent commission and all expenses.[93] Another major radio manufacturer, Atwater Kent, was recommending a broadly similar plan by 1929, based on deploying seven salesmen for intensive campaigns of three or four weeks, followed by the permanent retention of two or three to continue the work.[94] However, manufacturer-organized direct selling initiatives do not appear to have become firmly established before the depression curtailed such activity.

A 1928 *Radio Retailing* national survey of 109 dealers found that around 40 per cent of sales were made through canvassing, with those groups of retailers undertaking the highest, and lowest, sales being most reliant on canvassers. The survey concluded that, 'outside selling is more costly to the merchant and that its percentage cost is not reduced through increased volume to a figure comparable with the cost of inside selling'.[95] Scepticism intensified during the depression; a typical retailer comment being that, 'Too often...this makes money for everybody concerned except the dealer.'[96] Profits were said to be reduced by 'joy riders', who obtained a series of sets from various dealers on home demonstration with no intention of purchasing. One Atlanta dealer reported that each unsuccessful demonstration cost him $15 (when factors such as damage to cabinets and tube replacements were included), while only one in three resulted in a sale. The resulting costs (including at least $5 for each successful sale) wiped out almost all dealer profit.[97] A March 1930 *Radio Retailing* survey of 1,000 dealers broadly corroborated these figures; each successful and unsuccessful home demonstration being found to cost $4.51 and $13.43 respectively.[98]

Scott and Walker have examined the impact of direct sales on dealers' gross and net profits, using financial summaries for 100 dealers who provided their cost and revenue data to *Radio Retailing*.[99] This survey covered a particularly prosperous year for radio, 1928 (described as the most profitable to date). They found that selling expenditure offered a higher return on retailers' gross profits (before deduction of operating expenses) than either publicity or accommodation expenditure. However, once retailers' expenses had been deducted, the return on selling expenditure was much lower than that for either publicity or accommodation costs.

[93] Hagley, 2069/9/36, 'The Victor Resale Plan' (n.d., *c*.1928).

[94] '"Speciality selling"—the answer to sales slumps', *Radio Retailing* (Mar. 1929), 44–6.

[95] S. J. Ryan, '109 Radio Merchants Answer the Question—What of Selling Costs', *Radio Retailing* (Sept. 1929), 52–4 and 92.

[96] W. W. MacDonald, '4 Years in Business and Never Pushed a Doorbell', *Radio Retailing* (June 1934), 14–15 and 25 (14).

[97] Henry W. Baukat, 'It's a Sale—Not a Demonstration!', *Radio Retailing* (Mar. 1930), 18–19 and 58.

[98] 'It Costs $13.43 for Every Home Demonstration that Doesn't "Jell"', *Radio Retailing* (Mar. 1930), 45.

[99] Peter Scott and James T. Walker, 'Bringing Radio into America's Homes: Marketing New Technology in the Great Depression', *Business History Review*, 90 (2016), 251–76.

This suggests that retailers were right in perceiving that their direct selling activities were much more attractive for the manufacturer and wholesaler, who reaped the benefits but incurred no costs, than for themselves. However, while door-to-door selling may not have advantaged the retailer—compared to a situation where all local dealers abstained from canvassing—it does appear to have acted as a significant barrier to entry. Canvassing was a specialist activity, with substantial minimum costs for dedicated staff and vehicles, which were most efficiently employed in teams operating on a full-time (though perhaps temporary) basis. By reducing the pool of customers who purchased radios via conventional shopping, direct sales thus restricted the potential customer base for vendors who were not prepared to take on these costs. Moreover, authorized dealers for major radio brands had a competitive advantage in canvassing, as heavy manufacturer advertising boosted brand recognition and was often coordinated with retailers' direct sales campaigns—thus increasing the likelihood that the salesman would receive a positive reception. Thus, by deterring entry from dealers outside strong manufacturer-driven value chains, canvassing may have been of greater benefit to the specialist radio retailer than was evident from its contribution to net profits.

## THE DEPRESSION, THE 'MIDGET', AND THE TRANSFORMATION OF RADIO VALUE CHAINS

During the 1920s large manufacturers had generally avoided price competition, relying on strong brands and stressing quality and innovation.[100] However, price competition became much more important during the depression. Some 20 per cent of the five million radio sets produced in 1929 were said to be unsold at the end of the season, their liquidation putting 7,000 dealers out of business—a mortality rate that set the tone for the following years.[101] Manufacturers were also hit hard; according to *Fortune Magazine*, the number of radio set makers had declined from a peak of around 800 in 1926 to 150 in 1934.[102] Both large and small firms succumbed to the depression. Of the four leading set makers in 1929—RCA, Atwater Kent, Grigsby-Grunow, and Crosley—only RCA remained as a major player in radio manufacture. Moreover, this owed much to RCA's strong position in higher priced sets (which faced less vigorous price competition than the cheaper model classes during the depression), and, more importantly, its strengths in patents, components production, and broadcasting.

A new radio format, the 'midget' or 'compact', emerged from the depression market. Its appeal was based on price, while performance initially did not meet accepted industry standards. However, as radio now provided all-day entertainment, with an increasing element of afternoon soap operas, sports, and other 'talk' content, purity of sound reproduction was becoming less important, especially for

---

[100] Maclaurin, *Invention and Innovation*, 140.
[101] 'Philco', *Fortune Magazine*, 11, 2 (1935), 74–80 and 164–73 (164).
[102] Ibid., 75.

supplementary sets. Midget radios first appeared in California in 1929, and—as is often the case for new products that challenge incumbent formats—were initially produced by small start-ups that took advantage of the availability of cheap, externally sourced components.[103] Midgets were essentially 'market breakthroughs'— providing substantially higher customer value (for a segment of the market) using the industry's established core technology, rather than 'radical innovations' based on a substantially different technology.[104] The first midgets were stripped-down versions of standard radios in smaller cabinets; even in 1932, when Emerson pioneered the production of miniature components, these were more compact versions of those in conventional sets, rather than representing any radical new innovation (in contrast to later episodes of miniaturization, such as the transistor, or microchip).

Midget sales experienced rapid growth over the depression years, accounting for an estimated 60 per cent of all unit sales between 1 December 1932 and 1 May 1933.[105] During the 1930s their size and cost declined sharply (eventually retailing from under $10), while performance improved. An innovation initially widely viewed as a 'toy' or 'depression product' dominated unit sales by the end of the decade, showing dramatic improvements in quality that enabled it to challenge conventional radios for a progressively larger segment of the market.[106] Midget radio producers were also among the first radio firms to embrace the 'industrial design' movement, employing leading industrial designers to boldly differentiate their radio cabinets with striking designs, moulded from coloured plastic.[107] Meanwhile the radio market was experiencing a general trend towards lower unit prices, as shown in Table 5.4.

By radically reducing the minimum price of a receiver and offering the novel characteristic of portability, the midget's success upset the established industry structure and facilitated entry into the sector. These developments have strong parallels with the mobile phone industry, where economic recession at the beginning of this century depressed sales and triggered a shift in demand to low-price handsets. Marketing strategy thus shifted from quality and branding to aggressive pricing of entry-level phones, a submarket where firms outside the established industry proved more successful than the market leaders.[108] However, the midget also brought new life to a depressed market. By extending the market to supplementary

---

[103] Rajesh K. Chandy and Gerard J. Tellis, 'Organizing for Radical Product Innovation: The Overlooked Role of Willingness to Cannibalize', *Journal of Marketing Research*, 35 (1998), 474–87 (474); Chandler, *Inventing the Electronic Century*, 133–5.

[104] Chandy and Tellis, 'Organizing for Radical Product Innovation'.

[105] Peter L. Jensen, 'A New Major Development in Radio', *Radio Industries* (July–Aug. 1933), 56.

[106] Emerson Radio and Phonograph Co., *Small Radio: Yesterday and in the World of Tomorrow* (New York: Emerson, 1943), 34–6.

[107] Kazuo Usui, *The Development of Marketing Management: The Case of the USA, c.1910–1940* (Aldershot: Ashgate, 2008), 88–9.

[108] Claudio Giachetti and Gianluca Marchi, 'Evolution of Firms' Product Strategy over the Life Cycle of Technology-Based Industries: A Case Study of the Global Mobile Phone Industry, 1980–2009', *Business History*, 57 (2010), 1123–50; Michael L. Tushman and Philip Anderson, 'Technological Discontinuities and Competitive Environments', *Administrative Science Quarterly*, 31 (1986), 439–65.

household sets and for use in hotels, offices, and outdoor events, they helped maintain buoyant US radio sales long after market saturation in terms of household diffusion, with replacement demand amounting to only around two-thirds of radio sales even in the early 1940s.

Table 5.5 shows available evidence for market shares of the radio set market (in terms of unit sales). These are available only for two years, 1934 and 1940. The 1934 estimates in particular are subject to a substantial margin of error (being compiled by *Fortune Magazine* from various trade sources) but should at least show broad orders of magnitude. With the exception of RCA, the market leaders of 1940 were firms that were not major set makers in the 1920s, such as Philco, Zenith, and Emerson. Some had been active in the industry prior to 1929, but not typically as major receiver manufacturers. Crucially, their previous activity provided them with established distribution systems. For example, Philco—the leading set manufacturer of the 1930s—was a long-established electrical goods producer and a market leader in radio battery eliminators, but only entered receiver production in 1928 (capitalizing on its formidable distribution

**Table 5.5.** The leading radio set manufacturers, by unit sales, 1934 and 1940

| Company | 1934 | | 1940 | |
|---|---|---|---|---|
| | No. | % | No. | % |
| Philco | 1,250,000 | 29.8 | 1,675,000 | 14.2 |
| RCA | 500,000 | 11.9 | 1,700,000 | 14.4 |
| General Household Utilities (mainly autos) | 300,000 | 7.1 | — | 0.0 |
| Colonial (mainly for Sears Roebuck) | 300,000 | 7.1 | 650,000 | 5.5 |
| Crosley | 300,000 | 7.1 | 350,000 | 3.0 |
| Emerson (mostly midget sets) | 200,000 | 4.8 | 1,050,000 | 8.9 |
| GE (made by RCA in 1934) | 200,000 | 4.8 | 350,000 | 3.0 |
| Wells Gardiner (mainly for Montgomery Ward) | 200,000 | 4.8 | 200,000 | 1.7 |
| Zenith | 100,000 | 2.4 | 1,050,000 | 8.9 |
| Atwater Kent | 100,000 | 2.4 | — | 0.0 |
| Bosch | 100,000 | 2.4 | — | 0.0 |
| Galvin | | | 950,000 | 8.0 |
| Belmont | | | 550,000 | 4.6 |
| Noblitt Sparks | | | 400,000 | 3.4 |
| Stewart-Warner | | | 250,000 | 2.1 |
| Simplex | | | 250,000 | 2.1 |
| Electrical Research Laboratories | | | 250,000 | 2.1 |
| Sonora | | | 200,000 | 1.7 |
| Detrola | | | 175,000 | 1.5 |
| Farnsworth | | | 100,000 | 0.8 |
| Sparks Withington | | | 100,000 | 0.8 |
| All others | 650,000 | 15.5 | 1,584,000 | 13.4 |
| **Total** | 4,200,000 | 100.0 | 11,834,000 | 100.0 |

*Notes*: 1934 figures are compiled from conflicting trade sources and are possibly subject to a significant margin of error. Estimates include exports. Blank values denote 'unclassified' firms (possibly included in the 'All others' total).

*Sources*: 1934, 'Philco', *Fortune Magazine*, 11, 2 (1935), 74–80 and 164–73 (173); 1940, W. Rupert Maclaurin, *Invention and Innovation in the Radio Industry* (New York: Macmillan, 1949), 146.

network).[109] Similarly Emerson, which became the largest specialist producer of small radios, had been selling radios since 1924, but as a dealer in surplus equipment rather than as a manufacturer.[110]

Philco was the spectacular success story of the early 1930s, as shown in Table 5.6, which provides comparative radio sales for Philco, RCA, and the whole industry from 1929–41. Philco experienced a meteoric rise from around 9.2 per cent of all radios sold by American manufacturers in 1929 to a peak of just under a third of the industry's unit sales in 1934, followed by a continuous decline in market share which nevertheless still left them as the largest manufacturer in terms of output and value in 1940.

Philco followed an aggressive price-cutting strategy, evident as early as 1929, when they priced their sales leader at $129.50 to compete with a similar Majestic model selling at $137.50. They were also quicker to move into the table set market than the established industry leaders, introducing the Philco 'Baby Grand', in 1930 (a year before other major manufacturers entered this field) to provide a superior quality competitor to midget sets then selling for $59.50.[111] Then in 1932, when the yet smaller and cheaper 'peewee' variant of the midget reduced minimum retail prices to under $10, Philco responded after seven months (though, again, faster than the other big firms), with a slightly better version priced at $18.75.

Philco's success was also strongly linked to its development of strong value chains that reflected the new market conditions of the 1930s. Dealer loyalty was cemented by Philco's ability to avoid cutting list prices (and thus lumbering dealers with devalued stock) during the depression, owing to their advanced production planning system. Together with their price leadership strategy, this enabled Philco to achieve an impressive stock-turn. Philco claimed to have sales of $33 million in 1934 on an inventory of $2 million; an inventory turnover of 16.5 times a year, implying that the average Philco radio would be sold a little over three weeks after arriving in the store.[112]

Philco invested heavily in advertising and promotion (Fig. 5.2). In 1934 they employed seven divisional sales managers and fifty salesmen, to reach their 120 distributors (wholesalers, with a discount on list price of 55 per cent), 175 associate distributors (large retailers, with a 50 per cent discount), and 10,000 other dealers (with discounts of 40 or 46 per cent) 'who may be primarily in the radio business but are just as likely to be in the hardware business, the electrical business, the sporting-good business, the music business, or the drug business'.[113]

While Philco had built its initial success on low prices, it soon moved to challenge the broader radio market. From 1931 product strategy involved developing a comprehensive line of receivers, with a merchandising plan based on 'selling up' customers to the higher priced models. This 'model for every purse and purpose' strategy was famously pioneered by General Motors in the 1920s and was already being pursued by RCA. As a 1931 manual for RCA representatives noted: 'There

[109] Maclaurin, *Invention and Innovation*, 137–41.    [110] Ibid., 143–8.
[111] 'Philco', *Fortune Magazine*, 11, 2 (1935), 74–80 and 164–73 (166).
[112] Ibid., 79.    [113] Ibid., 80 and 164.

Table 5.6. Radio sales by Philco, RCA, and other manufacturers, units and dollar values, 1929–41

| Year | Philco sales | | RCA sales | | Industry sales | | Philco/Total | | RCA/Total | | Others/Total | |
|---|---|---|---|---|---|---|---|---|---|---|---|---|
| | Units | Values | Units | Values | Units | Values | Units | Values | Units | Values | Units | Values |
| 1929 | 408,000 | 23,000,000 | | | 4,438,000 | | 9.2 | | | | | |
| 1930 | 616,000 | 34,000,000 | | | 3,827,800 | | 16.1 | | | | | |
| 1931 | 977,000 | 34,000,000 | | | 3,420,000 | | 28.6 | | | | | |
| 1932 | 609,000 | 17,000,000 | | | 2,620,000 | | 23.2 | | | | | |
| 1933 | 963,000 | 23,000,000 | | | 3,806,000 | | 25.3 | | | | | |
| 1934 | 1,250,000 | 33,000,000 | 354,927 | 10,314,100 | 3,939,382 | 82,325,200 | 31.7 | 40.1 | 9.0 | 12.5 | 59.3 | 47.4 |
| 1935 | 1,500,000 | 46,740,000 | 371,746 | 11,838,100 | 5,516,749 | 115,554,400 | 27.2 | 40.4 | 6.7 | 10.2 | 66.1 | 49.3 |
| 1936 | 1,900,000 | 56,675,000 | 598,275 | 17,460,700 | 7,734,765 | 157,084,500 | 24.6 | 36.1 | 7.7 | 11.1 | 67.7 | 52.8 |
| 1937 | 1,550,000 | 51,904,000 | 603,661 | 19,574,900 | 7,498,416 | 151,990,000 | 20.7 | 34.1 | 8.1 | 12.9 | 71.3 | 53.0 |
| 1938 | 1,000,000 | 30,527,665 | 627,324 | 15,840,500 | 6,753,225 | 103,894,800 | 14.8 | 29.4 | 9.3 | 15.2 | 75.9 | 55.4 |
| 1939 | 1,500,000 | 45,421,078 | 1,170,399 | 20,871,172 | 10,266,884 | 144,929,400 | 14.6 | 31.3 | 11.4 | 14.4 | 74.0 | 54.3 |
| 1940 | 2,000,000 | 44,511,131 | 1,776,745 | 27,687,800 | 11,833,519 | 175,659,100 | 16.9 | 25.3 | 15.0 | 15.8 | 68.1 | 58.9 |
| 1941 | 2,100,000 | n.a. | 1,496,292 | 27,409,700 | 13,630,972 | 231,696,600 | 15.4 | n.a. | 11.0 | 11.8 | 73.6 | n.a. |

*Notes*: Values represent manufacturers' sales revenue rather than retail prices.

*Source*: Philco data, 1928–34, 'Philco', *Fortune Magazine*, 11, 2 (1935), 74–80 and 164–73 (166 and 170); 1935–40, John Paul Wolkonowicz, 'The Philco Corporation: Historical Review & Strategic Analysis' (unpublished MSc dissertation, Alfred P. Sloan School of Management, 1981), 39–53 and 99. RCA data (and industry value data from 1934), Hagley, 2069/9/49. Sales comparisons 1934–46, noted dated 2 Aug. 1945 (industry figures based on RCA royalty data). Industry unit sales, 1929–33, see Table 5.4.

# 'Of Course, We Can Own a Philco, John'

**Your Budget Will Permit You to Own A Philco --Because Philco's Low Prices Bring Perfect Radio Reception Within the Reach of Everyone.**

---

# Philco

**Offers Amazing Selectivity, Distance And Marvelous Tone**

Model 15

## Baby Grand

7 Tube Super-Heterodyne

Built with 7 Philco Balanced Tubes -4 Screen Grids, New Pentode Power Tube, New Electro - Dynamic Speaker. Beautiful walnut cabinet. Anti - "Y"-matched. Tone Control and Illuminated Station Recording Dial.

## $49.95

Complete With Tubes

Model 20

Baby Grand

9 Tube Super-Heterodyne

Indisputably greatest of all small radios, with real, big-set performance. Pointer Tone Control —Automatic Volume Control—New Electro Dynamic Speaker —Illuminated Station Recording Dial — New Pentode Power Tube. In American black walnut. Instrument Panel, matched butt walnut and ends of "V"-matched Oriental wood. Hand-rubbed finish.

## $69.50

Complete With Tubes

Your Nearest Philco Dealer Will Be Pleased to Show You These, or Any Other Philco Models You May Desire—Including Lowboys, Highboys, Lazy Boys, Grandfather Clock and Radio-Phonograph Models.

---

*NEW···*

## PHILCO RADIOS

### Thirteen Models

At a Price Range from

## $36.50 to $295.

# GABLE'S

11TH AVENUE BUILDING
FIRST FLOOR

**Fig. 5.2.** A 1932 Philco advert, stressing Philco's lower prices, together with a range that already encompassed thirteen models

*Source: Altoona Pennsylvania Tribune* (6 Jan. 1932). Reproduced with kind permission of Joe Haupt.

are many models in the RCA Victor Line, because there are many radio "markets". Models for every dealer and every radio prospect is, therefore, the RCA Victor motto. And the price range makes stepping-up the sale easy.'[114]

Philco's adoption of a broad product range strategy required establishing a reputation for quality, rather than just low prices. Philco vigorously pursued this via extensive magazine advertising and the early introduction of new industry innovations such as 'high fidelity'. By the start of the 1932–3 season Philco was launching twenty-six new models, with list prices ranging from $18.75 to $250. This strategy was soon copied by competitors, with Zenith introducing its 'Challenger' line for the 1933–4 season, competing with Philco on an almost model for model basis, backed up by a similarly aggressive marketing campaign.[115]

Major general or auto retailers, such as Montgomery Ward, Sears Roebuck, Firestone, Western Auto, Gamble's, and Goodyear, also took advantage of the shift from brand- to price-based competition by establishing retailer-based value chains, capitalizing on their strong retail brands and sales networks.[116] These acted as 'manufacturers without factories', selling under their own brands, but subcontracting all production to independent contractors.[117] In contrast to established manufacturer-driven value chains, which were based on heavy cumulative investments in building up dealer goodwill—and, therefore, high costs if manufacturers ceased to supply dealers (even temporarily)—retailers who developed their own brands faced much lower costs of switching suppliers or ceasing production. They had control over the key strategic assets of branding and design, and—as most manufacturers used similar production technologies—they could switch between different contractors on the basis of short-term cost considerations.[118] Even withdrawing from production altogether wasn't problematic, in times of adverse market conditions, as reliance on their strong retail brands, rather than specific product brands, made a resumption of sales when things improved relatively easy.

While such retailers prospered, the advent of the midget proved a disaster for the specialist radio dealer. Despite lower prices and profit margins, many retailers had initially welcomed the midget as something distinctive and novel in a depression market burdened by distress sales of surplus stock. Moreover, their lower prices and portability made them cheaper to sell and service than conventional radios.[119] As a 1930 article noted, they appeared to have answered the radio retailer's dream, 'no deliveries, no financing, no collection grief, no service. "Just one long, sweet process of fittin' em with tubes and passin' em over the counter to eager buyers."'[120]

---

[114] Hagley, 2069/3/5. 'The New RCA Victor-Line', Manual for Distributor Representatives, 1931–1932.

[115] Wolkonowicz, 'The Philco Corporation', 30–5.

[116] Raphael Kaplinsky and Mike Morris, *A Handbook for Value Chain Research* (Brighton: Institute of Development Studies, 2002) <http://www.ids.ac.uk/ids/global/pdfs/VchNov01.pdf>, 33.

[117] Maclaurin, *Invention and Innovation*, 148–9; Gary Gereffi, 'A Commodity Chains Framework for Analysing Global Industries', in Institute of Development Studies, *Background Notes for Workshop on Spreading the Gains from Globalisation* (1999) <http://www.ids.ac.uk/ids/global/conf/wkscf.html>, 1–2.

[118] Gary Gereffi, John Humphrey, and Timothy Sturgeon, 'The Governance of Global Value Chains', *Review of International Political Economy*, 12 (2005), 78–104.

[119] Emerson Radio and Phonograph Co., *Small Radio*, 28–30.

[120] 'Midgets hit the East', *Radio Retailing* (Aug. 1930), 56–7 and 65 (56).

Yet these characteristics opened up radio retailing to non-specialist stores, precipitating a dramatic decline for the specialist radio dealer. Despite a rise in US radio output from 4.44 million sets in 1929 to 6.03 million in 1935, employment in the 'household appliances, radio dealers' Census classification had fallen by 34.8 per cent, to 71,971. Dollar sales by stores in this group had declined by 53.4 per cent (compared with 32.2 per cent for all store sales); while the number of dealers had fallen by 26.3 per cent.[121] By reducing the need for home delivery and servicing, showrooms, and credit, the midget eroded the key differentiating advantages of the specialist dealer, effectively transforming a substantial sector of the radio market into a 'cash-and-carry' business, accessible to most general goods retailers.

Thus it was the weakness, rather than strength, of manufacturers' control over dealers, that undermined their long-term survival. Established manufacturers proved powerless to block midget radios, in contrast to British set makers, who suppressed the format throughout the 1930s (via a blacklist of non-conforming retailers—which was perfectly legal in the absence of any effective British anti-trust legislation).[122] In a depression market, specialist dealers had embraced what they believed to be a novelty and loss-leader, apparently unaware of the fundamental threat it posed to their business model.

## CONCLUSIONS

Within the first decade of entertainment broadcasting, radios had been transformed from complex, bulky, and expensive pieces of scientific apparatus, purchase and maintenance of which was mediated by salesmen who understood the mysteries of this new technology, into grand items of furniture (akin to the piano) and, finally, into compact, portable, and relatively inexpensive entertainment devices purchased over the counter. Radio retailing had similarly witnessed a dramatic transformation. Dealers in novel electrical components, sold to technically competent (or at least enthusiastic) early adopters, rapidly evolved into specialist niche consumer durable retailers, juggling the onerous requirements of trade-ins, time purchase contracts, servicing, and door-to-door canvassing, with the assistance of major manufacturers eager to secure their support. These specialist skills were, in turn, undermined by the introduction of the radically cheaper, 'no frills' midget radio format during the depression.

Like the refrigerator and washing machine, the radio of the early 1920s was an expensive mechanical novelty, requiring intensive advertising, considerable after-sales service, and costly door-to-door canvassing. By the late 1930s all three of these products had been largely transformed into 'staple' merchandise, increasingly marketed using standard retail channels and methods. However, while refrigerators and washing machines experienced this transition as an evolutionary process, with

[121] Sources: Radio output, Carter et al., *Historical Statistics of the United States*, vol. I, 667; vol. IV, 1027; store data, U.S. Dept. of Commerce, Bureau of the Census, *Sixteenth Census of the United States: 1940. Census of Business Volume 1. Retail Trade: 1939* (Washington: USGPO, 1943), 57.

[122] See Scott, 'When Innovation becomes Inefficient'.

new innovations tending to reinforce the first mover advantages of the leading firms and their established distribution networks, in radio it was marked by major disruptions to established industry structures and distribution channels.[123]

This has strong parallels with some modern high-tech durables, such as mobile phones. Development was characterized by rapid technological change, punctured by frequent 'technological discontinuities'—that made earlier vintages obsolete (for at least some market segments).[124] Such discontinuities can be 'competence-enhancing' (building on existing know-how within a product class) or 'competence-destroying'—creating new product subclasses that require different skills and competitive strengths. Competence-destroying discontinuities typically trigger new product class launches by firms outside the established industry, leading to rapid changes in industry structure and posing severe problems for established leaders.[125]

During the 1920s discontinuities in radio technology were generally of the competence-enhancing type, involving new circuits or features that could be most rapidly exploited by existing market leaders.[126] Conversely, the midget format constituted a competence-destroying discontinuity, competing on price, rather than quality. This posed a dilemma for market leaders with competencies based on quality, promotion, and branding. As predicted in the literature on technological discontinuities, this triggered both rapid firm entry and exit, with most leading manufacturers facing a rapid decline in market share, or liquidation.[127]

In common with more recent market breakthroughs, these changes had important implications for established relationships between manufacturers and their retailers.[128] Distribution networks based on cooperation failed to block the midget's introduction, owing to manufacturers' limited control over their dealers. Each typically sold several brands of radio and faced no contractual restrictions on stocking this new format. Nor could informal pressure achieve this end in an environment of sharply declining sales and prices. Yet, by embracing the midget radio, specialist dealers popularized a format that required substantially less marketing, servicing, and instalment credit and thus undermined their barriers to entry. Radio thus represents an important precursor of the modern pattern of disruptive technological change in high-tech durables sectors, with even the strongest manufacturers and distributors having to be forever vigilant for the next innovation that might threaten their competitive advantage.

---

[123] See Jonathan Rees, *Refrigeration Nation: A History of Ice, Appliances, and Enterprise in America* (Baltimore: Johns Hopkins University Press, 2013), 141–61; Robert Hoover and John Hoover, *An American Quality Legend: How Maytag Saved Our Moms, Vexed the Competition, and Presaged America's Quality Revolution* (New York: McGraw-Hill, 1993), 105–72.

[124] See Steven Klepper, 'Industry Life Cycles', *Industrial and Corporate Change*, 6 (1997), 145–81.

[125] Tushman and Anderson, 'Evolution'.

[126] These were available to all firms, with a short lag, owing to the industry's patent pool agreements; Sobel, *RCA*, 84–108; Maclaurin, *Invention and Innovation*, 132–6.

[127] Giachetti and Marchi, 'Evolution of Firms' Product Strategy'; Steven Klepper and Peter Thompson, 'Submarkets and the Evolution of Market Share', *Rand Journal of Economics*, 37 (2006), 861–86.

[128] See Tushman and Anderson, 'Evolution'.

# 6

# Britain's Inter-War Radio Industry

## INTRODUCTION

Radio experienced even faster diffusion in Britain than in the United States, representing both the first entertainment consumer durable and the first electronic, or even electrical, device to become ubiquitous in both middle- and working-class homes, with more rapid diffusion even than for mains electricity.[1] The stakes for control over the industry's profits were thus particularly high, one of the factors that led to it having the most contested value chain of any consumer durable covered in this book. Marconi initially used its monopoly over fundamental payments to extract huge rents from the set makers. It was in a much stronger position to do so than RCA, as Britain's legal system granted almost unrestricted powers to patent holders to exploit their monopoly rights as they saw fit. In the 1930s, when Marconi's fundamental patents began to expire, the two major producers of 'valves' (the British term for thermionic tubes used in radios) also sought to use patents to gain a measure of control over the industry—offering packages of radio patents to manufacturers in return for tying the manufacturer to buying their valves.

Such strategies could be expected to have resulted in domination of the industry by one or few firms with strong patent rights. Yet—in contrast to the gramophone industry, which became concentrated into two huge companies following market saturation in the 1930s—expectations by the market leaders of a similar trend in radio proved inaccurate.[2] In 1938 there were no less than eight firms supplying more than 5 per cent of the receiver market (by volume), four of which—Murphy, Bush, Ekco, and Pye—were specialist set makers. Meanwhile the two leading integrated radio and valve manufacturers, EMI and Philips-Mullard, controlled only 14.1 and 12.7 per cent of receiver output respectively.[3]

This and the following chapter show how specialist radio set manufacturers managed to avoid being driven out of business, or having most of their profits expropriated, by the big players. Given the importance of the battle for dominance of the radio value chain to the industry's production costs, industrial structure, and pricing, the current chapter focuses on this contest. The following chapter then explores in more depth how marketing and distribution networks were used to

---

[1] Sue Bowden and Avner Offer, 'Household Appliances and the Use of Time: The United States and Britain since the 1920s', *Economic History Review*, 47 (1994), 725–48 (729).

[2] J. J. Nott, *Music for the People: Popular Music and Dance in Interwar Britain* (Oxford: Oxford University Press, 2002), 26–32.

[3] See Figure 6.5.

create brand strength and thus allow independent firms such as Ekco, Pye, and Murphy to prosper, despite having to deal with patent royalties and a strongly oligopolistic, cartelized valve industry.

## BRITAIN'S BROADCASTING SYSTEM

As in the United States, military demand during the First World War had greatly accelerated both technical development and output growth for the infant British radio equipment industry. Meanwhile war surplus equipment and skills acquired during military service generated a substantial community of enthusiast radio 'hams', who constituted both an initial market for entertainment radio and a major source of early radio entrepreneurs.[4] However, for radio sales to expand beyond this enthusiast base required the development of regular entertainment broadcasting, that was initially blocked by the opposition of the Post Office—which had control over broadcast licensing.

Eventually public pressure led to an official change of heart. From May 1922 government representatives began discussions on broadcasting with interested manufacturers. Given unfavourable perceptions of the embryonic US broadcasting industry, there was a conscious attempt to avoid what was seen as an unregulated and sometimes chaotic American free market in the radio spectrum. The Post Office sought a broadcasting model that would foster cooperation between radio manufacturers and keep foreign sets out of the British market. They also sought to avoid any commercial monopoly over radio by Marconi (who was foreign-born and did not enjoy good relations with the British government) and to prevent American-style commercialism.[5]

Six leading radio manufacturers, (the 'Big Six': Marconi, British Thomson-Houston [BTH], GEC, Metropolitan-Vickers, Western Electric, and Radio Communication Co.) were encouraged to cooperatively develop a monopoly broadcasting system. However, financing broadcasting through advertising was ruled out—partly owing to opposition from national newspaper companies and press agencies. These had enormous political influence and made themselves a continual thorn in the flesh of the BBC when it eventually realized the full extent of its competitive threat. Even news and sports commentary was initially prohibited in order to appease them—though these restrictions were gradually relaxed.

Marconi (by far the most powerful interest among the radio companies), pushed for the new broadcaster to be a non-profit cooperative venture—to neutralize its impact on the balance of power between the major radio equipment manufacturers.[6] The British Broadcasting Company was thus constituted so as to provide a modest return to its shareholders, rather than seeking to maximize profits—a

[4] S. G. Sturmey, *The Economic Development of Radio* (London: Duckworth, 1958), 143–4.

[5] Michele Hilmes, *Networked Nations: A Transnational History of British and American Broadcasting* (London: Routledge, 2012), 38–9.

[6] Ibid., 39–42.

stance that paved the way for its reconstitution as a 'public corporation' (i.e. non-profit-making publicly owned utility) in 1927—with a mandate to inform, educate, and entertain.

From its foundation in October 1922 until 1938 the BBC was headed by the formidable John Reith, an austere Calvinist Scottish engineer, who did much to mould its character. Reith developed the BBC as a universal service, which would maintain high standards of broadcasting—a strategy underpinned by both its monopoly status and by independence from both commercial and (where possible) government pressures.[7] From the start the BBC developed on the basis of a unified national service, principally based in London.

Reith's vision involved taking the best culture (generally viewed as synonymous with metropolitan culture) to all corners of the nation. Programme content was mixed on each channel to avoid audiences segmenting according to their interests. Each offered a varied mix of drama, light entertainment, classical and 'light' music, talks, interviews, news, sport, and factual programmes (ranging from documentaries to gardening advice).[8] Yet the BBC tended to conceive the 'public' largely in terms of the middle and upper classes and had a strong bias towards 'highbrow' music and programming—justified partly by a belief that everyone would find classical music and Shakespearian plays accessible if sufficiently exposed to them. Some music forms were positively discouraged; for example while syncopated dance music was considered acceptable, jazz and other 'negro' music was deemed morally undesirable (while American music in general was frowned upon).

Yet during the mid to late 1930s growing competition from continental stations broadcasting in English—principally Radio Normandy and Radio Luxembourg—led the BBC to relax its 'elitist' approach somewhat, with a larger proportion of programmes aimed at a mass audience. The BBC also belatedly sought to expand regional broadcasting and thus soften its metropolitan bias. Thus by the time Reith left the BBC in 1938, he had already established much of its modern identity—combining a broad range of programming with an emphasis on quality. Comparisons with American broadcasting then, as now, were generally favourable to the British system (the main dissenters being the advertising agencies).

By 1938 the BBC had a staff of almost 5,000 and had become a major national institution.[9] Its impact on the nation it served was probably less than that of its American counterpart, given that Britain was a smaller, more centralized, and culturally and ethnically more homogeneous society, with a strong national newspaper industry. Nevertheless, the BBC played a crucial social and cultural role in creating a shared live national experience of news, drama, sport, and light entertainment. Its impacts on other entertainment media were also profound. For example, the BBC has been credited with creating a unified British music industry, by providing a popular national platform whereby all types of music (within certain bounds) were broadcast, acting as the most powerful music patron in the country, and—by

---

[7] Andrew Crisell, *An Introductory History of British Broadcasting* (London: Routledge, 1997), 18–19.
[8] Ibid., 29.    [9] Ibid., 30.

instantly popularizing songs—drastically reducing the turnover time for hit numbers.[10] While unable to entirely free itself of political censorship in news and current affairs coverage, it nevertheless strived to maintain impartiality and independence and avoided the excesses of both commercial broadcasting systems, as in America—and state-controlled systems, as in Germany.

The BBC was funded by a levy on sales of radio apparatus, averaging 15s per set (discontinued from July 1924), plus 50 per cent of revenue from the compulsory 10s per annum Post Office licences that all households with radios were obliged to purchase. The number of radio licences experienced rapid growth, to 2.18 million in 1926, 3.41 million in 1930, and 8.91 million in 1938.[11] Yet these figures do not fully reflect the number of households with radios, owing to substantial licence evasion. Estimates of UK radio ownership, for 1925, 1935, and 1939, indicate diffusion rates of 26.9, 72.2, and 86.5 per cent of households respectively, higher even than for the United States.[12] This appears counter-intuitive, given America's much higher real wages. However, there were strong regional variations in US radio ownership, from over 90 per cent in many north-eastern states in 1937 to under 50 per cent in several southern states.[13] The 1935 and 1939 British radio listening surveys also found that diffusion rates for working-class households were only around three percentage points below the national average, reflecting radio's status as a 'counter-status luxury', with utility varying inversely with income (as higher income groups have more substitutes for its entertainment services).[14]

Table 6.1 provides estimates of radio ownership in Britain and fifteen other countries in around December 1931, together with radio ownership per 100 population (calculated both on the basis of official figures and estimates that normalize the data for differences in reporting dates, while also taking account of estimated licence evasion). These show that Britain was second only to the United States in radio set ownership, both in absolute terms and relative to its population. Of the other countries in the table, only Germany came close to the UK in terms of numbers of radio sets (though not relative to population).

Britain's particularly rapid diffusion of radio listening, by international standards, reflected both its high per capita incomes and the quality of its broadcasting system. This contrasts with Weimar Germany, which developed a monopoly broadcasting system with superficial similarities to Britain's—being licensed and regulated by the Reichspost (Postal Ministry). However, the Reichspost's attitude

[10] Paddy Scannell and David Cardiff, *A Social History of British Broadcasting*, vol. I: *1922–1939: Serving the Nation* (Oxford: Blackwell, 1991), 181–4.

[11] 'The Radio Market—Present and Potential', *Wireless and Gramophone Trader* (28 Mar. 1931), 350–1; TNA, BT64/296, unsigned memorandum, 26 June 1945.

[12] Sources: 1925—Sturmey, *Economic Development*, 155; 1935—Bodleian Library, John Johnson Collection, Wireless Box 10, International Broadcasting Co., 'IBC Survey of Radio Advertising Penetration, 1935', unpublished report, Sept. 1935; 1939—'The Radio Market Analysed in Relation to Public Purchasing Power', *Wireless and Electrical Trader* (19 Aug. 1939), 232–3. For further discussion, see Peter Scott, 'When Innovation Becomes Inefficient: Reexamining Britain's Radio Industry', *Business History Review*, 88 (2014), 497–521.

[13] Source: 'Marketing statistics and sales...1937', *Radio Retailing* (Jan. 1938), 25–32 (32).

[14] D. S. Landes, *The Unbound Prometheus: Technological Change and Industrial Development in Western Europe from 1750 to the Present* (Cambridge: Cambridge University Press, 1969), 428.

**Table 6.1.** Radio ownership estimates for Britain and fifteen other countries, *c.*December 1931, ranked by ownership per 100 people

| Country | Estimate for | Number of radios | | Radios per 100 people | |
|---|---|---|---|---|---|
| | | Official | Possible* | Official | Possible* |
| United States | Apr. 1932 | 16,679,253 | 16,000,000 | 13.6 | 13.0 |
| United Kingdom | Dec. 1931 | 4,329,754 | 5,200,000 | 9.4 | 11.3 |
| Sweden | Dec. 1931 | 550,000 | 600,000 | 9.0 | 9.8 |
| Austria | Dec. 1931 | 450,272 | 500,000 | 6.7 | 7.4 |
| Germany | Dec. 1931 | 3,980,852 | 4,500,000 | 6.0 | 6.8 |
| Canada | Jan. 1932 | 571,898 | 600,000 | 5.5 | 5.8 |
| Australia | Feb. 1932 | 347,535 | 400,000 | 5.2 | 6.0 |
| France | 1930 | 2,000,000 | 2,000,000 | 4.9 | 4.9 |
| New Zealand | Feb. 1932 | 75,351 | 85,000 | 4.8 | 5.4 |
| Switzerland | Dec. 1931 | 149,000 | 160,000 | 3.7 | 4.0 |
| Norway | Dec. 1931 | 101,901 | 150,000 | 3.6 | 5.3 |
| Netherlands | Sept. 1931 | 278,891 | 280,000 | 3.5 | 3.5 |
| Czechoslovakia | Jan. 1932 | 397,591 | 500,000 | 2.7 | 3.4 |
| Belgium | Dec. 1931 | 199,000 | 275,000 | 2.5 | 3.4 |
| Japan | Mar. 1932 | 1,000,000 | 1,000,000 | 1.6 | 1.6 |
| Italy | Dec. 1931 | 250,000 | 500,000 | 0.6 | 1.2 |

*Notes*: Persons per radio calculated using nearest Census date to the estimate of radio numbers. * Including the best available estimates for illegally operated sets, adjusted by estimate to 31 Dec. 1931.

*Source*: Adapted from U.S. Department of Commerce, *Radio Markets of the World, 1932* (Washington: USGPO, 1932), 28–9.

towards programming was elitist even by BBC standards, providing information, education, but little in the way of entertainment, other than that of a very highbrow nature. Thus radio listening remained dominated by the middle classes throughout the Weimar period, many blue-collar workers regarding radio as not being worth the substantial slice of their discretionary income that equipment purchase and maintenance, plus licence fees, would take.[15]

Britain's ranking as the world's second-largest manufacturer of radios was based on its buoyant home market. British radio exports were not only lower than those of the United States (in absolute terms), but also, often, of Germany and the Netherlands. However, the territorial carve-up of radio patent rights meant that no countries enjoyed strong exports outside their patent monopoly areas. In 1937 American radio equipment exports amounted to £6.6 million, followed by the Netherlands with £4.3 million, Germany with £1.6 million, and Britain with £1.6 million. Meanwhile British radio equipment imports amounted to only £1.4 million.[16] However, these figures did little to dent the European market lead

---

[15] See Karl Christian Fuhrer, 'A Medium for Modernity: Broadcasting in Weimar Germany, 1923–1932', *Journal of Modern History*, 69 (1997), 722–53.

[16] 'World Wireless Trade. Some Highlights of the Export and Import Sides', *Wireless and Electrical Trader* (22 Oct. 1938), 115.

provided by Britain's domestic market, which brought its overall radio equipment sales (at factory gate prices) to around £19 million.[17] British radio productivity similarly lagged well behind the United States, but was good by European standards. American radio manufacturing labour productivity for 1935 has been estimated at around three times the British level, though German labour productivity was only around 70 per cent of that for the UK.[18]

## PRODUCTION SYSTEMS AND INDUSTRY STRUCTURE

Radio was unusual in reaching a mass market before the expiration of its fundamental patents.[19] This had important consequences for the British radio industry, owing to the UK's combination of an unusually strong intellectual property regime and the absence of any significant countervailing anti-trust legislation before the 1950s. This, in turn, reflected a socio-legal system developed to support Britain's dominant financial and mercantile business elites, which placed fundamental importance on private property rather than competition.

Patent royalties dominated the economics of the early industry. Prior to the launch of the BBC, Marconi rapidly consolidated its strong patent position in radio—buying out the entertainment rights of the other significant UK patent-holder, BTH. Marconi also gained exclusive British rights to radio patents held or subsequently developed by RCA—as a result of the agreement which led to its disposal of American Marconi. Further negotiations (also involving France and Germany) created a general international patent cartel, with Marconi, RCA, and the dominant firms in these other countries enjoying exclusive rights to the other companies' patents in their territories.[20]

In common with several other dynamic, science-based, industries—such as automobiles, aircraft, and, later, semiconductors and computer hardware and software—innovation in the radio sector was a cumulative process, with a small number of 'fundamental' patents providing the base on which future advances were developed. In such industries an uncompromising approach to prioritizing patent rights is viewed as particularly problematic for post-patent innovation

---

[17] Estimated using 1937 data for radio receivers and 1935 data for other radio equipment; UK, Board of Trade, *Final Report on the Fifth Census of Production and the Import Duties Act Enquiry, 1935, Part II* (London: HMSO, 1939), 307–11; UK, Board of Trade, *Final Report on the Census of Production for 1948, Volume 4* (London: HMSO, 1952), Section M, 7.

[18] Scott, 'When Innovation Becomes Inefficient', 499–500; L. Rostas, 'Industrial Production, Productivity, and Distribution in Britain, Germany, and the United States', *Economic Journal*, 53 (1943), 39–54 (46–8).

[19] U.S. Department of Commerce, *Radio Markets of the World, 1932* (Washington: USGPO, 1932), 18.

[20] William Rupert Maclaurin, *Invention and Innovation in the Radio Industry* (New York: Macmillan, 1949), 107; Robert Sobel, *RCA* (New York: Stein & Day, 1986), 21–35; Radcliffe Science Library, Oxford, Ms. Marconi [hereafter RSL, Marconi], 418, Marconi internal memorandum by W. Nicken (n.d., c.1938), 6–7.

compared to an 'open marketplace' for improvements.[21] Marconi capitalized on its control over fundamental patents to negate or reduce the threat from subsequent innovations. An internal company document noted that:

> By acquiring certain patents of early date the company has...been saved the expense of acquiring others of great technical merit but of later date. The Armstrong patent for the superheterodyne and super-regenerative circuits and also his earlier reaction patent were purchased by RCA at considerable cost. We were saved such expense because we owned the Franklin and Round patents for reaction and autoheterodyne and had acquired the Bolitho super-regenerative patent and had rights under the Levy super-heterodyne patents.[22]

Domestic producers (including the British plants of overseas multinationals) essentially served a captive home market. In 1935 the values of both radio receiver imports and exports were each equivalent to less than 3 per cent of British output.[23] Import duties and the protection offered to domestic firms by Marconi's international agreements were further buttressed by national agreements between manufacturers and distributors, prohibiting sales of imported equipment. Similarly, British exports were relatively unimportant. American sets, designed to prioritize range of reception and selectivity between stations, were said to be more suitable for contestable markets such as Australia and Argentina than British receivers (which focused on purity of reproduction, given Britain's good reception conditions).[24] Higher British prices were also a key factor—in 1935 the average unit price of exported British receivers was 93.6 per cent greater than that of imported sets.

Table 6.2 shows available data on UK production. While output estimates are available from 1926, examining trends over time is complicated by the different basis on which figures were compiled by trade and official sources. Trade data are limited to Radio Manufacturers Association (RMA) members and significantly underestimate total output by the 1930s, owing to the growth of non-member firms such as Philco. Meanwhile official estimates are based on factory gate values (which are roughly half the retail values on which the trade estimates are based). Furthermore, official data for valves show all sales external to the firm producing them, while trade data only include valves sold retail. This difference again becomes more important during the 1930s (as radio sets were often sold separately from valves during the 1920s). By 1937 radio receiver production had a factory gate value of £13.28 million, equivalent to retail sales of about £26 million, in addition to perhaps £10 million in retail sales of batteries, components, and valves—suggesting

[21] Louis Kaplow, 'The Patent–Antitrust Intersection: A Reappraisal', *Harvard Law Review*, 97 (1984), 1813–92; A. Carrier, 'Unravelling the Patent–Antitrust Paradox', *University of Pennsylvania Law Review*, 150 (2002), 761–854 (829–31).

[22] RSL, Marconi, 418, Marconi internal memorandum by W. Nicken (n.d., *c.*1938), 8.

[23] UK, Board of Trade, *Final Report on the Fifth Census of Production*, 307–11; UK, Customs and Excise, *Annual Statement, of trade of the United Kingdom, 1939* (London: HMSO, 1940), vol. II, 185 (imports), vol. III, 160–1 (exports).

[24] TNA, BT56/23, CIA1179/5, Department of Overseas Trade, memorandum on international position of wireless industry (n.d., *c.*October 1929); Sturmey, *Economic Development*, 221–2.

**Table 6.2.** The growth of UK radio equipment production, 1926–37

| Year | Total (£) | Complete receivers[a] | | | Radio valves | | | Batteries & accumulators | | Components[b] |
|---|---|---|---|---|---|---|---|---|---|---|
| | | No. | £ | £ per unit | No. | £ | £ per unit | No. | £ | £ |
| (1) Trade estimates—at retail prices | | | | | (valves sold retail) | | | | | |
| 1926 | 7,800,000 | | | | | | | | | |
| 1927 | 9,500,000 | | | | | | | | | |
| 1928 | 10,800,000 | | | | | | | | | |
| 1929 | 15,000,000 | | | | | | | | | |
| 1930 | 19,700,000 | 600,000 | 7,000,000 | 11.67 | 5,300,000 | 2,600,000 | 0.49 | 8,500,000 | 3,400,000 | 7,000,000 |
| 1931 | 29,800,000 | 1,258,197 | 12,500,000 | 10.00 | 6,000,000 | 3,250,000 | 0.54 | n.a. | 8,500,000 | 5,500,000 |
| 1932 | 36,627,425 | 1,436,849 | 19,323,000 | 13.45 | 4,653,100 | 2,854,425 | 0.61 | n.a. | 9,000,000 | 5,450,000 |
| 1933 | 22,568,000 | 967,800 | 14,092,000 | 14.56 | 2,275,000 | 1,256,000 | 0.55 | n.a. | 4,845,000 | 2,375,000 |
| (2) Official estimates—at factory gate prices | | | | | (valves sold externally) | | | | | |
| 1924 | | | | | | 1,508,000 | | | | |
| 1930[c] | | n.a. | 2,980,000 | | 5,625,000 | 1,516,000 | 0.27 | | | 3,343,000 |
| 1933[c] | | 1,281,100 | 8,040,000 | 6.28 | 9,288,000 | 2,102,000 | 0.23 | | | 2,463,000 |
| 1934 | | 1,756,900 | 12,043,000 | 6.85 | 11,108,000 | 2,204,000 | 0.20 | | | 1,991,000 |
| 1935 | | 1,849,800 | 12,229,000 | 6.61 | 11,777,000 | 2,215,000 | 0.19 | | 1,011,000[d] | 2,166,000 |
| 1937 | | 1,918,000 | 13,279,000 | 6.92 | | | | | | |

*Notes:* [a] Trade figures also include manufacturers' kits. All figures include radiograms. [b] All components, including loudspeakers and mains units. [c] The 1930 figures includes £36,000 of radio receivers, and £49,000 of components and parts, returned on schedules for trades not covered by the 1933 inquiry. A further £77,000 of wireless apparatus not separately distinguished has been attributed to 'all other components'; 1933 figure for radiograms based on 'electrical reproducers and radio-gramophones'. [d] Data are for wireless batteries only.

*Sources:* See Peter Scott, 'The Determinants of Competitive Success in the Interwar British Radio Industry', *Economic History Review*, 65 (2012), 1303–25 (1306).

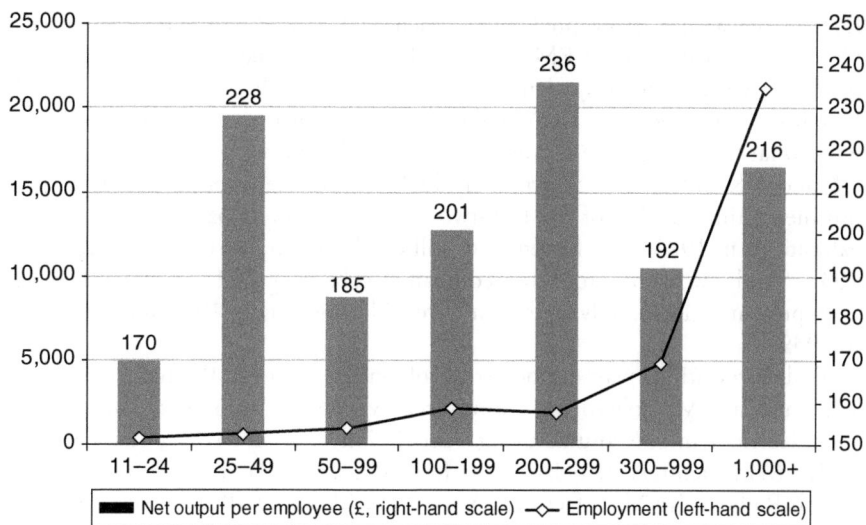

**Fig. 6.1.** Labour productivity and total employment by size of establishment (measured by numbers of workers), for British radio apparatus plants in 1935

*Note*: Excludes radio valve plants and establishments with ten or fewer workers.

*Source*: Board of Trade, *Final Report on the Fifth Census of Production and the Import Duties Act Enquiry, 1935* (London: HMSO, 1939), 330.

an average annual expenditure on radio equipment of around £2 18s per household, or 0.8 per cent of total consumer expenditure.[25]

As Figure 6.1 shows, production was relatively concentrated compared to, say, furniture. While there were some ninety-three establishments producing radio equipment (excluding valves and batteries/accumulators) in 1935, some 66 per cent of the industry's 32,000 workers were employed in eight plants of over 1,000 workers and a further 15 per cent in seven plants of 300–999 workers. Yet, in common with the American industry, there is no clear evidence of economies of scale. Plants with over 1,000 workers had a net output per worker of £216, only slightly above the sector's average of £211. Moreover, in common with the US radio equipment industry, labour productivity compared poorly to other manufacturing sectors. In 1935 average employment for establishments with eleven or more workers, in the British radio equipment industry (excluding valves) was 345.6, compared to 105.4 for all factory trades. Yet net output per employee, £211, was below the average for all factory trades (£229) or all electrical engineering (£231).[26]

As in America, relatively weak plant-level scale economies reflected the speculative nature of the industry. The bulk of annual sales represented new models, demand

[25] Total consumer expenditure based on Richard Stone and D. A. Rowe, *The Measurement of Consumers' Expenditure and Behaviour in the United Kingdom 1920–1938, Volume II* (Cambridge: Cambridge University Press, 1966), 143.

[26] UK, Board of Trade, *Final Report on the Fifth Census of Production and the Import Duties Act Enquiry, 1935, Part II*, 330; Final Summary Tables, 3.

for which was not easily predictable. Richard Haigh, English manager of the Gramophone Co. (part of EMI), reported that their major difficulty with radio production was estimating demand.[27] Similarly, British manufacturer V.Z. de Ferranti characterized radio as 'a highly speculative business... based on trying to guess what the public taste and demand will be'.[28] Another similarity between the US and UK industries was extremely high failure rates among manufacturers. Sturmey estimated that of the fifty-two set manufacturers participating at radio exhibitions in 1926, only fifteen were still exhibiting in 1931 and only seven by 1934. Similarly, of the fifty-seven companies exhibiting in 1931 which had not been present in 1926, only seventeen were still exhibiting in 1934 and only seven in 1939.[29]

Trade associations played a powerful role in the industry. By the beginning of 1924 a 'Valve Manufacturing Committee' was meeting under the auspices of the Electric Lamp Manufacturing Association, which changed its name to 'Valve Manufacturers Association' in June 1924. This later developed into the British Radio Valve Manufacturers Association (BVA) by 1926, which proved to be a tight and effective cartel.[30] BVA sought to enforce agreed list prices for valves, together with common discount structures and distribution terms for the trade, while blocking the sale of imported valves—whether sold separately on incorporated in radios.

Control was achieved via collective agreements with the other sections of the value chain—retailers, wholesale distributors, and set manufacturers. These included exclusivity clauses, prohibiting firms from handling valves not manufactured by BVA members.[31] Competition in the valve market was thus limited to performance, rather than price, one consequence of which was to stimulate technological innovation.[32] Like Marconi, the BVA justified its monopoly position to the wider trade in terms of protecting the home market from imports, while its behaviour was perfectly legal under British law.[33]

The National Association of Radio Manufacturers (open to any member of the British Broadcasting Company) had been established as early as 1923, followed shortly afterwards by the British Radio Manufacturers and Traders Association— mainly comprising the smaller manufacturers. In September 1926 these were merged into the Radio Manufacturers Association (RMA). This had a much larger membership than the BVA and weaker market power (as its broader membership

---

[27] 'Autolycus' (pseudonym), 'The All-Electric Advertising Man: Richard Haigh, English Manager of the Gramophone Company, Talks to Us about Radio (and Records)', *Advertising World* (Apr. 1934), 181–2 (182).

[28] Manchester Museum of Science and Industry, Ferranti collection [hereafter MMSI, Ferranti], 1996.10/10/1/1, V. Z. de Ferranti to A. E. Cutforth, 12 Jan. 1932.

[29] Sturmey, *Economic Development*, 166.

[30] Bodleian Library, Oxford, Gordon Bussey Collection [hereafter Bodleian, Bussey], Box 17, Part 2, 'The BVA a Personal Memoir' typescript by Michael Mason, former secretary of the Association, June 1986, 1.

[31] Ibid., 2.

[32] Keith Geddes and Gordon Bussey, *The Setmakers: A History of the Radio and Television Industry* (London: BREMA, 1991), 63–4.

[33] Leslie Hannah, *The Rise of the Corporate Economy* (London: Routledge, 1976), 42.

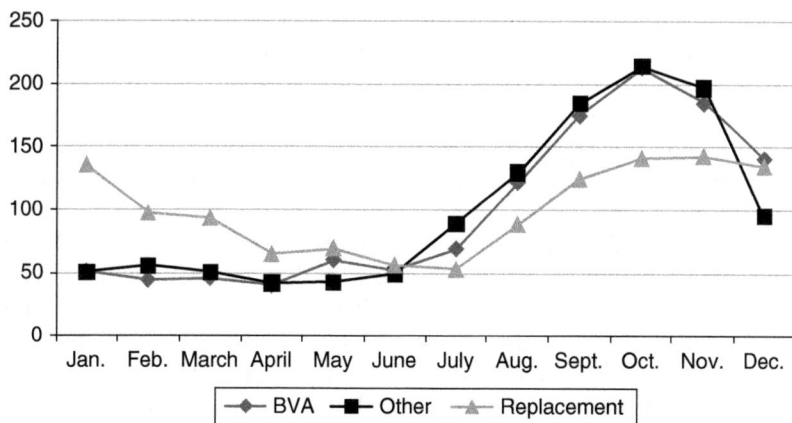

**Fig. 6.2.** Monthly output of valves used in radio production by BVA members, by other British set makers, and BVA replacement valve sales, as a percentage of mean monthly output (average for 1933 and 1934)

*Source*: Philips Company Archives, 882, England—Mullard Ltd (correspondence Loupart), Vol. 3, Mullard Statistical Department, statement (n.d., *c.*February 1935).

reflected divergent interests) though it succeeded in giving manufacturers a unified voice in negotiations with Marconi. It also played an active role in resale price maintenance (setting wholesalers' and retailers' discounts), and in industry-wide publicity activities. The RMA cooperated with the BVA, agreeing (from 1927) that its members would only use valves produced by BVA companies, in return for their support in blocking sales of foreign-manufactured sets.[34]

As in the United States, radio production and sales were highly seasonal. Figure 6.2 shows radio valves used in sets manufactured by BVA members (mainly large firms), valves sold to independent set makers, and valves sold retail for replacement use. Valves for new radios displayed a sharp autumn peak, followed by a long slack season (sales over January–June representing less than a quarter of the annual total). Annual model changes also contributed to highly seasonal production. Firms began developing new models from around July, to meet anticipated demand following the annual London 'Radiolympia' show. Unlike the main annual show for the British motor vehicle industry (another highly seasonal trade), which was timed to stimulate sales in the slack season, Radiolympia was held at the start of the new season (in September until 1931 and in the second half of August thereafter).[35] US radio exhibitions were also originally held in the autumn, though the first [US] Radio Manufacturers Association 'Radio Trade Exposition', in June 1927, broke this pattern and thereafter it became common to hold radio conventions in the early summer.[36]

[34] P. R. Morris, 'A Review of the Development of the British Thermionic Valve Industry', *Transactions of the Newcomen Society*, for 1993–4 (1994), 57–73 (60).

[35] Geddes and Bussey, *Setmakers*, 204.

[36] H. N. Cones, and J. H. Bryant, *Zenith Radio: The Early Years, 1919–1935* (Atglen, PA: Schiffer, 1997), 50; Ron Ramirez, *Philco Radio 1928–1942* (Atglen, PA: Schiffer, 1993), 53; 'July…a month of conventions', *Radio Retailing* (Aug. 1935), 47.

Attempts by some leading British set makers to move Radiolympia to an earlier date proved unsuccessful.[37] The RMA comprised dozens of set makers, whose collective agreement would be required for such a move. Each firm would have to modify their annual cycle of new model production and associated planning and, in an industry largely shielded from imports, many set makers felt little incentive to support a change which might benefit larger competitors more than themselves.[38]

As in the United States, radio manufacturers avoided the costs of having expensive machinery lying idle outside seasonal demand peaks by using labour-intensive techniques suitable for un/semi-skilled, often female, workers—many of whom were laid off early in the new year. Only 41.8 per cent of operatives in the 'radio apparatus, telecommunications equipment, gramophones, and electric lamps' sector were adult men (over eighteen) in 1937, compared to 57.3 per cent in other branches of electrical engineering.[39] The late 1920s witnessed the start of a trend towards line production methods, accompanied by the standardization of components and the mechanization of certain processes—though the trade remained very labour intensive.[40] As in the United States, demand for individual models was too unpredictable for mass production using special purpose machine tools and, while the economics of the industry do appear to have favoured large firms, this was not the result of technical economies of scale.

## PATENT ROYALTIES AND BRITAIN'S DISTINCTIVE PATH OF RADIO INNOVATION

The problems faced by Marconi in extracting the maximum 'rent' from its royalty monopoly were similar to a situation commonly studied in the economics literature, where a firm has a monopoly over a 'component' used in the manufacture of a product.[41] Firms purchasing this component might find ways of partially substituting it with components that are not controlled by the monopolist and are therefore likely to be cheaper. To prevent this, the monopolist can either integrate 'downstream' into assembly, or insist, as a condition of sale, that no such substitution can take place. The latter strategy is regarded as more difficult, as it entails considerable monitoring and enforcement costs. Meanwhile, costly innovations

---

[37] Christopher Saunders, *Seasonal Variations in Employment* (London: Longmans, 1936), 262–3.

[38] Margaret Graham, 'The Threshold of the Information Age', in A. D. Chandler and J. W. Cortada (eds.), *A Nation Transformed by Information* (Oxford: Oxford University Press, 2000), 137–75 (163).

[39] UK, Board of Trade, *Final Report on the Census of Production for 1948*, K/42; L/14; M/30; N/14; O13.

[40] Sturmey, *Economic Development*, 173.

[41] J. M. Vernon and P. A. Gordon, 'Profitability of Monopoly by Vertical Integration', *Journal of Political Economy*, 79 (1971), 924–5; R. Schmalensee, 'A Note on the Theory of Vertical Integration', *Journal of Political Economy*, 81 (1973), 442–9; F. R. Warren-Boulton, 'Vertical Control with Variable Proportions', *Journal of Political Economy*, 82 (1974), 783–802.

aimed at reducing the use of the monopoly input will also reduce the efficiency of the overall value chain.[42]

Marconi tried to block substitution away from its patents using a strategy that was to become common among holders of complementary patents, involving 'packaging' all patents under a single licence.[43] This was not justified in terms of strong technical complementarities between their thirteen packaged patents—as it was possible to produce a valve radio using only two of them (as revealed by the Brownie case, discussed later). Marconi's 'general licence' was based on the number of valves per receiver (though levied on the number of valve-sockets, as sets were often sold separately from valves). All complying British manufacturers were granted 'A2' licences, at a royalty of 12s 6d per valve-socket (taken as a proxy for the set's value).[44] The 'Big Six' were granted preferential royalties, while discounts were later introduced for manufacturers with annual payments over £5,000, with a sliding scale of reductions of 1s 6d to 2s 6d per valve-socket.[45]

Lower royalty payments gave the Big Six a substantial cost advantage in radio manufacture, while Marconi enjoyed a particularly strong cost advantage. However, these 'heavy electrical' firms, which—apart from GEC—had no background in consumer goods, proved too cumbersome to keep up with the rapid pace of technical change.[46] Marconi established a department for wireless production, which became the Marconiphone Co. in 1923. Despite access to Marconi's technical expertise, a loss of £184,811 was recorded in 1923 (including £96,500 written off for obsolescence). More serious losses followed, owing to recurring accumulations of obsolete stock. A 1927 Price Waterhouse Cooper report noted that orders were placed without first testing demand, and, despite most components being manufactured by another branch of Marconi, no effective efforts were made to cancel orders once problems became evident.[47]

Marconi ceased radio and valve production in 1928. Its Marconiphone subsidiary was sold to EMI—which had ambitions to become the dominant player in radio— together with half of Marconi's rights to the patent pool (which continued to be administered by Marconi). Most other members of the Big Six fared little better; 1928 losses on the merchandising and radio business of the BTH, Ediswan, Metro-Vick Supplies, and Hotpoint Electric Appliances companies amounted to £237,743.[48] By 1930 the only member of the Big Six still making radios was

---

[42] Oliver E. Williamson, *Markets and Hierarchies: Analysis and Antitrust Implications* (New York: Free Press 1975), 85; Warren-Boulton, 'Vertical Control'.

[43] Richard J. Gilbert and Michael L. Katz, 'Should Good Patents Come in Small Packages? A Welfare Analysis of Intellectual Property Bundling', *Journal of Industrial Organization*, 24 (2006), 931–52; William James Adams and Janet L. Yellen, 'Commodity Bundling and the Burden of Monopoly', *Quarterly Journal of Economics*, 90 (1976), 475–98.

[44] Morris, 'Review of the Development', 59.

[45] Sturmey, *Economic Development*, 45 and 215–19.     [46] Geddes and Bussey, *Setmakers*, 29.

[47] RSL, Marconi, 588, report on investigation of Marconi Wireless Telegraph Co. Ltd by Price Waterhouse & Co. and Cooper Brothers & Co., 20 Jan. 1927, folio section, 60–1.

[48] RSL, Marconi, 3024, 'Memorandum for Information of Directors of the Board of Associated Electrical Industries Ltd', July 1929.

GEC. Their failure to dominate radio production reflected the fact that this was an industry characterized by rapid technical progress, frequent design changes, and labour-intensive techniques, which limited the cost advantages of quantity production and gave agile specialist firms an advantage over cumbersome generalists.[49]

Early movers, including some of the Big Six, proved far more successful in dominating the valve industry—which became characterized by concentrated, cartelized production and very high margins. One unintended consequence of the Marconi royalty system was to stimulate a path-dependent process of technological innovation, which transferred some of Marconi's rents to the valve makers. It proved impossible to directly innovate around Marconi's patents, given Britain's combination of a strong intellectual property regime, in which fundamental patents were interpreted broadly, and the absence of anti-trust legislation to temper welfare losses from the exploitation of patent monopolies.[50] However, the form of the Maroni licence, based on the number of valves per set, enabled indirect innovation around the licence via the introduction of more complex valves. Early innovations involved increasing the amplification factor of each amplifying valve, while the 1930s saw the development of multi-functional valves.[51]

Valve makers invested heavily in producing more complex valves, enabling British radios to use progressively fewer valves than American sets of equivalent quality.[52] More complex and specialized valves also offered valve manufacturers increased potential for product differentiation (in a market where they could not compete on price, owing to BVA cartel rules). This reinforced the market power of both individual producers and the BVA, while reducing the threat from new market entrants (as rising complexity made valve design and manufacture progressively more difficult, while limiting interchangeability between different brands).[53] Interchangeability was further restricted by resisting the standardization of valve pin bases for fitting into radio-sockets.

These measures raised prices substantially compared to the simpler, interchangeable, American-type 'tubes', though as set makers saved more money on royalties than the premium they paid for multi-functional valves, overall costs were reduced.[54] A path-dependent process of technical change ensued, culminating in fundamental national differences in radio design.[55] This contributed to Britain's lower productivity compared to the United States. America's simpler tubes were cheaper to manufacture, owing to their wider tolerances and limits, and were produced in a narrower range of types in huge quantities, consequently lowering costs (despite requiring more tubes for a given quality of reception). By contrast the greater complexity of Britain's valves required production to close tolerances, at

---

[49] Sturmey, *Economic Development*, 148 and 167.

[50] For a discussion of the interaction between patent and anti-trust legislation, see Kaplow, 'Patent–Antitrust Intersection'; Carrier, 'Unravelling'.

[51] Morris, 'Review of the Development', 60–1.          [52] Sturmey, *Economic Development*, 223.

[53] Jerome Kraus, 'The British Electron-Tube and Semi-Conductor Industry, 1935–62', *Technology and Culture*, 9 (1968), 544–61 (547).

[54] See Scott, 'When Innovation Becomes Inefficient'; Morris, 'Review of the Development', 61.

[55] See Paul A. David, 'Clio and the Economics of QWERTY', *American Economic Review*, 75 (1985), 332–7; W. Brian Arthur, 'Competing Technologies, Increasing Returns, and Lock-in by Historical Events', *Economic Journal*, 99 (1989), 116–31.

substantially higher costs, while valve manufacturers were able to charge considerable mark-ups, owing to their strong cartel position and the limited compatibility between one firm's valves and another's.[56] Nevertheless, set manufacturers were prepared to pay the premium, as this was more than offset by lower royalties.

Following the expiration of the industry's fundamental patents, and the advent of price competition in the market for valve sales to set makers from the middle of 1934, the complex, high cost technical path of the British valve industry was gradually undermined. Rising imports played a major role in this process, accounting for about 20 per cent of total UK sales by 1937, despite the import restrictions, and making major inroads into the profitable replacement valve market.[57] Yet British valves remained markedly more complex and expensive than American tubes.[58] For example, the average unit price of tubes exported from the United States over 1935–7 was 1s 8d, compared to an average price for British tube exports in 1937 of 5s 4d.[59]

Radio manufacturers had long considered the 12s 6d per valve-socket royalty excessive, encouraging home construction of kit radios, or manufacture by firms sufficiently small to evade royalties. They also argued that British royalties were unreasonable given maximum German royalty charges of 2s 6d per valve-socket and zero charges in some European countries.[60] Opposition intensified during the late 1920s. Radio prices were falling (increasing the ratio of royalties to total costs), while Marconi found it impractical to pursue royalty evasion by consumers who built radios from kits, or manufacturers operating on a very small scale, placing compliant firms at a significant disadvantage. As Table 6.3 shows, standard royalties payable on a three-valve non-mains set rose from 7.5 per cent of the average retail price in 1924 to 8.2 per cent in 1926 and 11.0 per cent in 1928. As the prices shown are inclusive of essentials such as valves, batteries, and speakers—which were typically sold separately at this time—and retail prices were approximately double factory gate values, the impact on manufacturers' costs was well in excess of 20 per cent by 1928 (except for expensive newly introduced mains sets).

Moreover, by 1927 Marconi was pressing for a new licence, with royalties levied on each function of the new multi-stage valves.[61] The RMA formed a Royalty Committee in 1927, which pressed for a charge of 5 per cent of each radio's net selling price (with a lower percentage levy on more expensive sets, where cabinets formed a larger proportion of total costs, and a charge of 2s per valve-socket on very cheap sets). Marconi rejected any reduction and the RMA responded by launching a test case, using the opportunity created in 1928 when the Brownie

[56] Bodleian, Bussey, Box 18, G. R. M. Garratt, 'The Mullard Story. A Biography of S. R. Mullard and a History of Mullard Limited', unpublished manuscript, Part 5, 10–11.

[57] Morris, 'Review of the Development', 61.

[58] TNA, BT 64/279, 'Radio Valves', draft memorandum (n.d., *c.* Mar. 1946); Royal Mail Archives, London, POST 89/37, Ullswater Committee Paper No. 126, memorandum by Sir John Reith on broadcasting and the wireless trade, 19 Sept. 1936.

[59] 'World Wireless Trade: Some Highlights of the Export and Import Sides', *Wireless and Electrical Trader* (22 Oct. 1938), 115.

[60] Sturmey, *Economic Development*, 217.

[61] RSL, Marconi, 314, 'The Patents Position', document written in defence of Marconi's position, but not used, 17 July 1927.

**Table 6.3.** Marconi pool royalties as a proportion of the average estimated retail price of wireless sets, 1924–8

| | 1924 | | 1926 | | 1928 | | | | | |
|---|---|---|---|---|---|---|---|---|---|---|
| No. of valves | Price (£) | Royalties (%) | Price (£) | Royalties (%) | Price (£) | Royalties (%) | Price (£) | Royalties (%) | Price (£) | Royalties (%) |
| | | | | | Ordinary | | Mains | | Portables | |
| 1 | 12 | 5.2 | 8 | 7.8 | 3 | 20.8 | n.a. | n.a. | 5 | 12.5 |
| 2 | 18 | 6.9 | **14** | **8.9** | 9 | 13.9 | 19 | 6.6 | 10 | 12.5 |
| 3 | 25 | 7.5 | 23 | 8.2 | **17** | **11** | **26** | **7.2** | 19 | 9.9 |
| 4 | 29 | 8.6 | 38 | 6.6 | 26 | 9.6 | 33 | 7.6 | 25 | 10.0 |
| 5 | n.a. | na. | n.a. | n.a. | 29 | 10.8 | 50 | 6.3 | **25** | **12.5** |

*Notes*: Figures in bold show the sizes with the largest numbers of models produced. Estimates include costs of all essentials, such as valves, batteries, speakers, etc. Radios with over five valves are excluded. Royalties are based on the standard (12s 6d per valve-socket) Marconi royalty.

*Source*: Adapted from Gordon Bussey, *Wireless: The Crucial Decade. History of the British Wireless Industry 1924–34* (London: Peregrinus, 1990), 59–73.

Co. approached the Comptroller-General of Patents for a compulsory licence for two of Marconi's thirteen patents.

As the set Brownie wished to produce had only two valves and retailed at 25s, the royalty would have doubled the selling price, thus allegedly constituting an infringement of the Patents and Design Act 1919. Brownie's application explicitly challenged Marconi's package licensing approach; two of its five objections were that Marconi refused to grant separate licences for particular patents, and that royalties were payable on all valve-sockets, whether or not they involved Marconi patents.[62] However, British judicial decisions reflected the dominant 'liberal-conservative' political economy of the time, that had been developed to serve what was primarily a financial and mercantile economic elite, emphasizing property rights and avoiding state 'interference' in private property.[63] Following the logic of the liberal-conservative position, British common law had largely abandoned its traditional stance against 'restraints of trade' and any judicial actions which reflected this older approach were generally reversed by the higher courts.[64]

Judgement in the Marconi case was in line with this philosophy (in contrast to the United States, where both legislation and judicial decisions reflected a strong bias against anti-competitive practices).[65] In August 1928 the Comptroller-General found that Marconi's royalties were unreasonably high (recommending a charge equivalent to 10 per cent of the wholesale price, subject to minimum payments of 5s on the first valve-socket and 2s 6d on each additional valve-socket). However, he allowed Marconi to retain its general licence system. Yet even the level of fees was successfully appealed by Marconi at the High Court; Mr Justice

[62] Sturmey, *Economic Development*, 216–18.
[63] Nigel Harris, *Competition and the Corporate Society: British Conservatives, the State and Industry 1945–1964* (London: Routledge, 1972), 25.
[64] Hannah, *Rise of the Corporate Economy*, 42–3.
[65] See Scott, 'When Innovation Becomes Inefficient'.

Luxmoore ruled in June 1929 that Marconi was 'entitled to monopoly rights flowing from the ownership of patents it had acquired'.[66]

Louis Kaplow's 'ratio test' evaluates the conflicting social welfare benefits of intellectual property rights, and unrestricted competition, using the ratio between the reward the patentee receives when permitted to use a particular restrictive practice and the monopoly loss resulting from such exploitation (licensing practices which generate higher ratios being preferred).[67] Viewed from this perspective, Marconi's licensing system was clearly inferior to RCA's, discussed in Chapter 5. Marconi's royalties were both markedly higher and were levied on a flat-rate per valve-socket basis, rather than a proportion of the wholesale price. Charging a flat rate per valve-socket both reduced the proportionate impact of cost-reducing innovations on retail prices and created incentives for licensees to substitute single-function valves with multi-functional valves, which were more expensive to purchase (for equivalent functionality), but reduced royalty fees. This problem is recognized in the intellectual property literature, providing a justification for patents based on the final price of goods in which they are used (even where the end product is not subject to the patent).[68]

However, following the Comptroller-General's initial decision, many manufacturers had refused to pay more than the royalty suggested by that judgement, while some paid no royalties whatsoever. A joint investigation by RMA and Marconi estimated that these actions had reduced the average royalty per valve-socket for UK radio output from 11s 5d for the three years ending 30 September 1928 to only 5s 9d in 1929 (excluding Aeonic Radio; 4s 8d if it were included). The later addition of Philips to the figures, with annual radio sales equivalent to 100,000 valves, showed that a royalty necessary to maintain Marconi's current income—assuming all manufacturers complied—would be substantially less than 4s 8d.[69]

Marconi's royalty pool had thus faced sharply falling revenues, as shown in Figure 6.3, despite the fact that British radio production (expressed as an index of the number of valve-sockets[70] in total receiver output, set at 30 September 1928 = 100, with all years ending 30 September) had risen from 62.7 for 1926 to 75.3 in 1927, and an estimated 194.0 for 1929 (including an estimate for Aeonic Radio, which was not paying any royalty). Comparing patent pool income with these index numbers is problematic, as pool income data are only available for calendar years and valve-socket output data only for years ending 30 September. However, the figures suggest that, assuming royalty payments per valve-socket had remained at 1926 levels, Marconi's royalty income for 1928 would have been around £217,000, far in excess of its actual value (£167,000), while the figure for 1929 would have shown further strong growth, rather than a substantial decline.

While Marconi's eventual legal victory enabled it to press for both current and backdated royalty payments at the official 12s 6d level, this would have caused

[66] *The Times* (19 June 1929), 5.    [67] Carrier, 'Unravelling', 797–8.

[68] Kaplow, 'Patent–Antitrust Intersection', 1883–4.

[69] Philips Company Archives, Eindhoven [hereafter PCA], S1397, minutes of special meeting of the RMA Royalties Committee, 16 July 1929.

[70] Royalties were levied on the number of valve-sockets, rather than valves, to prevent manufacturers evading payment by selling receivers separately from valves.

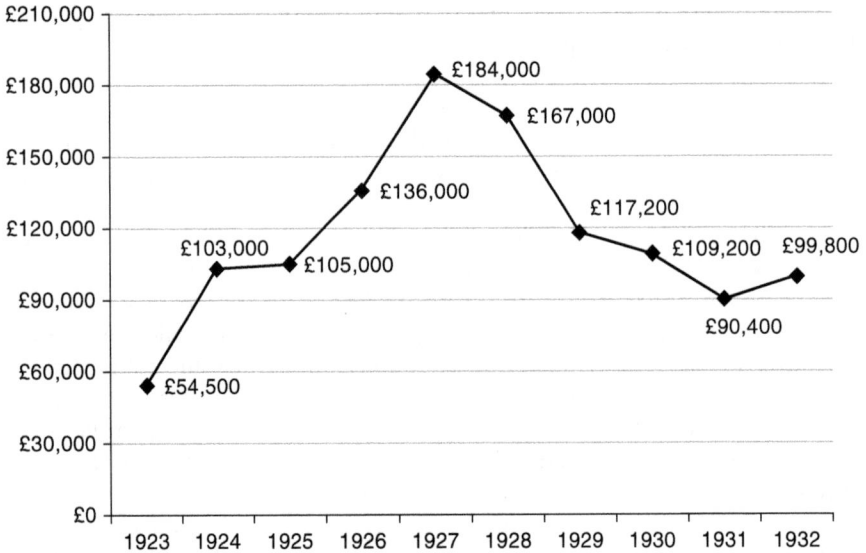

**Fig. 6.3.** Gross Marconi patent pool revenue for radio receivers and related apparatus, 1923–32

*Notes*: Before deduction of management expenses, bad debts, etc. From 1929 onwards receipts were divided equally between Marconi and EMI.

*Source*: Radcliffe Science Library, Marconi 418, internal memorandum, undated (*c.*1938).

serious financial difficulties for some firms. Moreover, Marconi appreciated that its key fundamental patents were soon to expire. From October 1929 it was possible to produce battery or DC sets in Britain without any patent infringement, while the expiry of the eliminator patent in December 1931 also made this possible for AC sets.[71] Marconi reacted by reopening negotiations with the RMA. A new 'A3'general licence was agreed, with royalties reduced from 12s 6d to 5s per valve-socket, though licensees were required to sign an agreement running for five years from 28 August 1929 and pay royalties on all their sets, regardless of whether they were covered by the patents.[72]

## RESTRUCTURING VALUE CHAINS IN THE 1930s

As Figure 6.4 shows, the inter-war radio industry can be divided into three broad phases. The first phase, from 1922–6, was dominated by rapid growth in demand for crystal sets, often assembled from components and kits. These cost only £2–£3 for a good set (and less for a home-constructed receiver) and required no batteries (as they received their power from the radio signal). However, crystal sets required headphones, were not well-suited to differentiating between radio signals, and

[71] Sturmey, *Economic Development*, 220.
[72] 'Reduced Royalties in New Pool Licence', *Wireless and Gramophone Trader* (22 July 1933), 74–5.

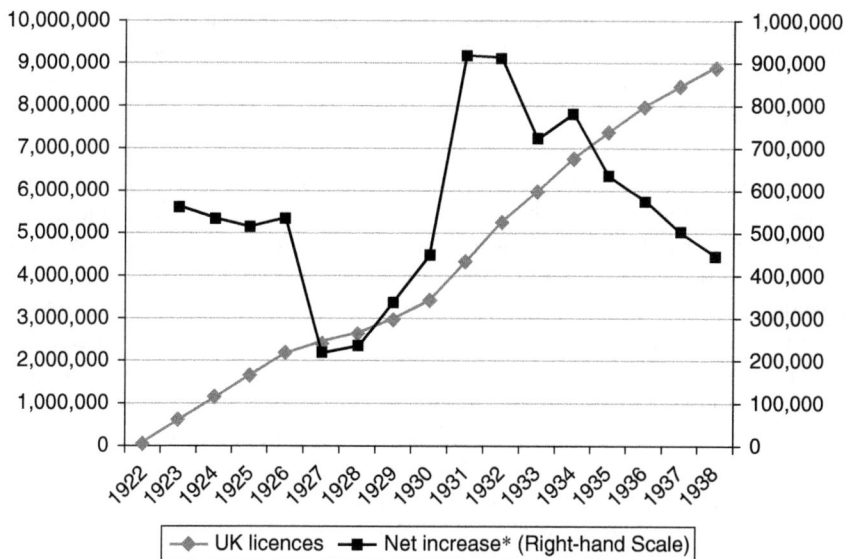

**Fig. 6.4.** Number of UK radio licences and net annual increase, 1922–38

*Notes*: All figures are for calendar years. *New licences minus licences not renewed.

*Sources*: 1922–30, 'The Radio Market—Present and Potential', *Wireless and Gramophone Trader* (28 Mar. 1931), 350–1; 1931–8, TNA, BT64/296, unsigned memorandum, 26 June 1945.

could not amplify weak signals. Meanwhile a good valve set cost at least £15, required a replacement high-tension battery every few months, weekly recharging of two to three accumulators providing the low-tension current to the valves, and frequent replacement of valves.[73]

The second phase, from 1927–31, witnessed the rapid displacement of the crystal set by the valve radio, boosted by a switch in broadcasting policy from a large number of small transmitters to a few high-power regional ones. Long-distance broadcasting suited valve sets, with high selectivity between channels.[74] By 1932 the industry had entered a third phase, market saturation, with replacement sets dominating sales; the Board of Trade estimated that replacement demand comprised 64 per cent of the total in 1935 and had reached 70 per cent by 1938.[75]

Over 1929–32 receivers were transformed from bulky, exposed apparatus requiring numerous essential 'accessories' into self-contained, mains-operated units.[76] Meanwhile radio production was transformed from a craft industry to one dominated by large-scale plants, using flow production methods. This was accompanied by some moves towards standardization of components and the

---

[73] Geddes and Bussey, *Setmakers*, 16–17.

[74] Gordon Bussey, *Wireless: The Crucial Decade. History of the British Wireless Industry 1924–34* (London: Peregrinus, 1990), 53.

[75] TNA, BT64/296, unsigned memorandum, 26 June 1945.     [76] Bussey, *Wireless*, 67.

mechanization of certain processes—though the trade remained very labour-intensive. Very small firms found it increasingly difficult to compete; the number of set manufacturers displaying at trade exhibitions declined from seventy-two in 1931 to fifty-four in 1934 and only twenty-nine in 1939.[77] Meanwhile, as the pace of technological change slowed over the 1930s, manufacturers increasingly focused on 'commercial innovations' concerning factors such as external appearance, ease of use, and the appearance of the tuning dial, rather than technical fundamentals.[78]

Although royalty payments fell substantially as a proportion of radio costs during the 1930s, the other major cost item, valves, proved less downwardly price-flexible, representing an increasing proportion of set makers' costs.[79] This reflected both the complexity of British multi-functional valves and the highly concentrated structure of the valve industry. According to a November 1932 estimate, Philips-Mullard (Philips and their subsidiary Mullard—the leading British valve manufacturer at the time it was acquired by Philips in 1926) supplied 41 per cent of British valves, Cossor 22 per cent, BTH 17.5 per cent, GEC 13 per cent, and EMI 6 per cent.[80] Valve manufacturers also accounted for a large proportion of receiver production—a BVA meeting of 29 April 1935 was informed that members were responsible for approximately 60 per cent of British radio sets (while separate estimates, based on valve-sockets, give figures of 46.3 and 51.5 per cent respectively in 1933 and 1934).[81]

Given the high mark-ups on valve sales, even to set makers, valve suppliers had a clear advantage in the receiver market—particularly if they chose to act as price leaders. Two multinational companies with established manufacturing competencies in consumer electronics—EMI and Philips—looked set to dominate the market. EMI faced a declining market for gramophones and records following the expansion of radio and was keen to establish a leading position in radio. In February 1934 Mullard's general manager, S. S. Eriks, recounted a recent conversation with EMI's managing director, Louis Sterling, who mentioned:

> that they were out to obtain a larger share of this market at all costs...they wish to put their sales of receivers in this country up to at least 400,000/450,000 sets out of an estimated total market of 1,200,000/1,400,000 sets in order to fill their factories and they will at a pinch be satisfied if they can do this during the next two or three years even at what they termed 'a progressive loss'.[82]

Philips also pursued an international policy of increasing receiver market share, based on an assumption that following market saturation fierce competition would lead to domination by a few major firms. It therefore continually reduced gross selling prices, whilst maintaining its discount to dealers, even at the cost of

---

[77] Sturmey, *Economic Development*, 166.       [78] Ibid., 174–9.
[79] PCA, 882, England—Mullard Ltd (correspondence Loupart), Vol. 1, S. S. Eriks to O. M. E. Loupart, 23 Apr. 1932.
[80] Ibid., Vol. 2, H. F. Van Walsam to S. R. Mullard, 1 Nov. 1932.
[81] Ibid., Vol. 3, report of BVA management meeting, 29 Apr. 1935, and Mullard Statistical Department statement (n.d., *c*.February 1935).
[82] PCA, S2729, S. S. Eriks to M. E. Loupart, 6 Feb. 1934.

squeezing its own profits.[83] Receiver sales in the UK and Ireland for Philips and its associated companies rose from 116,652 during the year 1933/4 to a peak of 252,843 during 1936/7.[84]

EMI, Philips, and another leading valve manufacturer, A. C. Cossor, became Britain's largest set makers, but nevertheless failed to dominate the market. A number of specialist set makers emerged during the late 1920s and early 1930s, which drew their main competitive advantage from innovative marketing. This encompassed the development of successful brands (symbolized by distinctive cabinet designs), intensive advertising, and strong cooperative links with retailers. Successful marketing gave them sufficiently strong bargaining positions with valve manufacturers and patent holders to negate most of their initial input cost disadvantages.

The 1930s witnessed a progressive reduction in the monopoly rents of both the Marconi pool and BVA, as the sector's fundamental patents expired. From the early 1930s Marconi faced serious competition from alternative patent pools, including Hazelpat, representing the patent resources of three American firms— Hazeltine Corporation, Philco, and Majestic Electric Co. Hazelpat joined the Marconi pool in September 1933, facilitating Philco's entry into the British market.[85] Of longer-term importance was the strategy of two major valve producers, Philips-Mullard and BTH, which, from around 1933, launched rival patent pools to Marconi, with access tied to purchasing valves from them.

For example, a draft agreement of 6 November 1935 between Mullard and McMichael Ltd stated that McMichael would buy valves for new radios exclusively from Mullard, at a price equal to the lowest Mullard charged any other manufacturer (excluding members of the BVA and Mullard's associated companies). Royalty payments would not exceed one-third of those for which McMichael were hitherto liable with Marconi, while Philips-Mullard indemnified McMichael against two-thirds of the cost of any litigation for patent infringement.[86] By this time McMichael produced around 40,000 radios per year, using 200,000 valves, which—even under these preferential terms—cost in excess of £40,000, or around 13.3 per cent of McMichael's turnover.[87] This strategy was broadly similar to that applied by RCA under the infamous Clause 9, discussed in Chapter 5.[88] While the presence of alternative patent pools tempered the market leverage advantages commonly associated with such tying arrangements, these nevertheless gave the two leading valve manufacturers considerable influence over manufacturers' set designs (indemnities against patent litigation only being granted for approved circuits).

[83] I. J. Blanken, *The History of Philips Electronics N.V*, vol. III: *The Development of N.V. Philips' Gloelampenfabrieken into a Major Electrical Group* (Zaltbommel, Netherlands: Nijhoff, 1999), 360–1.

[84] PCA, 81:87, financial ledger *c.* 1939. Financial years shown start in May.

[85] Sturmey, *Economic Development*, 224–6; Geddes and Bussey, *Setmakers*, 183; J. F. Wilson, *Ferranti: A History. Building a Family Business, 1882–1975* (Lancaster: Crucible, 2000), 252–3.

[86] PCA, 882, England—Mullard Ltd (correspondence Loupart), draft contract between Mullard and McMichael, 6 Nov. 1935.

[87] Ibid., S. S. Eriks to H. F. van Walsem, 26 Sept. 1935.

[88] Ibid., Vol. 3, N. Gunn to H. F. Van Walsem, 27 Apr. 1935.

Such tying strategies have the potential to extend monopoly power to the tied good market, by making continued operation unprofitable for rival producers of that good (if there are scale economies in its production).[89] Philips-Mullard were indeed motivated by a desire to increase their market power, though their ability to do so was limited by the presence of alternative patent pools. Marconi reacted to the new competition by introducing the A4 licence in June 1933, cutting the basic royalty from 5s to 2s 6d per valve-socket, with further reductions for large firms.[90] Meanwhile Phillips-Mullard's main rival in the market for valve sales to independent assemblers, BTH, also adopted a strategy of offering patent indemnities in return for tied valve sales.[91]

By April 1932 Philips-Mullard were considering price discrimination in favour of some assemblers who looked likely to be able to survive an anticipated competitive shake-out in the sector. Eriks noted that set makers' component costs had dropped rapidly and, given that valve manufacturers had proven more successful in resisting price cuts, valves comprised an increasing proportion of total receiver costs.[92] Meanwhile independent set makers were experiencing intense price competition from firms which integrated valve and set production and were thus tempted to turn to alternative valve suppliers such as Tunsgram (a Hungarian-based firm, which manufactured American-type valves and was refused admission to the BVA).[93] Offering preferential terms to certain larger set makers seemed a way forward:

> I have seen the costings of a few firms recently...they will have a very difficult run at VMA or near VMA prices, and although they would be very reluctant to give up their B.V.A. agreement, Tunsgram valves may at a pinch become attractive to those firms who do not particularly rely on the trade to sell their sets [such as retailers' brands]....unless we decide on such a policy...with a few...medium good Set Makers with whom we are on an intimate footing and tie them down by doing so we will of course accelerate the business going into the hands of the Valve/Set Makers and one or two manufacturers who are working so closely with Mazda [the BTH valve brand] that they can practically be regarded as such.[94]

Despite these attempts to extend control over the value chain by tying patent indemnities to the supply of valves, a number of major independent set makers were able to gain the upper hand in negotiations over access to patents and valves. They did so by developing distinctive brands, sufficiently popular to give them enough market share to make the rival patent pools vigorously compete for their custom.

[89] M. D. Whinston, 'Tying, Foreclosure, and Exclusion', *American Economic Review*, 80 (1990), 837–59.

[90] Sturmey, *Economic Development*, 231; 'Reduced Royalties in New Pool Licence', *Wireless and Gramophone Trader* (22 July 1933), 74–5. For radiograms an additional 2s 6d per valve-socket was charged on valves used in the gramophone circuit.

[91] PCA, 882, England—Mullard Ltd (correspondence Loupart), Vol. 3, S. S. Eriks to H. F. Van Walsem, 20 Jan. 1936.

[92] Ibid., Vol. 1, S. S. Eriks to O. M. E. Loupart, 23 Apr. 1932.

[93] J. W. Stokes, *70 years of Radio Valves and Tubes* (New York: Vestal, 1982), 223.

[94] PCA, S2729, S. S. Eriks to M. E. Loupart, 6 Feb. 1934.

From the middle of 1934 the BVA abandoned price-fixing on valve sales to manufacturers and thus extended the scope for price discrimination in favour of larger firms.[95] By doing so, they weakened their collective control over the radio value chain. An April 1935 BVA meeting noted that the largest set makers were beginning 'to dominate the Association rather than being controlled by it. These buyers seemed quite oblivious of the benefits which they had secured from the operations of the Association, such as the limitation of competition in set manufacture, the practical exclusion of imported sets, and so on.'[96]

There were attempts to reimpose price-fixing for valve sales to set makers, including a 1935 initiative from BTH. However, Eriks doubted that either this or a market-sharing arrangement would work, given the failure of previous initiatives and the growing market power of the large set makers. He also viewed their previous experience of non-price competition as being equally destabilizing—BTH had brought out new valves in rapid succession, forcing Mullard to do likewise. BTH also provided considerable technical assistance to some customers, practically designing sets for one or two firms, a policy which further tied them to its valve sales. Eriks believed that Mullard's recent policy of developing a more limited range of simpler valves would boost their efficiency and profits, especially given his perception that BTH had substantially higher production costs. His preferred strategy was to offer sufficiently attractive terms to important customers to capture their business, thus achieving a scale of production that would drive down unit costs and enable Philips-Mullard to further reduce their own radio production costs.[97]

This policy reflected the growing market power of major independent set makers: 'it will be extremely difficult, under present circumstances, to control the price of a business like Ekco's whatever we do...the price which one does not accept at one juncture appears attractive six or twelve months later'.[98] Ekco—one of the most successful independents—even began to manufacture their own valves, in an effort to further squeeze suppliers' prices. Philips-Mullard eventually capitulated to them, agreeing to both supply all Ekco's valve requirements at privileged rates and to purchase their valve-making equipment at a price which recouped Ekco's capital costs.[99]

## A PEOPLE'S RADIO?

As discussed in Chapter 5, the continued expansion of the US radio industry during the 1930s was largely due to the development of the new 'midget' radios. While these challenged the market for conventional radios, they also expanded it

---

[95] TNA, BT 64/279, 'Radio Valves', draft memorandum (n.d., *c.*Mar. 1946).

[96] PCA, 882, England—Mullard Ltd (correspondence Loupart), Vol. 3, report of a BVA management meeting, 29 Apr. 1935.

[97] Ibid., S. S. Eriks to H. F. van Walsem, 28 Sept. 1935; S. S. Eriks to H. F. Van Walsem, 20 Jan. 1936.

[98] Ibid., S. S. Eriks to C. M. E. Loupart, 23 Dec. 1935.

[99] Michael Lipman, *Memoirs of a Socialist Businessman* (London: Lipman Trust, 1980), 88–9.

to encompass sets that were supplementary to a household's main receiver, or were used in commercial venues such as hotels, offices, and garages. Moreover, these new sets were light enough to be carried to sports and other outdoor events, thus creating a substantial summer demand and reducing the strong seasonality in radio sales.[100] The development of cheap, lightweight, portable gramophones had mark-edly reduced seasonality in gramophone sales on both sides of the Atlantic, though in Britain a similarly portable radio was not to become available until after the Second World War.[101]

Midgets were initially of less attraction to British than to American listeners. Britain's monopoly radio system, broadcast on a network of high-power transmitters, provided particularly good reception.[102] Domestic demand thus prioritized pure sound reproduction rather than selectivity and range.[103] 'Midget' and other low-end American sets (which had poorer sound reproduction and were said to be used primarily for 'talk' radio) scored badly in this regard (especially the early models) though evidence suggests that, when available, they found a ready market. Kolster-Brandes (a subsidiary of International Telephone and Telegraph) produced a commercially successful two-valve set that had no difficulty picking up national and regional BBC stations.[104] American midget sets also sold well, despite the determined efforts of the UK industry to keep them out of the British market.[105]

Higher costs and valve makers' opposition inhibited Britain from introducing similarly small sets—priced sufficiently low to create a market beyond the house-hold's prime receiver. The advent of the midget had caused leading radio manufacturers much anxiety. This had also been the case in the United States, though, given Britain's lack of anti-trust legislation, it was much easier for the British trade associations to block this unwelcome innovation.

In June 1932 Eriks warned Philips' head office that: 'nothing will fritter away our profits quicker than having to keep pace with the Americans, also having regard to novelties they are introducing from time to time, as recently in Chicago'.[106] Yet imports of what he initially regarded as novelties were reaching Britain in significant numbers by the mid-1930s. In January 1934 *Wireless Trader* noted that these could be imported, duty-paid, at £3 8s per set and by June 1935 a three-valve midget was being advertised nationally at £3 5s by a major London store.[107] The British industry's main defence was the trade ban on American-type valves—as without a replacement supply, sets could not be kept working for any

---

[100] 'Marketing Statistics and Sales... 1937', *Radio Retailing* (Jan. 1938), 25–32 (26–7).

[101] Nott, *Music for the People*, 40–1.

[102] U.S. Department of Commerce, *Radio Markets of the World, 1932* (Washington, 1932), 95.

[103] TNA, BT56/23, Chief Industrial Advisor's Office, 'Electrical Industry—Exports—Position of Wireless Apparatus', undated memorandum, 1929.

[104] Geddes and Bussey, *Setmakers*, 173–7.

[105] PCA, 811.2 + S14.2, gegevens radio (Engeland), U.S. Dept. of Commerce, 'Radio Markets: United Kingdom', report, 6 July 1936, 8.

[106] PCA, 882, England—Mullard Ltd (correspondence Loupart), Vol. 1, S. S. Eriks to O. M. E. Loupart, 18 June 1932.

[107] 'The Menace of the Midget', *Wireless and Gramophone Trader* (6 Jan. 1934), 1; 'Still too Many American Sets', *Wireless and Gramophone Trader* (15 June 1935), 1.

length of time.[108] Legal action by the Marconi pool against importers, distributors, and retailers of American sets also had some impact, though importers circumvented this by dissolving companies threatened with litigation and commencing imports of a different model via a new company. The pool therefore began suing dealers as well as importers.[109]

From around 1936 attempts were made to produce lower-priced British sets, but within the constraints of the conventional table-top design, rather than the more radical American compact. In evidence to the Ullswater Committee, Sir John Reith noted Germany's success in producing a standardized, low-priced 'People's Set'.[110] British developments along these lines were recommended and a number of companies began to market lower-priced receivers. In 1936 Murphy introduced the B23 battery portable, priced at £6 7s 6d.[111] In the same year Philips launched a £6 6s superhet in response to the Committee's recommendations, reducing production costs to £2 10s by mounting the components directly onto the Bakelite case so as not to require chassis.[112]

However, the most enthusiastic response was from the British subsidiary of Philco, which vigorously marketed various 'People's Sets', including the three-valve battery B333 for £5 5s and mains versions from £6 6s, launched at the 1936 Radiolympia Exhibition. Although 130,000 Philco People's Sets had been sold by July 1937,[113] sales proved insufficient to justify a business plan based on low margins and very high throughput. Philco experienced a 'downfall' early in the trade recession of 1937/8, their attempt to benefit from long production runs resulting in a considerable overloading of the market and a breakdown of their distribution network.[114] At the start of the 1937/8 season Philco had taken the unusual step of raising prices for existing models (by 14.5 per cent for the B333).[115] Meanwhile restyling was rejected, owing to 'the strict utilitarian nature of the product'.[116] Carrying over an established model at a higher price was anathema to a market based on annual design changes (or model continuations at discounted prices), and produced a collapse in sales, transforming a 1936 profit of £102,815 into a 1937 loss of £111,504, while a reorganization which cut staff to one-third of 1937 levels failed to improve its position.[117]

---

[108] Geddes and Bussey, *Setmakers*, 183.

[109] PCA, 811.2 + S14.2, gegevens radio (Engeland), U.S. Dept. of Commerce, 'Radio Markets: United Kingdom', report, 6 July 1936, 8.

[110] Royal Mail Archives, POST 89/37, Ullswater Committee Paper No. 126, Memorandum by Sir John Reith on broadcasting and the wireless trade, 19 Sept. 1936.

[111] Joan Long, *A First Class Job! The Story of Frank Murphy, Radio Pioneer, Furniture Designer and Industrial Idealist* (Sheringham: Joan Long, 1985), 57.

[112] Geddes and Bussey, *Setmakers*, 185.

[113] *Philco News* (15 July 1937), 10.

[114] University of Reading, Museum of English Rural Life, J. H. Dunning collection, 'American Firms Manufacturing in Great Britain', file A, interview with Philco Radio Ltd, 5 Mar. 1954.

[115] *Philco News* (29 July 1937), 1.

[116] Carleton Dyer, 'Carl Dyer Speaks to You', *Philco News* (17 June 1937), 1.

[117] Guildhall Library, London, bound volumes of London Stock Exchange company reports for 1938 and 1939, statement by Carleton Dyer, circulated to Philco shareholders, 18 Feb. 1938; Philco Annual Report for year to 31 Dec. 1938 (20 Mar. 1939).

The various 'People's Sets' were roughly similar in size, weight, and appearance to their predecessors, with minimum prices more than double those of typical American midgets (and not greatly cheaper than conventional low-end British radios). As such, they were regarded by consumers mainly as competitors for the conventional set market, rather than fulfilling the supplementary functions of the much cheaper and more portable American midget. In a market which mainly served replacement demand, most consumers wanted a clearly superior set to their existing model and were thus not drawn to these cheaper models in sufficient numbers, while they had little impact in persuading the British public to adopt the American trend of the multiple set household.

## CONCLUSIONS

As Figure 6.5 shows, despite a considerable reduction in the number of radio manufacturers since the 1920s, no single firm or section of the industry had gained a dominant position in the radio receiver market by 1938. Three major valve manufacturers, EMI, Philips-Mullard, and Cossor, collectively comprised 36.7 per cent of receiver unit sales, though the largest, EMI, accounted for no

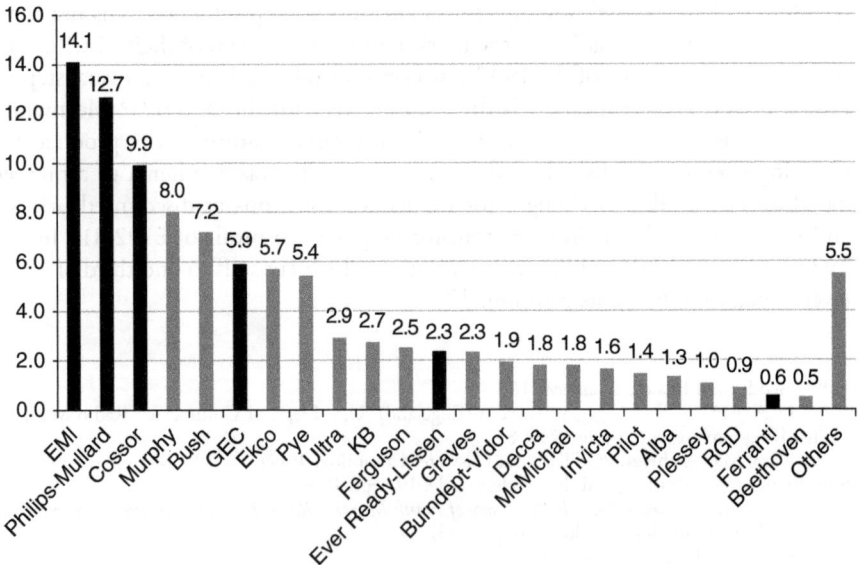

**Fig. 6.5.** Percentage distribution of 1938 radio set unit output, for Radio Manufacturers Association members

*Notes*: Highlighted columns represent members of the British Radio Valve Manufacturers Association. Total receiver production = 1,291,744 sets.

*Source*: Manchester Museum of Science and Industry, Ferranti collection, 1996.10/1/7/409, Radio Manufacturers Association statement for year ending 31 Dec. 1938 (n.d., *c*.1939).

more than 14.1 per cent. Meanwhile, of the eight firms with more than a 5 per cent market share, four—Murphy, Bush, Ekco, and Pye—were independent set makers and non-BVA members collectively accounted for the majority of all receiver production.

The failure of firms with initial cost advantages to gain long-term dominance of the British radio value chain illustrates the complex factors underpinning competitive success in the inter-war radio industry. Marconi had a major cost advantage during the 1920s owing to its patent monopoly, but nevertheless floundered in a market characterized by rapid obsolescence, annual model changes, and highly seasonal demand. The valve manufacturers, which enjoyed the most powerful market positions during the 1930s, generally fared better, reflecting their greater competencies in the logistics of new model development, in marketing, and in production. Yet these also failed to dominate an industry where product differentiation through branding was a major factor in competitive success. Tying valve sales to preferential royalties was used as a means to extend market control. However—given the presence of rival patent pools—the countervailing market power of independent firms with strong brands ultimately proved more important. Chapter 7 examines how these brands were developed and promoted by manufacturers and their retailers.

# 7

# British Radio Marketing, Distribution, and Retailing

## INTRODUCTION

The previous chapter emphasized the importance of strong brands in allowing set makers to gain sufficient market share to negotiate favourable terms with the valve manufacturers—who had sought to dominate the radio value chain. Meanwhile marketing-related weaknesses partially accounted for the failure of some firms with initial cost advantages to dominate the sector. This chapter explores the factors underpinning strong brands—effective marketing, distinctive designs, and strong links with distributors. It also examines two alternative channels of supply for radio reception that did not require purchasing a receiver—relay services and set rentals.

## THE RADIO VALUE CHAIN

Jefferys estimated that by 1938 there were some 400–450 wholesalers and 25–28,000 retail outlets who dealt with radios on at least an occasional basis, though those engaged substantially in the trade numbered only 80–100 wholesalers (with perhaps a further 75–100 branches or depots) and some 9–10,000 retailers.[1] However, a March 1937 RMA estimate put the figures somewhat higher, at around 30–40,000 retailers on manufacturers' lists, of whom around 15,000 were 'first-rate' dealers.[2] Most retailers were independents, accounting for an estimated 80–88 per cent of total sales, with multiples comprising a further 10–15 per cent, and department and cooperative stores only 2–5 per cent.[3] Retail price maintenance allowed local independent retailers to retain a strong market position in radio, particularly if they enjoyed a good reputation for after-sales service—in what was a particularly service-intensive trade.[4] As in the United States, radio retailers had to deal not only with problems of after-sales service, but with trade-ins, consumer credit, and

[1] J. B. Jefferys, *The Distribution of Consumer Goods: A Factual Survey of Methods and Costs in the United Kingdom in 1938* (Cambridge: Cambridge University Press, 1950), 299.

[2] MMSI, Ferranti, 1996.10/10/1/7/409, memorandum by Mr Beardsall, 5 July 1937.

[3] Jefferys, *Distribution of Consumer Goods*, 299.

[4] Keith Geddes and Gordon Bussey, *The Setmakers: A History of the Radio and Television Industry* (London: BREMA, 1991), 205.

highly seasonal demand. Seasonality slowed annual stock-turn; Jefferys estimated that radio wholesalers turned over their stock six to seven times per year and retailers five to six times (significantly below the six to eight times typical for other electrical appliance retailers).[5]

Retailers' discounts rose from 25 per cent of list prices in 1922–3 to 30 per cent over 1924–9 and 33.3 per cent during 1930–2.[6] From around 1933 a number of leading manufacturers successfully pushed for a reduction in retail discounts to 27.5 per cent, while many further reduced distribution costs by moving from wholesale to direct-to-dealer distribution.[7] However, discounts subsequently rose again and in 1938 retailers received 30–33.3 per cent (while authorized dealers and major multiples sometimes received significantly more generous terms).[8] Wholesalers (now restricted to only around 20–25 per cent of the trade) received an average discount equivalent to the retailer's margin plus 15–17.5 per cent. Meanwhile sets purchased in bulk by multiples and department stores and sold under their own brand names would carry margins of 40–45 per cent.[9]

Table 7.1 shows the value chain in radio production for a three-valve non-mains radio (the most common type of radio produced) in 1928. The data are based on a radio sold without valves (as was then normal practice). Unfortunately it is not possible to differentiate between raw materials, assembly, and other components costs, as firms varied markedly in the proportion of their components they produced in-house and sourced in the market.

Comparison with Table 5.2, showing the US radio value chain in the same year, demonstrates the much higher proportion of the retail value of radios that accrued

Table 7.1. The value chain for a three-valve non-mains radio in 1928

| Stages of value chain | Controlled by | % of retail price |
|---|---|---|
| Patents | Marconi | 11 |
| Design | Manufacturer | ( |
| Raw materials | Market | ( |
| Components | Market/manufacturer | (32 |
| Assembly | Manufacturer | ( |
| Valves | Valve makers | 12 |
| Wholesale distribution | Wholesalers | 15 |
| Retail distribution | Retailers | 30 |
| **Total** | | 100 |

*Note*: This assumes that valves were purchased separately from the radio by the final user.

*Sources*: Patent royalties and overall retail cost—see Table 6.3. Wholesale and retail margins, 'The Trend in Discounts', *Wireless and Gramophone Trader* (19 Mar. 1932), 338. Valve prices, T. C. H. Goring, 'The Growth of the Electronic Tube Industry', in *The Newcomen Society. History of Thermionic Devices, Conference Proceedings* (23 Apr. 1994), 41–62 (62) (read from graph).

[5] Jefferys, *Distribution of Consumer Goods*, 294 and 300.
[6] 'The Trend of Prices and Discounts', *Wireless and Gramophone Trader* (25 Mar. 1933), 328.
[7] 'Story of an Industry', *Wireless and Electrical Trader* (25 Mar. 1944), 342–8 (342).
[8] Jefferys, *Distribution of Consumer Goods*, 300.  [9] Ibid., 299–300.

to the patent holder (estimated at 11 per cent, compared to 4 per cent for an average American set, assuming no US patent royalty was paid on the tubes). Furthermore, despite the American set being assumed to have five tubes (roughly equivalent to a British set of three valves, given the greater number of functions incorporated into some valves), the purchase of valves for the British set constituted 12 per cent of the total cost to the consumer, compared to only 9 per cent for the US set. In each case the costs of design (excluding those aspects of internal design covered by patents), raw materials, other components, and assembly, are estimated at around 32 per cent of the retail price of the radio plus its tubes/valves. However, higher British royalties and valve costs left a lower margin for distributors and retailers to actively 'push' their products through intensive marketing. Thus wholesale and retail distribution (including their advertising expenditures) comprised only 45 per cent of the retail price in Britain, compared to 52.5 per cent in the United States.

Governance of the 1920s value chain was dominated by Marconi, who had control over key patents and determined their price, plus the ways in which these were combined with non-patented inputs (via its package licence, discussed in Chapter 6). However, this control was tempered by the valve makers, whose development of more complex, multi-functional valves both reduced manufacturers' patent liabilities and had some impact on internal set design. Manufacturers also had some control over internal design (within limits set by the patent holders) and controlled product differentiation—through branding, cabinet designs, 'features' (such as innovative tuning dials), and marketing. Moreover, set manufacturers constituted the chief source of governance over the distribution section of the value chain, determining list prices, discounts, and—from time to time—trade-in allowances and HP terms.

As shown in Chapter 6, during the 1930s the governance function of Marconi was weakened by the expiry of its fundamental patents and the development of rival patent pools. Meanwhile the largest valve manufacturers increased their governance role, by tying patent provision to valve purchase, under contracts which required set manufacturers to gain their approval for the receiver circuits used. However, successful set manufacturers experienced the greatest gains in value chain governance, typically developing authorized dealerships and direct-to-dealer distribution systems, while using their market power to negotiate favourable terms for valves and patent licences. All of this was dependent on their development of strong, successful brands. This process is examined in the following sections.

## VISUALLY DIFFERENTIATING THE BRAND—CABINET DESIGN

Promoting distinctive brands that would inspire consumer confidence and loyalty required cabinets which were both attractive and identified the brand at a glance, despite annual model changes. Cabinet design became particularly important during the 1930s, as radio manufacturers adopted broadly similar technical solutions to the problems of fidelity of reception, selectivity between stations, and sensitivity to radio signals. Manufacturers' promotional material still stressed technological improvements, but these increasingly involved 'commercial innovations' such as the display on the tuning dial, rather than technical fundamentals. Moreover, consumers treated radios as prized pieces of furniture, similar to the piano or cased clock of earlier times, which made outward appearance a key factor in their choice between brands and models.

In 1937 Nikolaus Pevsner singled out wireless cabinets as the only area of manufacturing where the best British models led the world in design.[10] Pye had introduced its distinctive fretwork rising sun over waves grille as early as 1927, which was capitalized on by its distinctively modernist advertising (see Fig. 7.1), though the specific design was said to have been copied from a cigarette case.[11] However, from the early 1930s several firms began to use leading professional designers, whose activities were integrated into the overall engineering design process.[12] The leading innovators were two recently established independent set makers, Murphy and Ekco (Fig. 7.2). Frank Murphy approached furniture designer Gordon Russell (a pioneer of high-quality functionalist furniture using mechanized techniques).[13] Gordon's brother, Dick, designed a set which produced a hostile reaction from Murphy's dealers (one christened it the 'Pentonville' on account of the prison-like speaker grill). Yet Murphy made a virtue out of this—as Dick Russell observed, 'One point that emerges from the various letters received is that the cabinet is either thoroughly disliked or thoroughly liked, and I think that this is an encouraging sign.'[14]

A similarly distinctive policy was followed by Ekco (which, like Murphy, was also noted for the high-quality, performance, and reliability of its sets). Ekco's chief engineer, John Wyborn, is said to have realized at an early stage that, 'once technical performance was taken for granted, styling and appearance would become the chief sales point'.[15] Capitalizing on their pioneering use of large Bakelite mouldings, Ekco held a design competition in 1932, which was won by leading British modernist designer Wells Coates and may also have provided their initial contact with other noted Ekco designers, including Serge Chermayeff, Jesse Collins, and Misha Black.[16] While Chermayeff's slightly more conventional Ekco 74 went into production first, in 1933, Wells' unprecedented circular design, introduced in 1934 as the AD65, proved their great breakthrough. Using Bakelite to produce a cabinet shape that would have been impossible in wood, Wells created both a design icon and one of the most popular radios of the 1930s—inspiring a

[10] Nikolaus Pevsner, *An Enquiry into Industrial Art in England* (Cambridge: Cambridge University Press, 1937), 101.

[11] Geddes and Bussey, *Setmakers*, 133.

[12] Gordon Russell, *Designer's Trade: Autobiography of Gordon Russell* (London: Allen & Unwin, 1968), 149–54; Fiona MacCarthy, 'Russell, Sir (Sydney) Gordon (1892–1980)', *Oxford Dictionary of National Biography*, Internet version.

[13] Russell, *Designer's Trade*, 147.

[14] R. D. Russell, 'The A24 Cabinet', *Murphy News* (4 Feb. 1934), 3–4.

[15] Michael Lipman, *Memoirs of a Socialist Businessman* (London: Lipman Trust, 1980), 70.

[16] Sheban Cantacuzino, *Wells Coates: A Monograph* (London: Fraser, 1978), 24.

**Fig. 7.1.** A distinctively modernist 1929 advert for the Pye Portable Radio, featuring its iconic 'sunrise over waves' motif

*Source*: Peter Scott collection.

# MURPHY

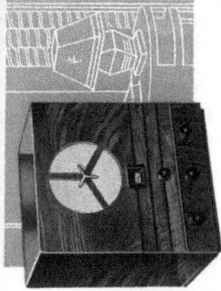

WE believe it is true to say that the first thing that impresses one when listening to a Murphy is the unusual beauty of tone.

When you have tested the set for yourself and found how easy it is to work, what volume and selectivity you have—then you will certainly be tempted to buy it.

And if you do buy it we think you will never regret your choice, because above all we aim to make Murphy sets reliable.

**MURPHY A.4.** This is a 4 valve all electric super-heterodyne receiver *for use on A.C. electricity only*. It is fitted with self-contained moving coil loudspeaker, and the cabinet is finished in Walnut and Rosewood. Single tuning control. Illuminated wavelength dial. Will receive British and many Continental stations. Very selective which extremely high quality of reproduction. Fitted with gramophone jack and extra loudspeaker sockets.
*Size 15½" high × 11½" wide × 10¼" deep.*

**MURPHY D.4.** Exactly the same in specification and performance as the A.4, but for use on D.C. electricity only.

**MURPHY B.5.** This is a 5 valve battery super-heterodyne receiver for use by those who have no electricity. Cabinet and specification as A.4 above.

Models A.4, D.4 or B.5.

Cash Price **£14.10.0** Hire Purchase Terms Available

**MURPHY A.8.** An 8 valve superheterodyne receiver for use on A.C. electricity only.

We know of no other set which has quite the same beauty of tone, gives such a choice of stations or is so simple to work.

This set is the only British set that is fitted with AUTOMATIC VOLUME CONTROL operated by a valve specially developed for Murphy Radio. The "fading" of foreign programmes is eliminated. All stations come in at about the same volume from a whisper to full power according to your choice. Moving Coil Loudspeaker, Walnut cabinet. Fitted with gramophone jack.
*Size 17" high × 24" wide × 13" deep.*

Cash Price **£24.0.0** Hire Purchase Terms Available

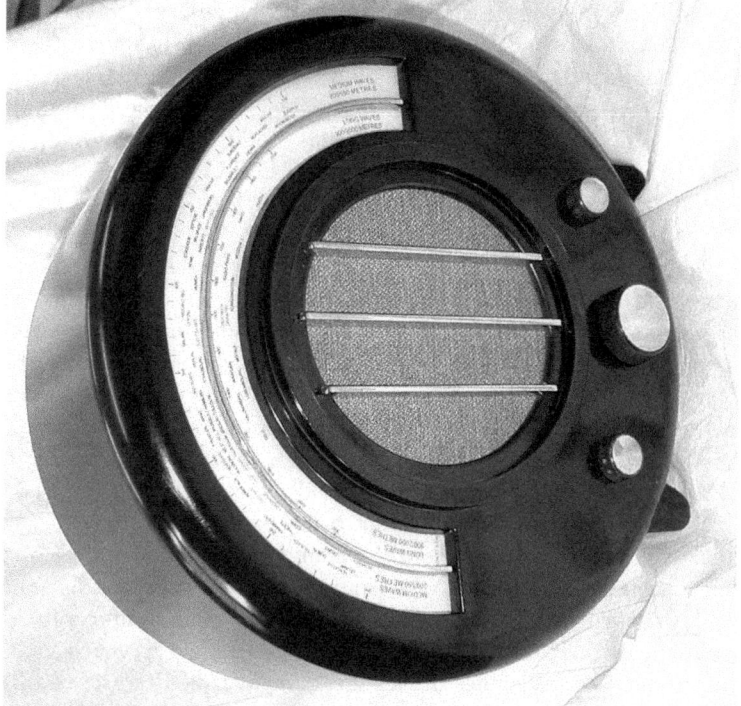

**Fig. 7.2.** Iconic British radio designs of the 1930s: Murphy A4 and A8 (left); Ekco AD 65 (right)

*Sources*: Murphy, Murphy Radio Catalogue, 1933 (reproduced by kind permission of Dave Grant); Ekco, generously provided by Southend Central Museum, Ekco collection.

range of circular Ekco receivers that greatly enhanced brand recognition.[17] As Pevsner noted, 'Chermayeff's and Wells Coates's models are conspicuous even in the worst shop window, and every child recognises them as Ekco sets.'[18]

## COMMUNICATING THE BRAND TO THE PUBLIC—MANUFACTURER ADVERTISING

While distinctive design assisted the development of a strong brand image, successful advertising was essential to communicating that image to the public. It was estimated that in 1935 manufacturers spent £1,100,000 on advertising for radio sets and radiograms, equivalent to 9.0 per cent of net sales (at factory gate values), compared to 4.16 per cent for all household equipment and entertainment goods.[19] Meanwhile radio sets, valves, components, accessories, batteries, and accumulators collectively accounted for 1.88 per cent of press display advertising, or 39.75 per cent of that for all household equipment and entertainment goods.[20]

Several leading figures in the British radio industry had backgrounds in advertising, including Frank Murphy, C. O. Stanley (who became Pye's chief executive), and Richard Haigh (English manager of EMI's Gramophone Co. subsidiary).[21] The advertising trade press criticized much radio advertising, due to its undifferentiated nature and lack of 'story'.[22] However, an advocate of the prevailing approach countered that similarities in the appearance and features of many radios were necessarily reflected in their advertising, while a straightforward picture of the receiver was better than contextual illustrations which might obscure important features.[23]

To examine the advertising strategies of the major radio brands, we have conducted a content analysis of every *Radio Times* radio/radiogram display advertisement over the peak October–December radio sales period, for 1931 and 1936 (excluding radios offered for coupons or rental), together with ads appearing in *The Times* for the whole of 1934 and 1938. Each insertion is classified separately (even those identical to previous ads) according to its most prominent single appeal. However,

[17] Ibid.; Fiona MacCarthy, 'Coates, Wells Wintemute (1895–1958)', *Oxford Dictionary of National Biography*, Internet version.

[18] Pevsner, *Enquiry into Industrial Art*, 106.

[19] Nicholas Kaldor and Rodney Silverman, *A Statistical Analysis of Advertising Expenditure and of the Revenue of the Press* (Cambridge: Cambridge University Press, 1948), 145–6. Similarly, Jefferys, *Distribution of Consumer Goods*, 300, estimated that in 1938 advertising comprised 9–10 per cent of manufacturers' sales revenue.

[20] Kaldor and Silverman, *Statistical Analysis*, 22.

[21] Joan Long, *A First Class Job! The Story of Frank Murphy, Radio Pioneer, Furniture Designer and Industrial Idealist* (Sheringham: Joan Long, 1985), 19–22; Mark Frankland, *Radio Man: The Remarkable Rise and Fall of C. O. Stanley* (London: Institution of Electrical Engineers, 2002), 20–23; 'Autolycus' (pseudonym), 'The All-Electric Advertising Man: Richard Haigh, English Manager of the Gramophone Company, Talks to us about Radio (and Records)', *Advertising World* (Apr. 1934), 181–2 (181).

[22] 'Crane' (pseudonym), 'Radio's Obscure Publicity', *Advertising World* (Sept. 1934), 44–46 (44); 'You Saw These Too', *Advertising World*, 67 (Aug.–Sept. 1935), 66–8 (67).

[23] V. Stanbridge Homewood, 'Radio's Efficient Publicity: A Reply to "Crane" by V. Stanbridge Homewood', *Advertising World*, 66 (Oct. 1934), 38–40 (40).

as many advertisements made multiple appeals, some could not be classified, because no single message dominated. Meanwhile others defied classification, as their main appeal was a general assertion of the brand's strength. Some 176 advertisements were identified, though for some companies the sample size was rather low and for these, additional press ads were examined for the 1930s using two ephemera collections held by the Bodleian Library (data for those companies with additional sampling are shown in bold in Table 7.2). This raised the overall sample size to 211 (with 196 for the fourteen classified companies). Advertising strategies were also checked against publicity brochures, using the National Library of Art's Ekco trade catalogue collection and the Bodleian's John Johnson collection.

Corroborating *Advertising World's* analysis, the majority of manufacturers focused on specific claims regarding the merits and characteristics of their receivers—though, while this approach may have produced criticism from some advertising pundits, this does not necessarily mean that it was ineffective. Meanwhile three of the largest radio manufacturers—Philips, Pye, and HMV—adopted policies of asserting the general strength of their brands, with slogans such as Philips' 'Tomorrow's Radio—Today' or Pye's 'The Greatest Modern Radio'. As Haigh noted in 1932, EMI used advertising to increase public awareness that '"His Master's Voice" means radio—and radio as good in quality as the records and gramophones which bear the dog-mark.'[24] Conversely, Kolster-Brandes adopted a price-leadership approach, which was also reflected in their brochures—'KB inexpensive radio is no mere catch phrase.'[25] This was assisted by their use of cheaper American-type valves, provided by their parent company, International Telephone and Telegraph Corporation.[26]

Three firms—Murphy, Bush, and Radio-Gramophone Development Co. (RGD)—used a 'conversational' approach. This was pioneered by Murphy during the early 1930s, in a campaign that received acclaim from both the radio and advertising trade. Founded in 1929 by the visionary, mercurial Frank Murphy—whose non-conformist socialist background strongly influenced his approach to business—Murphy Radio was one of the most innovative radio manufacturers of the 1930s. Murphy enjoyed a well-deserved reputation for excellence that encompassed technical quality and reliability, cabinet designs, and advertising.[27] Murphy Radio had produced some 214,178 sets by December 1935 with a total wholesale value of £2,363,000, and had spent £264,407 on advertising.[28] Rupert Casson (co-founder of Frank Murphy's former advertising agency, Arks Publicity) based the campaign around Murphy's visionary, eccentric personality and theories for making wireless simple and reliable, with adverts that featured a large photograph

[24] 'Autolycus' (pseudonym), 'All-Electric Advertising Man', 182.
[25] National Art library, Ekco trade catalogue collection, 'Koster-Brandes inexpensive radio', brochure (n.d., 1930s).
[26] J. W. Stokes, *70 years of Radio Valves and Tubes* (New York: Vestal, 1982), 205.
[27] Geddes and Bussey, *Setmakers*, 157–64.
[28] Hertfordshire Archives, Sir Frederic Osborn Archive (hereafter HA/SFOA), Murphy Radio Ltd, draft notes for prospectus by F. J. Osborn, 23 Apr. 1936.

Table 7.2. A content analysis of the main messages of 211 radio/radiogram press display advertisements during the 1930s

| | New model/ features | Price/value | Performance/reliability, simplicity | Special characteristics | Conversational | Difficult to classify | Total |
|---|---|---|---|---|---|---|---|
| **Specific brand claims** | | | | | | | |
| Cossor | | **3** | **2** | **2** | | **3** | **10** |
| Ekco | **3** | **1** | **5** | **3** | | **1** | **12** |
| Ferranti | **3** | **1** | **2** | **2** | | **5** | **13** |
| GEC | 4 | 1 | 6 | | | 4 | 15 |
| Lissen | | 1 | 4 | | | 1 | 6 |
| Marconiphone | | 3 | 6 | | | 2 | 11 |
| Philco | **3** | **3** | **2** | | | **1** | **9** |
| **General brand assertion** | | | | | | | |
| HMV | 1 | 5 | 16 | 7 | | 13 | 42 |
| Philips | 3 | 1 | 3 | | | 5 | 12 |
| Pye | | 1 | 1 | | | 10 | 12 |
| **Price appeal** | | | | | | | |
| Kolster-Brandes | | **9** | | | | | **9** |
| **Conversational approach** | | | | | | | |
| Bush | | | | | 7 | | 7 |
| Murphy | | | | | 26 | | 26 |
| RGD | | | 2 | | 8 | 2 | 12 |
| **Others** | | 3 | 3 | 5 | | 4 | 15 |
| **Total** | 17 | 31 | 52 | 19 | 41 | 51 | 211 |

Sources: Radio Times, October–December issues for 1931 and 1936; Times Digital Archive, all issues for 1934 and 1938. Figures in bold denote cases where a low sample size from these sources was boosted by adverts in the Bodleian Library's Bielik collection, boxes 6–9 and 16–17, and John Johnson collection, Wireless Box 1.

of Murphy and his pipe (Fig. 7.3).[29] His series of 'conversations' between Murphy and the public had precedents in the Mr Drage, Mr Everyman ads of the 1920s, but with the extra element of featuring an identifiable human being.[30]

Rather than talking up technical performance—in the superlatives typical of the period—Murphy used understated copy, often with a strong element of self-deprecating humour. For example, ads for their Russell-designed radios foreshadowed the celebrated 1960 VW Beetle 'Lemon' campaign, emphasizing their unusual and initially off-putting design (similar to 1940s utility furniture). An April 1934 advert bore the headline, "'…the longer you look at it the more you like it!'" followed by: 'There is a big disagreement of opinion about the A.24 Cabinet design and quite a lot of people think we ought to change it and given you "something that everybody will like". Well, I'm not going to change it, but I do think you are entitled to know why.'[31] Murphy then explained that Russell's ideal of beauty in machine-made furniture required some time for full appreciation, concluding with the statement that had headlined the ad. A candid, low-pressure, style inspired public confidence. As Casson noted, 'the advertising deals with realities, and not with the usual fantasies and extravagances. We talk…as frankly and naturally as though we were talking privately to an individual…We *discuss* problems and admit other points of view…We are not always on our dignity, and we don't mind printing a joke at our own expense.'[32]

Murphy used his conversational ads to address the public on a number of themes close to his heart. For example, a 1933 advert carried the headline, 'I dare not write home to Madge and tell her I've lost my job!' Murphy then explained that this was taken from a letter by one of the firm's workers, who had been given a week's notice, owing to the summer downturn in wireless demand. Similar adverts followed, urging the public to buy radios in the summer to avoid seasonal unemployment. One pledged the firm to 'spend thousands of pounds on advertising, at the time when it produces the least results. If anyone says this is a stunt to sell Murphy sets, then he is an ass.'[33] This successful appeal, like others dealing with contemporary topics, worked by creating a rapport through its frank and personal tone, which inspired public confidence.

Like the Mr Drage ads of the 1920s, Murphy used fresh adverts for each of his fortnightly conversations with the public, to keep the reader interested with a new and endlessly changing script.[34] As *Advertising World* noted, 'Whenever we saw that familiar head and pipe we were sure of reading a human, interesting and often extremely diverting piece of copy. So were the general public.'[35] Murphy's

[29] Long, *First Class Job!*, 34.
[30] See Peter Scott, 'Mr Drage, Mr Everyman, and the Creation of a Mass Market for Domestic Furniture in Interwar Britain', *Economic History Review*, 62 (2009), 802–27.
[31] Murphy Radio advert, *Radio Times* (6 Apr. 1934), reprinted in Long, *First Class Job!*, 70.
[32] C. R. Casson, 'Murphy Advertising, 1934', *Murphy News* (Nov. 1934), 3–4.
[33] Cited in E. S. Turner, *The Shocking History of Advertising* (Harmondsworth: Penguin, 1965), 185–6.
[34] 'Advertisers', *Advertising World* (June 1937), 33.
[35] 'You Saw These, Too', *Advertising World* (June 1937), 50–5 (52). Unfortunately Murphy's increasingly autocratic and capricious attitude towards his dealers (and his fellow directors) eventually led to problems which contributed to a decline in Murphy Radio's sales and the departure of Frank Murphy from the company in January 1937. Long, *First Class Job!*, 87–8 and 106; Geddes and Bussey, *Setmakers*, 165–7.

**I listened to a**

# MURPHY

## BUT I DIDN'T BUY ONE

THAT cheerful remark was made to me the other day, and this is how the gentleman went on:

"The fact is I can't afford a Murphy, but I wanted to get as near as I could to its naturalness of tone. So I listened to one of your sets and tested half-a-dozen other makes against it. In the end I chose a ——— and I reckon it's pretty good."

Well, it's nice to be told that our sets are "the standard by which other sets are judged," but we knew that already! We would rather the gentleman had *bought* a Murphy and *he* would have

been wiser to do so. "Pretty good" won't satisfy for long a man who wanted something better. Our claim is that *no* set generally available to the public has the naturalness of tone of a Murphy.

And our friend quite forgot another vital matter which he wasn't able to test—reliability. The proof of Murphy reliability lies in the price you can get for a second-hand Murphy.

With prices from £11 and Hire Purchase Terms available, the "can't afford it" argument just won't stand up. The fact is it is *cheaper* to buy a Murphy. I think I'll make a "slogan" of that phrase.

*Table Models from* £11. *Console Models from* £14 . 15s. *Radiogramophones from* £24 . 10s. *These prices do not apply in I.F.S.*

*Frank Murphy*

FOR THE NAME OF YOUR NEAREST MURPHY DEALER PLEASE WRITE TO MURPHY RADIO, LTD., WELWYN GARDEN CITY, HERTS.

**Fig. 7.3.** An August 1935 Murphy conversational advertisement
*Source*: Peter Scott collection.

conversational adverts were widely copied. For example, their rival Bush launched a broadly similar campaign, even including their own 'pipe-smoking man'—the popular radio broadcaster Christopher Stone acting as their public face.[36]

## THE BRITISH RADIO DEALER

Like radio manufacturers, many early radio stores were founded by amateur wireless enthusiasts who wanted to turn their hobby into a career (their skills commanding a premium in an era when radios required substantial after-sales service). Many also developed from existing retail businesses. Bicycle retailers were a major source of entrants to the early trade, often initially as a sideline. Like radio, the bicycle trade required workshops and a degree of mechanical knowledge, while two leading national radio wholesalers, Lugtons and Brown Brothers, had their origins in this sector and no doubt encouraged their retailer customers to consider this profitable new market. Others diversified into radio from related trades such as electrical or gas lighting suppliers, ironmongers, furnishers, and dealers in musical instruments and gramophones.[37]

Radio retailing was characterized by an unusually high proportion of independent retailers (rather than chain, department, or cooperative stores), principally owing to strong resale price maintenance that removed the price advantage of large-scale retailers. However, there were a few successful chains that sold radios as one of their major lines. The largest was Currys, with 135 branches in 1925 and 221 by 1938. Currys was a cycle dealer that diversified into radio equipment, though by the early 1930s radio dominated its overall sales. In addition to selling manufacturers' brands, Currys also manufactured radios from March 1931, initially via a subsidiary, Belcher Ltd.[38] Currys' largest competitor was J. & F. Stone Ltd, which dealt in radio equipment and lighting, heating, and cooking appliances. This firm had some 160 branches and, in 1936, formed Chain Stores Finance Trust Ltd to take over its HP business.[39] Max Stone Ltd operated a similar type of business, with over sixty branches run from their London head office. It also established a subsidiary, Stores Trust Ltd, to finance its HP agreements.[40] The only other radio and electrical retailer with more than fifty branches in 1939 was Lloyds Retailers Ltd.[41]

Data on the performance of British radio retailers are much scarcer than for their US counterparts. However, in 1934 Murphy conducted a survey of twenty-two authorized dealers. Their annual turnover per employee averaged £893, while turnover per square foot of selling space averaged £6 9s.[42] More broadly based data,

[36] Geddes and Bussey, *Setmakers*, 173.
[37] J. B. Jefferys, *Retail Trading in Britain: 1850–1950* (Cambridge: Cambridge University Press, 1954), 405–6; Geddes and Bussey, *Setmakers*, 32–3.
[38] Harry Lerner, *Currys: The First 100 Years* (Cambridge: Woodhead-Faulkner, 1984), 35–7 and 112.
[39] TNA, BT64/296, unsigned memorandum, 26 June 1945.
[40] Ibid.     [41] Jefferys, *Retail Trading*, 407.
[42] 'Factors in Retailing', *Murphy News* (29 June 1935), 3–4.

covering 125 of Murphy's 780 dealers, suggested that their average turnover for radio sets was £2,540 per annum, representing 82 per cent of total turnover (the balance being high tension batteries, valves, etc.).[43] Murphy later claimed that—on the basis of data collected from its dealers—rent, advertising, and canvassing made the following relative contributions to sales revenue: 'Turnover = 27.2 * Rent + 13.7 *Advertising cost + 8 * canvassing cost.'[44]

Murphy's identification of store location as by far the most important determinant of sales revenue appears at odds with the findings of the US dealer survey discussed in Chapter 5. However, this may reflect the fact that British people relied much more on public transport (which mainly radiates out from urban centres) than personal transport—the expansion of which had initiated a trend towards the suburbanization of US retailers by the 1930s. On the basis of these findings, Murphy sought to persuade dealers to move to central shopping pitches, which he termed the 'Woolworth site'.[45] Over a hundred dealers followed his advice, producing, according to Murphy's biography, a major increase in turnover.[46]

## PROMOTING THE BRAND TO THE TRADE

Radio manufacturers initially promoted their new sets to the trade (and to the public) principally via exhibitions, the most important of which was Radiolympia, held in September until 1931 and in the second half of August thereafter.[47] Until 1938 radio-frequency feeds were not provided at Radiolympia stands, thus visitors could not actually listen to the radios on display.[48] Some manufacturers lost confidence in the value of Radiolympia. Frank Murphy believed that it was not worth showing radios when people could not listen to them, that its audience was essentially London based, attendance figures were small relative to the national market, and it was held at the wrong time of year.[49] Instead he advocated retailer-based promotions, backed up by national press advertising.[50] Similarly, Philco did not exhibit at Radiolympia in 1935 but held a 'National Exhibition scheme' in September, with some 1,257 retailers staging their own store-based shows.[51]

Sets were initially supplied to dealers mainly through established wholesalers.[52] EMI was an exception, as it was able to extend its long-established system of direct supply relationships with HMV dealers to its new radio operations. EMI emphasized the importance of strong dealerships; as Haigh noted, radios 'aren't sold until they have been bought by *their* customer. Its *our* job to get people into the shops,

[43] Frank Murphy, 'About the Rent Theory', *Murphy News* (June 1935), 21–3.
[44] E. W. Kent, 'Distribution 1935 and 1936', *Murphy News* (11 Jan. 1936), 3–7 (3). Advertising refers to local advertising by the dealer.
[45] Long, *First Class Job!*, 85.      [46] Ibid.
[47] Geddes and Bussey, *Setmakers*, 204.      [48] Ibid.
[49] Frank Murphy, 'Olympia', *Murphy News* (5 Aug. 1933), 3.
[50] 'Your Radio Exhibition—is Here!', *Murphy News* (5 Aug. 1933), 4–5.
[51] 'Campaigns ', *Advertising World* (Feb. 1936), 79–83 (83).
[52] Geddes and Bussey, *Setmakers*, 204.

and then it's up to the dealers. And all of us here believe that a demonstration of our instruments is the finest possible means of clinching a sale.'[53] They therefore provided a variety of support and advisory services for dealers, including coordinating their advertising with them and providing training classes in radio servicing.[54]

Leading independents such as Ekco and Murphy followed EMI's example in providing a range of support services to dealers. Ekco's consumer advertising was supported by intensive publicity in the trade press, cooperative advertising with retailers in local papers, and generous supplies of sales aids and literature to dealers to win their cooperation and loyalty.[55] Its advertising agency, Willing Service, argued that the aim of their advertising, 'should be to direct the public to the radio dealer...once this has been achieved it is a comparatively easy matter for the dealer to effect the sale. These factors govern the policy behind every Ekco campaign, special attention being given at all times to strengthening and extension of dealer goodwill.'[56] Willing Service used simple, direct, copy and simple illustrations, based around the slogan, 'WHAT DO *YOU* THINK OF THE NEW EKCO RADIO?' Adverts offered £50 and a free EKCO receiver as a prize to people who witnessed a local dealer's EKCO demonstration and then wrote not more than 50 words answering this question.[57]

A 1932 leaflet advised dealers that, 'a definite "tie-up" between our advertising and your shop is essential if you are to enjoy the full benefit of the EKCO campaigns. This vital link is provided by the new range of EKCO Sales Aids and Window Display material...Because we are anxious for you to gain the maximum benefit from the EKCO advertising appropriation, we have spent thousands of pounds on new display material. Highly paid experts have designed the Window Displays and Sales Aids...their work is now at your service free of charge.'[58] The leaflet included examples of show cards, posters, etc. and showed how these could be used to create attractive window displays.

Murphy pursued a similar strategy, including launching an in-house journal, *Murphy News*, to communicate with their dealers, advise on various aspects of retail practice (such as window display, advertising, showrooms, service departments, accounting, management, and staff training), and coordinate advertising.[59] Murphy also used this to showcase the display items available free to dealers, including leaflets, show cards, posters, window display material, cinema slide shows, and adverts for fixing to the sides of dealers' vans. More expensive items, such as neon doorway signs, required some payment from the dealer. Murphy also engaged in cooperative advertising with dealers, from around 1933, for both press adverts and circulars.

[53] 'Autolycus' (pseudonym), 'All-Electric Advertising Man', 182.
[54] EMI Archives, file: Gramophone & radio manufacture 1931–7, 'The Marketing of Radio and Radio-Gramophones', address by Mr Godfrey to EMI branch managers' convention, March 1931.
[55] Southend Museum Service [hereafter SOUMS], file of uncatalogued material, Willing Service, 'Who's doing the EKCO Radio Advertising', brochure (n.d., *c.*1935).
[56] Ibid.     [57] Ibid.
[58] SOUMS, file of uncatalogued material, EKCO, 'Window Displays Sales-Aids and Literature 1932–3' (leaflet, 1932).
[59] *Murphy News* (issues for 1933–9).

Around 40 per cent of all Murphy stockists were reported to be participating in either their press advertising and/or circular schemes.[60]

By 1936 Philco were running a cooperative advertising programme whereby they contributed 25 per cent to the cost of retailer advertising previously approved by the distributor, while 25 per cent was paid for by the distributor and 50 per cent by the retailer (up to a certain maximum). The scheme covered newspaper adverts, posters and hoardings, and cinema advertising, which Philco regarded as the most effective media for dealer publicity. Philco also supplied advertising blocks, lay-outs, copy, and cinema slides for the campaign, free of charge.[61]

Murphy was the first of the independent set makers (firms without valve production interests) to develop direct links with their retailers, introducing a 'Limited Dealer Scheme' in October 1930, to eliminate wholesaler margins and ensure customers received adequate after-sales service.[62] Direct relationships with all Murphy retail outlets also made it easier to negotiate on issues such as trade discounts. In November 1932 Murphy asked their dealers to accept a 25 per cent discount instead of the standard 33.3 per cent so that (together with other economies, including a 10 per cent wage reduction for his workers) list prices could be reduced (from £19 19s to £12 10s for their A3A model). Following negotiations a discount of 27.5 per cent was agreed, reducing the price of the A3A to £13 10s.[63]

Murphy's actions set a precedent for other major manufacturers. During 1933 several leading set makers shifted from wholesaler distribution to direct-to-dealer schemes. Meanwhile nine firms agreed to standardize 27.5 per cent as their basic discount to dealers, reversing the previous trend of rising retailer discounts.[64] In June 1933 Pye switched to selling solely through 3,000 appointed retailers, justifying this in terms of the need to prevent price-cutting and ensure that dealers provided adequate after-sales service.[65] However, their selection was said to have been done in some haste, without the careful vetting employed by Murphy. Moreover, their wholesalers reacted by spoiling the market for the new retailers by dumping their stocks of Pye sets, resulting in a 30 per cent fall in sales for the two months following the switch relative to the same period in 1932.[66] Ferranti had also considered such a move, owing to perceptions that, while wholesalers performed their stocking, distribution, and accounting functions well, they failed to actively 'sell' Ferranti sets to retailers.[67] However, they do not appear to have followed through with this

[60] 'Advertisers', *Advertising World*, 69, 6 (June 1937), 33.

[61] 'Revision of Co-operative Advertising Scheme', *Philco News* (6 May 1937), 10.

[62] HA/SFOA, L1, Murphy Radio Ltd, draft notes for prospectus by F. J. Osborn, 23 Apr. 1936; Long, *First Class Job!*, 3.

[63] Long, *First Class Job!*, 75–7 and 114.

[64] 'The Trend of Prices and Discounts', *Wireless and Gramophone Trader* (25 Mar. 1933), 328–9; 'Story of an Industry', *Wireless and Electrical Trader* (25 Mar. 1944), 342.

[65] C. O. Stanley, 'Why we Switched to Direct Selling', *Business* (June 1934), 18–19.

[66] Frankland, *Radio Man*, 59.

[67] MMSI, Ferranti, 1996.10/10/1/7/409, C. P. Beardsall, 'Suggestions for a Reorganisation of the Radio Selling Force of the Company with a view to Obtaining High Efficiency at Reasonable Cost', report (5 Jan. 1933).

(possibly on account of their weak brand reputation).[68] Direct dealership schemes rapidly grew in popularity over the 1930s; the proportion of radios distributed through wholesalers fell from over 75 per cent in 1933 to only around 20–25 per cent by the late 1930s.[69]

Direct-to-dealer distribution undermined wholesalers' support for the Mutual Trading Agreement (MTA)—initiated in the autumn of 1931, which required wholesalers and retailers to respect manufacturers' terms regarding list prices, discounts, HP, and so forth. The MTA also prevented them from stocking the products of firms subject to radio trade boycotts—particularly foreign manufacturers. Originally signed by eleven manufacturers (responsible for about 80 per cent of British production) and 200 wholesalers, by June 1933 it encompassed forty-five manufacturers and 230 wholesalers.[70] In November 1932, under pressure from the Wireless Retailers Association, MTA signatories also agreed to boycott cooperative societies, unless undertakings were given that no dividend would be paid on the goods supplied. This eventually led the Cooperative Wholesale Society to introduce their own range of aptly named 'Defiant' radios (produced for the Cooperative Wholesale Society by Plessey).[71]

In March 1938 some 100 wholesalers withdrew from the MTA, which consequently broke down.[72] Shortly afterwards a meeting of radio manufacturers who still sold through wholesalers (attended by GEC, Decca, Ferranti, Ever Ready-Lissen, Philips, Burndept-Vidor, Whiteley, Alba, and RGD, with Kolster-Brandes and Ultra sending apologies), considered their position. The agreement's collapse would leave wholesalers free to distribute 'foreign-content' sets such as Philco, Pilot, Ferguson, and Sparton. It was agreed to offer wholesalers a new agreement whereby they confined their activities to RMA members' sets, any wholesaler declining to do so being boycotted by them. However, not surprisingly, the wholesalers rejected this ultimatum and it was reported that Philco were seeking their business. 'The Great Eastern Boys' (major wholesalers such as Hobday, Brown Brothers, and East London Rubber Co.) were said to believe that their interests would be better served by the foreign-content producers than by what was left of RMA's wholesale business.[73]

Despite the strength of trade boycotts, particularly strong brands could still operate outside the MTA framework, as shown by the example of Philco's UK subsidiary. In 1931 the BVA specifically refused to manufacture the US-type valves Philco wished to use, despite assurances that they were willing to fit a British valve base and fall into line with BVA list prices (which they considered too high), and

---

[68] Geddes and Bussey, *Setmakers*, 114.

[69] 'The Trend in Discounts', *Wireless and Electrical Trader* (19 Mar. 1932), 338; Jefferys, *Distribution of Consumer Goods*, 299; MMSI, Ferranti, 1996.10/10/1/7/409, memorandum by Mr Beardsall, 2 Apr. 1938.

[70] TNA, BT64/296, unsigned memorandum, 26 June 1945.

[71] Ibid.; John F. Wilson, Anthony Webster, and Rachel Vorberg-Rugh, *Building Co-operation: A Business History of the Co-operative Group, 1863–2013* (Oxford: Oxford University Press, 2013), 191–6; Geddes and Bussey, *Setmakers*, 178.

[72] TNA, BT64/296, unsigned memorandum, 26 June 1945.

[73] MMSI, Ferranti, 1996.10/10/1/7/409, memorandum by Mr Beardsall, 2 Apr. 1938.

trade discounts (which they considered too low). Philco therefore imported its valves, though it later began to purchase American-type valves from British suppliers. However, even in 1938 the BVA still refused to allow any Philco wholesaler to sell valves made by its members. Philco consequently eschewed participation in the various radio manufacturers' organizations, but nevertheless found numerous retailers (many regarded by the trade as not being first-rate dealers) who were prepared to stock its brand.[74]

As in the United States, home demonstration was a popular method of closing the sale. However, demonstrations were generally initiated by a customer's visit to the dealer's store, rather than through house-to-house canvassing.[75] Manufacturers vigorously promoted home demonstration. A Pye marketing leaflet advised prospective purchasers that:

> To appreciate the striking realism of the reproduction, the delightful simplicity of the controls, the extreme selectivity of the tuning, the remarkable range of programmes easily obtainable, demonstration is essential. And it is so easy to demonstrate the new Pye Twintriple Portable in your own home. See the effect of this beautiful instrument among your own furnishings, hear the irresistible quality of its reproduction on radio or on gramophone, experience for yourself the simplicity of operation and the ease of portability by requesting a home demonstration from your local Pye Service Agent.[76]

Kolster-Brandes tried selling radios door-to-door, from around spring 1930. They claimed to have noticed that their most entrepreneurial authorized dealers were circularizing or canvassing homes, offering free demonstrations. In addition to boosting turnover and reducing the magnitude of the summer sales slump, they argued that radios were obviously suited to direct selling, as their advantages were best illustrated by demonstration. They thus launched a 'Direct Sales *Assistance* Scheme', in cooperation with participating dealers (who accepted a lower margin on such sales to cover the cost of the service). Their salesmen—who presented themselves as employees of the local dealer—were sent out expressly, 'to sell three things—firstly the general idea of radio, then K-B radio, and finally K-B radio on hire purchase terms'.[77] As their sales supervisor, R. G. A. Staples, noted:

> The work of these men is to 'sell' their prospective customers on the benefits of *radio in the home* and it is from the demonstrations which the personality and persistence of these salesmen secure, that sales come. In other words, they are not merely taking orders from prospective buyers, but are *creating new business from a section of the public who have not yet realised the benefits of radio*...[78]

However, there is no evidence that door-to-door canvassing ever became widespread in Britain for radio, in contrast to vacuum cleaners, where this was the standard marketing channel for the leading brands (as discussed in Chapter 10). One reason

---

[74] 'Carl Dyer Speaks to You', *Philco News* (26 May 1938), 4.

[75] Geddes and Bussey, *Setmakers*, 204.

[76] Bodleian, Bussey, 'The Great New Radio. Radio with the Irresistible Tune', leaflet (n.d., *c.*1930).

[77] Quoted in 'Kolster-Brandes and Direct Selling', *Wireless and Gramophone Trader* (25 Apr. 1931), 87.

[78] Ibid. Emphasis in original.

may have been the relatively high costs of running a direct sales team, with motor vehicle, given Britain's higher petrol and vehicle taxes. While a vacuum cleaner could be manually hauled down the street by the salesman in its demonstration case, radios—comprising glass valves encased in wooden or Bakelite cabinets—were much more vulnerable to damage.

By the late 1930s, HP was estimated to account for around 70–75 per cent of radio sales, in line with other medium/high-value consumer durables.[79] Manufacturers provided HP facilities for dealers, but did not generally use HP terms as an instrument of inter-firm competition. Rapid technical obsolescence, and consequent low resale values led most radio manufacturers to avoid the longer HP terms prevalent in some consumer goods sectors, such as furniture and electrical appliances. As an EMI executive informed a 1931 branch managers' convention, while limiting their HP contracts to only twelve months could be seen as a disadvantage, 'the continued improvement in radio apparatus may make...longer credit periods traps for the unwary'.[80]

Dealers who used manufacturers' HP finance paid an 'accommodation fee' to the manufacturer, varying according to the length of the agreement and whether the dealer was partially or fully responsible for any losses incurred.[81] In July 1932 Ekco charged retailers an accommodation fee of 2.5 per cent, for which it took on responsibility for collecting instalments and all associated risks.[82] Some manufacturers' terms were less generous. For example, in 1934 Murphy offered its dealers HP facilities for contracts of twelve or eighteen months, with accommodation fees of 10 per cent and 15 per cent respectively.[83]

Manufacturers were keen to extend their control over dealers' HP terms, as they wanted to avoid HP being used as a means of cut-throat price competition, which might threaten dealers' ability to engage in promotional and after-sales service activities. Undercutting might involve 'no deposit' terms, or offering a full or partial refund of interest payments if all instalments were met promptly. Major set makers periodically worked collectively to stamp out such practices. For example, in the spring of 1936 fourteen leading manufacturers attempted to impose 'minimum' terms for HP contracts, for both dealers who accepted their finance and those who used independent sources. These covered the retail price (interest typically being added via a price mark-up), the minimum deposit (fixed at 5 per cent of the list price), and the maximum repayment period (eighteen months, or twenty-four months for sets costing over £15 15s). Sets sold on weekly payments would carry an annual interest charge of 10 per cent, plus one shilling per month of the hire period.[84]

[79] Jefferys, *Distribution of Consumer Goods*, 300.

[80] EMI Archives, file: Gramophone & radio manufacture 1931–37, 'The Marketing of Radio and Radio-Gramophones', address by Mr Godfrey to EMI branch managers' convention, March 1931.

[81] 'Hire-Purchase Stability', *Wireless and Gramophone Trader* (23 May 1936), 111–12.

[82] SOUMS, file of uncatalogued material, EKCO, 'Terms of Business and Hire Purchase System', leaflet for trade (July 1932).

[83] *Murphy News* (19 May 1934), 13.

[84] 'Hire-Purchase Stability', *Wireless and Gramophone Trader* (23 May 1936), 111–12; 'SMA Hire-Purchase Plan', *Wireless and Gramophone Trader* (23 May 1936), 130. Sets sold on monthly payments carried lower interest rates.

Such terms appear to have been consistent with prudent retailing practice. For example, in April 1937 Britain's largest radio retailer, Currys, resolved to limit HP terms to eighteen months, with a 5 per cent minimum deposit (and higher percentage minimums for items over £15). However, this was motivated by concerns regarding bad debts, rather than a wish to appease the manufacturers.[85] In March 1936 Murphy Radio estimated that while bad debts on radio HP amounted to only around 1 per cent of retail turnover, when other costs and interest charges were added Murphy's total costs would amount to at least 5 per cent of HP retail turnover. Costs incurred by their dealers on this HP business amounted to about the same proportion of turnover; thus an annual interest rate of 10 per cent per annum would be required just to break even.[86]

Another means of retailer competition via 'terms' was the offer of generous after-sales service. In April 1937 Currys' Executive Committee was informed that they were currently spending up to £40,000 per annum in wages and vehicle running expenses for service visits to wireless customers. It was noted that in the North of England their competitors were providing free service on radios purchased on HP, while in the South it would be easier to charge for service visits after the three months manufacturer's guarantee had expired.[87]

## ALTERNATIVES TO PURCHASE: WIRELESS RELAY SERVICES AND RADIO RENTALS

In 1932, in addition to households that had purchased complete radios for cash, there were some 70,000 that received broadcasts via relay subscriptions, and a larger number that had acquired their set by collecting cigarette coupons (some 320,000 'coupon sets' being distributed over 1931–2). Meanwhile home construction had not entirely died out, with around 500,000 home constructors' sets sold annually (excluding manufacturers' proprietary kits).[88]

Distribution of sets for cigarette coupons was officially terminated by a December 1933 decision of the Tobacco Trade Association to prohibit coupon trading,[89] while technological advances (especially new circuits, such as the super-het, which required calibrated instruments) steadily increased the quality gap between manufacturer-assembled and home-constructed receivers. Nevertheless, it was not a foregone conclusion that nineteen out of twenty households with radio services would obtain them via the purchase of home receivers. Two alternative modes of provision were developed during the inter-war years—relay services and rentals. The first fell fowl of lobbying by the radio industry, while the second

[85] LMA, Acc. 3485/007, Currys Ltd, Executive Committee minutes, 2 Apr. 1937.
[86] HA/SFOA, L1, note, 26 Mar. 1936.
[87] LMA, Acc. 3485/007, Currys Ltd, Executive Committee minutes, 16 Apr. 1937.
[88] 'Licences the Key to Actual Demand', *Wireless and Gramophone Trader* (25 Mar. 1933), 322–5 (324); '1931 Radio Production Reaches £29,750,000', *Wireless and Gramophone Trader* (19 Mar. 1932), 326–7.
[89] 'Story of an Industry', *Wireless and Electrical Trader* (25 Mar. 1944), 342.

established a small foothold in the market, which set a precedent for television rentals during the 1950s.

Monopoly radio broadcasting systems were most easily delivered via a series of high power transmitters, which provided particularly clear reception, for a very limited number of stations. Under such a system the distribution of the most popular channels via wireless relay services was a viable, low-cost means of household radio reception. Indeed, in some countries, such as the Netherlands, a substantial proportion of families listened in via wire relays. Similar systems were introduced in Britain, but with less success.

Wire relay services date back to the nineteenth century (using telephone lines to broadcast entertainment). In 1924 relay services were revived for radio programmes. Mr Maton, a Hythe-based radio retailer, arranged to relay BBC programmes from his own set to his neighbours using wires, for a small charge. The Post Office issued a special licence for relay operators in 1926 and by 1931 there were 132 exchanges and 43,889 subscribers—about 1 per cent of licence holders. The ratio of subscribers to licence holders peaked in 1935 at just over 3 per cent, though the absolute number of subscribers continue to edge upwards, totalling 256,000 by the end of 1938.[90]

Radio relays delivered programmes via loudspeaker terminal units. These provided good sound quality, virtually free of interference, in return for an installation fee and a small weekly payment (typically 1s 6d, plus a hire charge for the loudspeaker). Subscribers avoided both significant repair bills and the rapid depreciation typical of new radio sets. Families lacking mains electricity found them particularly attractive, as they offered the performance standards of a mains set. Their main disadvantage was that most relay services offered only two alternative programmes, though as most ordinary radios were unable to receive more signals with clarity this was often not considered a major problem.[91] Moreover, while choice was limited at any time, the programmes were often selected from the most popular available, sometimes encompassing as many as sixty to seventy stations each week.[92]

Radio relays were of particular attraction to low-income families, for whom the purchase and running costs of a good-quality modern radio were significant and who might find unexpected receiver repair and replacement bills problematic. Moreover, regular weekly payments were more suitable for working-class household budgeting, which was typically undertaken on a week-to-week basis.[93] The development of companies such as Rediffusion Ltd and Radio Central Exchanges Ltd (both founded in 1931), looked set to boost the growth of relay services, but

---

[90] R. H. Coase, 'Wire Broadcasting in Great Britain', *Economica*, 15 (1948), 194–220 (195); Mark Pegg, *Broadcasting and Society 1918–1939* (London: Croom Helm, 1983), 59–60.

[91] Coase, 'Wire Broadcasting'; Sturmey, *Economic Development of Radio*, 242–3.

[92] H. B. Boyd, 'Wireless Relay: A New and Thriving Industry', *Advertising World* (Nov. 1934), 50–51 (51).

[93] Royal Mail Archives, POST 89/36, Ullswater Committee, numbered papers 1–99. Paper No. 38, presented by the Relay Services Association of Great Britain (n.d., *c*.May 1935), 6; Pegg, *Broadcasting and Society*, 58.

this was thwarted by determined opposition from the radio industry and a lack of official support for this low-cost means of radio provision.

Radio manufacturers resented services that would compete with their products and the RMA thus lobbied government to curtail the spread of relays. Radio retailers were similarly antagonistic, lobbying local councils to reject applications for permission to take wires across public spaces. Local retailers also sometimes pressed their local authorities to grant them the concession to develop relays, as a defensive move so that they could ensure that the service was a failure and preserve their more lucrative receiver sales business. Yet some enterprising retailers made genuine efforts to develop successful relay services.[94]

In 1930 a new form of relay licence was introduced, which prohibited relay providers from broadcasting on their own account via relays. It also provided for compulsory purchase of wireless relay plant by the Post Office on the expiry of the licence (originally 1932, later extended to 1936), at a price which made no allowance for the value of the business as a going concern. This policy echoed that applied to the early private telephone companies (discussed in Chapter 12) and had the same effect—discouraging new investment.[95] The 1936 Ullswater Committee report on broadcasting recommended that radio relays should be taken over by the Post Office and control over programming transferred to the BBC. Government rejected this, but extended the licences of private relay services only until the end of 1939, while the unfavourable compulsory purchase terms were retained.[96]

Another option for those who could not afford outright purchase of a radio was renting. Several radio dealers identified this gap in the market. The leading player was Radio Rentals—founded by P. Perring-Toms, a Brighton radio dealer who began renting out sets in around 1930. By 1936 Radio Rentals was a public company with about 50,000 customers.[97] Renting offered both the advantages of spreading payments and an assurance of service—at a time when many sets were of limited reliability and dealers could not always be counted on to provide prompt and reliable servicing.[98] Renting was expensive, but less so than HP. For example one large, unnamed concern, whose terms were reviewed by *Wireless Trader* in December 1934, offered a 13 guinea set (said to be from last year's manufacturer's list) at rentals which fell from 2s 6d a week, in stages, to 2s 6d per month in the fifth year (corresponding to the average expected lifespan of a radio), for a 10s deposit.[99] In 1939 radios were still rented on similar terms.[100]

Radio rental schemes first came to the attention of the radio trade in around 1932, producing substantial opposition from mainstream dealers. These mainly

---

[94] Sturmey, *Economic Development of Radio*, 240.

[95] Coase, 'Wire Broadcasting', 199.      [96] Ibid., 207–14.

[97] UK, Monopolies Commission, *Thorn Electric Industries Ltd and Radio Rentals Ltd. A Report on the Proposed Merger* (London: HMSO, 1968), 15.

[98] 'The Common Sense of Renting', *Wireless and Gramophone Trader* (24 Mar. 1934), 1.

[99] 'The Economics of Renting', *Wireless and Gramophone Trader* (1 Dec. 1934), 1.

[100] 'Are Rentals a Proposition for Ordinary Retailers?', *Wireless and Electrical Trader* (13 May 1939), 190–4 (190).

continued to eschew rental business, which became concentrated in the hands of a few companies, the main players in addition to Radio Rentals being Rentertainments (London) Ltd, Central Equipment Ltd, and National Radio Hire Service. In May 1939 it was estimated that 230,000–250,000 people rented radios in Britain, compared to 256,000 relay subscribers in December 1938, the combined subscribers to both services thus constituting less than 6 per cent of households with radio licences.[101]

Renters appreciated the ability to upgrade their sets, the bulk of receivers being traded in for more up-to-date models before the end of the standard three-year rental term. They also appear to have valued the free maintenance service. The cost of replacement valves, components, and servicing sets rented for the full three-year term of typical contracts amounted to about £2 for the rental company.[102] This incentivized radio rental firms to supply receivers produced by firms with strong reputations for reliability, such as Ekco.

According to *Wireless Trader*, a set with an 'artificial' list price of around 12 guineas (equivalent to a conventional cash list price of around 11 guineas for an equivalent set sold by a normal dealer) would earn the company approximately £16 in rentals over the standard three-year period.[103] Comparing the purchase of this product at the equivalent cash list price of 11 guineas, and factoring in the service costs to the dealer (with no adjustment for any profit which a conventional dealer might make on these services), renting entailed a cumulative payment some 27.1 per cent above the retail price of the set over the first three years of the rental—which compares favourably with typical annual HP interest charges. Furthermore, renters also enjoyed greater flexibility in terms of either returning the set, or keeping it beyond three years (at a very low rental, or with ownership transferred to the renter at no additional cost).

## CONCLUSIONS

Major British radio manufacturers adopted broadly similar marketing techniques to promote their brands to the public, differentiate them from competitors, and generate loyalty both among final customers and their networks of authorized dealers. Those firms which were most successful either had strong production competencies based around integrating assembly, components production (including valves), and R&D—such as EMI and Philips—or strong branding competencies in cabinet design, advertising, and cementing cooperative relationships with dealers. Ekco and Murphy stand out as firms that combined excellence in the technical qualities of their radios, the distinctiveness of the cabinets in which they were encased, and strong marketing competencies. This gave them sufficient sales volume

---

[101] Ibid.; Pegg, *Broadcasting and Society*, 58–60.
[102] 'Are Rentals a Proposition for Ordinary Retailers?', *Wireless and Electrical Trader* (13 May 1939), 190.
[103] Ibid.

to reduce assembly costs to levels competitive with EMI and Philips. More importantly (given the very limited technical economies of scale in this sector, as discussed in Chapter 6), it gave them sufficient market power to negotiate favourable deals for component purchases (particularly valves) and patent licences, thus enabling them to be price competitive with the large, integrated manufacturers.

The British radio sector achieved remarkably high household diffusion rates compared to other new durables. However, the price and format in which radio was delivered to the public was not optimal from the perspective of, especially, lower-income listeners. Cheaper modes of delivery, such as American-style midget radios and wireless relays were blocked or constrained by a radio trade that could exert powerful collective pressure on non-conforming firms and, to some extent, central and local government, to block innovations that might undermine its preferred business model.

# PART III

# TOWARDS A MASS MARKET IN WHITE GOODS

'White goods' (labour-saving powered domestic appliances) have always been a lower priority for households than entertainment durables. In consequence, when compared to typical entertainment durables, their diffusion is generally characterized by long 'take-off' periods, slow growth rates, and long product cycles.[1] There are a number of reasons for this. Entertainment is generally seen as offering higher value than goods which reduce the quantity of housework by an equivalent unit of time (as reflected in the relatively high cost of much commercial entertainment, compared to a charlady's hourly wages, in this period). Meanwhile, labour-saving durables mainly impact on the utility of the housewife, while a radio or gramophone would provide entertainment to all family members (including the husband who—as breadwinner—had a major say in spending decisions involving high-ticket durables).

Moreover, as the following chapters show, with a few exceptions such as the gas cooker or electric iron, white goods were often not particularly attractive investments in terms of the labour they saved. They were expensive, often had much cheaper strong or medium substitutes, and their HP costs did not always compare very favourably with the alternative of daily paid help—especially given the greater flexibility of a 'daily', in terms of both the range of work that she could do and the ease with which her costs could be reduced or terminated if and when household circumstances required this.

White goods consequently faced strong consumer resistance and inertia. Manufacturers and retailers responded with 'push selling': household canvassing, demonstrations, and other strategies aimed at bringing their products to their consumers' homes or communities. For power-hungry appliances such as cookers, fires, and water heaters, the power utilities were key players. These were generally primarily interested in expanding power sales and offsetting industrial power demand peaks with consumer demand peaks later in the day. They therefore offered

---

[1] Sue Bowden and Avner Offer, 'The Technological Revolution that Never Was: Gender, Class, and the Diffusion of Household Appliances in Interwar England', in Victoria de Grazia and Ellen Furlough (eds.), *The Sex of Things: Gender and Consumption in Historical Perspective* (Berkeley, CA: University of California Press, 1996), 244–74 (250).

relatively generous terms to customers and played a significant quality control function—as they wanted their appliances to remain working in the home for as long as possible. An exception was the vacuum cleaner, where leading manufacturers took control of the marketing effort by employing armies of door-to-door salesmen. These firms offered much less attractive terms and employed marketing tactics that, in practice, were highly opportunistic and served to alienate customers both from the products in question and from the general idea of door-to-door selling.

Chapter 8 examines the general diffusion of electrical and gas-powered white goods in this period, focusing in particular on the marketing and sales activities of the utility providers, which dominated supply chains for most high-ticket white goods. Chapter 9 looks at the genesis of the portable household vacuum cleaner in the United States and the development of the door-to-door selling system by firms such as Hoover and Eureka. Chapter 10 then explores the introduction of this system to Britain, where—as in the United States—it was initially successful in generating rapid early diffusion, but was less so in sustaining that diffusion so as to create true mass markets. The chapter also explores the reasons behind growing popular hostility to door-to-door appliance-selling in Britain and shows how the system exploited not only the consumer, but the salesman.

# 8

# Bringing Power to the People
## Marketing Electric and Gas Labour-Saving Appliances

## INTRODUCTION

This chapter examines the marketing of 'white goods'—labour-saving appliances powered by electricity or gas. These form a diverse group of products in terms of price, functions, manufacturers, and whether they were 'installed' in houses or had merely to be plugged in. However, they share the common feature of distribution via two main channels—conventional store-based retailing, and sales through electricity or gas utilities, which marketed them both via their showrooms and through canvassing. The exception is the vacuum cleaner, which was mainly sold using armies of door-to-door salesmen trained and (effectively) employed by the manufacturer. This form of 'push' selling is examined separately in the two subsequent chapters of this section, which discuss the genesis of door-to-door vacuum sales in the United States and the introduction of similar 'pressure selling' in Britain.

Small labour-saving durables such as the electric iron, clock, fan, or toaster, were typically sold through shops, including both specialist electrical stores and more general retailers. Meanwhile power-hungry items such as cookers, refrigerators, water heaters, and wash boilers, that required delivery and, in most cases, installation, were sold mainly through specialist electrical contractor/retailers, some larger department stores, and, especially, the power utilities. Power supply concerns saw such appliances as key to building power sales and thus gaining productivity advantages from a larger and more even 'load'. Crucially, they also regarded these products as a key competitive weapon in their battle with their rival local utility provider (electricity/gas), at a time when a significant proportion of households used only one of these and most labour-saving appliances (including such unlikely candidates as refrigerators and irons) came in both electrical and gas-powered versions.

Utility providers were so keen to expand sales of these power-hungry durables that they sometimes offered extremely generous HP or hire terms and engaged in extensive promotional activity. As they earned significant revenue from the additional power consumption, they did not necessarily have to make a substantial profit directly from appliance trading. Given their central role in the development of the British market for appliances, this chapter examines the gas/electricity utility marketing battle in some detail. However, we first explore the nature of production systems and value chains in this sector, together with the range of appliances on offer.

## PRODUCTION SYSTEMS AND VALUE CHAINS

The market for white goods was small in relation to that for furniture or radio equipment. In 1938 consumers' expenditure on electrical appliances (excluding radios, radiograms, vacuum cleaners, and lamps) was estimated at only £5–6 million.[1] This was markedly lower than consumers' expenditure on gas appliances; the 1935 Census of Production found that gas cookers, ranges, and fires, including parts and fittings, had a factory gate value of £6,368,000, equivalent to a retail value of around £10,000,000.[2] However, even a combined consumers' expenditure on gas and electrical appliances of around £16 million was dwarfed by household furniture (£63–64 million in 1938), new private motor cars (£51–52 million), or radio equipment (around £36 million).[3]

Most household electrical appliances appear to have been manufactured using broadly similar production methods to those employed in radio—using moving assembly lines, but with un/semi-skilled assembly workers, rather than the special-purpose machine tools that characterized Fordist mass production. Economies of scale appear to have been relatively weak, as shown in Table 8.1, which summarizes data from the 1935 Census of Production for firms producing electrical heating and cooking apparatus. Labour productivity (as proxied by net output per worker) was highest in plants employing only 50–99 workers, while those employing over 500 workers had a net output per worker roughly equal to the sector as a whole.

The degree of concentration in the industry varied substantially by type of appliance, as shown in Table 8.2, which summarizes the results of a 1930 national survey of

Table 8.1. Output, employment, and productivity of electrical heating and cooking apparatus establishments in 1935

| Employees | No. of establishments | Gross output (£,000) | Net output (£,000) | No. of persons employed | Net output per person (£) |
|---|---|---|---|---|---|
| 11–24 | 5 | 44 | 15 | 94 | 158 |
| 25–49 | 5 | 81 | 27 | 190 | 141 |
| 50–99 | 5 | 190 | 92 | 349 | 263 |
| 100–199 | 7 | 470 | 225 | 993 | 227 |
| 200–399 | 4 | 429 | 206 | 1,255 | 164 |
| 500 + | 5 | 1,998 | 894 | 4,602 | 194 |
| Total | 31 | 3,212 | 1,459 | 7,483 | 195 |

*Notes*: Excludes firms employing fewer than eleven people. There were no firms in the 400–499 category.

*Source*: Board of Trade, *Final Report on the Fifth Census of Production and the Import Duties Act Enquiry, 1935, Part II* (London: HMSO, 1939), 336.

---

[1] J. B. Jefferys, *The Distribution of Consumer Goods: A Factual Study of Methods and Costs in the United Kingdom in 1938* (Cambridge: Cambridge University Press, 1950), 292–300.

[2] Cited in Political and Economic Planning, *Report on the Market for Household Appliances* (London: PEP, 1945), 67.

[3] Radios, see Table 6.2; cars and furniture, Jefferys, *Distribution of Consumer Goods*, 269–300 and 350.

**Table 8.2.** Distribution of electrical appliances by make, according to a 1930 household survey (% of households owning that appliance)

| Brand | Cookers | Fires | Irons |
|---|---|---|---|
| Belling | 9.8 | 14.8 | |
| GEC Magnet | 5.2 | 13.8 | 3.8 |
| Xcel | 3.6 | 1.8 | 2.8 |
| Creda | 2.6 | 2.5 | 1.6 |
| Metro-Vic | 2.0 | 1.1 | |
| Premier | 1.5 | 1.0 | 1.0 |
| Cleso | 1.5 | | |
| Eureka | 1.3 | | |
| Imperial | 1.0 | | |
| Valco | 1.0 | | |
| Hotpoint | | | 51.6 |
| Smoothwell | | | 11.2 |
| Cosmos | | | 2.7 |
| Revo | | | 2.5 |
| Ediswan | | | 1.7 |
| Electrolux | | | 1.5 |
| Gem | | | 1.3 |
| Ideal | | 17.1 | |
| Local power supply undertaking* | 1.8 | 22.3 | |
| All others | 68.7 | 25.6 | 18.3 |
| Total | 100.0 | 100.0 | 100.0 |

*Notes*: Firms with less than 1 per cent of the market for each good would appear in the 'all others' category. * Representing households which obtained their appliance from supply undertakings without knowing the maker's name.

*Source*: Bank of England Archives, SMT5/50, Lord & Thomas and Logan Ltd, 'Merchandising survey of Great Britain. Volume 5, Electrical Appliances (Domestic)', 1930, 52–4.

5,000 households wired for electricity. Electric cooker manufacture is shown to be extremely fragmented, with no brand representing more than 10 per cent of the market. Conversely electric fires were more highly concentrated, with three firms comprising around 46 per cent of all brands identified by households. Electric irons (a much cheaper item, with annual UK output valued at £56,000 in 1935, at factory gate values, compared to £1,454,000 for electric cookers, and £1,509,000 for electric heating apparatus) were highly concentrated, with Hotpoint serving around half the national demand.[4] The survey also found that no firm had a strong position across a broad range of household appliances.

Electrical appliances were sold through a wide range of outlets. The 1930 survey (which included vacuum cleaners as part of its sample) suggested that 40.2 per cent of electrical appliance owners purchased them from department stores, 38.3 per cent acquired them from a local electricity supply undertaking, 19.1 per cent from a local retail agent, 2.2 per cent from a canvasser, and only 0.2 per cent direct from the manufacturer. The importance of canvassers is almost certainly underestimated,

[4] For production data, see UK, Board of Trade, *Final Report on the Fifth Census of Production and the Import Duties Act Enquiry, 1935, Part II* (London: HMSO, 1939), 309.

given that these were frequently used by electricity supply concerns, department stores, and even local retailers, and therefore may have been partially included under these categories.[5] No similar data are available for gas appliances, though gas supply concerns appear to have played a much greater role in the provision of gas appliances than electrical utilities did for electrical goods, having established themselves as a key channel of appliance distribution before 1914.

Electricity and gas were supplied by monopoly local undertakings, reflecting their 'natural monopoly' characteristics and the need for statutory powers and regulation to lay mains in public thoroughfares. Local undertakings might be either privately owned or run by the council, though in almost all cases gas and electricity suppliers in any particular locality were under different ownership and control. Until 1919 municipal electricity suppliers were not permitted to deal in electrical appliances. The 1919 Electricity (Supply) Act empowered them to hire (but not yet to sell) appliances.[6] Their powers were subsequently extended under the Electrical Supply Act of 1926, which permitted municipal suppliers to sell fittings, apparatus, and wiring to their own customers and to cooperate with local electrical trades and contractors in such work.

Electrical goods' trade associations tried to take advantage of parliamentary scrutiny of the draft bill which became the 1926 Act to set up machinery for the enforcement of standard trade discounts and other terms of retail trading. Thus Clause 48, 'Sale of Fittings', which gave powers to local authorities (or contractors acting for them) to provide electric cabling and equipment to the public, stipulated that such sales would be at recognized trade prices. The same clause provided for the Electricity Commissioners to appoint a statutory committee, comprising representatives of electrical supply undertakings, together with contractors, manufacturers, and distributors of electrical apparatus, to adjudicate on recognized prices.

This 'Fair Trading Committee' was constituted in May 1927, to prepare a national agreement.[7] However, the electrical supply authorities proved unwilling to go further than accepting the policy of recognized prices in principle and it was not until May 1936 that a 'Fair Trading Policy' was formally adopted by the Council as the 'approved basis for trading in the Electrical Industry' and circulated for '*voluntary* adoption'.[8] Given that the code stipulated a trade discount for electricity supply undertakings equal to that offered to electrical contractors and retailers (despite the fact that electricity suppliers typically purchased direct from the manufacturer and had lower distribution costs than most retailers, on account of their

[5] Bank of England Archives, SMT5/50, Lord & Thomas and Logan Ltd, 'Merchandising Survey of Great Britain. Volume 5, Electrical Appliances (Domestic)' (1930), 51.

[6] Elizabeth Sprenger and Pauline Webb, 'Persuading the Housewife to Use Electricity? An Interpretation of Material in the Electricity Council Archives', *British Journal for the History of Science*, 26 (1993), 55–65 (59).

[7] Modern Records Centre, Warwick, Mss. 287/36, BEAMA archives [hereafter MRC, BEAMA], Arthur E. Lowe, *A History of the Electrical Fair Trading Policy* (London: Electrical Fair Trading Council, 1951), 2–3.

[8] Ibid., 4–5.

larger size), its compulsory adoption would have both raised costs to consumers and protected inefficient retailers and channels of supply.[9]

Following the 1926 Act many local electricity supply concerns opened elaborate showrooms to demonstrate appliances and, by buying direct from the manufacturer, were able to undercut competition from conventional retailers. Wholesalers were understandably annoyed, though by this time they were becoming increasingly marginalized in a broad range of consumer goods sectors. Contractors were also initially hostile, but often made cooperative arrangements with local supply authorities, whereby their customers used the supplier's showrooms to select fittings and equipment.[10] In the United States power companies had played a similar role in marketing appliances, using showrooms, demonstrations, advertising, and door-to-door canvassing. However, by the late 1930s many US electrical supply companies had withdrawn from this market, partly owing to vehement opposition from conventional appliance retailers.[11] Weaker retailer opposition in the UK may reflect the limited market for power-hungry durables in Britain, together with the gas supply concerns' traditionally dominant role in gas appliances provision.

Jefferys estimated that in 1938 only 25–30 per cent of household electrical goods were distributed through conventional wholesale channels, the rest going direct from manufacturer to retailer—be it an electrical supply undertaking; (comprising 10–15 per cent of distribution), or a conventional retail store or electrical contractor (55–65 per cent).[12] He also estimated that there were around 4–5,000 retail stores specializing in electrical goods, together with some 10,000 more which did some trade in this area (such as department stores, cooperatives, radio shops, and so forth).[13]

Resale price maintenance remained relatively strong in electrical goods—though supply undertakings often used their lower purchase and distribution costs to undercut list prices—often indirectly, via generous HP or hire terms. The average margin earned by wholesalers or factors in 1938 was said to be 15–17.5 per cent on the retail price. Electrical and other retailers, together with electrical contractors, were expected to receive a 25 per cent discount on the retail price under the code, regardless of whether they purchased through wholesalers or direct from the manufacturer. However, large retailers such as department stores and multiples obtained an additional quantity rebate of 10–15 per cent through buying direct from the manufacturer. Meanwhile supply authorities purchasing direct from the manufacturer received discounts of around 30–35 per cent.[14] A 1930 investigation

---

[9] MRC, BEAMA, Electrical Fair Trading Council, *British Electrical Industry Fair Trading Policy for the Home Trade*, 2nd edn. (London: Electrical Fair Trading Council, 1939).

[10] U.S. Department of Commerce, Bureau of Foreign and Domestic Commerce, *British Market for Domestic Electrical Appliances* (Washington, DC: USGPO, 1930), 10–11.

[11] U.S. Federal Trade Commission, *Report of the Federal Trade Commission Distribution Methods and Costs, Part IV* (Washington, DC: USGPO, 1944), 148.

[12] Jefferys, *Distribution of Consumer Goods*, 292.     [13] Ibid.

[14] Ibid., 293–4. All purchasers (except general stores, with small sales) were also entitled to settlement discounts from prompt payment.

of the British electrical goods market had found a similar discount structure, suggesting that discounts had remained stable over the 1930s.[15]

## THE PRODUCTS

A key characteristic of white goods is their joint consumption with power—generally electricity or gas. Britain had a very well-developed gas industry by 1920, while the diffusion of electricity distribution was hampered by both high charges and a lack of standardization. In the United States electricity supply was standardized as early as 1910, at 120 volt, 60-cycle alternating current, which proved of great value to manufacturers seeking to develop standardized products for a national market.[16] In 1925 the British Engineering Standards Association specified a 230 volt stand-ard for electrical supply (for alternating or direct current). However, there was no legal compulsion to follow these guidelines and in March 1927 bulb manufactures found that the standard voltage comprised only 24 per cent of national demand for 30-watt lamps.[17]

High power charges (both absolutely and relative to gas) constituted a formid-able barrier to the diffusion of electrical appliances throughout the inter-war period. As a 1930 survey of the British electrical appliances market noted, 'The principal handicap facing the manufacturer . . . is the unduly high cost of current . . . Electricity, except for lighting, is looked upon as a luxury by most people of normal means . . . with current at 6d. or 8d. a unit this view is justifiable.'[18] Electricity costs also varied widely by locality, even within the same region, thus further fragment-ing markets. In 1929 the price in pence per unit in London for domestic supply varied from 1.7 to 5.5; the price in Lancashire varied from 2.1 to 11.2 pence per unit; and in Yorkshire from 2.2 to 9.2 pence per unit.[19] The survey also noted the persisting problems arising from the lack of standardized voltage and the practice of wiring homes only for lighting (and low-power appliances that could be run from a light socket using an adapter).[20]

Household diffusion of electricity (and, earlier, gas) was generally led by its 'killer application'—lighting—which was often the main consideration for people weighing up the costs and benefits of wiring their homes. Electricity provided a brighter light and avoided the fumes and soot produced by the gas mantle, while the lower rates offered by electricity suppliers for lighting (rather than socket) power made it price competitive.[21]

[15] U.S. Department of Commerce, Bureau of Foreign and Domestic Commerce, *British Market for Domestic Electrical Appliances*, 6.

[16] Carroll Gantz, *The Vacuum Cleaner: A History* (Jefferson, NC: McFarland, 2012), 71.

[17] Bank of England Archives, SMT5/50, Lord & Thomas and Logan Ltd, 'Merchandising Survey', 2–3.

[18] Ibid., 1.      [19] Ibid., 68.      [20] Ibid., 1–2.

[21] Sue Bowden and Avner Offer, 'The Technological Revolution that Never Was: Gender, Class and the Diffusion of Household Appliances in Interwar England', in Victoria de Grazia and Ellen Furlough (eds.), *The Sex of Things: Gender and Consumption in Historical Perspective* (Berkeley: University of California Press, 1996), 244–74.

Other electrical labour-saving appliances typically diffused relatively slowly, even for wired households. These can be classified into three main groups, in terms of their characteristics and (to some extent) their diffusion. The first group, 'small appliances', covered a diverse range of products such as the electric iron, kettle, clock, fan, and hairdryer. These were typically sold through conventional retailers rather than power companies, as they had relatively low power consumption and did not require installation or delivery. Data on the household diffusion of such products are sparse, though diffusion appears to have been fairly rapid—although varying greatly according to the utility of the product and the availability of close substitutes. For example, by 1939 electric irons had spread to 77 per cent of wired homes—constituting the only electrical appliance (for which data are available) that had diffused to more than half such homes. Conversely, only 16 per cent had electric kettles, which offered few advantages over the much cheaper conventional kettle, heated on the range or oven.[22]

The next group of appliances substituted for functions traditionally undertaken by the coal range—space heating, cooking, and water heating (though many appliance owners continued to use the range for these in winter). These were more energy-intensive than small appliances, which made them particularly attractive to utility providers, while at the same time generating consumer resistance on the grounds of their heavy running costs.

Of this group, the cooker experienced the fastest diffusion, together with the greatest competition between local gas and electricity providers. Gas cookers were already widely diffused in British households before the First World War, making the task of persuading households to switch to electric cookers particularly difficult. Electric cookers were also subject to higher purchase and running costs than gas cookers, while also requiring expensive machine-bottomed pans for use on solid hot plates.[23] Moreover, gas was widely seen to have qualitative advantages for cooking, being faster and easier to regulate. A 1930 market research survey of 5,000 wired households (at a time when only one household in five had electricity) found that 11.5 per cent had electric cookers, while this figure had only risen to around 14 per cent of wired homes by 1939.[24] Gas dominated the nation's cooking; estimates suggest that by the end of 1938 there were around 9 million domestic gas cookers, compared to only 1.16–1.33 million electric cookers.[25]

Electric fires were more popular, with estimated diffusion rates to wired homes of 21 per cent in 1930 and 27 per cent in 1939.[26] These were typically used as a supplement to the coal fire, as plugged-in fires could be moved between rooms and used for short periods to avoid the work of setting a fire. In 1939 coal still

[22] Leslie Hannah, *Electricity before Nationalisation: A Study of the Development of the Electricity Supply Industry in Britain to 1948* (London: Macmillan, 1979), 208.

[23] Political and Economic Planning, *Report on the Supply of Electricity in Great Britain* (London: PEP, 1936), 77.

[24] Bank of England Archives, SMT5/50, Lord & Thomas and Logan Ltd, 'Merchandising Survey', 44–7; Hannah, *Electricity before Nationalisation*, 208.

[25] Political and Economic Planning, *Report on the Market for Household Appliances*, 67–9.

[26] Bank of England Archives, SMT5/50, Lord & Thomas and Logan Ltd, 'Merchandising Survey', 44–7; Hannah, *Electricity before Nationalisation*, 208.

dominated space heating, while gas accounted for no more than 5 per cent of room heating and electricity a still smaller proportion.[27]

Electric water heaters had reached less than 5 per cent of households by 1939.[28] People were chiefly deterred by their high running costs. For example, a 1930 study found that even those households which had installed electric water heaters were often deterred from using them for heating bath water by the prohibitive cost.[29] Gas water heaters delivered the same service at a markedly lower cost, but still made limited inroads in the face of the much cheaper alternative of heating water using a boiler connected to the coal fire. It was estimated that in 1938 not more than 20 per cent of homes had a gas water heater.[30]

Coal ranges created a good deal of additional housework, not only in attending to the fire (which could take up at least an hour each day where ranges were used for cooking and heating), but in the extra work inherent in cooking in the living room and doing food preparation and washing up in the scullery, not to mention cleaning up the soot and dirt. They also entailed unwanted space heating in summer, in order to serve their other functions. Yet, given coal's considerably lower cost, a large majority of working-class households still used a combination coal range for cooking, water heating, and space heating (at least in winter) until after the Second World War.

Gas was cleaner, more spatially and functionally divisible in use between space heating, water heating, and cooking, and more flexible in terms of both its range of uses and the speed with which it could be utilized and terminated. Electricity was still more flexible in its range of uses, but substantially more expensive. It was considered functionally superior to gas for lighting, but was widely deemed inferior for cooking. Meanwhile its cost severely limited its use among lower-income households as even a partial substitute for the range.[31] Coal had clear cost advantages; it was estimated that in 1939 the cost per useful therm for heating, for a family of four, was 1s 0.5d for coal (8.5d for anthracite), 1s 6d for gas, and 1s 9d for electricity. Meanwhile the all-in cost of hot-water generation over ten years (including installation, maintenance, and fuel) in 1938 was estimated at 3s 2.5d per week for a coal-fired back boiler, compared to a minimum of 3s 9.5d for gas and 4s 11d for electricity.[32]

The cost advantages of coal, or a combination of coal and gas technology, resulted in electricity consumption being strongly related to household income, as shown in Table 8.3. There were also substantial regional differences in the

[27] Political and Economic Planning, *Report on the Gas Industry in Great Britain* (London: PEP, 1939), 79.

[28] Hannah, *Electricity before Nationalisation*, 208.

[29] U.S. Department of Commerce, Bureau of Foreign and Domestic Commerce, *British Market for Domestic Electrical Appliances*, 15.

[30] 'Gas Advertising Review', *Gas Bulletin*, 17 (Jan. 1938), 2–4 (citing data from *Shelf Appeal*).

[31] Political and Economic Planning, *Report on the Supply of Electricity*, 84; Sue Bowden, 'The Market for Domestic Electric Cookers in the 1930s: A Regional Analysis' (unpublished PhD thesis, LSE, 1984), 26.

[32] Political and Economic Planning, *Report on the Gas Industry in Great Britain*, 80; Political and Economic Planning, *Report on the Market for Household Appliances*, 146.

**Table 8.3.** Relative uses of gas and electricity for domestic purposes by British households, classified by income (% of all households), *c.*1937

| Household income | Lighting | | Cooking | | Hot water | |
|---|---|---|---|---|---|---|
| | Gas | Electricity | Gas | Electricity | Gas | Electricity |
| Over £10 weekly (600,000 homes) | 3 | 97 | 70 | 20 | 25 | 13 |
| £4–10 (2,500,000 homes) | 23 | 77 | 80 | 13 | 25 | 3 |
| Below £4 (8,500,000 homes) | 52 | 48 | 70 | 5 | 18 | Very small |

*Notes*: Other fuels are not shown. For cooking and water heating many families used solid fuel in addition to gas and electricity. Ninety per cent of families were found to use coal as their main source of room heating.
*Source*: Eileen Murphy, 'Who are our prospects?', *Gas Salesman* (Mar. 1938), 133–5 (134).

technologies used for space heating, water heating, and cooking. A survey conducted by the Department of Scientific and Industrial Research during the Second World War found that 67 per cent of homes in the North of England used coal for cooking in winter and 53 per cent in summer. In the South, gas and electricity were found to be more commonly used for cooking, especially in the summer, but the kitchen range was still widely used for hot water supply (though less commonly than in Scotland, northern England, and the Midlands).[33]

The final class of durables were truly labour-saving—in that they substituted machinery for manual labour, rather than merely undertaking the functions of a coal-heated or manual appliance more conveniently. These included the vacuum cleaner (discussed in the following two chapters), the wash boiler, and the refrigerator. In contrast to the vacuum cleaner, neither the wash boiler nor refrigerator enjoyed substantial diffusion during this period. The 1930 market research survey mentioned earlier found that only 0.4 per cent of wired households had refrigerators; their diffusion remained negligible in 1939.[34]

While refrigerators had become popular in the United States, where a good proportion of the population already used ice boxes to keep food fresh (reflecting the much warmer summers in most of US states), British working-class housewives typically purchased perishables daily, leaving longer-term storage to the retailer.[35] Middle-class housewives had even less incentive to view refrigerators as 'labour-saving'—as they could have their groceries delivered, daily if necessary. Refrigerator ownership was also severely constrained by high running costs.

In 1936 there were only an estimated 62,000 electric refrigerators in domestic use. Indeed, it is likely that domestic electric refrigerators were outnumbered by gas refrigerators (which capitalized on lower running costs). While around 15,000 domestic electric refrigerators were sold nationally during 1936, some 13,000 gas

[33] Cited in Political and Economic Planning, *Report on the Market for Household Appliances*, 37.
[34] Bank of England Archives, SMT5/50, Lord & Thomas and Logan Ltd, 'Merchandising Survey', 51.
[35] Ibid., 44–7.

refrigerators were supplied to households just in the part of London covered by the Gas Light & Coke Company.[36] Like other gas concerns, Gas Light & Coke worked in cooperation with Electrolux (the only UK manufacturer of gas refrigerators) whose success appears to have been strongly linked to the gas utilities' marketing activities.

Electric washing machines constituted an even less well-developed market, cumulative national sales to the end of 1937 amounting to something over 50,000.[37] Running costs for washing machines were only moderately greater than for vacuum cleaners.[38] However, a 1930 study found that American washing machines introduced to the British market were priced too high to meet popular demand. Meanwhile public municipal wash houses provided an attractive alternative in many urban areas. Britain also had a very well-developed and efficient laundry industry, many companies having a network of depots where laundry was collected and delivered at reasonable rates. An electrical industry expert noted that houses using laundries were a difficult proposition for wash boiler sales, as they would be typically:

> working on the bare minimum of domestic staff, and that domestic staff is becoming increasingly independent...an electric washer in the home will not in such a household make any difference to the work of the mistress of the house, since she will not be doing the washing herself...But faced as she is with the domestic service problem already acute, it is extremely doubtful whether the average mistress would dare to thrust on to her independent staff extra work of this sort, even...with the assurance that work with an electric washing machine was very light.[39]

A survey conducted by the Department of Scientific and Industrial Research during the Second World War found that some 27 per cent of families had their washing done outside the home (either at commercial or communal laundries), with 22 per cent of families on incomes under £160 per annum, and 30 per cent of families on £160–300, doing so.[40] In addition to high purchase costs, many washing machines, while not of great size by American standards, were still too big for the average British scullery. Moreover, electrical supply companies showed little interest in providing washing machines on hire or HP, given their relatively low power consumption.[41]

Appliance sales were boosted by design improvements that added an element of technical obsolescence, though this was a much more gradual process than was the case for radio. Even the humble and ubiquitous electric flat iron began to

---

[36] 'Machinery in the Home', *Economist* (5 Feb. 1938), 279–80 (280).          [37] Ibid.

[38] A 1938 Edison Electric Institute study found that the annual kWh of electricity consumed in normal use were 24 for vacuum cleaners and 30 for washing machines, compared to 400 for refrigerators, 100 for radios, and 80 for flat irons. Cited in Smithsonian, Clark 201/2, data sheets compiled by Clark from Edison Electric Institute data.

[39] D. Winton Thorpe, 'The Sale of Load-Building Appliances: Cleaning and Washing Apparatus', *World Power* (June 1934), 316–18 (318).

[40] Cited in Political and Economic Planning, *Report on the Market for Household Appliances*, 192.

[41] U.S. Department of Commerce, Bureau of Foreign and Domestic Commerce, *British Market for Domestic Electrical Appliances*, 16.

be superseded from 1935 by an ergonomically designed model with variable thermostat and settings for different fabrics. However, given that these new irons initially cost between two and seven times the price of the old type, they served only a limited, high-end market prior to the Second World War.[42]

One general constraint on the diffusion of electrical durables was the reaction of the gas industry, which modified and extended its range of products to meet the competitive threat. Glendenning argues that the gas cooker of 1920 was virtually the same—in terms of external appearance and features—as that of 1895.[43] However, during the inter-war years, both the aesthetic appeal and functional characteristics of gas cookers improved rapidly. Traditional black cast-iron models were replaced with enamelled cookers in a variety of colours, incorporating improved features, such as oven heat control. These were both easier to clean and appeared more hygienic, meeting the needs of the new, more style-conscious, labour-saving kitchen. Britain's largest gas supplier, Gas Light & Coke Co., worked with gas appliance manufacturers to develop new, competitive models.[44]

An examination of housekeeping manuals (generally aimed primarily at lower-middle-class housewives) reveals that most 'white goods' were seen as being of limited value. For example, a 1935 *Pitman's* manual warned that, 'Some so-called "labour-saving" devices are not efficient in carrying out their intended purpose and are so difficult and intricate to manage that they are hindrances rather than helps.'[45] Their list of recommended devices consisted of such mundane items as stainless steel knives, aluminium or stainless steel pans, a gas copper, and hand-operated kitchen equipment such as egg-beaters and potato peelers. Significantly the only electrical item mentioned was the electric iron.

## EASY TERMS FOR POWER AND APPLIANCES

In 1938 fuel and light accounted for around 4.5 per cent of all personal expenditure, with coal comprising 55 per cent of this total, gas one-fifth, and electricity a little less than one-fifth.[46] Britain's electricity suppliers faced an uphill competitive struggle, given their much higher prices per unit of power and a formidable incumbent—the gas industry. Indeed, Britain had the highest per capita gas consumption of any industrialized country, with sales per consumer around 1.75 times

---

[42] 'Irons Can Make Good Profits for the Electrical Dealer', *Wireless and Electrical Trader* (10 June 1939), 295–7.

[43] Anne Glendenning, *Demons of Domesticity: Women and the English Gas Industry, 1889–1939* (Aldershot: Ashgate, 2004), 224.

[44] Stirling Everard, *The History of the Gas Light and Coke Company 1812–1949* (London: Benn, 1949), 346–8.

[45] Ruth Binnie and Julia E. Boxall, *Housecraft: Principles and Practice* (London: Pitman, 1935), 218.

[46] Richard Stone and D. A. Rowe, *The Measurement of Consumers' Expenditure and Behaviour in the United Kingdom 1920–1938, Volume I* (Cambridge: Cambridge University Press, 1954), 222. Estimates for gas and electricity include 'rentals' for fittings, etc.

greater than in the United States.[47] The 1930s witnessed an intense struggle between the gas and electricity supply industries for the household market and, in particular, the working-class market—which appeared to constitute the best arena for expanding power sales.

While gas faced a saturated domestic market in the 1930s, electricity experienced rapid diffusion from a relatively low base. The proportion of wired households in England and Wales rose from 7 per cent in 1920 to just over a third in 1930, and to 72 per cent by 1938, while sales of electricity to domestic customers increased from 2,111 million kWh in 1933 to 4,881 million in 1938. Consumption per domestic consumer increased much more modestly, from 468 to 579 million kWh; though consumption for purposes other than lighting expanded rapidly—from 168 to an estimated 279 kWh.[48] Diffusion was boosted by sharply falling prices, which fell from 6.5d per unit in 1920 to 4d in 1923 and less than 1.5d in 1938. In the battle for the working-class power market, cost was a prime consideration. As Hull's City Chief Electrical Engineer noted in 1933:

> Talk about convenience, cleanliness, comfort, labour-saving, etc., which is a really useful aid to selling electrical service to better-class houses, is of little, if any, value in the case of the small house. Total cost dominates the situation completely...In addition, the average tenant of a small house has no capital available for...outright purchase...wiring and apparatus must be provided by easy payments or hired.[49]

The first step towards building up a household's electricity consumption was getting it wired for electricity. 'Assisted wiring' schemes were introduced by electricity supply undertakings as a form of instalment purchase for electric cabling. The proportion of electrical undertakings operating assisted wiring schemes rose from a third in 1929 to 84 per cent in 1936, while repayment periods were often as long as ten or even fifteen years.[50] However, these were often limited to existing (rather than new) homes and to houses below a certain rateable value (often around £30); in keeping with the stated purpose of the scheme—to extend supply to low-income households.[51] Moreover they generally only covered lighting and a couple of low-power sockets; energy-hungry appliances such as cookers and water heaters entailed further installation costs.

During the 1930s electricity suppliers sought to entice customers to expand their use of electricity beyond lighting by offering generous terms for both electric power and power-using appliances. Two-part tariffs were introduced—comprising a standard quarterly charge (sometimes related to the consumer's ability to pay, for example by being based on the house's rateable value, number of rooms, or floor space) and a reduced rate for consumption beyond this limit. By 1936 some 86 per cent of electrical undertakings operated a two-part tariff and it was estimated in 1937 that

---

[47] Political and Economic Planning, *Report on the Supply of Electricity*, 4; 'Gas Produced or Sold in Important Countries of the World', BCGA, *Gas Bulletin*, 33 (Mar. 1933), 49.
[48] Bowden and Offer, 'Technological Revolution that Never Was', 260.
[49] J. N. Waite, 'Small Houses as a Market for Electricity', *World Power* (Jan. 1933), 10–13 (11).
[50] Hannah, *Electricity before Nationalisation*, 188.
[51] Bowden, 'The Market for Domestic Electric Cookers in the 1930s', 224–5.

some 35 per cent of domestic consumers were on these tariffs.[52] Two-part tariffs were introduced later to the gas industry, generally after the 1934 Gas Undertakings Act, which removed the severe statutory limitations on offering discounts to larger gas consumers.[53] Yet most gas suppliers still employed the flat-rate principle, with less than fifty undertakings operating two-part tariffs by the late 1930s.[54]

Two-part tariffs proved unpopular with working-class customers, as they penalized households with particularly low consumption and those with unstable earnings— who might find paying the fixed charge difficult during periods of reduced income.[55] Gas suppliers were legally obliged to offer flat rates to all customers, though electrical undertakings faced no such statutory controls and sometimes offered only two-part tariffs, with standing charges sufficiently high to deter many working-class households.[56] However, the tariffs sometimes also included the 'free' provision of cookers and other appliances.[57]

A key element in utility suppliers' marketing strategies was the use of generous hire or HP schemes, particularly for power-hungry appliances such as cookers, wash-boilers, and water and space heaters. Their main motivation was to increase power consumption by boosting the supply of appliances, rather than maximizing direct profits from equipment sales. Liberal hire or HP terms were often directed to expanding power sales to working-class households and were supported by aggressive direct marketing to overcome strong consumer inertia.[58] Recent econometric analysis has found that the provision of deferred payment mechanisms by electrical suppliers did boost electricity consumption, compared to localities where they were not available.[59]

Gas undertakings had traditionally provided cookers to customers on simple hire, though by 1930 they were beginning to introduce HP schemes.[60] Both gas and electricity suppliers appreciated the need to offer terms that suited the working-class weekly household budgeting cycle. In 1936 an electricity sales manager advised his colleagues that prepayment meters were usually essential for working-class families:

> because this type of consumer is not accustomed to save up sufficient money to meet the size of bill which it would be worth rendering by post. The weekly wage-earner

---

[52] Political and Economic Planning, *Report on the Supply of Electricity*, 76; 'Annual Survey of Domestic Appliances', *Electrical Trading* (Aug. 1937), 47–8 (47).

[53] Trevor I. Williams, *A History of the British Gas Industry* (Oxford: Oxford University Press, 1981), 75.

[54] Philip Chantler, *The British Gas Industry: An Economic Study* (Manchester: Manchester University Press, 1938), 125–6.

[55] Ibid., 127.

[56] Bowden and Offer, 'Technological Revolution that Never Was', 256.

[57] 'Service to Small Dwellings', *Electrical Trading* (Oct. 1935), 49–51 (50); Hannah, *Electricity before Nationalisation*, 206.

[58] Sue Bowden, 'Credit Facilities and the Growth of Consumer Demand for Electric Appliances in the 1930s', *Business History*, 32 (1990), 52–75 (53 and 63).

[59] Peter Scott and James T. Walker, 'Power to the People: Working-Class Demand for Household Power in 1930s Britain', *Oxford Economic Papers*, 63 (2011), 598–624.

[60] Bank of England Archives, SMT5/50, Lord & Thomas and Logan Ltd, 'Merchandising Survey', 48.

is...accustomed to pay as he goes, and the slot meter is, broadly speaking, the only means by which the gas industry, which has been catering for this class of business much longer than we have, has been able to collect revenue.[61]

HP terms became progressively more liberal during the decade, with contracts for expensive durables being extended for five to seven years in order to make appliances accessible to working-class households. Scattered evidence from individual companies suggests that the demand for electrical appliances was very elastic with respect to the liberality of HP terms. For example, Cannock Chase District Gas Co. perceived that its customers had difficulty keeping up payments on cookers sold on three-year HP terms. In 1935 they therefore selected four different types of cooker with an average cost (to the company) of £7 and offered them on six years' HP, at 1d per day. This resulted in an increase in cooker sales from 95 in 1934 to 454 in 1935 and 569 in 1936.[62] Similarly, the North Metropolitan Power Supply Co. (Northmet) found that when the price of washing machines was around 29 guineas or more, their annual sales never rose above one or two dozen per year. But the launch of a machine that could be marketed at below 20 guineas, supported by the company with HP terms and a planned sales campaign, increased unit sales to around 400 per annum.[63]

In addition to making appliances available on what were often very generous terms, the utilities also played an important product quality assessment function. As their primary aim was to boost power consumption, rather than profit directly from appliance sales, they had an incentive to select appliances with a reputation for reliability, long service lives, and low maintenance costs. For example, in May 1931 the County of London Electric Supply Co. considered how to expand installations of storage-type water heaters. Previous experience suggested that the first cost of these heaters, even when spread over two or three years via HP, precluded their extensive diffusion. Renting them on simple hire was considered more promising and Sadia were selected as the supplier, due to its strong, long-established reputation for product reliability (which their own experience had corroborated). The model in question was regarded as of such quality that its useful lifespan was estimated at twenty-five years or more.[64]

Electrical contractor/retailers also used HP, though this was typically financed by the manufacturer and offered on the manufacturer's standard terms.[65] By 1930 most leading British electrical goods manufacturers were offering HP credit (either directly, or through an HP finance house such as Electrical Manufacturers Finance Co. or The Equipment Trust Co.). Manufacturers often took responsibility for late or non-payment and, in many instances, received the instalments directly. Terms

---

[61] MMSI, ESI 73, British Electrical Development Association Inc., Annual report for Electricity Supply Sales Managers Conference, 30 Mar.–1 Apr. 1936, J. I. Bernard, 'Selling Electrical Service for the Small Household'.

[62] Charles Stewart, 'Sales Policy in a Mining Area', *Gas Salesman* (May 1937), 212–13.

[63] MMSI, ESI 73, British Electrical Development Association Inc., Annual report on Electricity Supply Sales Managers Conferences, 1938, 'Planned Selling' by G. E. Barrett (Northmet).

[64] LMA, 4278/01/280, County of London Electric Supply Co., memorandum to the Board, 19 May 1931.

[65] D. Winton Thorpe, 'The Sale of Load-Building Appliances: I. Electric Cookers', *World Power* (Sept. 1933), 129–32 (132).

generally involved a 10 per cent deposit and six to twenty-four monthly payments thereafter. For twelve monthly agreements, 5 per cent might typically be added to the cash price as interest.[66]

## CREATING NATIONAL BRANDS FOR FRAGMENTED UTILITY PROVIDERS

Both gas and electricity distribution constituted highly fragmented national markets comprised of local monopoly providers. In 1937 Britain had some 706 statutory gas undertakings, plus a further 544 small, non-statutory undertakings. Meanwhile, in March 1936 there were some 376 municipal electricity suppliers (providing around two-thirds of national supply), 247 private-sector electricity undertakings, and three joint electricity authorities. The largest suppliers served the major cities, for example London had both the largest national gas supplier— Gas Light & Coke Co.—which supplied 17 per cent of national gas consumption in 1935, and Britain's largest electrical supplier, Northmet.[67] Local power suppliers varied considerably in the extent to which they pushed appliance sales. For example, although 84 per cent of electrical undertakings offered assisted wiring schemes by 1936, 25 per cent of undertakings had no showrooms or hiring schemes and 20 per cent had no HP schemes; while over 40 per cent did not employ canvass-ers.[68] There were also considerable differences in pricing (and in effective interest rates). According to one 1939 estimate, the most expensive gas suppliers charged three times as much for supplying and installing appliances as the cheapest. Some undertakings were content to base charges on the purchase price from the manu-facturer, plus fixing and maintenance costs and interest on capital. Meanwhile others added a profit margin, which varied widely between suppliers.[69]

Sales policies were often strongly influenced by the generosity of the alternative utility provider. For example, in 1935 Rugby Corporation's Electricity Department introduced drastic reductions in the price of current and offered the latest models of domestic appliances at low simple hire rates: cookers from 2s 6d per quarter; fires and sink water heaters from 2s, wash boilers and immersion heaters from 3s, and bath water heaters from 5s—all wired free. Rugby Gas Co. reacted by offering gas cookers and fires on seven years' HP and wash boilers and water heaters on five years' HP. As they could not match the quarterly payments of the electricity com-panies, Rugby Gas Co. instead lowered their gas charges to one-third of a penny per unit (showing charges in units, as well as therms, to make them directly comparable with electrical appliances).[70]

---

[66] 'Have you Invited Manufacturers' Help for your Hire-Purchase Sales?', *Electrical Trading* (Oct. 1930), 48–50.

[67] Chantler, *British Gas Industry*, 28–9.

[68] Political and Economic Planning, *Report on the Supply of Electricity*, 76.

[69] National Gas Archive, R. J. Rogers, 'Further Aspects of the Retention and Development of the Domestic Load', paper presented at BCGA 29th annual conference, Brighton, 22–25 Apr. 1939.

[70] G. W. F. Cockayne, 'Fierce Competition Successfully Countered', *Gas Salesman* (Apr. 1937), 171–3.

The fragmented structure of the gas and electricity supply industries made national marketing strategies problematic. This was addressed by the establishment of the British Commercial Gas Association (BCGA) and the British Electrical Development Association (EDA) to coordinate their respective national marketing campaigns. These bodies organized and supported both press advertising and other promotional work, such as exhibitions and demonstrations.[71] Manufacturers provided a further national element to appliances marketing, via their direct consumer marketing activities and through cooperative activities with both individual suppliers and organizations such as the EDA and BCGA.

EDA and BCGA promotional strategies were relatively sophisticated, but often copied each other—for example, the adoption of 'Mr Therm' in 1931 as the gas industry's national mascot was shortly followed by the EDA's less successful 'I'm Electric' figure. Mr Therm was created by the newly formed publicity department of the Gas Light and Coke Co.—reflecting the industry leadership role taken by some of the largest gas and electricity supply concerns.[72] This cartoon-like figure, designed to anthropomorphize the live gas flame, rapidly became one of the most recognizable national brands of the 1930s and was employed in some innovative advertising—including cartoon strip adverts such as Figure 8.1.

Electricity and gas suppliers engaged in extensive print advertising, often using adverts prepared by either their national marketing organization or by manufacturers (Fig. 8.2). Until at least the mid-1930s, EDA focused its press adverts on middle-class publications such as the *Daily Mail*, *Daily Express*, *Good Housekeeping*, *Woman and Home*, and *Homes and Gardens*, while avoiding working-class women's magazines. Conversely, the gas industry was much more focused on the working-class women's press.[73] BCGA played a key role in generating advertising materials for gas undertakings, in addition to its national advertising campaigns. Their production department both supplied standard advertisements to gas suppliers and prepared bespoke adverts for their individual requirements. This constituted a valuable service for undertakings lacking their own publicity departments and helped foster unified and consistent marketing messages across the industry.[74] Show cards available in June 1930 included themes such as the potential gas appliances offered for increased leisure and home comfort ('USE GAS and HAVE LEISURE for the SUNNY HOURS'; 'WASHDAY LEISURE. USE A GAS WASH COPPER'); improved performance ('BE A GOOD COOK. USE GAS'; 'IF GAS COOKS YOUR FOOD PERFECT COOKING IS EASY AND LABOURLESS'); and lower cost.[75] The time-saving benefits of gas were most prominently featured, for example in leaflets bearing such titles as 'ESCAPING THE BLUES' and 'IF YOU HAD A REGIMENT OF SERVANTS...'.[76]

[71] W. Stewart, 'Advertisements Please', *BCGA Bulletin*, 35 (July 1936), 124–5.
[72] Everard, *History of the Gas Light and Coke Company*, 346.
[73] Bowden and Offer, 'Technological Revolution that Never Was', 267.
[74] Stewart, 'Advertisements Please'.
[75] BCGA, *Gas Bulletin*, 30 (June 1930), 110–11, examples of show cards recently designed by the association.
[76] 'New Leaflets', BCGA, *Gas Bulletin*, 31 (May 1931), 62.

**Fig. 8.1.** A 1933 cartoon-strip format Mr Therm advert, showing the advantages of gas heating in winter

*Source: Design for Today* magazine, 1933. Reproduced by kind permission of Mike Ashworth.

BCGA also produced a series of films during the mid-1930s. These included instructional films on topics such as cookery and kitchen planning, for use in gas suppliers' sales campaigns—screenings being accompanied by a compere who made sales points related to the film subject matter.[77] BCGA also commissioned a series of notable documentary films addressing social issues, with titles such as *Housing Problems* and *Enough to Eat*, which helped to develop a progressive image for a utility that was often seen as old-fashioned compared to electricity.

EDA promoted a vision of electricity providing cleaner, healthier homes: removing the soot created by coal and gas, eradicating remaining dirt with the vacuum cleaner, and halting the decay of food and the spread of germs via the refrigerator.[78] Its efforts were boosted by the Electrical Association for Women (EAW) launched in 1925 following an initiative by members of the Women's Engineering Society. EAW sought to educate women regarding the benefits of domestic electrical apparatus; by 1934 there were forty-seven local and regional EAW branches, each with a programme of activities.[79] Its success prompted the launch of the Women's Gas Council in 1935, with support of the gas industry, in an attempt to counter its influence.[80]

---

[77] 'Turning in to "National"', BCGA, *Gas Bulletin*, 36 (Nov. 1937), 147–50 (149).
[78] Sprenger and Webb, 'Persuading the Housewife to Use Electricity?', 62.
[79] Ibid., 60.     [80] Ibid., 64.

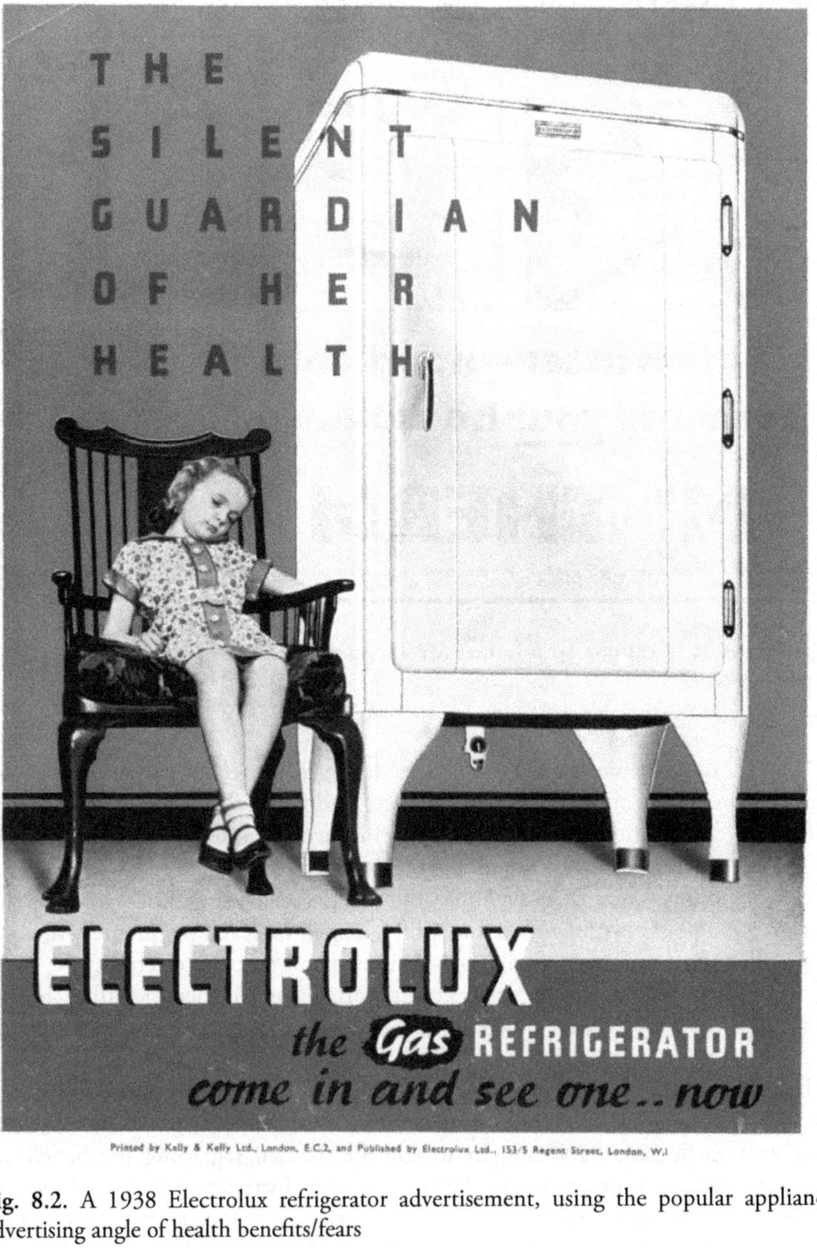

**Fig. 8.2.** A 1938 Electrolux refrigerator advertisement, using the popular appliance advertising angle of health benefits/fears

*Source: Electrolux News* (June 1938), 20. Peter Scott collection.

A 1930 U.S. Department of Commerce report was scathing about early efforts to market electrical appliances in Britain: 'Until recently electrical appliances in Great Britain were considered a luxury. When they were not sold as a luxury they were sold as a novelty. In fact, the word "electric" used in describing an appliance seems to have been a synonym for "expensive" in the minds of the public generally.'[81] The report added that in the past most advertising was confined to trade journals and only recently, led principally by the larger department stores, had any noticeable effort been made to reach the consumer (though it did acknowledge the propaganda work of the BEA and EAW).[82] Electricity supply industry campaigns were also criticized for focusing on the middle classes (especially before the mid-1930s), with themes such as how electrical appliances would make servants more efficient; how it would make them more content (and, thus, less liable to leave); and—of particular appeal to lower-middle-class households—the potential for dispensing with servants altogether.[83]

Electricity suppliers were particularly keen on promoting the concept of the professional housewife, which was aimed primarily at middle-class women. Advertising claimed that electrical appliances could take the hard work out of housework, allow women to reallocate their time towards motherhood and other 'caring' aspects of their housewife role, improve standards of cleanliness and hygiene, and reduce their dependence on paid help.[84] For example, in the 1920s EDA commissioned the propaganda film *Edward and Eda*, in which an engaged couple overcame the financial barriers to marriage by Eda volunteering to do her own housework with the aid of electric labour-saving appliances, rather than employing a domestic servant.[85]

In reality, the economics of middle-class household management were not nearly as favourable to the new consumer durables as such marketing suggested. For example, during the mid-1930s minimum monthly HP payments on a GEC electric washer and wringer were 18s 6d, while a more prestigious Hotpoint electric washer/wringer cost £1 3s 10d monthly over two years.[86] When their significant power costs are factored in, it is by no means clear that this constituted a better investment than employing a charlady (paid around 10d per hour) or the use of a commercial laundry. Moreover, these options would take care of washing tasks in their entirety, while washing, wringing, and ironing clothes remained a laborious chore for the housewife even with the aid of electrical machinery.[87]

## DEMONSTRATING APPLIANCES—SHOWROOMS, EXHIBITIONS, AND CANVASSING

As electricity suppliers began to extend their promotional activities to the working classes, they looked at what approaches had proved successful for other service

---

[81] U.S. Department of Commerce, Bureau of Foreign and Domestic Commerce, *British Market for Domestic Electrical Appliances*, 6.

[82] Ibid.    [83] Bowden and Offer, 'Technological Revolution that Never Was', 266–7.

[84] Ibid., 266.    [85] Hannah, *Electricity before Nationalisation*, 204.

[86] Peter Scott, collection, GEC, 'GEC Household Electrical Appliances', brochure (1936), 29; Hotpoint, '"Monday I Wash". A Book of Practical Information based on Tested Methods' (1935).

[87] For a fuller comparison of the relative costs and advantages of appliances and paid domestic labour during this period, see Peter Scott, *The Making of the Modern British Home: The Suburban Semi and Family Life between the Wars* (Oxford: Oxford University Press, 2013), 168–70.

sectors. As J. I. Bernard of Westminster Electric Supply Co. told the 1936 electricity supply sales managers' conference:

> the poorer sections of the community... need and expect the same 'personal attention' that they have been used to receiving from the rent collector, clothing club agent, etc.... The method of approach, therefore, must be essentially one of personal contact, the way having been paved beforehand by suitable publicity... in order to bring home... the fact that a scheme is being adopted for making electricity available to them on terms which they can afford to pay.[88]

Gas suppliers had pioneered many of the key techniques for personal contact with their consumers—showrooms, cookery demonstrations, instructional visits by gas 'home service' departments, and model gas-powered exhibition homes—prior to the First World War.[89] However, the intensity and sophistication of marketing campaigns increased markedly during the inter-war years, fuelled by growing competition between gas and electricity suppliers. A key element of this battle was presenting appliances to the customer, via exhibitions, showrooms (which could take the form of conventional retail showrooms, travelling showrooms, or show houses), demonstrations, and door-to-door canvassing.

In February 1934 an EDA representative suggested that local electricity undertakings should hold exhibitions every three years. He cited a recent EDA exhibition at Swansea which drew 36,000 people, with attractions that included an electric bungalow, a robot, and a talking film.[90] Fixed showrooms were also highly valued, though these must be 'accessible' to their target market, in terms of both their locations and the messages that their outward and inward appearance conveyed. This entailed avoiding 'anything that savours of an ornate or luxury atmosphere. In large towns this may mean that special showrooms are advisable, situated more in the working-class district and equipped in a plainer way than the central showrooms.'[91]

Electrical manufacturers assisted and encouraged electrical retailers with demonstrations. As a 1925 GEC brochure advised retailers:

> the surest way to effect sales of Domestic Electric Appliances is by means of practical demonstration. The public is still a little uncertain of the Electric method and quite a lot of old-fashioned prejudice yet remains. Demonstration is the means by which this may be overcome!... It is on the principle of the little boy wanting to see the wheels go round. Show your customers, by practical demonstration and explanation, what Electricity can do for them... they will understand it the better and desire it the more.[92]

---

[88] MMSI, ESI 73, British Electrical Development Association Inc., Annual report for Electricity Supply Sales Managers Conference, 30 Mar.–1 April 1936, J. I. Bernard, 'Selling Electrical Service for the Small Household'.

[89] Glendenning, *Demons of Domesticity*, 230.

[90] MMSI, ESI 73, British Electrical Development Association Inc., Annual report on Electricity Supply Sales Managers Conferences, 1934, paper on 'Organising a Local Electrical Exhibition' by Mr V. W. Dale, Electrical Development Association.

[91] MMSI, ESI 73, British Electrical Development Association Inc., Annual report for Electricity Supply Sales Managers Conference, 30 Mar.–1 April 1936, J. I. Bernard, 'Selling Electrical Service for the Small Household'.

[92] RSL, Marconi, 3780, GEC, 'A GEC Scheme for Popularising the Use of Domestic Appliances', brochure (Jan. 1925), 1–2.

To encourage dealer participation, GEC offered them a '"MAGNET" Domestic Outfit', consisting of an iron, toaster, kettle, and portable heater, for sale at £5 5s. This was to be publicized via a huge circularizing campaign, aimed at almost a million wired homes, inquiries being referred to the local '"MAGNET" Demonstrator'. The campaign was to be supported by press advertising in middle-class women's and lifestyle magazines such as *Homes and Gardens*, *Eve*, *Good Housekeeping*, *Ladies' Field*, *Ideal Home*, and *Vogue*. Participating dealers also received support via sales aids, such as leaflets overprinted with the dealer's name, show cards, window display items, and so forth. GEC also provided sales staff to show retailers how to conduct the demonstrations. In return, dealers were required to make various commitments, including stocking these appliances, arranging demonstrations of them, and displaying an 'Authorised "MAGNET" Demonstration' sign.[93]

Electrical goods manufacturers also assisted electricity suppliers with their showroom demonstrations. These were supported through advertising, window display, and canvassing materials—to drum up the audience—plus assistance with the actual showroom demonstrations. Meanwhile cooker demonstrations were also cross-promoted through the support of firms manufacturing flour, cake mixes, and so forth.[94]

Showing white goods in a realistic household setting was a popular method of exhibiting both gas and electric appliances. In 1925 GEC had opened the 'The "Magnet" Electric Home' (a public exhibition comprising a complete house) at its London headquarters on Holborn's Kingsway.[95] The City of Salford Gas Department ran a continuous succession of all-gas exhibition houses, each operating for three or four months, open throughout the week including Sundays (which produced more visitors than any other day).[96]

Electricity and gas suppliers were keen to secure business on new housing estates (ideally as the sole power provider), sometimes even offering incentives such as varying the service charge for supplying gas to a new estate according to the number of appliances installed.[97] Gas and electricity providers were also keen to kit out developers' show houses on new speculative estates with as many appliances as they could pack in.[98] In return, they were allowed to have a sales representative on hand to meet the large numbers of people who typically came to inspect show houses. They also offered cookery demonstrators for a week or so at around the point when the estate became half completed—a visitor attraction that boosted both their business and that of the estate developer.[99]

As in other areas of promotion, the gas industry was quick to counter new initiatives by the electrical concerns, and vice versa. For example, when the EDA

[93] Ibid.
[94] MMSI, ESI 73, British Electrical Development Association Inc., Annual report on Electricity Supply Sales Managers Conferences, 1934, paper on 'Value of Special Demonstrations', by W. B. Leigh.
[95] RSL, Marconi, 3780, GEC, 'The "Magnet" Electric Home', brochure (1925).
[96] 'All-Gas Houses are Good Publicity', BCGA, *Gas Bulletin*, 33 (May 1934), 78.
[97] J. Harwood, 'Selling Gas Apparatus on New Building Estates', BCGA, *Gas Bulletin*, 33 (Jan. 1934), 40–1.
[98] Ibid.     [99] Ibid.

launched an 'Electric Homes (Three Plug Points) campaign' for the first six months of 1931, using some fifty demonstration houses, BCGA countered by encouraging gas undertakings to mount similar campaigns for 'All-Gas' demonstration houses. The house developed by the Bristol Gas Company received over 2,000 visitors in its first week, including school visits from girls taking domestic science courses.[100]

During the early 1930s the Westminster Electric Supply Co. launched a campaign to sell electricity supply and appliances to the occupants of a block of 900 hitherto 'gas only' London County Council tenement flats. The gas company reacted by parking a travelling showroom right in the middle of the block and offering modern enamelled cookers on generous HP terms. Westminster Electric then placed a portable showroom about 100 yards away from that of the gas company.[101] Some years later, several electricity supply undertakings responded to local marketing of Electrolux gas refrigerators on 2s 6d per week HP terms by offering 3 cubic foot refrigerators on 2s 6d per week HP terms over five years. This gave them less than 7 per cent interest on the cash price over the whole five-year period (or approximately 1.4 per cent per annum), producing complaints of 'unfair trading' from local Chambers of Commerce—representing retailer/contractors.[102]

As one electricity sales executive noted, 'It is generally recognised that in connection with schemes for the sale, hire, or hire-purchase of electrical apparatus, demonstrations such as those carried out in consumer's homes or the weekly cooking demonstrations in showrooms are absolutely essential...and most undertakings have these demonstrations as a matter of course.'[103] Many gas concerns had 'Home Service' departments, which conducted cookery demonstrations, offered advice and recipes to individual customers, and assisted schools with domestic science classes. For example, Gas Light & Coke Co. expanded its staff of 'home service advisers' from twelve in 1922 to around fifty by the late 1930s.[104] It was estimated in 1937 that over 100,000 women a year attended their home service demonstrations, providing 'a subtle combination of entertainment, public education, domestic advice and advertising'.[105]

Appliances were also marketed door-to-door, via personal canvassing. Gas undertakings used their meter inspectors and maintenance engineers as canvassers, often paying them commission.[106] These had the advantage of guaranteed access to the house, while traditional canvassers sometimes found it difficult to gain

[100] 'Bristol Undertaking's Campaign', BCGA, *Gas Bulletin*, 31 (Feb.–Mar. 1931), 17.

[101] MMSI, ESI 73, British Electrical Development Association Inc., Annual report on Electricity Supply Sales Managers Conferences, 1934, W. Millner, 'An Intensive Campaign for Domestic Electrification in a Working-Class District'.

[102] MMSI, ESI 73, British Electrical Development Association Inc., Annual report on Electricity Supply Sales Managers Conferences, 1938, 'Planned Selling' by G. E. Barrett (Northmet), comment on paper by R. Mellor (Carlyle).

[103] MMSI, ESI 73, British Electrical Development Association Inc., Annual report on Electricity Supply Sales Managers Conferences, 1934, W. B. Leigh, 'Value of Special Demonstrations'.

[104] Glendenning, *Demons of Domesticity*, 266.

[105] Ibid., 269–72.

[106] E. J. Sutcliffe, 'How we do our Local Publicity', BCGA, *Gas Bulletin*, 30 (Sept. 1930), 138–40.

access in districts heavily worked by door-to-door salesmen.[107] Gas salesmen copied American door-to-door sales methods, including 'canned' (rehearsed) sales talk.[108] American salesmanship theory, such as the sociological approach based on the AIDA model (Attention, Interest, Desire, Action), had also diffused to British gas suppliers by the 1930s.[109] Door-to-door sales were often undertaken cooperatively with manufacturers. This allowed manufacturers' salesmen to introduce themselves as representatives of the gas undertaking—again increasing their chances of getting through the front door.[110]

Although gas and electricity suppliers' advertising generally avoided public criticism of the other's service, salesmen used more candid attacks. Gas salesmen would point to electrical power cuts, whereas gas supplies were not vulnerable to such interruption—as reflected in the slogan, 'Mr Therm never lets London down'.[111] Conversely electricity salesmen would talk of 'fumes', 'explosions', and 'dirt created by old-fashioned methods of lighting'.[112]

Salesmen were often paid via a combination of salary and commission. For example, in 1934 the North Eastern Supply Co. paid their fifty-two salesmen £3 per week plus 10s meal allowance, together with a commission of 2s 6d per KW for lighting and 1s per kW for any appliances sold, and a further commission of 5 per cent on HP, and 1.5 per cent on cash sales. They also used competitions between teams of salesmen as a motivational device.[113]

## CONCLUSIONS

Value chains for electrical and gas appliances appear to have been particularly favourable to the consumer. The power supply utilities that dominated sales of power-hungry appliances were mainly interested in expanding appliance ownership as a means of boosting their power sales. Consequently they were not only prepared to accept lower margins than those charged by conventional retailers, but also to engage in extensive promotional activity and offer generous 'easy terms' (HP or hire). Moreover, given that they were more interested in selling the power the appliances used than in boosting replacement sales, they had strong incentives to select appliances on the basis of reliability, long service lives, and value for money.

---

[107] Such resistance was noted by A. J. Garward of the Portsmouth Gas Company in a July 1931 talk to the Southern District Gas Salesmen's Circle—'Gas Salesmen's Circles. Southern District Meeting—Sub-Section "B"', BCGA, *Gas Bulletin*, 31 (July 1931), 102–4 (104).

[108] 'Selling Liquid Sunshine', *Gas Salesman*, 15 (May 1936), 139–41, summary of a talk by Edgar C. A. Bliault, managing director, National Gas Water Heating Co., to the North London Gas Salesman's Circle.

[109] Harold Whitehead, 'The Education Scheme', *Gas Salesman* (Jan. 1931), 36–8 (36).

[110] 'Selling Liquid Sunshine', *Gas Salesman*, 15 (May 1936), 139–41.

[111] Everard, *History of the Gas Light and Coke Company*, 348.

[112] National Gas Archive, G51:B15, W. A. Bishop, 'Meeting the Attack', notes of chairman's opening address to the London Circle of Gas Salesmen, 1934.

[113] MMSI, ESI 73, British Electrical Development Association Inc., Annual report on Electricity Supply Sales Managers Conferences, 1934, J. B. Kinnersley's discussion of article 'Outdoor Selling and Service Staffs', by Mr Pike, North Eastern Supply Co.

Yet appliance diffusion rates remained very low, owing to formidable demand-side obstacles. As noted earlier, people valued entertainment durables more highly than labour-saving ones (as an hour of entertainment was considered more valuable than an hour of labour saved). Moreover, labour-saving appliances reduced the work of the housewife, while—in an era when few women worked after marriage—it was often the husband who had to be persuaded that these were a worthwhile investment. Men typically worked 48 hours per week during this period, often under onerous supervision and work-pacing, together with weekly commuting times of perhaps two to four hours. Thus persuading even a consider- ate husband that his wife needed expensive machinery to lighten her work load was often an uphill task.

Nor did most married women have the option of using the time freed up by the new machinery to recoup its cost via paid work. Women had a low 'opportunity cost' of their time spent doing housework, as the most attractive jobs for women required full-time work, while part-time employment was often both low-paid and unpleasant (such as part-time domestic service, or work in a commercial laundry). Even full-time female workers generally received only around half the average wages of men in the same industries. Indeed, paying a charlady, or using a commer- cial laundry was not obviously poorer value for money than the new appliances. Moreover, appliance ownership conferred much less social kudos than the radio or new three-piece suite, which were prominently displayed in the parlour. Finally, the importance of consumer resistance and inertia should not be underestimated, given the entrenched nature of traditional social practices and routines associated with heating, cleanliness, and hygiene. 'Push' marketing offered one potential means of breaking down these barriers, a strategy employed, with considerable initial success, by the vacuum cleaner firms examined next.

# 9

# The Hard Sell

## Marketing Vacuum Cleaners in the United States

### INTRODUCTION

The vacuum cleaner was an archetypal 'new economy' product of the early twentieth century. It offered both major time savings and qualitative advantages over previous household cleaning methods—the brush, broom, and manual carpet sweeper. Its diffusion was dominated by strong, vigorously promoted brands. And it was aggressively sold door-to-door by armies of manufacturers' salesmen.

The sales techniques pioneered by vacuum cleaner manufacturers in the United States were to have a profound impact on the way vacuums were sold in Britain, and globally, being introduced to successive countries by multinationals such as Hoover and Electrolux (which still uses many of these in emerging markets, such as India). Yet vacuum cleaner marketing does not appear to have been an unambiguous success. In 1939 some 48.4 per cent of wired households and farms in the United States were estimated to have new vacuum cleaners, which constituted impressive diffusion relative to the UK, but lagged considerably behind the American diffusion of electric washing machines (59.6 per cent) and refrigerators (56.0 per cent).[1] Indeed, until the 1950s vacuum cleaners were generally viewed as a luxury item, accessible only to higher-income households.[2]

This chapter explores how the vacuum cleaner's distinctive product characteristics, which made it ideal for direct selling via demonstration, both provided an initial boost to sales and, eventually, acted to impede overall diffusion. Direct selling constituted an exceptionally high-cost distribution method, dominating the total costs of the vacuum cleaner value chain and driving up prices for vacuums sold via this method. However, it was particularly effective, with the firms that relied most heavily on direct sales still constituting the sector's market leaders in the late 1930s.

---

[1] Smithsonian, Clark, 55, 201/2, data sheets compiled by Clark from the January 1940 issue of *Electrical Merchandising*. These figures exclude sales of second-hand machines (other than those reconditioned and sold by the manufacturers).

[2] Carroll Gantz, *The Vacuum Cleaner: A History* (Jefferson, NC: McFarland, 2012), 87.

## PATENTS, TRADE ASSOCIATIONS, AND THE
## RESTRICTION OF COMPETITION

A suction carpet sweeper was patented in the United States as early as 1860, though there is no evidence that it was produced for sale. By 1876 carpet sweepers with manually generated suction and brush rolls were being commercially marketed, which, a leading authority argues, were technically vacuum cleaners.[3] British fairground engineer Hubert Cecil Booth is generally credited with inventing the *powered* vacuum cleaner, in 1901. Booth developed a huge petrol-powered cleaner, pulled by horses—attracting custom from the wealthy partly due to the amusement and novelty value of having the great contraption arrive at their house and then clean the carpets through hoses extended in through the doors and windows. Booth launched the British Vacuum Cleaner Co. (which later produced Goblin brand cleaners) to manufacture what were initially horse-drawn machines, available for hire.[4]

However, the activities of an American inventor, David T. Kenney, were to prove much more fundamental to the long-term evolution of the industry. In November 1901 (nine months after Booth's patent application) Kenney filed a patent for an 'apparatus for removing dust' which was granted in March 1907. This was the first patent to use a vacuum as the sole cleaning method, but for a system installed in buildings—powered by a steam-driven vacuum pump in the basement—with the suction action transmitted via pipes to each floor. Kenney purchased Booth's US patent application, thus avoiding any potential challenge to what proved to be the industry's fundamental patent. Kenney's patent covered the essential principle of all vacuum cleaners, the 'narrow nozzle'—sucking air through a narrow section of a broader tube to create a powerful vacuum that would draw in dirt. The patent's holder, the Vacuum Cleaner Company of New York, was successful in having the patent held valid and infringed in 1907 and by 1909 they had given up manufacturing in favour of exploiting a portfolio of vacuum patents, by granting licences to the major manufacturers.[5]

In 1911 four leading vacuum firms formed a defence association to fight the Kenney patents, reaching a deal in June 1912 whereby they accepted Kenney licences on a 2 per cent royalty basis.[6] These formed the core of what became the Vacuum Cleaner Manufacturers Association (VCMA), with membership restricted to the licensees of the fundamental (Kenney) patent. By 1924 there were nineteen direct licensees and six sub-licensees, all of whom were VCMA members.[7] Until the Kenney patents expired, in March 1924, it was difficult to operate in the sector without an original Kenney licence and VCMA membership thus encompassed all significant manufacturers.[8]

---

[3] Ibid., 35.      [4] Jane Furnival, *Suck, Don't Blow* (London: O'Mara, 1998), 10–11.

[5] Gantz, *Vacuum Cleaner*, 49–52.

[6] Kenney licence contract of 1912, reproduced in Federal Trade Commission, *Report on the House Furnishings Industry. Volume III: Kitchen Furnishings and Domestic Appliances* (Washington, DC: USGPO, 1925), 276; Gantz, *Vacuum Cleaner*, 75.

[7] Federal Trade Commission, *Report on the House Furnishings Industry*, xix.

[8] Gantz, *Vacuum Cleaner*, 92.

Over the two decades following the Kenney and Booth patent applications vacuum cleaners were transformed from large, cumbersome machines into portable, electrically powered devices suitable for the housewife. In 1905 the first self-contained portable electric vacuum cleaner was developed by a Dr William Noe of San Fransisco and by 1910 there was a significant number of US companies marketing carpet cleaners that relied primarily on powered suction. Subsequent innovation was reflected in other significant (though not fundamental) patents. For example, after hiring mechanical engineer Francis Mills Case in 1909, Hoover filed a patent in September 1910—for 'carpet agitation'—via a motor-driven rotary brush that produced a beating action as it passed over the carpet.[9] This gave Hoover a competitive advantage, through preventing other firms copying its motor-driven agitator and brush, until 1926.[10] Other leading manufacturers also invested heavily in innovation and patenting, enabling them to assert patent-protected product superiority; by May 1922 firms in the sector collectively held over 275 patents.[11]

During the lifetime of the Kenney patent interactions between the VCMA and the patent holders created an industry structure based on strong barriers to entry, high, relatively stable prices, and a considerable degree of cooperation between member companies. Clause 7 of the Kenney licence stated that the licensor would not grant any further licences without the consent of three-quarters of existing licensees. The trustee of the Kenney patents explained the rationale for this clause to the Federal Trade Commission (FTC) as follows: 'When the licensees got that contract they got it for the purpose of holding me down and keeping everybody out of the business.'[12] Indeed it was the policing of this provision that was the VCMA's principal function. Moreover, clause 14 of the Kenney licence stated that licences were not assignable to other parties by the licensee, unless the firm in question was to take over its entire vacuum business.[13]

This restriction of competition generated high profits. The FTC found that the average return on investment for eleven vacuum cleaner manufacturers was 36.2 per cent in 1920 and 20.6 per cent in 1921 (a depression year). These rates were much higher than those for other consumer durables industries; for example, thirty-five washing machine manufacturers surveyed by the Commission earned 22 per cent on their investment in 1920 and lost just under 0.5 per cent in 1921. The much larger profits of vacuum cleaner manufacturers were attributed to their ability to maintain prices, despite falling demand. The wholesale price index for washing machines fell by almost 20 per cent between its peak in late summer/early autumn of 1920 and December 1921, then remained stable during 1922 (retail prices closely following this trend). Conversely, vacuum prices were actually higher in 1921 than in 1920 and showed only insignificant declines in 1922.[14]

---

[9] Ibid., 53–67.     [10] Ibid., 96.

[11] VCMA minutes, 28 Oct. 1921, cited in Federal Trade Commission, *Report on the House Furnishings Industry*, 10–11.

[12] Federal Trade Commission, *Report on the House Furnishings Industry*, 7.

[13] Kenney licence contract of 1912, reproduced in Federal Trade Commission, *Report on the House Furnishings Industry*, 278.

[14] Federal Trade Commission, *Report on the House Furnishings Industry*, xx–xxi.

## PRODUCTION SYSTEMS, VALUE CHAINS,
## AND INDUSTRY STRUCTURE

Almost all the major US vacuum cleaner manufacturers were founded during the lifetime of the Kenney patent (generally during its first decade). Hoover owes its origins to James Murray Spangler, an asthmatic janitor, who devised a crude port-able electric vacuum in 1907. He sold the idea to his relative, W. H. 'Boss' Hoover, a leather-goods manufacturer in North Canton, Ohio, who started manufacturing cleaners in 1908.[15] Hoover was the US market leader for most of the inter-war period and was by far the most successful US vacuum firm in terms of overseas sales (assisted by a multinational strategy, with factories in Canada and, from 1932, Britain).

America's second most important vacuum manufacturer of the 1920s, Eureka, was established by the salesman Fred Wardell, who marketed the Eureka Model 1 from 1909 (originally produced via the Stecher Electric & Machine Co.) and, in 1910, founded the Eureka Vacuum Cleaner Co. in Detroit.[16] By the end of 1928 Eureka had some 625 factory employees and over 4,000 in total.[17] Another major inter-war vacuum manufacturer, the Frantz Premier Vacuum Cleaner Co., was also established in 1910, in Cleveland, Ohio, to market a cleaner designed by the inventor James Kirby. In 1915 it was acquired by General Electric and became the Electric Vacuum Cleaner Co., continuing to produce vacuums under the Frantz Premier brand until the Second World War.[18] By 1929 its plant occupied 1.5 acres, with a total floor space of 120,000 sq. ft., and the firm employed around 2,500 people. Their total sales rose from $3.45 million in 1922 to $6.25 million in 1927.[19]

In 1913 two founders of Premier, Clarence and Walter Frantz, formed a new company, the Apex Electric Manufacturing Co., to make vacuums and washing machines.[20] Meanwhile the P. A. Geiger Co. (established in 1905), began manufacturing vacuum cleaners in 1910 and by 1912 had switched production entirely to this product.[21] Most of the largest vacuum cleaner companies were based in Ohio; Hoover was headquartered in North Canton and Apex, Electric Vacuum Cleaner Co., and P. A. Geiger Co. in Cleveland, while Eureka was based in nearby Detroit.

Table 9.1 shows available data for vacuum cleaner sales/output, both in aggregate and for the two largest early manufacturers. Trade data on US sales are based on industry statistics collated by the VCMA and firm-level data for Hoover and Eureka. Census data are based on output, rather than sales, and thus overestimate sales within the United States (as they include exports). They also show values at factory gate, rather than retail prices. The data show a number of important trends. First, there is no sign of any 'take-off' in sales, as predicted by standard product diffusion models. Total unit sales for 1927 are not greatly above 1924

---

[15] Ibid., 15.      [16] Gantz, *Vacuum Cleaner*, 70.

[17] Moody's Investment Service, *Moody's Manual of Investments. American and Foreign. Industrial Securities* (New York: Moody's, 1929), 54.

[18] Gantz, *Vacuum Cleaner*, 70–6.      [19] Moody's Investment Service, *Moody's Manual*, 2980.

[20] Gantz, *Vacuum Cleaner*, 75.      [21] Ibid., 72.

**Table 9.1.** Estimates of US vacuum cleaner annual sales (units and dollar values), 1919–41

| Year | (A) Trade data (US sales) | | | | (B) Census data (output) | |
|------|--------|--------|---------|-----------|--------|-------------------|
| | Hoover | Eureka | Total | Total ($) | Total | Total ($, factory gate prices) |
| 1919 | 180,566 | | 702,000 | 42,120,000 | | |
| 1920 | 273,176 | | 1,024,167 | 61,450,000 | | |
| 1921 | 138,931 | 94,492 | 588,502 | 35,310,000 | 739,534 | 19,752,905 |
| 1922 | 172,097 | 132,995 | 745,873 | 44,752,000 | | |
| 1923 | 227,217 | 205,162 | 1,025,000 | 56,011,000 | 1,240,742 | 35,981,514 |
| 1924 | 210,223 | 243,497 | 943,600 | 63,633,900 | | |
| 1925 | 196,600 | 246,825 | 970,000 | 60,000,000 | 1,107,592 | 39,971,111 |
| 1926 | 189,874 | 272,617 | 1,065,000 | 65,000,000 | | |
| 1927 | 217,941 | 270,562 | 1,194,614 | 58,536,086 | 1,128,256 | 36,222,271 |
| 1928 | 205,592 | | 1,219,460 | 60,973,000 | | |
| 1929 | 189,859 | | 1,395,745 | 64,810,790 | 1,407,000 | 35,108,000 |
| 1930 | 168,067 | | 1,170,339 | 55,987,704 | | |
| 1931 | 133,859 | | 877,695 | 37,310,822 | 887,000 | 24,847,000 |
| 1932 | 123,895 | | 557,288 | 19,600,756 | | |
| 1933 | 104,125 | | 739,354 | 30,271,330 | 554,935 | 14,410,594 |
| 1934 | 124,728 | | 968,376 | 43,555,465 | | |
| 1935 | 147,384 | | 1,200,940 | 54,709,769 | 1,111,752 | 24,190,986 |
| 1936 | 168,939 | | 1,510,953 | 67,456,541 | | |
| 1937 | 201,275 | | 1,706,336 | 75,575,002 | 1,514,859 | 36,028,647 |
| 1938 | 162,278 | | 1,295,674 | 62,557,054 | | |
| 1939 | 201,677 | | 1,436,198 | 68,814,536 | 1,445,258 | 44,159,619 |
| 1940 | | | 1,743,443 | 81,195,409 | | |
| 1941 | | | 2,080,000 | 97,761,863 | | |

*Note:* Census data are for output rather than sales and values are at factory gate, rather than retail prices.

*Sources:* Eureka—Moody's Investment Service, *Moody's Manual of Investments. American and Foreign. Industrial Securities* (New York: Moody's, 1929), 54. Hoover, Hoover Historical Center [hereafter HHC], Hoover chronology by Lee P. Heinrich (undated, *c.*1940s). Industry-wide trade data: 1923 (units) and 1924–38 (units and value)—annual surveys of consumer durables sales published in *Electrical Merchandising*: (Jan. 1942), 607; (Jan. 1936), 2–3; (Feb. 1924), 4078. 1919–22 (units), U.S. Federal Trade Commission, *Report on the House Furnishings Industry. Volume III: Kitchen Furnishings and Domestic Appliances* (Washington, DC: USGPO, 1925), 14; 1919–23 (values), 'Five Years of Electric Vacuum Sales, by Quarters', *Electrical Merchandising* (Feb. 1924), 4098. Census data, U.S. Dept. of Commerce, Bureau of the Census, *Biennial Census of Manufactures* (Washington, DC: USGPO) for years 1927 (1930), 1061; 1933 (1936), 546; 1935 (1938), 1057; U.S. Dept. of Commerce, Bureau of the Census, *Fifteenth Census of the United States. Manufactures. 1929* (Washington, DC: USGPO, 1933), vol. 2, 1129; *Sixteenth Census of the United States. Manufacturers, 1939* (Washington, DC: USGPO, 1942), vol. 2, part II, 378.

levels, while sales do not return to 1929 levels until 1936. Second, the industry was relatively concentrated; Hoover and Eureka collectively enjoyed 40 per cent of US unit sales in 1921 and 41 per cent in 1927 (though their collective and individual market shares subsequently declined, partly owing to the rise of Electrolux).

The data also suggest that vacuum cleaner prices rose in real terms over the inter-war period. Between 1921 and 1927 (when general retail prices fell by about 3 per cent) the average factory gate price of a vacuum cleaner had risen from $26.7 to $32.1. Meanwhile the 1929–38 retail price data indicate that a fall in general retail

**Table 9.2.** US sales (units and retail values) of floor and hand-type vacuum cleaners, 1929–38

| Year | Floor type No. | Value | Unit price | Hand type No. | Value | Unit price | Hand as % of total | |
|------|------|------|------|------|------|------|------|------|
| | | | | | | | Units | Dollars |
| 1929 | 1,253,202 | 62,660,000 | 50 | 142,543 | 2,150,790 | 15.1 | 10.2 | 3.3 |
| 1930 | 960,343 | 52,818,865 | 55 | 209,996 | 3,168,839 | 15.1 | 17.9 | 5.7 |
| 1931 | 686,648 | 34,332,400 | 50 | 191,047 | 2,978,422 | 15.6 | 21.8 | 8.0 |
| 1932 | 447,056 | 17,882,240 | 40 | 110,232 | 1,718,516 | 15.6 | 19.8 | 8.8 |
| 1933 | 547,536 | 27,376,800 | 50 | 191,818 | 2,894,530 | 15.1 | 25.9 | 9.6 |
| 1934 | 722,367 | 39,720,185 | 55 | 246,009 | 3,835,280 | 15.6 | 25.4 | 8.8 |
| 1935 | 906,049 | 50,439,748 | 56 | 294,891 | 4,270,021 | 14.5 | 24.6 | 7.8 |
| 1936 | 1,149,492 | 62,359,941 | 54 | 361,461 | 5,096,600 | 14.1 | 23.9 | 7.6 |
| 1937 | 1,285,216 | 71,984,948 | 56 | 421,121 | 5,798,836 | 13.8 | 24.7 | 7.5 |
| 1938 | 1,005,800 | 59,704,300 | 59 | 291,730 | 4,282,596 | 14.7 | 22.5 | 6.7 |

*Sources*: Annual surveys of consumer durables sales published in *Electrical Merchandising*: (Jan. 1942), 607; (Jan. 1936), 2–3.

prices of about 18 per cent between these years was matched by a rise in average vacuum cleaner prices of 6.2 per cent. This is all the more surprising, given that there was a compositional shift in favour of hand-held vacuum cleaners (sometimes referred to as 'dusters'), as shown in Table 9.2.

Dusters were the sector's major product innovation of the inter-war period, but were supplementary to, rather than competitive with, traditional floor cleaners—being designed for furniture, stairs, small corners, and other ancillary tasks. It was common knowledge in the trade that attachments to floor cleaners for these purposes were not being used: 'in at least 75 per cent of the cleaners sold, the attachments are stored away, to be taken out at the most, two or three times a year... in many cases not to be taken out at all... their use involves too much time and effort ...'.[22] Hand cleaner sales increased from 10.2 per cent of all vacuum unit sales in 1929 to 22.5 per cent in 1938. Meanwhile the price of floor cleaners actually rose some 18 per cent in nominal terms between 1929 and 1938, equivalent to a real price rise of 44.6 per cent.

Vacuum manufacturing appears to have been more skill-intensive than radio production. Estimates for the mid-1930s indicate that wages in the sector were relatively high, while around three-quarters of factory employees were male.[23] Seasonality of production was significant, but not nearly as great as in radios. Figure 9.1 shows monthly industry data for vacuums leaving factories during 1928, compared with available data on the seasonality of US radio output (for

[22] Florence R. Clauss, 'Sell Them One More Cleaner', *Electrical Merchandising* (Jan. 1929), 64–7 (64).
[23] National Recovery Administration, *Code of Fair Competition for the Vacuum Cleaner Manufacturing Industry* (Washington, DC: USGPO, 1934), 451.

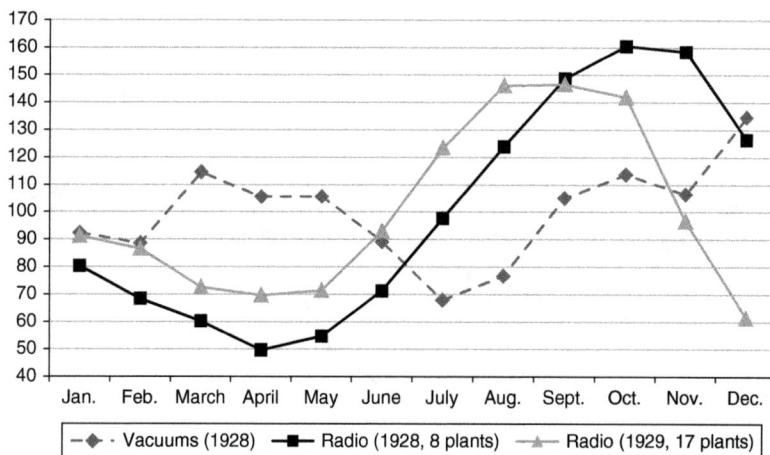

**Fig. 9.1.** Seasonality of production for American vacuum manufacturers in 1928, compared to American radio manufacturers in 1928 and 1929 (monthly output as a proportion of average monthly output in that year)

*Sources*: Vacuum cleaners: U.S. Department of Commerce, Survey of Current Business, No. 90 (Feb. 1929), 41 (based on VCMA data). Radio manufacturers: Caroline Manning, 'Fluctuations of Employment in the Radio Industry', *Bulletin of the Women's Bureau* No. 83 (Washington, DC: USGPO, 1931), 8.

1928 and 1929). Monthly vacuum cleaner output had a standard deviation of 18.1 percentage points, compared with 41.7 per cent for the 1928 estimate for radios and 31.4 per cent for the more broadly based 1929 radio estimate. This probably reflects the practice, common among American white goods manufacturers, of producing for stock and maintaining higher inventories of finished machines over the slack season (facilitated by slower product obsolescence than in radios).[24] As a result, vacuum firms appear to have avoided the seasonal pattern of hiring and firing evident in radio. Data submitted to the 1935 Census of Manufactures by Hoover indicate that their monthly employment never fell below 94 per cent of the annual average, though there was a wider variation in hours worked (see Fig. 9.2).

Relationships between factory costs, other manufacturers' costs, and profits for 1920 and 1921 are shown in Table 9.3, for eleven firms which supplied data to the FTC inquiry (classified by value of invested capital). These included all significant manufacturers.[25] Large firms are shown to have spent much more lavishly on marketing than their smaller counterparts. In 1922 the three largest firms, with average net sales of $3.6 million, had a ratio of selling expense to total costs of 29.4 per cent, compared to 16.2 per cent for the next four firms in the table, and only 6.6 per cent for the three smallest firms. The positive relationship between

---

[24] Federal Trade Commission, *Report of the Federal Trade Commission on Distribution Methods and Costs, Part IV* (Washington, DC: USGPO, 1944), 152.

[25] VCMA minutes, 28 Oct. 1921, cited in Federal Trade Commission, *Report on the House Furnishings Industry*, 18.

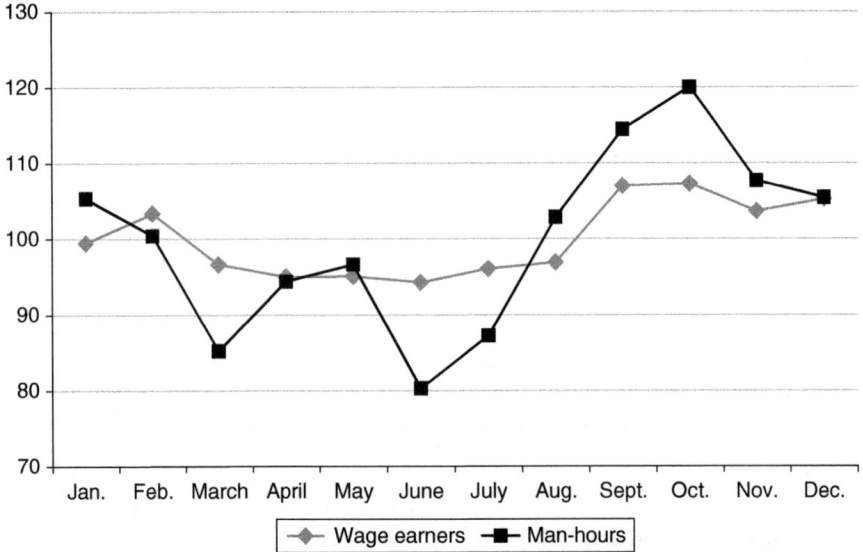

**Fig. 9.2.** Monthly employment at Hoover's North Canton plant (wage earners: number employed and man-hours), in 1935—percentage of average month

*Source:* US National Archives, Washington, RG29, Census of Manufacturers, 1935, Hoover Census of Production return for North Canton plant.

firm size and selling expense ratios is much clearer than for factory costs or general administration expenses (where the figures for medium and small firms are roughly similar).

Table 9.3 suggests that larger firms used the savings from any scale economies they reaped to invest more intensively in marketing and distribution, with the result that their profit margins were no larger than their smaller counterparts. This is corroborated by financial data for Eureka, shown in Table 9.4. Despite a rise in net sales from $3.1 million in 1921 to $12.8 million in 1927, unit prices rose, as reflected in net revenue per machine, which grew from $32.98 to $47.24. This appears to have been driven by a rise in costs and depreciation per machine, from $29.58 in 1923 to $39.00 in 1927. Until the mid-1920s this was accompanied by rising sales and profit rates, though by the end of the decade sales were stagnating and profits falling.

The FTC found that profit rates for vacuum cleaners were considerably higher than for ten other consumer durables it examined, partly owing to the use of the Kenney patent licence to block new entrants.[26] Meanwhile price competition between retailers was deterred by rigorous resale price maintenance; the major manufacturers refused supply or denied exclusive selling agency privileges to retailers that undercut their list prices.[27]

---

[26] Ibid.        [27] Ibid., 17.

**Table 9.3.** Sales, costs, and profits of eleven US vacuum cleaner manufacturers in 1920 and 1921 (grouped according to value of investment in 1920)

| Investment size | No. of firms | Average net sales | Percentage of net sales accounted for by: | | | | | | | Total |
| --- | --- | --- | --- | --- | --- | --- | --- | --- | --- | --- |
| | | | Factory cost of goods | Selling expense | General admin. expense | Total costs | Profit on goods sold | Net deductions | Net profit or loss | |
| **1920** | | | | | | | | | | |
| Over $1million | 3 | 6,288,643 | 52.9 | 25.7 | 8.3 | 86.9 | 13.1 | 1.2 | 11.9 | 100.0 |
| $500,000–$1 million | 4 | 3,087,113 | 72.3 | 11.9 | 6.4 | 90.6 | 9.4 | 2.9 | 6.5 | 100.0 |
| Under $500,000 | 4 | 987,374 | 74.0 | 6.3 | 6.0 | 86.3 | 13.7 | 1.7 | 12.0 | 100.0 |
| **Total** | 11 | 3,196,716 | 62.1 | 18.7 | 7.4 | 88.1 | 11.9 | 1.9 | 10.0 | 100.0 |
| **1921** | | | | | | | | | | |
| Over $1million | 3 | 3,631,861 | 45.1 | 29.4 | 12.7 | 87.1 | 12.9 | 0.6 | 12.2 | 100.0 |
| $500,000–$1 million | 4 | 2,337,044 | 65.9 | 16.2 | 8.0 | 90.1 | 9.9 | 3.4 | 6.5 | 100.0 |
| Under $500,000 | 4 | 594,496 | 66.0 | 6.6 | 9.2 | 81.8 | 18.2 | 3.7 | 14.6 | 100.0 |
| **Total** | 11 | 2,056,522 | 55.9 | 21.6 | 10.4 | 87.8 | 12.2 | 2.1 | 10.1 | 100.0 |

*Source:* Federal Trade Commission, *Report on the House Furnishings Industry. Volume III: Kitchen Furnishing and Domestic Appliances* (Washington, DC: USGPO, 1925), 305.

**Table 9.4.** Eureka Vacuum Cleaner Company sales revenue, costs, and profits

| Year | 1921 | 1922 | 1923 | 1924 | 1925 | 1926 | 1927 | 1928 | 1929* |
|---|---|---|---|---|---|---|---|---|---|
| Machines sold | 94,492 | 132,995 | 205,162 | 243,497 | 246,825 | 272,617 | 270,562 | n.a. | n.a. |
| Net sales ($) | 3,107,448 | 5,009,533 | 8,215,163 | 9,614,790 | 10,090,152 | 12,023,484 | 12,780,161 | 10,099,713 | 10,804,602 |
| Net revenue per machine | 32.89 | 37.67 | 40.04 | 39.49 | 40.88 | 44.10 | 47.24 | n.a. | n.a. |
| Costs & depreciation | n.a. | n.a. | 6,067,783 | 7,430,926 | 8,150,936 | 9,604,933 | 10,551,345 | 8,871,982 | 9,120,875 |
| Operating income | 439,082 | 710,352 | 2,147,380 | 2,183,864 | 1,939,216 | 2,418,551 | 2,228,816 | 1,227,731 | 1,683,727 |
| Costs per unit | n.a. | n.a. | 29.58 | 30.52 | 33.02 | 35.23 | 39.00 | n.a. | n.a. |
| Profit margin** | 14.13 | 14.18 | 26.14 | 22.71 | 19.22 | 20.12 | 17.44 | 12.16 | 15.58 |

*Notes:* All data are for calendar years *In 1929 Eureka took over all the common stock of its London dealer and the figures include its new London subsidiary. **As a proportion of sales, before deductions of fixed charges and federal taxes.

*Sources:* 1921–2, Hagley, 2069/9/16, Victor Talking Machine Co., Consignment selling, Victor Talking Machine Co. field survey, 1926–7. Reports of interview with Mr C. W. Phister, Eureka Vacuum Cleaner Co., 26 May 1927. 1923–9, Moody's Investment Service, *Moody's Manual of Investment*. American and Foreign. *Industrial Securities* (New York: Moody's), for years 1929, 54; 1930, 604.

## MARKETING AND DISTRIBUTION

Vacuum cleaner manufacturers were sales-driven companies. As Hoover's official history noted, 'the sales department is the most important part of an operation like this'.[28] Vacuum cleaner marketing was generally designed to do two tasks—to promote the advantages of vacuum cleaners over traditional cleaning methods and to assert the superiority of the brand over its competitors. Appeals to switch from manual cleaning methods included both labour-saving and hygiene claims. Cleaners were also sold on fear. As a 1936 manual for Eureka's salesmen and dealers noted:

> Diphtheria, measles, smallpox, scarlet fever, whooping cough and enteritis, account for over 75,000 deaths a year of children under 5 years of age. It's a terrible indictment of our carelessness and yearly sacrifices to dust. Young children are constantly at play on rugs and carpets where dust and germs are the thickest... This probably explains why growing children have so many diseases and why these diseases are so fatal... A child's life must not be sacrificed to an old, worn out cleaner or cheap brooms and carpet sweepers. The powerful Eureka is common sense insurance.[29]

Vacuum manufacturers mainly focused on non-price competition. This included trumpeting awards obtained in competitions at various international expositions, through statements designed to knock rival brands, and by stressing proprietary features. Hoover's principal selling point was its superior, patented cleaning system—'carpet agitation'—promoted with the slogan 'It Beats As It Sweeps As It Cleans' (coined by Gerald Page-Wood, the art director of Hoover's advertising agency, Erwin, Wasey & Company, in 1919).[30] This had a strong appeal to house-wives, since beating carpets to remove hidden dirt was part of the annual spring-cleaning ritual.[31]

In 1926, when the original agitator patents expired, Hoover introduced 'positive agitation'—with replaceable brushes and a rigid metal beater bar spir-alled around the roller to more efficiently remove dirt. This constituted an enduring firm-specific advantage and unique selling point for Hoover.[32] The advantages of this system over rival models appear to have been substantial, with independent testing laboratories showing greater cleaning efficiency than cleaners using suction only, or suction plus a brush.[33] Such achievements were underpinned by heavy investments in research and development. Hoover's

---

[28] Frank G. Hoover, *Fabulous Dustpan: The Story of the Hoover* (Cleveland, OH: World Publishing, 1955), 161.

[29] McLean County Museum of History, Bloomington, IL, Eureka Williams Electrolux Archive [hereafter McLean Eureka Archive], Folder 2, 'The Eureka Salesman', manual for Eureka dealers and salesmen, 1936, 31.

[30] Ibid., 128.

[31] Hoover, *Fabulous Dustpan*, 111–12, 128; Hoover Ltd, *On Judging a Vacuum Cleaner* (leaflet, n.d., *c.*1936).

[32] Hoover, *Fabulous Dustpan*, 96–7.

[33] HHC, Filing Cabinet 78.033#52, Ford, Bacon & Davis, 'Report, Business and Sales Operations, The Hoover Company, North Canton, Ohio', 14 Feb. 1940 [hereafter Ford, Bacon & Davis report], vol. 1, 118.

Experimental Department, established in 1919 to test materials and conduct R&D, employed 100 people by 1938.[34]

Eureka stressed its variety of innovative attachments, including paint spraying and hair drying functions.[35] Despite a pronounced slowing in basic product innovations, firms were still emphasizing new mechanical features during the 1930s. For example, in July 1932 Hoover introduced a headlight to its Model 750 (originally as an optional extra) to reveal dirt in dark corners. By the mid-1930s vacuum firms were also following the lead of the automobile industry in employing leading industrial designers, such as Henry Dreyfuss, Raymond Loewy, and Lurelle Guild. These developed distinctively modern designs, such as the Apex MW (1934) and the Hoover 825 (1936)—with a classic modern design, placing the headlight so as to dramatically illuminate the Hoover logo.[36]

There was also a strong element of negative promotion, via attacks on the characteristics of rival brands (but generally without specific mention of brand names, to avoid litigation). Hoover had coined the word 'Bojack' as a generic term for competitors' machines, which they could use without fear of the libel laws.[37] Hoover had, in turn, been on the receiving end of much negative advertising from suction-only cleaners, which asserted that cleaners with a beating action (i.e. Hoovers) damaged carpets.

Aggressive price competition between the major firms was rare, but not unknown. In 1923 Eureka introduced a new Model 9 upright cleaner, with a sales price that undercut Hoover's by almost 50 per cent.[38] Model 9 had the same horsepower as its Hoover competitor, but was a third lighter and sported superior features. This proved to be Eureka's bestseller of all time, allowing them to temporarily become the market leader. Hoover countered with its Model 700, introduced in 1926 to great acclaim—the first model to include its 'positive agitation' system. This enjoyed considerable success, despite being priced at $75 without tools (or $87.50 with them included), making it the most expensive cleaner on the market. Thus technical superiority appears to have been more important than price—particularly for firms that sold door-to-door and made their sales pitch principally on the superiority of their product over all rival brands.

Electrolux, which replaced Eureka as Hoover's main rival in the 1930s, took a different approach to asserting product superiority, emphasizing ease of use. For most of the decade it was the only significant 'tank type' cleaner on the US market. Independent market research found that it was perceived as being easier to carry, easier to use with attachments, easier to clean furniture without moving the cleaner, easier to dispose of dirt, less noisy, and 'not so hard on rugs'. Moreover, the researchers found that Electrolux's ease of use features were more obvious to housewives than Hoover's greater cleaning efficiency, which was substantial, but not so apparent to the user.[39]

---

[34] HHC, undated Hoover chronology by Lee P. Heinrich, 73.
[35] Gantz, *Vacuum Cleaner*, 78.       [36] Ibid., 104–8.
[37] Hoover, *Fabulous Dustpan*, 206.       [38] Gantz, *Vacuum Cleaner*, 92–3.
[39] HHC, Ford, Bacon & Davis report, vol. 1, 119–20.

Vacuum cleaner brands were promoted via intensive advertising. For example in 1928 the sector was estimated to have invested some $1,001,595 in national magazine advertising alone, led by Hoover ($415,100), Premier Duplex ($251,700), and Eureka ($147,400).[40] Vacuum cleaner manufacturers also engaged in newspaper and other local advertising, often cooperatively with their dealers. Hoover was an early advocate of cooperative advertising. For example, a 1911 magazine produced for Hoover dealers had items on preventing objections, 'sales helps' (marketing materials) available from its 'Dealer's Cooperation Department', and the results of their recent dealer sales contest.[41] Hoover also used competitions between its dealers to stimulate promotional activities such as window displays; these had become a regular fixture of its dealer marketing calendar by the early 1920s.[42]

## DOOR-TO-DOOR SELLING

Economist Philip Nelson famously divided products into 'search goods', such as clothing, which he defined as goods that can be assessed with a fair degree of accuracy by inspection during the shopping process, and 'experience goods'. The latter have a value that can only be accurately assessed through 'post-purchase experience' (through their use), on account of difficulties in evaluating characteristics such as performance and durability via inspection.[43] Vacuum cleaners were classic experience goods—both their general advantages over manual cleaning and, especially, the relative merits of specific brands, could only be adequately assessed through experience (and, even then, imperfectly). Yet, as many sales were to first-time purchasers, customers often had little or no direct experience and had to rely on indirect experience, such as the advice of friends or information from advertisements.

As Nelson noted, actions that limit pre-purchase information-gathering by consumers will necessarily concentrate sales and enhance producers' market power.[44] Salesmen could both pre-empt the information-gathering process that might normally precede purchase (by approaching prospects before they had considered acquiring a cleaner) and substitute their own assertions regarding performance and superior attributes. Moreover, vacuum cleaners were a low priority for most households. Customers typically prized entertainment durables more highly, from both a functional and a status perspective (partly owing to the vacuum being stored out of sight). They were also extremely expensive, implying a high monetary cost to each hour of working time saved.

Both Hoover and Eureka's early success were strongly linked to direct sales. In December 1908, shortly after Hoover had entered the vacuum business, they placed

---

[40] Crowell Magazines, *National Markets and National Advertising 1929* (Crowell Magazines, 1929), 114.

[41] HHC, 'Hoover Sweepings', 1, 7 (1911).

[42] HHC, '38 Dealers Share Cash Prizes', *Hoovergrams* (Feb. 1923), 9.

[43] Phillip Nelson, 'Information and Consumer Behaviour', *Journal of Political Economy*, 78 (1970), 311–29.

[44] Ibid., 317.

an advert in the *Saturday Evening Post*, offering readers a Hoover on ten days' free trial. Orders received were then used to drum up dealerships. Each Hoover was shipped to a retailer in the nearest town, with instructions to deliver the Hoover to the customer, collect the payment after the free trial period, and keep the commission. If the customer refused delivery or returned the Hoover, the store was instructed to keep it as a demonstration model and become a Hoover dealer.[45]

Hoover moved to direct sales in around 1910, after observing that their retailers were not pushing Hoovers any more than the other products they stocked. They initially placed a salesman in each store, who would work for the dealer but be paid by Hoover—what became known as the 'resale system'. The dealer's commission was reduced from 33.3 per cent to only 15 per cent; the remaining 18.3 per cent paying the salesman and the costs of his training and management. In 1920 Hoover still sold primarily through dealers, having only 650 'resale men' (plus eighty division and district managers), for its 4,800 dealers.[46] However, from 1921 it began to move to a strategy of house-to-house canvassing (rather than only going to people's homes if asked for a demonstration).[47]

Eureka was also quick to organize and train a door-to-door salesforce.[48] By 1912 they were offering a free ten-day home trial of their machines, a technique they continued to use into the 1920s.[49] In 1927 their national sales operation comprised four regional divisions, managing thirty branch territories. Each territory was in turn structured into a wholesale section (serving the conventional store trade) and a retail section—selling under the resale system.[50] At this time Eureka employed 2,835 men in its outside sales organization, while its total factory workforce numbered 625. In other words, it took 4.5 people to sell the output of each production worker (excluding the contribution of the independent retailers with whom their salesforce collaborated).[51]

Recruiting salesmen was problematic. Ford, Bacon & Davis (a firm of consultant engineers, employed by Hoover in 1939 to examine their operational efficiency) found that some 90 per cent of applicants for Hoover salesmen's jobs were people without money, who desired security, and only considered sales work because they could not find a job offering a similar *guaranteed* income. Conversely, 'Men who have been successful as salesmen in other lines will not take a job selling vacuum cleaners as they consider it beneath them. The public is inclined to look down on the work…so the fear of ridicule on the part of applicants is one of the principal things to be overcome.'[52] Selling vacuums lacked the romance of high-profile 'masculine' products (such as cars) and was considered more distasteful even

[45] Hoover, *Fabulous Dustpan*, 100–3.

[46] HHC, undated Hoover chronology by Lee P. Heinrich, 78.

[47] Douglas E. Eberhart, 'William Henry Hoover: His Life, His Business, His Success' (unpublished BA thesis, Princeton University, 1985), 85.

[48] McLean Eureka Archive, Box 3, *Eureka Morning News* (13 Feb. 1928), 1.

[49] McLean Eureka Archive, Box 3, copies of Eureka adverts in the *Saturday Evening Post* (9 March 1912 and 1914) and *Ladies Home Journal* (Sept. 1924), 148.

[50] Hagley, 2069/9/16, Victor Talking Machine Co., Consignment selling, Victor Talking Machine Co. field survey, 1926–7. Reports of interview with Mr C. W. Phister, Eureka Vacuum Cleaner Co., 26 May 1927.

[51] Ibid.        [52] HHC, Ford, Bacon & Davis report, vol. 1, 156–7.

than washing machines—which in turn were more distasteful to sell than refrigerators or radio sets. Ford, Bacon & Davis ranked vacuum selling just ahead of 'relief', with the activities of the Work Progress Administration being cited as a major factor making it harder to recruit salesmen.[53]

In common with most sectors selling high-ticket consumer products door-to-door, the major vacuum cleaner manufacturers developed systematic salesforce training, management, and monitoring systems, equipping their salesmen with rehearsed arguments and advice on sales psychology, while supporting their efforts with extensive consumer advertising.[54] In June 1924 Hoover introduced a 'standard' vacuum demonstration for its resale men, with the production of *The Hoover Sale*, a booklet setting out twenty-eight separate steps to the demonstration, said to have been compiled from contributions by its salesforce. In 1932 the company sought further standardization, via a new 'Standard Way' plan of predetermined sales steps.[55] By 1936 Hoover's sales manual provided forty-seven pages of sales advice, largely consisting of step-by-step sales dialogue.[56] Salesmen were told to deal with prospects, 'who are not aware of their need' for a new cleaner as follows:

> overwhelm them with dirt, the evidence of their need. Show them the dirt beyond the reach of their present cleaners, the need of Cleaning Tools—Dirt Traps everywhere. This causes dissatisfaction with their cleaners—makes them want The Hoover. A complete, rousing, enthusiastic, impressive demonstration will disclose the need and create desire, and closing logic will mould favourable decision.[57]

Hoover also emphasized the importance of persistent demonstration. Its sales manual advised them to:

DEMONSTRATE TO SELL

Demonstrate with assurance that you are rendering a genuine service.

Demonstrate the inefficiency of her cleaner by getting large quantities of dirt. Prove that her cleaner will not get the dirt.

Demonstrate the value of The Hoover up and the value of her cleaner down. We arrive at values by comparisons.

Demonstrate with an enthusiasm to overcome all resistances.

...

Demonstrate long and hard. If cleaning one rug does not bring the sale, clean another—keep demonstrating.

...

Demonstrate with a sale in mind. Do not accept 'No' as final. Fight for that sale. Turn on the heat! Demonstrate to sell![58]

---

[53] Ibid.

[54] Walter A. Friedman, *Birth of a Salesman: The Transformation of Selling in America* (Cambridge, MA: Harvard University Press, 2004), 195–6.

[55] HHC, Harry Frease et al., 'The History of the Hoover Company', unpublished typescript (n.d., c.1940s), 129 and 188.

[56] Hoover Co., *Steps to the Hoover Sale* (North Canton, OH, 1936).     [57] Ibid., 5.

[58] Ibid.

Hoover dealers were instructed to 'Sell the need first. Prove the inefficiency of your prospect's cleaning method.'[59] This involved a variety of 'tests', including the 'Positive Agitation Test', where the salesman would tap the rug with a screw driver to show the need for beating; the 'Bag Screen Test' (where the salesman would ask the housewife to clean an area of carpet with her own cleaner and would then clean it again with his demonstration Hoover, to show how much dirt remained); and the 'Kapoc-Yarn Test' (to show that the Hoover could remove dirt without damaging the carpet).[60] Salesmen were given sheets of step-by-step dialogue to deal with customer objections such as, 'I'll think it over', 'Can't afford', or 'I'll buy later'. Where the sale was not closed, they were advised to call back at a later date to make a second attempt.[61] Hoover even attempted to use their advertising to provide dialogue to housewives, in arguing the case for purchasing a Hoover with their husbands, as shown in Figure 9.3.

Eureka similarly provided salesmen with tactics for combating prospects' objections. For example, '"Can't afford" – "Want to Look Around"' should be countered by 'an emotional appeal based on germs—moths—the child—home is a woman's workshop—etc.'[62] Their salesmen were trained to undertake a demonstration, with steps, 'so arranged as to lead the prospect through all the motions and mental reactions necessary to the final decision to purchase'.[63] This followed standard contemporary selling practice, dividing the sales process into four stages. Part one—establishing the need; part two—convincing the prospect that Eureka was the right cleaner to buy; part three—reinforcing the need by demonstrating the attachments; and part four—emphasizing the need to combat moth destruction—'"play" on fear'. Salesmen were told to attempt a 'trial close' after each part, as different prospects reacted differently to the various steps.[64]

By 1927 an estimated 95 per cent of Eureka's sales were coming from house-to-house activities. An average Eureka salesman, paid on a combination of salary and commission, achieved around six sales per month.[65] However, there was a major gap between the earnings of the 'average' and the 'typical' vacuum cleaner salesman, as illustrated in a sales plan for a new local sales team proposed by Charles G. Groff, president of Electrolux's New York subsidiary. Taking into account differences in ability and experience, a successful team, in business for a month, would ideally comprise:

One man selling 20 or more [per month].
Four top men selling an average of 4 per week.
Eight medium men selling an average of 2 per week.
Nine below-average men selling 1 per week.
Three new men selling 1 each for the month.[66]

[59] Ibid., 10.          [60] Ibid., 14–15.          [61] Ibid., 44.
[62] McLean Eureka Archive, Folder 2, 'The Eureka Salesman', manual for Eureka dealers and salesmen, 1936, 34.
[63] Ibid., 35.          [64] Ibid.
[65] Hagley, 2069/9/16, Victor Talking Machine Co., 'Consignment Selling', Victor Talking Machine Co. field survey, 1926–7. Reports of interview with Mr C. W. Phister, Eureka Vacuum Cleaner Co., 26 May 1927.
[66] British Library, Charles R. Groff, *Observations of Management: Confidential Report for Electrolux Executives* 1, 1 (1932), 7.

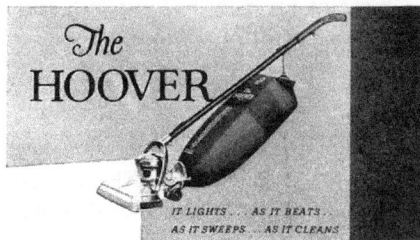

**Fig. 9.3.** A 1934 Hoover ad seeking to provide the housewife with convincing arguments regarding the 'need' for a new vacuum

*Source*: Peter Scott collection.

They would thus achieve total sales of around 200 cleaners—a good result for the firm. Yet almost half the staff would sell one or fewer cleaners per week, and only 20 per cent would earn what could be regarded as a reasonable white-collar income. Hoover took a ruthlessly Darwinistic approach to this problem. After initial training, only those salesmen who had met or exceeded their sales quota were called back in for further training. As the company's official history notes, they aimed at: 'continually sharpening up [only] those who were already the best. The less successful salesmen automatically dropped out of their own volition because income was based on sales. They would be replaced by stronger men.'[67]

The poor reputation of vacuum selling, together with its variable and typically low remuneration, created major problems of staff turnover. In 1939 Hoover's labour turnover ranged from 100 per cent per annum for their 1,500 leading salesmen—who generated 80 per cent of sales—to about 500 per cent for the other salesmen on their list. The 1,500 leading salesmen earned around $31 per week, while others regarded as 'productive' about $13 per week. However, the rest, numbering some 2,500–3,000, sold only around one cleaner per month, on which they would earn around $13 per month.[68]

The major firms made continued efforts to redress problems of poor motivation, which threatened both salesmen's productivity and retention. By 1911 Hoover were already using salesmen's contents as a key motivational device, based on sales relative to a 'quota' set by the firm.[69] Salesmen soon became subjected to a proliferation of contests, with individual and team prizes, together with a rapid succession of bulletins and flyers, touting the success of top salesmen and encouraging greater sales efforts. Pressure to achieve targets sometimes led salesmen to use dubious or even criminal tactics. Eureka employed a detective who travelled across the United States, checking on their salesforce. He was reported to occasionally run into 'some crookedness', though the losses incurred were described as 'inconsequential'.[70] Nevertheless, such tactics acted to increase customer resistance to the salesman's call.

In common with the radio sector, vacuum cleaner sales were heavily reliant on consumer credit and entailed a substantial and increasing element of trade-in business. Given the high costs of vacuum cleaners, instalment finance was an integral element of the door-to-door sales formula. In 1922 Hoover had set up a dealer finance plan with Commercial Investment Trust Inc. for its dealers and by 1923 almost 80 per cent of Hoovers were sold on instalments.[71] A 1936 Hoover manual told salesmen to show the affordability of instalment credit by presenting it in terms of daily and weekly costs:

> The Hoover Company and the (Dealer's store) are so enthusiastic over this new and beautiful ensemble, and so anxious that you may enjoy its many benefits that they

---

[67] Hoover, *Fabulous Dustpan*, 158.        [68] HHC, Ford, Bacon & Davis report, vol. 1, 9.
[69] HHC, 'Hoover Sweepings', 1, 9 (1911), 21.
[70] Hagley, 2069/9/16, Victor Talking Machine Co., 'Consignment Selling', Victor Talking Machine Co. field survey, 1926–7. Report of interview with Mr C. W. Phister, Eureka Vacuum Cleaner Co., 26 May 1927.
[71] HHC, 'Greater Profits for all Hoover Dealers who use the Hoover (C.I.T.) Finance Service', *Hoovergrams* (Oct. 1923), 8–9.

have permitted me to offer it to you for only $1.50 a week. Why, that is only 20c a day, the price of a magazine or bus fare down town and back.[72]

Trade-ins were less problematic for the vacuum industry than for the radio or automobile trades, largely owing to good cooperative relations between the major vacuum manufacturers. By 1927 six leading vacuum firms—Hoover, Eureka, Premier, Apex, Royal, and Western Electric, had a joint arrangement whereby trade-ins were returned to their original manufacturer for reconditioning and then sold to a wholesaler of refurbished vacuum cleaners.[73] The average trade-in allowance on all vacuum cleaner brands on Eureka's preferred list (these six firms) during 1926 was $6.72. For makes outside this list Eureka would salvage them if possible and otherwise scrap them. However, they offered such a low allowance on these 'lesser makes' that, in conjunction with the preferred list arrangement and the high proportion of sales conducted without trade-ins, the overall charge for trade-ins against their entire production was only 40 cents per instrument.[74]

Manufacturers also incentivized their salesmen to keep trade-in allowances as low as possible. Eureka stood the full cost of any trade-in allowances up to $5; 50 per cent of the excess over $5 on allowances from $5–10 (the remainder being borne by the salesman); and made no further contribution for allowances over $10. Some firms, including Hoover, also began to recondition traded-in models of their own cleaners and sell them through their retail dealers, as discussed in the following section.

## SALES STRATEGY DURING THE DEPRESSION AND ITS AFTERMATH

The depression witnessed a substantial fall in vacuum cleaner sales. From 1929 to 1933 unit sales of floor-type vacuum cleaners declined from 1,253,000 to 548,000, in contrast to refrigerators and washing machines, which had recovered beyond their 1929 unit sales.[75] However, the industry generally managed to maintain list prices, despite sharp falls in the prices of most other durables, and witnessed relatively few corporate liquidations.

The main casualty was Eureka. By 1930 direct sales accounted for the bulk of Eureka's market, with an army of over 4,000 door-to-door salesmen working on a straight commission basis. These were supported by thirty-five major branch offices in large US cities, and 100–150 sub-branches (sales offices) which ran the customer credit, stocked inventories, and supervised those retailers that worked with

---

[72] Hoover Company, 'Steps to the Hoover Sale', manual, 1936, 25.
[73] Hagley, 2069/9/16, Victor Talking Machine Co., 'Consignment Selling', Victor Talking Machine Co. field survey, 1926–7. Reports of interview with Mr C. W. Phister, Eureka Vacuum Cleaner Co., 26 May 1927.
[74] Ibid.     [75] See Table 9.1.

Eureka under the resale plan.[76] Around 50 per cent of sales were made directly, around 25 per cent under the resale plan, and the remainder by dealers who purchased cleaners outright from the factory.

Eureka's direct sales proved particularly expensive, owing to the heavy costs of their branch network, inventories, and instalment accounts. These impacted on the prices of all their machines, even those sold through conventional retail channels—as it was impractical to charge one price to final customers purchasing from a door-to-door salesman and a lower price for the same models sold through stores.[77] During the depression high costs were translated into huge losses. Eureka's sales had peaked in 1927, at $12,780,000, generating a profit of $1,806,198. However, a sharp fall in sales during the depression, to $4,297,000 in 1931, brought losses of $1,163,096.[78]

Eureka only survived by closing its sub-branches, ending all direct instalment selling, slashing its branch office staff, and focusing on sales via the resale system and through 'distributor-dealers' who paid their own salesmen's commission and acted as wholesalers for local retailers. This gave the company a small profit of $18,420 for the first six months of 1932, but on a drastically reduced turnover of only $1,360,360 for the whole of 1932.[79] Despite some recovery in the following years, Eureka never regained the market share it had enjoyed in the 1920s. In 1941 its vacuum cleaner sales represented only 7 per cent of the industry total.[80]

Depression conditions had made direct selling more challenging. Evidence suggests that consumer resistance to door-to-door salesmen was already building by the late 1920s. For example, in around 1929 Eureka adverts began to promote their salesman as well as their products: 'Welcome the Eureka Man, who comes to your door on a mission of helpfulness. Let him show you the latest and best in home sanitation methods.'[81] Customer resistance intensified markedly during the depression. In addition to many 'prospects' having lower and/or less secure incomes, large numbers of unemployed men had swollen the ranks of salesmen and complaints mounted from people who felt besieged by them. Surveys found that in some neighbourhoods householders received between twelve and seventeen calls in a single afternoon.[82]

---

[76] 'Eureka Vacuum Cleaner Company. Discontinuance of Branches and Sub-branches (case)' [hereafter 'Eureka...(case)], in *University of Michigan, School of Administration, Announcement 1934–35* (Ann Arbor, MI: University of Michigan, 1934), 79–82 (79).

[77] United States, Temporary National Economic Committee, *Investigation of Concentration of Economic Power Monograph No. 1. Price Behavior and Business Policy* (Washington, DC: USGPO, 1940), 146.

[78] 'Eureka', in *University of Michigan, School of Administration, Announcement*, 79–82 (79–80).

[79] O. Fred Rost, *Distribution Today* (New York: McGraw-Hill, 1933), 113; Moody's Investment Service, *Moody's Manual of Investments. American and Foreign. Industrial Securities* (New York: Moody's, 1931), 1350.

[80] 'Eureka Williams. Its Oil Burners are still Selling Easily but for Vacuum Cleaners the Buyer's Market is Here Again', *Fortune* (Dec. 1947), 108–90 (108 and 111–12).

[81] McLean Eureka Archive, Box 3, 'There had to be a Better Way', Eureka advert (n.d., *c.*1929).

[82] Rost, *Distribution Today*, 113–15; 'Eureka...(case)', 81–2.

This reflected the prevailing orthodoxy that, 'Selling vacuum cleaners is largely a matter of man-power.'[83] Hoover subscribed to this view, though Ford, Bacon & Davis noted that Hoover's sales over 1929–38 correlated much better with the index of industrial production than with the size of their salesforce. They also identified a sharp decline in Hoover's salesforce productivity, from an average of 1.54 cleaners sold per man per week in 1929 to only 0.95 in 1937, as shown in Table 9.5, which they largely attributed to increased customer resistance.

Yet both Ford, Bacon & Davis and industry experts interviewed by *Electrical Merchandising*, found that direct selling still appeared to be the key to success in this sector (in contrast to refrigerators and washing machines, which were rapidly becoming transformed into staple 'over-the-counter' merchandise). Total 1933 vacuum sales were said to be almost completely down to four companies: Hoover, Electrolux, Airway, and Premier. The first three companies sold direct to the customer, while direct sales also dominated Premier's aggregate sales. The success of Airway in achieving large sales through door-door selling, despite raising its prices, was said to have exerted a strong demonstration effect on other manufacturers.[84] A 1940 US government investigation attributed the success of direct vacuum sales, despite higher costs (and consequently prices), to the effectiveness of home demonstrations in persuading the housewife, 'that she is eliminating only part of the dirt from her home with her carpet sweeper or old cleaner'.[85]

However, the 1930s did witness some expansion in retailer own-brand vacuums—a trend also evident for other consumer durables, such as radios and refrigerators. As in the radio sector, production was often undertaken by leading manufacturers,

**Table 9.5.** Productivity of Hoover salesmen in 1929 and 1937

| Year | 1929 | 1937 |
| --- | --- | --- |
| Number of cleaners sold | 189,755 | 200,663 |
| Number sold by Hoover salesmen | 149,189 | 194,990 |
| Number of salesmen on list | 1,859 | 3,937 |
| Cleaners sold per man per week | 1.54 | 0.95 |
| Average unit price | 79.43 | 73.84 |
| Retail billings per man per week ($) | 123.00 | 70.00 |
| Commission rate (per cent; net, after trade-in participation) | 18.00 | 20.02 |
| Commission per man per week ($) | 22.10 | 14.01 |
| Real value of commission per man-week ($) | 22.10 | 15.83 |

*Source*: HHC, Filing Cabinet 78.033#52, Ford Bacon & Davis, 'Report. Business and Sales Operations, The Hoover Company, North Canton, Ohio', 14 Feb. 1940, vol. 1, 87 and 162.

[83] E. A. Holmberg, 'Cleaners Need a New Deal', *Electrical Merchandising* (June 1932), 38–9 and 55 (38–9).
[84] 'Electrical Merchandise Review and Forecast', *Electrical Merchandising* (Jan. 1934), 29–33 (31).
[85] United States, Temporary National Economic Committee, *Investigation of Concentration of Economic Power*, 140.

working on contract. A 1944 Federal Trade Commission (FTC) report found that, of ten vacuum manufacturers surveyed, five undertook some manufacture for distributors' brands in addition to their manufacturer-branded production.[86]

Contract manufacture offered a means for firms such as Hoover, which focused on the upper end of the market, to supply the lower-price segments without compromising its brand. Hoover had been exploring ways of doing so from the late 1920s. Around the start of 1928 it launched an initiative to sell factory rebuilt traded-in Hoovers via its dealers (with a ninety-day guarantee). Hoover claimed that these machines were completely 'torn down', with all worn parts replaced and each machine polished, re-enamelled, and equipped with a new cord, dirt bag, brush, furniture guard, and belt.[87] This also helped it address the rising cost of trade-ins, in what was rapidly becoming a saturated market (sales that involved accepting trade-ins accounted for an average of 70.7 per cent of Hoover's annual sales over 1931–8).[88]

In 1937 Hoover launched another initiative to tap the lower-price market, introducing the 'Norca' vacuum cleaner, designed for 'over-the-counter' sales by department stores. This was similar to the Hoover Model 300, but had a brush roll rather than an 'agitator'. In 1938 cosmetically differentiated versions of the Norca floor and hand cleaner models were provided as own-brands for the Allied Mercantile Corporation and in 1939 an own-brand floor cleaner was developed for the Jordan Marsh Company of Boston.[89]

Yet Ford, Bacon & Davis found that Hoover's principal difficulties lay not in its market segmentation, or in its use of direct selling, but in its failure to efficiently structure its downstream value chain so as to make it competitive with other firms, especially its principal rival, Electrolux. Formed in 1919 by the merger of two Swedish firms, Svenska Elektron AB and Lux AB (which had already commenced manufacturing vacuum cleaners before the First World War), Electrolux had opened a New York sales and service office in 1924. However, it only became a significant player in the US market in 1933, when it opened a US factory in Old Greenwich, Connecticut.[90]

The consultants found that Hoover's profits, in relation to gross investment applicable to operations, averaged 4.2 per cent over 1936–8, compared to 48.0 per cent for Electrolux (that distributed only through salesmen) and 18.0 per cent for Maytag (America's leading washing machine manufacturer, that sold only through normal retail channels).[91] Hoover's operating profits and return on investment were also low relative to other consumer durables' firms for which data were available. This was not, primarily, a problem of scale. Using data provided by Hoover, they showed that Hoover's operating profit rate failed to rise for annual unit

---

[86] Federal Trade Commission, *Report on Distribution Methods*, 155–6.

[87] HHC, 'Rebuilt Hoovers Spell Profit', *Hoovergrams* (Apr. 1928), 3–4 and 15.

[88] HHC, Ford, Bacon & Davis report, vol. 2, Exhibit 33.

[89] HHC, Harry Frease et al., 'The History of the Hoover Company', unpublished typescript (n.d., c.1940s), 228 and 231.

[90] Gantz, *Vacuum Cleaner*, 93–4.          [91] HHC, Ford Bacon & Davis report, vol. 1, 10.

sales above 210,000 (and declined beyond around 225,000) owing to the disproportionate increase of certain selling expenses (such as bonuses), which outweighed any scale economies in production.[92]

As Table 9.6 shows, the report identified generous retailer discounts under the resale system as the main factor depressing Hoover's operating profits compared to Electrolux. Hoover's dealers received 15.8 per cent of the retail price of each vacuum sold under this system, while Electrolux had no dealer costs. Furthermore, although Electrolux provided a higher percentage commission to its salesmen, it spent considerably less on supporting their activities through advertising, promotion, training, and supervision.

A 15.8 per cent commission was found to be excessive compared to the services dealers provided under the resale system—letting Hoover use their names, allowing salesmen to solicit demonstrations in store, stocking inventory, dealing with instalment credits, and bearing part of the cost of any machines that reverted back to them. Hoover's brand managers believed that they could secure the same sales volume without dealer participation and it was noted that Electrolux had built up its sales volume without involving retailers.[93]

More generally, Hoover was found to have a high-cost distribution structure in relation to other significant vacuum manufacturers. Ford, Bacon & Davis estimated that in 1939 approximately 45 per cent of all new vacuums were distributed via dealers, 38 per cent were sold direct to the consumer with no dealer role, and the balance represented Hoover—which was alone in still using direct sales with dealer assistance.[94] As Table 9.7 shows, pricing strategy in the sector was mainly determined by choice of distribution channels, rather than production costs, given that manufacturing cost was a relatively small element of retail price. This was even true within Hoover. Their Norca cleaner (sold through dealers only, at a retail price of $39.75, which had been set relatively high to avoid too great a difference in price between it and the Hoover 305), had a manufacturing cost of $8.76, while the Hoover 305, on which it was based, cost $8.67 to manufacture, but sold for $52.50.[95]

Those firms using dealer channels exclusively had the lowest retail prices ($43–$49.50 for their median models), while Eureka, which sold principally through dealers but still had some direct sales activity, charged $58. Meanwhile firms that sold wholly or principally through direct sales charged $69–$71.00, while Hoover, which had the most costly distribution method, charged the highest prices in the sector (though not sufficient to offset its higher costs). Moreover, Hoover's high cost structure restricted the commission it could offer salesmen; Electrolux, Airway, and Rex Air, which used direct sales, all had markedly higher commission rates.[96]

The report attributed the long-run trend of rising vacuum cleaner prices (in contrast to falling costs for other consumer durables) to the sector's high distribution costs, which ate up any cost savings from product or process innovations: 'The two leading companies...are selling by methods which necessitate prices

[92] Ibid., 3–6.　　[93] Ibid., 72.　　[94] Ibid., 98.　　[95] Ibid., 100.
[96] Ibid., 100 and 161.

**Table 9.6.** A comparison of the value chains for Hoover and Electrolux in 1938 (% of retail price)

| Costs | Hoover | Electrolux |
|---|---|---|
| Manufacturing | 22.6 | 20.0–22.6 |
| Dealer discounts | 15.8 | 0.0 |
| Sales management & administration | | |
| Branch and district sales organization | 12.9 | n.a. |
| Other | 12.1 | n.a. |
| **Total** | 25.0 | 23.5–25.0 |
| Sales support activities | | |
| Sales personnel education | 1.0 | 0.0 |
| Sales promotion | 0.9 | 0.5 |
| Advertising | 3.6 | 1.0 |
| Supervision | 7.2 | 3.0 |
| **Total** | 12.7 | 4.5 |
| Salesmen's remuneration | 21.7 | 27.5 |
| **Total costs** | 97.8 | 75.5–79.6 |
| Operating profit | 2.2 | 20.4–24.5 |

*Note*: Electrolux's costs are estimates by the consultants.

*Source*: HHC, Filing Cabinet 78.033#52, Ford Bacon & Davis, 'Report. Business and Sales Operations, The Hoover Company, North Canton, Ohio', 14 Feb. 1940, vol. 1, 71.

**Table 9.7.** Channels of distribution for the leading US vacuum cleaner firms in 1939

| Firm | Distribution channels | Retail price ($) |
|---|---|---|
| Hoover | Direct with dealer assistance | 73.50 |
| Electrolux | Direct | 69.00 |
| Eureka | Dealer and direct | 58.00 |
| General Electric | Dealer | 43.00 |
| Airway | Direct | 71.00 |
| Royal | Dealer | 49.50 |
| Premier | Direct and dealer | 70.00 |
| Singer | Direct | 69.50 |
| Westinghouse | Dealer | 47.00 |

*Note*: Prices are for the median models for each firm.

*Source*: HHC, Filing Cabinet 78.033#52, Ford Bacon & Davis, 'Report. Business and Sales Operations, The Hoover Company, North Canton, Ohio', 14 Feb. 1940, vol. 1, 98 and 100.

approximately twice as high as those possible under other available methods of distribution.'[97] Yet it did not recommend a switch to normal retail channels in order to cut prices, given that firms that had followed this strategy had failed to either match the sales of Hoover and Electrolux, or achieve Electrolux's high profit rate. Interviews with retailers had shown no evidence of a trend towards increased retailer sales. Indeed, most dealers perceived that vacuums were unusual

[97] Ibid., 102.

in that home demonstrations were key to sales—by demonstrating the inefficiency of the housewife's existing cleaner (which was less evident than for an old refrigerator, washing machine, or radio). They also noted that psychological obsolescence was a less important motivation for replacement purchase, as the cleaner was kept out of sight in the closet.[98]

The consultants argued that, while cleaner models without distinctive features had to be sold over the counter and compete on price, those with such features could most profitably be sold directly. Meanwhile, Hoover's policy of developing their Norca over-the-counter brand, together with sales to dealers of rebuilt Hoovers ('Specials') allowed them to tap the over-the-counter market that their branded new cleaners were priced out of.[99] It thus appears that Hoover's problems of low profitability stemmed from its attachment to the outdated resale system, rather than from its reliance on direct selling.

## CONCLUSIONS

The product life-cycle model suggests that new products move from a novelty phase characterized by high promotion costs, limited scale economies, and high prices, to a 'mature' phase where they become 'staple' products, with low prices and distribution costs. However, both nominal and real (inflation-adjusted) prices for vacuum cleaners rose over the inter-war period, driven by a high cost, but effective distribution system. This model underpinned the enduring competitive advantage of the market leaders (with the exception of Eureka, whose decline appears to have been linked to managerial difficulties).[100] In 1937 the top four vacuum manufacturers were estimated to account for some 70 per cent of the total US market (by value), a lower level of concentration than for refrigerators (77 per cent for models of 6 cubic feet or over and 69 per cent for smaller models), but greater than that for washing machines (53 per cent) and far higher than for radio.[101] Moreover, the hierarchy of major firms had remained remarkably stable compared to other household durables. Of the top eight vacuum cleaner brands in 1939 (see Table 9.7), all but Electrolux were already major firms in the sector by the early 1920s.

However, from the perspective of long-term market growth the direct sales system proved to be something of a trap for the industry, as profitability required prices beyond the budgets of a large proportion of households. Thus, as Figure 9.4 shows, household diffusion of new vacuum cleaners fell below that of washing machines by the mid-1930s and, shortly after, behind that of refrigerators. Yet from the perspective of the individual firm, a successful direct sales programme

---

[98] Ibid., 103.     [99] Ibid., 104.

[100] 'Eureka Williams. Its Oil Burners are still Selling Easily but for Vacuum Cleaners the Buyer's Market is Here Again', 108 and 111–12.

[101] United States, Temporary National Economic Committee, *Investigation of Concentration of Economic Power*, 163.

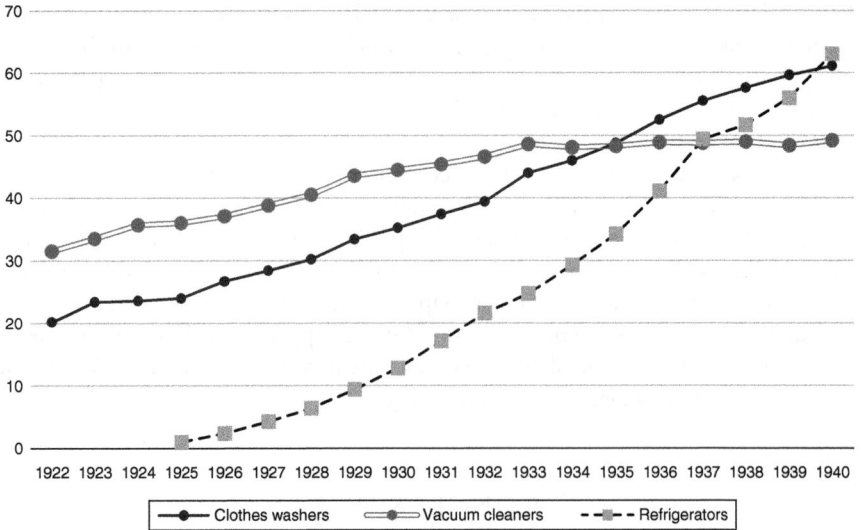

**Fig. 9.4.** National diffusion of vacuum cleaners, refrigerators, and electric washing machines (percentage of US homes with these appliances), 1922–41

*Source*: '50 Years of Statistics and History', *Merchandise Week*, 104, 9 (28 Feb. 1972), 21–54 and 110–60.

proved a major competitive advantage, enabling it to get to the customer before she realized that she was in the market for a vacuum. The direct sales system thus proved remarkably resilient. Finally, as the contrasting profitability of Hoover and Electrolux shows, restructuring value chains so as to lower distribution costs by cutting out the retailer completely could have a major impact on profitability and competiveness.

# 10

## 'Pushing' Vacuum Cleaners in Inter-War Britain

### INTRODUCTION

Marketing vacuum cleaners in the UK largely followed US practice, being strongly influenced by the pioneering activities of Hoover's British subsidiary. This represented a genuine innovation in British retailing. While door-to-door selling had long been used by firms marketing financial services (typically insurance and contractual savings), together with low-value goods (by peddlers, 'Scotch drapers', and similar itinerants), there had been no real tradition of selling expensive branded durable goods in this way. The nearest precedent had been door-to-door sales of Singer sewing machines, from the 1860s. However, Singer's sales strategy had involved a continuing relationship between salesman and household—as the salesman was also responsible for collecting HP payments (on which they obtained a further commission)—thus tempering opportunism during the sales pitch.[1] Conversely, this new brand of salesman had no further contact with his customers after the initial sale.

Vacuum cleaner firms established a new form of direct selling in Britain, which was to be of enduring importance during the post-1945 decades for durable goods and services such as double glazing, home improvements, and encyclopaedias—developing a well-deserved reputation for sharp practice. As in the United States, the popularity of direct selling among suppliers was based on its effectiveness, demonstrated by its success in achieving rapid diffusion of vacuum cleaners, relative to other 'high-ticket' labour-saving appliances. There were an estimated 2.3 million household vacuum cleaners in 1939, in around 30 per cent of British homes wired for electricity. This compares with diffusion rates to wired homes of only 3.6 per cent for electric clothes wash boilers, 6.3 per cent for electric water heaters, 2.3 per cent for electric refrigerators, and 16.8 per cent for electric cookers (none of which were suitable for household demonstration by a salesman travelling on foot).[2] Similarly, 1938 consumers' expenditure on vacuums, estimated at

---

[1] See Robert Bruce Davies, *Peacefully Working to Conquer the World: Singer Sewing Machines in Foreign Markets, 1854–1920* (New York: Arno, 1976), 63–6. Singer also tempered potential opportunism by salesmen through paying salary as well as commission and by withholding part of their commission as a safeguard against dishonesty.

[2] *Sources*: Political and Economic Planning, *The Market for Household Appliances* (London: PEP, 1945), 211–12.

between £5 million and £5.5 million, almost equalled the £5–6 million spent on all other electric household appliances (excluding radios, radiograms, and lamps).[3]

Unlike the United States—where door-to-door salesmen were generally accepted as part of the retail culture—in Britain this system encountered much greater public opposition. As a 1930 US Department of Commerce report on the British market noted, 'The average English householder dislikes very much to be hurried into a decision by "high pressure" sales methods, especially in his own home.'[4] Intensified consumer resistance, together with lower typical household incomes, smaller homes, and greater use of alternatives to carpets (such as linoleum or parquet flooring) contributed to vacuum cleaner salesmen having an even more difficult task in Britain than in the United States. Only a small minority managed to earn an acceptable living and many salesmen reacted by engaging in sharp practice, both through desperation and often, in a conscious attempt to turn the tables on their employers.

## PRODUCTION SYSTEMS AND VALUE CHAINS

Despite Britain being a pioneer in developing the powered vacuum cleaner, the inter-war British market was dominated by the subsidiaries of two overseas-based multinationals, Hoover and Electrolux. Hoover had marketed cleaners in Britain as early as 1912. However, it was not until 1919 that it set up a British sales branch, headed by Malcolm C. Dizer. Dizer had previous managerial experience in the UK, having established a London retail outlet for the US stationery firm Dennison Manufacturing Co. in around 1912. Having returned to the United States during the First World War, H. W. Hoover offered him the job of setting up its British sales operation. Following a visit to Hoover's North Canton headquarters to learn the firm's methods, he arrived in Britain around the beginning of March 1919, with $10,000 and 2,000 Hoovers.

As some of the imported Hoovers were the wrong voltage for particular areas of Britain (which had no standard voltage at this time), a British electrical engineer, C. B. Colston, was hired as a consultant and, shortly afterwards, was appointed as Hoover's Chief Engineer.[5] By the end of the year he had assumed direct control of Hoover's resale organization and in 1920 he became general manager, with a seat on the board. Following Dizer's departure in 1927, Colston became managing director of Hoover's British subsidiary and under his leadership it became one of the largest vacuum cleaner manufacturing and sales operations outside North America.[6]

[3] J. B. Jefferys, *The Distribution of Consumer Goods: A Factual Study of Methods and Costs in the United Kingdom in 1938* (Cambridge: Cambridge University Press, 1950), 292–300.

[4] U.S. Department of Commerce, Bureau of Foreign and Domestic Commerce, *British Market for Domestic Electrical Appliances* (Washington, DC: USGPO, 1930), 8–9.

[5] HHC, Filing Cabinet, 'Foreign plants 11-45, 78.034', file on 'Perivale England Plant, 1933', Interview with Mr Tribute, 12 Nov. 1965, unsigned.

[6] HHC, 'History Hoover Ltd Perivale', file, historical note by Helen Magraw, 1985.

After the First World War, Hoover had transformed its Canadian assembly operation into a factory, to gain superior access to Britain and its empire. Canadian production both avoided import duties and capitalized on national sentiment favouring home-produced goods ('AN EMPIRE PRODUCT' being prominently displayed on the chassis badge). Hoover opened a small UK factory for assembling Canadian parts, though it was not until 1931 that it decided to move to full manufacture, precipitated by Britain's gold standard departure and its adoption of a 33.3 per cent tariff.

Hoover found that, even though cleaners imported from Canada benefited from empire preference, it now made financial sense to produce them in the UK.[7] A review of foreign-based competitors, conducted by Hoover UK in December 1931, showed that apart from Thor, which imported 10,000–12,000 machines annually, other US firms each imported less than 2,000 machines per year. This made it impractical for Hoover's US competitors to justify the costs of setting up full manufacture in the UK. Meanwhile, Electrolux had announced that it was considering moving to complete manufacture at its Luton factory, while the Danish firm Tellus and another European importer, C.C.A., were considering setting up UK factories. Hoover therefore decided to commence UK manufacture, both to outflank US importers and prevent European firms with UK factories from gaining a competitive advantage.[8]

Fronted by offices that constitute one of the finest surviving British examples of Art Deco architecture, its new factory in Perivale, West London, grew to employ 1,733 people by 1938.[9] This undertook both assembly and components manufacture; a 1933 Hoover had some 340 separate parts, all of which—apart from the castings, electric wire, and mains cable—were manufactured at Perivale.[10] Hoover's Perivale factory was well equipped for staff welfare, facilities including a social club, sports grounds, free medical care, and a staff canteen.[11]

Moving to full production cemented Hoover's position as the UK market leader, with annual sales of 211,814 cleaners in 1938 (valued at £2,302,849).[12] Moreover, Hoover found it cost-effective to use its British subsidiary's Perivale factory to supply the whole of the British Empire (excluding Canada) and continental

---

[7] HHC, 'History Hoover Ltd Perivale', undated historical notes on Hoover UK.

[8] HHC, 'High Spots Hoover Ltd, H.W.H', file, 'Manufacturing in England versus Canada', unsigned memorandum, 7 Dec. 1931.

[9] National Archive for Electrical Science and Technology, London, Sir Walter Charles Puckey papers, [hereafter, NAEST, Puckey papers], 146/1/1, 'Hoover Production Facts and Figures, 1938–1950', report, 1950; Wendy Hitchmough, *Hoover Factory: Wallis, Gilbert and Partners* (London: Phaidon, 1992), 20.

[10] 'The opening of the new Hoover factory and offices at Perivale', *Domestic Appliances* (May 1933), 296–9 (296).

[11] NAEST, Puckey papers, 146/1/1, 'Hoover production facts and figures 1938–1950', report, 1950. These included some 760 hourly paid men, 257 hourly paid women, 350 male 'staff', and 366 female 'staff'; Hitchmough, *Hoover Factory*, 20.

[12] Sue Bowden, 'Colston, Sir Charles', in David J. Jeremy (ed.), *Dictionary of Business Biography: A Biographical Dictionary of Business Leaders Active in Britain in the Period 1860–1980* (London: Butterworths, 1984), vol. 1, 755–9 (756); NAEST, Puckey papers, 146/1/1, 'Hoover Production Facts and Figures, 1938–1950', report, 1950. The 1938 sales-value figure also includes accessories.

Europe.[13] It appears to have been reasonably successful. With the exception of the Netherlands and New Zealand, export sales of the British Hoover company in 1937 and 1938 to British Empire markets, and to those European markets where Hoover UK had subsidiaries, were generally much greater than total US vacuum exports to those countries.[14]

Hoover's major rival in the British market was the Swedish firm Electrolux. While Hoover had championed the upright loose-bag cleaner, Electrolux became the international market leader in cylinder vacuum cleaners. Electrolux (which also manufactured refrigerators) had opened a British factory in Luton in 1927. Electrolux vacuums were significantly cheaper than Hoovers and were thus more popular with retailers who sold vacuums over the counter.[15]

Table 10.1 shows official and trade estimates for national production, imports, exports, and sales of vacuum cleaners. The large difference in the two production estimates for 1930 is probably due to the inclusion in the 1931 trade estimate of some cleaners, such as Hoovers, which were then manufactured overseas but assembled in Britain (the trade estimate for production being roughly equal to the official estimate for sales). Despite vigorous growth until the mid-1930s, sales appear to have stagnated during the second half of the decade. According to a trade estimate, just prior to the Second World War national sales were about 400,000 per year (roughly equal to the 1935 trade estimate in Table 10.1), while the number in use had reached 2.3 million.[16]

As in the United States, the most distinctive feature of vacuum cleaner value chains was downstream distribution. Jefferys estimated that in 1938 only 25–30 per cent of vacuum cleaners passed through wholesalers. Meanwhile 5–10 per cent were sold direct from manufacturer to consumer and 60–70 per cent technically passed from manufacturer to 'retailer' (including electricity supply undertakings) and then to the consumer. However, about two-thirds of sales direct to retailers were generated by door-to-door salesmen employed by the manufacturers, under the resale system.[17] Electricity suppliers accounted for around 15 per cent of national vacuum cleaner sales in the late 1930s and department stores averaged about 5 per cent. Meanwhile the multiples had 3–5 per cent of the market (an unusually low figure compared to other categories of electrical goods) and the co-ops 1 per cent.[18]

In common with US experience, door-to-door selling proved a relatively high-cost means of distribution, requiring high price mark-ups.[19] As Sir Basil Smallpeice (Hoover's chief accountant at Perivale) recalled:

> The standard cleaner complete with accessory dusting tools cost us about £7 to import.... We sold it for £21, a mark-up of 200 percent. The cost of selling was £11,

[13] HHC, 'History Hoover Ltd Perivale', file, historical note by Helen Magraw, 1985.

[14] HHC, Ford, Bacon & Davis report, vol. 1, 203.

[15] Bank of England Archives, SMT5/50, Lord & Thomas and Logan Ltd, 'Merchandising survey of Great Britain. Volume 5, Electrical Appliances (Domestic)', 1930, 53–8.

[16] Political and Economic Planning, *Market for Household Appliances*, 211.

[17] Jefferys, *Distribution of Consumer Goods*, 297.    [18] Ibid.

[19] Everett R. Smith, 'The Economic Future of House-to-House Selling', *Harvard Business Review*, 4 (Apr. 1926), 326–33 (326); Victor P. Buell, 'Door-to-Door Selling', *Harvard Business Review*, 32 (May/June 1954), 113–23 (118).

Table 10.1. Annual British production and sales estimates for vacuum cleaners, 1930–6

| Year | (A) Official estimates | | | | | | (B) Trade estimates | | |
|------|------------|-----------|------------------------|---------|------------------|----------|------------|-----------|------------------------|
| | Production | Value (£)* | Value per cleaner (£)* | Exports | Retained imports | Sales** | Production | Value (£) | Value per cleaner (£) |
| 1930 | 37,550 | 524,198 | 13.96 | 3,237 | 140,130 | 174,443 | 175,000 | | |
| 1931 | | | | | | | 195,000 | | |
| 1932 | | | | | | | 220,000 | | |
| 1933 | 247,333 | 2,112,224 | 8.54 | 15,744 | 20,681 | 252,270 | 252,000 | 2,112,000 | 8.38 |
| 1934 | 318,039 | 2,541,132 | 7.99 | 16,931 | 11,205 | 312,313 | 318,000 | 2,540,000 | 7.99 |
| 1935 | 409,345 | 3,287,040 | 8.03 | 27,813 | 13,150 | 394,682 | 363,000 | 3,119,000 | 8.59 |
| 1936 | | | | | | | 400,000 | | |

*Notes:* *Ex-works value. **'Sales' (units sold) data based on production plus retained imports minus exports.

*Sources:* Political and Economic Planning, *The Market for Household Appliances* (London: PEP, 1945), 211; Imperial Economic Committee, *Twenty-ninth Report: A Survey of the Trade in Electrical Machinery and Apparatus* (London: HMSO, 1936), 79; *Electrical Trading* (Mar. 1938), 69.

of which £8 covered door-to-door selling, distribution, and administration. The other £3 went to the retailer, who took the risk of the buyer defaulting. This left us with £3 profit, which was nearly half what the cleaner cost us—though it was only a modest 14 percent on turnover.[20]

These figures appear broadly typical for the sector; Political and Economic Planning found that the average ex-works value of a British vacuum in the 1930s, around £8, corresponded to an average retail price of around £15 to £20.[21] Similarly, Hoover's commission to retailers of 14 per cent (according to both Smallpeice's calculations and Table 10.2) corroborates Jefferys' estimates that retailers selling vacuums on orders obtained through salesmen received a margin of between 12.5 and 20 per cent (averaging nearer the lower end of this range).[22] Smallpeice later received the American company's cost sheets, showing that manufacturing costs were less than £4; thus its profit was also £3 per cleaner, in addition to the English subsidiary's £3. When the Perivale factory got into regular production, it was able to match American costs, earning the £3 manufacturing mark-up as well as the £3 distribution profit. Thus, as Smallpeice noted, 'in essence the economics of the business...were [that]...it cost £11 to market and £4 to make, and the company netted a £6 profit—a return of 150 percent on [manufacturing] cost'.[23]

Table 10.2 shows Hoover's value chain, based on these data. Hoover's sales and marketing costs are shown to be double its manufacturing and related costs, while the retailer's role earned them a fee equivalent to 14.3 per cent of the retail price. Yet, as in the United States, the retailer's participation in the sales process was typically limited to lending their name to the sales effort, managing the HP contracts (on terms set by Hoover), dealing with arrears and defaults, and, sometimes, stocking and delivery of the cleaner. The generosity of retailer remuneration is illustrated by data for the Manchester department store Kendal Milne & Co.—one of Hoover's largest retail collaborators, with sales of £351,565 over the five and a half years to July 1938.[24] Kendal Milne & Co. accrued significant arrears on HP contracts for these Hoovers: of 12,000 accounts in operation in July 1938, 2,000 were in arrears of two months or more (including 622 for six to twelve months and 451 for over twelve months).[25] However, as Table 10.3 shows, Kendal Milne's total costs of managing its Hoover HP contracts, net of interest payments on these contracts, reduced its gross margin (14.3 per cent of the cleaner's retail price) by a mere 0.7 percentage points.

In sum, the resale system relied on high sales expenditures to sell a product for around five times its production costs, in the process accruing attractive net margins for Hoover and, especially (in relation to its limited role in the process),

[20] Basil Smallpeice, *Of Comets and Queens* (Shrewsbury: Airlife, 1981), 13.

[21] Political and Economic Planning, *Market for Household Appliances*, 211.

[22] Jefferys, *Distribution of Consumer Goods*, 297–8. A 25 per cent mark-up was applied in approximately two-thirds of cases and 33 per cent for the others.

[23] Smallpeice, *Of Comets and Queens*, 13.

[24] Harrods Company Archive, London, HF9/3/7, 'Hoover Statistics at 30 July 1938', 29 Sept. 1938.

[25] Harrods Company Archive, HF9/3/6, Harrods Ltd, notes on accounts for half year ended 31 July 1936, note on Kendal Milne and its Hoover trade, 10 Aug. 1936.

**Table 10.2.** The value chain for Hoover UK in the 1930s (% of retail price)

| Stages of value chain | Controlled by | % of retail price |
|---|---|---|
| Patents | Hoover | ( |
| Design | Hoover | ( |
| Raw materials | Market | ( |
| Components | Hoover* | (19.0 |
| Assembly | Hoover | ( |
| Distribution etc. (manufacturer) | Hoover | 38.1 |
| Distribution etc. (retailer) | Retailer** | 14.3 |
| Manufacturer's profit | Hoover | 28.6 |
| Total | | 100.0 |

*Notes*: *A very small proportion of components were purchased externally. **See text for the retailer's specific functions under the resale system. This item includes both the retailer's costs and profits.
*Sources*: See text.

**Table 10.3.** Kendal Milne & Co.'s Hoover business, 30 January 1933–30 July 1938

| | £ | % |
|---|---|---|
| Total sales for 5.5 years | 351,565 | n.a. |
| Standard commission | 44,766 | 12.7 |
| Special allowance on purchases | 5,617 | 1.6 |
| **Total commission** | 50,383 | 14.3 |
| HP interest | 28,779 | 8.2 |
| HP costs | | |
| Estimated office expenses | 10,550 | 3.0 |
| Estimated interest on average book debts at 3% p.a. | 16,000 | 4.6 |
| Actual bad debt written off | 4,779 | 1.4 |
| Total | 31,329 | 8.9 |
| Net margin (including HP) | 47,833 | 13.6 |

*Source*: Harrods Archives, HF9/3/7, Kendal Milne & Co., 'Hoover Statistics at 30 July 1938', 29 Sept. 1938.

collaborative retailers. However, this system considerably raised prices for the consumer. Moreover, there was another party who typically fared badly—the army of door-to-door salesmen who Hoover and the other leading vacuum cleaner manufacturers employed to sell their products.

## MARKETING

Britain's vacuum cleaner market had more price variation between brands than the US market, though as in America it was generally the large companies who sold the higher-price models. An analysis of the sales of electrical and non-electrical vacuum cleaners by eight leading London department stores in around 1929 noted twelve different makes of electrical machines on sale, at prices varying from £5 12s 6d to £22 1s. Meanwhile, there were seven different makes of non-electrical machines (which constituted a third of all sales), ranging in price from £2 5s to

£5 5s.[26] List prices were rigidly enforced by individual manufacturers, who also generally sought to avoid price competition with rival brands.[27] Despite the development of lower-priced cleaners by less well-known firms whose cheapest models were priced at £5 10s to £5 15s in 1931 and £3 to £4 in 1938 (with one firm, Brown Brothers Ltd, marketing two models at below £3), prices for leading brands showed remarkable stability. A comparison of models listed both in 1933 and 1938 shows that while some prices were lower, a large proportion had not changed at all.[28]

As in the United States, Hoover was both the market leader and the firm which charged the highest unit prices. Hoover's prices remained relatively stable throughout the inter-war period (indicating a significant increase in real terms); a high-powered Hoover sold at around £20 from the early 1920s to the late 1930s.[29] Hoover openly acknowledged its high prices. An article on its new Perivale factory (subsequently reprinted as corporate publicity material) noted that, 'the Hoover is at once the highest-priced article in its field, *and* the biggest seller. To parallel such a position one would have to imagine Rolls Royce selling more cars than Austin or Morris. The Hoover is a heartening phenomenon in these days, when the tendency in so many industries has been rather to stampede the public on price.'[30]

However, Hoover did move some way towards countering competition from cheaper models, launching the lower-powered 'Junior' in 1935, priced at £10 15s (plus £2 2s 6d for dusting tools).[31] The Junior immediately achieved high sales, without eating into the market of its larger cousin, which suggests that price had previously been a major factor limiting Hoover's market. Its success facilitated an expansion in Hoover's salesforce from 1,409 in 1934 to 3,000 in 1935 and almost 4,000 in 1936.[32]

As in the United States, firms focused on non-price competition, particularly emphasizing ancillary functions or 'features'. For example, Electrolux claimed superior adaptability for cleaning upholstery, furnishings, and curtains (although Hoovers had additional dusting tools for these purposes). Electrolux also asserted that its cleaner's reverse action made it suitable for paint-spraying, and even claimed that it

> purifies the very air by passing it through an impregnated pad. The whole of the air in the room can be thus 'changed' in a few minutes by the Electrolux. Stuffiness and the

[26] U.S. Department of Commerce, Bureau of Foreign and Domestic Commerce, *British Market for Domestic Electrical Appliances*, 13.

[27] Jefferys, *Distribution of Consumer Goods*, 297.

[28] *Electrical Trading* (Mar. 1933), 68–9; (Mar. 1938), 73–4.

[29] Gunnersbury Park Museum, London, 82.85/4, *The Hoover 'Success' Family Magazine* (Apr. 1922), 3, notes a price of £19 15s for a Hoover (having been reduced by £5 5s). *Electrical Trading* (Mar. 1933), 68–9, lists the Hoover 750 at £19 19s and the Hoover 900 at £26 5s; while *Electrical Trading* (Mar. 1938), 73–4, lists the Hoover 875 at £19 19s and the Hoover 160 at £23 3s.

[30] 'The Hoover Factory in the Making', *Domestic Appliances* (Jan. 1933), 167–8 (168) (emphasis in original).

[31] Hoover advertisement, *The Times* (Feb. 1935), 11, col. E.

[32] HHC, 'History Hoover Ltd Perivale', undated historical notes on Hoover UK.

smell of stale tobacco disappear, and a refreshing odour of cleanliness is wafted through the house. Electrolux is the safest home and health insurance against colds, influenza and all diseases carried by germs.[33]

It is doubtful whether most of these ancillary features were much utilized by the typical purchaser. As a 1930 U.S. Department of Commerce report on the British market noted, 'Practically all of the machines have different types of attachments for different purposes, but the majority of them are too complicated for the average British maid, so they are seldom used... many machines turned in as partial payment for a new model have attachments that have never been used.'[34]

For most households, vacuum cleaners were not a high priority. In 1938 the social research organization, Mass Observation, asked 200 volunteer observers (predominantly lower-middle-class, but with a significant proportion of upper-working-class people) about the main drawbacks in their everyday lives.[35] Eighteen per cent of men and 31 per cent of women mentioned lack of electric appliances (though vacuum cleaners were only mentioned by 6 per cent of women and 4 per cent of men). Yet, in response to the question, 'What would you do with an extra £100 a year?', electrical equipment (excluding radios and gramophones) was given top priority by only 3 per cent of both men and women.[36]

From the consumer's perspective, there were strong practical reasons for according them low priority. Vacuum cleaners and other labour-saving appliances brought much less social prestige than investment in highly visible display items, such as new furniture (which was prioritized by more than twice the number of households that mentioned electric goods), a larger house (more space also received higher priority in the survey), or a radio, gramophone, or new car (all of which were ranked above electric appliances). Manual carpet sweepers, which could be bought for as little as 10–20 shillings during the 1930s, provided a much cheaper (though markedly less efficient) alternative.[37] Another alternative was the charwoman (increased domestic help receiving the same priority as electric goods), whose employment also conferred more social prestige.[38]

Nor were the cost advantages over domestic help at all clear-cut. A 1935 survey of fifteen women found that they spent an average of 15.5 hours per week on domestic cleaning (including both regular cleaning and more intensive work during the annual spring clean).[39] Monthly payments on a £20 cleaner would be around £1, while it would also incur power costs (claimed by Hoover in 1936 to

---

[33] Geffrye Museum, Electrolux Ltd, *The Cleaner Cleaner* (undated leaflet).

[34] U.S. Department of Commerce, Bureau of Foreign and Domestic Commerce, *British Market for Domestic Electrical Appliances*, 14.

[35] University of Sussex, Mass Observation Archive [hereafter MOA], File Report A10, 'Reactions to Advertising', Dec. 1938.

[36] It appears that respondents wrote in their top priorities, rather than being presented with a range of options. Electrical equipment ranked thirteenth.

[37] Prices taken from: Peter Scott collection, John Noble Ltd, *John Noble's Ideal Club Catalogue* (Manchester: John Noble, 1935), 360; Manchester Mutual Trading Association Ltd, *Mutual Clubs Catalogue A.38* (Manchester: Mutual Trading Association, n.d., *c.*1938), 271.

[38] MOA, File Report A10, 'Reactions to Advertising', Dec. 1938.

[39] Cited in Political and Economic Planning, *Market for Household Appliances*, 26–7.

be around a penny per hour).[40] Total monthly costs would thus be sufficient to employ a charwoman (paid around 10d per hour) for six hours per week to do the heavier cleaning.[41] Charwomen were also much more flexible in their range of household tasks and—despite the sharp decline in the employment of indoor servants—it was common for lower-middle-class households to employ part-time help.[42] After the two years or so of the HP agreement had elapsed the vacuum would become a much cheaper option (incurring only power costs and servicing charges of six shillings per year, exclusive of parts).[43] Yet, until then, its HP costs constituted a substantial and inflexible financial commitment, whereas the charwoman's employment could be terminated if the need arose.

Another key feature of vacuum cleaner marketing, via both door-to-door and conventional retailing, was heavy reliance on HP, which accounted for an estimated three-quarters of sales in 1938.[44] Down-payments varied from 10s to £1 (generally towards the higher end of this range), with monthly instalments generally spread over one to three years.[45] Given that a cleaner marketed by one of the leading brands typically cost the equivalent of several weeks' wages for a clerk or skilled worker, credit facilities proved key to making vacuums more widely affordable. As with other consumer durables, manufacturers offered retailers support with HP credit, often through arrangements with independent HP finance houses. HP contracts on vacuum cleaners were generally of fairly short duration, compared to furniture or power-hungry white goods, and had higher minimum deposit requirements. As such, the vacuum cleaner sector shared the features of the radio and motor vehicle trades in that HP terms were generally not used as a means of inter-firm competition.

Manufacturers' print advertising was mainly used to support direct sales, boosting brand recognition.[46] The leading brands were extensively advertised, though the sector's ratio of advertising spend to sales was lower than for some other durables. According to estimates for 1935, advertising to final consumers was estimated to be equivalent to 3.1 per cent of manufacturers' net sales, markedly lower than for radios (90 per cent), refrigerators (7.7 per cent), cookers, heaters, and grates (4.0 per cent), and cars (3.7 per cent).[47] They also engaged in substantial trade advertising. Hoover UK (which employed the London branch of Erwin Wasey, the parent company's advertising agency) used advertising to cement cooperative

[40] Peter Scott collection, Hoover Ltd, *On Judging a Vacuum Cleaner*, leaflet (n.d., c.1936).

[41] Elizabeth Craig, *Keeping House with Elizabeth Craig* (London: Collins, 1936), 203.

[42] Philip Massey, 'The Expenditure of 1,360 British Middle-Class Households in 1938–39', *Journal of the Royal Statistical Society*, 105 (1942), 159–96, indicated an average weekly expenditure on domestic help in 1938–9 of 43s 5d.

[43] Hoover recommended servicing every six months, at three shillings per visit. Peter Scott collection, Hoover guarantee, 19 Jan. 1939.

[44] Jefferys, *Distribution of Consumer Goods*, 298.

[45] 'Have You Invited Manufacturers' Help for Your Hire-Purchase?', *Electrical Trading* (Oct. 1930), 48–50.

[46] U.S. Department of Commerce, Bureau of Foreign and Domestic Commerce, *British Market for Domestic Electrical Appliances*, 9.

[47] Nicholas Kaldor and Rodney Silverman, *A Statistical Analysis of Advertising Expenditure and of the Revenue of the Press* (Cambridge: Cambridge University Press, 1948), 144–7.

relations with its dealers. These received a regular bulletin, including proofs of current advertising adapted for their use and information concerning window displays, show cards, and other promotional materials available from Hoover.[48] During 1921 customer advertisements were directly linked with dealer display, using illustrations that were also suitable for dealers' windows.[49]

Consumer advertising focused on a number of key themes, including both the general merits of vacuum cleaners (labour-saving, hygiene, substituting for domestic servants, and so forth) and the specific advantages of the brand in question (Fig. 10.1). As such, it served primarily to support the door-to-door salesman. The three main overseas-based firms in the British market—Hoover, Electrolux, and Thor (General Electric)—had introduced vacuum direct selling. Conversely, most British manufacturers had initially used conventional distribution channels.[50] GEC (producers of Magnet cleaners) appears to have avoided direct sales throughout the inter-war period.[51] Similarly, until the late 1930s, Vac-Tric adopted a policy of selling only via retailers and electricity supply undertakings, prohibiting their salesmen from making direct calls on the public.[52] Yet the intensity of competition from firms using direct sales deterred many retailers from stocking vacuums, while some developed their own door-to-door sales teams.[53] By 1938, Vac-Tric had switched to direct sales, though (almost uniquely among cleaner firms) it supplemented its salesmen's commission payments with a genuine salary (rather than a drawing account against commission earnings).[54]

Hoover appears to have been the first firm to sell vacuums door-to-door on a significant scale.[55] A few Hoovers had been sold in the UK via agents from 1912, though even after Hoover set up a British sales office in 1919, it initially sold through conventional retail channels. Hoover initially targeted major London department stores, signing an agreement with Selfridges on 2 April 1919 and, shortly afterwards, Harrods, and Waring and Gillow. By 1920 it had recruited some 700 retailers.[56]

However, Hoover soon moved to the resale system, assigning each dealer a representative who canvassed and demonstrated cleaners in customers' homes. This was financed by offering a lower retail discount than was customarily allowed on consumer durables (20 per cent, rather than 30 per cent), with the 10 per cent saving being spent on the resale staff (8 per cent) and their training and support

[48] HHC, Filing Cabinet, 'Foreign plants 11-45, 78.034', file on 'Perivale England Plant, 1933', 'The history of Hoover Limited. Vol. 1. The first three years 1919–1921', 26.

[49] Ibid., 27.

[50] TNA, BT56/43, memorandum on electrically operated vacuum cleaners for the Chief Industrial Advisor's office by W. Hall, 2 Jan. 1931.

[51] Bodleian, Marconi, GEC Board minutes, Apr. 1919–Sept. 1939, and GEC *Magnet* staff magazine, 1932–9.

[52] 'Vac-Tric Vacuum Cleaners' (display advertisement), *The Times* (27 Nov. 1934), 20, col. E.

[53] Gerald Carr, 'Selling Vacuum Cleaners with a Difference', *Electrical Trading* (Mar. 1937), 71.

[54] *Bognor Regis Post* (19 Feb. 1938), 12.

[55] TNA, BT56/43, memorandum on electrically operated vacuum cleaners for the Chief Industrial Advisor's office by W. Hall, 2 Jan. 1931.

[56] HHC, Filing Cabinet, 'Foreign plants 11-45, 78.034', file on 'Perivale England Plant, 1933', 'The history of Hoover Limited. Vol. 1. The first three years 1919–1921', 3.

These sunny days have

𝒯he HOOVER

REGISTERED TRADE MARK

It BEATS... *as it Sweeps... as it Cleans*

—*and get more out of life!*

COUPON TO:— HOOVER, LTD., DEPT. O.5.
PERIVALE . GREENFORD . MIDDLESEX
Please send particulars of the new "Jubilee" Hoover
Cleaners at prices from £10 . 15 . 0.

NAME_____

ADDRESS_____

_____

**Fig. 10.1.** A 1935 advert, showing the leisure opportunities created by the labour-saving Hoover

*Source*: Reproduced by kind permission of Neil Baylis.

(2 per cent). The 20 per cent discount was subsequently reduced to 14 per cent and, by 1939, 13 per cent.[57] Direct sales required considerable manpower; by 1939 Hoover claimed to have Britain's largest salaried outside salesforce.[58]

Retailers, particularly department stores and electrical supply utilities, assisted the direct sales drive by hosting in-store demonstrations (in keeping with their broader policies of showcasing new consumer durables), providing 'leads' for salesmen (presumably using information from customer accounts), and hosting in-store promotions. Using the retailer's name when calling on prospects also increased the salesman's chances of getting through the front door.[59]

Electrolux (which was using door-to-door sales in Britain by 1924) adopted a slightly different system to Hoover's—using female canvassers to arrange household demonstrations, followed up by a visit from the salesman.[60] This gender segmentation both reflects the overwhelmingly masculine orientation of direct-sales work and the heavy physical labour involved in hauling a heavy cleaner, plus tools and case, around the streets.[61]

A 1930 market research report found that 35.6 per cent of surveyed homes with vacuums had Hoovers, 18.9 per cent had Electrolux cleaners, and the only other brands with more than a 5 per cent estimated market share were Goblin (5.6 per cent) and Thor (5.5 per cent). Yet nine further brands were enumerated (each with market shares of 1.3–4.3 per cent) and 12.7 per cent of households owned brands with even lower market shares, indicating that there was a long tail of small manufacturers.[62] Market concentration appears to have increased during the 1930s; by 1938 Hoover claimed to account for over half the money spent on electric cleaners in Britain.[63]

## THE DOOR-TO-DOOR SALESMAN

Although there were only around 6–7,000 British vacuum salesmen in 1938, a far higher number had entered the trade over the 1930s, probably well in excess of 100,000, owing to chronic labour turnover. High labour turnover was common

---

[57] Ibid., 7–8 and 17; Ford, Bacon & Davis report, vol. 1, 111.

[58] Bowden, 'Colston, Sir Charles', 757.

[59] U.S. Department of Commerce, Bureau of Foreign and Domestic Commerce, *British Market for Domestic Electrical Appliances*, 9; Harrods advertisement, *The Times* (18 Nov. 1920), 9, col. E; TNA, BT56/43, memorandum on electrically operated vacuum cleaners for the Chief Industrial Advisor's office by W. Hall, 2 Jan. 1931.

[60] Museum of London Archive, interview with Sam Tobin, for Gavin Weightman and Steve Humphries, *The Making of Modern London, 1914–1939* (London: Ebury, 1984); Electrolux advertisement, *The Times* (17 Mar. 1924), 19, col. A.

[61] Julian MacLaren-Ross, *Of Love and Hunger* (London: Wingate, 1947), 104. For example, few women were employed as commercial travellers; Michael French, 'Commercials, Careers, and Culture: Travelling Salesmen in Britain, 1900s–1930s', *Economic History Review*, 58 (2005), 352–77 (368–9).

[62] Bank of England Archives, SMT5/50, Lord & Thomas and Logan Ltd, 'Merchandising survey of Great Britain. Volume 5, Electrical Appliances (Domestic)', 1930, 53.

[63] HHC, 'History Hoover Ltd Perivale', undated historical notes on Hoover UK.

in direct selling.[64] Yet Hoover's British salesforce turnover was 500 per cent (significantly higher than for its US parent), the average salesman lasting less than two and a half months.[65] This reflected low and unstable earnings. Details given by Hoover to the Chief Industrial Advisor's office in February 1932 provide an insight into the size, structure, and productivity of its salesforce. Some 1,300 salesmen, 400 supervisory salesmen, forty district sales managers, and five branch sales managers together sold 45,000 machines per year, with a retail value of £852,000.[66] Thus the average salesman sold fewer than twenty-six cleaners per year, compared to around sixty-five for each member of its US salesforce in 1927.[67] Low average sales, probably mainly reflecting Britain's markedly lower average household incomes, may be a key factor in the more negative image of the vacuum cleaner salesman in the UK than in the United States—from the perspective of both the public and the salesmen themselves.

A Hoover salesman drew £2 weekly in advance of a £3 commission (a rate of 14 per cent, equal to that received by the collaborative retailer) when he sold a cleaner. If he ran up a deficit of £8 his employment was terminated.[68] Based on the 1931 turnover and salesforce data, a Hoover salesman's earnings would typically be only £2 to £3 a week (a sum corroborated by salesmen's testimonies), putting them in a wage bracket well below that of other 'white-collar' workers and among the lower ranks of manual workers. Moreover, sales were subject to substantial seasonal variation, as illustrated by Hoover's 1938 monthly sales data, in Figure 10.2. The standard deviation of monthly sales is 23.2 per cent of the average month's sales. Seasonal variation broadly followed the American pattern, with the exception of a particularly strong peak in March—the month of the traditional British 'spring clean'. Although seasonality was weaker than in radio, a salesman making an average of one sale per week over the year would nevertheless struggle during seasonal troughs to avoid the £8 deficit that would lead to his being fired.

Salesmen employed by other vacuum companies appear to have had similarly low incomes; there is no strong evidence that particular firms were regarded as offering markedly better earnings than their rivals. Hoover's competitors generally paid higher percentage commissions (for cleaners with lower selling prices) but did not enjoy Hoover's particularly strong brand image. Furthermore, unlike Hoover, most did not pay any retainer.

---

[64] For estimates for the United States, see Walter A. Friedman, *Birth of a Salesman: The Transformation of Selling in America* (Cambridge, MA: Harvard University Press, 2004), 183; Buell, 'Door-to-Door Selling', 117.

[65] Smallpeice, *Of Comets and Queens*, 14. Contemporary sources indicate that it was common for salesmen laid off by one company to find employment with another, though companies did not usually rehire salesmen whom they had previously dismissed.

[66] TNA, BT56/49, Chief Industrial Advisor's file regarding Hoover's proposal to set up UK production, note, signed C.L.W., 8 Feb. 1932, and 'Confidential Report' from Hoover, 27 May 1932. It is not clear whether the value given for sales included accessories and replacement parts as well as cleaners.

[67] Carroll Gantz, *The Vacuum Cleaner: A History* (Jefferson, NC: McFarland, 2012), 88.

[68] Smallpeice, *Of Comets and Queens*, 14.

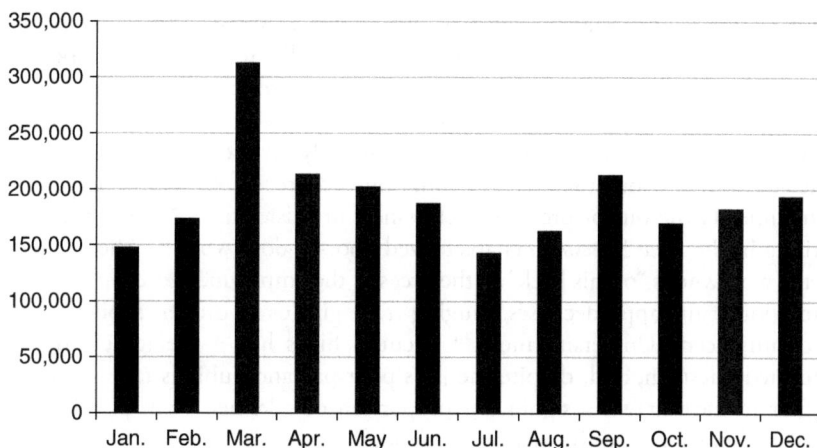

**Fig. 10.2.** Hoover's monthly UK sales of cleaners and tools, 1938 (£)

*Source*: National Archive for Electrical Science and Technology, London, Sir Walter Charles Puckey papers, 146/1/1, Table of Hoover's monthly UK cleaner and tools sales, 1938 and 1947–51 (n.d., *c.*1951).

Chronic labour turnover necessitated a constant stream of new salesmen. These were mainly recruited through small ads in local newspapers. As a former vacuum salesman writing in the *New Statesman* noted: 'In a London daily of the sober type readers may have noticed scores of attractively worded "smalls" which offer a man of ambition, energy and unquestioned integrity (and preferably with a public school education) the prospect of an important executive post in some rapidly expanding sales organisation.'[69] For example, one January 1935 issue of the *Times* contained ten such ads; a typical entry claimed, 'Four figure incomes are being earned by men on our sales staff. We are prepared to engage and train men of personality and appearance without previous selling experience.'[70]

Another less common route into the profession was via salesmanship courses. For example, Harold Marshall, a former quarry worker, enrolled with the Woolis Atwood Training College, responding to an ad in the *Yorkshire Evening Post* that began, 'Would you like to earn £1,000 a year?' The course cost fifteen guineas, but the college promised to find him employment, which turned out to involve selling vacuums for a US firm, on commission only.[71]

Many potential applicants were put off when they discovered the true nature of the job; selling door-to-door was widely regarded as a residual occupation for people who could not find other employment. However, given the mass unemployment of the early 1930s there was no shortage of applicants. As in the United States, firms tended to apply only the most basic selection procedures, relying

[69] A.B.C. [pseudonym], '"Sales Representative"', *New Statesman and Nation* (21 May 1938), 863–4 (863); Julian MacLaren-Ross, *Collected Memoirs* (London: Black Spring, 2004), 186.

[70] *The Times* (17 Jan. 1935), 3, col. A.

[71] British Library, London, National Sound Archive, Millennium Memory Bank, C900/19547/C1, Interview with Harold Marshall.

on the commission system to weed out the poorer salesmen.[72] Smallpeice characterized Hoover's average recruit as, 'no salesman really; to him it was work, when
jobs of any kind were hard to come by. He managed to sell half-a-dozen Hoovers
to people he knew and then called it a day.'[73]

Vacuum salesmen were perhaps the most socially diverse occupational group in
inter-war Britain; but they had in common a degree of economic desperation,
sometimes borne out of previous recklessness or misfortune. A former salesman
writing in the *New Statesman* characterized door-to-door work as: 'the last refuge
of the man who is "on his back"... the dregs of the employment exchanges, crooks
and a lot of unhappy declassés, ranging from gigolos to broken rubber-planters
and "unplaced" University men'.[74] Vacuum firms had a preference for well-
educated salesmen, and, despite the job's poor pay and dubious reputation, they
appear to have drawn a significant proportion of salesmen from people with a
public school and/or university background.[75]

The attraction of unsuccessful middle-class men to this form of employment
reflected its ambiguous social status. Commercial travellers, while being among the
lowest ranks of the middle class, were nevertheless clearly members of that class in
terms of both income and status.[76] Thus, salesmanship as a generic occupation was
more respectable for penniless public school men than better-paid manual work.
Yet door-to-door sales rapidly developed much more negative connotations. As an
Electrolux salesman noted in his Mass Observation diary report, following a visit
to see his mother: 'She was proud of me (God only knows why)[.] "Yes, Len is a
salesman in London," she doesn't know I sell vacuum cleaners door to door.'[77]

There is little information on the origins and recruitment of female canvassers,
but they appear to be characterized by the same relatively broad social background
and economic desperation as their salesmen colleagues.[78] For example, Fanny
Cradock (who went on to be one of Britain's first celebrity TV chefs) was the
daughter of a corn merchant and had attended boarding school. Yet, being wid-
owed shortly after marriage at the age of 17, she found herself penniless, with a
young son. She took a variety of casual and short-term jobs, and after working in
the bargain basement of Selfridges during the Christmas rush, switched to vacuum
cleaners, working on commission only (with her son locked in their bed-sitting
room waiting to be fed on her return).[79]

[72] Buell, 'Door-to-Door Selling', 117.          [73] Smallpeice, *Of Comets and Queens*, 14.
[74] A.B.C. [pseudonym], ' "Sales Representative" '.
[75] See Peter Scott, 'Managing Door-to-Door Sales of Vacuum Cleaners in Interwar Britain',
*Business History Review*, 82 (2008), 761–88.
[76] French, 'Commercials, Careers, and Culture', 354–6.
[77] MOA, Day survey 379, 12 July 1937.
[78] Vacancies for female canvassers were advertised in the quality daily papers and generally asked
for women of smart appearance, for example *The Times* (2 May 1923), 3; (8 Apr. 1929), 3; (11 Sept.
1935), 3.
[79] Fanny Cradock, *Something's Burning: The Autobiography of Two Cooks* (London: Putnam 1960),
86–8; Paul Levy, 'Cradock, Phyllis Nan Sortain [Fanny] (1909–1994)', *Oxford Dictionary of National
Biography* (Internet version).

Hoover UK closely modelled its salesmen's training on that of its American parent. In September 1920 three of the firm's key managers, including C. B. Colston, were sent to the United States to attend the sales training programme and on their return Colston was tasked with organizing a similar programme. The course originally ran for two weeks and included technical and service matters, as well as salesmanship.[80] Later sales innovations adopted by the US parent were rapidly extended to the UK. For example, in autumn 1933 members of Hoover's US Sales Education Department were sent to London to provide Hoover UK with seven weeks' instruction in their new 'Standard Way' sales formula, with H. W. Hoover in attendance to oversee dissemination.[81]

The writer Julian Maclaren-Ross (who joined Hoover in the late 1930s) recalled that the first day of classes covered the 'Three Types of Dirt'. On the second day the students were introduced to 'The Science of Positive Agitation, which may be summed up by our slogan It Beats as It Sweeps as It Cleans, and which is the only satisfactory method for combating all three types of dirt'.[82] They were subsequently taught how to assemble the machine, conduct a demonstration, and make a sale. Students typically took turns being the salesman and the prospect. Sam Tobin, who started work with Hoover in 1938, recalled that they were given a script to learn, which they followed almost to the letter.[83] On graduation, a representative from head office would typically visit to inspire confidence, 'encourage everybody to be "hundred percenters" (everything must be 100 percent) and extend prospects of an almost aggressive profusion of badges, ties, china tea-sets, trips to Ostend and cups as an added inducement to "big sales"'.[84] They might then receive their first drawing account payment and be sent into the field.

Selling involved long days of repetitive, laborious work. A common ploy, following American practice, was to offer to leave the machine in the house 'for a few days', so that the housewife might come to regard it as indispensable by the time the salesman returned. This entailed trekking back to the branch office for a second machine, dragging the heavy display case back to the street, and then repeating the process. Then, if a housewife had been won over, a repeat call had to be made in the evening, to try to talk the husband into agreeing to the purchase.[85]

Yet the most difficult task was getting through the door. Houses with servants proved particularly challenging. As a 1930 US Deptartment of Commerce report on the British market noted, 'In homes where servants are employed there is very little personal contact between the head of the house and the tradesmen, since one

[80] HHC, Filing Cabinet, 'Foreign plants 11-45, 78.034', file on 'Perivale England Plant, 1933', 'The history of Hoover Limited. Vol. 1. The first three years 1919–1921', 22.

[81] HHC, 'Standard Way Goes Overseas', *Hoover Manager* (Oct. 1933), 4.

[82] MacLaren-Ross, *Collected Memoirs*, 186. This sales pitch was paralleled in Hoover's promotional literature, e.g. Peter Scott collection, Hoover Ltd, 'Dirt—and How to Get Rid of It', leaflet (n.d., c.1930s).

[83] Museum of London Archive, interview with Sam Tobin, for Weightman and Humphries, *Making of Modern London*.

[84] A.B.C. [pseud.], '"Sales Representative"', 864.

[85] Ibid.; Museum of London Archive, interview with Sam Tobin, for Weightman and Humphries, *Making of Modern London*.

member of the staff is usually responsible for purchasing many of the household supplies...tradesmen's entrances...prevent easy approach to the head of the house.'[86] Calling at the tradesman's entrance was futile, as the maid's standard response was that she had no authority to grant an interview with the madam of the house. Meanwhile calls at the front door were usually ignored. Sam Tobin solved this problem (on the advice of a veteran colleague) by coming equipped with clipboard and paper and what looked like an impressive roll of cash (comprising a couple of pound notes and some stage money). He would then knock at the door, look at the house number, knock again, and invariably see a curtain twitch. At this point, he started to count the money, looking at the number and at the board, which usually led the housewife to answer the door, 'because they thought they were going to get something for nothing'.[87]

When the door was opened, a typical pitch was: 'Good morning madam, I represent the North Metropolitan Electrical Power Supply Company, and I've been told to offer you my service, which is to clean one of your carpets, and some of your furniture with the latest Hoover cleaner.'[88] If the salesman managed to get through the door, he would proceed with the demonstration. Housewives usually raised a series of objections to buying, for which salesmen had ready answers (often learned at the training school). For example, if she said she couldn't afford it, the salesman might look out the window and say, 'Well I see you got a nice lawn there madam, no doubt your husband cuts it with a modern cylinder type lawn mower....Well surely he wouldn't expect to cut it with shears would he[?] Not now....And does he expect you then to sweep this carpet with an old fashioned sweeping brush[?] I think not.'[89] Similarly, resistance to buying on HP might be countered with the phrase, 'After all, you wouldn't pay your maid a year's wages in advance, would you?'[90]

In addition to being articulate, a successful salesman was expected to have the vital qualities of energy, confidence, and enthusiasm.[91] However, the practicalities of selling vacuums door-to-door acted to progressively undermine morale, as the job entailed making calls that most often produced a curt 'no thank you,' or having the door slammed in the salesman's face. Salesmen were lucky to even get as far as the demonstration and, even then, only a very small number resulted in sales. A common feature of salesmen's testimonies is reference to depression and despondency during periods of low sales, often leading to a downward spiral that eventually resulted in their being fired or simply giving up.

In some cases, disillusionment set in almost at once. Writer Bill Naughton had been recruited by a manufacturer of manually powered vacuum cleaners in 1930, at a time when he was a young unemployed labourer, in chronic poverty. He and another new recruit were each given a postcard with six names and addresses for

---

[86] U.S. Department of Commerce, Bureau of Foreign and Domestic Commerce, *British Market for Domestic Electrical Appliances*, 8–9.

[87] Museum of London Archive, interview with Sam Tobin, for Weightman and Humphries, *Making of Modern London*.

[88] Ibid.        [89] Ibid.        [90] MacLaren-Ross, *Of Love and Hunger*, 7.

[91] Friedman, *Birth of a Salesman*, 42.

demonstrations, and had high hopes. Yet, 'the optimism, the excitement, the big talk, and the feeling of purpose' evaporated once they began to knock on the six doors and found that the demonstration bookings had been fabricated by the canvasser.[92] Similarly, Howard Stone soon discovered that his allocated sales territory in Leigh-on-Sea had been 'flogged and flogged and flogged again' by salesmen. Morale was knocked by unpleasant incidents that punctuated days without sales. For example, on one occasion, feeling depressed after having had many doors slammed in his face, Stone knocked on the side door of a house that opened to reveal a huge dog bounding towards him. After the dog was restrained, Stone began his speech, which was cut short by the door slamming in his face. He walked on to what he thought was the side door to the next house, unaware that he had in fact gone around to the back door of the same house. To his horror, when it opened, the same dog charged at him.[93]

Even salesmen who were initially successful and were held up as exemplars to their colleagues often fell into depression when sales proved elusive. Sam Tobin, who had been awarded Hoover's Bronze Star for sales, described a frequent scenario:

> Many, many times you knocked on doors, and you got no answer, or you got the door slammed in your face... if you [were] following around people that were trying to sell the *News of the World, The People,* and... various other publications and also the Electrolux man and the Goblin man and the Thor man and all the other vacuum cleaner sellers, well you'd got no hope at all.... [S]o once more you just retired to the local park, or to the cinema until the day's work time had finished, and then you'd report back to the office, foot sore, weary, and thoroughly fed up.[94]

## MOTIVATING THE SALESMAN

Vacuum cleaner firms tried various techniques to motivate their sales staff, mainly building on US practice. These included regular bulletins. For example, a surviving issue of the *Hoover 'Success Family' Magazine*, for April 1922, contains inspirational essays, poems, stories from salesmen, and other features under the common theme of 'More demonstrations mean more commission'. It dangled the carrot of high potential earnings: 'A large number of resalemen have received cheques of £10 to £12 and £15 per week during the last few weeks. Have you received yours yet? It lies within your grasp, and we will be more pleased than you when cheques of this size are counted amongst the smallest we have to sign.'[95]

Vacuum firms drew on the military model of managerial organization, which had been popular in US direct selling since the Civil War.[96] Former army, navy, or

---

[92] Bill Naughton, *A Roof Over Your Head* (London: Pilot, 1945), 19–20.

[93] Essex Record Office, Essex Sound and Video Archive, SA 20/1/48/1, interview with Howard Stone, conducted by Ted Haley, 7 Sept. 1983.

[94] Museum of London Archive, interview with Sam Tobin, for Weightman and Humphries, *Making of Modern London.*

[95] Gunnersbury Park Museum, 82.85/4, *Hoover 'Family Success' Magazine* (Apr. 1922), 2.

[96] Friedman, *Birth of a Salesman*, 36.

RAF officers were strongly represented in the ranks of sales managers.[97] Hoover even awarded 'medals' to successful salesmen, similar in design to First World War medals, for campaigns with titles such as 'Spring Manoeuvers', 'Hoover War', and 'Hoover Crusade'.[98] An ethos of vigorous competition was encouraged by posting the turnover of each salesman in the local sales office and launching frequent competitions between both individual salesmen and sales teams.[99] Regular motivational dispatches were sent to salesmen, including one-page fliers displaying inspirational messages that echoed the motivational slogans posted in sales offices.[100] Electrolux salesman H. L. Lacey even resorted to creating his own slogans, which he pinned to the wall of his bed-sitting room: 'THE 2nd EFFORT TO RECOVERY COMMENCES JULY 10th' and 'A SUCCESSFUL SALESMAN REQUIRES SELF DISCIPLINE'. To these admonishments, he appended the underlined warning, 'I MUST NOT FAIL'.[101]

Hoover also employed a more idiosyncratic motivational device—the collective singing of company songs (adapted from popular tunes). These had long been used by its US parent to boost morale at sales conventions and meetings; they were also sometimes used as a promotional device, featuring in cinema and radio advertising.[102] Their UK subsidiary also embraced this technique; local sales teams periodically received an inspirational talk over pints of bitter and snacks, rounding off the evening with a selection of 'Hoover songs', such as:

> Buy, buy, you need a Hoover,
> Cleaning for you.
> Buy, buy, make all your dreams
> Of leisure come true
> Buy, buy, your life is fleeting
> Just let the Hoover do all your beating
> Now it's the time,
> Buy, buy, I'm here you,
> I'm to serve you,
> Buy madam, sign![103]

Yet salesmen's testimonies indicate that the gap between the company's presentation of their job and the day-to-day reality only served to further alienate them. As one former salesman noted, the humiliation, loss of nervous energy, and sense of utter futility that resulted from badgering unwilling and often hostile housewives, day after day, was only magnified by the final irony of receiving, at the end of a week without sales (or, therefore, pay), 'a chatty "sales bulletin", charged with ponderous bonhomie and talk of cups and bonuses'.[104]

---

[97] A.B.C. [pseud.], ' "Sales Representative" ', 864; MacLaren-Ross, *Of Love and Hunger*, 114.

[98] Peter Scott collection, Hoover awards made to W. H. Newsome, 1930–6.

[99] Interview with Cyril K. Jaegar, conducted by the author on 21 Aug. 2006.

[100] MOA, Day survey 425, 12 June 1937.　　　[101] MOA, Day survey 379, 12 July 1937.

[102] Frank G. Hoover, *Fabulous Dustpan: The Story of the Hoover* (Cleveland, OH: World Publishing, 1955), 142–3; Jane Furnival, *Suck, Don't Blow* (London: O'Mara, 1998), 17.

[103] Museum of London Archive, interview with Sam Tobin, for Weightman and Humphries, *Making of Modern London*; see also MacLaren-Ross, *Of Love and Hunger*, 36.

[104] A.B.C. [pseud.], ' "Sales Representative" ', 864.

Hoover's resale system constrained Hoover UK from giving its salesmen a higher commission rate, as it allotted around 14 per cent of the retail price to the dealer. Hoover's British managers regarded this as excessive (a view later corroborated by the consultants Hoover USA brought in to look at its operations in 1939, discussed in Chapter 9). In May 1937 C. B. Colston had tried to persuade H. W. Hoover:

> that there was one method by which Selling Costs could be very substantially reduced, and that was by getting better Salesmen—by paying them a very much better rate of commission. If the rate of commission was so attractive that men were looking for jobs with Hoover Limited rather than Hoover Limited having to look for men... then the process of weeding out became a much simpler thing.[105]

C. B. Colston then suggested that they might follow the plan of British Hoover's Belgian sales subsidiary, where all sales made directly by Hoover salesmen required no commission payments to dealers. E. L. Colston (Hoover UK's sales director), then explained 'at very great length' that in Europe the dealer was often more of a handicap than an asset and was not essential to instalment credit provision as, after the first four months of the agreement, the finance company took responsibility for the loan.[106] However, this argument appears to have fallen on deaf ears (though it may account for a marginal reduction in dealer commission at some point in the late 1930s, from 14 to 13 per cent). In 1937 Hoover UK also engaged the industrial psychologist G. H. Miles as its research officer, with a brief to find ways to reduce its rapid salesforce turnover. Unfortunately Miles and his staff were not able to resolve this problem.[107]

## OPPORTUNISTIC BEHAVIOUR AND CONSUMER RESISTANCE

Rapid labour turnover and a geographically dispersed workforce prevented any collective opposition by salesmen to what were widely perceived as exploitative conditions. Instead, resistance mainly took the form of various 'fiddles', partly borne out of desperation or opportunism, but also from a desire to turn the tables on their employers.[108] In contrast to the competitive ethos managers sought to engender, salesmen's testimonies indicate a strong sense of occupational solidarity (even between salesmen from rival companies). This acted both to promote a common consciousness of exploitation by their employers and to legitimize the methods by which they could increase their earnings at their employers' expense—information about various scams commonly being shared among salesmen.[109]

---

[105] HHC, 'High Spots Hoover Ltd, H.W.H', file, memorandum of discussion with Mr H. W. Hoover, C. B. Colston, and E. L. Colston, 18 May 1937.

[106] HHC, 'High Spots Hoover Ltd, H.W.H', file, 'Manufacturing in England versus Canada', unsigned memorandum, 7 Dec. 1931.

[107] HHC, Filing Cabinet, 'Foreign plants 11-45, 78.034', file on 'Perivale England Plant, 1933', Interview with Mr Tribute, 12 Nov. 1965, unsigned.

[108] 'Intensive Door-to-Door Salesmanship', *Hire Traders' Record* (June 1936), 3.

[109] Interview with Cyril K. Jaeger, conducted by the author on 21 Aug. 2006.

Frauds often grew from behaviour initially regarded as a temporary bending of the rules to get through periods of low earnings. For example, Hoover salesmen needed to make ten demonstrations per week to receive their £2 retainer. But this proved problematic in districts facing heavy canvassing, where housewives had learned not to let the salesman through the door. Names and addresses couldn't simply be made up, in case they were checked by the supervisor. Sam Tobin resolved this problem by knocking on a door and asking, 'Does Mrs MacWilliams live here?' The housewife might reply, 'No, my name is Brown.' He would then add, 'Well perhaps Mrs MacWilliams lives at number 80', which would usually lead the housewife to reveal the name of her neighbour.[110] Another, simpler, method was to take names and addresses from the local directory.[111]

Sometimes supervisors would turn a blind eye to this practice, or even assist. A Mass Observation day diary entry by E. Neilson recorded the morning's meeting with his supervisor, where they wrote up the report for Hoover and collaborated in bringing his four demonstrations up to the requisite ten.[112] Some people would play the system in a more calculated manner. Rather than engaging in any real sales activity, they made up fictitious demonstrations, so that they could draw the £2 retainer for four weeks, before being fired.[113]

Trade-in deals also proved fertile territory for scams. Tobin recalled that, on receiving a Hoover Junior in part exchange for a larger model, a salesman would typically make up the £2 difference between the full and the trade-in price from his own pocket and then sell the machine to one of his prospects. Conversely, if a housewife told him that she would like to buy a cleaner but didn't have the deposit, he would go to the local market and buy a second-hand cleaner in very poor condition, claiming that this had been traded in. Thus, if he sold the prospect a Junior he would earn 30s commission, in return for spending 10s or less, a clear profit of £1.[114] Again, supervisors would often turn a blind eye or even collaborate. MacLaren-Ross was fired from Hoover after a new branch manager learned that he had sold a traded-in cleaner to a prospect. The deal had in fact been instigated by his supervisor, who took half the money but used him to make the actual sale, to divert responsibility should the arrangement be discovered.[115]

Part exchange scams sometimes developed into outright frauds. For example, in 1936 P. Maybury was charged with fraudulently obtaining £3 4s from the local agents for an unnamed vacuum manufacturer. He had reported a sale, claiming the housewife had provided a machine in part exchange. The firm advanced him the part exchange value, but the purchaser later denied signing the agreement, stating that she had allowed him to take away the cleaner because he told her he could sell

---

[110] Museum of London Archive, interview with Sam Tobin, for Weightman and Humphries, *Making of Modern London*.

[111] MacLaren-Ross, *Of Love and Hunger*, 4.　　　[112] MOA, Day survey 425, 12 June 1937.

[113] A.B.C. [pseud.], '"Sales Representative"', 864.

[114] Museum of London Archive, interview with Sam Tobin, for Weightman and Humphries, *The Making of Modern London*.

[115] MacLaren-Ross, *Collected Memoirs*, 109.

it for 40s. The bench, stressing Maybury's public school education, bound him over for six months.[116]

While salesmen's accounts universally present such behaviour as an attack on their employers, in reality it often impacted most severely on the customer. For example, a number of county court cases involved firms claiming 'depreciation' charges of around half the price of cleaners that had been returned without, in some cases, the tissue the machine was wrapped in even being opened.[117] Defendants typically reported that they believed the machine was left with them on trial and that they had been deceived into signing the contract. As depreciation charges were specified in the HP contract, the judge generally had no option but to find in favour of the firm. However, several set monthly payments at only one penny—thus extending them over a hundred years or more. Judges also used these opportunities to denounce the door-to-door system and the manufacturers who used it. For example, in 1937 Judge Leigh condemned a salesman's methods as typical of what was 'going on all over the county. People who are comparatively ignorant...are being bamboozled into signing documents they do not understand, and entering into contracts to buy things they do not want.'[118]

Frauds were sometimes quite ambitious. For example, in 1936 Archie Friday stood trial at the Old Bailey on four charges of obtaining money under false pretences by forging signatures on HP agreements, while fellow salesman George Gutteridge was accused of conspiring with him to obtain money from vacuum dealer Robert Edwards. Edwards had employed them to sell cleaners, on commission only. Friday had hired two female canvassers, whom he allegedly instructed to 'get in as many dud sales as you can', adding that he would change firms before this came to light. He received almost £300 commission on bogus contracts, costing Edwards around £500–£600. Friday received nine months' imprisonment: the judge noted the complicity of a large number of people, obviously in on the fraud, who were fortunate not to be in the dock and who treated the matter 'as a huge joke'.[119]

The 1930 US Department of Commerce investigation into the British market noted numerous complaints regarding unscrupulous behaviour by door-to-door salesmen, prompting MPs to call for restrictive legislation.[120] By the mid-1930s adverse public reaction was so strong that even the Hire Traders Protection Society (the main trade association for HP dealers) had begun to publicly denounce vacuum manufacturers for abuses their salesmen were forced by poverty to perpetrate. As an article in their journal noted, relying on commission for their daily living led salesmen to do 'many things which a living wage would never allow to be schemed'.[121]

---

[116] 'Vacuum Cleaner Fraud', *Hire Traders' Record* (Oct. 1936), 8.
[117] For example, 'Penny a Month in H.P. Claims', *Hire Purchase Journal* (May 1938), 8.
[118] 'Just 120 Years to Pay Instalments!', *Hire Traders' Record* (Mar. 1937), 5.
[119] 'Commission on Bogus Orders', *Hire Traders' Record* (1 Feb. 1936), 4–5.
[120] U.S. Department of Commerce, Bureau of Foreign and Domestic Commerce, *British Market for Domestic Electrical Appliances*, 9.
[121] 'Intensive Door-to-Door Salesmanship', *Hire Traders' Record* (June 1936), 3.

# PARTNER

*in a business that sells
leisure to housewives*

HE is one of a team of salaried Hoover men—a partner in the greatest electric cleaner organization in the country. He and his fellows are helping to build a world in which freedom from drudgery plays a bigger part.

That is why hundreds of thousands of housewives remember these men as friends, as men who have done them a really good turn. Ask a Hoover owner yourself — not one would go back to the old work-ridden days.

Then why, oh why, do *you* still slave away at back-breaking jobs that leave you tired out before lunch-time? Why do you put up with that old and inefficient cleaner? Trade it in, in part exchange. For only 10/- down and 4d. a day you can have your Hoover.

Take a firm stand. Give the Hoover man a hearing. NOW—before Spring Cleaning!

## The HOOVER

*It* BEATS... *as it* Sweeps... *as it* Cleans

*Coupon*

to Hoover Ltd., Dept. H.1, Perivale, Greenford, Middx. Please send me without obligation your booklet describing all Hoover Electric Cleaners.

NAME

ADDRESS

*The*
HOOVER JUNIOR
**10/**- DOWN
Cash Price £10.15
Cleaning Tools
£2.2.6

**Fig. 10.3.** The Hoover salesman as portrayed by the firm
*Source: Times* (27 Jan. 1938), 9, col E.

**"Good afternoon, Mrs. Bennington. Here I am again."**

**Fig. 10.4.** The Hoover salesman as depicted by *Punch*

Source: *Punch* (28 Dec. 1938), 723. Reproduced courtesy of Punch Ltd.

Adverse publicity strengthened consumer resistance. Meanwhile, the growing intensity of canvassing acted to educate the consumer in the art of saying no to the salesman's call. Thus, despite an attempt by Hoover in the late 1930s to promote its salesmen as 'friends' who had done hundreds of thousands of housewives 'a really good turn' (Fig. 10.3), getting past the front door was becoming increasingly difficult (Fig. 10.4). Meanwhile, declining unemployment reduced the supply of good-quality sales recruits. Sales campaigns began to falter. In March 1939 Hoover's British managing director reported a decline in annual profits from £419,807 to £338,515, which he ascribed to an expansion of its salesforce to meet what the company expected to be a difficult year, but which had failed to produce a corresponding increase in sales.[122]

---

[122] 'Hoover Limited', *The Times* (16 Mar. 1939), 25.

National vacuum-cleaner sales in the late 1930s, of around 400,000 per annum, were no higher than during the middle of the decade. Industry commentators talked of market saturation, as by 1938 replacement demand was estimated to account for around three out of every eight cleaners purchased (based on an estimated lifespan of six to eight years).[123] Yet the estimated 2.3 million cleaners in use by 1939 represented only around 30 per cent of wired homes, or 52 per cent of households in the middle-class income range (over £250 per annum).[124]

## CONCLUSIONS

Door-to-door selling had enabled vacuum cleaner manufacturers to rapidly expand sales to levels that sustained national marketing operations, by directly addressing consumer resistance and inertia. However, it appears to have been less effective in the UK than in America, owing to lower incomes, more cost-effective alternatives (particularly domestic help), and greater consumer resistance. Rising consumer resistance in turn reflected the typically low incomes of vacuum salesmen, which often led them to engage in sharp and sometimes unlawful practice—which was widely publicized and brought the system into disrepute. Hoover's UK management identified one promising means to resolve this impasse—the termination of the dealer's role in the sales process—which could have boosted salesmen's earnings either through increasing commissions per sale, or by lowering prices (thus increasing unit sales). However, the US parent was strongly committed to its resale system and by 1940, when the parent company's consultants identified dealer commission as the weak link in its US operation, Britain was at war and Perivale had switched production from vacuums to munitions.

---

[123] 'The Replacement Market', *Electrical Trading* (Mar. 1938), 69.
[124] Political and Economic Planning, *Market for Household Appliances*, 211–12 and 355.

# PART IV

# BRITAIN'S MASS MARKET 'FAILURES'—CARS AND TELEPHONES

This final section examines two sectors where Britain considerably lagged behind the United States in mass market diffusion—automobiles and telephones. Britain's 'failure' in automobiles is often exaggerated. Despite not achieving America's mass-market diffusion, Britain had the second-largest motor vehicle industry in the world and—in common with the other major car-producing nations—it relied heavily on the home market. Moreover, car manufacture was atypical in that it was one of the very few consumer durables for which true 'Fordist' mass production methods—replacing skilled labour with special-purpose machine tools—was successfully applied anywhere in the world before 1939. Even there the costs of the machine tools were so great that only the largest three US car manufacturers achieved sufficient output to make Fordism economical—though for high volumes it provided such steep scale economies that these were able to slash prices to levels well below the minimum for any British car.

Telephones were a clearer British failure. Throughout the inter-war years the diffusion of the British telephone network and its utilization lagged not only behind the United States and Canada but also Australia, New Zealand, Denmark, Sweden, Norway, and Switzerland. This was closely linked to public ownership of the network from 1912. However, rather than reflecting bureaucratic inefficiencies or the other problems popularly attributed to nationalized industries, the key impediment was Treasury control over Post Office spending on the telephone service. The Treasury had long pursued a rigid economic orthodoxy based around three classical 'pillars': the gold standard (by which sterling's value was linked to gold at a constant exchange rate and, therefore, to all other currencies that were convertible into gold); minimal, balanced, government budgets; and free trade. The second and third pillars were important chiefly because they supported the first, gold standard, pillar. For example, increased public spending commitments might make it more difficult for the Treasury to cut spending when deflationary policy was deemed necessary, to support either sterling's gold parity or the smooth running of the international gold standard system.

The Treasury had thus traditionally opposed increased public expenditure, even if that expenditure constituted directly profitable investment (as in the case of the telephone service) or provided a high investment return to the British economy overall (as with road building). By the 1920s the gold standard system was in severe crisis, as the First World War had forced a break with Britain's pre-1914 gold standard parity, while wartime inflation had substantially eroded the value of sterling compared to that gold parity. War expenditure had also drained much of Britain's foreign currency and gold reserves. More fundamentally, the war had led to major dislocations in trade patterns and the imposition of growing trade barriers by overseas countries, which undermined the viability of the international gold standard system. In an ultimately unsuccessful attempt to restore the international gold standard, the Treasury and Bank of England pushed through savage domestic deflation, first to restore sterling to the gold standard at its pre-war parity and then (after this was achieved, in 1925) to maintain it at what proved to be an overvalued exchange rate.

Britain was eventually forced to abandon the gold standard in September 1931, after which the pound depreciated to a more realistic value, generating a substantial economic recovery (in contrast to Bank of England and Treasury predictions of economic disaster if the policy was abandoned). Nevertheless, the Treasury and Bank of England remained wedded to low, balanced, government budgets, arguing that this was necessary to maintain 'confidence' in the British economy (despite the fact that most other major industrial nations were pursuing much more active stimulus policies to combat the world depression).

As the following chapters show, the Treasury doctrine of balanced, minimal government budgets had major detrimental impacts on the development of both the telephone network and the motor vehicle industry. The Treasury vehemently opposed investment in the telephone service, until a political storm eventually tempered its ability to do so. It had longer-term success in holding back the diffusion of the car in Britain by imposing petrol and vehicle taxes that were considerably higher than those for other car-producing nations, while at the same time preventing any major expansion in road building to meet the needs of the rapidly growing volume of road traffic. Depressing expenditure on consumer durables, in order to support sterling, the City, and Britain's international role, was a policy that the Treasury and Bank of England applied more generally, and brutally, during the 1950s and 1960s, with devastating results for Britain's consumer durables industries, as discussed in this book's final chapter.

# 11

## Failure to Accelerate
### Britain's Stalled Mass Market for Cars

### INTRODUCTION

From an international perspective, the inter-war car industry was a British success story. By the late 1920s Britain ranked only second to the United States as the leading producer of, and market for, automobiles.[1] The number of cars manufactured in Britain rose from just under a third of the European total in 1925 and 1929 to 43 per cent in 1937. And while the United States, Canada, and France never managed to regain their 1929 levels of car production before the Second World War, Britain overtook its 1929 output in 1933 and had doubled it by 1937.[2] Yet Britain's car industry was always dwarfed by the United States. British production was equivalent to less than 4 per cent of American output in 1925 and 1929 and, despite the Great Depression, only 9.7 per cent in 1937, when it peaked at 379,300 cars.[3]

Britain's high car output (by European standards) was based on home demand. As with most consumer durables, international trade in cars was not extensive during the inter-war era, given the high tariff regimes operating in most countries. In 1936 only 17.7 per cent of all cars produced in the UK were exported, though even this proportion was higher than the ratios of exports to domestic production for the United States, Germany, or France.[4]

Jefferys estimated consumers' expenditure on new private cars in 1938 at £51–52 million, a substantially greater sum than for radios or household appliances and equivalent to more than 80 per cent of consumers' furniture expenditure.[5] However, while consumers' expenditure was high, it was not deep—car ownership was limited to only around 15.4 per of UK households even in 1938, compared to

---

[1] William M. Park, *Automotive Industry and Trade of Great Britain and Ireland*, United States Dept. of Commerce, Bureau of Foreign and Domestic Commerce, Trade Promotion Series No. 63 (Washington, DC: USGPO, 1928), 1.

[2] George Maxcy and Aubrey Silberston, *The Motor Industry* (London: George Allen & Unwin, 1959), 14 and 39.

[3] Susan Bowden, 'Demand and Supply Constraints in the Inter-War UK Car Industry: Did the Manufacturers Get it Right?', *Business History*, 33 (1991), 241–67 (244) (based on Society of Motor Manufacturers and Traders data).

[4] Bowden, 'Demand and Supply Constraints', 244–5.

[5] J. B. Jefferys, *The Distribution of Consumer Goods: A Factual Study of Methods and Costs in the United Kingdom in 1938* (Cambridge: Cambridge University Press, 1950), 350. Estimate excludes purchases by firms and government departments.

about 44 per cent in the United States by the mid-1930s.[6] This chapter examines why the British automobile sector failed to 'take off' into mass market diffusion. A number of important factors are highlighted, including lower British wages relative to the United States; punitive vehicle and petrol taxation; and the high unit production costs incurred in serving a market too small to justify Fordist mass production techniques. However, a more fundamental reason was the low priority given to car ownership by most people, in a relatively small, densely populated, and highly urbanized island nation with well-developed public transport networks.

## PRODUCTION SYSTEMS AND PRODUCT INNOVATION

Patents were relatively unimportant in motor vehicles—either as a means of limiting competition or extracting rents from manufacturers. Maxcy and Silberston argued that it was not difficult to manufacture components which were substantially similar to existing ones without patent infringement—as evidenced by the absence of significant motor vehicle patent litigation in either the UK or United States.[7]

Conversely, production methods were a key factor determining costs and—in contrast to most industries examined in this study—were strongly influenced by the ability to tap truly mass markets. In September 1922 Herbert Austin and his new finance director, Ernest Payton, visited the United States to discover how American manufacturers were able to deliver a car from their works at a price roughly equal to what Austin would pay for the material inputs.[8] They visited several major manufacturers, including Ford and General Motors, together with some components and tool producers. Austin concluded that low US costs were strongly linked to heavy expenditure on machine tools, but that such expenditure required high output volumes:

> Of course it might be argued that the big outputs warrant this large expenditure, as the cost per car is probably lower than with us, but on the other hand, without this complete and costly equipment the low cost per car could not be obtained, and as the equipment has to be provided beforehand the first essential is the decision to provide the equipment.[9]

Henry Ford had famously driven down the price of American automobiles in the years immediately before the First World War by replacing artisanal labour with a system based around expensive machinery (and, later, single-purpose machine tools), interchangeable parts, work-pacing using moving conveyor belts, and the

---

[6] Sources: for UK see note 126; United States: Karen A. Kopecky and Richard M. H. Suen, 'A Quantitative Analysis of Suburbanization and the Diffusion of the Automobile', *International Economic Review*, 51 (2010), 1003–37 (1006).

[7] Maxcy and Silberston, *Motor Industry*, 126.

[8] Source: MRC, 226/AU/1/1/1, Austin Motor Co. Board minutes, insert, Herbert Austin, 'Visit of the Chairman & Mr E. L. Payton to the USA' (n.d., *c.*October 1922).

[9] Ibid.

specialization of each worker's role into simple, repetitive tasks. During the 1920s General Motors and Chrysler adopted modified Fordist strategies, producing a range of cars with shared components and machine tools. These three companies (the 'Big Three') dominated the US motor vehicle industry, as no other manufacturer could achieve the minimum sales volume for Fordist mass production (which was, in turn, a prerequisite for competition in the US volume car market).[10]

No British car manufacturer of this era achieved the volume output to justify true Fordist mass production. Yet the British car industry nevertheless flourished, owing to its home market being protected both by tariffs and by a tax system that favoured smaller cars than those popular in the United States. A 33.3 per cent tariff on the landed cost of imported cars was introduced during the First World War, under the McKenna duties. This tariff continued throughout the inter-war period and provided a substantial element of protection for the British industry. Meanwhile Britain's tax system drove down the size of British cars. In 1921 the government abolished petrol tax, replacing it with a vehicle tax of £1 per unit of horsepower per annum. Both this and a relatively high petrol tax (reintroduced in 1928 at 4d per gallon and raised to 8d per gallon from 1931) encouraged the purchase of small cars, which were also cheaper to garage and insure.[11]

British firms responded by developing lower horsepower high compression engines. From 1925 to 1934 the average taxable horsepower of British cars fell from 13.90 to 11.90, thereafter stabilizing at around that level.[12] These cars were sufficiently powerful for British roads, but not for the rougher terrain of less densely populated countries such as the United States, Canada, and Australia.[13] The tax thus differentiated British cars from their American counterparts in terms of size and engine characteristics, simultaneously protecting the British industry and hampering exports.[14] The protection to the home market provided by this tax appears to have been considerable. Following a reduction in the horsepower tax from £1 to 15s per horsepower in the April 1934 budget (with the new rate coming in to effect at the beginning of 1935) there was an immediate boom in car imports from the United States. The number of cars imported during the first three months of 1935 was some 347 per cent higher than the first three months of 1934, while relative US/UK car prices and exchange rates hardly changed.

Foreman-Peck, Bowden, and McKinlay estimate that, taking into account other factors influencing the demand for cars (including the general boost to demand arising from the tax cut), the 25 per cent tax reduction was responsible for a 300 per cent increase in American imports relative to home-produced car sales. From this they extrapolate that the complete removal of the tax might have increased

[10] Daniel M. G. Raff, 'Making Cars and Making Money in the Inter-War Automobile Industry: Economies of Scale and Scope and the Manufacturing behind the Marketing', *Business History Review*, 65 (1991), 721–53.

[11] Political and Economic Planning, *Motor Vehicles* (London: PEP, 1950), 65.

[12] The Clarks Archive, Street, 2/12, Sampson Clark & Company Ltd, 'Business Development Bulletin. The Motor Car Industry', market research report, 1938, 3.

[13] Park, *Automotive Industry*, 6.

[14] 'Progress of the Industry', *Economist* (7 Dec. 1935), 1134–6.

American and Canadian car imports from a 1935 level equivalent to 4 per cent of home-produced cars sold in the UK, to around 36 per cent. This would have had a devastating impact on the UK motor industry (though they suggest that this is almost certainly an overstatement, as the short-run impact of the change was likely to be greater than its long-run impact).[15]

Moves towards a more concentrated industry generated scale economies. The number of car-producing firms fell from eighty-eight in 1922 to thirty-one in 1929, with Morris and Austin accounting for 60 per cent of production and Singer a further 15 per cent.[16] The 12 horsepower Morris-Cowley and the smaller Austin Seven (introduced in 1915 and 1922 respectively) both achieved relatively long production runs over the 1920s and were credited as having facilitated the introduction of elementary mass production techniques by these firms, which boosted their price competitiveness and consequent ability to drive out many smaller producers. Yet neither had an average output by the late 1920s of much over 50,000 cars per year.[17]

Production of the Austin Seven was based on a strategy of high volumes and small profit margins (within the constraints of Austin's financial difficulties during the 1920s)—using the continuous flow production methods Austin had observed in the United States. Austin introduced Britain's first moving car assembly lines, for both chassis and car bodies. However, he struggled to keep some of the specialized machine tools fully employed, given his limited output and recurring production bottlenecks. Nevertheless, these innovations led to a major increase in productivity, the number of employees per car per week falling from fifty-five in 1922 to only ten in 1927.[18] Overall, however, British cars were estimated in 1928 to be almost 50 per cent more expensive than their American counterparts.[19]

The motor industry was subject to substantial production seasonality (though not nearly as severe as in the radio sector), as shown in Figure 11.1. Taking the average ratio of output for each month, relative to annual output for that year, for the three years 1929–31, gives a standard deviation of monthly output of 25.9 per cent. Production peaked in February at 146 per cent of the monthly average and remained above the monthly average until July, when it dipped sharply to 58 per cent of the average. Sales then recovered in the autumn, boosted by the annual Motor Show (originally held in November, then—from 1924—in October), which saw most of the year's new model launches.[20]

Retailer stock-turn for cars was relatively low, estimated by Jefferys at three to four times per year for retailers other than main dealers, compared to four to five times for multiple furniture chains or five to six times for radio retailers.[21] This probably mainly reflects the fact that seasonality was both substantial and predictable,

[15] James Foreman-Peck, Sue Bowden, and Alan McKinlay, *The British Motor Industry* (Manchester: Manchester University Press, 1995), 74–6.

[16] Maxcy and Silberston, *Motor Industry*, 13–15 and 99.    [17] Ibid., 99.

[18] Roy Church, *Herbert Austin: The British Motor Car Industry to 1941* (London: Europa, 1979), 97–100.

[19] Park, *Automotive Industry*, 35.    [20] Political and Economic Planning, *Motor Vehicles*, 67.

[21] Jefferys, *Distribution of Consumer Goods*, 353.

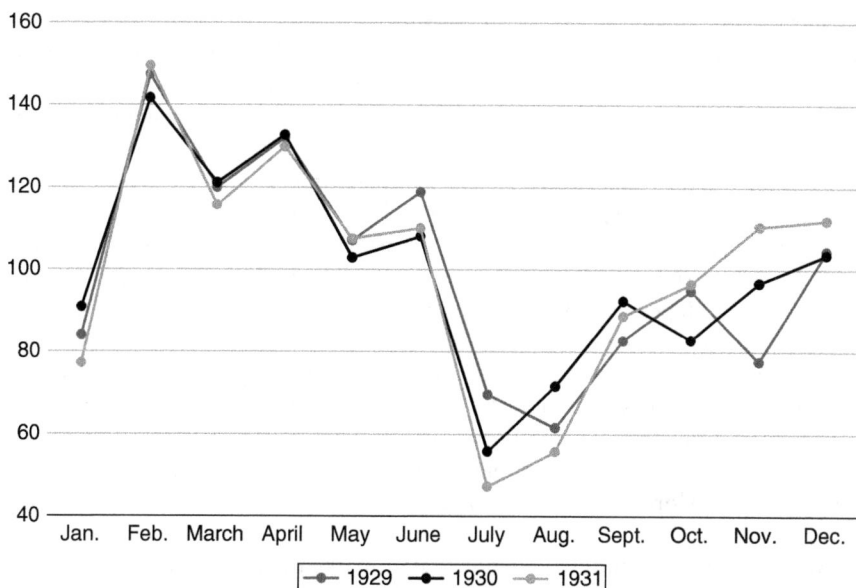

**Fig. 11.1.** Estimated monthly production of private cars and taxi cabs in Britain as a percentage of monthly average, 1929–31

*Source*: Bank of England Archives, EID9/35, note, 7 Nov. 1932.

so retailers could cooperate with manufacturers by taking stocks in advance of sales in order to smooth manufacturers' output, without running high risks of not being able to sell them (which had led to hand-to-mouth ordering policies in radio retailing, where demand was less predictable).

The second half of the 1920s witnessed rapid technological development for the car. For example over the two years to May 1929 the proportion of new private cars that were closed-top models almost doubled from 41.87 to 82.12 per cent.[22] However, this further raised the costs of fully mechanized mass production. In 1932 Vauxhall's sales director, A. F. Palmer Phillips, informed visitors from the Bank of England that the introduction of all-metal (rather than metal and fabric) bodied cars had increased tooling-up costs for each new model. He estimated that the capital costs for its own new model (including extending its premises) would amount to £500,000 for that season.[23]

The 1929–32 recession witnessed a major shift in the composition of demand in favour of small cars, boosted by the reintroduction of petrol tax. The proportion of new cars with engines of 10 horsepower or less increased from around a quarter

[22] Society of Motor Manufacturers and Traders, *The Motor Industry of Great Britain, 1929* (London: SMMT, 1929), 43.

[23] Bank of England Archives, EID9/35, two notes of visit to Vauxhall Motors, both dated 14 Nov. 1932.

in 1928 to 60 per cent in 1933 and remained at around that figure for the rest of the decade. This market was, in turn, roughly equally split between 8 and 10 horse-power vehicles.[24] The 1930s also witnessed the growing importance of foreign-owned car producers and the associated rise of the South East as a major production centre. Ford's Dagenham plant began production in 1932, while General Motors' acquisition of the small Luton-based manufacturer Vauxhall (in line with its general European strategy of acquiring individual companies in order to build on these firms' existing reputations), rapidly transformed it into one of the 'Big Six'.[25]

The six largest firms (Morris, Austin, Ford, Vauxhall, Standard, and Rootes) accounted for 90 per cent of production by 1939.[26] Moreover, they achieved com-plete domination of the small car market; by 1939 Jowett was the only independ-ent manufacturer selling an 8 horsepower car.[27] D. G. Rhys notes that the degree of concentration shown in Table 11.1 underestimates the importance of the Big Six, as some firms in the 'Others' category were either part of larger groupings or had a common controlling shareholder with a member of the Big Six. For example, the figures for Morris omit MG, Wolseley, and Riley, which were part of Morris's 'Nuffield group'.[28]

Yet the British car industry demonstrated markedly less firm concentration in the 1930s than either the United States or the major European car manufacturing nations.[29] Moreover, the market was very fragmented at the level of the individual model. In 1928 Morris moved away from his two-model production policy, in favour of a 'car for every need' strategy, facilitated by his acquisition of the Wolseley Motor Company (which aimed at a higher market segment) the previous year. By 1933 the Nuffield group's car output spanned twenty-three basic models and twelve engines, while both Austin and Ford each produced seven models and four engines.[30] The number of car models in production by the ten largest manufactur-ing groups (controlling over 90 per cent of the market) rose from forty-six in the 1929–30 model year to sixty-four in 1933–4, and more than eighty by 1939.[31] As Table 11.2 shows, by 1933 customers were faced with a wide range of car models, spanning a broad price range, even within a specific horsepower class.

This trend was accompanied by a switch in the emphasis of competition from price to quality, performance, and styling within individual price brackets, partly driven by perceptions of market saturation. 'Price-model competition' led to annual model changes (a strategy employed in the United States from the 1920s),

[24] Maxcy and Silberston, *Motor Industry*, 100.

[25] For GM's European strategy, see Andrea Hiott, *Thinking Small: The Long, Strange Trip of the Volkswagen Beetle* (New York: Ballantine, 2012), 80.

[26] Maxcy and Silberston, *Motor Industry*, 13–15 and 99.      [27] Ibid., 106.

[28] D. G. Rhys, 'Concentration in the Inter-War Motor Industry', *Journal of Transport History*, 3 (1976), 241–64 (250–1).

[29] Bowden, 'Demand and Supply Constraints', 261.

[30] Roy Church, 'Mass Marketing Motor Cars in Britain before 1950', in Richard S. Tedlow and Geoffrey Jones (eds.), *The Rise and Fall of Mass Marketing* (London: Routledge, 1993), 36–57 (43–4).

[31] 'The British Motor Industry. I—Private Cars', *Economist* (21 Oct. 1933), 755–6; D. G. Rhys, *The Motor Industry: An Economic Survey* (London: Butterworths, 1972), 13; Maxcy and Silberston, *Motor Industry*, 15.

**Table 11.1.** Percentage shares of British car production, for major firms, 1929–39

| Year | Morris | Austin | Ford | Vauxhall | Standard | Rootes | Others | Total (%) | Total (thousands) |
|------|--------|--------|------|----------|----------|--------|--------|-----------|-------------------|
| 1929 | 34.8 | 25.3 | 3.8 | 0.8 | 3.3 | 3.0 | 29.1 | 100.0 | 182.3 |
| 1930 | 34.4 | 32.2 | 6.1 | 5.1 | 4.4 | 4.8 | 13.0 | 100.0 | 169.6 |
| 1931 | 27.4 | 24.2 | 2.4 | 4.5 | 7.5 | 4.8 | 29.2 | 100.0 | 158.9 |
| 1932 | 29.4 | 23.5 | 6.0 | 4.5 | 10.2 | 6.4 | 20.1 | 100.0 | 171.2 |
| 1933 | 19.9 | 20.2 | 13.2 | 5.0 | 6.2 | 6.4 | 29.2 | 100.0 | 220.7 |
| 1934 | 23.7 | 23.3 | 12.4 | 7.0 | 6.9 | 7.0 | 19.8 | 100.0 | 256.8 |
| 1935 | 29.7 | 21.9 | 15.7 | 8.0 | 7.0 | 7.5 | 10.3 | 100.0 | 325.1 |
| 1936 | 27.3 | 21.3 | 20.4 | 5.8 | 8.9 | 8.6 | 7.7 | 100.0 | 367.2 |
| 1937 | 25.3 | 20.9 | 20.5 | 7.4 | 8.9 | 8.7 | 8.3 | 100.0 | 379.3 |
| 1938 | 23.6 | 20.4 | 17.5 | 10.4 | 9.9 | 10.2 | 8.0 | 100.0 | 341.0 |
| 1939 | 24.2 | 21.9 | 13.2 | 9.4 | 11.5 | 9.8 | 10.0 | 100.0 | 305.0 |

*Source*: D. G. Rhys, 'Concentration in the Inter-War Motor Industry', *Journal of Transport History*, 3 (1976), 241–64 (246).

**Table 11.2.** Number of makes and retail price ranges of British cars by horsepower class, *c.*April 1933

| Horse power | No. of makes | No. of catalogued body types | Retail price range From: | To: |
|-------------|--------------|------------------------------|--------------------------|-----|
| 8 | 5 | 22 | 100 | 395 |
| 9 | 4 | 18 | 159 | 315 |
| 10 | 9 | 35 | 148 | 385 |
| 12 | 19 | 75 | 165 | 650 |
| 14 | 9 | 33 | 195 | 448 |
| 15 | 4 | 12 | 180 | 465 |
| 16 | 12 | 53 | 235 | 1975 |
| 17 | 5 | 20 | 275 | 695 |
| 24 | 5 | 21 | 190 | 895 |

*Note*: Special bodies mounted on the above chassis by makers other than the chassis manufacturers are excluded.

*Source*: Bank of England Archives, EID9/35, enclosure in letter, A. F. Palmer Phillips, Sales Director, Vauxhall Motors, to Ministry of Transport, 29 Apr. 1933.

new introductions usually occurring at the autumn Olympia Show. These both increased production costs and cut production runs. However, Britain did not follow the US route of employing leading industrial designers to accelerate psychological obsolescence. While Herbert Austin had recruited the Italian engineer Ricardo Burzi in 1929 to restyle his cars in support of his new annual model change policy, the UK industry generally showed little interest in the industrial design movement.[32]

---

[32] Church, 'Mass Marketing Motor Cars', 49–50.

This new emphasis on market segmentation and psychological obsolescence weakened the potential for true mass production. In 1938 the 'Big Six' produced forty different types of engine, while their chassis and car bodies showed even greater product differentiation.[33] In 1939 the Nuffield group alone produced some eighteen basic car types. Their manufacturing technique was described by PEP as 'flexible'. The number of designs of each component made in the works was often too large for separate machines to be assigned to each, preventing Nuffield from switching from general-purpose to special-purpose machine tools.[34] There was also a growing emphasis on bought-in components, which further weakened the scale economies of the largest firms. The upshot was a marked reduction in both model-level and in firm-level market concentration among the two or three largest manufacturers—in contrast to the United States, where Fordist production techniques led to a progressive concentration of output among the Big Three.[35]

## THE BRITISH CAR VALUE CHAIN

Component manufacture and final assembly was generally much more integrated in motor vehicles than in, for example, radio. The much larger number of moving parts in a car and the necessity of fitting components to very close tolerances (to avoid leakage of oil, water, or petrol) meant that modifications to any one component were more likely to require modifications to others. However, moves towards mass production during the 1930s were accompanied by increased reliance on externally sourced components, with some major car plants, such as Vauxhall, becoming assemblers rather than full manufacturers.[36]

There is no evidence of strong rents in the British automobile value chain (other than those imposed externally on car owners by the Treasury). Car manufacturers operated on small net margins; one contemporary estimate put the trading profit per vehicle in 1936 at £10 for Austin, £15 for Morris, £8 for Standard, £9 for Ford, and £24 for Vauxhall, at a time when a mid-range car sold for between £150 and £200.[37] These figures are broadly in line with Holden's estimates of profits for Vauxhall, Morris, and Austin, shown in Table 11.3.

However, contrary to Maxcy's and Silberston's argument that strong price stability for volume car models produced by the 'Big Six' during 1929–39 reflected benchmarking their prices against competitors, rather than systematic collusion, collusion did take place—at least on an informal and ad hoc basis.[38] For example, in July

[33] Bowden, 'Demand and Supply Constraints', 263.

[34] Political and Economic Planning, *Motor Vehicles*, 27.

[35] Church, 'Mass Marketing Motor Cars', 44.

[36] Len Holden, *Vauxhall Motors and the Luton Economy 1900–2002* (Woodbridge: Boydell, 2003), 54.

[37] 'More but Dearer Motors', *Economist* (10 July 1937), 62–3; Clarks Archive, 2/12, Sampson Clark & Company Ltd, 'Business Development Bulletin. The Motor Car Industry', market research report, 1938, 60.

[38] Maxcy and Silberston, *Motor Industry*, 100–6.

**Table 11.3.** Profits for Vauxhall, Morris, and Austin, 1931–8 (£ per unit)

| Year | Vauxhall | | Morris | | Austin |
|------|----------------|---------------|----------------|---------------|---------------|
| | Trading profit | Actual profit | Trading profit | Actual profit | Actual profit |
| 1931 | 20 | 4 | 17.2 | 5.6 | 24 |
| 1932 | 22 | 7 | 19.2 | 10.9 | 23 |
| 1933 | 31 | 16 | 19.1 | 11.0 | 18 |
| 1934 | 34 | 21 | 20.0 | 14.1 | 19 |
| 1935 | 31 | 21 | 14.9 | 11.2 | 15 |
| 1936 | 34 | 24 | n.a. | n.a. | 16 |
| 1937 | 32 | 19 | n.a. | n.a. | 14 |
| 1938 | 27 | 12 | n.a. | n.a. | 14 |

*Source*: Len Holden, *Vauxhall Motors and the Luton Economy 1900–2002* (Woodbridge: Boydell, 2003), 64.

1933 Herbert Austin reported to his board that meetings with several car manufacturers had led to agreements not to reduce prices for the 1933/34 season, under an understanding that also prohibited offering better terms and 'Olympia Banquets' (corporate hospitality) to agents.[39]

Both vertical and horizontal cooperation in the industry was partly organized through its trade associations. The Society of Motor Manufacturers and Traders (SMMT) was founded in 1902, principally to avoid manufacturers being obliged to show cars at a multitude of exhibitions. It became the organizer of the annual Motor Show and developed a monopoly on organizing motor trade exhibitions, prohibiting its members from showing cars at rival trade shows, or entering them in trials not sanctioned by the SMMT. It also fostered component standardization, via a series of technical committees. Another key function was to exert some degree of control over the wholesale and retail trades.[40] In 1906 SMMT formed an agents' section, for dealers, and in 1910 the Motor Trade Association (MTA) was formed to enforce retail price maintenance. MTA operated outside the formal SMMT structure to gain the legal protection for collective action afforded by 'trade union' status, thus enabling it to put firms flouting price maintenance on a 'stop list' of companies with whom MTA members were prohibited from trading.[41]

In the UK, as in the United States, no significant car manufacturer pursued a strategy of full vertical integration for its distribution network. Instead cars were sold through independent distributors and dealers. Some major manufacturers, such as Rover, Singer, Triumph, and Humber, had started as bicycle manufacturers. This may have influenced them in following the precedent of the bicycle trade, which, by

[39] Source: MRC, 226/AU/1/1/2, Austin Motor Co. Board minutes, 26 July 1933.

[40] G. C. Allen, *British Industries and their Organisation* (London: Longman, 1933), 199; Political and Economic Planning, *Motor Vehicles*, 41.

[41] K. C. Johnson-Davies, *The Practice of Price Maintenance with Particular Reference to the Motor Industry* (London: Iliffe, 1955), 2–4; Roy Church, 'The Marketing of Automobiles in Britain and the United States before 1939', in Akio Okochi and Koichi Shimokawa (eds.), *Development of Mass Marketing: The Automobile and Retailing Industries* (Tokyo: University of Tokyo Press, 1981), 59–87 (70).

the 1890s, had developed a distribution system of appointed authorized agents, who both conducted sales and took responsibility for maintenance and repairs.[42]

While practice varied somewhat between manufacturers, there were four broad types of distributors for new cars, all of which sold some cars directly to the public. These collectively provided around 13,000 retail selling points for new cars. The top tier of the distribution pyramid were the 'main dealers' (estimated at 900–1,000 in 1938).[43] Main dealers, sometimes called distributors, were given exclusive territories by a manufacturer (around the size of a county) together with an annual quota of new vehicles. They were required to maintain showrooms, demonstration cars, and workshops, together with a stock of new cars and parts. They were also tasked to manage wholesale distribution in their area (where they enjoyed a monopoly on sales to other dealers) and to provide dealers with cars and spare parts.[44] Main dealers were required to pay a deposit on all cars ordered, with the balance due on delivery. This facilitated production planning by manufacturers, who developed direct salesforces to communicate and coordinate with them.[45]

'Dealers' (numbering around 2,500 in 1938) were appointed to cover an exclusive territory within that of the main dealer. They were given a quota of cars and parts and were obliged to maintain showrooms, a workshop, and demonstration cars. Dealers were allowed to sell to 'retail dealers' (numbering 3,500), and 'casual dealers' (numbering 6,000), in addition to the general public. Retail dealers were also required to stock cars and spare parts and provide service facilities, but could only sell to final consumers. Casual dealers differed from retail dealers in that they were not under any obligations to stock new cars.[46] Jefferys estimated the proportion of 1938 retail sales through these various channels as follows:

From main dealer direct to consumer 30–35 per cent
From main dealer—to dealer—to consumer 40–45 per cent
From main dealer—to retail dealer or casual dealer—to consumer 10–15 per cent
From main dealer—to dealer—to retail or casual dealer—to consumer 10–15 per cent[47]

Dealers' margins remained relatively stable over the inter-war years. A British government report found that in 1926 retailers' margins varied from 12.5–20 per cent (plus rebates for volume sales).[48] A 1928 US study stated that English manufacturers offered discounts of 17.5–20 per cent (presumably including the main dealer's margin), while American cars were distributed in Britain at higher discounts—of 22–25 per cent.[49] Jefferys found that in 1938 main dealers received a discount of 17.5–20 per cent off the retail price, plus a volume rebate of 2.5–3 per cent on net purchases

---

[42] Church, 'Marketing of Automobiles', 62.
[43] Kenneth Richardson, *The British Motor Industry 1896–1939* (London: Macmillan, 1977), 222.
[44] Jefferys, *Distribution of Consumer Goods*, 350.
[45] Richardson, *British Motor Industry*, 222.
[46] Jefferys, *Distribution of Consumer Goods*, 351.        [47] Ibid.
[48] UK, Parliament, Committee on Industry and Trade, *Further Factors in Industrial and Commercial Efficiency. Being Part II of a Survey of Industries* (London: HMSO, 1928), 110–11.
[49] Park, *Automotive Industry*, 19.

(providing a cumulative discount of 21–23 per cent). They then allowed dealers a discount of 17.5–20 per cent (the majority offering 17.5 per cent). The dealer also received a volume discount averaging around 1.5–2 per cent. Meanwhile main dealers typically allowed retail dealers discounts of 17.5 per cent, plus a volume discount of 1–1.5 per cent. Casual dealers were given discounts that varied from 10–17 per cent (typically between 10 and 15 per cent), with no volume discount.

Thus main dealers' wholesale margins varied from 10–12 per cent on sales to casual dealers, to 3.75–4 per cent on sales to 'dealers'. Where cars were provided to retail dealers or casual dealers from the main dealer indirectly via 'dealers', the dealer typically allowed a discount of 17.5 per cent for retail dealers and 10–15 per cent for casual dealers. Retail dealers also received a volume rebate of 0.5–1 per cent, giving the 'dealer' an average margin of 2–3 per cent on such sales, compared to 7–7.5 per cent on sales to casual dealers. Retail dealers earned an average margin of 17.5 per cent on sales and casual dealers 12.5 per cent.[50]

## PRODUCER MARKETING

During the 1920s competition focused on developing smaller cars that were cheaper to both buy and to run (especially given Britain's horsepower-based vehicle tax system). Manufacturers capitalized on their models' low horsepower by reflecting this in their names, such as the Morris Eight and the Austin Seven.[51] The Austin Seven—the outstanding success story of the 1920s—achieved public acceptability for the small car. Despite being unusual both in terms of its small size and its distinctive design when it was launched in 1922, the Seven was widely praised for its reliability and performance (demonstrated by a strong record of sporting success). However, it remained the butt of many jokes on account of its small size, as shown in Figure 11.2. The Seven heralded a new era of cheaper motoring, more suited to the lower-middle classes, who had hitherto been restricted to the motorbike (often with sidecar).[52] The introduction of elementary mass production techniques enabled Austin to reduce the price of the Seven from £225 at the time of its launch to £130 by 1929.[53] The late 1920s and early 1930s witnessed attempts to further lower the minimum price of a new car, with successful new small models such as the Morris Minor (1929) and Ford Eight (1932).

In contrast to the vigorous price competition in the 1920s, the 1930s witnessed relative price stability and a focus on style, service, and quality.[54] During the recessionary years of 1930–2 replacement demand dominated new car sales and after 1933 replacement sales comprised around half the total.[55] This gave manufacturers a significant incentive to accelerate model changes, to hasten psychological

---

[50] Jefferys, *Distribution of Consumer Goods*, 352–3.
[51] Jonathan Wood, *Wheels of Misfortune: The Rise and Fall of the British Motor Industry* (London: Sidgwick & Jackson, 1988), 43.
[52] Richardson, *British Motor Industry*, 83.    [53] Rhys, *Motor Industry*, 303.
[54] Ibid., 306.    [55] Political and Economic Planning, *Motor Vehicles*, 61.

# "JUST DUCK YER 'EAD, MISTER, THEN I CAN DRIVE RIGHT OVER YER!"

**Fig. 11.2.** An example of one of the many cartoons of the era, parodying the small size of the Austin Seven

*Source*: Peter Scott collection (postcard, n.d., *c*.1929).

obsolescence.[56] Thus the focus of competition moved from price to quality and variety within particular price brackets.

British car manufacturers began to follow the practice (already well established in the United States) of making model changes every few years, interspersed with annual 'face-lifts' for existing models, to cosmetically differentiate them from their predecessors.[57] Even Austin and Morris adopted broad model range strategies in the 1930s, eroding the scale advantages on which they had built their earlier success.[58] Towards the end of the 1930s Ford and Morris moved away from yearly model changes, using 'Series' models (with each series lasting several years). Annual model changes accentuated seasonal production downturns and lay-offs in the run-up to the autumn Motor Show and the next round of new models.[59]

In 1938 manufacturers' distribution costs (including administrative selling costs, warrantees, and advertising) were said to average 7–8 per cent of retail sales revenue, almost half of which represented advertising.[60] This is roughly in line with a 1935 estimate, which put manufacturers' total UK advertising expenditure for private motor vehicles at £1,650,000, or 3.7 per cent of net sales.[61] Comparing contemporary estimates of annual press advertising spend by the Big Six in 1938 and the number of cars produced by each firm in that year indicates that the American-owned manufacturers, Vauxhall and Ford, had substantially higher press advertising budgets (£10.30 and £7.00 per car sold) than the largest British-owned firms (£5.90 for Morris, £4.90 for Austin, and £4.10 for Standard). These figures are, of course, inflated slightly by sales of items other than cars, and exclude non-press advertising, though this is unlikely to substantially distort the general pattern.[62]

Motoring journalism provided much low-cost publicity, targeted at an enthusiast audience.[63] William Morris capitalized on this by hiring motoring journalist Miles Thomas in January 1924 as the publicist for Morris Motors. One of his first tasks involved starting an in-house magazine *The Morris Owner*, 'to consolidate the family feeling among owners of Morris cars'.[64] This was sold through Morris agents as well as conventional retail channels. Thomas was also active in drumming up editorial coverage in the press about the activities of Morris Motors and its chief executive.[65] This strategy had long been pursued by Austin, which had launched the in-house magazine *Austin Advocate* to promote its cars as early as 1911.[66] Austin also reaped much low-cost publicity from the appeal of the Austin Seven to the sporting market, having designed a car with excellent performance and an engine that lent itself to tuning.[67]

[56] Maxcy and Silberston, *Motor Industry*, 138.    [57] Church, 'Marketing of Automobiles', 68.
[58] Maxcy and Silberston, *Motor Industry*, 108–9.    [59] Rhys, *Motor Industry*, 305.
[60] Jefferys, *Distribution of Consumer Goods*, 353.
[61] Nicholas Kaldor and Rodney Silverman, *A Statistical Analysis of Advertising Expenditure and of the Revenue of the Press* (Cambridge: Cambridge University Press, 1948), 147.
[62] Sources: press advertising, F. P. Bishop, *The Economics of Advertising* (London: Robert Hale, 1944), 95; car output, Rhys, 'Concentration in the Inter-War Motor Industry', 246.
[63] Park, *Automotive Industry*, 18.
[64] Miles Thomas, *Out on a Wing: An Autobiography* (London: Michael Joseph, 1964), 128–9.
[65] Ibid., 140.    [66] Church, *Herbert Austin*, 90.
[67] R. J. Wyatt, *The Austin Seven: The Motor for the Million 1922–1939* (Newton Abbot: David & Charles, 1982), 27.

## DOWNSTREAM DISTRIBUTION AND MARKETING

The importance of strong dealer networks, and good dealer relationships, are illustrated by the case of Ford. In 1911 Ford began assembling cars in Britain and by 1913 his Trafford Park plant constituted the largest car factory in Europe, producing 6,138 cars annually, more than the combined output of the five largest British automobile producers.[68] However, an increasingly intransigent and autocratic attitude towards his British plant—even refusing to modify Model Ts to include right-hand steering wheels until 1919—progressively undermined Ford's market position.[69] Moreover, Ford alienated his dealers, imposing an American-style franchise system on them in 1919, when Ford's market position in Britain was already coming under pressure.

Under the new system all agents were required to have direct contracts with Ford, who would allocate them sales quotas, and require them to carry large stocks (sometimes sent without dealer orders), which had to be paid for on delivery.[70] Ford dealers were also prohibited from stocking other firms' cars (a significant problem, given that Ford's Model T did not meet the needs of a large segment of the British market). This precipitated the departure of some two-thirds of Ford's 1,200 dealers, a torrent of indignation in the trade press, and a substantial weakening of their distribution base.[71] A heavy-handed approach towards the remaining dealers, including 'dumping' vehicles on them to boost sales, together with the horsepower tax and high British fuel duties, effectively stalled the first attempt to create a British mass car market.[72]

Ford's competitors soon began to incorporate elements of his approach, but were more tactful and aware of the limitations of their bargaining power. For example, Ford's 1919 introduction of a standard scale of charges for repairs by its dealers was followed immediately by Austin and, in 1923, by Morris.[73] The 1920s also witnessed increasing pressure on dealers not to stock the cars of other firms, or, at least, those of direct competitors.[74] However, a 1928 report advised US auto firms that in Britain, 'exclusive representation is rarely ever obtainable... it is not uncommon to find the larger and more important firms handling 8 or 10 makes of cars. Even small dealers will hold the local agency for four or five different makes.'[75] Exclusive representation became more common in the 1930s, boosted by the extensive model range policies of most major manufacturers. For example, Austin gradually moved to insisting that its dealers sold only Austin cars, assisted by broadening his model range.[76]

---

[68] Steven Tolliday, 'The Rise of Ford in Britain: From Sales Agency to Market Leader, 1904–1980', in Hubert Bonin, Yannick Lung, and Stephen Tolliday (eds.), *Ford: The European History 1903–2003*, vol. 2 (Paris: P.L.A.G.E., 2003), 7–57 (11); Church, 'Mass Marketing Motor Cars', 39.

[69] Church, 'Mass Marketing Motor Cars', 39.

[70] Bernard Julien, 'Ford's Distribution Network in Europe: Recent Developments in the Context of the History of Automobile Retailing', in Bonin, Lung, and Tolliday (eds.), *Ford*, 417–42 (421).

[71] Church, 'Marketing of Automobiles', 71.     [72] Tolliday, 'Rise of Ford', 13–18.

[73] Church, 'Marketing of Automobiles', 78.     [74] Richardson, *British Motor Industry*, 222.

[75] Park, *Automotive Industry*, 18.     [76] Richardson, *British Motor Industry*, 116.

Contracts between British manufacturers and distributors, and between distributors and the various tiers of subsidiary dealers, were usually granted and renewed annually. These specified the retail price to be charged, trade discounts, the dealer's territory, and the repair and other services that must be provided.[77] Customers desired a good network of service and repair facilities, with a ready supply of replacement parts. Manufacturers thus sought to exert control over both the availability and quality of service points by tying service facilities to dealerships in order to cement brand loyalty.[78]

Contracts were typically signed at the time of the Motor Show—when dealers could gauge the likely demand for the new models. They included estimates of the number of cars which were expected to be sold in that territory.[79] However, British manufacturers never had anything like the same degree of coercive power over their dealers as was enjoyed by their American counterparts. Britain had a more fragmented market, together with a strong tradition of dealers stocking multiple car makes. Moreover, British dealers paid for their cars on delivery (in contrast to the US system of distributors' credit, which provided manufacturers with greater leverage regarding the amount of stock they could oblige dealers to hold).[80] The 1928 Bureau of Foreign & Domestic Commerce report noted that:

> distributor and dealer contractual arrangements are...respected more in the breach than in the observance. Owing to the highly competitive market conditions, some of the English manufacturers stock distributors or dealers on a consignment basis, a business practice which is, however, not followed by any of the American firms represented in the British market...If, owing to unforeseen circumstances, a bad selling season, or other inadvertence, the contract cannot be lived up to...particularly with reference to the estimated number of cars to be sold, it is rare that the manufacturer...takes summary measures against the dealer.[81]

Manufacturers nevertheless wanted dealers to hold substantial inventories of vehicles—to smooth production and reduce their own inventory costs. One way to achieve this was to offer dealers protection against list price reductions. By the late 1920s the standard distributor's contract stipulated that:

> In the event of a reduction in the advertised price...the company undertakes to credit the distributor with the difference between the old and the new retail price less his discount for all new, unused, and unregistered cars held in stock by the distributor on the date of the announcement of such reduction, provided such...cars have been purchased from the company not more than 90 days prior to the announcement of the reduction.[82]

In addition to holding inventories, dealers were also central to manufacturers' production planning, as a source of sales data. By the early 1930s British car manufacturers required weekly returns and reports from their dealers. Together with the growing

---

[77] Political and Economic Planning, *Motor Vehicles*, 38.    [78] Allen, *British Industries*, 200.

[79] Park, *Automotive Industry*, 18–19; Church, 'Marketing of Automobiles', 72.

[80] P. W. S. Andrews and Elizabeth Brunner, *The Life of Lord Nuffield* (Oxford: Blackwell, 1955), 116.

[81] Park, *Automotive Industry*, 19.

[82] Standard distributor's contract, reproduced in Park, *Automotive Industry*, 47.

proportion of credit business, this imposed what one major distributor described as 'an over abundance of clerical work'.[83] However, such paperwork considerably aided accurate production planning—as shown by the experience of Vauxhall.

Vauxhall had access to the considerable marketing expertise of its GM parent and by the 1930s had adopted GM's practice of requiring regular stocks and sales figures from dealers, to plan and coordinate production.[84] Bank of England officials who visited Vauxhall in November 1932 noted the importance placed on planning and budgetary control, including using both its own sales and production data and, recently, an exchange of data between car producers (though this was done unofficially, as not all SMMT members were prepared to cooperate). Vauxhall examined daily figures for production, performance, and sales, which it then compared with the previous year and its budget estimates. Palmer Phillips mentioned that an ex-employee, who Vauxhall had considered expensive at a salary of £400, was now receiving £1,500 from Singer because he had introduced Vauzhall's forecasting methods which—it was claimed—he had shown little interest in while at Vauxhall.[85]

Vauxhall had also introduced the special simplified dealer accounting system originally developed for its US parent's Chevrolet dealerships. It was claimed that, in addition to direct benefits to Vauxhall, this had more than doubled the proportion of Vauxhall dealers who were making what was regarded as an adequate profit. The system both assisted dealers in keeping proper accounts (owing to its simplicity) and provided them with 'target' levels for performance and cost indicators such as the optimum amount of capital, stock, rent, wages, and so forth for any given sales volume.[86]

Vauxhall also supplied its dealers with an analysis of the market potential of their territories and a monthly sales and stocking programme to reflect this, so that each dealer knew what his benchmark performance should be. Palmer Phillips claimed to have found that ' "averages" established by statistical research have caused a complete revision of manufacturers' ideas as to which were the efficient dealers'.[87] A rebate on sales for which statistics were returned within seven days was offered as an incentive to dealers to get their data in on time.[88]

Manufacturers also used their annual dealer agreements to ensure an adequate level of dealer promotional expenditure. A standard clause in contracts obliged the distributor to:

> affix to his premises in a conspicuous position a sign approved by the company stating that he is a distributor of ... and shall advertise the ... cars effectively in the local newspapers. The total amount to be expended by the distributors in such local newspaper

[83] Bank of England Archives, EID9/35, letter, Albert Brand, Brand Bros., Automobile Agents and Distributors, to J. A. C. Osborne, Statistical Section, Bank of England, 12 July 1932.

[84] Holden, *Vauxhall Motors*, 77.

[85] Bank of England Archives, EID9/35, two notes of visit to Vauxhall Motors, both dated 14 Nov. 1932.

[86] Bank of England Archives, EID9/35, letter, Albert Brand, Brand Bros., Automobile Agents and Distributors, to J. A. C. Osborne, Statistical Section, Bank of England, 12 July 1932.

[87] Ibid.        [88] Ibid.

advertising during the existence of this agreement shall not be less than £2 for each car estimated for in the schedule herein. This advertising shall be exclusive...and shall not mention any other make of car. The distributor agrees to mail to the company at the end of each month printed copies of each...advertisement run during the said month, together with the rates paid.[89]

As in other sectors, manufacturers also worked cooperatively with their dealers, for example by offering to pay a proportion of their advertising costs.[90] Manufacturers also assisted dealers with after-sales service. From the 1920s several set up service schools to train dealers in car maintenance.[91] For example, in 1932, following a suggestion by the Institute of Motor Salesmanship, Austin established the Austin Sales Training Centre at Longbridge, offering a month's training—to follow on from the Institute's existing three-month courses, held at its London headquarters. It also ran a system of visiting lectures at various sales territories.[92]

## TRADE-INS AND HIRE PURCHASE

Most people who acquired a car during this period purchased it second-hand. By 1928 trade-ins were already estimated to feature in at least 75 per cent of new car sales.[93] During the 1930s the average life of a private car was estimated at around eight years, during which time it might, typically, have changed hands at least three times. Thus both the stock and annual sales of second-hand cars was substantially greater than for new cars.[94] By the late 1930s an estimated 700,000 used cars were sold annually to final users, with a total value of perhaps £50 million (around £70 per car), compared to 300,000 new cars, for over £60 million (over £200 per car). Second-hand cars were said to represent an important part of turnover for a large proportion of motor dealers, especially smaller ones.[95]

Trade-ins might be resold by the dealer directly or (especially in the case of main distributors) sold on to 'used-car specialists', often at a loss. A buoyant second-hand car market thus supported new car sales—presenting a problem for higher horse-power cars, which were costly to run and thus unattractive to people looking for a cheap car.[96] It was claimed that during the inter-war period dealers were, on average, having to accept at least two used cars in part-exchange for every new one sold, as the first (better) used car was only resaleable via a further trade-in deal.[97] This posed a major problem for resale price maintenance; as one prominent distributor informed the Bank of England's statistical section, 'I shall be glad to know how you

---

[89] Standard distributor's contract, reproduced in Park, *Automotive Industry*, 45–6.
[90] Source: MRC, Warwick, Mss 226/AU/1/1/2, Austin Motor Co. Board minutes, 28 Oct. 1931.
[91] Church, 'Marketing of Automobiles', 78.    [92] Church, *Herbert Austin*, 92.
[93] 'The British Motor Industry. II—Present Position and Prospects', *Economist* (14 July 1928), 60–1.
[94] 'Marketing and Distribution', *Economist* (7 Dec. 1935), 1131–2.
[95] 'The Second-Hand Car', *Economist* (17 Sept. 1938), 531–3.
[96] Ibid.    [97] Johnson-Davies, *Practice of Price Maintenance*, 27.

would arrive at the actual value of the [new car] sale. Would you require the actual selling price of the car or the amount of cash actually drawn on the deal.'[98]

From the dealer's perspective, trade-ins involved either estimating the price for which each traded-in car could be sold without loss, or offering more—as a method of covert price-cutting. This was a high-risk strategy, dealers sometimes finding themselves with substantial capital frozen in used cars bought at excessive prices.[99] In common with the radio trade, manufacturers vehemently opposed price cutting via trade-ins, fearing that it might erode dealers' promotional and after-sales service activities and thus damage their entire value chain.

As early as 1922 Herbert Austin regarded price-cutting as 'a serious matter...in spite of the efforts of the M.T.A.'[100] By 1924 Morris Motors was also voicing concern and taking steps to police its dealers' behaviour.[101] The 1928 US report on the British car market found an enormous amount of price-cutting by dealers, usually in the form of splitting commissions. Prospective purchasers were said to 'shop around, playing off one dealer against another until a rock-bottom price was obtained'.[102]

From 1927 the MTA attempted to control trade-ins, via lists of specified used-car prices. However, price-cutting via trade-ins continued to grow, and by 1933 was said to have depressed dealers' profits to such an extent that many were being driven out of business or forced to cut back on activities such as servicing. Dealers sought higher margins from manufacturers, to improve their financial viability, but manufacturers proved unwilling to concede them during a falling market.

In 1933 the MTA launched the 'Nemesis' scheme, local traders being encouraged to report price-cutting competitors to the MTA, who would then refer the case back to the local MTA division, without divulging the name of the complainant. However, this plan proved problematic and later that year the MTA Council set up a 'Joint Committee of Vehicle Manufacturers and Retailers' to seek a way forward. Its May 1934 report recommended the publication of a 'National Used Car Price Book' with maximum trade-in prices. The MTA was reconstituted the following year, with manufacturers having a two-thirds majority on its council and all committees. Henceforth all manufacturers' contracts with distributors and dealers required MTA membership and conformance to MTA rules. Non-compliant dealers could be fined or suspended from the MTA (thus losing their ability to sell new cars). This scheme was only partially successful, but did act to significantly reduce price competition. Meanwhile maximum 'Book' prices became standard prices, meaning that careful owners gained no price advantage when trading-in their cars.[103]

[98] Bank of England Archives, EID9/35, letter, Albert Brand, Brand Bros., Automobile Agents and Distributors, to J. A. C. Osborne, Statistical Section, Bank of England, 12 July 1932.

[99] 'The British Motor Industry. II—Present Position and Prospects'.

[100] Source: MRC, 226/AU/1/1/1, Austin Motor Co. Board minutes, insert, Herbert Austin, 'Visit of the Chairman & Mr E. L. Payton to the USA' (n.d., c.October 1922), 8–9.

[101] Andrews and Brunner, *Life of Lord Nuffield*, 122.

[102] Park, *Automotive Industry*, 20.

[103] Johnson-Davies, *Practice of Price Maintenance*, 6 and 28; 'The Second-Hand Car', *Economist*; Rhys, *Motor Industry*, 334–6.

HP terms were much less open to dealers' covert price competition, owing to greater control by the manufacturers. HP sales of motor vehicles in Britain have been traced back to 1903, but only appear to have been developed on a systematic basis from the 1920s.[104] Herbert Austin had arranged credit terms for his dealers with the Industrial Corporation Ltd from 1921, enabling them to borrow at only 3 and 4 per cent and thus hold larger stocks.[105] During his 1922 US visit Austin was informed that around 75 per cent of American car sales were on credit or time-payment and that most of the large companies either had their own finance corporations, or arrangements with a specialist finance company. Austin considered that a similar system was inevitable in Britain and, 'the concern which ... puts into operation, a really efficient scheme in this direction, will have a very big advantage over those that leave the question of credit to their agents, who, in most cases, have no means of knowledge to enable them to do the work satisfactorily'.[106]

American auto manufacturers had originally expected their dealers to both organize consumer credit and pay cash deposits on all orders in advance of delivery, which inevitably imposed a major strain on their finances. Auto sales finance companies were developed from 1913 to remedy this, building on the precedents of finance companies for other consumer durables, such as pianos. In 1915 the Guarantee Securities Corporation was launched, pioneering a successful business model of both financing instalment credit and loaning money to dealers for their vehicle purchases.[107]

Continental Guaranty founded a British subsidiary, United Dominions Trust (UDT), in 1919. This offered a US-style 'stocking plan', whereby UDT provided money for dealers to take normal quotas of cars even during the winter slack season. This in turn enabled manufacturers to avoid seasonal cutbacks in production and thus obtain the benefits of capacity output.[108] UDT initially tried to win round the retailers, but ran into some dealer resistance to credit sales, together with competition from other credit providers offering better terms.[109] However, switching its marketing focus to the manufacturers proved more successful. After signing contracts with Austin and Morris in 1924, many other car manufacturers followed suit, each receiving a specially designed brochure for mailing to their dealers.[110] Morris had already sought to develop HP facilities, in order to standardize his dealers' HP terms, but was happy to collaborate with UDT as this would require less capital. Their UDT credit facility was partly financed by advances from Morris Motors, which had a veto over contracts.[111] Some major London car dealers

---

[104] Lloyds Bank Archive, S/10/d/3, Augustus Muir and Mair Davies, 'United Dominions Trust. The History of an International Banking and Finance Group', unpublished typescript history, 19.

[105] Church, *Herbert Austin*, 90–1.

[106] Source: MRC, 226/AU/1/1/1, Austin Motor Co. Board minutes, insert, Herbert Austin, 'Visit of the Chairman & Mr E. L. Payton to the USA' (n.d., *c.*October 1922), 8.

[107] Lendol Calder, *Financing the American Dream: A Cultural History of Consumer Credit* (Princeton, NJ: Princeton University Press, 1999), 187–94.

[108] Lloyds Bank Archive, S/10/d/3, Augustus Muir and Mair Davies, 'United Dominions Trust. The History of an International Banking and Finance Group', unpublished typescript history, 1–37.

[109] Ibid., 18.    [110] Ibid., 44.

[111] Andrews and Brunner, *Life of Lord Nuffield*, 118.

financed their own HP credit, though once UDT and its competitors were firmly established a handful of London-based finance companies accounted for most of the rest of British automobile HP.[112]

UDT's success during the 1920s was partly based on its development of a formal system of credit risk assessment. Each motor dealer was given a confidential 'credit rating', while a system of assessing the credit-worthiness of car purchasers, according to their occupation, was also developed. For example, men receiving a regular salary were seen as superior risks to many professions characterized by volatile earnings (though there were exceptions, such as doctors, who were regarded as being trustworthy regardless of their reliance on prompt payment by their patients). Owner-occupation was also seen as an indicator of a good credit risk.[113]

In London and some other large British cities an estimated 60–65 per cent of passenger cars were said to be sold on HP by 1928.[114] Terms were typically 25 per cent deposit and monthly instalments spread over twelve to eighteen months (though these were sometimes extended to two years).[115] British motor vehicle HP terms were among the best available in Europe and were more favourable than those in the United States (where a deposit equal to one-third of the cash price was required and maximum contract lengths were limited to twelve months until the early 1930s, extended to eighteen months by 1934).[116] A 1928 American study noted that while British HP contract lengths seemed unduly long, they were necessary to provide affordability. Moreover:

> Owing to the ease of obtaining credit and other information regarding a prospective purchaser, the manufacturers and finance companies maintain these long terms can be successfully granted without undue risk. In an old-established community like Great Britain there is less likelihood of a purchaser violating any agreement whereby his credit and standing in the community is adversely affected. If he...moves to a new district his reputation follows him without difficulty.[117]

Terms were nevertheless onerous from the consumer's perspective. This reflected the fact that cars were highly valuable and extremely portable (and thus good targets for theft), while also being subject to unusually rapid depreciation and considerable risks of damage or even write-offs in accidents. Finance agreements thus typically specified a minimum deposit of 25 per cent.[118] American families found car purchase to be much more 'affordable', owing to higher average incomes and, crucially, lower car prices. Bowden and Turner estimated that average monthly payments (excluding finance charges) in 1931 would have been £10.97 in the UK

[112] Foreman-Peck, Bowden, and McKinlay, *British Motor Industry*, 71.
[113] Lloyds Bank Archive, S/10/d/3, Augustus Muir and Mair Davies, 'United Dominions Trust. The History of an International Banking and Finance Group', 63.
[114] Park, *Automotive Industry*, 20.     [115] Ibid., 22.
[116] Sue Bowden and Paul Turner, 'The Demand for Consumer Durables in the United Kingdom in the Inter-War Period', *Journal of Economic History*, 53 (1993), 244–58 (252–5).
[117] Park, *Automotive Industry*, 22.
[118] Bowden and Turner, 'Demand for Consumer Durables', 253.

but only £4.52 in the United States, as lower US car prices more than compensated for their more restrictive credit terms.[119]

## CONSUMPTION AND DIFFUSION

Austin claimed to have designed the Austin Seven for 'the man in the street...who, at present, can only afford a motor cycle and sidecar, and yet has the ambition to become a motorist'.[120] However, with an initial price of £225, Austin's 'man' was clearly a member of the established middle classes.[121] Nevertheless, the high volume sales achieved by the Austin Seven and Austin's consequent ability to incorporate elementary mass production techniques played an important direct and demonstration role in lowering minimum car purchase costs.

Between 1924 and 1935 retail prices for private cars fell by almost 50 per cent. Running costs also fell (excluding taxes). Petrol costs declined from 1s 6.5d per gallon (exclusive of tax) in 1924 to significantly less than a shilling in 1937. Meanwhile cars had become markedly more fuel-efficient, tyres were both cheaper and longer-lasting, and the costs of garages and servicing had also fallen.[122] Moreover, the car market had become increasingly focused on the lower price bands. In 1936 Chrysler's statistician, R. J. Shillady, estimated that some 38.8 per cent of British cars sold at £150 or less, while 36.0 per cent sold at between £150 and £200. The bulk of remaining new car registrations, 13.3 per cent, sold for £205–250, leaving only 11.9 per cent in the higher price categories.[123]

The motorcycle had appeared to offer an attractive cheaper alternative to the car, but its relative popularity was already waning by the mid-1920s, as shown in Figure 11.3, and by the late 1920s motorcycle ownership was in absolute decline, falling to just over half its 1927 level by 1938.[124] The 1930 Road Traffic Act, which imposed compulsory third-party insurance on motorcycles, had led many owners to switch to small cars, given their advantages of protection from the elements, carrying multiple passengers, and higher social status.[125]

In 1938 there were some 2,045,400 cars registered in the UK, more than double the 997,900 registered in 1928. However, after allowing for families with more than one car (estimated at 100,000 in 1935), cars are estimated to have diffused to only around 15.4 per cent of UK households.[126] One key constraint was affordability.

---

[119] Ibid., 255.     [120] Wyatt, *Austin Seven*, 21.     [121] Ibid., 22.

[122] 'Motoring at Easter', *Economist* (28 Mar. 1937), 686–7.

[123] Clarks Archive, No 2/12, Sampson Clark & Company Ltd, 'Business Development Bulletin. The Motor Car Industry', market research report, 1938, 60.

[124] Church, *Herbert Austin*, 81–2; Wyatt, *Austin Seven*, 51.

[125] 'Progress of the Industry', *Economist* (7 Dec. 1935), 1134–6.

[126] Car registrations taken from Bowden, 'Demand and Supply Constraints', 245, based on SMMT data. Number of households estimated using figures for number of private households in England and Wales (Marion Bowley, *Housing and the State 1919–1944* (London: George Allen & Unwin, 1945), 269), grossed up using the ratio of the UK to England and Wales population in 1941. Multiple car ownership estimated from 'Progress of the Industry', *Economist* (7 Dec. 1935), 1132–4. The calculation assumes that these owned only two cars per household.

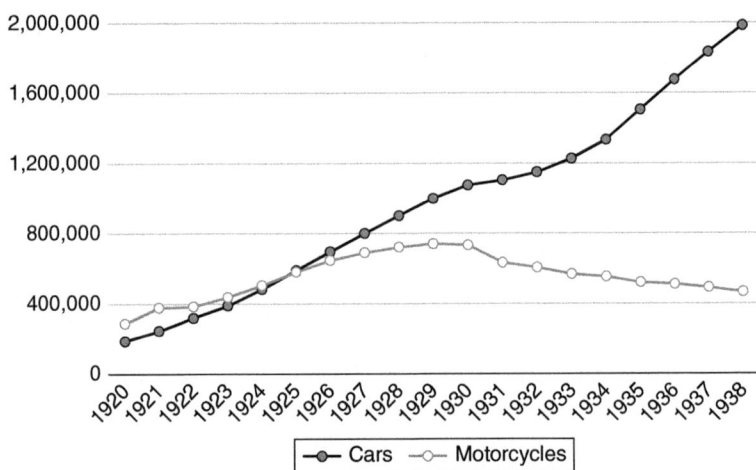

**Fig. 11.3.** Number of private cars and motorcycles in use in the UK, 1920–38
*Source*: Society of Motor Manufacturers and Traders, *The Motor Industry of Great Britain, 1939* (London: SMMT, 1939), 63.

In 1926 the SMMT had estimated the minimum income necessary for car owner-ship at £450 (though it accepted that some car owners would have lower incomes), which implied a potential car ownership of 835,000, compared to the 580,000 cars currently registered. However, SMMT acknowledged that a continued fall in car prices, together with improving economic conditions and the expanding used-car market, might eventually make them available for people in the £250–300 income class.

Three years later SMMT revised its minimum income boundary down to around £400, partly owing to the expansion of HP finance (and, no doubt, influ-enced by the fact that car ownership had already expanded beyond its original market projection). However, it noted that the key constraint was 'maintenance costs, particularly garaging and taxation, that ... are keeping the motor car beyond the reach of income classes which in the United States, Australia, or New Zealand are able to own and run cars'.[127] The minimum threshold income was again revised during the late 1930s, the industry assuming that ownership was limited to families with annual incomes of at least £250 (around 2.5 million), which suggested that the market was nearing saturation. However, PEP argued that many people on lower incomes (such as single men) must have been able to afford a small car, perhaps bought second-hand.[128]

In October 1938 the *Economist* proposed that British manufacturers might follow the German model of developing a 'People's car', 'devoting a whole factory

---

[127] Society of Motor Manufacturers and Traders, *Motor Industry of Great Britain, 1929*, 43–5; Society of Motor Manufacturers and Traders, *The Motor Industry of Great Britain, 1926* (London: SMMT, 1926), 15–16.
[128] Political and Economic Planning, *Motor Vehicles*, 58.

to the manufacture of one model, and...standardising that model in essentials for several years...to compete effectively with American cars'.[129] However, this ignored the fact that more modest previous attempts to launch a utility car had proven unsuccessful, at least in terms of direct profits. In 1931 Morris launched an austerity version of the Morris Minor, priced at only £100, but did not find a ready market. Customers were deterred by its austere appearance, perhaps preferring second-hand versions of more prestigious models to a new utility car. Miles Thomas considered this a useful publicity stunt, drawing in customers for the higher-price (and higher margin) variants of the Morris Minor: 'No one wants to keep down with the Jones's.'[130] Similarly, in 1934, when Austin launched its first £100 car—the Austin Seven Opal two-seater—it sold very few, with most customers opting for its more expensive four-seater saloon models.[131]

Ford made a more determined effort, cutting the price of its Ford Eight by 13 per cent in October 1935, to £100 (20 per cent below its rivals). The price was held at this level for almost two years, resulting in an increase in Ford's market share for cars of 8 horsepower and under from 22 per cent in 1935 to 43 per cent in 1937. However, this could be interpreted as a defensive reaction to the launch of the Morris Eight at the end of 1934, which proved to be the most successful British car of the 1930s and cut deep into Ford's market share for this class. Indeed, given that Ford's increased sales following this move were largely offset by the price reduction, they proved more successful in gaining market share than in increasing profits. The UK market thus appears to have been insufficiently price-elastic to justify a low-price, Fordist-style mass production strategy, a conclusion that Ford may have reached in 1938, when it raised the price of the Ford Eight by a higher margin than that of its competitors (reducing its price advantage from 20 to 10 per cent).[132]

There were good economic reasons why a reduction in the minimum price of a new car from around £125 to £100 would attract relatively few new customers into the market. As the *Economist* had noted in 1927, the chief factor holding back car ownership was not the capital cost, which had already fallen to less than £150 for a new car, or as little as £50 for a second-hand model, nor the running costs in terms of fuel (before tax) and tyres. The major barrier constituted 'standing charges' and depreciation. They gave the example of a light car, used for non-professional purposes, that had been driven for 6,300 miles over twelve months at a cost of £113—of which taxation accounted for 11 per cent, insurance for 9 per cent, garaging for 11.5 per cent (which was stated to be unusually cheap), and depreciation (said to be on the heavy side in the estimate) for 44 per cent. Thus running expenses, net of taxation, accounted to only 25 per cent of all costs (Fig. 11.4). A second example involved a three-year-old car, run for six months of the year only, and garaged on the owner's premises. Total annual costs (including depreciation), for 5,070 miles, still amounted to £78, of which running expenses (net of taxation) and repairs represented only 34 per cent. Thus overall car ownership costs

---

[129] 'Motor Economics', *Economist* (15 Oct. 1938), 119–20.
[130] Thomas, *Out on a Wing*, 168.     [131] Wyatt, *Austin Seven*, 138 and 145.
[132] Maxcy and Silberston, *Motor Industry*, 100–3.

**Fig. 11.4.** A September 1935 Austin Seven advert emphasizing low running costs
*Source*: Peter Scott collection.

represented around £1 10s to £2 per week, a considerable sum if not justified by some business use.[133]

Running costs remained high throughout the inter-war years. Total standing charges on a typical 8 horsepower car during the late 1930s have been estimated at £32.35, while its annual running costs would amount to an additional £24.75; the total annual costs of £57.10 being more than a third of the purchase price.[134] A 1938 market research report gave a larger total annual cost figure (including depreciation) for a car bought new for £130, of £93 per annum over five years. It also found that a second-hand car would also incur running costs of around this level over five years, given its higher maintenance expenses and greater fuel consumption.[135]

High road and petrol taxes reflected the Treasury's view of motor vehicles as 'luxuries' rather than as an important growth industry which might boost the economy, both through direct effects and by increasing mobility. Motor vehicles constituted a lucrative source of taxation, yielding 10 per cent of government revenue during the late 1930s.[136] This imposed an onerous burden on car owners. For the financial year to March 1929 (a year after the reintroduction of petrol duty) the total tax take from vehicle and petrol taxes, £39 million, was equivalent to around £20 per motor vehicle (£30 if motorcycles are excluded)—more than six weeks' wages for a typical highly-skilled manual worker.[137] British motor vehicle taxation was also particularly onerous by international standards, as shown in Table 11.4.[138]

Given this strong revenue flow, it seems surprising that the Treasury did not wish to encourage car ownership. However, its major concern was to avoid roads expenditure becoming a major, continual claim on government funds, which might prove difficult to restrain at times when deflationary policy was deemed necessary in order to support sterling. The Treasury proved particularly successful in curtailing roads expenditure during the 1930s, depressing it below 1930 levels for most of the decade. It also successfully blocked motorway development (assisted by a politically powerful rail lobby that was particularly concerned by the amount of freight switching from rail to road). Thus, while the United States, Germany, Italy, Belgium, the Netherlands, and Canada all had motorway programmes by the late 1930s, the first British motorway was not opened until 1957. Meanwhile road conditions deteriorated markedly in relation to traffic volumes; in central London average motor vehicle speeds were lower in 1938 than for horse-drawn vehicles thirty years earlier.[139]

However, British consumers also appear to have given motorized personal transport much lower priority than their US counterparts. In America the car had

[133] 'The British Market for Motor Cars', *Economist* (15 Oct. 1927), 640–1.

[134] Bowden, 'Demand and Supply Constraints', 247.

[135] Clarks Archive, No 2/12, Sampson Clark & Company Ltd, 'Business Development Bulletin. The Motor Car Industry', market research report, 1938, 52–3.

[136] Political and Economic Planning, *Motor Vehicles*, 66.

[137] 'The Position of the Motor Industry', *Economist* (11 May 1929), 1034–5.

[138] See also Political and Economic Planning, *Motor Vehicles*, 66.

[139] D. J. Dyos and D. H. Aldcroft, *British Transport: An Economic Survey from the Seventeenth Century to the Twentieth* (Leicester: Leicester University Press, 1969), 369–70.

**Table 11.4.** Comparison of private car taxation, based on 8,000 miles driven per annum, *c.*1937

| Major car-producing countries | Average horsepower of cars in use | Average total tax per year (£)* | Average tax per 100 cc (shillings)* |
|---|---|---|---|
| Great Britain | 12 | 26.35 | 35 |
| USA | 27 | 7.05 | 4 |
| Canada | 27 | 7.05 | 4 |
| Germany | 14 | 15.75 | 18 |
| France | 14 | 19.12 | 22 |
| **Major overseas markets for British cars** | | | |
| Australia | 20 | 20.54 | 16.5 |
| New Zealand | 14 | 15.77 | 18 |
| South Africa | 20 | 15.21 | 12 |

*Notes:* *'Tax' includes all direct taxes, fuel tax, insurance, sales taxes, and driving licences. The predominant car in each country is taken as the standard.

*Source:* Clarks Archive, 2/12, Sampson Clark & Company Ltd, 'Business Development Bulletin. The Motor Car Industry', market research report, 1938, 3. Based on SMMT data.

become a 'counter-status luxury' in the 1920s, with lower-income families being prepared to make major sacrifices for car ownership. The manager of a Muncie, Indiana automobile finance company informed the 1925 *Middletown* survey that a working man earning $35 weekly was frequently prepared to devote one week's salary each month to car ownership, often at the cost of cutting back on 'necessities', including food.[140] As one of their lower-income respondents explained: 'We don't have no fancy clothes when we have the car to pay for...The car is the only pleasure we have.'[141] A follow-up survey of 1935 found that even families on relief saw the car as a necessity: 'People give up everything in the world but their car.'[142]

## CONCLUSIONS

The British government had protected Britain's car industry to an extent unparalleled for other manufactured goods, through a combination of tariffs and a horsepower tax that made imported cars of standard design uncompetitive in British markets. Conversely, the Treasury's imposition of high vehicle and petrol taxes, together with its staunch opposition to roads expenditure, had a substantial negative impact on the diffusion of the automobile. Even in 1938 private cars were still seen as primarily luxury products, for the leisure of that small section of the population who could afford their heavy running costs.

[140] Robert S. Lynd and Helen M. Lynd, *Middletown: A Study in American Culture* (New York: Harcourt, Brace & Co., 1929), 105 and 254–6.
[141] Ibid., 256.      [142] Ibid., 265.

However, it is unlikely that, even if Britain had matched the road taxes and ratios of roads expenditure to GDP of the other major car-producing nations, there would have been a ready market for a 'utility' car. Britain's high population density, high urbanization, and (partly as a consequence) very well-developed public transport networks, simply made the car less important to personal mobility. This was evident even before the spread of the automobile. In 1901 there were only around 3.3 million horses in Britain, compared to over 24 million in the United States, while Britain's accumulated stock of horse-drawn road vehicles was smaller than the number of such vehicles produced annually in the United States.[143]

Americans had welcomed the Model T as a machine which liberated them from isolation—in a nation where most people were rural or small-town dwellers—and a work-horse to get product to market or themselves to work. Britain had a much lower proportion of farmers and rural dwellers than the United States, Canada, or France. The section of the population who undertook business travel (other than to and from a fixed place of work and excluding professional drivers) tended to be specific white-collar occupations such as doctors, estate agents, journalists, and commercial travellers. For such occupations, the importance of visible status symbols was such that many would have preferred to take a taxi rather than to drive to a client in the cheapest car on the market. Britain therefore appears to have lacked a sufficiently large customer base for the type of cheap, reliable, car pioneered by Ford before the First World War and being prototyped by some European car-makers in the 1930s (such as the Volkswagen Beetle and Citroen 2CV).

[143] Leslie Hannah, 'Logistics, Market Size, and Giant Plants in the Early Twentieth Century: A Global View', *Journal of Economic History*, 68 (2008), 46–79 (50–1).

# 12

## Failure to Connect
### The Slow Diffusion of the Telephone

### INTRODUCTION

Despite being an important pioneer of telephone technology, Britain's record in developing a telephone network up to 1939 can only be considered a failure. Compared to the United States, Canada, Australia, and several Western European countries, Britain's telephone system was characterized by slow diffusion, high charges, and an often, at best, apathetic approach to market expansion on the part of its monopoly service provider. This was closely linked to the nationalization of the service in 1912. However, as this chapter will show, rather than being the result of factors commonly associated with public sector provision (such as bureaucratic inertia or administrative inefficiency), the reasons behind the poor development of the telephone service were much simpler—opposition in principle by the Treasury to any activities that might give rise to long-term spending commitments on the part of the British state.

The Treasury's stranglehold on the telephone service eventually became the subject of vigorous political controversy, compelling government to relax Treasury control over telephone development. This allowed the General Post Office (GPO) to actively market the telephone service, develop more attractive tariffs, and expand the use of the telephone system beyond its relatively narrow base of mainly business-related calls. However, even the most ardent advocates of an expanded network found it difficult to imagine that the telephone might eventually become a mass market service, encompassing the lower strata of the middle class and even some sections of the working class.

This chapter explores the constraints facing Britain's early telephone network and the campaign during the 1930s to expand telephone utilization and diffusion, together with its achievements and limitations. It also examines how the phone was used by the British public. The telephone system is shown to have been largely used for relatively brief conversations, dominated by commercial transactions or—in the case of residential customers—organizing the 'business' of the household. Most involved information too urgent for transmission by mail or telegraph. Using the telephone for more general purposes, such as social calls, was inhibited by high British charges. However, the very low proportion of extended calls suggests that there was also a cultural aversion to having in-depth discussions on the phone among a population who had not generally 'grown up' with the phone habit.

# EVOLUTION OF THE TELEPHONE NETWORK
# AND THE CONSEQUENCES OF
# TREASURY CONTROL

The commercial exploitation of the telephone began in the United States in 1877. A year later the first British telephone company was established—The Telephone Company Ltd, using Alexander Graham Bell's patents, while the Edison Telephone Co., using different patents, was established in 1879. These amalgamated within a year to form United Telephone Co.[1] Fearing competition with its telegraph service, the Post Office launched a legal challenge to the new companies on the grounds that telephone was a 'telegraph' (in the context of the Telegraph Acts, which gave the Postmaster General a monopoly on telegraph business) and the companies had violated the Post Office's monopoly in sending 'telegrams'. In December 1880 judgement was found in favour of the Post Office, forcing the private companies to come to terms in a deal where they paid royalties for the right to operate services, while the GPO retained the sole right to develop the lucrative trunk line business.

This legal decision had a substantial negative impact on the early diffusion of the service. The Post Office maintained a tight rein over the industry and, under an agreement of 1901, took the right to purchase the assets of the private companies without any additional payment for goodwill when their licences expired in 1911. They were duly purchased for £12.5 million in 1912, nationalizing UK mainland telephone services (with the exception of municipal undertakings in Hull and Portsmouth). Meanwhile, restrictions the Post Office had placed on the private companies, combined with disincentives for new investment after it became clear that they were to be nationalized, had contributed to a much lower telephone diffusion rate than for most countries with similar per capita incomes.[2] The First World War and immediate post-war period saw severe under-investment in the telephone network, in common with other areas of government-sponsored infrastructure development. By the early 1920s the system was held in 'public contempt', due to long delays, poor reliability, and congested trunk lines.[3] As late as 1925 the Post Office found it necessary to suspend canvassing in many areas, and even reject some subscriptions, owing to capacity problems.[4]

The Post Office made modest financial surpluses on its telephone services from 1923, averaging 3.91 per cent over 1923–39.[5] Moreover, as discussed later, economies of scale would have made lower charges practicable without adversely affecting

---

[1] Arthur Hazlewood, 'The Origins of the State Telephone Service in Britain', *Oxford Economic Papers*, 5 (1953), 13–25 (14).

[2] Laszlo Solymar, *Getting the Message: A History of Communications* (Oxford: Oxford University Press, 1999), 100–12.

[3] TNA, T161/245, Cabinet memorandum C.P. 304/25 by W. Mitchell-Thomson, Postmaster General, 24 June 1925.

[4] Ibid.

[5] BT Archive, London [hereafter BT Archive], reference library, *Post Office Telecommunications Statistics* (Mar. 1949), 24.

long-term profitability. Yet Post Office policy was constrained by tight Treasury controls on its investment. Constituted as a Department of State, under a minister, the Postmaster General, the Post Office enjoyed no special dispensation to take account of its commercial functions. Treasury pressure to constrain public expenditure often overrode commercial considerations, as with other areas of government infrastructure provision, such as road development.[6]

During the 1920s the Treasury explicitly argued that telephone investment should be constrained in pursuit of its general deflationary macroeconomic strategy of cutting public expenditure, to support Britain's return to the gold standard at its pre-war parity and then defend what proved to be an over-valued exchange rate. In July 1925 the Chancellor of the Exchequer, Winston Churchill, argued in a Cabinet memorandum that Post Office requirements must be subordinated to 'those of the Treasury. They cannot be treated as a separate entity, bearing no relation to the general scheme of government finance.'[7] This policy also found support among a few senior and influential figures within the Post Office, such as its autocratic, conservative secretary, Evelyn Murray.[8]

When Post Office capital expenditure next came up for review, in 1928, the Treasury was still smarting from the 1925 settlement, where Cabinet eventually approved most of the investment the Post Office had requested. General macroeconomic arguments were now backed up by specific criticisms of the service. The need to extend diffusion was challenged, given that 'important' business traffic was already catered for. Although the Post Office was prohibited from press advertising, the Treasury attacked it as being extravagant for employing canvassers.[9] The validity of the Post Office's accounting system, which showed a significant surplus on telephone expenditure, was also challenged—despite the fact that it had been adopted on Treasury advice.[10] The Treasury proposed that for the next ten years the Post Office should raise prices on telephone calls and lower charges for telegraphs in order to divert traffic to its loss-making telegraph service.[11] However, boosting telegraph traffic appears to have been a rationalization for a minimal investment policy, rather than a specific Treasury aim.

Not surprisingly, diffusion continued to lag behind other nations with similar per capita incomes (as shown in Table 12.8). In 1930 Britain had 4.3 telephones per 100 population, compared to 16.4 in the United States, 14.0 in Canada, 10.7 in New Zealand, 9.8 in Denmark, 8.0 in Australia, 7.3 in Switzerland, 6.7 in

---

[6] Howard Robinson, *Britain's Post Office: A History of Development from the Beginnings to the Present Day* (Oxford: Oxford University Press, 1953), 247; Peter Scott, 'Public Sector Investment and Britain's Post-War Economic Performance: A Case Study of Roads Policy', *Journal of European Economic History*, 34 (2005), 391–418.

[7] TNA, T161/245, Cabinet memorandum C.P. 325(25), Winston Churchill, 6 July 1925.

[8] Duncan Campbell-Smith, *Masters of the Post: The Authorised History of the Royal Mail* (London: Penguin, 2012), 272–9; D. C. Pitt, *The Telecommunications Function in the British Post Office: A Case Study of Bureaucratic Adaption* (Westmead: Saxon House, 1980), 52–3.

[9] TNA, T162/281, internal Treasury memorandum for Richard Hopkins, signed R.R.S., 7 Mar. 1928; unsigned Treasury memorandum, 18 Apr. 1928.

[10] TNA, T162/281, W. Mitchell-Thomson to Winston Churchill, 8 May 1928.

[11] TNA, T162/281, internal Treasury memorandum for Richard Hopkins, signed R.R.S., 7 Mar. 1928; letter, Winston Churchill to W. Mitchell Thomson, 11 Apr. 1928.

Norway, and 5.1 in Germany. By 1937, while Britain's figure had risen to 6.4, its international ranking was broadly similar (having overtaken only Germany). Telephone diffusion was considerably higher in London than in the rest of Britain. In 1936 the City and County of London had a telephone density of over 16 per 100 population. Outer London had a density in excess of 12, while a number of major cities, including Manchester, Birmingham, Glasgow, Southampton, Leeds, and Bristol, had densities of below 7.[12]

High line rentals and call charges contributed to slow diffusion. The inter-war years witnessed substantial price reductions for some expanding technologies, such as radio, electricity supply, and, in the 1920s, cars. In contrast, phone call charges remained relatively stable except over very long distances (though telephone rentals were moderately reduced). Meanwhile business users dominated total subscriptions. In 1923 (the first full year of separate British business and residential tariffs) there were some 807,000 business 'stations' with phones, only 175,719 households, and 13,917 'call offices' (public phones). By 1934 (when new, lower tariffs were introduced) the number of business stations had reached 1.5 million and by 1939 had expanded further to 1.9 million, representing annual growth rates of 6.04 and 4.85 per cent respectively. Residential subscriptions expanded to 625,000 in 1934 and 1.19 million in 1939, representing annual growth rates of 12.95 and 13.87 per cent respectively. Meanwhile the number of call centres had experienced modest absolute growth, to 41,185 in 1934 and 49,518 in 1939.[13]

While capacity constraints and promotional restrictions limited diffusion, the main deterrent from the subscriber's perspective was high charges.[14] These remained relatively stable over the inter-war period, as shown in Tables 12.1 and 12.2. Between July 1922 and 1939 business rentals declined only moderately in real terms, by 5.2 per cent in London, 7.8 per cent in Britain's other four largest cities—Birmingham, Glasgow, Liverpool, and Manchester (hereafter four large cities)—and 10.7 per cent in the rest of the country. Residential rentals experienced somewhat larger real falls over the same period, of 15.7, 19.6, and 24.3 per cent respectively.[15] However, while short and very long distance call charges also declined significantly from July 1922 to 1939, charges for many medium distances (25–100 miles) actually rose in real terms.

Public pressure for a more expansionary telephone development programme eventually led to a change in government policy. Telephone equipment manufacturers argued that the Treasury's failure to differentiate between productive and unproductive expenditure had led to an expensive, underdeveloped system.[16]

---

[12] BT Archives, J. Innes, 'Present-Day Problems in Telephone Administration' (Part II) *Telephone Sales Bulletin*, 4, 9 (Sept. 1938), 134–6 (135).

[13] BT Archive, reference library, *Post Office Telecommunications Statistics* (Mar. 1949), 2 and 4.

[14] See Table 12.8 for an international comparison of gross earnings per phone, and per conversation, in 1923.

[15] Series deflated using retail price index; Lawrence H. Officer and Samuel H. Williamson, 'Six Ways to Compute the Relative Value of a U.K. Dollar Amount, 1270 to present', MeasuringWorth, 2009 <https://www.measuringworth.com/ukcompare/>.

[16] UK Parliament, Committee of Enquiry on the Post Office, 1932, *Report* (Cmd 4149 of 1932), para. 25.

**Table 12.1.** Examples of charges for a three-minute intermediate rate phone call, July 1922–39

| Date | Charges by mileage (d) | | | | | | | |
|---|---|---|---|---|---|---|---|---|
| | 0–5 | 7.5–10 | 10–12.5 | 25–35 | 35–50 | 75–100 | 100–125 | 150–200 |
| July 1922 | 1.25 | 3.5 | 4.5 | 10 | 13 | 24 | 28 | 42 |
| July 1923 | 1.25 | 3 | 4 | 10 | 13 | 24 | 28 | 42 |
| July 1924 | 1.25 | 3 | 3 | 9 | 12 | 24 | 28 | 42 |
| October 1929 | 1.25 | 3 | 3 | 9 | 12 | 24 | 27 | 39 |
| October 1934 | 1.25 | 3 | 3 | 9 | 12 | 24 | 24 | 30 |
| May 1936–39 | 1 | 3 | 3 | 9 | 12 | 24 | 24 | 30 |

*Source*: BT Archives Reference Library, Post Office, *Post Office Telecommunications Statistics* (Dec. 1957), 39–42.

**Table 12.2.** Quarterly telephone rental charges, April 1921 to end 1939

| Date | | Quarterly rental, exclusive line (£): | | |
|---|---|---|---|---|
| | | London* | Four large cities** | Rest of country |
| April 1921–June 1922 | | 2.13 | 2.00 | 1.88 |
| July 1922–June 1923 | Business | 2.13 | 2.00 | 1.88 |
| | Residential | 1.75 | 1.63 | 1.50 |
| July 1923–Sept. 1934 | Business | 2.00 | 1.88 | 1.75 |
| | Residential | 1.63 | 1.50 | 1.38 |
| Oct. 1934–Sept. 1936 | Business | 1.90 | 1.75 | 1.60 |
| | Business, small user | 1.60 | 1.45 | 1.30 |
| | Residential | 1.30 | 1.15 | 1.00 |
| Oct. 1936–39 | Business | 1.78 | 1.63 | 1.48 |
| | Business, small user | 1.48 | 1.33 | 1.18 |
| | Residential*** | 1.30 | 1.15 | 1.00 |

*Notes*: *10 mile radius. **Birmingham, Glasgow, Liverpool, Manchester (7 mile radius). ***From this point on residential subscribers received a 'free' call allowance of 50 penny units per quarter.
*Source*: As for Table 12.1.

The Post Office's conservative development policy also came under attack during the Liberal Party's 1929 election campaign.[17] However, public criticism from an insider, Lord Wolmer (an Assistant Postmaster General in the previous Conservative government) in a series of autumn 1929 *Times* articles, was particularly influential. Wolmer claimed that urban telephone charges in Sweden, Switzerland, Italy, and Belgium were less than half those in Britain, while those in Denmark, Germany, and Norway were slightly more than half. British rural rates were also shown to be markedly higher than in other countries, while the cost of a 200 mile trunk call was 4s 6d in Britain, compared to 10d in Sweden, 1s 10d in Germany,

---

[17] Pitt, *Telecommunications Function*, 47–9.

and 4s 4d in the United States. High costs were said to reflect low diffusion rates, which were in turn the product of an expensive, poor quality, service, lacking effective marketing.[18]

A December 1931 memorial to the Prime Minister, signed by some 320 MPs, succeeded in securing the appointment of a Committee of Enquiry, under Lord Bridgeman, which generally upheld Wolmer's criticisms.[19] High phone tariffs were found to stem partly from low utilization rates which, in turn, reflected limited diffusion. This raised costs, owing to economies of scale in infrastructure provision and utilization. The system had thus failed to capitalize on positive network externalities that linked the utility derived from subscription (and, therefore, utilization rates and unit costs) to the size of the network.[20] Furthermore, plant costs were found to be unnecessarily high, due to excessively stringent construction standards for cabling in thinly populated areas (whereas aerial cables were widely used in the United States). The Committee recommended increased financial autonomy for the Post Office, but rejected proposals to transfer the service to a statutory corporation. These recommendations were largely accepted by government and following the report the GPO's administrative structure was thoroughly reorganized, with the introduction of more attractive tariffs and the launch of an active marketing campaign.

## THE TELEPHONE VALUE CHAIN

The British telephone system had a peculiar value chain, owing to the pervasive influence of the Treasury over its operations. The Treasury's overriding aim to minimize costs (and therefore any potential government expenditure commitments), led to scrutiny of, and interference in, all aspects of the telephone service, including pricing, marketing activities, and even whether the GPO should aim to expand the telephone service. Under the Treasury was the GPO, a department of state subject to a variety of political pressures that acted as constraints on the normal business imperatives of profit maximization. The GPO had a national monopoly over British telephone services (with the exception of the municipally owned Hull telephone service). In addition to owning and controlling the telephone service and its infrastructure, the GPO had its own factories for equipment production. However, after the First World War these were largely confined to production and repair work to assess the tender prices of private manufacturers.

Private equipment suppliers operated in a strongly collusive environment, which no doubt added to the costs of the service. Prior to 1920–1 their main

[18] Lord Wolmer, 'Post Office and the Public. The System at Fault, I—Costly Telephones', *The Times* (30 Sept. 1929), 17; Lord Wolmer, 'Post Office and the Public, II—How the Money is Lost', *The Times* (1 Oct. 1929), 13.

[19] J. H. Robertson, *The Story of the Telephone: A History of the Telecommunications Industry of Britain* (London: Pitman, 1947), 244; Committee of Enquiry on the Post Office, 1932, *Report*, para. 5.

[20] See, for example, Paul de Bijl and Martin Peitz, *Regulation and Entry into Telecommunications Markets* (Cambridge: Cambridge University Press, 2002), 31.

trade association, the Telephone Cable Manufacturers Association (TCMA)—which accounted for about 95 per cent of UK telephone cable production in 1920—operated a price ring, unbeknown to the Post Office. Contracts were covertly rigged so that their selected firm would quote the lowest price and get the contract. From 1920–30 prices for supplying cables for local lines were negotiated with the industry, via short-term price agreements that had the effect of limiting the access of non-TCMA firms.

Negotiations with collusive manufacturers also formed the basis of telephone exchange ordering. In 1923, having selected the Strowger step-by-step director automatic telephone exchange system, the 'London Agreement' allocated orders for this system to four firms who agreed to pool their patents: Automatic Telephone Manufacturing Co. (the developer of the Strowger system), Standard Telephones and Cables, Seimens Brothers Ltd, and GEC. Each was allocated a fixed proportion of GPO orders. In 1928, these firms (together with Ericsson Telephones Ltd, which had joined the agreement in 1927) suggested that they could offer a lower price if a steady stream of orders was guaranteed, an initiative that resulted in the first 'Bulk Supply Agreement' (BSA), covering 1928–33. Under this agreement manufacturers were allowed to organize the allocation of orders, subject to the Postmaster General's agreement.[21] Other BSAs were made during the 1930s, covering coils, batteries, transmission equipment, cordage, and telephone subscribers' apparatus.[22]

In 1930, when the GPO was coming under severe pressure regarding the prices and quality of the telephone service, it also reconsidered its arrangements with the cable manufacturers and proposed increasing the access of manufacturers outside the TCMA. TCMA countered by suggesting a ten-year bulk supply agreement. The Post Office agreed, signing a BSA for cables in 1931. However, unlike the telephone exchange BSA, the TCMA succeeded in excluding access to non-member firms without offering any reduction in their existing prices. BSAs were credited with accelerating standardization, though—given the elimination of competition—their impact on innovation is likely to have been less positive. They also appear to have substantially raised prices; the termination of some BSAs during the 1950s was followed by sharp falls in contract prices.[23]

Construction and maintenance of the telephone network was undertaken by a combination of Post Office staff and independent contractors, the bulk of the work being contracted out (direct labour accounting for only one-fifth of capital expenditure on GPO constructional work during the early 1930s). Critics of the Post Office claimed that this work was undertaken less efficiently than in some other countries. However, the 1932 Bridgeman report found that intensive study

---

[21] James Foreman-Peck, 'Competition and Performance in the UK Telecommunications Industry', *Telecommunications Policy*, 9 (1985), 215–28 (217–25).

[22] BT Archives website <http://www.btplc.com/Thegroup/BTsHistory/1912to1968/1923.htm>.

[23] Foreman-Peck, 'Competition and Performance', 225; Monopolies and Restrictive Practices Commission, *Report on the Supply of Insulated Electric Wires and Cables* (London: HMSO, 1952), 39–43.

of these costs had led to reductions of between 30 and 40 per cent and that the inefficiencies had been common to both direct labour and contracted-out work.[24]

It thus appears that the extraction of 'rents' through collusion between equipment suppliers (and possibly contractors) significantly raised the costs of providing the telephone service. However, these impediments on realizing the potential of network economies to bring down unit costs as the service expanded were relatively unimportant compared to the dead hand of the Treasury—through opposing proposals to introduce more attractive tariffs and seeking to constrain expansion and prohibit active marketing of the service.

## ATTEMPTS TO EXPAND THE TELEPHONE SERVICE

Even ignoring Treasury funding restrictions, the complex relationship between telephone charges, customer numbers, calls per phone, 'network' benefits, and overall profitability, posed difficult pricing problems for the Post Office. Costs which were directly attributable to each subscriber, such as the customer's telephone and line, metering, and billing, were ideally covered by a fixed charge per period of time, i.e. a rental. One model for dealing with other costs was the railway pricing policy of 'what the traffic will bear', which provided a justification for higher charges for business than for residential subscribers.

Many costs were also dependent on peak, rather than general, traffic—as equipment and staff required for demand peaks would be idle at other times. There was thus a powerful rationale for higher peak charges, both to reflect service costs and to move some traffic to less busy periods. A final complicating factor was that the telephone system displayed classic network benefits, the value of a telephone depending on the number of subscribers. This provided a justification for both 'promotional' tariffs and permanent reductions in charges to accelerate diffusion.[25]

Economic theory suggests that, in the absence of special conditions, monopolists will find it optimal to use a two-part tariff with a fixed access charge that fully captures consumer surplus, plus charges per unit of use equivalent to marginal cost.[26] However, given elastic demand, providers have incentives to set access charges at below marginal cost, in order to capitalize on the positive network effects associated with increased membership of the system.[27] The Post Office used a two-part tariff, with residential line rentals set slightly below average costs (effectively cross-subsidized by higher business rentals, a practice which was also common in North America).[28]

---

[24] Committee of Enquiry on the Post Office, 1932, *Report*, 13.

[25] Arthur Hazlewood, 'Pricing as Applied to Telephone Service', *Review of Economic Studies*, 18 (1950–1), 67–78 (71–7).

[26] See, for example, de Bijl and Peitz, *Regulation and Entry*, 29.

[27] Wouter Dessein, 'Network Competition in Nonlinear Pricing', *Rand Journal of Economics*, 34 (2003), 593–611 (595).

[28] BT Archives, TCB 298/14, Telephone Charges Committee 1934, 'Report on Rental etc. Reductions, 1934'; Jean-Guy Rens, *The Invisible Empire: A History of the Telecommunications Industry in Canada, 1846–1956* (Montreal: McGill-Queen's University Press, 2001), 283–8.

**Table 12.3.** Subscribers classified by value of quarterly local calls (% of total subscribers), based on an analysis conducted in 1933

| Business users | | | | Residential users | | | |
| --- | --- | --- | --- | --- | --- | --- | --- |
| Local calls up to: | Provinces | London | UK | Local calls up to: | Provinces | London | UK |
| 2s 6d | 6.8 | 2.8 | 5.3 | 2s 6d | 10.5 | 7.9 | 9.2 |
| 5s | 17.3 | 7.9 | 13.8 | 5s | 28.9 | 23.6 | 26.3 |
| 7s 6d | 27.5 | 13.6 | 22.4 | 7s 6d | 47.0 | 39.3 | 43.2 |
| 10s | 36.9 | 19.9 | 30.6 | 10s | 61.9 | 52.9 | 57.5 |
| 12s 6d | 45.0 | 25.9 | 37.9 | 12s 6d | 72.6 | 63.8 | 68.3 |
| 15s | 51.8 | 31.7 | 44.3 | Over 12s 6d | 27.4 | 36.2 | 31.7 |
| Over 15s | 48.2 | 68.3 | 55.7 | | | | |
| Total (%) | 100.0 | 100.0 | 100.0 | Total (%) | 100.0 | 100.0 | 100.0 |
| (No.) | 430,000 | 237,000 | 667,000 | (No.) | 228,000 | 207,000 | 435,000 |

*Note:* Based on exchanges with over 200 working lines.

*Source:* BT Archives, POST 1222/482, note by G. H. Taylor, 4 Oct. 1933, and accompanying tables.

Nevertheless, rentals were still beyond the reach of most residential customers. From July 1923 to October 1934 annual provincial line rentals were £5 10s for residential customers and £7 for business subscribers. Rates in London were £1 per annum higher, while rates in Britain's four other largest cities were 10s above the general rate (reflecting the higher proportion of calls made at local rates in densely populated urban centres and higher capital costs for some plant). High rentals reflected installation costs; it was estimated that the capital cost of an average exchange line, telephone, and associated plant, was about £70, representing an annual cost, including maintenance and depreciation, of £5–6 (though such costs were subject to economies of scale).[29]

Table 12.3 shows a 1933 analysis of business and residential subscribers, classified by their quarterly value of local calls. Comparison with Table 12.1 shows that (excluding trunk calls) quarterly rentals dominated overall phone bills for a majority of both business and residential users, while a substantial proportion of callers made relatively little use of the system for outgoing local calls relative to the fixed cost of the line rental. In January 1933 a GPO official estimated that some 70 per cent of residential subscribers made fewer than 600 calls per year.[30] Lower line rentals could thus be expected to substantially boost subscriptions.

The Bridgeman report concluded that high charges were the result of 'the low calling rate which, in turn, is partly due to the low telephone density; but it is difficult to see how...[these] can be raised substantially unless they are given the preliminary impetus of a reduction in rates, even though this reduction might cause initial losses in some cases'.[31] Telephone equipment manufacturers lobbied for the introduction of a 'party line' service, which had proved successful overseas

[29] A. C. Belgrave, *Telephone Service*, Post Office Green Paper No. 37 (London: Post Office, 1937), 7–9.
[30] BT Archives, POST 122/482, letter, L. Simon to H. Buckland, 20 Jan. 1933.
[31] Committee of Enquiry on the Post Office, 1932, *Report*, 12.

and might broaden residential diffusion beyond its upper-middle-class base. This reflected American experience, where party lines accounted for 55.6 per cent of US household phones in 1929 and 3.4 per cent of business phones. These had enabled the American Bell Telephone Co. to reduce its cheapest residential phone rates to around 2 per cent of industrial workers' wages by the mid-1920s.[32] As a report on a 1930 Post Office research visit to the United States noted, party lines had made phone use 'habitual with all grades of the people in America... The telephone is not regarded as a luxury, but is looked upon as a necessity in all ranks of life... The application form for a ticket to use the New York Library calls upon the applicant to state "Name", "Address" and "Telephone Number".'[33] Party lines also proved key to working-class adoption of the telephone in Canada during the 1920s, boosting both diffusion and sociability uses—'meeting on the lines'.[34]

Yet British discussions regarding a party line service quickly rejected considerably lower rentals, owing to fears that many existing subscribers might switch to this service.[35] Planning shifted to the more limited aim of attracting potential subscribers with low demand for outgoing calls, rather than using party lines to draw in socio-economic groups currently priced out of the market. Analysis of provincial business subscribers showed that 40 per cent originated less than 10s worth of local calls per quarter, while a study of three provincial districts indicated that 55–60 per cent of low-use business subscribers were shopkeepers, doctors, dentists, and nurses, who mainly used the phone for incoming calls.[36]

The new service was announced on 27 December 1933, branded as 'Group Service' to avoid the implications of lack of privacy associated with the term 'party line' (other members were prevented from listening in on conversations and each customer had their own ringing signal).[37] Tariffs were offered via both the Post Office's traditional 'message rate' and on 'measured rates'—which including 10s worth of 'free' calls. The message rates included a discount on standard quarterly line rentals of between 23.1 and 28.6 per cent for business users (depending on location) and between 30.8 and 36.4 per cent for residential users. Under both tariffs subscribers paid 1d more than the standard rate, for calls of 4d or less. Charges under the group service and standard tariffs were equal when subscribers made about 120 local calls per quarter under the message rate and about 150 under the measured rate.[38] Yet group service did not prove popular and in December 1938 it was decided that it should be allowed to 'die out', sales staff being instructed not to recruit new subscribers.[39] The archives do not discuss

---

[32] Claude S. Fischer, *America Calling: A Social History of the Telephone to 1940* (Berkeley, CA: University of California Press, 1992), 110.

[33] BT Archives, TCB 306/21, report of visit to the USA by Messrs. Comersall & Wilby, examining installation of subscribers' services, organization, etc. for Engineer-in-Chief, Post Office, 1930.

[34] Michele Martin, 'Communication and Social Forms: The Development of the Telephone, 1876–1920', *Antipode*, 23 (1991), 307–33 (319–20); Rens, *Invisible Empire*, 283–8.

[35] BT Archives, POST 122/482, note by G. H. Taylor, 20 Jan. 1933.

[36] BT Archives, POST 122/482, note by G. H. Taylor, 4 Oct. 1933.

[37] BT Archive, POST 122/482, letter, G. H. Taylor to district managers, 27 Dec. 1933.

[38] BT Archives, POST 122/482, circular to district managers by G. H. Taylor, 19 Jan. 1934.

[39] BT Archives, POST 122/482, letter, initialled T.J., 13 Dec. 1938.

why the service failed, though by 1936 some of its attractive features had been incorporated into the standard tariff. Many customers may also have resented the higher call charges.

Reductions in standard charges proved more important in boosting subscriptions. By 1934 cost-reducing technical improvements, together with rising traffic, had considerably raised the telephone surplus, with further substantial rises projected. It was also recognized that trunk calls were relatively expensive compared to most European countries, particularly over longer distances; a morning rate call costing 7d over a distance of 15–20 miles cost 2s for 50–75 miles, 3s at 100–125 miles, and 4s 6d for 150–250 miles. Meanwhile calls exceeding 75 miles generated considerable profits, ranging from about 80 per cent over costs for 75–100 miles, to well over 125 per cent for longer distances—the relatively heavy phone traffic between London and the industrial districts of Lancashire and Yorkshire earned around 140 per cent over cost. Moreover, long-distance traffic was sufficiently smaller than medium distance calls to suggest that it was being stifled by the high charges.[40]

All charges for calls over 100 miles were reduced; for example, morning London–Birmingham rates fell from 3s to 2s 6d, while morning rates from London to the main industrial areas of Lancashire and Yorkshire fell from 4s 6d to 3s. Maximum charges for intermediate rate calls were halved to 3s 6d, and maximum night rates were drastically reduced from 4s 9d to only 1s, to stimulate social calls and non-urgent business traffic.[41] Rental charges, found to be the dominant factor deterring new customers, were also reduced, as shown in Table 12.2. Monthly rather than quarterly billing was introduced, to attract subscribers who budgeted on a monthly basis and did not wish to build up debts over a longer period—i.e. lower and middle income salaried workers and small businesses. A new small business tariff was also launched, with a lower rental, compensated for by higher call charges (until the number of calls reached a certain level). This was seen as potentially attractive to small businesses which had limited outward calls but derived considerable advantage from being on the phone.[42] However, several Post Office sales managers argued that the connection charge would inhibit potential subscribers.[43]

May 1936 witnessed some further, more moderate, charge reductions, mainly involving 'morning' (9 a.m.–2 p.m.) calls for distances over 35 miles.[44] Rates were further modified in October 1936. The 'free radius'[45] was extended from two to three miles and residential subscribers were given a block of fifty free calls—to

[40] BT Archives, TCB 298/14, Telephone Charges Committee 1934, Report on trunk charges, 2 Aug. 1934.

[41] BT Archives, TCB 325/EH66, GPO leaflet, 'Reduced Charges for Long-Distance Telephone Trunk Calls', 1934.

[42] BT Archives, TCB 298/14, Telephone Charges Committee 1934, 'Report on Rental etc. Reductions, 1934', 1934.

[43] BT Archives, POST 33/4812, Sales Conference proceedings, 4–5 July 1934, comments by Learoyd (North-western region); Mr Adams (North-eastern); Mr Reid (Glasgow); and Mr Humphries (South Wales) on G. R. Taylor, 'The Revised Telephone Charges. The Development Expected and the Responsibility of the Sales Staff to Achieve it'.

[44] BT Archives, TCB 310/11, GPO, 'Cheaper Trunk Calls', pamphlet, 1936.

[45] The radius over which calls could be made without incurring any excess mileage charge.

attract customers who feared bills of an unknown, and possibly high, value.[46] This was not seen as being similarly attractive to businesses, which instead received a lower line rental.[47]

The tariff reductions received an enthusiastic reception from the press and public and generated considerable growth in telephone traffic and subscriptions. During the eight months following the October 1934 reductions, long-distance trunk traffic (over 75 miles) rose by around 16 per cent for daytime, and 204 per cent for night-time, calls. Meanwhile trunk calls of below 75 miles rose by 10 per cent for day, and 28 per cent for night, traffic.[48] The new charges also accelerated the growth of subscriptions. Business line growth rose by 34 per cent per annum (from 17,400 to 23,400 per annum), but residential line growth was boosted from 21,500 to 102,300 per annum—an increase of 376 per cent—suggesting very high price elasticity for residential consumers.[49] The October 1936 reductions further accelerated the growth of the service.[50] The absence of further significant tariff reductions after 1936 may be due to the growth in subscribers exceeding the capacity of the Post Office's installation service. A rapid rise in the waiting list for phone connection in the early months of 1937 became so severe that the GPO found it expedient to place restrictions on their canvassers in certain areas.[51]

The network had also experienced substantial technical upgrading during the 1930s, including the introduction of 'no delay' trunk calls (where the caller waited to be put through by the operator, rather than having to book a call in advance), the introduction of new services such as the speaking clock and the spread of automatic exchanges (which served only 4.1 per cent of telephones in 1925, but rose to 40.9 per cent by 1935 and 60.3 per cent by 1940).[52]

## MARKETING THE TELEPHONE

While the Post Office was prohibited from using print advertising for the telephone during the 1920s, the telephone equipment manufacturers took up this role, forming the Telephone Development Association (TDA) in May 1924. This body combined promotional activity for the telephone service with lobbying for a more aggressive approach to expanding the telephone network and seeking out new customers.[53] TDA both used print advertising and drummed up editorial

[46] BT Archives, J. Innes, 'Present-Day Problems in Telephone Administration', *Telephone Sales Bulletin*, 4, 8 (Aug. 1938), 118–20 (118); BT Archives, 'Things to Come', *Telephone Sales Bulletin*, 2, 12 (Dec. 1936), 178–82 (180).

[47] BT Archives, TCB 298/14, Traffic Charges Committee report to the Postmaster General, 29 Apr. 1936.

[48] BT Archives, TCB 298/16, Telephone Charges Committee, report on minor concessions, 1935.

[49] Innes (Aug. 1938), 'Present-Day Problems', 118.

[50] BT Archives, 'Things to Come', 178; extract of talk to London sales staff by Controller of Sales.

[51] Innes (Sept. 1938), 'Present-Day Problems', 135.

[52] W. F. Shepherd, 'Residence Expansion in the British Telephone System', *Journal of Industrial Economics*, 14 (1966), 263–74 (265).

[53] Robertson, *Story of the Telephone*, 191–3.

publicity (something that, as in other industries, was facilitated by direct advertising spend in the publications concerned).[54] They also organized exhibition displays and other promotional and propaganda efforts. Whilst being deeply critical of the GPO's failure to popularize the telephone service, TDA nevertheless developed a working relationship with the GPO. The two organizations cooperated with exhibitions and work with schools, while TDA found sales leads for them, placing a detachable postcard in its leaflet 'Why aren't you on the telephone?', that could be completed and sent to the local GPO contract office.[55]

TDA residential consumer publicity emphasized the social value of the phone. For example, one 1930 leaflet, distributed at the Ideal Home Exhibition and aimed at middle-class suburban housewives, noted that:

> Life is fuller than ever of exciting possibilities when there's a 'phone in the house—of enjoyment, of happiness, of sheer fun. Parties, trips, meetings—they can all be arranged in a minute or two...And where there's a telephone loneliness can never be. No woman can feel solitary when she can pick up the 'phone and chat to a friend. A husband is never out of reach, friends are never beyond your call, that feeling of dreariness and helpless isolation can never sweep over you.[56]

In 1930 the Postmaster General Clement Attlee bowed to public pressure for the Post Office to conduct its own print advertising. However, cut-backs during the depression meant that a significant publicity campaign was not launched until autumn 1932, as part of a wider reorganization following the Bridgeman Committee's recommendations, led by Sir Kingsley Wood (Postmaster General from November 1931 to June 1935). The new National Government wanted to modernize the Post Office, reducing the degree of direct political (and Treasury) control so that its services, especially telecommunications, could be developed more effectively.[57] The move to an active publicity policy can be dated to the establishment of the GPO's Telephone Publicity Committee in 1931, which was chaired by the Postmaster General and included both senior internal marketing-related staff and several eminent external marketing and business authorities, including Sir William Crawford (founder of the advertising agency W. S. Crawford Ltd), Sir Frances Goodenough (controller of the Gas Light & Coke Company), and, most influentially, Sir Stephen Tallents of the Empire Marketing Board.[58]

Tallents, who served on the Post Office's Telephone Publicity Committee (later renamed the Post Office Publicity Committee) from 1931, and was appointed as its first Controller of Public Relations in August 1933, was the moving spirit behind the new marketing programme. Tallents was responsible for a number of key marketing and PR innovations, drawing on his earlier experience at the recently

[54] Ibid.

[55] Michael Heller, 'The Development of Integrated Marketing Communications at the British General Post Office, 1931–39', *Business History*, 58 (2016), 1034–54 (1038–9).

[56] BT Archives, POST 33/1875, TDA leaflet, 'The Ideal Home is on the Phone' (1930).

[57] Scott Anthony, *Public Relations and the Making of Modern Britain: Stephen Tallents and the Birth of a Progressive Media Profession* (Manchester: Manchester University Press, 2012), 101.

[58] Heller, 'Development of Integrated Marketing Communications', 1039.

defunct Empire Market Board and redeploying some of its key artistic and marketing resources, including its Film Unit.

The Post Office's publicity programme initially concentrated on telephones. Tallents described its aims as being chiefly, 'to make the Post Office "alive" to the public; to present it as a National Institution—modern, up-to-date, in close touch with the community and inspired with a desire to serve'. Selling telephones and other services was only a secondary purpose, and the campaign approached this, 'not quite in the commercial sense but rather in the sense of inducing the community to take the greatest advantage of the great variety of services available'.[59]

In July 1931, when the Post Office's Telephone Publicity Committee held its first meeting, the GPO had a telephone sales organization based around 700 contract officers, who conducted door-to-door canvassing and personal selling to the public, supported by promotional leaflets and circulars that were mailed to prospective and current customers and distributed through Post Offices. These often included coupons that could be sent to the Post Office, requesting additional information—providing leads for their salesmen.[60] Canvassers remained a key part of the GPO's promotional machinery, publicity being viewed as 'preparation of the ground for the salesman's personal effort'.[61]

The Telephone Publicity Committee considered that newspapers, and then periodicals, should be prioritized. This was partly because adverts including coupons (or codes specific to the particular newspaper) generated sales inquiries that could be traced back to the relevant publication. Such inquiries also had good conversion rates into orders: 'Approximately 40% of the inquiry forms received [from press adverts] produce orders. It is the ability to key advertisements and results which makes newspaper advertising valuable as compared with other media.'[62] Conversely, keying was not considered practicable for poster advertising: 'We want names and addresses and posters do not produce these.'[63] Partly as a consequence, poster advertising played a relatively small part in the GPO's telephone and wider advertising campaign, generally being restricted to 'free' sites such as Post Office buildings and vans.[64]

An initial policy of confining newspaper advertising to national titles produced protests from local and regional newspaper interests. Some attempted to 'blackmail' the Post Office for paid advertisements, on the grounds that they were already providing free advertising for them, via their news features.[65] Like most PR men,

[59] BT Archives, POST 33/4812, Sales Conference proceedings, 4–5 July 1934, Sir Stephen Tallents, 'The Post Office Publicity Programme'.

[60] Heller, 'Development of Integrated Marketing Communications', 1038.

[61] BT Archives, POST 33/4812, Sales Conference proceedings, 4–5 July 1934, G. R. Taylor, 'The Revised Telephone Charges. The Development Expected and the Responsibility of the Sales Staff to Achieve it'.

[62] BT Archives, TCB664/4, conference of district managers, 10–11 May 1932, item 2, 'Publicity', paper by A. G. Highet, Headquarters.

[63] Ibid.

[64] BT Archives, POST 33/4812, Sales Conference proceedings, 4–5 July 1934, Sir Stephen Tallents, 'The Post Office Publicity Programme'.

[65] BT Archives, TCB664/4, conference of district managers, 10–11 May 1932, item 2, 'Publicity', paper by A. G. Highet, Headquarters.

one of Tallents' principal jobs was to encourage favourable editorial coverage. The introduction of frequent press conferences and an open door to journalists had succeeded in increasing editorial coverage of the GPO from 36,000 column inches in 1933 to 56,000 in 1934.[66] Concentrating adverts in particular national news-papers was defended internally on the grounds that, 'To be effective newspaper advertising must be continuous and single insertions are not paying propositions. The guiding principles of all advertising are Simplicity, Domination, and Repetition.'[67] However, Post Office sales managers in the northern provinces advocated greater use of the provincial press, given that the market penetration of national papers declined significantly with distance from London.[68] By summer 1934 local news-paper advertising had been initiated, though on a more restricted basis than its national advertising (for example, to mark the opening of a telephone exchange or Post Office shop, or to publicize new telephone tariffs).[69]

The Post Office viewed exhibitions as valuable for goodwill advertising, 'demon-strating the technical skill and the vast organisation behind telephone service'.[70] Following successful telephone exhibitions during the early 1930s, including a large stand at the Ideal Home Exhibition, the GPO received many invitations from large department stores to stage smaller exhibitions on their premises, a num-ber of which were accepted. By May 1932 it was also looking into renting empty shops in prominent positions, to act as telephone display and order-taking stations.[71] This was developed into a policy of opening 'Post Office Shops' in dif-ferent centres, for periods of a month or six weeks, taking a temporary lease of a vacant shop which would then be used for both sales and display activities. Shops opened in London's Strand, Nottingham, Plymouth, Scarborough, and Ipswich in 1933 attracted audiences of 400,000, 148,666, 108,710, 109,108, and 50,709 respectively.[72] However, the Post Office did not adopt the travelling showrooms used extensively by the gas and electricity supply utilities.[73]

The new PR efforts included a 'Telephone Week', at the beginning of October 1934, to publicize the new, cheaper telephone tariffs. Some 270,000 posters, 500,000 postcards, together with newsreels, lectures, editorial publicity in news-papers and on the BBC, and other media (including the launch of the temporary

[66] Anthony, *Public Relations*, 116; BT Archives, TCB 350, Stephen Tallents, *Post Office Publicity*, Post Office Green Paper No. 8 (1935), 17.

[67] BT Archives, TCB664/4, conference of district managers, 10–11 May 1932, item 2, 'Publicity', paper by A. G. Highet, Headquarters.

[68] See, for example, BT Archives, POST 33/4812, Sales Conference proceedings, 4–5 July 1934, comments by Mr Rushton (North-western region) and Mr Broderick (Belfast) on G. R. Taylor, 'The Revised Telephone Charges. The Development Expected and the Responsibility of the Sales Staff to Achieve it'.

[69] BT Archives, POST 33/4812, Sales Conference proceedings, 4–5 July 1934, Sir Stephen Tallents, 'The Post Office Publicity Programme'.

[70] BT Archives, TCB664/4, conference of district managers, 10–11 May 1932, item 2, 'Publicity', paper by A. G. Highet, Headquarters.

[71] Ibid.

[72] BT Archives, TCB 350, Stephen Tallents, *Post Office Publicity*, Post Office Green Paper No. 8 (1935), 16; Anthony, *Public Relations*, 101–4.

[73] BT Archives, POST 33/4812, Sales Conference proceedings, 4–5 July 1934, Comment by Mr Semper (London) on Sir Stephen Tallents, 'The Post Office Publicity Programme'.

shops, together with displays in local Post Offices) were used in an integrated media campaign to popularize the telephone.[74] This built on the longer-term 'Come on the Phone' campaign, launched in 1933 with the aim of making the British people (or at least those comfortably within the ranks of the middle classes) view the telephone as a necessity rather than a luxury, by fostering a national 'telephone-mindedness'.[75] Tallents sought to further cultivate telephone-mindedness by the development of new services such as Directory Enquiries, the Speaking Clock (Fig. 12.1), and 999, together with a May 1935 initiative to provide, in conjunction with the King's Silver Jubilee of the following year, a public telephone kiosk in every mainland village that had a Post Office.[76]

The Post Office was also a key innovator in the use of promotional films. Following the dissolution of the Empire Marketing Board in 1933, the GPO took on its Film Unit (having worked with it since 1932) and produced a series of celebrated documentary and other short films. These were designed for showing in commercial cinemas, Post Office shops, schools, social institutions, and other venues.[77] Several early films highlighted the telephone service, including the 1934 comedy short *Pett and Pott. A Fairy Story of the Suburbs.*[78] This contrasted the phone-minded Petts with the snobbish servant-keeping Potts. Mr Pett, 'Family Solicitor' is shown leaving an office next to that of Mr Pott, 'Debt Collector', setting up the two characters in a similar manner to the 'Mr Tenant, Mr Owner' Abbey Road Building Society ads discussed in Chapter 4.

However, the period of vigorous and innovative marketing proved relatively short-lived, with the Treasury patiently waiting in the wings until the political spotlight had moved on and it could regain control. Tallents had expanded the GPO's publicity apparatus from five people to thirty-six (to the chagrin of the Treasury, who complained regarding the cost). When Wood was replaced as Postmaster General by Major G. C. Tryon in June 1935, coinciding with declining political support for Post Office modernization, such complaints were given more weight and Tallents's term at the Post Office came to an end.[79] While the expansion and promotion of the service remained much more vigorous than during the 1920s, the era of dynamic marketing was drawing to a close.

## HOUSEHOLD CONSUMPTION AND WELFARE

The Bridgeman report noted the link between slow telephone diffusion and the popular British view of the telephone, 'as a purely utilitarian adjunct, rather than

[74] Anthony, *Public Relations*, 101–4; Heller, 'Development of Integrated Marketing Communications', 1041–4.

[75] Heller, 'Development of Integrated Marketing Communications', 1041.

[76] BT Archives, TCB 298/16, Telephone Charges Committee, report on minor concessions, 1935.

[77] BT Archives, POST 33/4812, Sales Conference proceedings, 4–5 July 1934, Sir Stephen Tallents, 'The Post Office Publicity Programme'.

[78] BT Archives, TCB 350, Stephen Tallents, *Post Office Publicity*, Post Office Green Paper No. 8 (1935), 16.

[79] Anthony, *Public Relations*, 116.

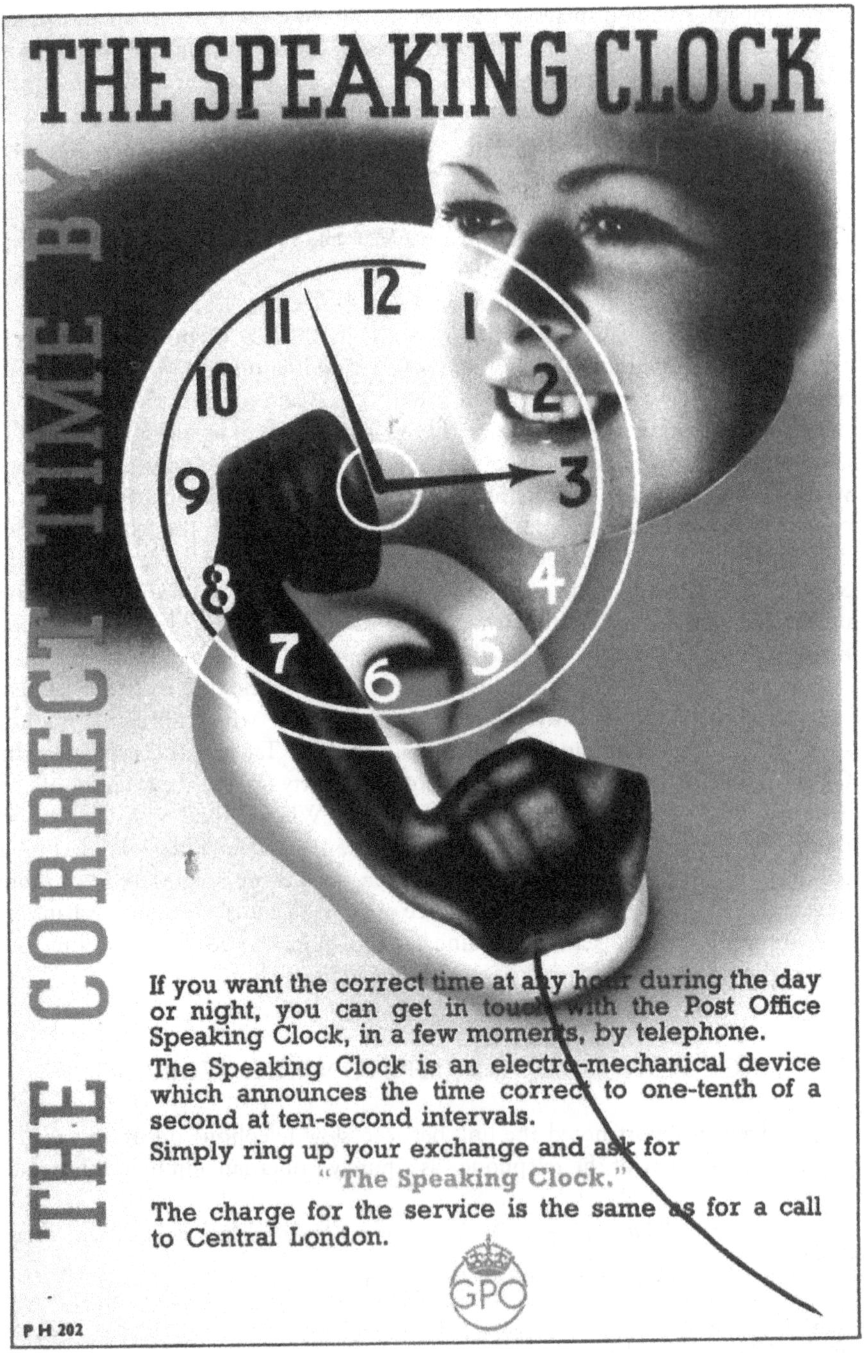

**Fig. 12.1.** An example of the strikingly modernist graphic art style of GPO publicity—a 1936 leaflet for the new Speaking Clock service

*Source*: Reproduced by kind permission of BT Archives.

as an amenity of life…An examination of comparable statistics in London and New York shows that after business hours the calling rate in New York is maintained at a far higher level than in London.'[80] In the United States some 42 per cent of households had telephones by 1929 and though subscriptions fell during the depression they had recovered to over 40 per cent by 1939. Telephones were found in most middle-income American homes (especially outside the South) and perhaps a third or less of working-class households.[81] Conversely, in the UK the phone was only widely diffused in households with incomes over £500 per year (the top 5 per cent of the income distribution).[82]

GPO research showed that by September 1934 around 20 per cent of households with annual incomes of over £1,000 had no telephone, which was attributed to their being, 'old-fashioned and prejudiced against it'.[83] Similarly, the fact that around 65 per cent of households with incomes of £500–1,000 had no telephones was ascribed to insufficient marketing efforts. Conversely, it was estimated that over 80 per cent of households with incomes of £350–500, and over 90 per cent on £250–350, lacked telephones and for these groups affordability was seen as the key factor.

In 1936 the Controller estimated that all households with annual incomes over £500 could be expected to become subscribers over the next twenty years, as would almost all households on £350–500, for whom the cost represented 1–1.5 per cent of household income. Conversely households on £250–350 (numbering over 600,000 in 1936, around 2.3 times the size of the over £500 group) were not seen as good prospects, especially at the bottom end of this range, where the cost of service would represent about 2 per cent of household income.[84] Only around 50 per cent of this group were expected to become subscribers over the following two decades. Meanwhile higher-income working-class households, on £200–250 per year (numbering more than 750,000, with subscription rates of around 3 per cent in 1934), were only expected to achieve a diffusion rate of 10 per cent by 1956. Households with incomes under £200 (the bulk of the UK population), were not viewed as a significant potential market, even on a twenty-year time horizon.[85]

Evidence regarding socio-economic diffusion in the late 1930s is available from the two national household expenditure surveys for working-class and for middle-class families, discussed in Chapter 2. The middle-class survey corroborates the Post Office's findings that subscription was concentrated among households on incomes over £500. Families with head of household incomes of £250–350 spent only 5.5d per week on telephones and telegrams, equivalent to 0.34 per cent of

[80] Committee of Enquiry on the Post Office, 1932, *Report*, 12.
[81] Fischer, *America Calling*, 53.
[82] It was estimated that in 1937 there were some 635,500 households with incomes in excess of £10 per week, equivalent to 5.2 per cent of all families.
[83] BT Archives, 'Things to Come', 180; extract of talk to London sales staff by Controller of Sales.
[84] Based on data for the distribution of individual incomes in 1938; Robert Bacon, George S. Bain, and John Pimlott, 'The Economic Environment', in A. H. Halsey (ed.), *Trends in British Society since 1900* (London: Macmillan, 1972), 64–96 (91).
[85] BT Archives, 'Things to Come', 180–1.

household expenditure. This amounted to £1 4s per year, while annual phone rentals were at least £4 (see Table 12.2)—suggesting that for most households this expenditure represented public phones and telegrams. For those on £350–500 per year, phone and telegram expenditure rose to £3 4s per year, indicating that only a minority had telephones. For the final two groups (with main incomes of £500–700 and over £700) annual telephone/telegraph expenditure was £6 19s and £15 10s per year respectively, indicating high diffusion.

The working-class survey aggregated telephone and telegram expenditure with postage costs. However, as Table 12.4 shows, comparison of the two highest working-class income groups, and the two lowest income groups in the middle-class survey (which have broadly similar household expenditures to each other), suggests very limited working-class telephone use. The top two working-class groups devoted roughly similar proportions of household expenditure to post and telecommunications to the spending on postal costs alone by middle-class families on similar incomes, suggesting very low working-class telephone expenditure. The author's analysis of 170 life histories for working-class people who moved to new owner-occupied or council estates over the inter-war period corroborates this; only one mentions having a telephone in the house before the Second World War.[86] The expenditures are sufficiently low to suggest that most working-class families made relatively little use even of public telephones, as would be expected, given that few of their friends and family would be on the system.

By 1938 there were some 1,089,000 residential 'stations' in Britain, indicating that the top 5 per cent of the income distribution probably still accounted for around half of all residential subscribers. Telephones were much more widely diffused among businesses. By late 1936 business subscribers had risen to almost 800,000, leaving 750,000 firms without a telephone. These were mainly micro-businesses, such as tradesmen, boarding houses, farms, and small shops.[87]

In a paper presented to the December 1928 Post Office District Managers' conference, A. E. Coombs argued that, in contrast to the well-developed business telephone traffic: 'The social call is...still in its infancy. It occupies today much about the same place in the general scheme of things that the business call did in pioneer telephone days...it is looked upon more as a luxury than as a necessity.'[88] GPO advertising also portrayed the telephone as primarily a means of business communication. For example, in 1936 the Post Office produced two leaflets, 'The Telephone in Business' and a more general leaflet, 'Come on the Telephone'.[89] 'The

---

[86] UK Data Service, SN5085, Peter Scott, 'Analysis of 170 Biographical Accounts of Working Class People Who Moved into Owner-Occupation or Suburban Council Housing during the Inter-War Period, 1919–1939' (2005) <https://discover.ukdataservice.ac.uk/doi/?sn=5085#>. These data were collected from a variety of sources, including oral history archives, autobiographies, and contemporary interviews.

[87] BT Archives, 'Things to Come', 182.

[88] BT Archives, TCB 664/2, A. E. Coombs, 'Ways and Means of Accelerating the Development of Social Telephone Traffic', in 'Report of Proceedings at District Managers' Conference', 11–12 Dec. 1928, 1–5 (1).

[89] BT Archives, TCB 318/PH2, 'The Telephone in Business', c.1936; PH3, 'Come on the Telephone', c.1936.

**Table 12.4.** An analysis of working-class* telephone, telegram, and postage expenditure, 1937–8 and lower-middle-class expenditure, 1938–9

| Mean weekly household expenditure (shillings per week) | Telephone + telegram | Post | Telephone, telegram, & post | Family size | Wage/salary earners | Ratio of 'disposable' to total income** |
|---|---|---|---|---|---|---|
| Working-class survey | % of total household expenditure | | | No. | No. | % |
| 32.5 | | | 0.33 | 2.52 | 1.15 | 18.0 |
| 45.8 | | | 0.42 | 3.21 | 1.19 | 21.8 |
| 55.2 | | | 0.47 | 3.32 | 1.24 | 24.0 |
| 65.3 | | | 0.45 | 3.49 | 1.35 | 26.0 |
| 74.8 | | | 0.50 | 3.56 | 1.52 | 28.4 |
| 84.8 | | | 0.49 | 3.80 | 1.69 | 29.5 |
| 94.6 | | | 0.48 | 3.82 | 1.78 | 31.1 |
| 105.1 | | | 0.52 | 4.24 | 2.15 | 32.1 |
| 114.4 | | | 0.50 | 4.28 | 2.36 | 33.6 |
| 124.7 | | | 0.52 | 4.56 | 2.71 | 32.8 |
| 134.8 | | | 0.55 | 4.74 | 2.55 | 37.8 |
| 180.8 | | | 0.59 | 4.71 | 2.91 | 46.3 |
| Middle-class survey | | | | | | |
| 136.0 | 0.34 | 0.57 | 0.90 | 2.98 | 1.17 | 44.5 |
| 173.4 | 0.71 | 0.55 | 1.26 | 3.39 | 1.25 | 49.5 |
| 227.8 | 1.17 | 0.49 | 1.66 | 3.56 | 1.26 | 51.0 |
| 321.7 | 1.85 | 0.51 | 2.36 | 3.97 | 1.30 | 55.8 |

*Notes*: *Excluding agricultural workers. **Disposable income is proxied by household expenditure, net of spending on housing, food, clothing, fuel, and light.

*Sources*: Working-class households: TNA, LAB17/7, 'Weekly Expenditure of Working-Class Households in the United Kingdom in 1937–38', report, Ministry of Labour and National Service, July 1949, sections III and VI. Middle-class households: Philip Massey, 'The Expenditure of 1,360 British Middle-Class Households in 1938–39', *Journal of The Royal Statistical Society*, 105 (1942), 159–96 (169).

Telephone in Business' emphasized the growing importance of the telephone as a tool of business communication, while the more general leaflet emphasized the telephone's importance to organizing the 'business' of the household:

> The telephone to-day is not a luxury. It may well be a necessity. It will almost certainly be an economy. It will save you money and may make you money. It will save you from wasting time and money on journeys, when a telephone message would do just as well. It will secure for you business opportunities which, but for your phone, would be offered to others. It will bring to you and your household invitations which would otherwise go elsewhere. It will be a constant insurance against the day of sickness or emergency.[90]

[90] BT Archives, TCB 318/PH3, 'Come on the Telephone', *c*.1936, 2.

Despite the fact that telephone messages, unlike written communications, leave no permanent record, we have unusually rich and direct data on the uses of the British telephone network from two major covert surveys of telephone users, conducted by the Post Office in 1936 and 1938. The 1936 survey (hereafter London residential survey) involved monitoring 4,383 telephone conversations originating from London residential lines. The 1938 survey (hereafter national trunk call survey) involved monitoring national[91] 'demand' (not pre-booked) trunk calls from 2 p.m. to 9.30 p.m. daily over the week beginning Monday 13 June. Some 10,896 calls were observed, representing approximately 1.5 per cent of total demand traffic. These were coded according to:

(a) When the call was made.
(b) The type of line from which the call originated—business, residential, or 'call office'.
(c) The gender of the caller and the called party.
(d) The occupational status of the caller (for business calls).
(e) The type of call (personal or business).
(f) The length of conversation.
(g) The chargeable distance 'step' (band).
(h) The subject of conversation.
(i) The dominant purpose of the call.
(j) Whether an appointment was made.
(k) The degree of urgency.[92]

Both surveys showed that typical conversations were of short duration. The mean length of call for the London residential survey was only 2.43 minutes, with 52.7 per cent of conversations concluded within 90 seconds and 74.6 per cent in under three minutes; only 10.7 per cent continued beyond 5.5 minutes. The national trunk call survey found slightly longer durations; only 12.4 per cent of calls between 2 p.m. and 7 p.m. and 7.2 per cent between 7 p.m. and 9.30 p.m. lasted for less than 90 seconds, while 52 and 56.4 per cent of afternoon and evening calls respectively were concluded in less than three minutes. However, more than three-quarters of calls lasted less than five minutes, and over 85 per cent less than six minutes.[93] Britain thus had a surprisingly small proportion of conversations of the length that would be expected for business telephone 'meetings' or for sociability uses.

Table 12.5 shows London residential survey calls, classified by subject and dominant purpose. Some 57.8 per cent were for 'business' purposes (defined so as to also include households contacting businesses). These mainly concerned shopping; services (such as betting, personal and domestic services, and hairdressing); and calls to doctors and other professionals. Calls in the commerce, manufacturing,

---

[91] Comprising thirty provincial centres, plus the London Trunk Exchange. Comparisons by the investigators with other available data indicated that this constituted a representative sample.
[92] BT Archives, TCB 309/2, Sales Investigation Report No. 22, June 1938.
[93] Ibid.

and financial categories—which were more likely to involve strictly business purposes, made up only a very small proportion of 'business' calls. Almost half of all calls categorized as 'business' involved placing orders for goods and services, while the next most important category concerned inquiries regarding goods and services.

The 1938 national trunk call survey found that week-day use of the trunk service was dominated by business lines. These originated some 84.5 per cent of calls from 2 p.m. to 7 p.m. on Monday–Friday, with 'call offices' (public phones) contributing a further 7.9 per cent and residential lines only 7.6 per cent. Furthermore, it was noted that had the analysis been extended to the morning period, the dominance of business lines would have been even greater. Conversely, residential lines made

Table 12.5. Analysis of 4,383 residential telephone conversations originating in the London area, c. June 1936

| Subjects | % | Purpose | % |
|---|---|---|---|
| **Business** | | **Business** | |
| Retail | 23.83 | Orders | |
| Professional | 4.62 | Re Goods & services | 28.04 |
| Services: | | On management aspect | 0.66 |
| Betting | 3.54 | Offers | 0.18 |
| Personal & domestic | 2.51 | Inquiries | |
| Hairdressing | 2.28 | Re goods & services | 9.65 |
| Other services | 7.18 | On management aspect | 4.45 |
| Commerce | 2.13 | Report | |
| Manufacturing | 1.44 | Re Goods & services for sale | 4.79 |
| Financial | 0.73 | On management aspect | 3.58 |
| Business uncertain | 9.55 | Business uncertain | 6.46 |
| **Total business** | 57.81 | **Total business** | 57.81 |
| **Social** | | **Social** | |
| Personal & private affairs | 22.00 | Instructions | |
| Health & welfare | 4.08 | About family & close friends | 0.73 |
| Invitations | 3.56 | About other people | 0.25 |
| Congratulations | 0.14 | About things & arrangements | 3.03 |
| Bad news | 0.14 | Inquiry | |
| Fire, police, ambulance | 0.00 | About family & close friends | 4.24 |
| Other emergencies | 0.02 | About other people | 1.51 |
| Travelling & journeys | 0.57 | About things & arrangements | 12.26 |
| Sport & recreation | 2.19 | Report | |
| Social gatherings | 1.25 | About family & close friends | 2.14 |
| Other social & uncertain | 5.82 | About other people | 0.64 |
| | | About things & arrangements | 6.80 |
| | | Gossip | 5.43 |
| | | Social uncertain | 2.74 |
| **Total social** | 39.77 | **Total social** | 39.77 |
| Totally uncertain | 2.42 | Totally uncertain | 2.42 |
| **Grand total** | 100.00 | **Grand total** | 100.00 |

*Source*: BT Archives, TCB 298/17. Telephone Charges Committee (1936), paper No. 6, 1 July 1936.

up 42.0 per cent of calls after 7 p.m., compared to 30.9 per cent from business lines and 27.1 per cent from call offices. Given that morning rate calls comprised around 42 per cent of all call traffic, 'intermediate rate' (afternoon) calls around 34 per cent, and evening calls only 24 per cent, the overall dominance of long-distance calls by business lines was considerable.

Tables 12.6 and 12.7 examine the distribution of calls in the national trunk call survey over the full week of the survey, by subject and 'dominant purpose'. The survey revealed both the dominance of business calls in overall traffic and the extent of segmentation between daytime business and evening social calls. Some 87.7 per cent of calls from business lines before 7 p.m. concerned business topics, while these also accounted for 45.8 per cent of residential calls and 48.7 per cent of calls from public phones. Thus, in the afternoon and early evening, just over one call in five was a social call. Conversely after 7 p.m. social calls dominated all types of line and while 29.0 per cent of all evening calls originated on business lines, over 70 per cent of these were for social purposes.

The dominant business uses of the telephone were broadly similar to those identified by Graeme Milne for the early adopters of this technology before 1911.[94] Business trunk calls were found to mainly involve managers or their clerks and assistants discussing commerce or services, while the 'dominant purpose' of most such calls concerned trading activities. Post Office promotional material had highlighted the value of the telephone as an instrument for trading: 'Without so much as moving from your chair you can place orders, sell your goods, confirm prices, open up new selling areas, introduce yourself to new clients hundreds of miles away. You can obtain immediate answers to enquiries. You can save yourself the time, the cost and the inconvenience of travel.'[95] Commercial and trading activities, together with transport and communications, were often conducted over significant distances, even if involving communications within the boundaries of the firm. Conversely, much manufacturing, for example, was conducted on the same site as the firm's headquarters and intra-firm communications would thus typically involve internal phone networks.

The London residential survey found that the main subjects of social calls were personal and private affairs, health and welfare, and invitations. These were chiefly calls to organize the social 'business' of the household—the main 'dominant purposes' involving inquiries about 'things and arrangements, etc.' or reports regarding these. The national trunk call survey also found that a large proportion of social conversations concerned family and close friends. For example, in addition to their dominance of 'personal and private affairs', some 90 per cent of calls classified as 'health and welfare' involved inquiries or reports about family members or close friends.[96] 'Gossip' constituted the dominant purpose of only 5.43 per cent of all calls in the London residential survey and, in the national trunk call survey, 1.0 per cent

[94] Graeme J. Milne, 'British Business and the Telephone, 1878–1911', *Business History*, 49 (2007), 163–85.

[95] BT Archives, TCB 325/EHA 81, brochure, 'The Speediest Way of Doing Business! By Telephone', c.1927.

[96] BT Archives, TCB 309/2, Sales Investigation Report No. 22, June 1938.

**Table 12.6.** National trunk call survey conversations, classified by type of line and subject of conversation (% of total)

| Type of line | Business | | Residential | | Call office | | Total | |
|---|---|---|---|---|---|---|---|---|
| **Time of day** | 2–7 | 7–9.30 | 2–7 | 7–9.30 | 2–7 | 7–9.30 | 2–7 | 7–9.30 |
| **A: Business** | | | | | | | | |
| Financial | 3.1 | 0.4 | 0.8 | 0.2 | 0.9 | 0.1 | 2.6 | 0.2 |
| Fishing, agriculture, mining | 0.4 | 0.1 | 0.1 | 0.1 | 0.2 | 0.0 | 0.3 | 0.0 |
| Manufacturing | 4.9 | 0.6 | 1.2 | 0.3 | 1.3 | 0.3 | 4.0 | 0.3 |
| **Commerce** | **38.2** | **8.7** | **12.3** | **3.4** | **11.2** | **3.0** | **32.1** | **4.8** |
| Produce | 4.0 | 1.6 | 1.3 | 0.3 | 1.2 | 0.2 | 3.3 | 0.7 |
| Manufactured goods | 25.0 | 3.1 | 5.1 | 1.1 | 6.1 | 1.7 | 20.6 | 1.8 |
| Food, drink, tobacco | 2.2 | 1.3 | 2.7 | 1.0 | 1.5 | 0.3 | 2.2 | 0.9 |
| Other commerce | 7.0 | 2.7 | 3.2 | 1.0 | 2.4 | 0.8 | 6.0 | 1.4 |
| **Services** | **26.8** | **14.8** | **21.6** | **11.5** | **24.1** | **9.0** | **25.9** | **11.9** |
| Personnel, domestic, & accommodation | 2.8 | 5.2 | 6.6 | 9.8 | 2.6 | 4.8 | 3.2 | 7.2 |
| Theatres & entertainment | 0.8 | 1.1 | 1.1 | 0.5 | 0.5 | 0.2 | 0.8 | 0.6 |
| Betting | 2.0 | 0.2 | 3.0 | 0.1 | 2.7 | 0.2 | 2.2 | 0.1 |
| Press | 4.7 | 2.8 | 4.6 | 0.2 | 7.9 | 0.8 | 5.1 | 1.2 |
| Road transport | 3.5 | 3.1 | 1.2 | 0.2 | 6.4 | 1.5 | 3.5 | 1.4 |
| Other transport | 4.8 | 0.6 | 1.3 | 0.2 | 0.6 | 0.3 | 4.0 | 0.3 |
| Other services | 8.2 | 1.8 | 3.8 | 0.5 | 3.4 | 1.2 | 7.1 | 1.1 |
| Professional (doctor, etc.) | 2.3 | 1.5 | 3.1 | 0.8 | 1.4 | 0.2 | 2.3 | 0.8 |
| Retail | 0.4 | 0.1 | 1.0 | 0.1 | 0.2 | 0.0 | 0.4 | 0.1 |
| Business uncertain | 11.6 | 3.2 | 5.7 | 2.4 | 9.4 | 2.1 | 10.7 | 2.6 |
| **Total business** | **87.7** | **29.4** | **45.8** | **18.8** | **48.7** | **14.7** | **78.4** | **20.7** |
| **B: Social** | | | | | | | | |
| Personal & private affairs | 4.5 | 35.9 | 20.7 | 38.5 | 20.0 | 41.6 | 8.1 | 38.5 |
| Health & welfare | 1.2 | 11.9 | 10.1 | 17.0 | 8.1 | 14.5 | 3.0 | 14.8 |
| Invitations | 0.7 | 2.6 | 2.9 | 4.0 | 1.3 | 2.2 | 1.1 | 3.1 |
| Congratulations | 0.1 | 0.7 | 0.5 | 1.5 | 0.2 | 0.5 | 0.1 | 1.0 |
| Bad news | 0.5 | 1.1 | 3.0 | 1.4 | 1.3 | 1.5 | 0.9 | 1.4 |
| Emergencies | 0.1 | 0.0 | 0.0 | 0.2 | 0.2 | 0.0 | 0.1 | 0.1 |
| Travelling & journeys | 3.1 | 13.3 | 10.9 | 12.3 | 14.8 | 18.7 | 5.3 | 14.4 |
| Sport & recreation | 0.4 | 0.5 | 0.8 | 0.6 | 0.5 | 0.2 | 0.5 | 0.5 |
| Social gatherings | 0.2 | 0.4 | 0.7 | 0.3 | 0.8 | 0.3 | 0.3 | 0.3 |
| Other & uncertain | 1.5 | 4.2 | 4.6 | 5.4 | 4.1 | 5.8 | 2.2 | 5.2 |
| **Total social** | **12.3** | **70.6** | **54.2** | **81.2** | **51.3** | **85.3** | **21.6** | **79.3** |
| **Grand total** | 100.0 | 100.0 | 100.0 | 100.0 | 100.0 | 100.0 | 100.0 | 100.0 |
| **Grand total (No.)** | 4,678 | 1,328 | 744 | 1,961 | 655 | 1,292 | 6,077 | 4,581 |

*Note*: The analysis excludes 238 calls, the purposes of which were totally uncertain.

*Source*: BT Archives, TCB 309/2, Sales Investigation Report No. 22, June 1938.

**Table 12.7.** National trunk call survey conversations, classified by type of line and dominant purpose (% of total)

| Type of line | Business | | Residential | | Call office | | Total | |
|---|---|---|---|---|---|---|---|---|
| Time of day | 2–7 | 7–9.30 | 2–7 | 7–9.30 | 2–7 | 7–9.30 | 2–7 | 7–9.30 |
| **Business** | | | | | | | | |
| Orders | | | | | | | | |
| For goods & services | 16.2 | 6.3 | 10.6 | 5.6 | 7.6 | 2.9 | 14.6 | 5.1 |
| On management aspect | 3.3 | 0.9 | 1.3 | 0.5 | 2.0 | 0.7 | 2.9 | 0.7 |
| Offers | | | | | | | | |
| Re sale accepted | 1.5 | 0.5 | 0.8 | 0.2 | 0.2 | 0.2 | 1.2 | 0.3 |
| Re sale not accepted | 1.3 | 0.2 | 0.7 | 0.1 | 0.2 | 0.1 | 1.1 | 0.1 |
| Inquiries | | | | | | | | |
| About goods & services | 19.5 | 5.5 | 10.4 | 5.9 | 6.7 | 3.1 | 17.0 | 5.0 |
| On management aspect | 11.6 | 3.1 | 5.2 | 0.9 | 6.3 | 1.6 | 10.3 | 1.7 |
| Reports | | | | | | | | |
| About goods & services | 18.1 | 5.0 | 8.2 | 2.4 | 12.9 | 2.2 | 16.4 | 3.1 |
| On management aspect | 11.5 | 6.2 | 6.0 | 1.7 | 9.0 | 2.8 | 10.6 | 3.3 |
| Business uncertain | 4.7 | 1.7 | 2.6 | 1.5 | 3.8 | 1.1 | 4.3 | 1.4 |
| Total business | 87.7 | 29.4 | 45.8 | 18.8 | 48.7 | 14.7 | 78.4 | 20.7 |
| **Social** | | | | | | | | |
| Instructions | | | | | | | | |
| About family & close friends | 0.3 | 1.2 | 0.9 | 1.5 | 0.5 | 0.6 | 0.4 | 1.2 |
| About other people | 0.0 | 0.5 | 0.4 | 0.1 | 9.3 | 0.2 | 0.1 | 0.2 |
| About things & arrangements | 1.4 | 4.4 | 2.8 | 5.6 | 4.9 | 3.8 | 1.9 | 4.7 |
| Inquiries | | | | | | | | |
| About family & close friends | 2.1 | 17.1 | 9.8 | 21.7 | 9.2 | 20.4 | 3.8 | 20.0 |
| About other people | 0.4 | 0.9 | 1.9 | 1.8 | 0.8 | 0.6 | 0.6 | 1.2 |
| About things & arrangements | 2.3 | 10.0 | 8.6 | 13.6 | 8.2 | 8.8 | 3.7 | 11.2 |
| Report | | | | | | | | |
| About family & close friends | 1.3 | 10.5 | 9.7 | 11.5 | 8.1 | 14.6 | 3.1 | 12.0 |
| About other people | 0.2 | 0.5 | 1.6 | 1.2 | 0.3 | 0.8 | 0.4 | 0.8 |
| About things & arrangements | 3.3 | 17.0 | 14.5 | 15.1 | 13.8 | 22.4 | 5.8 | 17.7 |
| Gossip | 0.5 | 7.4 | 2.4 | 7.4 | 3.2 | 10.8 | 1.0 | 8.4 |
| Social uncertain | 0.5 | 1.1 | 1.6 | 1.9 | 2.0 | 2.6 | 0.8 | 1.9 |
| Total social | 12.3 | 70.6 | 54.2 | 81.4 | 60.3 | 85.6 | 21.6 | 79.3 |
| **Grand total** | 100.0 | 100.0 | 100.0 | 100.2 | 109.0 | 100.3 | 100.0 | 100.0 |
| **Grand total (No.)** | 4,678 | 1,328 | 744 | 1,961 | 655 | 1,292 | 6,077 | 4,581 |

*Source and notes*: As for Table 12.6.

of calls over 2 p.m.–7 p.m. and 8.4 per cent of evening calls. Truly social uses of the phone thus appear to have been of relatively minor significance prior to the Second World War.

While only 7.2 per cent of calls in the London residential survey were classified as of immediate urgency (where some action or response was required within 15 minutes) a further 57.4 per cent were regarded as 'relatively urgent' and only 35.4 per cent were non-urgent (i.e. business that could be conducted through, for example, the post). The 1938 survey found that calls of immediate urgency comprised around 7.5 per cent of business and residential calls, and 10 per cent of all office calls, before 7 p.m., and an even lower proportion of evening calls. Conversely, relatively urgent calls comprised around two-thirds of calls from business lines and call offices, and around half the calls from residential lines, before 7 p.m.; their relative importance again declining after 7 p.m. Daytime uses of the phone network thus appear to have been mainly justified by the need for rapid communication, though after 7 p.m. non-urgent calls dominated all types of line.

Thus, even in the late 1930s the telephone was still mainly used for purposes identified in studies of the pre-1914 period—short, instrumental calls conveying relatively urgent information on matters such as trading and organizing the economic and social business of the household.[97] Yet in the United States and Canada sociability uses, such as 'voice visiting' (extended general conversations with distant friends and family) were increasingly emphasized in telephone promotion from the early 1920s—by which time rising sociability use had been evident for some years.[98]

The economic advantages of broadening telephone use beyond instrumental functions were recognized in Britain, as its high proportion of business phone lines, together with a low proportion of non-business calls, resulted in a high ratio of peak to average traffic. As the Bridgeman report noted, 'The slow growth of the telephone habit in this country and the disposition to regard the use of the instrument as a purely utilitarian adjunct, rather than as an amenity, of life, have a not unimportant effect on telephone costs.'[99] Further evidence that there had been no major transition towards the use of the phone as a more general instrument of communication is provided in Table 12.8, which shows Britain's international ranking in terms of telephone diffusion and use in 1923 and 1937. Britain ranked fifteenth among the seventeen countries shown in terms of telephone communications per capita in 1923 and twelfth in 1937. In terms of phones per 100 population it ranked higher—eleventh in 1923 and ninth in 1937. However, in terms of conversations per telephone, Britain does particularly poorly, ranking fifteenth in both 1923 and 1937 and experiencing an actual reduction in phone utilization. On any of these criteria, telephone use was unusually low, given Britain's high GDP per capita.

---

[97] Milne, 'British Business', 179; Robert M. Pike, 'Kingston Adopts the Telephone: The Social Diffusion and Use of the Telephone in Urban Central Canada, 1876–1914', *Urban History Review*, 18 (1989), 32–47 (39–42).

[98] Fischer, *America Calling*, 262–3; Martin, 'Communication and Social Forms', 319–20.

[99] Committee of Enquiry on the Post Office, 1932, *Report*, para. 26.

**Table 12.8.** Britain's phone use compared with seventeen other countries for 1923 and 1937

| | Communications per capita: | | | Phones per 100 population | Conversations per telephone | Gross earnings per: | |
|---|---|---|---|---|---|---|---|
| | Telephone | Telegram | Total | | | Phone ($) | Call (cents) |
| **A: 1923** | | | | | | | |
| Canada | (195.1) | (1.4) | (196.5) | 11.0 | (1535.4) | 43.14 | |
| USA | 184.5 | 1.7 | 186.2 | 13.7 | 1333.8 | 48.49 | 3.64 |
| New Zealand | (178.9) | (4.9) | (183.8) | 8.3 | (1770.6) | | |
| Denmark | 123.7 | 0.7 | 124.4 | 8.7 | 1418.4 | | |
| Norway | 109.6 | 1.6 | 111.2 | 6.1 | 1788.5 | | |
| Sweden | 95.8 | 0.7 | 96.5 | 6.7 | 1427.8 | 48.71 | 3.41 |
| Austria | 46.2 | 0.8 | 47.0 | 2.1 | 2230.2 | 61.17 | |
| Netherlands | 44.5 | 0.8 | 45.3 | 2.7 | 1646.7 | 50.71 | 5.74 |
| Australia | 44.3 | 2.9 | 47.2 | 5.0 | 883.2 | | |
| Hungary | 37.7 | 0.6 | 38.3 | 0.9 | 4029.5 | | |
| Switzerland | 34.6 | 0.8 | 35.4 | 4.6 | 751.4 | 48.69 | 6.48 |
| Germany | 31.1 | 0.9 | 32.0 | 3.8 | 825.9 | | |
| Japan | 30.0 | 1.0 | 31.0 | 0.8 | 3683.0 | 54.46 | 1.48 |
| France | 20.8 | 1.5 | 22.3 | 1.5 | 1369.7 | | |
| UK | 20.4 | 1.4 | 21.8 | 2.5 | 805.6 | 58.18 | 7.22 |
| Belgium | 19.4 | 0.7 | 20.1 | 1.5 | 1283.9 | | |
| Czechoslovakia | 13.7 | 0.3 | 14.0 | 0.7 | 1821.5 | | |
| **B: 1937** | | | | | | | |
| Canada | 236.0 | 1.1 | 237.1 | 11.90 | 1976.0 | | |

| Country | | | | |
| --- | --- | --- | --- | --- |
| USA | 220.2 | 1.6 | 221.8 | 15.09 | 1454.8 |
| New Zealand | | | | 11.97 | |
| Denmark | 182.6 | 0.4 | 183.0 | 11.25 | 1626.9 |
| Sweden | 170.5 | 0.7 | 171.2 | 11.75 | 1448.5 |
| Norway | 101.1 | 1.2 | 102.3 | 7.61 | 1324.3 |
| Austria | 96.0 | 0.2 | 96.2 | 4.12 | 2324.4 |
| Australia | 83.4 | 2.5 | 85.9 | 8.71 | 954.8 |
| Japan | 71.4 | 0.9 | 72.3 | 1.82 | 3895.2 |
| Switzerland | 70.2 | 0.4 | 70.6 | 10.26 | 682.3 |
| Netherlands | 50.6 | 0.4 | 51.0 | 4.65 | 1083.5 |
| **UK** | **46.4** | **1.2** | **47.6** | **6.41** | **721.6** |
| Germany | 40.1 | 0.2 | 40.3 | 5.31 | 751.2 |
| Belgium | 37.9 | 0.7 | 38.6 | 4.70 | 803.0 |
| France | 23.2 | 0.7 | 23.9 | 3.70 | 627.3 |
| Hungary | 19.8 | 0.2 | 20.0 | 1.65 | 1191.9 |
| Czechoslovakia | 18.7 | 0.3 | 19.0 | 1.43 | 1292.5 |

*Notes*: 1923 figures are partly estimated, for gross earnings per telephone in the Netherlands and number of telephone conversations in Austria and the Netherlands. Figures in brackets are for 1926 for Canada and 1927 for New Zealand (the first years with available data). 1937 telephone conversations and telegrams data for Czechoslovakia are for 1936.

*Source*: American Telephone and Telegraph Co., *Telephone Statistics of the World* (New York: AT&T, issues for 15 June 1925; 1 June 1928; 1 June 1929; 15 Mar. 1939).

The table illustrates the stability of rankings for most countries. The same six nations have the highest rankings in both years, in terms of both telephone diffusion and calls per capita. All of these had established their international lead in telephone diffusion well before the First World War and were characterized by high utilization rates. The table also shows gross revenue per telephone and per conversation for eight countries in 1923 (AT&T did not compile these data for later years). Britain had the highest gross revenue per phone of any country shown, though the difference is most marked in terms of revenue per conversation, which was twice as high in Britain as in the United States or Sweden. Given the relative stability of British phone charges, it seems unlikely that this price gap narrowed over the inter-war period.

High British charges and Treasury-imposed investment constraints can account for the slow diffusion of telephone lines, but do not provide a full explanation of the absence of significant social use of the telephone. Face-to-face meetings would often entail significant time and travel costs, which would have outweighed the marginal cost to an existing subscriber of an extended telephone conversation. A reluctance to conduct such meetings by phone is unlikely to stem from some fundamental British cultural aversion to this medium, since countries with strong cultural links to Britain, such as Canada, New Zealand, and Australia, had high telephone utilization.

The explanation may lie in the fact that using the phone for in-depth conversations involves social learning—as much normal face-to-face communication is non-verbal. Those countries with the highest phone use in the 1930s had already experienced several decades of widespread middle-class telephone diffusion. Systems such as the party lines of the United States and Canada facilitated social learning, by providing communication between those sharing the line at zero extra cost. An analogous process appears to have occurred in Sweden, Norway, and Denmark. In all three countries the introduction of the telephone was characterized by low charges and the spread of cooperatives, where subscribers built their own lines using iron wire to lower costs, paying a small annual fee for exchange service and maintenance. H. L. Webb, writing in 1911, argued that these facilities introduced the 'telephone habit...into the life of the Scandinavian peoples to an extent unapproached in other Continental countries'.[100]

Evidence from the United States and Canada also suggests that party line facilities played a major role in embedding sociability uses of the phone system into the 'habitus' of subscribers.[101] While such trends appear to have preceded the active marketing of sociability uses, telephone providers subsequently became keen to stress them in promotional material. In Britain, by contrast, higher charges and lower diffusion rates had reduced the scope for social learning. Moreover, the Post

[100] H. L. Webb, *The Development of the Telephone in Europe* (London: Electrical Press, 1911).

[101] See Fischer, *America Calling*, 47–8; Martin, 'Communication and Social Forms', 319–20; Rens, *Invisible Empire*, 283–8; Pierre Bourdieu, *Distinction: A Social Critique of the Judgement of Taste* (London: Routledge & Kegan Paul, 1984), 243.

Office's frustrations that the 'telephone habit' was not catching on in Britain could not be addressed until the prohibition on press advertising was lifted in the 1930s.

## CONCLUSIONS

Of all the sectors examined in this study, the telephone service was the least successful in moving towards a mass market, both in terms of the proportion of families with phones and, especially, in comparison with other countries. During the 1930s there had been a concerted attempt to develop a more expansionist marketing policy, involving not only extensive promotion but lower charges and an improved service. Yet residential diffusion remained largely confined to the top 5 per cent of the population until the late 1930s. Moreover, the dominant uses of the telephone system remained largely consistent with the functions its initial promoters had envisaged sixty years earlier. High call charges deterred 'frivolous' conversations during a period when even many households in the middle ranks of the middle class perceived themselves to be operating within tight budgets. However, the very low proportion of extended calls, even for business users, suggests that there were also other factors prohibiting the widespread use of the phone for more complex discussions than trading activities or imparting factual information. While party lines had educated many Americans and Canadians in the art of conversing about complex or intimate matters using this purely verbal medium, even those British people who had grown up with a phone in the house were acutely aware of the cost of each call and thus developed telephone habits based on brief, informational calls.

This, in turn, suggests that the utility derived from telephone subscription in Britain did not extend much beyond that accruing from its use as a niche communication medium for relatively urgent information. Utility can be modelled as a function of the number of calls made, the number received, the mean length of call, the subjective value assigned to each call, and the value attached to having a phone subscription regardless of expected usage (for reasons such as social prestige or use in emergencies). In the late 1930s the number of calls per subscriber was below that in the mid-1920s, calls were still typically of short duration, and they mainly involved relatively urgent instrumental messages. There is thus little evidence of a major increase in the utility derived from telephone subscription over the inter-war period, while the real price of the service had also changed relatively little since the early 1920s. In 1939 the Post Office was still struggling to extend the appeal of the telephone beyond its niche uses or make it a 'necessity' for families in the £250–500 income range, which constituted the bulk of the British middle class.

# 13

## Conclusions

### INTRODUCTION

This chapter first discusses the distinctive features of the British inter-war consumer durables revolution, analysing the production, consumption, and marketing characteristics of the sectors reviewed in the previous chapters and the ways these interacted to enable some durables (such as furniture, modern suburban housing, and radio) to diffuse relatively rapidly, compared to others, such as white goods, cars, and telephones. The chapter then moves on to examine the impacts of the different supply-side strategies in influencing diffusion rates. This highlights the importance of financial liberalization, advertising (especially that aimed at changing public perceptions of the importance and accessibility of the good, together with the legitimacy of purchasing it on credit), and differences in value chains. This section also compares Britain's experience with the three-phase model of marketing evolution identified by Richard Tedlow.

We then briefly review the impacts of the inter-war consumer durables revolution on both the industries concerned and on households—with a particular focus on the working and lower-middle classes. Finally, we take the story forward to the early post-1945 decades, to explain why Britain was transformed from Europe's leading producer of consumer durables in 1939 to a country whose durable goods industries were in crisis and decline by the 1970s.

### A VERY BRITISH CONSUMER DURABLES REVOLUTION

During the inter-war period Britain had succeeded in creating true 'mass' (though not universal) markets for furniture, new owner-occupied housing, and electronic entertainment durables. Britain had also witnessed a major extension in demand for certain white goods, including modern gas and electric cookers, vacuum cleaners, and a range of small appliances such as irons, clocks, and fans. Conversely, some goods considered 'necessities' by many American households, such as cars, telephones, and refrigerators, had experienced only slow diffusion, which had generally not penetrated beyond the middle ranks of the middle classes by 1939.

To assess the factors behind this very different pattern of diffusion in Britain, compared to the United States and Canada, Tables 13.1–13.3 examine the interaction between the production characteristics, consumption characteristics, and marketing strategies of each sector. Table 13.1 summarizes production characteristics. The first column looks at the impacts of patent royalties in raising costs. These were substantial for radios (especially in the 1920s), but less so in other sectors. The next examines 'complexity' which encompasses such things as the number of components required to assemble the good, the number of different processes in its manufacture/construction, and (for the telephone service) the need for complex infrastructure. Technical scale economies are then shown. These were relatively high in cars (though not nearly so much as in the United States, where the largest firms used Fordist production methods) and in telephones (owing to network effects), but were relatively weak for the other sectors.

The next three columns look at the potential for long production runs, which is influenced by the extent to which the product could be standardized at the firm level, the speed of product innovation/obsolescence, and the frequency of model changes. Furniture was subject to low standardization and rapid model changes, as firms felt it necessary to offer a wide range of designs and change these frequently. Housing was inherently difficult to standardize (despite firms using the same range of house designs across different estates) but was subject to slower changes in design. Radios were subject to rapid, unpredictable technical progress and policies of annual model launches, while white goods were subject to more gradual technical and 'cosmetic' change, as were telephones. Cars experienced a slowdown in technical change during the 1930s, though the introduction of annual cosmetic 'face-lifts' acted as a brake on production runs.

Finally the table shows unit costs, with any dominant factors in the previous columns determining these costs being highlighted. Of the four sectors with particularly high unit costs, three—housing, cars, and telephones—owed high costs primarily to the complexity of the product. For furniture, high costs were driven by a combination of weak scale economies, short production runs (the result of limited standardization and rapid design changes), and high downstream transport and inventory costs, owing to their bulky nature and vulnerability to damage in transit. The practice of marketing furniture in suites, rather than as individual items, also raised 'unit' prices.

Table 13.2 looks at the characteristics of these products from the consumer's perspective. Here cost is broken down into two elements—first (i.e. purchase) costs and running costs. Furniture had high purchase costs but low running costs (largely limited to cleaning and repairs). Housing also had high purchase costs, but running costs that were moderate (and low, relative to purchase costs)—for maintenance and so forth. Radios and white goods were in a medium cost bracket for purchase and (generally) for running costs—though particularly power-hungry appliances such as refrigerators and electric water boilers could be very expensive to run. Cars and (to a lesser extent) telephones were towards the high end of the cost spectrum, particularly for running costs—a particular problem with the telephone, as the cost of calls was not known until the quarterly bill arrived.

The next two columns examine the value to the consumer, decomposed into value in use and status value. Furniture, housing, and radios scored high on both counts. In comparison, white goods (apart from a few items, such as gas cookers,

**Table 13.1.** Production characteristics of case-study sectors

| Product | Patents | Complexity | Technical scale economies | Standardization | Product innovation | Model changes | Unit cost |
|---|---|---|---|---|---|---|---|
| Furniture | Weak | Medium | Weak | Low | Slow | Rapid | High |
| Housing | Weak | High | Weak | Low | Slow | Slow | High |
| Radios (USA) | Strong | Medium | Weak | High | Rapid | Rapid | Medium |
| Radios (UK) | Strong | Medium | Weak | High | Rapid | Rapid | Medium |
| White goods (major appliances) | Moderate | Medium | Weak | High | Moderate | Moderate | Varied |
| Vacuums (USA) | Moderate | Medium | Weak | High | Moderate | Moderate | Medium |
| Vacuums (UK) | Moderate | Medium | Weak | High | Moderate | Moderate | Medium |
| Cars | Moderate | High | Strong | High | Moderate | Rapid | High |
| Telephones | Varied* | High | Strong | High | Moderate | Slow | High |

*Notes*: *For patent royalties, the telephone sector is designated as 'varied', as patents were important in facilitating collusion between some equipment suppliers to raise prices (see the example of automatic telephone exchange equipment in Chapter 12).

*Sources*: Chapters 3–12.

**Table 13.2.** Consumption characteristics of case-study sectors

| Product | First cost | Running cost | Use value | Status value | Substitutes | Priority |
|---|---|---|---|---|---|---|
| Furniture | High | Low | **High** | **High** | Strong | High |
| Housing | High | Medium | **High** | **High** | Strong | High |
| Radios (USA) | **Medium** | Medium | **High** | **High** | Weak | High |
| Radios (UK) | **Medium** | Medium | **High** | **High** | Weak | High |
| White goods (major appliances) | Varied | Medium | Varied | Low | **Strong** | Low |
| Vacuums (USA) | Medium | Medium | Medium | Low | **Medium** | Medium |
| Vacuums (UK) | Medium | Medium | Medium | Low | **Strong** | Low |
| Cars | High | **High** | Medium | High | **Strong** | Low |
| Telephones | Medium | **High** | Low | Medium | **Strong** | Low |

*Sources*: Chapters 3–12.

that had already reached the mass market) had only a moderate use value relative to these other goods and a low status value—as they were usually placed out of sight of the neighbour calling at the door, in the kitchen or under the stairs. The table then looks at substitutes. Furniture and owner-occupied housing had strong substitutes, in the form of second-hand or repurposed furniture and rented housing. Radios had weak substitutes in terms of entertainment than could be instantly accessed, while most live entertainment was much more expensive per hour of use. White goods had strong substitutes—in the form of paid daily domestic help, the coal range (combining the functions of space heating, water heating, and cooking, at a low running cost), and market-based services such as grocers' home delivery services and commercial laundries. Paid help was cheaper in Britain than in the United States, while Britain's higher urbanization increased access to market-based substitutes, making substitution easier in Britain than in America.

Finally the table looks at the priority consumers attached to the various durables. New furniture and modern suburban owner-occupied housing enjoyed high priority, despite the presence of close substitutes. They had both high use and status value and, moreover, sent a clear signal to the wider world that the family was buying into a cluster of modern 'respectable' values based around hygiene, domesticity, and the family.[1] Meanwhile radio enjoyed high use and status value and had only weak substitutes—leading to a rate of household diffusion that was unprecedented for any consumer durable. As the table highlights, these four classes of goods shared the common characteristic of both high use and status value. In contrast, low priority goods did not rank highly in either of these categories (with the exception of the car, where its high status value was outweighed by exceptionally heavy running costs). Moreover, in Britain these goods faced strong substitutes, so it is hardly surprising that households accorded them low priority.

---

[1] Jan De Vries, *The Industrious Revolution: Consumer Behaviour and the Household Economy, 1650 to the Present* (Cambridge: Cambridge University Press, 2008), 189.

**Table 13.3.** Marketing characteristics of case-study sectors

| Product | Price mark-ups | Branding | Dominant value chains | Dominant distribution channel | Credit | Diffusion |
|---|---|---|---|---|---|---|
| Furniture | High | Strong | Retailer-led | Retailer | **Liberal** | Rapid |
| Housing | Low | Weak | Integrated | Direct/agent | **Liberal** | Rapid |
| Radios (USA) | Moderate | Strong | Relational | Retailer | Short | Rapid |
| Radios (UK) | Moderate | Strong | Relational | Retailer | Shot | Rapid |
| White goods (major appliances) | Low–moderate | Weak | Retailer-led | Power supplier | Liberal | Slow |
| Vacuums (USA) | High | Strong | Integrated | **Canvasser** | Short | Medium |
| Vacuums (UK) | High | Strong | Integrated | **Canvasser** | Short | Medium |
| Cars | Low | Strong | Relational | Retailer | Short | Slow |
| Telephones | Moderate | Moderate | Integrated | Canvasser | None | Slow |

*Sources*: Chapters 3–12.

Table 13.3 then looks at marketing strategies. Price mark-ups were relatively moderate for all sectors other than furniture (where high mark-ups funded liberal consumer credit) and vacuums (where they financed the extremely high costs of sending an army of door-to-door salesmen to market them to one consumer at a time). Branding was generally strong, with the exception of the telephone (where it improved markedly in the 1930s), housing, and white goods (excluding vacuums)—where many families were guided by the power company's recommendation or stocking policy, rather than the manufacturers' brand name.

The next column examines value chains, which have been simplified to focus on the relationships between production and distribution. In housing, vacuums, and telephones, there was a strong degree of integration between production and distribution. In furniture and power-hungry white goods, retailer-driven value chains predominated, run respectively by the high street furniture chain stores and the power supply companies—which made the key decisions regarding what goods would be offered to the public, and on what prices and credit terms. Retailer dominance was particularly strong in furniture, where most suppliers were reduced to the status of contractors. Meanwhile in radios and cars relational value chains were developed with independent franchised retailers which were offered a variety of incentives and support to conform to the manufacturer's retail policy. These were sectors where after-sales service was particularly important, and manufacturers placed a premium on dealers who would offer a good level of service, stock replacement parts, and refrain from price-cutting, either overtly or through generous trade-in or HP terms.

All the sectors examined were mainly or wholly conducted without the presence of the conventional wholesaler and his mark-up (even in cars, where 'main dealers' conducted both wholesale and retail functions). Furniture, radios, and cars were sold mainly through retailers; houses were sold either by the builder's direct salesforce and/or through estate agents; vacuums and phones were sold mainly through canvassers; and power companies used a mix of canvassers and showrooms to sell major appliances. Credit liberalization is shown to have applied only to a minority of the sectors examined, with car, vacuum, and radio firms all being careful to avoid competitively liberalizing credit terms. The exceptions are housing and furniture (where liberal credit was essential to 'affordability') and white goods sold through power companies, which were more interested in making money on the power the appliances consumed than on their direct sales.

Motor vehicles had a similar problem of affordability to furniture and housing, but did not follow their path of progressively liberalizing credit (though British HP terms were markedly more liberal than in the United States). There are obvious reasons for this. Cars are notoriously vulnerable to theft, or to being written off in crashes. More importantly, high running costs placed a limit on affordability that could not be seriously reduced even by markedly longer HP contracts.

Finally, the table looks at diffusion rates, with the key drivers of diffusion in previous columns (and in Table 13.2) being highlighted. High use and status value gave housing and furniture particularly high priority, while liberal consumer credit markedly lowered the affordability hurdle, thus culminating in rapid diffusion (especially given that for these goods purchase was strongly bunched around the new household formation stage of the family life cycle). Radios also offered particularly high use value to the consumer and—despite the impact of patent royalties in raising prices—were sufficiently cheap to be affordable even on conventional HP terms, again resulting in rapid diffusion.

In contrast, white goods had relatively low value to the consumer (particularly from a status angle) and close substitutes that were price competitive. They thus enjoyed low priority and diffused only slowly. Vacuum cleaners might have followed the same path, except for the innovation of door-to-door sales by salesmen trained by the manufacturers, who used hard-sell tactics to 'push' their products to consumers who had not previously accorded them high priority. In contrast, the power supply companies sought to develop long-term relationships with households and thus generally avoided high-pressure tactics. High-pressure canvassing enabled vacuum manufacturers to achieve medium levels of diffusion despite selling goods that consumers accorded low priority, paving the way for generations of door-to-door salesmen who would harass housewives with offers of double glazing, encyclopaedias, and other goods that they hadn't known they had needed.

## DRIVERS OF THE CONSUMER DURABLES REVOLUTION

Richard Tedlow identified three broad phases of marketing in the United States.[2] The first phase constituted fragmented domestic markets, owing to the absence of an integrated transport and communications infrastructure, which generally prevented the development of national brands and national advertising. Profit maximization

---

[2] Richard S. Tedlow, *New and Improved: The Story of Mass Marketing in America* (Oxford: Heinemann, 1990).

thus often involved what later became known as a 'skimming strategy'—keeping margins and prices high and serving only higher-income customers. The second phase, which Tedlow dates from the closing years of the nineteenth century, saw the creation of a national mass market, owing to the completion of the railroad and telegraph network.

Tedlow found that 'mass production demanded mass marketing'.[3] In his second phase firms were able to capitalize on scale economies and switch from a high-margin strategy to a 'penetration strategy', selling as many units as possible and making profits on volume rather than margins. This phase witnessed the rise of giant firms—sometimes manufacturers and sometimes retailers—that vigorously promoted their brands via national marketing and coordinated their value chains in order to reduce supply bottlenecks and increase the chain's systemic efficiency. Tedlow's third phase saw the development of market segmentation, with manufacturers differentiating their products to meet the different requirements of, and values placed on them by, different market segments. This phase emerged at different times for different markets, being pioneered in automobiles during the 1920s but not becoming important in some sectors until the 1950s.[4]

One of the key findings of this book is that in Britain mass marketing often preceded true mass production—reflecting Britain's much smaller geographical size and higher population density (which had led to the emergence of national markets well before 1914). The furniture chain stores that reached out to a broad working-class market from the 1920s typically contracted out their orders to a variety of large and small retailers, often for the same designs. Similarly the mass marketing of modern suburban homes was undertaken against the background of a fragmented housing development sector, which still used essentially craft methods. Radios and white goods were more standardized in design, but were not produced on 'Fordist' mass production lines—with special-purpose machinery taking the place of skilled labour—either in Britain or the United States. The extremely high tooling-up costs for such machinery made it uneconomic at this time, especially given that most assembly tasks in sectors such as radios could be undertaken cost-effectively by unskilled or semi-skilled labour using hand operations or simple, general-purpose tools.[5] Of the British case studies examined here, only in cars is there evidence of strong manufacturing scale economies, though even here the costs of Fordist methods generally proved prohibitive, given the size of the British market.

While Fordist mass production technologies were not appropriate to the nature of the production processes for these industries (or, for cars, the size of the British market), there were other instances where either diffusion and/or consumer welfare was limited by factors over which producers (at least those that dominated their industry value chains) had real discretion. High radio patent royalties (supported

[3] Ibid., 18.     [4] Ibid., 4–8 and 345–8.
[5] See Peter Scott and Nicholas Ziebarth, 'The Determinants of Plant Survival in the U.S. Radio Equipment Industry during the Great Depression', *Journal of Economic History*, 75 (2015), 1097–127.

by a socio-legal system that placed almost no constraints on patent holders from exploiting their monopoly position) drove up the costs of radio sets, both directly and by encouraging expensive innovation to reduce patent fees. This had relatively little impact on radio diffusion rates—given the great value people placed on their entertainment services—but did act to raise costs to the consumer. Actions by the radio trade to block low-cost radio formats, such as the midget radio, and to hamper the growth of radio relay services, had similar impacts. Britain's slow adoption of standardization for electrical components and for mains voltage (again influenced by its strong socio-legal tradition of non-interference in private property) had a more general impact in slowing the diffusion of electrical goods—as a unified national market required unified national standards.

There was also active state obstruction to the growth of some durables sectors. The Treasury raised costs and reduced consumer utility (as reflected in quality of service) for those durables which required state-funded infrastructure provision—cars and telephones—in order to minimize domestic spending commitments that might get in the way of its international priorities. This was achieved by heavy car and petrol taxes, plus high telephone charges (relative to other industrialized countries), together with persistent attempts to severely constrain government road and telephone infrastructure investment to very low levels (when judged against either other countries with similar per capita incomes, or the revenue government received from these sectors).

Meanwhile aggressive door-to-door selling in the vacuum cleaner sector boosted sales (especially during the early stage of diffusion), but encouraged opportunistic behaviour by salesmen that led to heavy costs for consumers who fell foul of their sharp practice. Even in the absence of fraud, assertive door-to-door selling had a negative welfare impact in that it persuaded people to buy goods that they did not consider to be a high priority before the salesman's call (and, in many cases, after the salesman had left with their signature on the contract). Moreover, the very high costs of this form of marketing greatly reduced value for money to the consumer compared to goods sold through conventional retail channels.

Yet this study has shown that the demand side of the durables diffusion equation was generally at least as important as the supply side. One of our key aims has been to discern whether there was a clear shift in consumer preferences in favour of durables, even after taking account of the 'price' impacts of credit liberalization. This was certainly the case, but—given the tight budgets on which most households were working—the 'revolution' was concentrated on those goods towards the top of the priority list. This mainly involved modern housing, furniture, and radio sets—together with a few other items not examined in this study that offered great utility relative to their cost (such as electric lighting and bicycles). Housing and furniture were items that both involved very high costs and could be bought in a range of quantities (if housing is viewed in terms of floor and garden space) and qualities, while consumers' choices in these areas were integral to demonstrations of status and 'distinction', both between the working and middle classes and within various segments of those classes. Households across the 'mass market' income spectrum thus typically invested heavily in them relative to their incomes, with even lower-middle-class families often perceiving their budgets to be strained by their acquisition.

Paying off the house mortgage and HP instalments on furniture and a radio might fully commit a new household's finances for four or more years, by which time they would typically have several dependent children and thus face a new 'crisis' of expenditure. Under these circumstances it is hardly surprising that the consumer durables revolution did not generally extend to items such as power-hungry white goods (with the exception of the gas cooker), let alone telephones and cars. Fundamentally, there was still a very strong income constraint on household choices, which made expanding durables purchases beyond a few high priority goods difficult even for people with stable and relatively well-paid jobs, such as teachers, commercial travellers, and clerks.

Britain enjoyed relatively rapid diffusion of those goods people prioritized— modern suburban housing, new suites of furniture, and radio entertainment, which diffused markedly faster than could be explained by changes in real incomes or relative prices. Conversely, in contrast to their US counterparts, they largely rejected refrigerators, washing machines, cars, and phones, which offered less value for money, especially given the presence of acceptable (if imperfect) cheaper substitutes. Such substitution was much weaker in the United States, as fewer people enjoyed access to public transport to and from their place of work, relatively cheap domestic labour, local commercial laundry services, or shops that would deliver provisions on the day they were ordered.

## CONSTRAINTS ON AND IMPACTS OF THE CONSUMER DURABLES REVOLUTION

In retrospect the surprising thing is not how limited but how extensive Britain's inter-war consumer durables revolution was, given the unfavourable macroeconomic background. This was an era of mass unemployment. The Great Depression of 1929–32 was a worldwide phenomenon, but much of the unemployment of the 1920s was inflicted on the British people by its own government's policy of severe deflation to restore and then support Britain's return to the gold standard at an over-valued pre-war parity.

Britain had come out of the First World War with substantial war debts, while war finance had necessitated the liquidation of a large part of its overseas investment portfolio, seriously weakening Britain's invisible balance and role as international creditor. Meanwhile, Britain's established patterns of exports—dominated by international financial services and shipping, together with its 'staple industries' of coal, textiles, iron and steel, and shipbuilding—had also been severely disrupted. This made it very difficult for the UK to continue its previous role of managing the international gold standard, with sterling as the world's key currency. Meanwhile the United States and, to a lesser extent, France, had emerged as important financial creditors, with money markets competing with London. However, neither the United States nor France proved willing to prioritize the gold standard over their own internal stability, either individually or in cooperation with Britain. Meanwhile, the war had represented a huge shock to the international financial system, disrupting patterns of international trade and finance in such a way that the system had become inherently much more difficult to manage.[6]

Nevertheless, the 1918 Cunliffe Committee on Currency and Foreign Exchanges after the war (which was dominated by banking interests) recommended that Britain should take action to re-establish the gold standard through deflationary policy—reducing government spending and raising interest rates. However, war-time inflation, followed by a vigorous post-war boom, had raised prices to such a level that deflationary policies would have to be so severe as to risk massive unemployment and serious social unrest. Government waited until November 1919 (by which time fears of serious social unrest during demobilization had subsided) before raising interest rates, cutting expenditure, and thereby generating a major slump. Despite the onset of mass unemployment, deflation was continued to pave the way for restoration of the gold standard at its pre-war parity in April 1925. Meanwhile unemployment among workers subject to national insurance had rocketed to 17.0 per cent in 1921 and only fell below 10 per cent for a single year during the rest of the decade (1927, when it dipped to 9.7 per cent).[7]

Following the restoration of the gold standard in April 1925, Britain struggled with a substantially over-valued currency that hit its price-sensitive staple industries and the northern regions of Britain that were reliant on them, with particular severity. This marked the start of the 'north–south' divide in unemployment and prosperity, that has remained a feature of British economic development ever since. Sterling and the UK balance of payments came under repeated pressure, which was intensified following the onset of the international depression from autumn 1929. This culminated in a collapse of international confidence in sterling in August 1931, leading the new National Government to abandon the gold standard on 19 September.

Leaving the gold standard precipitated one of the strongest recoveries from the world depression of any major industrialized country, though Bank of England and Treasury officials never gave up their hopes of a return to gold—and thus continued their opposition to increased public spending on infrastructure such as roads or the telephone network. They also vigorously opposed rearmament expenditure, which both undermined Britain's credibility in negotiations to seek a peaceful settlement with Germany and left Britain ill-equipped to defend itself when war finally broke out. Even as late as 1938 Britain's defence expenditure was less than 7 per cent of national income, compared to Germany's 23 per cent.[8]

High inter-war unemployment, especially in Britain's northern regions, is likely to have had a major negative impact on consumer durables expenditure, especially

---

[6] For a fuller discussion, see Peter Scott, *Triumph of the South: A Regional Economic History of Britain During the Early Twentieth Century* (Aldershot: Ashgate, 2007), 69–70.

[7] W. R. Garside, *British Unemployment 1919–1939: A Study in Public Policy* (Cambridge: Cambridge University Press, 1990), 5.

[8] Mark Thomas, 'Rearmament and Economic Recovery in the Late 1930s', *Economic History Review*, 36 (1983), 552–79 (554).

for the working classes. In addition to the large numbers unemployed, many more lived in real fear of unemployment, either because they worked in sectors connected with the staple export industries, or lived in regions where high unemployment spilled over into sectors dependent on the local economy. Data on regional patterns of consumer durables diffusion are very scarce (apart from cars and phones, which were almost entirely restricted to the middle classes). However, the data in Figure 4.2, on private sector house-building, provide a good indication of the north–south divide. New inter-war private houses, as a proportion of each British region's 1931 population, varied from 9.96 per cent in the South East to only 2.13 per cent in Scotland, 3.72 per cent in Wales, and 5.00 per cent in England's northern region.

Yet despite this, the consumer durables boom did have profound impacts on the lives of many, if not most, members of the lower-middle and working classes. The radio was present in almost every home (apart from, perhaps, those of agricultural workers and the long-term unemployed) by 1939, opening up a world of popular and classical music, comedy, drama, news, and documentaries that were now accessible even to the illiterate and were free from the savage political bias of most popular newspapers. The bicycle provided cheap personal local transport, while new suites of furniture, available on the 'never never' allowed people to create a modern domestic environment that was superficially similar in appearance to that of more affluent households—at least in their front room.

Meanwhile, there was a major boom in modern suburban housing, typically with three bedrooms, integrated bathrooms and water heating systems, mains electricity, and gardens. While only 18 per cent of British (non-agricultural) working-class families were owner-occupiers by 1939, working-class participation was substantial relative to the number of people forming new households during the 1930s—house purchase generally occurring within a couple of years of marriage. Many more families experienced moves to housing with broadly similar characteristics, on suburban council estates. A recent study has estimated that around 25 per cent of non-agricultural British working-class households moved to modern suburban housing over the inter-war years, with 13 per cent taking the municipal housing route, 9 per cent the owner-occupation route, and perhaps 3 per cent renting privately developed suburban houses.[9] Middle-class participation was much more substantial—though this probably had a weaker impact on lifestyles, as the homes they moved from already had larger rooms, internal plumbing, and (sometimes) gardens.

Together, the new consumer durables (especially new suburban housing) created a distinctively 'modern' lifestyle, based around domesticity, the family, hygiene, mobility, and longer-term time horizons. Access to this lifestyle was unequal across the classes, according to such factors as education and level and stability of income. However, distinctions between the working and lower-middle classes had become much less profound than was the case in 1914, reflected in dress (with the suits

---

[9] Peter Scott, *The Making of the Modern British Home: The Suburban Semi and Family Life between the Wars* (Oxford: Oxford University Press, 2013), 10.

working men bought from Burton's, or the dresses that working-class women purchased from Marks & Spencer, being superficially similar to those worn by their middle-class counterparts); aspirations (within the constraints of their incomes and class status); and even the topics on which people could comfortably converse. In addition to the profound effect of the radio in giving people a shared experience of information, entertainment, and (to the extent to which it was culturally accessible) education, other areas of media such as the expanding women's press, also brought values and lifestyles that would have earlier been restricted to middle-class readers to large numbers of working-class people by the 1930s.

Despite the mass unemployment of the inter-war years, the Britain of 1939 was a country of markedly higher real wages, a dramatically improved housing stock, liberal consumer credit, and an increasing business philosophy that 'Mr Everyman' was the target market, rather than 'Mr Middle Class'. Britain had also developed a strong position as a manufacturer of consumer durables—second only to the United States—with the world's second-largest motor vehicle and radio industries, the first regular high-definition television service (from 1936), over 70 per cent of households wired for electricity (in England and Wales), and an expanding, if—by American standards—low diffusion of electrical appliances.[10] Britain had established itself as one of the world's leading nations in terms of both access to and production of consumer durables. What could possibly go wrong?

## EPILOGUE: BRITAIN'S POST-WAR CONSUMER DURABLES INDUSTRIES—DEATH BY WHITEHALL?

The early post-war years are often viewed as something of a golden age for the working classes in Britain, partly due to, the creation of a comprehensive welfare state by the 1945–51 Labour governments which was followed by an era of mass affluence under the Conservative administrations of 1951–64. In reality, by the 1960s Britain was falling behind leading industrialized countries in consumer durables ownership. For example, in 1957 less than 10 per cent of British homes had refrigerators, compared to 11 per cent in Italy, 12 per cent in France, 14 per cent in West Germany, 25 per cent in Denmark, 26 per cent in New Zealand, and rates of 50 per cent or more in Sweden, Australia, Canada, and the United States.[11] Even in cars, where Britain had been the world's second-largest producer during the 1930s (and where long lifespans masked Britain's deteriorating relative position), ownership in 1965 stood at only 164 per 1,000

---

[10] For the diffusion of electric wiring, see Sue Bowden and Avner Offer, 'Household Appliances and the Use of Time: The United States and Britain since the 1920s', *Economic History Review*, 47 (1994), 725–48 (745).

[11] Jonathan Rees, *Refrigeration Nation: A History of Ice, Appliances, and Enterprise in America* (Baltimore, MD: Johns Hopkins University Press, 2013), 179.

population, compared to 387 in the United States, 268 in Canada, 272 in New Zealand, 254 in Australia, 232 in Sweden, and 197 in France.[12]

Contrary to some popular accounts, there had never been a consensus among policy-makers that post-war economic policy should prioritize domestic reconstruction and Keynesian full-employment policy. An influential coalition of Bank of England and Treasury officials (including Cameron Cobbold, deputy governor of the Bank of England from 1945–9 and governor from 1949–61) advocated an economic policy based around restoring sterling's credit-worthiness—in the face of Britain's huge war debts—through savage deflation. John Maynard Keynes criticized this group for prioritizing international 'obligations' over the wartime commitment to build a fairer society—which would amount to a repetition the 1920s gold standard episode—though his direct influence was ended with his untimely death in April 1946.[13] However, in the immediate post-war period the Bank of England's 'sterling first' policy was seen as flying in the face of political realities by both the Labour and Conservative parties—which was dramatically confirmed by Labour's landslide 1945 election victory. Cobbold and his colleagues were left to bide their time until the political climate turned in their favour.

They had to wait six years, until a Conservative government was elected in October 1951, with a commitment to replace planning and regulation with a more free-market approach. Yet market liberalization did not extend to consumer durables. The Korean War provided the Treasury and Bank of England with an opportunity to introduce restrictions on domestic sales of durables, to economize on metals, and switch production to armaments. This was achieved by new regulations on HP sales (limiting contract lengths and minimum deposits) in the January 1952 budget.[14] These were used in conjunction with changes in Purchase Tax (a sales tax that was originally introduced in 1940 and became increasingly focused on consumer durables) to depress home demand for household durables and vehicles.

By the mid-1950s the Treasury recognized that defence and resource-saving arguments in favour of HP controls were no longer valid.[15] However, the Bank of England and the Treasury's Overseas Finance Division regarded the controls as particularly useful tools of 'financial repression' to cut consumer demand at any given interest rate. This assisted their forceful championship of a policy of sterling liberalization (and eventual full convertibility) that would require domestic demand to be periodically squeezed in order to avoid runs on sterling, given Britain's high debts and low currency reserves. The Bank now proved successful in pushing this agenda, becoming so confident that the burden of any pressure on sterling could be addressed via measures to depress domestic demand that, even

[12] B. R. Mitchell, *International Historical Statistics: Europe 1750–1993* (London: Macmillan, 1998), 89–90 and 739–42; B. R. Mitchell, *International Historical Statistics: The Americas, 1750–1988* (London: Macmillan, 1993), 62–3 and 590–2; B. R. Mitchell, *International Historical Statistics: Africa, Asia & Oceania, 1750–1988* (London: Macmillan, 1998), 66 and 765.

[13] See Scott Newton, 'Keynesianism, Sterling Convertibility, and British Reconstruction 1940–1952', in Ranald Michie and Philip Williamson (eds.), *The British Government and the City of London in the Twentieth Century* (Cambridge: Cambridge University Press, 2004), 257–75 (262–3).

[14] F. R. Oliver, *The Control of Hire Purchase* (London: Allen & Unwin, 1961), 177; Hansard, 29 January 1952, Cols. 58–9.

[15] TNA, T233/1587, 'Control of Credit for Hire Purchase', memorandum, 28 May 1954.

without overseas support, it moved to substantially liberalize controls on the transferability of external sterling holdings in March 1954, while also reopening the London gold market. This increased Britain's vulnerability to runs on the pound by creating a large market for transferable sterling, traded at an observable and unprotected exchange rate. Moreover, external holders were particularly sensitive to any downward pressure on sterling that might lead to their assets being blocked unless they converted them into a safer currency.[16] So yet more financial repression was required, to maintain their confidence.

HP regulations were subject to frequent changes, which durables manufacturers were not informed of in advance. Controls were suspended in July 1954, reintroduced in February 1955, tightened substantially in July 1955 and again in February 1956 (when they were extended to furniture for the first time). Then on 15 September 1958, with sterling strong and recession looming, HP controls were relaxed, followed by their suspension six weeks later. However, liberalization was short-lived. The Chancellor had responded to rising unemployment and a strong 1959 balance of payments by what proved to be a recklessly expansionist budget that (like many economic adjustments of the period) came too late in the economic cycle to have the desired impact.[17] In consequence HP controls were reimposed at the end of April 1960, precipitating a severe contraction in new HP credit for durable goods.[18] Even the Treasury (which typically sought to downplay the impact on HP controls) was forced to privately admit that, 'The situation is potentially a serious one... production in the next twelve months... [could] be at a rate 40–50 per cent lower than the levels to which it had been reduced in July and August.'[19] HP and Purchase Tax continued to be used as key instruments of macroeconomic 'stop–go' policy during the 1960s (though with less drastic changes in the intensity of controls).

Consumer durables manufacturers and retailers resented what they saw as the arbitrary designation of their sectors for demand management, but were particularly aggrieved by the sudden and unanticipated changes to HP restrictions and Purchase Tax rates that played havoc with production schedules. Heavy involvement in munitions production during the Second World War had accelerated the introduction of mass production techniques in these sectors, making economies of scale much more important to efficiency and international competitiveness.[20] However, such arguments cut no ice with a Treasury that subordinated the needs of domestic industry to its major long-term aims of defending sterling and restoring Britain to its former status as a leading financial and trading nation. The consumer

---

[16] William A. Allen, *Monetary Policy and Financial Repression in Britain, 1951–59* (Basingstoke: Palgrave Macmillan, 2014), 46 and 72.

[17] Samuel Brittan, *Steering the Economy: The Role of the Treasury* (London: Secker & Warburg, 1969), 139–41.

[18] Source: Aubrey Silberston, 'Hire Purchase Controls and the Demand for Cars', *Economic Journal*, 73 (1963), 32–53 (51), based on Board of Trade data.

[19] TNA, T230/660, 'The Consumer Durables Industries and the BREMA Memorandum', undated note, c. October 1960.

[20] Margaret Wray, 'Household Durables and the "Squeeze"', *Westminster Bank Review* (Aug. 1957), 5–9 (5–6); TNA, BT233/1586, 'The Permanent Control of Hire Purchase Terms', memorandum (n.d., c. 1954).

durables sectors thus persistently failed to secure a stable tax and HP regulation framework suitable for mass production, or even long-term planning. As a June 1960 Federation of British Industries (FBI) memorandum noted:

> production over the past decade in the domestic appliance industry, which is particularly vulnerable to such [credit restriction] measures, presents a bewildering pattern, reflecting the violent changes in demand...with slumps following booms in seemingly endless rotation...Artificial booms...created by the release of pent-up demand, are as much to be deplored as slumps.[21]

Government officials also privately acknowledged this. A 1963 working party on HP controls noted that when they were lifted production could not be expanded quickly enough to meet pent-up demand, leading to a boom in imports. Conversely, additions to capacity to meet rising demand could prove worthless following their unanticipated reimposition. Meanwhile the resulting failure to achieve economies of scale raised unit costs and hit competitiveness both at home and overseas.[22]

One notable victim was the motor vehicle industry, which accounted for almost one million workers in 1960 (including components, garage, and repair servicing), around 5 per cent of industrial production, and 16 per cent of UK visible exports.[23] In addition to very strict HP controls compared to other leading producers, the 60 per cent Purchase Tax on the wholesale price of cars (equivalent to around 50 per cent of the retail price) was far higher than the sales taxes on cars imposed by the major European car-producing nations in 1957 (6 per cent in Germany; 7 per cent in Italy; and 24 per cent in France), while the burden of other car taxes was also high by international standards.[24]

The various 'stop' phases of government stop–go policy had seen increases in HP controls on cars (sometimes in conjunction with Purchase Tax rises) that had left the industry working well below capacity and generated substantial unemployment and short-time working.[25] They had also substantially raised unit costs; in 1957 Ford estimated that home sales of British cars were around 25 per cent less (and overall production 14 per cent less) owing to Purchase Tax alone—sufficient to increase British unit production costs by at least 10 per cent. These problems were seen as particularly ominous given Britain's proposed participation in the European Free Trade Area—which threatened more vigorous competition in home

---

[21] MRC, 200/F/3/E3/10/1, 'Hire Purchase Controls', unsigned memorandum, 29 June 1960.

[22] See, for example, TNA, T230/660, draft report of the Working Party on Hire Purchase Controls, 22 Oct. 1963, 12.

[23] TNA, T230/2310, note on representations from the Society of Motor Manufacturers and Traders, 23 Feb. 1961.

[24] TNA, BT213/72, Ford Motor Co., 'Purchase Tax on Motor Vehicles', memorandum submitted to the Board of Trade, Feb. 1957.

[25] TNA, T229/724, Society of Motor Manufacturers and Traders, 'Purchase Tax', memorandum, 24 Sept. 1952; Bank of England Archives, C40/690, 'Short-Term Working in the Motor Industry', unsigned note, 5 Mar. 1956; TNA, T230/2310, note on representations from the Society of Motor Manufacturers and Traders, 23 Feb. 1961.

markets.[26] Similar problems were evident in household durables. In September 1960 the FBI's director-general informed the Board of Trade that, as a result of intensified HP controls, domestic sales of leading durables manufacturers had fallen by 30–40 per cent.[27]

One standard Treasury response to industry complaints involved exhortations to focus on exports. In fact, HP restrictions were widely regarded as acting to depress exports and (during boom phases of the stop–go cycle) encourage imports. Domestic producers lacked the capacity to meet the sudden surges in demand when controls were eased, while the periodic imposition of restrictions made British goods less competitive by increasing unit costs and slowing new model development.[28]

Despite strong evidence of these devastating impacts, Treasury officials took comfort in the buoyant state of national employment.[29] However, within the affected industries the restrictions were having substantial negative impacts on employment, labour productivity, and labour relations. For example, employment in furniture and upholstery fell from 142,000 in 1954 to 125,700 by April 1958.[30] Moreover, in the domestic appliances and motor vehicle sectors much unemployment was disguised by hoarding skilled labour.[31] Then in boom phases firms were often forced to rely extensively on overtime to meet orders, given their depressed capacity.

In the television industry (where Britain had been a leading pioneer) HP restrictions and Purchase Tax distorted home demand in favour of lower model standards, such as smaller screen sizes, that were often unsuitable for export markets. Pressure to provide lower-cost sets also led British manufacturers to produce models of less attractive cosmetic design and fewer 'features' than were demanded in major overseas markets.[32] Moreover, the frequent unanticipated changes in the restrictions made it very difficult to plan output, achieve economies of scale, or sell the full production runs of current models before they became obsolete (given the rapid pace of technical change in the sector)—problems that led to EMI's exit from television production and the demise of Ekco, Murphy, and, eventually, Pye, as independent firms.[33]

---

[26] TNA, BT213/72, Ford Motor Co., 'Purchase tax on motor vehicles', memorandum submitted to the Board of Trade, Feb. 1957.

[27] MRC, 200/F3/E3/10/1, letter, Sir Norman Kipping, FBI Director-General, to Sir Richard Powell, Board of Trade, 15 Sept. 1960.

[28] TNA, BT258/437, draft Board of Trade evidence on Hire Purchase for the Radcliffe Committee, 6 Sept. 1957.

[29] TNA, T230/660, note by R. L. Hall, 13 Oct. 1960.

[30] TNA, BT258/437, 'Hire Purchase Control on the Furniture Industry', draft memorandum by President, Board of Trade, 9 July 1958.

[31] MRC, 292/660/91/2, 'Hire Purchase', Labour Party Study Group on Control of Industry memorandum, Mar. 1958; TNA, BT103/728, 'House of Commons: Hire Purchase', memorandum, 10 Mar. 1956.

[32] MRC, Mss. 200/F/3/E3/10/4, 'Hire Purchase Controls—Radio and Television Products. Special Considerations', BREMA memorandum, Sept. 1960.

[33] For a more detailed discussion, see Peter Scott and James T. Walker, 'The Impact of "Stop-Go" Demand Management Policy on Britain's Consumer Durables Industries, 1952–1965', *Economic History Review* (forthcoming).

The credit squeezes had a number of lasting impacts on the consumer durables sectors, including deteriorating industrial relations. As a 1960 FBI memorandum noted, when controls were eased the resulting spikes in production fostered 'exceptionally high earnings accentuated by incentives and overtime which...inculcates a sense of false values and creates a most difficult situation when earnings are subsequently depressed...it is virtually impossible to maintain good relations, sound incentive schemes, or to organise satisfactory training and promotion if the company is forced by violent changes in demand to a policy of "hire and fire"'.[34] This cycle of overtime and short-time working has been identified as an important factor fostering the labour militancy that became a growing feature of the auto sector from this time.[35]

Stop–go policy (together with the Treasury and Bank of England's general opposition to public infrastructure investment) also had other impacts on Britain's durables sectors. For example, in addition to high UK Purchase Tax, vehicle taxes, and petrol taxes (relative to other industrialized countries), the British car industry was also impeded by a severe reduction in road transport investment, even compared to the 1930s.[36] A 1957 official survey found that the UK had the lowest proportion of total investment in transport and communications of Western European nations examined, despite having the highest traffic densities in Europe.[37] This was especially true for roads investment. Despite the fact that in 1954 the number of vehicles per road mile in Britain was by far the highest in Europe at 22.3,[38] in 1955 the UK spent 0.09 per cent of national income on roads, compared to 0.69 per cent by France and 0.75 per cent by West Germany.[39] Meanwhile UK annual road investment per head of population during 1953–5 was £0.27, compared with figures for other Western European countries ranging from £1.10 (Italy) to £5.40 (Finland).[40] The Treasury appreciated the economic case for roads expenditure, but found this easier to block than other areas of expenditure that enjoyed higher political priority.[41]

Stop–go policy also severely restricted house-building (both private and municipal). The Conservatives' very public pledge to build 300,000 houses per year was quietly abandoned during the mid-1950s credit squeeze. Council house-building was restricted by reducing the loan sanction for local authority borrowing for this purpose and raising the interest rates at which they could borrow. Meanwhile, the Treasury covertly restricted building society mortgage lending, by keeping building

[34] MRC, 200/F3/E3/10/1, 'Hire Purchase Controls', unsigned memorandum, 29 June 1960.

[35] Jonathan Wood, *Wheels of Misfortune: The Rise and Fall of the British Motor Industry* (London: Sidgwick & Jackson, 1988), 97.

[36] See Peter Scott, 'Public Sector Investment and Britain's Post-War Economic Performance: A Case Study of Roads Policy', *Journal of European Economic History*, 34 (2005), 391–418.

[37] TNA, T230/351, 'Economic Survey of Europe in 1956—part II European Transport Problems', Statistical Working Party on Long-Term Survey of Transport memorandum, 9 Apr. 1957.

[38] John Tetlow and Anthony Goss, *Homes, Towns and Traffic*, 2nd edn. (London: Faber, 1968), 73.

[39] 'Speeding the Road Programme', *Financial Times* (30 Apr. 1957).

[40] TNA, T228/621, 'Road Investment in an Expanding Economy', memorandum submitted to Chancellor of Exchequer by British Road Federation, Nov. 1958.

[41] TNA, T229/686, J. A. C. Robertson to Mr Blaker, 8 Apr. 1954.

society interest rates (for deposits and mortgages) sufficiently low, relative to other rates, that building societies were starved of funds and found it necessary to ration lending in order to maintain adequate reserves. This policy—which was never made public—continued during the 1960s and 1970s, producing a severe reduction in long-term housing investment, relative to both other Western European countries and to Britain's record in the 1930s.[42]

The cumulative impacts of HP restrictions, punitive Purchase Tax rates, and other measures designed to rein in consumer expenditure on durables and housing impacted most severely on working-class households, whose access to consumer durables and decent housing was strongly influenced by their prices and credit terms. It was estimated in 1959 that consumer HP debt in Britain amounted to only around £12 per capita, a much lower figure than in the United States (£49), Australia (£32), or Canada (£33).[43] As a Board of Trade memorandum acknowledged, restrictions largely impacted through, 'suddenly making it more difficult for poor people to obtain goods...when the same goods were readily available to people able to pay cash', or to white-collar workers with access to bank loans or department store accounts.[44] In effect, it was the poorest sections of society who were having to shoulder most of the burden of economic adjustment so that Britain could have a strong sterling and a rapidly growing financial services sector.

The persisting consequences of Britain's policy of active discrimination against consumer durables producers contributed substantially to their relative decline, culminating in an absolute decline from the 1970s. This, in turn, had negative impacts on the regions where these sectors were concentrated: most notably the West Midlands, where GDP per capita fell from 104 per cent of the British average in 1961 to 89.5 per cent in 2001.[45] Judgement on the wider long-term impacts of these policies depends on whether an economy strongly biased towards a narrow base of financial and business services and related industries is inherently more unstable than the more broadly based economies of Germany, France, and Italy—which have consistently supported their manufacturing sectors. The next financial crisis may provide us with at least a partial answer to this question.

[42] Peter Scott and James T. Walker, 'The Origins of the British Housing Crisis: "Stop-Go" Policy and the Restriction of Private Residential House-Building', unpublished paper.

[43] Ralph Harris, Arthur Seldon, and Margot Naylor, *Hire Purchase in a Free Society* (London: IEA, 1959), 54.

[44] TNA, BT233/1586, 'The Permanent Control of Hire Purchase Terms', memorandum (n.d., *c.*1954); T230/660, draft report of the Working Party on Hire Purchase Controls, 22 Oct. 1963, 17–18; BT258/477, note by Board of Trade, I.M. 2, 9 Sept. 1957.

[45] See Frank Greary and Tom Stark, 'Whatever Happened to Regional Inequality in Britain in the Twentieth Century?', *Economic History Review*, 69 (2016), 215–28 (221).

# Bibliography

## ARCHIVAL SOURCES (TOGETHER WITH ABBREVIATIONS USED)

**Netherlands**
Philips Company Archives, Eindhoven [PCA].

**United Kingdom**
Bank of England Archives [BEA], files C40/690; EID9/35; and SMT5/50.
Barclays Bank Group Archive, Wythenshawe [BBGA] Class 1023, Woolwich Building Society papers.
Bexley Local Studies and Archive Centre, London [Bexley Local Studies], oral history transcripts and estates brochures.
Bodleian Library, Oxford, Biellik collection.
Bodleian Library, Oxford, Gordon Bussey Collection [Bodleian, Bussey].
Bodleian Library, Oxford, John Johnson Collection.
British Library, Charles R. Groff, *Observations of Management: Confidential Report for Electrolux Executives* 1, no. 1 (1932).
British Library, National Sound Archive, Millennium Memory Bank recordings.
BT Archive, London [BT Archive], archives and reference library collections.
Building Societies Association Library, London [BSA Library], records of predecessor organizations.
Centre for Oxfordshire Studies, Oxford, oral history collections.
Circa Trust (Construction Industry Resource Centre Archive), Stroud, George Wimpey archives.
Clarks Archive, Street, 2/12, Sampson Clark & Company Ltd, 'Business Development Bulletin. The Motor Car Industry', market research report, 1938.
EMI Archives, London, file, 'Gramophone & Radio Manufacture 1931–37'.
Essex Record Office, oral history collections.
Geffrye Museum Library, London [GM], furniture and appliances brochure collections.
Guildhall Library, London, bound volumes of London Stock Exchange company reports.
Gunnersbury Park Museum, London, ephemera and oral history collections.
Harrods Company Archive, London, records in class HF9/3.
HBOS Archives, Edinburgh, Halifax Building Society papers.
Hertfordshire Archives, Sir Frederic Osborn Archive [HA/SFOA].
Lloyds Bank Archive, S/10/d/3, Augustus Muir and Mair Davies, 'United Dominions Trust. The History of an International Banking and Finance Group', unpublished typescript history.
London Metropolitan Archives [LMA], Papers of the Abbey Road Building Society; County of London Electric Supply Co.; Curry's Ltd.
Manchester Museum of Science and Industry [MMSI], ESI 73, British Electrical Development Association papers; Ms. 1996, Ferranti papers.
Mass Observation Archive, University of Sussex [MOA], Day Surveys and File Reports.
Modern Records Centre, Warwick [MRC], files: 200/F/3/E3/10/1; 200/F/3/E3/10/4; 226/AU/1/1/1-2; 287/36; 292/660/91/2.

Museum of Domestic Design and Architecture, University of Middlesex [MoDA], collections of estate developers' and furniture retailers' promotional literature.

Museum of London Archive, oral history and autobiographical materials.

National Archive for Electrical Science and Technology, London, Sir Walter Charles Puckey papers [NAEST, Puckey papers].

National Archives, Kew [TNA], files in the BT 56, 64, 103, 213, 233, 258; CAB 27; HLG 29, 56; LAB 17; LCO 2; and T 161, 162, 228, 229, 230, 233 classes.

National Art Library, London, trade catalogues collection.

National Gas Archive, Manchester, gas industry archives and trade journal collections.

Nuffield College, Oxford, Nuffield College Social Reconstruction Survey Archive, [NCSRS].

Peter Scott collection (ephemera collection held privately by the author).

Radcliffe Science Library, Oxford, Marconi Archives [RSL, Marconi].

Royal Mail Archives, London, POST 89/36–37, Ullswater Committee papers.

Royal Pharmaceutical Society Library Archives, IRA 1996.417, 'Survey of Retail Organisation and Trends', O. W. Roskill, 5 July 1939.

Southend Museum Service [SOUMS], Ekco papers.

University of East Anglia Archives [UEA], Pritchard papers.

University of Reading, Museum of English Rural Life, J. H. Dunning collection.

Women's Library, London Metropolitan University, Women's Group on Public Welfare papers (this archive has been relocated to the London School of Economics Library since the time of the research).

**United States**

Hagley Museum Library, Wilmington, Delaware [Hagley], MS 2069, RCA Victor records; David Sarnoff Technical Library [Hagley, Sarnoff].

Hoover Historical Center, North Canton, Ohio [HHC], Hoover Company records.

McLean County Museum of History, Bloomington, Illinois, Eureka Williams Electrolux Archive [McLean Eureka Archive].

Smithsonian National Museum of American History, Washington, DC, Lemelson Center Archives, Clark Collection [Smithsonian, Clark].

US National Archives, Washington, DC, records in the RG29 and RG234 classes.

WEB-BASED/DIGITAL SOURCES

BT Archives website <http://www.btplc.com/Thegroup/BTsHistory/1912to1968/1923.htm>.

Gereffi, Gary, 'A Commodity Chains Framework for Analysing Global Industries', in Institute of Development Studies, *Background Notes for Workshop on Spreading the Gains from Globalisation* (Brighton: Institute of Development Studies, 1999) <http://www.ids.ac.uk/ids/global/conf/wkscf.html>.

Kaplinsky, Raphael and Morris, Mike, *A Handbook for Value Chain Research* (Brighton: Institute of Development Studies, 2002) <http://www.ids.ac.uk/ids/global/pdfs/VchNov01.pdf>.

Officer, Lawrence H. and Williamson, Samuel H., 'Six Ways to Compute the Relative Value of a U.K. Dollar Amount, 1270 to Present', MeasuringWorth, 2009 <https://www.measuringworth.com/ukcompare/>.

*Oxford Dictionary of National Biography* <http://www.oxforddnb.com/>: MacCarthy, Fiona, 'Coates, Wells Wintemute (1895–1958)'; MacCarthy, Fiona, 'Russell, Sir (Sydney) Gordon (1892–1980)'; Levy, Paul, 'Cradock, Phyllis Nan Sortain [Fanny] (1909–1994)'.

UK Data Service, SN5085, Peter Scott, 'Analysis of 170 Biographical Accounts of Working Class People Who Moved into Owner-Occupation or Suburban Council Housing during the Inter-War Period, 1919–1939' (2005) <https://discover.ukdataservice.ac.uk/doi/?sn=5085#>.

## UNPUBLISHED THESES AND DISSERTATIONS

Bowden, Sue, 'The Market for Domestic Electric Cookers in the 1930s: A Regional Analysis', PhD thesis (LSE, 1984).

Bundock, J. D., 'Speculative Housebuilding and Some Aspects of the Activities of the Suburban Housebuilder within the Greater London Outer Suburban Areas 1919–1939', MPhil thesis (University of Kent, 1974).

Constable, Lynne, 'An Industry in Transition: The British Domestic Furniture Trade 1914–1939', PhD thesis (Brunel University, 2000).

Eberhart, Douglas E., 'William Henry Hoover: His Life, His Business, His Success', BA thesis (Princeton University, 1985).

Eoyang, Thomas, 'An Economic Study of the Radio Industry in the United States of America', PhD thesis (Columbia University, 1936).

Giles, Margaret Judith, 'Something That Bit Better: Working-Class Women, Domesticity, and "Respectability", 1919–1939', DPhil thesis (University of York, 1989).

Lomax, S. F., 'The Department Store and the Creation of the Spectacle, 1880–1940', PhD thesis (University of Essex, 2005).

McCulloch, A. D., 'Owner-Occupation & Class Struggle: The Mortgage Strikes of 1938–40', PhD thesis (University of Essex, 1983).

Ryan, Deborah, 'The Daily Mail Ideal Home Exhibition and Suburban Modernity, 1908–1951', PhD thesis (University of East London, 1995).

Speight, George, 'Building Society Behaviour and the Mortgage Lending Market in the Interwar Period: Risk-Taking by Mutual Institutions and the Interwar House-Building Boom', DPhil thesis (University of Oxford, 2000).

Wolkonowicz, John Paul, 'The Philco Corporation: Historical Review & Strategic Analysis', MSc dissertation (Alfred P. Sloan School of Management, 1981).

Worden, Suzette A., 'Furniture for the Living Room: An Investigation of the Interaction Between Society, Industry, and Design in Britain from 1919 to 1939', PhD thesis (Brighton Polytechnic, 1980).

## OFFICIAL PUBLICATIONS

**United Kingdom**

Board of Trade, *Final Report on the Fifth Census of Production and the Import Duties Act Enquiry, 1935* (London: HMSO, 1939).

Board of Trade, Working Party Reports, *Furniture* (London: HMSO, 1946).

Board of Trade, *Final Report on the Census of Production for 1948, Volume 4* (London: HMSO, 1952).

Business Statistics Office, *Historical Record of the Census of Production, 1907–70* (London: HMSO, 1978).

Customs and Excise, *Annual Statement of Trade of the United Kingdom, 1939* (London: HMSO, 1940).

Glass, D. V. and Grebenik, E., *The Trend and Pattern of Fertility in Great Britain. A Report on the Family Census of 1946*, Papers of the Royal Commission on Population, Volume 6 (London: HMSO, 1954).

House of Commons, *Parliamentary Debates*, CCCXXX (1937), cols. 731–40.

House of Commons, *Parliamentary Debates*, CDXCV (1952), cols. 58–9.

Imperial Economic Committee, *Twenty-Ninth Report: A Survey of the Trade in Electrical Machinery and Apparatus* (London: HMSO, 1936).

Monopolies Commission, *Thorn Electric Industries Ltd and Radio Rentals Ltd. A Report on the Proposed Merger* (London: HMSO, 1968).

Monopolies and Restrictive Practices Commission, *Report on the Supply of Insulated Electric Wires and Cables* (London: HMSO, 1952).

Parliament, Committee Appointed by the Local Government Board and the Secretary of State for Scotland to Consider Questions of Building Construction in Connection with the Provision of Dwellings for the Working Classes in England and Wales, and Scotland, and Report upon Methods of Securing Economy and Despatch in the Provision of Such Dwellings, *Report* (Cd. 9191 of 1918).

Parliament, Committee of Enquiry on the Post Office, 1932, *Report* (Cmd 4149 of 1932).

Parliament, Committee on Industry and Trade, *Further Factors in Industrial and Commercial Efficiency. Being Part II of a Survey of Industries* (London: HMSO, 1928).


**United States**

Manning, Caroline, 'Fluctuations of Employment in the Radio Industry', *Bulletin of the Women's Bureau*, No. 83 (Washington, DC: USGPO, 1931).

National Recovery Administration, *Code of Fair Competition for the Vacuum Cleaner Manufacturing Industry* (Washington, DC: USGPO, 1934).

Park, William M., *Automotive Industry and Trade of Great Britain and Ireland*, United States Dept. of Commerce, Bureau of Foreign and Domestic Commerce, Trade Promotion Series No. 63 (Washington, DC: USGPO, 1928).

Temporary National Economic Committee, *Investigation of Concentration of Economic Power Monograph No. 1. Price Behavior and Business Policy* (Washington, DC: USGPO, 1940).

U.S. Department of Commerce, *Survey of Current Business*, No. 90 (Feb. 1929).

U.S. Department of Commerce, *Merchandising Problems of Radio Retailers in 1930* (Washington, DC: USGPO, 1931).

U.S. Department of Commerce, *Radio Markets of the World, 1932* (Washington, DC: USGPO, 1932).

U.S. Dept. of Commerce, Bureau of the Census, *Biennial Census of Manufactures* (Washington, DC: USGPO) for 1927 (1930); 1933 (1936); 1935 (1938).

U.S. Department of Commerce, Bureau of the Census, *Fifteenth Census of the United States. Manufactures. 1929, Vol. 2* (Washington, DC: USGPO, 1933).

U.S. Department of Commerce, Bureau of the Census, *Sixteenth Census of the United States: 1940. Census of Business Volume 1. Retail Trade: 1939* (Washington, DC: USGPO, 1943).

U.S. Department of Commerce, Bureau of the Census, *Sixteenth Census of the United States: 1940. Manufacturers 1939, Vols. 1 & 2* (Washington, DC: USGPO, 1942).

U.S. Department of Commerce, Bureau of Foreign and Domestic Commerce, *British Market for Domestic Electrical Appliances* (Washington, DC: USGPO, 1930).

U.S. Dept. of Commerce, Bureau of Foreign and Domestic Commerce, 'Merchandise Problems of Radio Retailers in 1930', *Travel Information Bulletin No. 778* (Washington, DC: USGPO, 1931).

U.S. Federal Trade Commission, *Report of the Federal Trade Commission on House Furnishing Industries. Vol. 1: Household Furniture* (Washington, DC: USGPO, 1923); *Volume III: Kitchen Furnishings and Domestic Appliances* (Washington, DC: USGPO, 1925).

U.S. Federal Trade Commission, *Report of the Federal Trade Commission Distribution Methods and Costs, Part IV* (Washington, DC: USGPO, 1944).

## OTHER PRINT REFERENCES

'50 Years of Statistics and History', *Merchandise Week* (28 Feb. 1972), 21–54 and 110–60.

'1931 Radio Production Reaches £29,750,000', *Wireless and Gramophone Trader* (19 Mar. 1932), 326–7.

A.B.C. [pseudonym], '"Sales Representative"', *New Statesman and Nation* (21 May 1938), 863–4.

Adams, William James and Yellen, Janet L., 'Commodity Bundling and the Burden of Monopoly', *Quarterly Journal of Economics*, 90 (1976), 475–98.

'Advertisers', *Advertising World* (June 1937), 33.

Aitken, Hugh G. J., *The Continuous Wave: Technology and American Radio 1900–1932* (Princeton, NJ: Princeton University Press, 1985).

'All-Gas Houses are Good Publicity', BCGA, *Gas Bulletin*, 33 (May 1934), 78.

Allen, G. C., *British Industries and their Organisation* (London: Longmans, 1933).

Allen, Gordon, 'Building to Sell', in Ernest Betham (ed.), *House Building 1934–1936* (London: Federated Employers' Press, 1934), 137–53.

Allen, William A., *Monetary Policy and Financial Repression in Britain, 1951–59* (Basingstoke: Palgrave Macmillan, 2014).

American Telephone and Telegraph Co., *Telephone Statistics of the World* (New York: AT&T, issues for 15 June 1925; 1 June 1928; 1 June 1929; 15 Mar. 1939).

Andrews, P. W. S. and Brunner, Elizabeth, *The Life of Lord Nuffield* (Oxford: Blackwell, 1955).

Angel, David P. and Engstrom, James, 'Manufacturing Systems and Technological Change: The U.S. Personal Computer Industry', *Economic Geography*, 71 (1995), 79–102.

'Annual Survey of Domestic Appliances', *Electrical Trading* (Aug. 1937), 47–8.

Anthony, Scott, *Public Relations and the Making of Modern Britain: Stephen Tallents and the Birth of a Progressive Media Profession* (Manchester: Manchester University Press, 2012).

'Are Rentals a Proposition for Ordinary Retailers?', *Wireless and Electrical Trader* (13 May 1939), 190–4.

Aris, Stephen, *The Jews in Business* (London: Jonathan Cape, 1970).

Arthur, W. Brian, 'Competing Technologies, Increasing Returns, and Lock-in by Historical Events', *Economic Journal*, 99 (1989), 116–31.

Ashworth, Herbert, *The Building Society Story* (London: Franey, 1980).

Astbury, B. E., 'The "Snatch-Back" System Menace', [letter] *The Times* (16 Dec. 1937), 15.

Aston, C. W., *Hire-Purchase Accounts and Finance* (London: Gee, 1930).

'Autolycus' [pseudonym], 'The All-Electric Advertising Man: Richard Haigh, English Manager of the Gramophone Company, Talks to Us about Radio (and Records)', *Advertising World* (Apr. 1934), 181–2.

Bacon, Robert, Bain, George S., and Pimlott, John, 'The Economic Environment', in A. H. Halsey (ed.), *Trends in British Society since 1900* (London: Macmillan, 1972), 64–96.

Bain, Joe S., *Barriers to New Competition* (Cambridge, MA: Harvard University Press, 1962).

Baines, Dudley and Johnson, Paul, 'In Search of the "Traditional" Working Class: Social Mobility and Occupational Continuity in Interwar London', *Economic History Review*, 52 (1999), 692–713.

Ball, Michael, *Housing Policy and Economic Power: The Political Economy of Owner-Occupation* (London: Methuen, 1983).

Barger, Harold, *Distribution's Place in the American Economy since 1869* (Princeton, NJ: NBER 1955).

Bateman, R. A., *How to Own and Equip a House* (London: Bateman, 1925).

Baukat, Henry W., 'It's a Sale—Not a Demonstration!', *Radio Retailing* (Mar. 1930), 18–19 and 58.

Belgrave, A. C., *Telephone Service*, Post Office Green Paper No. 37 (London: Post Office, 1937).

Bellman, Harold, *The Thrifty Three Millions: A Study of the Building Society Movement and the Story of the Abbey Road Society* (London: Abbey Road Building Society, 1935).

Benson, John, *The Rise of Consumer Society in Britain, 1880–1980* (London: Longman, 1994).

Bentley, Ian, 'The Owner Makes his Mark: Choice and Adaption', in Paul Oliver, Ian Davis, and Ian Bentley, *Dunroamin: The Suburban Semi and its Enemies* (London: Pimlico, 1981), 136–53.

Binnie, Ruth and Boxall, Julia E., *Housecraft: Principles and Practice* (London: Pitman, 1935).

Bishop, F. P., *The Economics of Advertising* (London: Robert Hale, 1944).

Blanken, I. J., *The History of Philips Electronics N.V.*, vol. III: *The Development of N.V. Philips' Gloelampenfabrieken into a Major Electrical Group* (Zaltbommel, Netherlands: Nijhoff, 1999).

Bolling, C. L., *Hire Purchase Trading* (London: Pitman, 1935).

Bondfield, Margaret, *Our Towns: A Close-Up* (London: Oxford University Press, 1944).

Borden, Neil H., *The Economic Effects of Advertising* (Chicago, IL: Irwin, 1942).

Bourdieu, Pierre, *Distinction: A Social Critique of the Judgement of Taste* (London: Routledge & Kegan Paul, 1984).

Bourke, Joanna, *Working Class Cultures in Britain 1890–1960: Gender, Class and Ethnicity* (London: Routledge, 1994).

Bowden, Sue, 'Colston, Sir Charles', in David J. Jeremy (ed.), *Dictionary of Business Biography: A Biographical Dictionary of Business Leaders Active in Britain in the Period 1860–1980* (London: Butterworths, 1984), vol. I, 755–9.

Bowden, Sue, 'Credit Facilities and the Growth of Consumer Demand for Electric Appliances in the 1930s', *Business History*, 32 (1990), 52–75.

Bowden, Sue, 'Demand and Supply Constraints in the Inter-War UK Car Industry: Did the Manufacturers Get It Right?', *Business History*, 33 (1991), 241–67.

Bowden, Sue and Offer, Avner, 'Household Appliances and the Use of Time: The United States and Britain since the 1920s', *Economic History Review*, 47 (1994), 725–48.

Bowden, Sue and Offer, Avner, 'The Technological Revolution that Never Was: Gender, Class and the Diffusion of Household Appliances in Interwar England', in Victoria de Grazia and Ellen Furlough (eds.), *The Sex of Things: Gender and Consumption in Historical Perspective* (Berkeley, CA: University of California Press, 1996), 244–74.

Bowden, Sue and Turner, Paul, 'The Demand for Consumer Durables in the United Kingdom in the Interwar Period', *Journal of Economic History*, 53 (1993), 244–58.

Bowley, Marion, *Housing and the State 1919–1944* (London: George Allen & Unwin, 1945).

Boyd, H. B., 'Wireless Relay: A New and Thriving Industry', *Advertising World* (Nov. 1934), 50–1.

Boyer, George R., 'Living Standards 1860–1939', in Roderick Floud and Paul Johnson (eds.), *The Cambridge Economic History of Modern Britain*, vol. II: *Economic Maturity, 1860–1939* (Cambridge: Cambridge University Press, 2004), 280–313.

'Bristol Undertaking's Campaign', BGCA, *Gas Bulletin*, 31 (Feb.–Mar. 1931), 17.

Brittan, Samuel, *Steering the Economy: The Role of the Treasury* (London: Secker & Warburg, 1969).

Broadberry, S. N. and Crafts, N. F. R., 'Britain's Productivity Gap in the 1930s: Some Neglected Factors', *Journal of Economic History*, 52 (1992), 531–58.

Buell, Victor P., 'Door-to-Door Selling', *Harvard Business Review*, 32 (May/June 1954), 113–23.

'Building Societies since 1925', *Economist* (1 July 1939), 10–11.

Burnett, John, *A Social History of Housing 1815–1885*, 2nd edn. (London: Methuen, 1986).

Bussey, Gordon, *Wireless: The Crucial Decade—History of the British Wireless Industry 1924–34* (London: Peregrinus, 1990).

Calder, Lendol, *Financing the American Dream: A Cultural History of Consumer Credit* (Princeton, NJ: Princeton University Press, 1999).

'Campaigns', *Advertising World* (Feb. 1936), 79–83.

'Campaigns: In Furniture Field, Sex is Exclusively a Smart's Affair', *Advertising World*, 70, 3 (Mar. 1938), 55–6.

Campbell-Smith, Duncan, *Masters of the Post: The Authorised History of the Royal Mail* (London: Penguin, 2012).

Cantacuzino, Sheban, *Wells Coates: A Monograph* (London: Fraser, 1978).

'Carl Dyer Speaks to You', *Philco News* (26 May 1938), 4.

Carnevali, Francesca, 'Fashioning Luxury for Factory Girls: American Jewelry, 1860–1914', *Business History Review*, 85 (2011), 295–317.

Carnevali, Francesca and Newton, Lucy, 'Pianos for the People: From Producer to Consumer in Britain, 1851–1914', *Enterprise and Society*, 14 (2013), 37–70.

Carpenter, Niles, 'Attitude Patterns in the Home-Buying Family', *Social Forces*, 11 (1932), 76–81.

Carr, Gerald, 'Lost Chances in New Houses', *Electrical Trading* (Feb. 1937), 57–8.

Carr, Gerald, 'Selling Vacuum Cleaners with a Difference', *Electrical Trading* (Mar. 1937), 71.

Carrier, A., 'Unravelling the Patent–Antitrust Paradox', *University of Pennsylvania Law Review*, 150 (2002), 761–854.

Carter, S. B., et al., *Historical Statistics of the United States: Earliest Times to the Present. Millennial Edition* (Cambridge: Cambridge University Press, 2006).

Casson, C. R., 'Murphy Advertising, 1934', *Murphy News* (Nov. 1934), 3–4.

'Catchpenny Furnishing Offers. National Chains May Attempt to Stop Supplies', *Cabinet Maker* (24 July 1937), 103.

Chandler, Alfred D., *Strategy and Structure: Chapters in the History of the Industrial Enterprise* (Cambridge, MA: MIT Press, 1962).

Chandler, Alfred D., *Inventing the Electronic Century: The Epic Story of the Consumer Electronics and Computer Industries* (New York: Free Press/Macmillan, 2001).

Chandy, Rajesh K. and Tellis, Gerard J., 'Organizing for Radical Product Innovation: The Overlooked Role of Willingness to Cannibalize', *Journal of Marketing Research*, 35 (1998), 474–87.

Chantler, Philip, *The British Gas Industry: An Economic Study* (Manchester: Manchester University Press, 1938).

Chirui, Maria Concetta and Jappelli, Tullio, 'Financial Market Imperfections and Home Ownership: A Comparative Study', Università Degli Studi di Salerno, Centre for Studies in Economics and Finance Discussion Paper No. 44 (2000).

Church, Roy, *Herbert Austin: The British Motor Car Industry to 1941* (London: Europa, 1979).

Church, Roy, 'The Marketing of Automobiles in Britain and the United States before 1939', in Akio Okochi and Koichi Shimokawa (eds.), *Development of Mass Marketing: The Automobile and Retailing Industries* (Tokyo: University of Tokyo Press, 1981), 59–87.

Church, Roy, 'Mass Marketing Motor Cars in Britain before 1950', in Richard S. Tedlow and Geoffrey Jones (eds.), *The Rise and Fall of Mass Marketing* (London: Routledge, 1993), 36–57.

Clarke, Sally, 'Closing the Deal: GM's Marketing Dilemma and its Franchised Dealers, 1921–41', *Business History*, 45 (2003), 60–79.

Clauss, Florence R., 'Sell Them One More Cleaner', *Electrical Merchandising* (Jan. 1929), 64–7.

Cleary, E. J., *The Building Society Movement* (London: Elek, 1965).

Coase, R. H., 'Wire Broadcasting in Great Britain', *Economica*, 15 (1948), 194–220.

Cockayne, G. W. F., 'Fierce Competition Successfully Countered', *Gas Salesman* (Apr. 1937), 171–3.

Cohen, Deborah, *Household Gods: The British and their Possessions* (New Haven, CT: Yale University Press, 2006).

'Combined Craftsmanship of 42 Men and Women Required in Assembling of One Crosley Five Tube Model 5-50', *Crosley Broadcaster* (15 Dec. 1926), 9.

'Commission on Bogus Orders', *Hire Traders' Record* (1 Feb. 1936), 4–5.

Cones, Harold N. and Bryant, John H., *Zenith Radio: The Early Years, 1919–1935* (Atglen, PA: Schiffer, 1997).

Coopey, Richard, O'Connell, Sean, and Porter, Dilwyn, *Mail Order Retailing in Britain: A Business and Social History* (Oxford: Oxford University Press, 2005).

Cradock, Fanny, *Something's Burning: The Autobiography of Two Cooks* (London: Putnam 1960).

Craig, Elizabeth, *Keeping House with Elizabeth Craig* (London: Collins, 1936).

'Crane' [pseudonym], 'Radio's Obscure Publicity', *Advertising World* (Sept. 1934), 44–6.

Crisell, Andrew, *An Introductory History of British Broadcasting* (London: Routledge, 1997).

Cross, Gary S., *Time and Money: The Making of Consumer Culture* (London: Routledge, 1993).

Crossley Jr, Powel, 'Ten Commandments to 16,000 Dealers', *The Radio Dealer* (Apr. 1926), 52–3.

Crowell Magazines, *National Markets and National Advertising 1929* (Crowell Magazines, 1929).

'Current Furniture Advertising', *Cabinet Maker* (23 Aug. 1930), 326–8.

*Daily Express* Publications, *The Home of Today* (London: *Daily Express*, 1934).

David, Paul A., 'Clio and the Economics of QWERTY', *American Economic Review*, 75 (1985), 332–7.

Davidson, Caroline, *A Woman's Work is Never Done: A History of Housework in the British Isles, 1650–1950* (London: Chatto & Windus, 1982).

Davies, Glyn, *Building Societies and their Branches: A Regional Economic Survey* (London: Franey, 1981).

Davies, Robert Bruce, *Peacefully Working to Conquer the World: Singer Sewing Machines in Foreign Markets, 1854–1920* (New York: Arno, 1976).

Davis, Ian, 'A Celebration of Ambiguity: The Synthesis of Contrasting Values', in Paul Oliver, Ian Davis, and Ian Bentley, *Dunroamin: The Suburban Semi and its Enemies* (London: Pimlico, 1981), 77–103.

Davis, Martin, *Every Man His Own Landlord: A History of the Coventry Building Society* (Warwick: Coventry Building Society, 1985).

de Bijl, Paul and Peitz, Martin, *Regulation and Entry into Telecommunications Markets* (Cambridge: Cambridge University Press, 2002).

De Vries, Jan, *The Industrious Revolution: Consumer Behaviour and the Household Economy, 1650 to the Present* (Cambridge: Cambridge University Press, 2008).

Dessein, Wouter, 'Network Competition in Nonlinear Pricing', *Rand Journal of Economics*, 34 (2003), 593–611.

'Dispute over Hired Furniture', *Furniture Record* (18 Feb. 1927), 310.

'Does House-to-House Selling Really Pay?', *Radio Merchandising* (July 1925), 57–8.

Douglas, Alan, *Radio Manufacturers of the 1920's*, vol. I: *A-C Dayton to J. B. Ferguson Inc.* (New York: Vestal, 1989); vol. II: *Freed-Eisemann to Preiss* (New York: Vestal, 1989); vol. III: *RCA to Zenith* (New York: Vestal, 1991).

Duguid, Paul, 'Brands in Chains', in Teresa Da Silva Lopes and Paul Duguid (eds.), *Trademarks, Brands, and Competitiveness* (London: Routledge, 2010), 138–64.

Dunlop, W. R., 'Retail Profits', *Economic Journal*, 39 (1929), 357–70.

Dyer, Carleton, 'Carl Dyer Speaks to You', *Philco News* (17 June 1937), 1.

Dyos, D. J. and Aldcroft, D. H., *British Transport: An Economic Survey from the Seventeenth Century to the Twentieth* (Leicester: Leicester University Press, 1969).

Edwards, Clive, *Turning Houses into Homes: A History of the Retailing and Consumption of Domestic Furnishings* (Aldershot: Ashgate, 2005).

Edwards, Clive, 'Buy Now—Pay Later. Credit: The Mainstay of the Retail Furniture Business?', in John Benson and Lauran Ugolini (eds.), *Cultures of Selling: Perspectives on Consumption and Society since 1700* (Aldershot: Ashgate, 2006), 127–52.

Eichengreen, Barry, 'The British Economy between the Wars', in Roderick Floud and Paul Johnson (eds.), *The Cambridge Economic History of Modern Britain*, vol. II: *Economic Maturity 1860–1939* (Cambridge: Cambridge University Press, 2004), 314–43.

'Electrical Merchandise Review and Forecast', *Electrical Merchandising* (Jan. 1934), 29–33.

Emerson Radio and Phonograph Co., *Small Radio: Yesterday and in the World of Tomorrow* (New York: Emerson, 1943).

'Eureka Returns to Speciality Selling', *Electrical Merchandising* (July 1933), 25.

'Eureka Vacuum Cleaner Company. Discontinuance of Branches and Sub-branches (case)', in *University of Michigan, School of Administration, Announcement 1934–35* (Ann Arbor, MI: University of Michigan, 1934), 79–82.

'Eureka Williams. Its Oil Burners are Still Selling Easily but for Vacuum Cleaners the Buyer's Market is Here Again', *Fortune* (Dec. 1947), 108–90.

Everard, Stirling, *The History of the Gas Light and Coke Company 1812–1949* (London: Benn, 1949).

'Factors in Retailing', *Murphy News* (29 June 1935), 3–4.

Feinstein, Charles, *National Income, Expenditure, and Output in the United Kingdom, 1855–1965* (Cambridge: Cambridge University Press, 1972).

Feinstein, Charles, 'What Really Happened to Real Wages? Trends in Wages, Prices, and Productivity in the United Kingdom, 1880–1913', *Economic History Review*, 43 (1990), 329–55.

'Finance Companies Re-enter the Field', *Radio Retailing* (Oct. 1935), 20.

Finn, Margot C., *The Character of Credit: Personal Debt in English Culture, 1740–1914* (Cambridge: Cambridge University Press, 2003).

Fischer, Claude S., *America Calling: A Social History of the Telephone to 1940* (Berkeley, CA: University of California Press, 1992).

'Five Years of Electric Vacuum Sales, by Quarters', *Electrical Merchandising* (Feb. 1924), 4098.

Foreman-Peck, James, 'Competition and Performance in the UK Telecommunications Industry', *Telecommunications Policy*, 9 (1985), 215–28.

Foreman-Peck, James, Bowden, Sue, and McKinlay, Alan, *The British Motor Industry* (Manchester: Manchester University Press, 1995).

Fox, Stephen, *The Mirror Makers: A History of Advertising and its Creators* (New York: Morrow, 1984).

Fox-Smith, V. R., *Hire Purchase Organization and Management* (London: Pitman, 1932).

Frankland, Mark, *Radio Man: The Remarkable Rise and Fall of C. O. Stanley* (London: Institution of Electrical Engineers, 2002).

French, Michael, 'Commercials, Careers, and Culture: Travelling Salesmen in Britain, 1900s–1930s', *Economic History Review*, 58 (2005), 352–77.

Friedman, Walter A., *Birth of a Salesman: The Transformation of Selling in America* (Cambridge, MA: Harvard University Press, 2004).

Fuhrer, Karl Christian, 'A Medium for Modernity: Broadcasting in Weimar Germany, 1923–1932', *Journal of Modern History*, 69 (1997), 722–53.

'Furnishing—Out-of-Income Ads', *Cabinet Maker* (10 Oct. 1925), 49–50.

Furnival, Jane, *Suck, Don't Blow* (London: O'Mara, 1998).

Gantz, Carroll, *The Vacuum Cleaner: A History* (Jefferson, NC: McFarland, 2012).

Garside, W. R., *British Unemployment 1919–1939: A Study in Public Policy* (Cambridge: Cambridge University Press, 1990).

'Gas Advertising Review', *Gas Bulletin*, 17 (Jan. 1938), 2–4.

'Gas Produced or Sold in Important Countries of the World', BGCA, *Gas Bulletin*, 33 (March 1933), 49.

'Gas Salesmen's Circles. Southern District Meeting—Sub-Section "B"', BGCA, *Gas Bulletin*, 31 (July 1931), 102–4.

Geddes, Keith and Bussey, Gordon, *The Setmakers: A History of the Radio and Television Industry* (London: BREMA, 1991).

Gereffi, Gary, Humphrey, John, and Sturgeon, Timothy, 'The Governance of Global Value Chains', *Review of International Political Economy*, 12 (2005), 78–104.

Gerth, Ruth, 'The Rational Approach to the Problem of Radio Design', *R.M.A. Engineer*, 2 (1937), 27–30.

'"Getting Across" in Advertising', *Furnishing Trades Organiser* (21 Nov. 1921), 421.

Giachetti, Claudio and Marchi, Gianluca, 'Evolution of Firms' Product Strategy over the Life Cycle of Technology-Based Industries: A Case Study of the Global Mobile Phone Industry, 1980–2009', *Business History*, 57 (2010), 1123–50.

Gilbert, Richard J. and Katz, Michael L., 'Should Good Patents Come in Small Packages? A Welfare Analysis of Intellectual Property Bundling', *Journal of Industrial Organization*, 24 (2006), 931–52.

Gittins, Diana, *Fair Sex: Family Size and Structure, 1900–39* (London: Hutchinson, 1982).

Glendenning, Anne, *Demons of Domesticity: Women and the English Gas Industry, 1889–1939* (Aldershot: Ashgate, 2004).

Gold, J. R. and Gold, M. M., '"A Place of Delightful Prospects": Promotional Imagery and the Selling of Suburbia', in L. Zonn (ed.), *Place Images in Media: Portrayal, Experience, and Meaning* (Savage, MD: Rowman & Littlefield, 1990), 159–82.

Gold, J. R. and Gold, M. M., '"Home at Last!" Building Societies, Home Ownership and the Imagery of English Suburban Promotion in the Interwar Years', in John R. Gold and Steven V. Ward (eds.), *Place Promotion: The Use of Publicity and Marketing to Sell Towns and Regions* (Chichester: Wiley, 1994), 75–92.

Gomery, Douglas, *A History of Broadcasting in the United States* (Malden, MA: Wiley-Blackwell, 2008).

Goring, T. C. H., 'The Growth of the Electronic Tube Industry', in *The Newcomen Society. History of Thermionic Devices, Conference Proceedings* (23 Apr. 1994), 41–62.

Gower, L. C. B., 'Building Societies and Pooling Agreements: The Borders Case and its Consequences', *Modern Law Review*, 3 (1939), 33–47.

Graham, Margaret, 'The Threshold of the Information Age', in A. D. Chandler and J. W. Cortada (eds.), *A Nation Transformed by Information* (Oxford: Oxford University Press, 2000), 137–75.

Greary, Frank and Stark, Tom, 'Whatever Happened to Regional Inequality in Britain in the Twentieth Century?', *Economic History Review*, 69 (2016), 215–28.

Grebler, Leo, Blank, David M., and Winnick, Louis, *Capital Formation in Residential Real Estate* (Princeton, NJ: Princeton University Press, 1956).

Greenfield, Jill and Reid, Chris, 'Women's Magazines and the Commercial Orchestration of Femininity in the 1930s: Evidence from *Woman's Own*', *Media History*, 4 (1998), 161–74.

Hannah, Leslie, *The Rise of the Corporate Economy* (London: Routledge, 1976).

Hannah, Leslie, *Electricity before Nationalisation: A Study of the Development of the Electricity Supply Industry in Britain to 1948* (London: Macmillan, 1979).

Hannah, Leslie, 'Logistics, Market Size, and Giant Plants in the Early Twentieth Century: A Global View', *Journal of Economic History*, 68 (2008), 46–79.

Harris, Nigel, *Competition and the Corporate Society: British Conservatives, the State and Industry 1945–1964* (London: Routledge, 1972).

Harris, Ralph, Seldon, Arthur, and Naylor, Margot, *Hire Purchase in a Free Society* (London: IEA, 1959).

Harris, Richard, *Building a Market: The Rise of the Home Improvement Industry, 1914–1960* (Chicago, IL: University of Chicago Press, 2012).

Harwood, J., 'Selling Gas Apparatus on New Building Estates', BCGA, *Gas Bulletin*, 33 (Jan. 1934), 40–1.

'Have you Invited Manufacturers' Help for your Hire-Purchase Sales?', *Electrical Trading* (Oct. 1930), 48–50.

Hazlewood, Arthur, 'Pricing as Applied to Telephone Service', *Review of Economic Studies*, 18 (1950–1), 67–78.

Hazlewood, Arthur, 'The Origins of the State Telephone Service in Britain', *Oxford Economic Papers*, 5 (1953), 13–25.

Heller, Michael, 'The Development of Integrated Marketing Communications at the British General Post Office, 1931–39', *Business History*, 58 (2016), 1034–54.

Helper, Susan, 'Strategy and Irreversibility in Supplier Relations: The Case of the US Automobile Industry', *Business History Review*, 65 (1991), 781–824.

Hilmes, Michele, *Radio Voices: American Broadcasting, 1922–1952* (Minneapolis, MN: University of Minnesota Press, 1997).

Hilmes, Michele, *Networked Nations: A Transnational History of British and American Broadcasting* (London: Routledge, 2012).

Hilton, John, *Rich Man Poor Man* (London: Allen & Unwin, 1938).

Hiott, Andrea, *Thinking Small: The Long, Strange Trip of the Volkswagen Beetle* (New York: Ballantine, 2012).

'Hire Purchase Abuses', *The Times* (11 Dec. 1937), 9.

'Hire Purchase Bill—1. Case for the Bill', *Economist* (16 Apr. 1938), 145–6.

'Hire Purchase Finance—II', *Economist* (14 Apr. 1934), 819–20.

'Hire-Purchase Stability', *Wireless and Gramophone Trader* (23 May 1936), 111–12.

'Hire Purchase. Systems to Meet a Growing Demand on the Part of the Public', *Cabinet Maker* (17 Sept. 1927), 621–2.

Hitchmough, Wendy, *Hoover Factory: Wallis, Gilbert and Partners* (London: Phaidon, 1992).

Holden, Len, *Vauxhall Motors and the Luton Economy 1900–2002* (Woodbridge: Boydell, 2003).

Holmberg, E. A., 'Cleaners Need a New Deal', *Electrical Merchandising* (June 1932), 38–9 and 55.

Homewood, V. Stanbridge, 'Radio's Efficient Publicity. A Reply to "Crane" by V. Stanbridge Homewood', *Advertising World*, 66 (Oct. 1934), 38–40.

Hoover Co., *Steps to the Hoover Sale* (North Canton, OH, 1936).

Hoover, Frank G., *Fabulous Dustpan: The Story of the Hoover* (Cleveland, OH: World Publishing, 1955).

Hoover, Robert and Hoover, John, *An American Quality Legend: How Maytag Saved Our Moms, Vexed the Competition, and Presaged America's Quality Revolution* (New York: McGraw-Hill, 1993).

'H.P. Firm Denies Responsibility', *Hire Purchase News* (26 Feb. 1931), 1.

Hughes, A. and Hunt, K., 'A Culture Transformed? Women's Lives in Wythenshawe in the 1930s', in A. Davies and S. Fielding (eds.), *Workers' Worlds: Cultures and Communities in Manchester and Salford, 1880–1939* (Manchester: Manchester University Press, 1992), 74–101.

'Intensive Door-to-Door Salesmanship', *Hire Traders' Record* (June 1936), 3.

'Irons can Make Good Profits for the Electrical Dealer', *Wireless and Electrical Trader* (10 June 1939), 295–7.

Issacharoff, Ruth, 'The Building Boom of the Interwar Years: Whose Profits and Whose Cost?', in Michael Harloe (ed.), *Urban Change and Conflict* (London: CES, 1978), 280–325.

'It Costs $13.43 for Every Home Demonstration that Doesn't "Jell"', *Radio Retailing* (Mar. 1930), 45.

Jackson, Alan A., *Semi-Detached London: Suburban Development, Life, and Transport, 1900–39*, 2nd edn. (Didcot: Wild Swan, 1991).

Jefferys, J. B., *The Distribution of Consumer Goods: A Factual Study of Methods and Costs in the United Kingdom in 1938* (Cambridge: Cambridge University Press, 1950).

Jefferys, J. B., *Retail Trading in Britain, 1850–1950* (Cambridge: Cambridge University Press, 1954).

Jensen, Peter L., 'A New Major Development in Radio', *Radio Industries* (July–Aug. 1933), 56.

Jevons, Rosamond and Madge, John, *Housing Estates: A Study of Bristol Corporation Policy and Practice between the Wars* (Bristol: Arrowsmith, 1946).

Johnson, Paul, *Saving and Spending: The Working-Class Economy in Britain 1870–1939* (Oxford: Oxford University Press, 1985).

Johnson-Davies, K. C., *The Practice of Price Maintenance with Particular Reference to the Motor Industry* (London: Iliffe, 1955).

Jones, Stephen G., *Workers at Play: A Social and Economic History of Leisure 1918–1939* (London: Routledge, 1986).

'Judge on Canvassers', *Hire Traders' Record* (May 1926), 2.

Julien, Bernard, 'Ford's Distribution Network in Europe: Recent Developments in the Context of the History of Automobile Retailing', in Hubert Bonin, Yannick Lung, and Stephen Tolliday (eds.), *Ford: The European History 1903–2003*, vol. 2 (Paris: P.L.A.G.E., 2003), 417–42.

'July...a Month of Conventions', *Radio Retailing* (Aug. 1935), 47.

'Just 120 Years to Pay Instalments!', *Hire Traders' Record* (Mar. 1937), 5.

Kaldor, Nicholas and Silverman, Rodney, *A Statistical Analysis of Advertising Expenditure and the Revenue of the Press* (Cambridge: Cambridge University Press, 1948).

Kaplinsky, Raphael, 'Globalisation and Unequalisation: What can be Learned from Value Chain Analysis?', *Journal of Development Studies*, 37 (2000), 117–46.

Kaplinsky, Raphael and Manning, Claudia, 'Concentration, Competition Policy and the Role of Small and Medium-Sized Enterprises in South Africa's Industrial Development', *Journal of Development Studies*, 35 (1998), 139–61.

Kaplow, Louis, 'The Patent–Antitrust Intersection: A Reappraisal', *Harvard Law Review*, 97 (1984), 1813–92.

Kent, E. W., 'Distribution 1935 and 1936', *Murphy News* (11 Jan. 1936), 3–7.

Kimber, Philip, 'Retailers! Look Natural Please!', *Advertiser's Weekly* (28 Feb. 1930), 316 and 348.

Kirkham, Pat, Mace, Rodney, and Porter, Julia, *Furnishing the World: The East London Furniture Trade 1830–1980* (London: Journeyman, 1987).

Klepper, Steven, 'Industry Life Cycles', *Industrial and Corporate Change*, 6 (1997), 145–81.

Klepper, Steven and Thompson, Peter, 'Submarkets and the Evolution of Market Share', *Rand Journal of Economics*, 37 (2006), 861–86.

'Kolster-Brandes and Direct Selling', *Wireless and Gramophone Trader* (25 Apr. 1931), 87.

Kopecky, Karen A. and Suen, Richard M. H., 'A Quantitative Analysis of Suburbanization and the Diffusion of the Automobile', *International Economic Review*, 51 (2010), 1003–37.

Koppes, Clayton R., 'The Social Destiny of the Radio: Hope and Disillusionment in the 1920s', *South Atlantic Quarterly*, 68 (1969), 363–76.

Kraus, Jerome, 'The British Electron-Tube and Semi-Conductor Industry, 1935–62', *Technology and Culture*, 9 (1968), 544–61.

Kuznets, Simon, *National Income and Capital Formation 1919–1935* (New York: NBER, 1937).

Laing, John, 'Increased Mortgages on Builders' Guarantees', in Ernest Betham (ed.), *House Building 1934–1936* (London: Federated Employers' Press, 1934), 86–91.

Landes, D. S., *The Unbound Prometheus: Technological Change and Industrial Development in Western Europe from 1750 to the Present* (Cambridge: Cambridge University Press, 1969).

Langlois, Richard N., 'External Economies and Economic Progress: The Case of the Microcomputer Industry', *Business History Review*, 66 (1992), 1–50.

Lee, Frank L., 'The Changes in Building Society Practice to Meet Changed Business Conditions', *Building Societies Gazette* (Oct. 1936), 934–40.

Lerner, Harry, *Currys: The First 100 Years* (Cambridge: Woodhead-Faulkner, 1984).

'Licences the Key to Actual Demand', *Wireless and Gramophone Trader* (25 Mar. 1933), 322–5.

Lipman, Michael, *Memoirs of a Socialist Businessman* (London: Lipman Trust, 1980).

London Information Service, *Statistical Review of Press Advertising* (1933–7).

London School of Economics, *The New Survey of London Life and Labour*, vol. II: *London's Industries* (London: P. S. King, 1931).

London School of Economics, *The New Survey of London Life and Labour*, vol. IX: *Life and Leisure* (London: P. S. King, 1935).

Long, Joan, *A First Class Job! The Story of Frank Murphy, Radio Pioneer, Furniture Designer and Industrial Idealist* (Sheringham: Joan Long, 1985).

Lynd, Robert S. and Lynd, Helen M., *Middletown: A Study in American Culture* (New York: Harcourt, Brace & Co., 1929).

MacDonald, W. W., '4 Years in Business and Never Pushed a Doorbell', *Radio Retailing* (June 1934), 14–15 and 25.

'Machinery in the Home', *Economist* (5 Feb. 1938), 279–80.

MacLaren-Ross, Julian, *Of Love and Hunger* (London: Wingate, 1947).

MacLaren-Ross, Julian, *Collected Memoirs* (London: Black Spring, 2004).

Maclaurin, W. Rupert, *Invention and Innovation in the Radio Industry* (New York: Macmillan, 1949).

'Major and H.-P. Judge Speaks of Repudiated Contract', *Hire Traders' Record* (Oct. 1935), 4–5.

Mann, H. U., 'Selling in the Home Multiplies Desire', *Radio Retailing* (May 1930), 22–4.

Marchand, Roland, *Advertising the American Dream: Making Way for Modernity, 1920–1940* (Berkeley, CA: University of California Press, 1985).

'Marketing and Distribution', *Economist* (7 Dec. 1935), 1131–2.

'Marketing Statistics and Sales…1937', *Radio Retailing* (Jan. 1938), 25–32.

Marshall, Howard, *Slum* (London: Heinemann, 1933).

Marteau, Fernand A., 'The Drage Way and the Smart Reply: Inside Story of Two Furnishing Houses' Campaigns', *Furniture Record* (19 Mar. 1926), 465.

Martin, Michele, 'Communication and Social Forms: The Development of the Telephone, 1876–1920', *Antipode*, 23 (1991), 307–33.

Mason, Tony, 'Football', in Tony Mason (ed.), *Sport in Britain: A Social History* (Cambridge: Cambridge University Press, 1989), 146–86.

Massey, Philip, 'The Expenditure of 1,360 British Middle-Class Households in 1938–39', *Journal of the Royal Statistical Society*, 105 (1942), 159–96.

Maxcy, George and Silberston, Aubrey, *The Motor Industry* (London: George Allen & Unwin, 1959).

Mellers, Wilfrid and Hildyard, Rupert, 'The Interwar Years', in Boris Ford (ed.), *The Cambridge Cultural History*, vol. VIII: *Early Twentieth-Century Britain* (Cambridge: Cambridge University Press 1992), 27–45.

'Midgets Hit the East', *Radio Retailing* (Aug. 1930), 56–7 and 65.

Milne, Graeme J., 'British Business and the Telephone, 1878–1911', *Business History*, 49 (2007), 163–85.

Minshull, C. B., 'The Importance of the No Warranty Clause in Agreements', *Hire Purchase Trading* (July 1934).

Mitchell, B. R., *International Historical Statistics: The Americas, 1750–1988* (London: Macmillan, 1993).

Mitchell, B. R., *International Historical Statistics: Africa, Asia & Oceania, 1750–1988* (London: Macmillan, 1998).

Mitchell, B. R., *International Historical Statistics: Europe 1750–1993* (London: Macmillan, 1998).

Moody's Investment Service, *Moody's Manual of Investments. American and Foreign. Industrial Securities* (New York: Moody's, volumes for 1929 and 1931).

'More but Dearer Motors', *Economist* (10 July 1937), 62–3.

Morris, P. R., 'A Review of the Development of the British Thermionic Valve Industry', *Transactions of the Newcomen Society,* for *1993–94* (1994), 57–73.

'Motor Economics', *Economist* (15 Oct. 1938), 119–20.

'Motoring at Easter', *Economist* (28 Mar. 1937), 686–7.

Murphy, Eileen, 'Who are our Prospects?', *Gas Salesman* (Mar. 1938), 133–5.

Murphy, Frank, 'Olympia', *Murphy News* (5 Aug. 1933), 3.

Murphy, Frank, 'About the Rent Theory', *Murphy News* (June 1935), 21–3.

National Electrical Manufacturers Association, *The Radio Market* (New York: NEMA, 1928).

Naughton, Bill, *A Roof Over Your Head* (London: Pilot, 1945).

Nelson, Phillip, 'Information and Consumer Behaviour', *Journal of Political Economy*, 78 (1970), 311–29.

'New Leaflets', BGCA, *Gas Bulletin*, 31 (May 1931), 62.

Newton, Scott, 'Keynesianism, Sterling Convertibility, and British Reconstruction 1940–1952', in Ranald Michie and Philip Williamson (eds.), *The British Government and the City of London in the Twentieth Century* (Cambridge: Cambridge University Press, 2004), 257–75.

Nott, J. J., *Music for the People: Popular Music and Dance in Interwar Britain* (Oxford: Oxford University Press, 2002).

O'Connell, Sean, *The Car and British Society: Class, Gender, and Motoring, 1896–1939* (Manchester: Manchester University Press, 1998).

O'Connell, Sean and Reid, Chris, 'Working-Class Consumer Credit in the UK, 1925–60: The Role of the Check Trader', *Economic History Review*, 58 (2005), 378–405.

Oliver, F. R., *The Control of Hire Purchase* (London: Allen & Unwin, 1961).

Olney, Martha L., 'Credit as a Production-Smoothing Device: The Case of Automobiles, 1913–1938', *Journal of Economic History*, 49 (1989), 377–91.

Olney, Martha L., *Buy Now, Pay Later: Advertising, Credit, and Consumer Durables in the 1920s* (Chapel Hill, NC: University of North Carolina Press, 1991).

'Order for Return to Trader', *Hire Traders' Record* (2 May 1932), 3–4.

Page Jr, Leslie J., 'The Nature of the Broadcast Receiver and its Market in the United States from 1922 to 1927', in Lawrence W. Lichty and Malachi C. Topping (eds.), *American Broadcasting: A Source Book on the History of Radio and Television* (New York: Hastings House, 1975), 467–72.

Palmer, Gladys L. and Stoflet, Adam M., *The Labour Force of the Philadelphia Radio Industry in 1936*. Philadelphia Labour Market Studies Report No. P-2 (Philadelphia, PA, 1938).

Pegg, Mark, *Broadcasting and Society 1918–1939* (London: Croom Helm, 1983).

'Penny a Month in H.P. Claims', *Hire Purchase Journal* (May 1938), 8.

Pevsner, Nikolaus, *An Enquiry into Industrial Art in England* (Cambridge: Cambridge University Press, 1937).

'Philco', *Fortune Magazine*, 11, 2 (1935), 74–80 and 164–73.

Pike, Robert M., 'Kingston Adopts the Telephone: The Social Diffusion and Use of the Telephone in Urban Central Canada, 1876–1914', *Urban History Review*, 18 (1989), 32–47.

Pinto, E. H., *The Craftsman in Wood* (London: Bell, 1962).

Pitt, D. C., *The Telecommunications Function in the British Post Office: A Case Study of Bureaucratic Adaption* (Westmead: Saxon House, 1980).

Planck, Robert C., 'Her Ladyship, the Radio Customer', *The Radio Dealer* (Oct. 1925), 155–6.

Plant, Arnold and Fowler, R. F., 'Operating Costs of Department Stores', reports for the Retail Distributors Association, Bank of England, and London School of Economics, final report for year ending 31 Jan. 1938 (1939), and for year ending 31 Jan. 1939 (1940).

Political and Economic Planning, *Report on the Supply of Electricity in Great Britain* (London: PEP, 1936).

Political and Economic Planning, *Report on the Gas Industry in Great Britain* (London: PEP, 1939).

Political and Economic Planning, *The Market for Household Appliances* (London: PEP, 1945).

Political and Economic Planning, *Motor Vehicles* (London: PEP, 1950).

Pollard, Sidney, *The Development of the British Economy 1914–1950* (London: Edward Arnold, 1962).

'Progress of the Industry', *Economist* (7 Dec. 1935), 1132–6.

Raff, Daniel M. G., 'Making Cars and Making Money in the Interwar Automobile Industry: Economies of Scale and Scope and the Manufacturing behind the Marketing', *Business History Review*, 65 (1991), 721–53.

Ramirez, Ron, *Philco Radio 1928–1942* (Atglen, PA: Schiffer, 1993).

Ravetz, Alison, *Council Housing and Culture: The History of a Social Experiment* (Abingdon: Routledge, 2001).

'Reduced Royalties in New Pool Licence', *Wireless and Gramophone Trader* (22 July 1933), 74–5.

Rees, Jonathan, *Refrigeration Nation: A History of Ice, Appliances, and Enterprise in America* (Baltimore, MD: Johns Hopkins University Press, 2013).

Reich, Leonard S., 'Research, Patents, and the Struggle to Control Radio: A Study of Big Business and the Uses of Industrial Research', *Business History Review*, 51 (1977), 208–35.

Reid, Hew, *The Furniture Makers: A History of Trade Unionism in the Furniture Trade* (Oxford: Malthouse, 1986).

Rens, Jean-Guy, *The Invisible Empire: A History of the Telecommunications Industry in Canada, 1846–1956* (Montreal: McGill-Queen's University Press, 2001).

'Retail Advertising', *Cabinet Maker* (31 Oct. 1925), 195–6.

'Revision of Co-operative Advertising Scheme', *Philco News* (6 May 1937), 10.

Rhys, D. G., *The Motor Industry: An Economic Survey* (London: Butterworths, 1972).

Rhys, D. G., 'Concentration in the Inter-War Motor Industry', *Journal of Transport History*, 3 (1976), 241–64.

Richardson, Kenneth, *The British Motor Industry 1896–1939* (London: Macmillan, 1977).

Roberts, Robert, *The Classic Slum: Salford Life in the First Quarter of the Century* (Manchester: Penguin, 1971).

Robertson, J. H., *The Story of the Telephone: A History of the Telecommunications Industry of Britain* (London: Pitman, 1947).

Robinson, Howard, *Britain's Post Office: A History of Development from the Beginnings to the Present Day* (Oxford: Oxford University Press, 1953).

Rost, O. Fred, *Distribution Today* (New York: McGraw-Hill, 1933).

Rostas, L., 'Industrial Production, Productivity, and Distribution in Britain, Germany, and the United States', *Economic Journal*, 53 (1943), 39–54.

Routh, Guy, *Occupation and Pay in Great Britain 1906–60* (Cambridge: Cambridge University Press, 1965).

Russell, Gordon, *Designer's Trade: Autobiography of Gordon Russell* (London: Allen & Unwin, 1968).

Russell, R. D., 'The A24 Cabinet', *Murphy News* (4 Feb. 1934), 3–4.

Ryan, S. J., '109 Radio Merchants Answer the Question—What of Selling Costs', *Radio Retailing* (Sept. 1929), 52–4 and 92.

Ryan, S. J., 'Expenses, 29.5%, Profit, 8.2%. Part II of Radio Retailing's Co-operative Industry Survey of the Costs of Selling Radio', *Radio Retailing* (Oct. 1929), 56–60 and 96.

Salter, W. E. G., *Productivity and Technical Change* (Cambridge: Cambridge University Press, 1960).

Saunders, Christopher, *Seasonal Variations in Employment* (London: Longmans, 1936).

Scannell, Paddy and Cardiff, David, *A Social History of British Broadcasting*, vol. I: *1922–1939: Serving the Nation* (Oxford: Blackwell, 1991).

'Scathing Comments by Judge', *Hire Purchase News* (22 Jan. 1931), 2.

Schmalensee, R., 'A Note on the Theory of Vertical Integration', *Journal of Political Economy*, 81 (1973), 442–9.

Scott, Peter, 'The Twilight World of Interwar Hire Purchase', *Past & Present*, 177 (2002), 195–225.

Scott, Peter, 'Public Sector Investment and Britain's Post-War Economic Performance: A Case Study of Roads Policy', *Journal of European Economic History*, 34 (2005), 391–418.

Scott, Peter, *Triumph of the South: A Regional Economic History of Britain during the Early Twentieth Century* (Aldershot: Ashgate, 2007).

Scott, Peter, 'Did Owner-Occupation Lead to Smaller Families for Interwar Working-Class Households?' *Economic History Review*, 61 (2008), 99–124.

Scott, Peter, 'Managing Door-to-Door Sales of Vacuum Cleaners in Interwar Britain', *Business History Review*, 82 (2008), 761–88.

Scott, Peter, 'Marketing Mass Home Ownership and the Creation of the Modern Working Class Consumer in Interwar Britain', *Business History*, 50 (2008), 4–25.

Scott, Peter, 'Mr Drage, Mr Everyman, and the Creation of a Mass Market for Domestic Furniture in Interwar Britain', *Economic History Review*, 62 (2009), 802–27.

Scott, Peter, 'The Determinants of Competitive Success in the Interwar British Radio Industry', *Economic History Review*, 65 (2012), 1303–25.

Scott, Peter, *The Making of the Modern British Home: The Suburban Semi and Family Life between the Wars* (Oxford: Oxford University Press, 2013).

Scott, Peter, 'When Innovation Becomes Inefficient: Reexamining Britain's Radio Industry', *Business History Review*, 88 (2014), 497–521.

Scott, Peter and Newton, Lucy, 'Advertising, Promotion, and the Rise of a National Building Society Movement in Interwar Britain', *Business History*, 54 (2012), 399–423.

Scott, Peter and Spadavecchia, Anna, 'Did the 48-Hour Week Damage Britain's Industrial Competitiveness?', *Economic History Review*, 64 (2011), 1266–88.

Scott, Peter and Walker, James T., 'Power to the People: Working-Class Demand for Household Power in 1930s Britain', *Oxford Economic Papers*, 63 (2011), 598–624.

Scott, Peter and Walker, James T., 'Working Class Household Consumption Smoothing in Interwar Britain', *Journal of Economic History*, 72 (2012), 797–825.

Scott, Peter, and Walker, James T., 'Bringing Radio into America's Homes: Marketing New Technology in the Great Depression', *Business History Review*, 90 (2016), 251–76.

Scott, Peter and Walker, James T., 'The Impact of "Stop–Go" Demand Management Policy on Britain's Consumer Durables Industries, 1952–1965', *Economic History Review* (forthcoming).

Scott, Peter and Walsh, Peter, 'Patterns and Determinants of Manufacturing Plant Location in Interwar London', *Economic History Review*, 57 (2004), 109–41.

Scott, Peter and Ziebarth, Nicolas, 'The Determinants of Plant Survival in the U.S. Radio Equipment Industry During the Great Depression', *Journal of Economic History*, 75 (2015), 1097–127.

Seafire, William, 'The Cold War's Hot Kitchen', *New York Times* (24 July 2009), A25.

'Selling Liquid Sunshine', *Gas Salesman* (May 1936), 139–41.

'Service to Small Dwellings', *Electrical Trading* (Oct. 1935), 49–51.

Shepherd, W. F., 'Residence Expansion in the British Telephone System', *Journal of Industrial Economics*, 14 (1966), 263–74.

Silberston, Aubrey, 'Hire Purchase Controls and the Demand for Cars', *Economic Journal*, 73 (1963), 32–53.

'SMA Hire-Purchase Plan', *Wireless and Gramophone Trader* (23 May 1936), 130.

Smallpeice, Basil, *Of Comets and Queens* (Shrewsbury: Airlife, 1981).

Smith, Everett R., 'The Economic Future of House-to-House Selling', *Harvard Business Review*, 4 (Apr. 1926), 326–33.

Smulyan, Susan, *Selling Radio: Commercialization of American Broadcasting, 1920–34* (Washington, DC: Smithsonian Institution, 1994).

Sobel, Robert, *RCA* (New York: Stein & Day, 1986).

Society of Motor Manufacturers and Traders, *The Motor Industry of Great Britain* (London: SMMT, 1926, 1929, and 1939 issues).

Solymar, Laszlo, *Getting the Message: A History of Communications* (Oxford: Oxford University Press, 1999).

Soutar, M. S., Wilkins, E. H., and Florence, P. Sargant, *Nutrition and Size of Family. Report on a New Housing Estate—1939* (London: George Allen & Unwin, 1942).

'"Speciality Selling"—The Answer to Sales Slumps', *Radio Retailing* (Mar. 1929), 44–6.

Speight, George, 'Who Bought the Inter-War Semi? The Socio-Economic Characteristics of New-House Buyers in the 1930s', University of Oxford, Discussion Paper in Economic and Social History, No. 38 (Dec. 2000).

Sprenger, Elizabeth and Webb, Pauline, 'Persuading the Housewife to Use Electricity? An Interpretation of Material in the Electricity Council Archives', *British Journal for the History of Science*, 26 (1993), 55–65.

Stanley, C. O., 'Why We Switched to Direct Selling', *Business* (June 1934), 18–19.

Stewart, Charles, 'Sales Policy in a Mining Area', *Gas Salesman* (May 1937), 212–13.

Stewart, W., 'Advertisements Please', BCGA, *Gas Bulletin*, 35 (July 1936), 124–5.

'Still Too Many American Sets', *Wireless and Gramophone Trader* (15 June 1935).

Stokes, J. W., *70 years of Radio Valves and Tubes* (New York: Vestal, 1982).

Stolper, W. F., 'British Monetary Policy and the Housing Boom', *Quarterly Journal of Economics*, 56 (1941), i–iv and 1–170.

Stone, Richard and Rowe, D. A., *The Measurement of Consumers' Expenditure and Behaviour in the United Kingdom 1920–1938, Volume 1* (Cambridge: Cambridge University Press, 1954).

Stone, Richard and Rowe, D. A., *The Measurement of Consumers' Expenditure and Behaviour in the United Kingdom 1920–1938, Volume II* (Cambridge: Cambridge University Press, 1966).

'Story of an Industry', *Wireless and Electrical Trader* (25 Mar. 1944), 342–8.

Strasser, Susan, *Satisfaction Guaranteed: The Making of the American Mass Market* (New York: Pantheon, 1989).

Sturmey, S. G., *The Economic Development of Radio* (London: Duckworth, 1958).

Sugarman, David and Rubin, G. R., 'Towards a New History of Law and Material Society in England 1750–1914', in G. R. Rubin and David Sugarman (eds.), *Law, Economy and Society, 1750–1914: Essays in the History of English Law* (Abingdon: Professional Books, 1984), 1–186.

Sugden, F. E., 'Hire Purchase and the Law', *Hire Purchase Journal*, 1 (1937), 6–7.

Sutcliffe, E. J., 'How we do our Local Publicity', BGCA, *Gas Bulletin*, 30 (Sept. 1930), 138–40.

Szreter, Simon, *Fertility, Class and Gender in Britain, 1860–1940* (Cambridge: Cambridge University Press, 1996).

Tebbutt, Melanie, *Making Ends Meet: Pawnbroking and Working-Class Credit* (London: Methuen, 1984).

Tedlow, R. S., *New and Improved: The Rise of Mass Marketing in America* (Oxford: Heinemann, 1990).

Tetlow, John and Goss, Anthony, *Homes, Towns and Traffic*, 2nd edn. (London: Faber, 1968).

Thorpe, D. Winton, 'The Sale of Load-Building Appliances: I. Electric Cookers', *World Power* (Sept. 1933), 129–32.

Thorpe, D. Winton, 'The Sale of Load-Building Appliances: Cleaning and Washing Apparatus', *World Power* (June 1934), 316–18.

Tirole, Jean, *The Theory of Industrial Organization* (Cambridge, MA: MIT Press 1988).

Todd, Selina, *Young Women, Work, and Family in England 1918–1950* (Oxford: Oxford University Press, 2005).

'The British Market for Motor Cars', *Economist* (15 Oct. 1927), 640–1.

'The British Motor Industry. I—Private Cars', *Economist* (21 Oct. 1933), 755–6.

'The British Motor Industry. II—Present Position and Prospects', *Economist* (14 July 1928), 60–1.

'The Common Sense of Renting', *Wireless and Gramophone Trader* (24 Mar. 1934), 1.

'The Economics of Renting', *Wireless and Gramophone Trader* (1 Dec. 1934), 1.

'The Hire Purchase Bill: Different Viewpoints', *Hire Purchase Journal*, 2 (Jan. 1938), 16–18.

'The Hoover Factory in the Making', *Domestic Appliances* (Jan. 1933), 167–8.

'The Menace of the Midget', *Wireless and Gramophone Trader* (6 Jan. 1934).

'The Opening of the New Hoover Factory and Offices at Perivale', *Domestic Appliances* (May 1933), 296–9.

'The Position of the Motor Industry', *Economist* (11 May 1929), 1034–5.

'The Radio Market Analysed in Relation to Public Purchasing Power', *Wireless and Electrical Trader* (19 Aug. 1939), 232–3.

'The Radio Market—Present and Potential', *Wireless and Gramophone Trader* (28 Mar. 1931), 350–1.

'The Replacement Market', *Electrical Trading* (Mar. 1938), 69.

'The Second-Hand Car', *Economist* (17 Sept. 1938), 531–3.

'The Trend in Discounts', *Wireless and Electrical Trader* (19 Mar. 1932), 338.

'The Trend of Prices and Discounts', *Wireless and Gramophone Trader* (25 Mar. 1933), 328–9.

Thomas, Mark, 'Rearmament and Economic Recovery in the late 1930s', *Economic History Review*, 36 (1983), 552–79.

Thomas, Miles, *Out on a Wing: An Autobiography* (London: Michael Joseph, 1964).

Tolliday, Steven, 'The Rise of Ford in Britain: From Sales Agency to Market Leader, 1904–1980', in Hubert Bonin, Yannick Lung, and Stephen Tolliday (eds.), *Ford: The European History 1903–2003*, vol. 2 (Paris: P.L.A.G.E., 2003), 7–57.

Trentmann, Frank, *Empire of Things: How We Became a World of Consumers, from the Fifteenth Century to the Twenty-First* (St Ives: Allen Lane, 2016).

Trumbull, J. G., 'Regulating for Legitimacy: Consumer Credit Access in France and America', paper presented at the 2011 Economic History Association meeting, Boston.

'Tube Suits Against RCA Settled by Cash and License Grants to 21 Claimants', *Radio Retailing* (Oct. 1931), 66.

Turner, E. S., *The Shocking History of Advertising* (Harmondsworth: Penguin, 1965).

'Turning in to "National"', BGCA, *Gas Bulletin*, 36 (Nov. 1937) 147–50.

Tushman, Michael L. and Anderson, Philip, 'Technological Discontinuities and Competitive Environments', *Administrative Science Quarterly*, 31 (1986), 439–65.

Usui, Kazuo, *The Development of Marketing Management: The Case of the USA, c.1910–1940* (Aldershot: Ashgate, 2008).

'Vacuum Cleaner Fraud', *Hire Traders' Record* (Oct. 1936), 8.

Vallance, A., *Hire Purchase* (London: Thomas Nelson, 1939).

Vernon J. M. and Gordon, P. A., 'Profitability of Monopoly by Vertical Integration', *Journal of Political Economy*, 79 (1971), 924–5.

Waite, J. N., 'Small Houses as a Market for Electricity', *World Power* (Jan. 1933), 10–13.

Walter, Sydney J., 'British Building Society Methods of Publicity and Advertising', *Building Societies Gazette* (Sept. 1931), 664–9.

Walton, J. K., 'Towns and Consumerism', in Martin Daunton (ed.), *The Cambridge Urban History of Britain*, vol. III: *1840–1950* (Cambridge: Cambridge University Press, 2000), 715–44.

Walvin, James, *The People's Game: The History of Football Revisited* (Edinburgh: Mainstream, 2000).

Warner Browne, A., 'Interview with Mr Drage', *Cabinet Maker* (5 Nov. 1927), 293.

Warren-Boulton, F. R., 'Vertical Control with Variable Proportions', *Journal of Political Economy*, 82 (1974), 783–802.

Watkins, E. S., *Credit Buying* (London: Laidlaw & Laidlaw, 1939).

Webb, H. L., *The Development of the Telephone in Europe* (London: Electrical Press, 1911).

Weightman, Gavin and Humphries, Steve, *The Making of Modern London 1914–1939* (London: Sidgwick & Jackson, 1984).

Wellings, Fred, *British Housebuilders: History & Analysis* (Oxford: Blackwell, 2006).

Westby-Nunn, E., 'The New Hire Purchase Law Based on the New Hire Purchase Act, 1938', *International Accountants Journal*, 9 (1939), 13–20.

'What Does the Public Want?', *Radio Retailing* (Oct. 1929), 51.

'What Will the Tube Decision Mean to the Trade?', *Radio Retailing* (Mar. 1929), 52–3 and 83.

Whinston, M. D., 'Tying, Foreclosure, and Exclusion', *American Economic Review*, 80 (1990), 837–59.

Whitehead, Harold, 'The Education Scheme', *Gas Salesman* (Jan. 1931), 36–8.

Williams, Trevor I., *A History of the British Gas Industry* (Oxford: Oxford University Press, 1981).

Williamson, Oliver E., *Markets and Hierarchies: Analysis and Antitrust Implications* (New York: Free Press, 1975).

Willmott, Phyllis, *Growing Up in a London Village: Family Life between the Wars* (London: Owen, 1979).

Wilson, Charles, *First With the News: The History of W.H. Smith 1792–1972* (London: Jonathan Cape, 1985).

Wilson, John F., *Ferranti: A History. Building a Family Business, 1882–1975* (Lancaster: Crucible, 2000).

Wilson, John F., Webster, Anthony, and Vorberg-Rugh, Rachel, *Building Co-operation: A Business History of the Co-operative Group, 1863–2013* (Oxford: Oxford University Press, 2013).

Wolmer, Lord, 'Post Office and the Public. The System at Fault, I—Costly Telephones', *The Times* (30 Sept. 1929), 17.

Wolmer, Lord, 'Post Office and the Public. II—How the Money is Lost', *The Times* (1 Oct. 1929), 13.

Wood, Jonathan, *Wheels of Misfortune: The Rise and Fall of the British Motor Industry* (London: Sidgwick & Jackson, 1988).

Wood, William W., *Selling to the Home Market: A Guide to its Management* (London: Lockwood, 1954).

Woods, Robert, *The Demography of Victorian England and Wales* (Cambridge: Cambridge University Press, 2000).

'World Wireless Trade: Some Highlights of the Export and Import Sides', *Wireless and Electrical Trader* (22 Oct. 1938), 115.

Wray, Margaret, 'Household Durables and the "Squeeze"', *Westminster Bank Review* (Aug. 1957), 5–9.

Wyatt, R. J., *The Austin Seven: The Motor for the Million 1922–1939* (Newton Abbot: David & Charles, 1982).

'You Saw These Too', *Advertising World*, 66 (Oct. 1934), 42–8.

'You Saw These Too', *Advertising World*, 67 (Aug.–Sept. 1935), 66–8.

'You Saw These, Too', *Advertising World* (June 1937), 50–5.

Young, Michael and Willmott, Peter, *Family and Kinship in East London* (Harmondsworth: Penguin, 1957).

'Your Radio Exhibition—is Here!' *Murphy News* (5 Aug. 1933), 4–5.

'Your Sales Program for 1929', *Radio Retailing* (Feb. 1929), 36–7.

# Index